PLUNKETT'S SPORTS & RECREATION INDUSTRY ALMANAC 2024

The only comprehensive guide to the sports & recreation industry

D1800184

Jack W. Plunkett

Published by:
Plunkett Research®, Ltd., Houston, Texas
www.plunkettresearch.com

PLUNKETT'S
SPORTS & RECREATION INDUSTRY
ALMANAC 2024

Editor and Publisher:
Jack W. Plunkett

Executive Editor and Database Manager:
Martha Burgher Plunkett

Senior Editor and Researchers:
Isaac Snider

Editors, Researchers and Assistants:
Charles Bui
Atticus Emig
Annie Paynter

Information Technology Manager:
Rebeca Tijiboy

Special Thanks to:
ESPN
Forbes Magazine
International Health, Racquet & Sportsclub
Association (IHRSA)
National Basketball Association (NBA)
National Collegiate Athletic Association (NCAA)
National Football League (NFL)
National Hockey League (NHL)
NFL Players Association
Major League Baseball Association (MLB)
U.S. Bureau of Labor Statistics
U.S. Department of Commerce
U.S. International Trade Administration

Plunkett Research®, Ltd.
P. O. Drawer 541737, Houston, Texas 77254 USA
Phone: 713.932.0000   Fax: 713.932.7080
www.plunkettresearch.com

Plunkett Research®, Ltd.
P. O. Drawer 541737
Houston, Texas 77254-1737
Phone: 713.932.0000, Fax: 713.932.7080 www.plunkettresearch.com

<u>**ISBN13 #**</u> **978-1-64788-005-7 (eBook Edition # 978-1-62831-997-2)**

Limited Warranty and Terms of Use:

PLUNKETT'S SPORTS & RECREATION INDUSTRY ALMANAC 2024

CONTENTS

Introduction		**1**
How To Use This Book		**3**
Chapter 1: Major Trends Affecting the Sports & Recreation Industry		**7**
1)	Introduction to the Sports & Recreation Industry	8
2)	NFL (National Football League): The Biggest Money in U.S. Sports	10
3)	Broadcasting Fees, Digital Access and Investment Savvy Boost MLB (Major League Baseball)	11
4)	NBA (National Basketball Association) Goes Global	12
5)	NHL (National Hockey League) Expands	13
6)	Television Rights Contracts Bring in Lucrative Revenues for Major Sports Leagues	14
7)	Soccer (Football) Leagues Around the World Reap Significant Revenues and Sponsorships	14
8)	New Sports Stadiums Launched in the U.S./Stadium Sponsorships Offset Costs	16
9)	NCAA College Sports Are Immense Revenue Generators, Thanks to Broadcast Rights	16
10)	Student Athletes Eligible for Endorsement Fees/ Fight for Compensation and Benefits	17
11)	Golf Is a Major Sports Sector/PGA (Professional Golf Association) Plans to Merge with LIV	18
12)	Tennis Is a Massive Global Sport for Professionals and Amateurs Alike	19
13)	Fantasy Sports Post Growth, with 60 Million Players	20
14)	eSports: Electronic Games Become Spectator Sports	21
15)	Sports Betting Gains Traction with Online Betting	21
16)	Sports Equipment Manufacturers Offer the Latest High-Tech Advantages	22
17)	Wearable Sensors Track Exercise Data/Apparel and Shoe Manufacturers Adopt Technologies	23
18)	Sports Agents Are Indispensable/Sports Marketing Booms in China	25
19)	Sports Licensing Heats Up	25
20)	New Video Game Console Technologies and Features Boost Sales	26
21)	Virtual Reality/Augmented Reality and 3-D Games Create Opportunities in the Tech Industry/Immersion Games to Grow	28
22)	Aging Baby Boomers Will Cause Significant Changes in the Leisure Sector, Including Sports and Activity-Based Travel	29
23)	Athletic Footwear Sales Boom, Drawing Big Names from Athletes to Designers	30
24)	The Vast Majority of Shoes Sold in the U.S. Are Made Elsewhere	31
25)	3-D Printing and Robotics Revolutionize Manufacture of Shoes and Fabrics	31
26)	Exercise Apparel Sales Rise/Athleisure Clothing Sales Soar	32
27)	Sports Equipment and Social Media Converge	33
28)	The Future of the Sports Industry Will Be Shaped by Technologies and Demographics	33
Chapter 2: Sports & Recreation Industry Statistics		**35**
	Sports & Recreation Industry Statistics and Market Size Overview	36
	Global Sports Industry Revenues, 2020-2022	37
	Selected U.S. Sports Industry Revenues: 2015-2021	38
	Sports Industry, Estimated Sources of Revenue & Expenses, U.S.: 2016-2021	39

Continued on the next page

U.S. Spectator Sports, Performing Arts & Related Industries, Breakdown of Expenses: 2018-2021 **40**
Estimated Monthly Sporting Goods Stores Retail Sales, U.S.: 1992- March 2023 **41**
Overview of the Media Contracts of the Four Big Sports Leagues **42**
Sports Industry Employment by Business Type, U.S.: 2019-2023 **43**

Chapter 3: Important Sports & Recreation Industry Contacts
Addresses, Telephone Numbers and Internet Sites **45**

Chapter 4: THE SPORTS & RECREATION 400:
Who They Are and How They Were Chosen **73**
Index of Companies Within Industry Groups **74**
Alphabetical Index **84**
Index of U.S. Headquarters Location by State **88**
Index of Non-U.S. Headquarters Location by Country **91**
Individual Profiles on each of THE SPORTS & RECREATION 400 **93**

Additional Indexes
Index of Hot Spots for Advancement for Women/Minorities **506**
Index by Subsidiaries, Brand Names and Affiliations **508**

A Short Sports & Recreation Industry Glossary **523**

INTRODUCTION

PLUNKETT'S SPORTS & RECREATION INDUSTRY ALMANAC is designed as a general source for researchers of all types.

The data and areas of interest covered are intentionally broad, ranging from the various types of businesses involved in sports and recreation, to the teams and leagues that make up professional sports of all types, to an in-depth look at the major firms (which we call "THE SPORTS & RECREATION 400") within the many segments that make up the sports industry.

This reference book is especially intended to assist with market research, strategic planning, employment searches, contact or prospect list creation and financial research, and as a data resource for executives and students of all types.

PLUNKETT'S SPORTS & RECREATION INDUSTRY ALMANAC takes a rounded approach for the general reader and presents a complete overview of the sports and recreation field (see "How To Use This Book").

THE SPORTS & RECREATION 400 is our unique grouping of the biggest, most successful corporations in all segments of the sports, leisure and recreation industry. Tens of thousands of pieces of information, gathered from a wide variety of sources, have been researched and are presented in a unique form that

can be easily understood. This section includes thorough indexes to THE SPORTS & RECREATION 400, by geography, industry, sales, brand names, subsidiary names and many other topics. (See Chapter 4.)

Especially helpful is the way in which PLUNKETT'S SPORTS & RECREATION INDUSTRY ALMANAC enables readers who have no business background to readily compare the financial records and growth plans of sports companies and major industry groups. You'll see the mid-term financial record of each firm, along with the impact of earnings, sales and strategic plans on each company's potential to fuel growth, to serve new markets and to provide investment and employment opportunities.

No other source provides this book's easy-to-understand comparisons of growth, expenditures, technologies, corporations and many other items of great importance to people of all types who may be studying this, one of the fastest growing industry sectors in the world today.

By scanning the data groups and the unique indexes, you can find the best information to fit your personal research needs. The major companies in sports and recreation are profiled and then ranked using several different groups of specific criteria. Which firms are the biggest employers? Which companies earn the most profits? These things and much more are easy to find.

In addition to individual company profiles, a thorough analysis of trends in sports, leisure and recreation sectors is provided. This book's job is to help you sort through easy-to-understand summaries of today's trends in a quick and effective manner.

Whatever your purpose for researching the sports field, you'll find this book to be a valuable guide. Nonetheless, as is true with all resources, this volume has limitations that the reader should be aware of:

- Financial data and other corporate information can change quickly. A book of this type can be no more current than the data that was available as of the time of editing. Consequently, the financial picture, management and ownership of the firm(s) you are studying may have changed since the date of this book. For example, this almanac includes the most up-to-date sales figures and profits available to the editors as of mid-2023. That means that we have typically used corporate financial data as of late-2022.

- Corporate mergers, acquisitions and downsizing are occurring at a very rapid rate. Such events may have created significant change, subsequent to the publishing of this book, within a company you are studying.

- Some of the companies in THE SPORTS & RECREATION 400 are so large in scope and in variety of business endeavors conducted within a parent organization, that we have been unable to completely list all subsidiaries, affiliations, divisions and activities within a firm's corporate structure.

- This volume is intended to be a general guide to a vast industry. That means that researchers should look to this book for an overview and, when conducting in-depth research, should contact the specific corporations or industry associations in question for the very latest changes and data. Where possible, we have listed contact names, toll-free telephone numbers and internet sites for the companies, government agencies and industry associations involved so that the reader may get further details without unnecessary delay.

- Tables of industry data and statistics used in this book include the latest numbers available at the time of printing, generally through 2022. In a few cases, the only complete data available was for earlier years.

- We have used exhaustive efforts to locate and fairly present accurate and complete data. However, when using this book or any other source for business and industry information, the reader should use caution and diligence by conducting further research where it seems appropriate. We wish you success in your endeavors, and we trust that your experience with this book will be both satisfactory and productive.

Jack W. Plunkett
Houston, Texas
July 2023

HOW TO USE THIS BOOK

The two primary sections of this book are devoted first to the sports industry as a whole and then to the "Individual Data Listings" for THE SPORTS & RECREATION 400. If time permits, you should begin your research in the front chapters of this book. Also, you will find lengthy indexes in Chapter 4 and in the back of the book.

THE SPORTS & RECREATION INDUSTRY

Chapter 1: Major Trends Affecting the Sports & Recreation Industry. This chapter presents an encapsulated view of the major trends that are creating rapid changes in the sports, leisure and recreation industry today.

Chapter 2: Sports & Recreation Industry Statistics. This chapter presents in-depth statistics including an industry overview.

Chapter 3: Important Sports & Recreation Industry Contacts – Addresses, Telephone Numbers and Internet Sites. This chapter covers contacts for important government agencies, industry organizations and trade groups. Included are numerous important Internet sites.

THE SPORTS & RECREATION 400

Chapter 4: THE SPORTS & RECREATION 400: Who They Are and How They Were Chosen. The companies compared in this book were carefully selected from the sports industry, largely in the United States. Many of the firms are based outside the U.S. For a complete description, see THE SPORTS & RECREATION 400 indexes in this chapter.

Individual Data Listings:
Look at one of the companies in THE SPORTS & RECREATION 400's Individual Data Listings. You'll find the following information fields:

Company Name:
The company profiles are in alphabetical order by company name. If you don't find the company you are seeking, it may be a subsidiary or division of one of the firms covered in this book. Try looking it up in the Index by Subsidiaries, Brand Names and Selected Affiliations in the back of the book.

Industry Code:
Industry Group Code: An NAIC code used to group companies within like segments.

Types of Business:
A listing of the primary types of business specialties conducted by the firm.

Brands/Divisions/Affiliations:

Major brand names, operating divisions or subsidiaries of the firm, as well as major corporate affiliations—such as another firm that owns a significant portion of the company's stock. A complete Index by Subsidiaries, Brand Names and Selected Affiliations is in the back of the book.

Contacts:

The names and titles up to 27 top officers of the company are listed, including human resources contacts.

Growth Plans/ Special Features:

Listed here are observations regarding the firm's strategy, hiring plans, plans for growth and product development, along with general information regarding a company's business and prospects.

Financial Data:

Revenue (2022 or the latest fiscal year available to the editors, plus up to five previous years): This figure represents consolidated worldwide sales from all operations. These numbers may be estimates.

R&D Expense (2022 or the latest fiscal year available to the editors, plus up to five previous years): This figure represents expenses associated with the research and development of a company's goods or services. These numbers may be estimates.

Operating Income (2022 or the latest fiscal year available to the editors, plus up to five previous years): This figure represents the amount of profit realized from annual operations after deducting operating expenses including costs of goods sold, wages and depreciation. These numbers may be estimates.

Operating Margin % (2022 or the latest fiscal year available to the editors, plus up to five previous years): This figure is a ratio derived by dividing operating income by net revenues. It is a measurement of a firm's pricing strategy and operating efficiency. These numbers may be estimates.

SGA Expense (2022 or the latest fiscal year available to the editors, plus up to five previous years): This figure represents the sum of selling, general and administrative expenses of a company, including costs such as warranty, advertising, interest, personnel, utilities, office space rent, etc. These numbers may be estimates.

Net Income (2022 or the latest fiscal year available to the editors, plus up to five previous years): This figure represents consolidated, after-tax net profit from all operations. These numbers may be estimates.

Operating Cash Flow (2022 or the latest fiscal year available to the editors, plus up to five previous years): This figure is a measure of the amount of cash generated by a firm's normal business operations. It is calculated as net income before depreciation and after income taxes, adjusted for working capital. It is a prime indicator of a company's ability to generate enough cash to pay its bills. These numbers may be estimates.

Capital Expenditure (2022 or the latest fiscal year available to the editors, plus up to five previous years): This figure represents funds used for investment in or improvement of physical assets such as offices, equipment or factories and the purchase or creation of new facilities and/or equipment. These numbers may be estimates.

EBITDA (2022 or the latest fiscal year available to the editors, plus up to five previous years): This figure is an acronym for earnings before interest, taxes, depreciation and amortization. It represents a company's financial performance calculated as revenue minus expenses (excluding taxes, depreciation and interest), and is a prime indicator of profitability. These numbers may be estimates.

Return on Assets % (2022 or the latest fiscal year available to the editors, plus up to five previous years): This figure is an indicator of the profitability of a company relative to its total assets. It is calculated by dividing annual net earnings by total assets. These numbers may be estimates.

Return on Equity % (2022 or the latest fiscal year available to the editors, plus up to five previous years): This figure is a measurement of net income as a percentage of shareholders' equity. It is also called the rate of return on the ownership interest. It is a vital indicator of the quality of a company's operations. These numbers may be estimates.

Debt to Equity (2022 or the latest fiscal year available to the editors, plus up to five previous years): A ratio of the company's long-term debt to its shareholders' equity. This is an indicator of the overall financial leverage of the firm. These numbers may be estimates.

Address:

The firm's full headquarters address, the headquarters telephone, plus toll-free and fax numbers where available. Also provided is the internet address.

Stock Ticker, Exchange: When available, the unique stock market symbol used to identify this firm's common stock for trading and tracking purposes is indicated. Where appropriate, this field may contain "private" or "subsidiary" rather than a ticker symbol. If the firm is a publicly-held company headquartered outside of the U.S., its international ticker and exchange are given.

Total Number of Employees: The approximate total number of employees, worldwide, as of the end of 2022 (or the latest data available to the editors).

Parent Company: If the firm is a subsidiary, its parent company is listed.

Salaries/Bonuses:

(The following descriptions generally apply to U.S. employers only.)

Highest Executive Salary: The highest executive salary paid, typically a 2022 amount (or the latest year available to the editors) and typically paid to the Chief Executive Officer.

Highest Executive Bonus: The apparent bonus, if any, paid to the above person.

Second Highest Executive Salary: The next-highest executive salary paid, typically a 2022 amount (or the latest year available to the editors) and typically paid to the President or Chief Operating Officer.

Second Highest Executive Bonus: The apparent bonus, if any, paid to the above person.

Other Thoughts:

Estimated Female Officers or Directors: It is difficult to obtain this information on an exact basis, and employers generally do not disclose the data in a public way. However, we have indicated what our best efforts reveal to be the apparent number of women who either are in the posts of corporate officers or sit on the board of directors. There is a wide variance from company to company.

Hot Spot for Advancement for Women/Minorities: A "Y" in appropriate fields indicates "Yes." These are firms that appear either to have posted a substantial number of women and/or minorities to high posts or that appear to have a good record of going out of their way to recruit, train, promote and retain women or minorities. (See the Index of Hot Spots For Women and Minorities in the back of the book.) This information may change frequently and can be difficult to obtain and verify. Consequently, the reader should use caution and conduct further investigation where appropriate.

Glossary: A short list of sports and recreation industry terms.

Chapter 1

MAJOR TRENDS AFFECTING THE SPORTS & RECREATION INDUSTRY

Major Trends Affecting the Sports & Recreation Industry:

1) Introduction to the Sports & Recreation Industry
2) NFL (National Football League): The Biggest Money in U.S. Sports
3) Broadcasting Fees, Digital Access and Investment Savvy Boost MLB (Major League Baseball)
4) NBA (National Basketball Association) Goes Global
5) NHL (National Hockey League) Expands
6) Television Rights Contracts Bring in Lucrative Revenues for Major Sports Leagues
7) Soccer (Football) Leagues Around the World Reap Significant Revenues and Sponsorships
8) New Sports Stadiums Launched in the U.S./Stadium Sponsorships Offset Costs
9) NCAA College Sports Are Immense Revenue Generators, Thanks to Broadcast Rights
10) Student Athletes Eligible for Endorsement Fees/ Fight for Compensation and Benefits
11) Golf Is a Major Sports Sector/PGA (Professional Golf Association) Plans to Merge with LIV
12) Tennis Is a Massive Global Sport for Professionals and Amateurs Alike
13) Fantasy Sports Post Growth, with 60 Million Players
14) eSports: Electronic Games Become Spectator Sports
15) Sports Betting Gains Traction with Online Betting
16) Sports Equipment Manufacturers Offer the Latest High-Tech Advantages
17) Wearable Sensors Track Exercise Data/Apparel and Shoe Manufacturers Adopt Technologies
18) Sports Agents Are Indispensable/Sports Marketing Booms in China
19) Sports Licensing Heats Up
20) New Video Game Console Technologies and Features Boost Sales
21) Virtual Reality/Augmented Reality and 3-D Games Create Opportunities in the Tech Industry/ Immersion Games to Grow
22) Aging Baby Boomers Will Cause Significant Changes in the Leisure Sector, Including Sports and Activity-Based Travel
23) Athletic Footwear Sales Boom, Drawing Big Names from Athletes to Designers
24) The Vast Majority of Shoes Sold in the U.S. Are Made Elsewhere
25) 3-D Printing and Robotics Revolutionize Manufacture of Shoes and Fabrics
26) Exercise Apparel Sales Rise/Athleisure Clothing Sales Soar
27) Sports Equipment and Social Media Converge
28) The Future of the Sports Industry Will Be Shaped by Technologies and Demographics

1)   Introduction to the Sports & Recreation Industry

The sports business means many different things to different people. This is a truly global industry, and sports stir up deep passion within spectators and players alike in countries around the world. To one person, sports are a venue for gambling; to another, they are a mode of personal recreation and fitness, be it skiing, cycling, running or playing tennis. To businesspeople, sports provide a lucrative and continually growing marketplace worthy of immense investment. To athletes, sports may lead to high levels of personal achievement, and to professionals, sports can bring fame and fortune. To facilities developers and local governments, sports are a way to build revenue from tourists and local fans. Sports are deeply ingrained in education, from elementary through university levels. Perhaps we cannot state with confidence that sports enrich the lives of all of us, but they certainly entertain a huge swath of the world's population. In addition to economic impact, the largest single effect that sports create is that of gripping entertainment: hundreds of millions of fans around the globe follow sports daily, whether via radio, television, printed publications, online or in person, as spectators or participants.

Sports are big business. Combined, the "Big 4" leagues in America, the National Football League (NFL), National Basketball Association (NBA), the National Hockey League (NHL) and Major League Baseball (MLB), brought in about $42.5 billion in revenue during 2022, but that's just the tip of the iceberg. On a very broad basis, including related services, a reasonable estimate of the total U.S. sports and recreation market for 2022 would be $587.7 billion yearly (and $1.6 trillion for the entire world).

Also, the sports industry is so complex, including ticket sales, licensed products, sports video games, collectibles, sporting goods, sports-related advertising, endorsement income, stadium naming fees and facilities income, that it's difficult to put an all-encompassing figure on annual revenue.

When researching numbers in the sports industry, be prepared for apparent contradictions. For example, the NFL receives vastly more money each year for TV and cable broadcast rights than MLB, despite the fact that MLB teams play about 10 times more games each year than NFL teams.

When the astonishing variety of sports-related sectors is considered, a significant portion of the workforce in developed nations such as the U.S., UK, Australia and Japan rely on the sports industry for their livelihoods. Official U.S. Bureau of Labor

Statistics figures as of end of year 2022 found that 603,500 Americans work in fitness centers, 50,300 in snow skiing facilities, 70,600 in bowling centers and 401,000 at country clubs or golf courses. In total, approximately 1.4 million Americans work directly in amusement, sports and recreation sectors. Another 66,700 work in the wholesale trade of sporting goods, and 308,400 in retail sporting goods stores. Sports, recreation and related supplies and services have been among the greatest new job engines over the past several years.

While it may not seem like it to the casual observer, the sports sector is constantly evolving in terms of personal tastes, popular games and technologies. In fact, the personality and popularity of a top athlete can have a tremendous impact on the current popularity of a particular sport—NBA basketball megastar LeBron James, who was recruited for the league directly out of high school, being a superb example with his extremely positive impact on basketball both at home and abroad. Lance Armstrong, at the peak of his popularity as a Tour de France winner, had an immense impact on the sport of cycling.

Physical fitness activities have been showing substantial growth in popularity in recent years. There has been significant growth in elliptical motion trainers, running/jogging, and stationary cycling done in groups ("spinning"). Participation in fitness classes like Zumba, boot camps and yoga also has been growing.

The Physical Activity Council is a consortium of sports industry groups. Its 2022-edition report tracked participation in hundreds of activities during the past year. The group's extensive survey showed that only 76.3% of Americans aged 6+ participate in physical activities, ranging from golf and walking to fitness clubs and organized team sports.

Meanwhile, many enigmas remain obvious in sports and recreation. For example, the number of people playing golf in America has been dropping over the long term, although audiences for televised golf events remain very large, and golf participation increased during the worst of COVID. Then there's the fact that big audiences have been watching high-stakes poker tournaments on television recently. Does that qualify as sports broadcasting? It's certainly a game. Moreover, thanks to the internet, fantasy sports teams and online betting on sports events are soaring. Meanwhile, electronic games have become one of the world's fastest-growing industries, generating tens of billions of dollars in annual, global revenues including software, game consoles, mobile games and game subscriptions. In the minds of many people, competing against other electronic games players is a sporting activity, so much so that live electronic game competition now draws large crowds willing to buy tickets to watch top pros compete in person. This type of organized electronic game play is now referred to as eSports. Related leagues, tournaments and sponsors are growing quickly. Earnings can be very substantial for top players. On an amateur level, eSports are beginning to be recognized as legitimate sports activities at some schools. Dedicated eSports stadiums can be found in Germany, China and the U.S.

One of the strongest, long-term growth trends in the recreation business has been in fitness-related activities. In the U.S. alone, 40,000 health clubs enjoyed 64.2 million members, prior to the Coronavirus pandemic. Members visited their clubs an average of about 100 days each year. Another 45 million Americans use exercise machines in their homes, according to Plunkett Research estimates. Tens of millions of surviving baby boomers, with time and money on their hands plus a growing concern about their quality of life, will boost the health club and home exercise sectors further. (Sports and leisure revenues from the Baby Boomer segment will grow quickly. For example, "pickleball," a racquet and ball game played on a court about one-quarter the size of a tennis court, is soaring in popularity with senior citizens.)

Globally, Plunkett Research estimates that there are 200,000 gyms/health clubs. Brazil, a very body-conscious nation and home of Rio de Janeiro's famous beach culture, is second only to the U.S. in the total number of health clubs.

Evolving technologies and fashions have an immense impact on sales of sporting goods within specific sectors. Sporting goods makers are constantly trying to create reasons for consumers to buy new equipment. Golf club makers adopt new technologies with great success. Snow ski and board makers use new technologies as soon as they become available. Additionally, ski gear manufacturers introduce new fashions, new colors and new styles yearly in an effort to get consumers to buy new or buy up, regardless of whether significant new technologies are involved. Nanotechnology, with the ability to provide components with tremendous strength at very low weight, is being featured in new equipment to a growing degree, including tennis rackets. Likewise, carbon fibers are increasingly

seen in the construction of upper-end equipment, including fine bicycles.

The types of electronic technology applied to sporting apparel and sporting goods is becoming much more advanced, as sensors are being embedded that wirelessly gather information through sophisticated accelerometers. Nike's Nike+ brand is a major success in this arena, enabling users to set goals, see real-time exercise results and upload exercise histories to www.nikeplus.com from their smartphones and other devices. Eventually, the sports industry will see widespread use of remote wireless sensors in virtually all types of sporting equipment, from tennis rackets to bicycles to golf clubs and even apparel such as swimsuits. Sports participants are going to want to be as totally connected to personal electronics during their recreational activities are they are in all other aspects of their lives.

Meanwhile, the media used to deliver sports and sports related information is evolving quickly. Sports coverage is one of the most widely viewed categories online. At the same time, digital TV recording devices, such as TiVo, are enabling fans to watch events according to their own schedules.

Some of the biggest opportunities in the sports industry today lie in providing exciting, high-value opportunities for sports fans, such as high-tech recreational gear at reasonable prices; eSports, spectator sports ticket packages that represent good value; exercise/fitness services that appeal to aging baby boomers; subscriptions that enable online and mobile viewing of events as well as online home exercise classes; and equipment and apparel that provide high value and exciting design. Globally, over the long term, the industry has tremendous upside potential in rapidly developing consumer markets such as China, India and Mexico.

In the U.S., the increased legalization of sports betting, particularly online and mobile, is spurring rapid growth in the sports sector as a whole. Thanks to a 2018 ruling by the Supreme Court, the 50 states and the District of Columbia are free to legalize and regulate sports on their own. By mid-2023, roughly two-thirds of states had cleared some form of betting on sports. Restrictions vary greatly by state. Some allow only in-person betting, while others restrict betting to lower level games and collegiate events. The fact that states can earn significant levels of taxes and fees from such betting, combined with consumer demand, will encourage the level of activities allowed to expand and cause this industry to continue to grow rapidly.

2) NFL (National Football League): The Biggest Money in U.S. Sports

The National Football League (NFL) is the world-famous American professional football league, with 32 teams organized in two conferences: the American Football Conference and the National Football Conference. The NFL has an 18-week regular season (and a three-week preseason) which runs from August through January, culminating in the Super Bowl championship game between the leaders of each conference in February.

The NFL is a global sports business giant. *Forbes* magazine's list of NFL teams had an average value of approximately $4.47 billion in 2022, up from $3.5 billion in 2021 and $3.0 billion in 2020. (In comparison, *Forbes* found a $2.32 billion average team value in Major League Baseball (MLB); a $2.86 billion average in the National Basketball Association (NBA); and a $1.03 billion average in the National Hockey League in 2022). In the United States, the NFL continues to command by far the greatest revenue, plays in the largest and most expensive stadiums and amasses more viewers than any other sport. This is all the more remarkable in light of the fact that the NFL plays far fewer games per season than the MLB or the NBA.

NFL team valuations were boosted considerably in 2022 with the sale of the Denver Broncos to Walmart heir Rob Walton and his daughter and son-in-law for $4.65 billion. The most recent team sales previously were the Carolina Panthers in 2018 for $2.28 billion and the Buffalo Bills in 2014 for $1.4 billion.

The most valuable franchise in the NFL by far is the Dallas Cowboys, valued at $8 billion, according to *Forbes*. The team is owned by Jerral ("Jerry") Jones. The New England Patriots were valued in second place, followed by the Los Angeles Rams and the New York Giants.

The Cowboys are number one in this category due to the revenues of their enormous, relatively new stadium, savvy broadcasting and advertising agreements, and a hometown full of loyal and wealthy ticket holders. The team's stadium, completed in 2009 at a cost of $1.15 billion, seats 80,000 fans in normal configuration and can be reconfigured to hold as many as 110,000 people for special events. It was the largest domed stadium in the world when completed. It features opening glass doors on each end of the stadium that are 180 feet wide by 120 feet high. The opening dome roof measures 410 feet long by 256 wide. The structure has 315 luxury suites which lease for roughly $200,000 to $500,000 per season. The Cowboys sold their stadium naming rights in July 2013 to AT&T, making it AT&T Stadium. The deal is worth nearly $20 million yearly.

The $1.1 billion U.S. Bank Stadium of the Minnesota Vikings opened in June 2016. The structure is designed to seat 65,000 fans (with possible expansion to 72,000 for major events), has 131 suites, 8,000 club seats and 430 concessions. The Atlanta Falcons moved into their new $1.5 billion Mercedes-Benz Stadium in the 2017-18 season. Meanwhile, the Los Angeles Rams doubled in value (reaching $2.9 billion) in 2016 when the team moved from St. Louis. Its $4 billion mixed-use stadium complex, SoFi Stadium, opened in September 2020 in Inglewood, California.

FedEx Stadium, home to the Washington Football Team (formerly the Washington Redskins), affords the franchise $207 million from FedEx over 27 years for naming rights, averaging about $7.6 million per year. Other deals include Reliant Stadium, home of the Houston Texans, which brings in $10 million per year in naming rights; a $400 million, 25-year deal for the Giants and Jets stadium with MetLife; the Levi's Stadium which is home to the San Francisco 49ers for $220 million for 20 years; and Phillips Arena, home of the Atlanta Hawks and Thrashers, which reaps $9.3 million per year for naming rights.

NFL revenues reached about $16 billion during the 2022-2023 season, per Plunkett Research estimates. The business model established in the NFL stipulates partial revenue sharing among teams and a player free-agency system. For the entire NFL, broadcast rights, licensed merchandise and certain other revenue streams are shared evenly among the teams. The result of the NFL league's strategy is a tight group of teams which, regardless of each team's individual value and record, all have a chance to hire top players and to win. Each team is able to recruit and pay top talent so that fans never know from game to game, season to season which team will win the Super Bowl.

Another revenue stream for the NFL comes from major sponsorship deals with companies such as Verizon, PepsiCo and Microsoft. A league-wide, national sponsorship can cost more than $100 million yearly, and such sponsorships generated about $1.88 billion for the league during the 2022-2023 season according to IEG's Sponsorship Intelligence Database. The funds are split equally among the league's 32 teams.

A potential revenue generator is the NFL's attempt to drum up interest in foreign markets. An International Division for the league has been established, and a modest number of regular season games are being played outside the U.S., including five in the 2023-24 season, three in London and two in Frankfurt.

3) Broadcasting Fees, Digital Access and Investment Savvy Boost MLB (Major League Baseball)

Major League Baseball (MLB) is a professional baseball league in North America. The league has 30 teams that play in two conferences, the National League and the American League. A season consists of 162 games played over approximately six months, usually late March through October. The season ends with the best-of-seven games World Series played between the champions of each conference.

After an off-season lockout in early 2022, MLB adopted a new collective bargaining agreement which introduced advertising jersey patches and helmet decals as new sources of revenue. The league has also expanded its playoff season and struck new streaming deals.

Baseball was long considered by some observers to be a slow-paced game. This deterred some fans from buying game tickets. The average game in 2022 required three hours and six minutes. Bear in mind that this was an average; some games ran much longer. Starting in 2023, new rules were introduced that were very effective in speeding up the game and making it more exciting. A large "pitch clock" is now on the field, allowing pitchers only 15 seconds to get the ball away (20 if runners are on base). Likewise, new rules make batters speed up their play. The bags marking each base are now larger, giving runners who try to "steal" a base a larger target and a shorter distance to run. By the summer of 2023, the average game time was down to about 2 hours and forty-six minutes. Game play is much livelier as well.

The New York Yankees are by far the richest club in baseball, valued in 2022 at $6.0 billion (followed by the Los Angeles Dodgers), according to *Forbes* magazine. Not only does the Yankees' stadium garner staggering revenue in regular season tickets and luxury suites, it also brings in about $85 million yearly in sponsorship deals with PepsiCo, Bank of America, MasterCard and Delta Air Lines. In addition, the Yankees own a regional sports channel, YES Network, one of the most profitable regional networks in the U.S. (The team formerly owned 20% of the network with the remaining 80% held by 21st Century Fox, the latter of which was purchased by the Walt Disney Co. The Yankees then bought Disney's stake for $3.47 billion in March 2019.)

Eight-year broadcasting agreements with Fox, TBS and ESPN are in place that average $52 million per season for each of the league's 30 teams from 2012 through 2021. Starting in 2022, new six-year agreements with the three networks will average about $60.1 million per season per team (augmented by local TV deals worth $40 million minimum per team). ESPN's total contract value will be $3.85 billion; Fox, $5.1 billion; and TBS, $3.75 billion.

Lucrative local TV deals also include an $8.35 billion, 25-year deal for the Los Angeles Dodgers and a $2.5 billion, 28-year deal for the Seattle Mariners. In addition, the Philadelphia Phillies signed a $5 billion, 25-year agreement with Comcast for cable coverage beginning in the 2016 season.

SPOTLIGHT: MLBAM (The MLB's advanced online game video technology)

Major League Baseball Advanced Media (MLBAM) owns and operates the league's web site, www.mlb.com, which was the first to master streaming online technology that allows it to broadcast live games on its site. MLBAM began with an initial $80 million investment by all 30 MLB clubs, which is being repaid through hefty annual dividends. The site includes all out-of-market games. In addition, BAM sells $80 million in MLB merchandise yearly, such as hats, jerseys and signed balls.

Other content owners are looking to MLBAM to distribute content. ESPN uses it to handle online distribution, while HBO's online video service HBO Now is powered by it. World Wrestling Entertainment uses MLBAM to operate its over-the-top (OTT) service (so called because it delivers video content without a cable TV subscription).

MLBAM spun-off its BAMTech unit, which focuses on non-baseball related revenue such as the digital and television rights to National Hockey League (NHL) games, for which MLBAM paid $600 million earlier in 2015. BAMTech was expected to eventually bring in billions of dollars in revenues from strategic partners including Walt Disney Co., Apple and other video distributors. However, in 2017, Walt Disney Co. acquired a majority ownership of BAMTech for $1.58 billion.

Success both on the field and off for particular teams is spread across the entire league thanks to a revenue-sharing system by which all 30 teams in baseball must abide. Teams with revenue above the league average must make payments (worth the difference between the team's actual revenue and the league average) that are split among teams with revenue lower than the average figure. As a result, lower-revenue teams such as the Oakland Athletics, Miami Marlins and Tampa Bay Rays have increased their operating incomes.

Revenue sharing is an attempt to even the playing field between franchises. Otherwise, wealthy teams with the capital to pay big salaries (such as the Yankees and the Red Sox) could easily dominate the league, winning year after year by forming very expensive dynasties. The idea is that with shared revenue, less wealthy teams have the wherewithal to attract (and pay top salaries to) leading players. The goal is to achieve parity, making almost any team capable of winning the World Series and therefore bringing more excitement to the game. The average player salary in 2023 was $4.9 million, up 11.1% from 2022, according to an Associated Press (AP) study.

Big data has come to baseball in the form of Statcast, a number-crunching system designed to evaluate speed, movement and trajectories of both players and baseballs. Two systems are utilized, one developed by ChyronHego that tracks and photographs players, and another from TrackMan that tracks balls. A third camera is used to shoot the field as a whole. When combined, the "triple threat" affords TV commentators the ability to create stunning visual displays to illustrate plays. Statcast also is a powerful recruiting and coaching tool. Up-and-coming players' abilities can be quickly analyzed, as can established players' performance. For example, Houston Astro pitcher Collin McHugh's curveball was measured and shown to have a very fast spin. When coached to throw the pitch more often, McHugh became a star player.

4) NBA (National Basketball Association) Goes Global

The National Basketball Association (NBA) is a professional basketball league in North America comprised of 30 teams. The league has two conferences, the Eastern Conference and the Western Conference, with each of those divided into three divisions. A standard season has 82 games, which allows each team to play the other teams in their conference eight times. The NBA season begins in late October and ends in April, with the NBA finals played in June after a series of playoffs. Basketball is a fast-paced game with an intimate feeling to it, as the court upon which it is played is relatively small, compared to the fields of baseball, soccer and football. The number of seats at a professional basketball facility is typically only one-quarter of those found in a football stadium.

Team values have skyrocketed since 2011, when no franchise was valued at even $1 billion. A seven-year collective bargaining agreement was signed in late 2016 which allowed for hikes in average salaries (from $5 million to more than $9 million).

As of late 2022, San Francisco's Golden State Warriors were the NBA's most valuable franchise, valued at $7 billion. The Warriors play in the state-of-the-art Chase Stadium, on an 11-acre site in the Mission Bay neighborhood. The 18,000 seat stadium was completed in 2019 at a cost of $1.4 billion. The Warriors were followed in total team value by the New York Knicks and the Los Angeles Lakers.

The Los Angeles Lakers signed a 20-year deal with Time Warner Cable worth an average of $200 million per year starting with the 2012-13 season. TNT and ESPN/ABC retained and extended their rights to air NBA games under a new $23.4 billion, nine-year contract beginning with the 2017-18 season.

For decades, basketball's greatest talents have played for the NBA, with team rosters made up of more and more players from outside the U.S. in recent years. In the 2023 draft, the San Antonio Spurs used their number one pick for 19-year-old, 7 foot 4 inch French phenom Victor Wembanyama.

As of the opening of the 2021-22 season, the NBA had 121 international players from 40 countries and territories. The league has also pushed to establish offices and programs in many countries, most especially China, where an estimated 300 million people play the sport, according to the Chinese Basketball Association. The NBA has been actively recruiting in China for years (former Houston Rockets center Yao Ming, who is currently the head of the Chinese Basketball Association, is an example), but in an ambitious move, the Association established a new league there after the conclusion of the 2008 Summer Olympics.

NBA China is endorsed by all 30 North American teams and has $253 million in financial backing from ESPN (a division of The Walt Disney Co.), Bank of China Group Investment, Legend Holdings Limited, Li Ka Shing Foundation and China Merchants Investments. Collectively, this group owns 11% of the enterprise. The NBA has a large, well designed store on a major street in downtown Shanghai that sells NBA-logoed merchandise and apparel. The store is decorated with massive posters of NBA players. In addition, NBA merchandise is sold at approximately 200 branded stores and more than 5,000 licensed retail outlets in China.

The NBA runs the Chinese Basketball Association Dongguan Basketball School and NBA Training Center, where elite 12- to 17-year old players train. The league owns and operates a $1.5 billion, 2,300 acre sports and entertainment complex outside Beijing where visitors can train in a fitness center, play one-on-one with a virtual LeBron James and dine in a hoop-themed restaurant and kid's zone.

SPOTLIGHT: The WNBA

The Women's National Basketball Association (WNBA) is a professional basketball league comprised of 12 teams. The teams are organized into the Eastern and Western conferences. The WNBA season is made up of 40 games per team, starting each year in May and ending in September or early October with the WNBA finals, in which a championship team emerges in a best-of-five-games series.

The WNBA was expected to generate between $180 million and $200 million in combined league and team revenue in 2023 according to Bloomberg. In early 2022, the league received a $75 million investment funded by team owners, the NBA, Nike and other investors. The funds are earmarked for brand elevation and marketing and globalization. As of early 2023, the Seattle Storm was the league's most valuable team after selling minority stakes to 15 investors and bringing total value up to $151 million, according to *The Wall Street Journal.*

Games are aired on ESPN and ABC (both owned by Disney) in a deal that will expire in 2025. Streaming coverage is available on Amazon Prime Video and on CBS streaming platforms. Starting in 2023, Friday night games are being aired by Scripps' Ion network.

The last expansion franchise in the league was the Atlanta Dream in 2008. WNBA commissioner Cathy Engelbert recently announced her aim to have at least one additional franchise in operation by late 2025.

---

5) NHL (National Hockey League) Expands

A National Hockey League (NHL), operating in the U.S. and Canada, is made up of 32 teams which, on the surface, look equally promising, since teams across a broad spectrum of profitability have managed to win the Stanley Cup in recent years. The Coronavirus pandemic, and its restrictions on movement across the U.S.-Canada border, resulted in a realignment of the league in 2021 into four divisions: North, East, Central and West (with all of the Canadian teams in the North division). All games in the regular season will now be played by teams within their divisions. The top four teams in each division will make the playoffs.

The wealthiest teams are typically in Canada and some northern U.S. states. In addition to the Rangers, these teams include the Toronto Maple Leafs, the Montreal Canadiens, the Chicago Blackhawks and the Boston Bruins. They have the most lucrative broadcast rights and the nicest arenas boasting luxury seats and plush club seats. Further south and west, where hockey is more of an acquired taste, the picture is very different.

Revenue sharing in the NHL sees predominantly Canadian teams ponying up the lion's share. Some owners charge that underperforming franchises intentionally keep their revenues under the sharing threshold so as not to contribute. Subsidies paid by high-revenue teams to lower-end rivals are capped at $150 million.

The NHL attracts the smallest fraction of television audiences when compared to other sports, such as football, baseball and basketball. The league is attempting to reach a younger audience through an online service called GameCenter Live. The service affords subscribers the ability to watch almost any NHL game live on its web site in addition to full-length replays.

The big news in the NHL is the creation of an expansion team in Las Vegas, Nevada, the first expansion in 16 years. Owner Bill Foley paid a $500 million expansion fee to establish the team, which began playing in the 2017-18 season in a new T-Mobile Arena, built by MGM Resorts International and AEG, which operates the venue. A second expansion team, the Seattle Kraken, began play in the 2021-2022 season. They play in the Climate Pledge Arena in the Pacific Division in the NHL's Western Conference.

6) Television Rights Contracts Bring in Lucrative Revenues for Major Sports Leagues

Television rights to NFL games are big business. After 35 years of airing *Monday Night Football*, ABC lost the weekly slot, beginning with the 2006 season, to cable sports company ESPN, although the program ultimately remains under its original corporate umbrella since both ABC and ESPN are owned by the Walt Disney Company. Disney is paying dearly for the privilege.

New deals to air NFL games were announced for 2023-33. Disney's deal for *Monday Night Football* on Disney-owned ESPN amounts to $2.55 billion per year. ESPN's deal includes the rights to air 500 additional hours of programming and expands ESPN's digital rights to stream *Monday Night Football* on ESPN+. Fox's deal is an annual average of about $2.03 billion per year for the Sunday afternoon NFC league package through 2033, while CBS agreed to pay an annual average of about $1.85 billion for the Sunday afternoon AFC package (NFC teams tend to be in larger markets with larger numbers of fans, hence the difference in fees). Fox previously aired Thursday night games for $660 million per year, but the new rights awarded Thursday nights to Amazon Prime for $1.32 billion per year (the first time a streaming service will exclusively air a full NFL package). NBC is spending $1.71 billion per year for Sunday night games. The overall cost to air NFL games during the 2023 to 2033 period amounts to approximately $105 billion. In the previous package (which expires in 2021), CBS, Fox, NBC and Disney paid $43.1 billion. In addition, YouTube TV is paying approximately $2 billion per year to air a Sunday Ticket subscription package starting with the 2023-24 season. Meanwhile, the NFL Network (a cable and satellite network owned by the NFL) airs approximately 13 games and 27 studio shows and it is staffed with dozens of on-air announcers and analysts.

Television viewership of NFL games had been dropping. Super Bowl LX, which aired in February 2021, had had 91.63 million viewers, down from 2020's 100.45 million, according to Nielsen. (The game aired on CBS, which reported that while TV viewership was sharply down, streaming coverage was watched across a record-breaking 5.7 million unique devices, up from 3.4 million devices in 2020 and 2.6 million in 2019.) However, Super Bowl LXI, which aired in February 2022, averaged an audience of 112.3 million, including 101.1 million TV viewers and 11.2 million streaming viewers.

Meanwhile, prime time U.S. broadcast rights for Major League Baseball (MLB) are locked up by Fox, which negotiated a seven-year, $3.5 billion deal starting with the 2014 post-season. In late 2018, Fox announced an extension of the deal through 2028 worth an estimated $5.1 billion. MLB also has a seven-year, $5.6 billion contract with ESPN through 2021 and a smaller ($2.8 billion) agreement for limited games with Turner Broadcasting for 13 regular season Sunday games through 2021.

The National Basketball Association (NBA) began an eight-year, $7.5 billion deal with ABC, ESPN and Turner in the 2008-09 season. That deal was extended in 2014 for nine years and $24 billion ($2.7 billion per year). The NBA also broadcasts games through NBA TV.

Soccer is the sport that attracts the most TV viewers on a global basis. Top teams and leagues are posting phenomenal growth largely due to lucrative television contracts.

In recent years, ESPN had lost millions of TV subscribers as increasing numbers of viewers cancelled their cable and/or satellite subscriptions. The network dropped from a high of almost 100 million households during 2011 to less than 80 million by 2020. This is a result of the so-called "cord-cutting" trend, where many consumers are opting-out of expensive monthly cable contracts that offer hundreds of channels—most of which they don't watch. Instead, they are subscribing to smaller bundles of channels or viewing on internet-based platforms. At the same time, ESPN has recently been paying ever-higher fees to leagues for rights to broadcast major sporting events. Another effort, ESPN+ is a parallel streaming app similar to one offered by HBO. The service launched in April 2018, and had 25.3 million subscribers as of the end of the second quarter of 2023.

7) Soccer (Football) Leagues Around the World Reap Significant Revenues and Sponsorships

The sport of soccer (known as football outside of the U.S.) has a massive global following. According to the World Population Review, the sport has approximately 3.5 billion fans and 250 million players across 200 countries. There are a significant number of valuable professional leagues around the world. Top leagues include English Premier League (which has 20 teams in the UK); La Liga (20 teams in Spain); Bundesliga (18 teams in Germany); Ligue 1

(20 teams in France); and Major League Soccer or MLS (27 teams in the U.S.). Latin America is home many leagues as well including the Argentine Primera Division (26 teams) and Campeonato Brasileiro Serie A (20 teams). International competition is overseen by the International Association Football Federation (FIFA), which has 211 affiliated associations and organizes championship World Cup tournaments each year.

Forbes' 2022 top 30 list of the world's most valuable soccer teams is headed by Real Madrid at $6.07 billion. A major factor in the teams' remarkable growth is significant increases in broadcasting revenue as more fans tune in around the globe.

As in American sports teams, global soccer players have reaped rewards from owners with deep pockets who are willing to write astronomical contracts for top talents. For example, Cristiano Ronaldo, currently playing for Al-Nassr earned $136 million in 2022, including salary, bonuses and endorsements.

Wealthy teams such as Spain's Real Madrid, England's Manchester United and Germany's Bayern Munich not only have the capital to pay multi-million-dollar salaries to star players, they also have the cash and the clout to form lucrative sponsorship alliances with Adidas-Salomon, Nike and other apparel manufacturers. Barcelona, for example, has a ten-year, $1.25 billion agreement with Nike that empowers the apparel maker to handle all of the team's merchandising on a global basis starting in 2018.

Poorer teams haven't the wherewithal to strike such deals, and they gamble seriously by trying to play the top-salary game. A losing season means revenue losses in the millions due to lower ticket sales and lost television revenue, as well as the very real possibility of sliding from first league status into the second league.

Savvy team owners are well aware of the challenges before them and are taking steps to safeguard their investments. Player contracts are beginning to include clauses relating compensation to performance. Owners have also been increasing stadium seating and adding luxury boxes to attract higher ticket prices, as well as recruiting young, international talent as opposed to established (and therefore expensive) players. Young players can work together over time to build a cohesive team, while players from foreign countries such as China open marketing opportunities on a global scale. For example, Sun Jihai played for Manchester City and

then Sheffield United, while Dong Fangzhuo played for Manchester United, attracting hundreds of millions of Chinese viewers of televised games. Both have since retired after finishing their careers playing for Chinese teams.

In May 2021, Britain's Premier League signed a $7 billion renewal deal with Sky Sports, BT Sport, Amazon Prime Video and BBC Sport through 2024-2025. This is only the beginning of the league's broadcasting revenue since it has contracts with networks in many other nations around the world.

While European soccer (in Europe and other regions the game is referred to as "football" or "futball") generates more than $12 billion annually in revenue, roughly 400 first division teams throughout the region are fighting for a piece of it. Only those elite qualifiers for the two main championship tournaments at the end of the season, the UEFA Champions League and the UEFA Cup, have the opportunity to score big when it comes to revenue and profits. According to global accounting firm Deloitte Touche Tohmatsu, teams making it to these championships can add more than $50 million to their annual revenue.

European teams are targeting fans (and revenue) in the U.S. The Barcelona team, for example, opened a residential training center in Arizona and is planning to create a team based in California within the National Women's Soccer League. Billionaire Sheikh Mansour, owner of the Manchester City team, launched the New York City FC in 2015. A number of European teams play in the U.S. during the offseason to amass U.S. fans and earn appearance fees.

In May 2022, Russian oligarch Roman Abramovich was forced to sell his Chelsea Football Club after the British government placed sanctions on his business interests in response to Russia's invasion of Ukraine. The team sold for a record $3.2 billion to a U.S. consortium headed by Todd Boehly, a part owner of the Los Angeles Dodgers.

In the U.S., Major League Soccer (MLS), although it has nowhere near the financial eminence and prestige of soccer in other regions of the world, is enjoying a modest success, boosted significantly in 2019 by the U.S. women's team's win of the 2019 World Cup. Energy drink maker Red Bull spent $100 million to buy New York's MetroStars and promptly changed the team's name eponymously to the Red Bulls. In addition, Soccer United Marketing, a commercial soccer promotion company holding promotion rights for the MLS and for other leagues, sold U.S. broadcast rights for MLS and U.S. National

Team Matches to ESPN in an eight-year agreement to run from 2015 through 2022. EPSN, NBC and Univision will collectively pay approximately $90 million per year over the period (about three times the value of MLS' previous deals with the broadcasters).

America's MLS has 29 teams with an overall average attendance in 2023 of 21,992 per game, up 5% from 2022 according to Soccer Stadium Digest. The league puts complicated salary caps on each team. In 2023, this was set at $5,210,000 per team, as the maximum amount, in total, allowed as a budget for the entire roster of a team's 20 senior players. A smaller, additional budget is allowed for 10 non-senior players.

8) New Sports Stadiums Launched in the U.S./Stadium Sponsorships Offset Costs

American sports stadiums have historically been built using large amounts of local taxpayer dollars, voted in by fans willing to bear part of the burden for hosting a professional team. Demand for new, climate-controlled facilities with cutting edge video and sound systems and ever-widening selections of dining venues continues to grow in major cities in the U.S. and elsewhere.

In Arlington, Texas, the Texas Rangers baseball franchise replaced its 22-year-old stadium with a new $1 billion ballpark, featuring a retractable roof, just as the Coronavirus pandemic of 2020 began. The cost is being split between the team and the city of Arlington. The Atlanta Braves also built a new facility to replace the 1996 Turner Stadium (built for the Summer Olympics of that year) called SunTrust Park, as did the Atlanta Falcons football team. Mercedes-Benz agreed to pay the Falcons $345 million over 30 years for naming rights to the new $1.5 billion stadium, which is also used by the Atlanta United soccer team.

Although bond initiatives continue to pay substantial amounts towards funding new stadiums, teams and the cities who host them have had to look to specific taxes for additional sources of cash. In some cases, funds come from a slice of sales taxes on tourist activities. For example, Reliant Stadium, home of the Houston Texans football team, is supported by an additional 2% tax on city hotels and a 5% tax on car rentals.

Funding can be and is raised by selling seat rights to season ticket holders in addition to multi-million-dollar stadium naming rights. The U.S. Bank Stadium, which is home to the Minnesota Vikings

and was completed in June 2016, spent $348 million in state funds, $150 million in Minneapolis municipal funds and $550 million from the Vikings (U.S. Bank is spending as estimated $220 million over 20 years for the naming rights).

Yet another twist to stadium finance is packaging a stadium within a larger complex that also includes offices, retail and commercial space. San Diego's PetCo Park incorporates a renovated 95-year-old office building, a condominium tower and a sandy "beach" play area in its 26-block ballpark redevelopment area.

Some cities vote against public funding, putting the burden on the teams. In the case of the move of the St. Louis Rams back to its original home city of Los Angeles (announced in early 2016), a new $4.25 billion stadium complex called the Los Angeles Stadium and Entertainment District at Hollywood Park is being paid for partly by the team owners, Stan and Ann Walton Kroenke, who are investing $1.6 billion in the project. In total, the complex holds the 70,240-seat SoFi Stadium (which can be configured up to 100,000 seats for special events), a 6,000-seat performance venue, more than 1.5 million square feet of retail and office space, 2,500 homes, a 300-room hotel and 25 acres of park space. The stadium is home to the Los Angeles Rams and Chargers and opened in September 2020. It hosted Super Bowl LVI in 2022 and is scheduled to host the College Football Championship Game in 2023 and the Opening and Closing Ceremonies of the Olympic Games in 2028.

9) NCAA College Sports Are Immense Revenue Generators, Thanks to Broadcast Rights

American universities that are members of the National Collegiate Athletic Association (NCAA) can bring in very lucrative revenues, particularly if that have top football teams. Of the top ten schools by football revenues for 2022, Ohio State led the pack with $251.6 million in total revenue, followed by the University of Texas with $239.3 million, Alabama with $214.4 million and Michigan with $210.7 million, according to the NCAA.

Growth in television rights helps to fund the largest university sports programs, such as lucrative agreements between NCAA conferences (like the SEC and PAC-12) and major broadcasters. For example, in mid-2022, Fox, CBS and ESPN signed a deal with the Big Ten conference to televise football games for more than $7 billion from July 1, 2023, through the end of the 2029-30 athletic year. The deal's payout will be between $80 million and $100 million per school per year. Also, major media agreements are in place between broadcasters and the NCAA for rights to air each year's extremely popular college bowl football playoffs and championships, and for a wide range of other events.

The University of Texas created the Longhorn Network in August 2011, the first sports cable TV network devoted exclusively to athletics at one school. The network is backed by a 20-year deal worth $300 million, and is a partnership between the University, ESPN (owned by Walt Disney) and IMG College, a division of IMG Worldwide, a global sports and media company.

The big revenue-producing sports are football and, at a distant second, men's' basketball. OSKR calculated data for the New York Times, based on information from the U.S. Department of Education, that found that football (including donations and other revenue sources), brings in at least 65% of total revenue at major athletic programs. In effect, revenue generated by football and men's' basketball helps subsidize another 18 sports played on the college level. In addition to ticket revenues and booster and alumni club dues, many schools attract multimillion-dollar endowments and donations from alumni and other supporters who are sports fans.

Huge budgets fund top salaries for winning coaches as well as state of the art athletics facilities. As of early 2023, the highest paid coach was the University of Alabama's Nick Sabin, who earns $10.9 million in salary for running the football program. Clemson's Dabo Swinney was second ($10.54 million) followed by Georgia's Kirby Smart ($10.25 million). Even coaches for less popular sports are paid well at the largest schools, such as the $250,000 per year paid to a coach for a softball program.

The NCAA includes more than 1,000 members, each categorized into one of three divisions. Division I teams, for example, are required to sponsor at least seven sports for men and seven for women (or six for men and eight for women). Several other regulations and requirements must be met at various Division levels. Sports involved range from bowling and fencing to field hockey, golf, gymnastics, wrestling and more. The NCAA itself, operating on behalf of its member universities, had fiscal 2022 revenue of $1.14 billion. That revenue was generated primarily by television and marketing rights fee, with the balance generated by the annual championships, investments and membership fees.

There is a great divide between the largest conferences, such as the Southeastern (SEC) and the Big 12, and the smaller conferences. Schools in the big conferences typically have much higher television ratings and earn far greater revenue, sometimes inconsistent with performance. That kind of power may set the top conferences above NCAA restrictions on operations, such as limits on scholarships, the use of agents and advisors and limits on the amount of contact allowed with top athlete prospects.

10) Student Athletes Eligible for Endorsement Fees/ Fight for Compensation and Benefits

In October 2019, the state of California passed the Fair Pay to Play Act, under which all student athletes are free to accept contracts for payment for use of their names, images or likenesses (NIL). In June 2021, the U.S. Supreme Court unanimously ruled that NCAA limits on college athlete compensation violates U.S. antitrust law. The ruling opened the door for U.S. states to decide when and how athletes may sign endorsement deals with third parties. The ruling also allows colleges to recruit athletes by offering education-related compensation such as scholarships for graduate or vocational schools, computer equipment and study abroad programs in addition to limited cash awards (expected to be around $6,000).

The NCAA officially changed its policy regarding student compensation in mid-2021. Students may employ agents to assist them with contract negotiations. In fact, consulting firms such as Opendorse and MatchPoint have launched to handle student endorsement deals.

Businesses, from restaurant chains to sporting goods manufacturers to internet providers, big and small, are signing deals with student athletes in droves. Deals range from six-figure endorsement deals between national brands and star athletes from big schools to local businesses hiring community college athletes for small marketing campaigns (including social media promotions) in exchange for small fees, free products or gift cards.

In 2022, after winning the NCAA men's basketball title, the Kansas Jayhawks team went on a six week "KU Basketball Barnstorming Tour," earning a collective $1 million for signing autographs, auctioning memorabilia and performing shoot-arounds. The tour was organized by a sports collective, a business with no connections to the University of Kansas or its athletic department. According to the Business of College Sports, 37 of

65 schools in the five wealthiest athletic conferences have at least one collective.

On the small end, The Vitamin Shoppe (a nutritional supplements retailer with about 800 outlets in the U.S. and Canada) worked with OpenSponsorship (a sports marketing consultancy) to find 14 college athletes from a variety of different sports to promote products on social media. Each athlete was compensated with about $100 worth of free products such as performance supplements and Vitamin Shoppe shake bottles.

Meanwhile, in June 2023, the California State Legislature passed the College Athlete Protection Act, which, if fully enacted, would require college sports programs to share their revenues with the athletes. This could include minimum pay plus benefits. Per the act, player's incomes would be based on a formula where one-half of a pool of funds is set aside for male athletes each year, and the another half set aside for females. The money would then be distributed (above a baseline and after the cost of scholarships is deducted) along complicated lines, depending in part on which programs generated the money.

Payouts-per-player could be very substantial, particularly at schools with massive television rights income. Up to $25,000 per player would be paid out promptly, with the balance set aside until the players complete their college degrees. The NCAA threatened to boycott California schools if the legislation is eventually passed. Whatever the outcome, this is likely only the beginning of intense, U.S.-wide activism for payments to athletes. On the down-side, college athletic programs state that the law would cut deeply into school funds available for less popular sports, such as fencing, that prepare athletes for Olympic events.

11) Golf Is a Major Sports Sector/PGA (Professional Golf Association) Plans to Merge with LIV

The sport of golf is thought to date back to 15th Century Scotland. Its popularity spread quickly among the leisure class of the time, with King James IV of Scotland thought to have been the first golf-playing monarch. The game quickly spread on a regional and then global basis, and became accessible over time to a wider and wider base of players and fans. Today, it is a massive global income generator for golf properties, professional players and equipment makers alike.

Established in 1916, the Professional Golfers' Association (PGA) has 28,000 members who play or teach golf for at least part of their personal incomes. The PGA Tour was organized to conduct major golfing events at the highest level.

Professional golf is organized by gender. The LPGA Tour (Ladies Professional Golf Association) was founded in 1950 and oversees professional tournaments played by elite women players from around the world. Today, the LPGA also operates LPGA Professionals, a group of 1,800 members dedicated to teaching, coaching and golf facility management.

Professional golf tours rely to a large extent on attracting corporate sponsors anxious to reach the highly prized demographics of typical Tour fans. Generally the fans are between the ages of 40 and 65. Fans who become ticket holders to these events have above-average incomes and are prime targets for corporate marketing departments. A title sponsorship, that is, the highest level of sponsorship that puts a company's name on an event may require a corporate investment of $7 to $10 million or more. There is a lot of history here: the first U.S. Open Championship was held at the Newport, Rhode Island Golf Club in 1895.

Typically, each tour event operates as a charity, returning all net proceeds to various causes. The amount of money donated by each year by the PGA Tour tops $200 million. The LPGA Foundation was established in 1991 to encourage and educate young women in golf.

To its fans, golf is not only fun and challenging to play as amateurs, it is also fascinating as a spectator sport where the world's top players vie for titles and prize money. Golf courses are often sited in beautifully landscaped country clubs that photograph extremely well. The intensity of tournament play combined with attractive surroundings enable tournament organizers to reap generous fees from broadcasters. Tournament players can win very substantial amounts, with leading winners topping $10 million yearly. In addition, they typically earn even higher amounts in yearly endorsement fees. Over time, top players have earned lasting star quality (and substantial wealth), including Tiger Woods, Arnold Palmer and Greg Norman. LPGA winnings can be very substantial, as well, with the annual prize purse topping $100 million.

Both the PGA and LPGA have been emphasizing international expansion, including the PGA's World Golf Championship tournaments which have been played on five continents.

In Europe, the European Tour operates a highly successful golf tour program, lately known as the DP

World Tour. By 2021, a stiff, international competitor emerged, determined to become a major factor in the golf tour market, the LIV Golf League. In the fall of 2021, Saudi Arabia's Public Investment Fund (PIF) announced its investment of $200 million in LIV. Former number-one ranked golfer Greg Norman was the founding CEO of the company. LIV signed up a stellar roster of top players, attracting them with immense guaranteed incomes. The new league committed $225 million in total prize purses across eight events in 2022. The first LIV event, played at the Centurion Club in St. Albans outside London in June 2022, featured prominent PGA players such as Dustin Johnson and Phil Mickelson. The PGA Tour responded promptly by suspending 17 players, including Johnson and Mickelson. As a result, several players sued the PGA Tour. The PGA Tour also increased prize money in its tournaments and offers players a guaranteed minimum of $500,000 per year.

A major lawsuit between the PGA Tour and LIV was launched, that undoubtedly would have taken many years and immense costs to resolve. Partly to end the litigation, in June 2023 the PGA Tour and LIV announced plans to merge. The proposed deal would combine LIV with the PGA Tour's commercial and business rights with a third entity, the DP World Tour. The combined business would operate on a for-profit basis. As of mid- 2023, the deal was under scrutiny by regulators including the U.S. Department of Justice.

Elsewhere, the United States Golf Association (USGA), which operates the U.S. Open, the U.S. Women's Open and other tournaments each year, also receives major sponsorships.

When it comes to golf tournaments, hospitality is the operative word. Hospitality tents are erected all around tournament courses in which clients and top employees of participating corporations were wined and dined throughout the tournaments. Tournament activities for sponsor-guests vary from a day of professional-amateur play, in which wealthy aficionados can buy a round partnered with a pro, to up-close viewing of three days of play, usually ending on a Sunday when the winner takes the third and final round. Corporate sponsors, whether title sponsors or those on lower levels, line up to pay for the privilege of association with golf.

Amateur play soared during the Coronavirus pandemic, offering socially distanced, outdoor play. Rounds played in the U.S. in December 2020 were up 37% compared to the previous month. Equipment sales rebounded as well.

The PGA is hoping to boost amateur interest with its Play Golf America program, which includes free lessons, as well as links on its web site to a network of courses and facilities that cater to new players; and the First Tee program, which hosts under-privileged kids from urban environments. In addition, the game of golf got an excellent global boost by returning to the Summer Olympics starting in Brazil in 2016.

G\Some golf resorts in the U.S. are building nine-hole courses of shorter length, with par-three holes to attract vacationers and casual players who are short on time. For example, the Cradle is a 789-yard course adjacent to the storied Pinehurst course in North Carolina. It's typically packed with players of all levels, from rank beginners to serious golfers who want to add some holes after playing the full 18 holes next door at Pinehurst. Another perk on some new short courses and elsewhere are golfboards, which are motorized scooters with wheels and designed like surfboards. Riders store their golf bags on the front, grasp a front mounted handle and lean into turns to "surf" the course.

12) Tennis Is a Massive Global Sport for Professionals and Amateurs Alike

Tennis is a global sport with a very wide following. For spectators, it is an intimate viewing opportunity, as it is played on a relatively small court. It is also a quick-paced, easy-to-understand and exciting game that is extremely well suited to television viewing. Thus, the tennis sector gains substantial revenues from broadcasting rights. For professionals who do well in major tournaments, global fame and very substantial incomes are possible. Meanwhile, amateurs are readily able to participate on their local courts and at their tennis clubs.

While some tennis play is mixed-gender, particularly mixed doubles, the professional side of tennis is largely organized along gender lines. The Association of Tennis Professionals (ATP) is the top men's professional tennis circuit, organizing well-sponsored tournaments with generous prize purses. The ATP Tour showcases the world's top male players. The Women's Tennis Association (WTA) is the top women's professional tennis group, with major sponsorships and a global viewing audience.

The four annual Grand Slam tournaments are professional play at the highest level for both men and women. They include the Australian Open, French Open, Wimbledon and U.S. Open. Elsewhere, the ATP Finals and WTA Finals tournaments attract the top-ranking players from the two Tours. Tournament play includes both singles and doubles games. Top tournaments offer multi-million dollar prizes to the top winners. Other important yearly events include the Madrid Open, Monte-Carlo Masters, Miami Open and the Indian Wells (California) Masters.

Tennis has a vast fan and player base worldwide. The sport is easy to enter as a beginner, and it can be quite inexpensive when played on public courts, such as those widely available throughout the U.S. In fact, tennis can be one of the least expensive of all amateur sports. Amateur players participate for fun and exercise, and some compete intensely in local clubs and tournaments. Like the golf sector, tennis has spawned a significant, global industry for the design, manufacture and distribution of apparel and equipment. Tennis also continually adopts new technologies to enhance player performance and spectator experiences. Innovations such as Hawkeye technology for line calls and wearable devices for player monitoring have become part of the sport.

The United States Tennis Association (USTA) has roots in the establishment of the American Lawn Tennis Association (ALTA) in 1881. ALTA was created by a group of tennis enthusiasts who sought to standardize the rules of the game and to organize competitions. It was renamed the USTA in 1975. In the early years, the USTA primarily focused on organizing national championships and fostering the growth of tennis across the U.S. One of the most notable developments during this period was the creation of the U.S. National Championships, which later became known as the U.S. Open. The first U.S. National Championships were held in 1881, at the Casino in Newport, Rhode Island, for men's singles. Women's singles were added in 1887. The USTA opened its Arthur Ashe Stadium in Flushing Meadows (outside of New York City) in 1997, with a massive seating capacity of 23,200 fans.

Likewise, the UK and Europe are huge markets for tennis, as well as home to many of the world's top-ranked players and famous tournaments. Countries like Spain, Switzerland and Germany have produced numerous tennis champions. Players from India are now among the world's best professionals. In the UK, the first Wimbledon championship was held in 1877, and a women's championship was added in 1994. Doubles were added in 1913. British tennis fans spread the sport throughout the British Empire. Wimbledon is run by the All England Lawn Tennis and Croquet Club (its subsidiary named AELTC runs the annual Wimbledon tennis tournament). Its games are played on grass outdoor

courts, with a small number of retractable roofs available, particularly over the main "Centre Court." Today, the Wimbledon championships are among the most watched of all broadcast sporting events.

As in golf, sponsorships and television broadcast rights play a vital role in the tennis industry's finances. Companies and brands partner with tournaments, leagues and individual players to gain exposure and promote their products. Television networks and streaming platforms acquire broadcast rights to televise matches, generating significant revenue and expanding the sport's reach.

13) Fantasy Sports Post Growth, with 60 Million Players

Fantasy sports leagues, in which amateurs ("gamers") choose professional players to participate in virtual ("fantasy") teams are a huge success. Revenues are generated through league fees, transaction fees, web hosting, prize fees and challenge games. Gamers follow their chosen players' on-field, real-life statistics throughout the season. Many bet against their friends' teams, contributing to a pool of money. At the end of the season, the fantasy team with the best statistics wins the pot. The practice began in the early 1980s among baseball fans and has expanded to a wide variety of sports, both professional and amateur, including football.

An estimated 60 million gamers participated in the U.S. and Canada as of 2023, according to the Fantasy Sports & Gaming Association (FSGA). Online firms that enable and host these fantasy teams reap big revenues from gamers.

Players early-on paid a fee to fantasy site operators, but many leagues now allow play free of charge. Revenues come from the sale of draft guides, expert analysis and advertising. Operators typically pay licensing fees of 5% to 10% of revenues for the rights to professional players' names and statistics. The largest of the operating companies pay substantial yearly fees for these rights. For Major League Baseball alone, millions of fantasy players participate, subscribing to any of a dozen fantasy sports magazines, hundreds of web sites (some free and some fee-based) and hundreds of amateur blogs.

Leading fantasy sites include FanDuel and DraftKings. FanDuel, early in its development, raised venture capital in a funding round led by units of Time Warner and Comcast, Inc. DraftKings raised venture capital led by Fox Networks Group.

At least 40 states have passed laws to regulate or legalize fantasy sports contests. In some cases, the states claim that the fantasy contests are actually gambling, while fantasy sports firms counter that their games are, in fact, legal, because they require skill, not just luck.

In 2018, the U.S. Supreme Court ruled that the 50 U.S. states may determine on a per-state basis whether or not off-site betting on sports events is allowed. This is expected to accelerate betting in many parts of the U.S. on nearly all types of sports activities.

14) eSports: Electronic Games Become Spectator Sports

Big news in video games is the growing number of enthusiasts who are interested in gathering to watch other people play them. Gaming as a spectator sport is attracting viewers in the millions, most of whom pay for the privilege. According to Newzoo BV, 532 million people were expected to either watch video game competitions or participate in game play by individuals in 2022 on a global basis, up 8.7% from 2021. eSports were expected to generate $1.38 billion in global revenue in 2022. Media rights and sponsorship were expected to generate $837.3 million in 2022, or 60% of the total market. By 2023, the total audience is expected to rise to 646 million and revenue to $1.6 billion.

eSports are particularly popular in China, where 26% of Chinese internet users watch eSports at least once per month as of early 2020, which is about twice the rate in the U.S. and Western Europe, according to research group Ampere Analysis.

In late 2014, Amazon acquired Twitch Interactive, Inc., an internet video channel for broadcasting and watching people play games, for $970 million. By early 2022, Twitch had 140 million monthly active users compared to only 55 million in 2015. 71 million hours of content are viewed daily.

Sports arenas and other entertainment venues are hosting sell-out games tournaments. College campuses in the U.S. are joining eSports leagues. Turner Broadcasting System, in partnership with WME/IMB, established a league for videogame players and fans which has become ELeague. The league broadcasts games on TBS, Twitch.tv, YouTube and Esporte Interativo in Brazil.

Online videos of game players are proliferating in a practice referred to as the "Let's Play" series of screen shots and video footage of people at play (e.g. Let's Play Minecraft, Let's Play Grand Theft Auto, Let's Play Star Wars Battlefront 2). Let's Players on YouTube are attracting subscribers in the millions, including a Swedish player named Felix Kjellberg

(who uses the YouTube handle PewDiePie). Manufacturers are beefing up prize money to attract more gamers, thereby prolonging a game's lifespan and extending its reach.

A major business initiative at games industry giant Activision Blizzard is called Overwatch, a console-gaming subscription service with tens of millions of subscribers. The Overwatch League sells tickets to fans who watch teams competing at live events, as well as TV broadcasting of this competition.

eSports are in the mainstream on college campuses where teams are competing in tournaments for tuition money and other prizes. As competition (and prize money) grows, a niche for videogame coaches has opened up, both on college campuses and in other tournament play. For example, Riot Games, Inc. runs tournaments in which 116 teams compete worldwide, and each of those teams has at least one coach on staff, with salaries of between $30,000 and $50,000 annually.

Special stadiums dedicated to eSports games are being built around the world. In late 2018, the city of Arlington, Texas opened a 100,000 square-foot complex named Esports Stadium Arlington. This is a logical investment by the city, as it is already the home of the stadiums of both the Texas Rangers MLB team, and the Dallas Cowboys NFL football team. A firm called Allied Esports International has planned or opened several eSports stadiums, including locations in the U.S. (California and Las Vegas), as well as cities in China and Germany.

15) Sports Betting Gains Traction with Online Betting

In 2018, the U.S. Supreme Court ruled that the 50 U.S. states may determine on a per-state basis whether or not off-site betting on sports events is allowed. This is accelerating betting in many parts of the U.S. on nearly all types of sports activities. Advanced technologies could boost this trend. For example, fans could place bets online using their smartphones while they watch a game on TV or at a stadium. Leagues may be big beneficiaries because betting could boost audiences and viewer engagement. Sophisticated betting systems might allow fans to bet on the results of sub-segments of games—for example, the number of "outs" a baseball pitcher throws in a given inning or game. A very wide range of betting options may be possible.

As of early 2023, 37 U.S. states and the District of Columbia had legalized sports betting. Some states restrict betting to casinos, while others allow online wagering (including using mobile devices). U.S. gamblers placed $16 billion in bets on Super Bowl LVII, "the largest single-event legal handle in American sports betting history" according to the American Gaming Association. More than 68 million Americans placed bets on the NCAA March Madness basketball tournament in 2023.

A number of companies have capitalized on the trend, including Penn National Gaming, Inc., which acquired a 36% stake in Barstool Sports, a sports and pop culture blog in January 2020. Penn National has exclusive rights to use the Barstool brand in sports betting products. Meanwhile, FanDuel and Paddy Power Betfair owner Flutter Entertainment PLC acquired The Stars Group in May 2020, creating a major player in online poker and sports betting.

Washington D.C.'s Capital One Arena became the first U.S. sports venue to house a sports booking agency. Stadium owner Monumental Sports & Entertainment partnered with British gambling operator William Hill PLC to complete the project, which includes a two-floor bar and restaurant.

Growing numbers of media companies are investing in gambling. For example, Sinclair Broadcast Group, Inc. rebranded its U.S. regional Fox Sports networks as Bally Sports Marketing (Bally is a well-known name in hotel-casinos.) Sports betting content such as odds and picks are to be integrated into broadcasts.

16) Sports Equipment Manufacturers Offer the Latest High-Tech Advantages

Major strides have been made in sports equipment technology, especially in golf. Equipment manufacturers such as Callaway Golf, Wilson Golf and Titleist spend millions of dollars on developing new, cutting-edge clubs, balls and accessories that offer hope to those who want to increase distance and precision while lowering handicaps. Manufacturers are hoping to lure customers by developing new, game-changing equipment.

With regard to golf equipment, high-tech tools range from gauges that can plot a golfer's distance from the hole using GPS, to room-size simulators that can recreate course conditions from famous courses around the world. The SkyCaddie by SkyHawke Technologies is a GPS that measures distance coordinates for almost 30,000 courses around the world. The expensive Vector Pro Launch Monitor System by Accusport uses infrared light and twin cameras to measure ball spin and speed and perform

video swing analysis. On the super luxury end, the Indoor Resort by TruGolf is a simulator with a tee area, a high resolution video screen and software that can double as a home theater and as a simulator for cycling, car racing and shooting. Available in home and commercial models, the simulator runs between can cost tens of thousands of dollars and offers realistic simulation of play on courses such as Northern California's Pebble Beach and Scotland's St. Andrews.

Data-driven technology is behind the Arccos Caddie platform (www.arccosgolf.com), a system using sensors that screw into the top of each golf club shaft and measures variables relating to a golfer's swing, such as speed and distance. The data is beamed to a smartphone app on which users can analyze their shots. The system can be paired with the Arccos Caddie app, which has a built-in range finder and plots a clear path to the hole (even if that path is obscured by trees or other course elements). The app can also make club selection recommendations based on temperature, wind velocity, topography and distance to the whole. Similar shot-tracking technology is available from Game Golf (www.gamegolf.com).

Until recently, most sales of golf equipment occurred in pro shops on golf courses. There was little competition and prices remained high. However, with the growing availability of golf equipment in discount stores and the advent of golf superstores located in malls and strip centers, golfers are taking their equipment business off the links. Of course, the internet is providing even more competition, not only for new equipment, but also for used equipment on auction sites such as eBay. The National Golf Foundation reports that non-course retailers take in 80% of the dollars spent on equipment in the U.S.

SPOTLIGHT: TopGolf

TopGolf International, Inc. (www.topgolf.com) offers a practice range concept that takes driving practice to a whole new level. There are 70 TopGolf Game Centers (three in the UK, one each in Australia, Mexico and the United Arab Emirates and 64 in the U.S.), that offer driving bays from which up to five players tee off, aiming for targets that range in distance from 20 to 240 yards. Balls are equipped with microchips that broadcast exact positions, earning players points depending upon where their balls land. Each bay is equipped with a flat screen monitor that tracks points. The centers also offer food and bar service on call, as well as pros who are available for lessons, pro shops with equipment and attire for sale, and miniature golf courses for children.

The centers attract not only hard-core golfers, but people young and old who are looking for entertainment, as well as companies that bring their staffs for team building exercises. Each TopGolf facility costs between $5 and $7 million to build, and generates revenues through sales of memberships, in addition to revenues from games, food and beverage, retail sales, mini golf, events and lessons. As of mid-2021, new U.S. locations were planned or under construction in Los Angeles, California; Ft. Meyers and St. Petersburg, Florida; Baltimore, Maryland; and Colorado Springs, Colorado; among others. In March 2021, TopGolf was acquired by Callaway Golf for $2.6 billion.

Tennis is getting a technological boost with new, smart equipment to help players improve. For example, a racket called Play Pure Drive made by Babolat captures data such as impact strength, ball speed and the number and type of each shot hit. The data is analyzed by an accompanying smartphone app.

Another new tennis technology is analysis by PlaySight Interactive Ltd.'s Smart Court, which uses high-definition cameras and digital-imaging technology to record everything a player does on the court. Players can review their performance and adjust accordingly for improvements.

17) Wearable Sensors Track Exercise Data/Apparel and Shoe Manufacturers Adopt Technologies

The big news in sports equipment is wearable sensors that can measure anything from heart rates to speed achieved to physical exertion. Sensors are being embedded in all kinds of apparel, shoes and accessories. This sector will evolve very quickly by adopting the latest breakthroughs in the Internet of Things (IoT) and machine learning, in order to capitalize on data generated by device wearers.

A private company called Catapult Sports makes a matchbook-sized GPS device called Vector that professional and amateur athletes wear to measure performance. The firm also offers the ClearSky local positioning system (LPS) and the Catapult One athlete monitoring system. The devices are paired with analytical software capable of tracking multiple athletes both indoors and out. Catapult acquired sports monitoring device company GPSports.

Sporting goods manufacturers such as Nike are using sensors to entice customers. Nike and other shoemakers, including Adidas, have long offered sensors that can be worn on running shoes to collect data on steps, mileage or calories burned. Nike provides a technology called Nike+ that is incorporated in certain running shoes and can communicate with Apple or Android smart phones. Users can see total running time, distance, pace and calories burned. It can provide feedback during the run to let the runner know whether or not personal goals are being met. If you don't want to buy the special shoes, you can buy standalone sensors that can be attached to your favorite shoes from other makers. The Nike FuelBand (a wristband that can track a user's walking, dancing, basketball playing and many other activities via a built-in accelerometer) was a pioneer in this field. However, after a few short years Nike dropped the band itself while maintaining the underlying technology. Nike now makes its Fuel software available to outside firms for incorporation in a wide variety of activity trackers. Nike's Fuel Band was widely admired but did not rack up impressive sales. One of the trends causing the firm to change gears was the development of the Apple Watch. Nike Fuel is now available as an Apple Watch app.

GPS company TomTom offers a watch with a large screen and built-in GPS. Nikeplus.com enables users to upload complete running and workout information, compete with friends, store personal exercise history and find popular running routes. A large number of TomTom editions are available specifically for golfers, hikers and participants in other types of activities.

The system can also be used by people using exercise equipment indoors. Compatible cardio machines such as treadmills, elliptical machines and stationary bikes made by firms such as LifeFitness, Precor and Cybex have ports to which iPods can be connected to record pace, time and distance. In addition, iTunes is featuring upbeat music for workouts, favorite playlists from famous athletes and even real-time voice feedback during exercise. The sensor and transmitter retail at a modest price. The result has been a massive online running community, with millions of members. Members can post comments about their runs, share tips and engage in friendly competition to see who makes the best time for a given distance or track.

Eyewear is also utilizing sensors for a variety of uses. Luxottica's Oakley offers athletes the Radar Pace sunglasses and attached earphones with a voice-activated system that tracks heart rate, power output, speed, cadence, distance and times, while it partners with Intel for data analysis. The OrCam MyEye integrates glasses with earphones and cameras that read text to assist the visually impaired. Vuzix's smart glasses are Android-based wearable computers for industrial and medical applications, with the ability to take still photos, record and playback video, track timed events and link to other devices such as smartphones.

Apparel and fabrics are also being redesigned to incorporate sensors or at least provide connectivity to personal electronics. Textronics, Inc. makes fabric with circuitry, sensors and a functional component woven in that render the material capable of sending signals to heart rate monitors, which are popular among serious athletes. Textronics makes a sports bra under the NuMetrex brand which senses the wearer's heart rate and communicates that data to a wrist monitor. The bras free female athletes from wearing separate heart rate monitor straps and sensors.

Adidas has been innovating with sensors as well. Its latest effort is a line of smart products under the miCoach brand, including fit smart, a wristband which measures heart rate, calories, pace and speed, distance and stride rate; smart run, which is an all-in-one running watch; smart ball, a soccer training ball embedded with a sensor that measures speed, spin and strike force; x_cell, a wearable sensor that measures vertical movement in addition to heart rate and running speed; speed cell, an on-shoe sensor; and the Adidas heart rate monitor with strap. Most Adidas miCoach sensors link to selected smartphones. OMsignal, a Montreal-based company, makes machine-washable t-shirts that measure the wearer's heart rate, breathing and body temperature.

Fitness apparel maker Under Armour invested $710 million buying fitness app companies MapMyFitness, MyFitnessPal and Endomondo.

MapMyFitness is U.S. firm that offers an app aimed at runners and cyclists. MyFitnessPal is a calorie counting app with a massive community of users. Endomondo is a European app for logging exercise data for a variety of sports. Analysts expect Under Armour to develop clothing that tracks and analyzes fitness data.

Another twist on wearable electronics is the use of conductive fibers, which are typically substrate fibers such as cotton, polyester or nylon coated or embedded with electrically conductive elements. The result is lighter and more flexible than using metal wires as conductors, making it easily wearable and washable. Conductive fibers can be used in a wide variety of applications, including in military uniforms (which can power equipment), RFID tags in clothing and sensors in active wear that can measure heart rate and distance covered.

Internet Research Tip:

For more about conductive fibers, see the web site for the Conductive Fibers Manufacturing Council, www.cfibermfg.com.

The Massachusetts Institute of Technology (MIT) announced the founding of the Advanced Functional Fabrics of America Institute (AFFOA), a public-private consortium of manufacturers, universities, agencies and companies to accelerate innovation in high-tech, U.S.-based manufacturing involving fibers and textiles. AFFOA includes dozens of universities, industry members, manufacturers and startup incubators across 29 U.S. states and Puerto Rico.

Electronic components, which are becoming smaller and smaller, are now easily incorporated into articles of clothing. Industrial applications for wearable electronics will also evolve. For example, police officers, soldiers and emergency medical technicians may benefit from the ability to see up-to-date data on a wearable dashboard such as Google Glass, while built-in cameras and microphones may exchange vital real-time information with experts and analysts in remote locations. This could move remote collaboration in highly critical situations to a new level.

SPOTLIGHT: CuteCircuit

London-based CuteCircuit is a fashion house that produces women's and men's clothing made of fabric embedded with micro-electronics that create changing, lighted patterns, shapes and texts. CuteCircuit projects include the Sound Shirt, with micro-actuators embedded in the fabric that receive music transmissions that the wearer can feel; and the Hug Shirt, which captures the strength, duration and location of touches such as hugs and actuators that recreate the sensations. CuteCircuit produces custom clothing through its Haute Couture line, and offers ready-to-wear through its website, cutecircuit.com.

18) Sports Agents Are Indispensable/ Sports Marketing Booms in China

Sports agency, as we know it today, was largely defined by the efforts of the late superagent Mark McCormack, who founded International Management Group with a handshake deal to represent golfer Arnold Palmer. McCormack and his company, which later become known as IMG Worldwide, pioneered the negotiation of highly lucrative contracts for top athletes. World-class athletes can earn millions of dollars yearly by excelling in their sports, but they can also multiply their incomes significantly by endorsing products, participating in special events and speaking to groups. According to *Forbes,* Argentine soccer star Lionel Messi garnered $130 million through salary, winnings and endorsements, making him the number one highest paid athlete in the world in 2022.

Sports agents make this possible by serving athletes in an ever-increasing number of ways. From contract negotiation to endorsement deals to special event planning to investment planning to personal handling, agents have become indispensable to top athletes in every sport.

McCormack was the first to arrange endorsements, signing Palmer as a spokesperson for everything from golf clubs to motor oil to the Lear Jet. McCormack planned and executed golf tournaments, selling rounds of golf played with Palmer to executives around the world for hefty fees. The golfer was a highly paid inspirational speaker for many years. At the end of his career, long after Palmer's official retirement, he still earned $20 million a year from deals struck by IMG.

From golf, McCormack's IMG branched out into 10 other sports, plus modeling and the arts. The firm also launched a television production division and established IMG College which has the marketing rights to for more than 200 collegiate institutions for licensing, sponsorships, ticketing, publishing and seating. Meanwhile, in 1995, four former IMG agents, including Ariel Emanuel, formed the Endeavor Talent Agency. Endeavor and competing firm William Morris Agency merged to form WME in 2009. WME went on to form a strategic partnership with investment company Silver Lake Partners three years later.

In December 2013, IMG was acquired by WME and Silver Lake Partners for $2.3 billion. The latest chapter in the powerhouse agency story was the 2017 establishment of Endeavor LLC, which is now the parent firm for the entire WME and IMG business.

Outside the U.S., China is a hotbed of opportunity for sports marketing. China's growing middle class is being exposed to talented athletes from around the world. These athletes and their agents are looking for ways to tap the growing Chinese market. While Yao Ming, a native of China, has long been a familiar face in Chinese ads and at personal appearances, athletes including Serena Williams, LeBron James and Kobe Bryant are doing the same.

19) Sports Licensing Heats Up

In late 2019, The National Football League Players Association, the Major League Baseball Players Association and RedBird Capital Partners LLC founded OneTeam Partners to manage the portrayal of player names, images and likenesses. OneTeam not only helps players market themselves, but also invests revenue generated by that marketing into new business ventures. The players associations earn tens of millions of dollars yearly from licensing deals with videogame publishers and trading card companies. RedBird made an initial investment of $125 million in OneTeam and owns about a 40% stake in the firm. The players associations own the remaining 60%.

SPOTLIGHT: Fanatics, Inc.

Fanatics, Inc. is an online retailer of licensed sports merchandise. Customers can purchase items via online sites through the Fanatics (Fanatics.com), FansEdge (FansEdge.com), Kitbag (Kitbag.com) and Majestic (MajesticAthletic.com) brands. The firm also offers a collection of sports collectibles and memorabilia through Fanatics Authentic (FanaticsAuthentic.com).

Fanatics operates more than 300 online and offline partner stores, including the ecommerce business for all major professional sports leagues (NFL, MLB, NBA, NHL, NASCAR, MLS, PGA, Premier League); major media brands (NBC Sports, CBS Sports, FOX Sports); and more than 200 collegiate and professional team properties. In addition to ecommerce, the company's capabilities include multichannel-integrated event and team retail across all leagues and major events such as Kentucky Derby, Ryder Cup and NHL's Winder Classic. NFLSHOP.ca is an ecommerce platform for Canadian NFL fans. Fanatics comprises an innovative vertical ecommerce business model that allows the company to quickly design, manufacture and distribute fan gear, jerseys, headwear and hardgoods. Fanatics Betting and Gaming offers a global database for online sports betting and gaming. Candy Digital by Fanatics is a next-generation digital collectibles company, bringing together digital artists, designers and technologists to develop a broad range of non-fungible tokens (NFTs). Candy Digital's immersive ecosystem allows fans and collectors to purchase, trade and share officially licensed NFTs. Fanatics is headquartered in Florida, and is privately-owned by Kynetic, LLC. The firm has other headquarter locations in California, USA; Manchester, U.K.; and Tokyo, Japan. In January 2022, Fanatics acquired Topps' trading cards and collectibles business, both the physical and digital divisions.

20) New Video Game Console Technologies and Features Boost Sales

Game Console History: Sony's PlayStation 2, released in the fall of 2001, was the first unit to play DVDs and audio CDs while offering top-of-the-line high-tech gaming. By mid-2007, PlayStation 2 had sold 115 million units worldwide, and the company dropped its retail price from $179 to $129, thereby extending the sales life of the unit.

Microsoft was hoping to break Sony's dominance in the market with its Xbox, which was released in November 2001 (with a $500 million marketing budget). Xbox was a major step in the company's attempt to revolutionize home entertainment in the same way that PCs revolutionized the office. The unit is a combination of some of the functions of a high-end PC, complete with high-speed internet port and a powerful graphics chip. Xbox Live, Microsoft's online gaming subscription service, was launched in November 2003 and had 52 million members by mid-2017. It provides gamers anywhere in the world with the ability to play against each other using the internet, and it has evolved into a key component to the video gaming experience.

Sony's PlayStation 3 (PS3) went on sale with great fanfare in November 2006. Sony saw sales surge when prices were reduced in 2009 and again in late 2011. PS3 includes a high-definition DVD player using the Sony standard called Blu-ray. This was a bold move since, in 2006, the entertainment industry was still undecided as to which DVD technology would be embraced by the buying public. Sony was actually taking a loss on the DVD player included in PS3 in order to market Blu-ray technology and soften the blow for movie watchers who would have to buy high-definition versions of their favorite DVDs. The gamble paid off since Blu-ray became a high-definition format of choice.

The debut of Microsoft's $4-billion enhanced game console, the Xbox 360, was a major milestone in video gaming. Released for sale at midnight, November 22, 2005, Xbox 360 was a completely redesigned product. The high-end model has a wireless controller, cables for TV connection, a DVD player, a removable hard drive and a complimentary pass to Xbox Live. The console includes ports for attaching digital cameras or portable music players. The Xbox 360, with its three-core 3.2-gigahertz custom chip from IBM, has been a big hit. The software giant hopes that the popularity of its game systems will spur sales of its other consumer products.

Nintendo, the third key player in video game sets, has been a powerful competitor. Its hand-held game player Nintendo DS (first released in 2004) was the best-selling game machine in the U.S. at the end of 2007. By the end of 2009, total DS units sold worldwide had reached 125.1 million. Meanwhile, in a vigorous attempt to hold on to its top spot and to compete with Sony's PSP, Nintendo launched a small player in 2005, the Game Boy Micro. Modestly priced, it is barely four inches wide and two inches tall. It had a leg up over other portable devices because it is compatible with more than 700 games designed for earlier Game Boy models.

Next, Nintendo released its revolutionary game system, Wii (pronounced "wee"), in 2006, which has been an immense success. Equipped with a state-of-the-art wireless controller and moderately priced, the system provides gamers with sensory-enhanced playing. The controller communicates with sensors (mounted near a television) that respond to the player's body movements. A fishing game, for example, causes the controller to "tug" on the player's hand when a fish is hooked, and the player can then "jerk" on the controller like a fishing pole to reel the catch in. While many new games have been developed for Wii, the new technology also works with long-time game favorites including *Pokémon*, *Mario Bros.* and *The Legend of Zelda.*

For 2010, the big news in electronic games was the November launch of Microsoft's Kinect add-on for Xbox 360. Kinect is a sensory-enhanced system that reacts to body gestures, designed to compete head-on with Wii. Kinect also reacts to users' voice commands. It is revolutionary because, unlike Wii, it does not require the use of a handheld controller. Instead, Kinect incorporates a motion-sensing camera. This device definitely raises consumers' expectations for future machines. Through Kinect, Xbox Live users enjoy YouTube functionality, DVR and TV capability plus the ability to use voice controls. Microsoft acquired Canesta, a manufacturer specializing in semiconductors used in 3-D technology, in late 2010 to further enhance Kinect's three-dimensional experience. Most of the world's major game developers created new games for Kinect. Microsoft sold 8 million units in Kinect's first 60 days on the market, far exceeding its expectations.

Microsoft announced an upgrade to the Xbox 360 console in late 2011 that allows subscribers to watch a variety of mainstream TV programming from providers such as HBO, Verizon FiOS and Comcast Xfinity. Perhaps more importantly, users with Kinect will have the ability to search for programming with voice commands and hand signals. The technology is one step closer to freeing consumers from TV set-top boxes. Microsoft reports that Xbox Live users spent more time watching videos or listening to music than playing games in 2012, and it has released dozens of apps or upgrades to Xbox specifically targeting non-gamers.

Microsoft launched the Xbox One, in November 2013. Xbox One integrates gaming with cable or satellite television and Skype-based voice chatting. (Microsoft owns Skype.) It offers voice control in addition to a motion-sensing camera that works with the Kinect operating system to respond to user gestures. The console is not backwards compatible with Xbox 360 games. Microsoft, like all console makers, has made continuous improvements to the Xbox One's software since the initial launch, including better chat and social functions, improved media player functionality and changes to its DVR features. Another console, the Xbox One S debuted in early 2017, and is 40% smaller than the Xbox One.

Microsoft launched the Xbox One X in November 2017. The unit offers 4K graphics and high-fidelity virtual reality, through eight CPU cores and six teraflops of GPU power.

Nintendo earned headlines with the launch of a 3-D version of its DS game player. Unveiled at the 2011 Electronic Entertainment Expo in Los Angeles, California, the device comes with two screens, one capable of 3-D viewing and the other a standard 2-D. The Nintendo 3DS creates the illusion of depth by placing a parallax barrier in front of a liquid-crystal display which makes a 3-D effect possible without the game player having to wear special glasses.

Sony's response to Nintendo's new 3DS was the late 2011 release of a new hand-held unit called PlayStation Vita (formerly codenamed Next Generation Portable, or NGP). The unit has a five-inch, organic light-emitting diode (OLED) touch-screen display, a rear touch panel and wireless network connectivity. The buzz about Vita is its ability to offer gamers full-scale playing that's portable, as well as mobile access to Sony's full line of entertainment products (including movies, music and games). In addition, Sony is offering PlayStation games on a variety of portable devices such as smartphones and tablet computers running Google's Android operating system.

Meanwhile, Sony's PlayStation 4 (PS4) also launched in time for the Christmas season of 2013. Its new features included the ability to play games streamed over the internet in a practice called "cloud streaming." Games (including games from PlayStation 3) can be played from the cloud, but also from optional discs. In late 2016, Sony released the PlayStation 4 Pro console, with 4K display resolution and more processing power than PS4, just in time for the holiday season. The console's latest versions are the PS4 Slim and the PS4 Pro.

Nintendo released the first of the so-called "eighth generation consoles" in November 2012 with the Wii U. The system builds on the Wii's motion control innovations with high-definition graphics and a controller that features touch screen capabilities. The controller also has the ability to play some games after the connected television has been turned off. The Wii U is backwards-compatible with Wii games.

Later Game Console Releases: The all-new $499 Microsoft Xbox Series X was released on November 10, 2020. Capabilities include 8K resolution support, a solid-state drive (similar to that in Sony's PlayStation 5) for faster load times and frame rates of up to 120 frames per second. Games are streamed via Microsoft's xCloud service rather than downloading full copies. For optimum play, the new console requires a 4K TV that can run games at 120 Hz, which only the latest sets, such as the $1,400 LG CX, offer. The smaller $299 Xbox Series S, also released in November 2020, plays games at 1440p at 60 frames per second. Both units sold out quickly and as of early 2021, many gamers were still watching for restock notices from retailers.

In March 2017, Nintendo released Switch, which acts as both a mobile and home console game. Switch, which retails for about $300, sold 2.74 million units in its first month on the market. At the same time, the well-reviewed *The Legend of Zelda: Breath of the Wild* game for Switch was released which sold more copies on retailer GameStop in early 2017 than units of the Switch player. A stripped-down version of the Switch console was introduced in late 2019 at a lower price-point. Nintendo announced that no new Switch unit would be released in 2020, but the company did launch the Nintendo Switch OLED in late 2021, with a seven-inch OLED screen and enhanced audio.

The newest Sony console, PlayStation 5 (PS5), launched in November 2020. The unit features a solid-state drive, 8K television support, an 8-core AMD chipset, 3D audio and backward compatibility with PS4 games and PSVR hardware. According to Sony, 4.5 million PS5 units were shipped worldwide in 2020.

Xbox Series X and PS5 offer ray tracing, a ground-breaking graphical technology that significantly improves the way light and shadows appear on gaming screens. The same technology is used by video and film makers when combining real action with computer-generated (CG) content. It uses an algorithm to trace the path of light and then simulates the process in which the light interacts with virtual objects, resulting in highly realistic effects. Nvidia, Microsoft and AMD are all working on ray tracing technology. The latest consoles all enable users to access cloud-based games, individually or via subscription.

21) Virtual Reality/Augmented Reality and 3-D Technologies Create Opportunities for the Tech Industry/Immersion Games to Grow

Virtual Reality (VR): One of the most closely watched developments in the technology sector, especially in electronic games, is virtual reality, or "VR." In addition to gaming, potential major uses for VR include training/education as well as entertainment in general. Growth will be boosted by the ability to connect VR and augmented reality (AR) devices to IoT.

California-based Oculus VR headsets make virtual reality seem startlingly lifelike. Its Oculus Rift S headset makes stereoscopic 3-D gaming players using PCs feel immersed in the game, using some components that are commonly found in smartphones and tablets. This is sometimes referred to as "immersion" gaming. The Oculus Go headset requires no PC, no wires and no controller, while the Oculus Quest headset works with an app and a game controller.

Facebook acquired Oculus VR for $2 billion in March 2014. Today's Meta Quest headsets (originally developed by Oculus) bring a realistic feeling to virtual meetings and entertainment, in addition to the obvious advantages for games. Meta planned to release its latest headset, Quest 3, in 2023.

Sony's virtual reality headset, the PlayStation VR, was released in October 2016. Another virtual reality headset is HTC Corporation's Vive. Its price tag includes two wireless controllers and two base stations for 360-degree room-scale motion-tracking.

Google has had a major focus on the potential of VR since 2014. It was the lead investor in a $542 million funding round for Magic Leap, Inc., the developer of an eyeglass-based device that can project computer generated images over real settings (a twist on VR called augmented reality). The Magic Leap One device was released in early 2019.

Microsoft's 3D offering, HoloLens, made its debut in 2015. Another device that promises augmented reality, HoloLens imposes holograms over real views. The headset is designed to allow users to play electronic games, build 3D models and conduct immersive videoconferencing. Microsoft offers a HoloLens Commercial Suite for organizations and a Development Edition for individual developers. In late 2019, Microsoft released Hololens 2, a next generation version designed for the enterprise sector with a wider field of view and hand and eye-tracking.

Microsoft's artificial intelligence capabilities (including its collaboration with OpenAI), its cloud computing platform Azure, its business enterprise tools and its video gaming products all have massive potential to work together with the HoloLens product to create highly innovative services and add-on tools. Microsoft's Windows operating system supports VR headsets from a variety of manufacturers including Acer, Dell, HP, Lenovo Group and Samsung. Samsung's HMD Odyssey headset, for example, features OLED displays and includes headphones and a built-in microphone.

VR equipment sales have seen a disappointing adoption rate, particularly among video gamers, as of early 2023. Sony launched PlayStation VR2 in February 2023, despite sales of its earlier version (PlayStation VR) coming in at only about 5 million units between 2016 and 2019 (less than 10% of the number of traditional PlayStation gaming consoles sold during the same period). Meta Platforms' sales of its Quest VR headsets have been similarly lackluster. Part of the problem is the relatively high cost. HTC and Samsung have also been developing VR sets.

Augmented Reality (AR): AR is a technology that superimposes computer-generated, digital images on a real-time view, creating a composite view. For example, health technicians may use smart glasses, with AR installed, to see the location of a patient's veins before drawing blood, or technicians may wear smart glasses to see schematics and instructions relating to nearby equipment that needs fixing. AR equipment currently available includes Microsoft's HoloLens 2 headset (at about $3,500) and Lenovo's ThinkReality A3 smart glasses (at about $1,500).

SPOTLIGHT: AR Boosts Online Retail

Online shoppers are embracing AR as a way of "trying on" clothing, accessories, cosmetics and more, by imposing images of items for sale on their own faces or bodies captured by cameras on their mobile devices. Warby Parker, for example, has long offered an app on which online shoppers see different glasses frames on their digital faces. Cosmetics retailers Ulta Beauty and MAC Cosmetics launched an AR shoppable filter from Snapchat in February 2022. Snapchat parent Snap, Inc. reported that as of mid-2022, 200 million people were utilizing AR on a daily basis. The company commissioned a study from Deloitte Digital that concluded that online shoppers who use AR had a 94% higher conversion rate than those without.

The Coronavirus pandemic accelerated the adoption of AR since social distancing requires people to stay far apart. Business travel virtually shut down for several months and will likely continue to be curtailed even as businesses reopen. AR technology allows team members to interact from a distance. For example, due to a global curtailment of travel, an Intel engineer in Germany was unable to fly to a chip plant in Arizona that needed his expertise. Intel relayed a video to the engineer of real-time work at the plant via AR goggles, and he was able to walk the plant workers through a vital

repair. Volkswagen AG's Porsche subsidiary reported that use of AR glasses in U.S. service departments more than tripled during the pandemic when technicians got virtual help from counterparts in different cities and different countries. Other sectors that are embracing the technology include health care and defense.

Apple, Inc. was investing heavily in both VR and AR technology. Its headset, called Vision Pro, is expected to offer an 8K display for each eye and has an anticipated release in early 2024 at a price of about $3,500. The company also offers certain AR features on iPhones which, as early as 2018, were equipped with cameras that enable composite images, and it offers tens of thousands of AR apps in its store. Among the more popular AR features for iPhones are the ability to transform a screen within Snapchat with special effects—such as tropical flowers or a star-filled sky. Arki enables users to visualize projects and designs in 3D. The app from eyeglasses retailer Warby Parker utilizes AR to enable users to virtually see, on their faces onscreen, a pair of glasses that they are considering. VR apps for interactive learning are also available. For example, JigSpace enables an in-depth view of a coral reef, and the ability to visualize a machine such as a jet engine from the inside out. Another retailer, IKEA, has an AR-featured app that enables the user to visualize pieces of specific furniture in their homes.

VR and AR uses are stretching far beyond gaming. Surgeons can practice complicated techniques before cutting into patients (Medivis is a pioneer in this field). Corporate training is another area where VR is coming into play. Wal-Mart, Inc., for example, now utilizes VR training in all 200 of its training centers, which serve 140,000 new hires per year.

22) Aging Baby Boomers Will Cause Significant Changes in the Leisure Sector, Including Sports and Activity-Based Travel

The term "Baby Boomer" generally refers to someone born in the U.S. or Europe from 1946 to 1964. The term evolved to describe the children of soldiers and war industry workers who were involved in World War II. When those veterans and workers returned to civilian life, they started or added to families in large numbers. As a result, the Baby Boom generation is one of the largest demographic segments in the U.S. Some Baby Boomers have already reached retirement age. In 2006, the first of the boomers reached 60, a common early retirement age. In 2011, millions began to turn traditional retirement age (65) for the first time. Eventually, the aging of Baby Boomers will result in extremely rapid growth in the senior portion of the population.

The Baby Boom segment will have distinct requirements that should be considered by businesses that want to succeed in evolving markets. A major consideration is the fact that many boomers will attempt to reap the health benefits of exercise for the first time in years, if not for the first time in their lives. Aerobic activity will become vital to those who want to maintain healthy lifestyles, but activities and equipment must be adapted to aging bodies. For example, leaders in the bicycle marketplace are introducing a growing number of models that enable older riders to sit more upright, while leaning over less. Bicycle seats and suspension that are kinder to older bodies will sell well.

One new sport gaining popularity among Americans aged 55 and over is pickleball, a sport played on a small court using wood and graphite rackets and plastic balls. The smaller courts are easier on aging joints than tennis.

Firms that design and make equipment for high-impact or repetitive-motion sports will be striving to create equipment that is easier on older joints and muscles. For example, golf clubs or tennis rackets that have bigger sweet spots or provide more power with less effort in the stroke are logical products for this market.

Lower-impact sports and exercise will gain in favor. Swimming, power walking and day hiking should all have bright futures, as should the firms that manufacture equipment for these activities. Exercise and gym equipment makers will do well to make lines of equipment adapted to, or specifically for, older users. For example, instruction labels on gym equipment will need to have larger font sizes so that the type will be easy for older eyes to read. Softer, more ergonomic grips on weights and other gym equipment make sense. Activities that are easy for older people to enter for the first time will prosper in this market. Pilates and yoga, when taught in a manner suitable for stiffer, older bodies, could continue to boom.

Travel and tours centered on sports and recreation activities will continue to do well, especially where at least some venues are tailored to appeal to older participants. The massive number of affluent, retired consumers will be looking for healthy activities and recreation on their travels. Tours that combine cycling, hiking, walking and other activities of moderate intensity are good fits in

this market, and demand will grow sharply. Tours that combine hiking or cycling with luxury accommodations or unique lodging in pristine remote settings (including the rapidly growing trend of ecotourism) will find large numbers of customers. Sporting goods manufacturers would do well to provide sponsorships and test equipment to tour operators and should seek ways to offer seminars and sports instruction that fit neatly with the growing activity-based tour business. They will do especially well to target the 60+ age segment with marketing, products and services tailored to that group.

Tours that offer participation in cultural activities, environmental projects and educational opportunities will also enjoy soaring growth. Many travelers want to do much more than relax or shop while on tours—they want to get to know and understand the local people, help solve local problems and enrich their own lives in the process.

A select set of seniors can be extremely active and athletic. Older athletes are competing in senior and "masters" events, often setting startling records of speed and endurance. Many athletes in their 60s are either discovering exceptional ability for the first time or nurturing and toning up athletic prowess that they haven't taken time to use in decades. Runners, tennis players, swimmers, cyclists and track and field participants well past 50, 60 and even 70 years of age are performing well (sometimes brilliantly). For example, Jeanne Daprano, a former third grade schoolteacher, entered masters track events for the first time in her late 40s. In her seventieth year, she became the first woman to break the seven-minute mile past age 70, running the distance in 6:46.91. At age 75, in 2012, she set world records in her age bracket for runs of 400 meters, 800 meters and one mile.

23) Athletic Footwear Sales Boom, Drawing Big Names from Athletes to Designers

Athletic shoes have long been sporting the names and endorsements of famous professional athletes, particularly basketball legend Michael Jordan. Nike's line of Air Jordan shoes has been the top selling shoe brand of all time. Other athletes in the Nike stable include LeBron James, Kevin Durant, Giannis Antetokounmpo and Carmelo Anthony. This trend to sell a shoe under an athlete's name is called "marquee footwear."

A new twist to marquee footwear is that which sports a famous designer's name instead of an athlete's. Stella McCartney, a high-fashion designer and daughter of former Beatle Paul McCartney, began collaborating with Adidas in 2005 for hip athletic shoes and clothing. Another designer/athletic shoe partnership was that between traditional shoemaker Cole Haan and its former parent Nike. The combination resulted in a line of comfortable street shoes called Cole Haan Nike Air.

Prices for top basketball shoes are in the hundreds of dollars, with a few collectible models topping $1,000. Of course, there are cheaper, more fashionable alternatives on the market which are attracting teen consumers especially. One big leader in the trend toward chic athletic footwear is Germany-based Puma. Puma, which experienced dismal sales in the 1980s while Nike leaped to the top of the market, is enjoying a renaissance. The company has focused on style and fashion, aided by designers such as Germany's Jil Sander and American supermodel-turned-yoga guru Christy Turlington. Although Puma's sales figures are still dwarfed by heavy hitters like Nike and Reebok, it continues to do well.

Nike overhauled its computerized supply systems to increase efficiency and focused on international markets for soccer and fashion shoes and apparel. (Nike gets more than one-half of its revenues from markets outside the U.S.) Nike's marketing budget is legendary, including multimillion dollar sports star endorsement deals.

24) The Vast Majority of Shoes Sold in the U.S. Are Made Elsewhere

U.S. retail stores specializing in shoes sold $40.6 billion in goods during 2022, per U.S. Census Bureau reports, up significantly from $27.0 billion in 2020. (This number does not include the massive number of shoes sold in department stores, in sporting goods stores and on internet sites like Zappos.)

According to the American Apparel & Footwear Association (www.aafaglobal.org), Americans purchase more than 2.2 billion pairs of shoes yearly. About 98% of those shoes are imported, and China is one of the most important sources. (However, as wages and other costs are rising in China, manufacturing is starting to migrate to lower cost nations such as Vietnam and Cambodia.) Major Chinese shoe manufacturers include Yue Yuen Industrial Holdings Ltd., Li Ning Co. Ltd. and Belle International Holdings Ltd. One long-term result of the Coronavirus pandemic may be a desire by shoe brands to spread their manufacturing base over a wider range of nations in order to be less reliant on China.

While a handful of manufacturers, such as Allen-Edmonds (a high-end maker of men's shoes), are able to maintain factories in the U.S., domestic manufacturing is all but dead. Another exception is New Balance. This maker of high-end running and athletic shoes operates five factories in the U.S. While New Balance gets much of its inventory from overseas factories, the firm has taken an interesting position with its manufacturing philosophy. It is the only major running shoe brand that continues to operate plants in the U.S., while its major competitors, such as Nike and Reebok, get most or all of their shoes from Asia.

25) 3-D Printing and Robotics Revolutionize Manufacture of Shoes and Fabrics

With the advent of 3-D printers, advanced software and robots in factories, shoes and clothing can be made more quickly and efficiently than ever before. Nike launched a revolutionary new running shoe called the Flyknit. The 5.6-ounce, high tech shoe is made from synthetic yarn, using a machine that knits together the upper part of the shoe, which is then attached to the sole. This process not only produces a lighter-weight shoe (which running enthusiasts have long awaited) with less manufacturing waste, the Flyknit requires far less labor since it has 35 fewer pieces to assemble than comparable shoes.

The savings may make it possible for Nike to have the Flyknit manufactured in the U.S. While still more expensive than production overseas, the company will spend less on shipping and fulfill orders more quickly to meet demand. Nike also offers Nike By You, a customizable shoe option both in stores and online.

Adidas, the German shoe and athletic apparel manufacturer, has a new facility called Speedfactory in the town of Anspach, Germany with robots and 3-D printers. The plant has a capacity of 500,000 pairs of athletic shoes per year. Adidas built a similar facility near Atlanta, Georgia, USA in 2018. However, as of late 2019, the firm closed both the German and American facilities to focus on production in Vietnam and China.

Brooks, a shoe manufacturer based in Seattle, Washington, is utilizing HP's FitStation biomechanical measuring system for its new bespoke shoes. The system makes a 3-D scan of customer's feet while in motion, enabling Brooks to make shoes of ideal density for up to 30 zones of the foot.

Carbon, Inc. (www.carbon3d.com) is a 3-D printer manufacturer in California that has made athletic shoe soles for Adidas. Carbon's process employs a technology called digital light synthesis, which uses software to control chemical reactions, resulting in the "growth" of parts based on liquid polymers. The technology produces 12 classes of materials including heat-resistant cyanate ester for use in automotive and aerospace parts and elastomers that are used in shoes. Another company, Betabrand (www.betabrand.com), partners with shoe and accessory manufacturer Li and Fung to combine crowdsourcing with 3-D digital rendering. Website visitors vote on popular styles, with winners becoming available in as little as five days.

SPOTLIGHT: Garment Factory Automation

While many industries are automating, with robots replacing workers in factories, the garment industry has been somewhat protected by the complexity of cutting and sewing. The work has remained in the hands of millions of factory workers around the world. However, Steve Dickerson, a professor at the Georgia Institute of Technology and the founder of a startup called SoftWear Automation, built and patented a robotic sewing machine in 2012. The machines, called Sewbots, use high-speed photography that captures up to 1,000 frames per second to track material as it is sewn. Software analyzes the photographs fast enough to make tiny adjustments necessary to switch positions when necessary and even feed fabric into the sewing machine when needed.

A materials-handling system called LOWRY was developed to pick up pieces of fabric and move them to other machines for buttonholes, zippers or related finishing tasks. Tianyuan Garments Co. in eastern China was recently opened a $20 million factory staffed by approximately 330 robots built by SoftWear Automation. As more garment factories automate and are freed from cost of labor issues, look for more companies to relocate production to areas where the bulk of their customers reside.

---

26) Exercise Apparel Sales Rise/ Athleisure Clothing Sales Soar

While Americans (as well as residents of many other countries from Mexico to China) have been putting on weight, they have also developed a keen interest in sports apparel and workout gear to wear at the gym and in other leisure activities. This is one of the fastest-growing product categories in the apparel and shoe sector. Athletic apparel is increasingly worn as streetwear as well, in a trend called "athleisure." During the very casual work-from-home trend launched by the Coronavirus, this type of apparel got a huge boost.

Sports apparel is divided into several categories including branded athletic apparel, performance apparel, fitness apparel and branded activewear. Plunkett Research estimates that for 2022, men's and women's activewear and sports apparel sales reached $72 billion in the U.S. Brands in the sector include lululemon athletica, Athleta (which was acquired by Gap, Inc. in 2008), Lucy (acquired by VF Corporation in 2007) and Adidas by Stella McCartney.

Sports and fitness apparel are big hits with consumers in Asia. For example, in China's major cities, including Beijing and Shanghai, major brands have very high visibility and consumer acceptance. In the malls and biggest shopping districts, large stores are devoted to Nike, Adidas and other global brands. Chinese consumers are eager to be attached to Western sports and sports figures. NBA (the U.S.-based National Basketball Association) has large stores in China dedicated to basketball fashions and accessories, and immense graphics of American basketball stars are visible from streets and sidewalks.

Athleisure is putting the squeeze on sales of support garments such as girdles, body shapers and control-top panty hose. More women are choosing the comfort of yoga pants over confining slacks, dresses or skirts worn over flattering shapewear. Shapewear companies are scrambling to reinvent themselves. For example, SPANX hired former Nike head of apparel Jan Singer to revamp the company's products, focusing more on lighter, more comfortable everyday wear such as jeans, underwear and bathing suits. SPANX has opened a small number of retail stores in addition to its wholesale business, and it is making products for men as well as women.

Growth in China will likely continue, as the Chinese government hopes to see a significant increase in its sports industry by 2025. National as well as local leaders are working to promote sports races and tournaments, build new arenas and support television stations to cover events. Regulatory barriers to sports equipment and apparel companies are being lifted.

Adidas has long-term plans to increase the number of stores that sell its products in China, with today's total around 12,000 locations. The company is also establishing soccer programs in 20,000 Chinese elementary and middle schools over three years, training 50,000 teachers and operating a national summer soccer camp. Adidas is hoping to promote soccer in China as effectively as the NBA has promoted basketball in that nation. However, it remains to be seen what slowdown in the Chinese sports and athletic apparel sector may occur as a result of the Coronavirus pandemic.

SPOTLIGHT: lululemon athletica, inc.

One of the biggest growth stories in exercise apparel is Canada-based retailer lululemon. Known for high quality, and high priced, yoga and exercise apparel, the company has been growing at a blazing speed while maintaining impressive profit margins. The firm has more than 600 corporate-owned stores in 18 countries. Even more impressive were its financial results. The stores enjoy one of the highest retail sales per square foot rates in the apparel industry, at $2,000. The firm has done a remarkable job of building a community around its stores, with free yoga lessons and a strategy that sees sales personnel as educators about lifestyle and apparel, while it has attracted legions of professional fitness instructors to act as ambassadors in gyms for lululemon apparel.

---

27) Sports Equipment and Social Media Converge

As people spend more and more time on social media sites and apps, it is not surprising that they would interact with friends and others while exercising or playing team sports. Equipment makers have an excellent opportunity to build hardware and software into their products in a way that will enable users to connect with others.

An excellent example is Peloton Interactive, Inc., which is a stationary bike and treadmill designer and producer of live-streaming, instructional indoor classes. While the firm sells its highly popular, proprietary equipment, its real business model is based around subscription fees paid by users of those bikes. The firm's virtual cycling classes initially revolved around the in-house designed, Peloton Bike. The Peloton Bike is a sophisticated, carbon steel and aluminum stationary bike that is integrated with a 21.5-inch full HD 1080p, wireless-ready, Bluetooth-ready, touchscreen console. The console includes two stereo speakers and a front-facing camera. The interface allows the bike's rider to participate in studio cycling classes with highly qualified instructors, from the comfort and convenience of the rider's own home and own schedule. The result is a very high quality, boutique-style fitness class

delivered via live streaming to the home. Through their monthly subscription fee, users of the Peloton Bike have access to a variety of classes covering various moods and styles. Additionally, there are over ten daily live rides streamed from the firm's NYC studio, whereby a user can ride along with a real class, as well as thousands of on-demand rides users can access through the Peloton Bike's interactive console, filtered by instructor, type, length, difficulty or as previously saved favorite rides. More recently, Peloton launched the Peloton Tread treadmill for running classes and the Peloton Guide, which superimposes images of the user lifting weights along with data about reps performed, calories and effort expended alongside the televised class coach.

Other exercise/social media combinations include the Fitbit community and Nike+. These communities unite people, who use wearable sensors to track their activities, with apps and web sites where they can compare distances and intensities, share nutrition and diet information and cheer each other on. Many other firms now offer compelling workout equipment with access to digital classes embedded.

28) The Future of the Sports Industry Will Be Shaped by Technologies and Demographics

Several factors will drive significant changes in the global sports industry over the long-term. These include demographics, technology and the regulatory environment, as well as consumer habits and interests.

To begin with, a rising middle class in nations like India, China and Indonesia are likely to enjoy growing incomes that will enable them to indulge in pastimes like viewing sports on newly acquired widescreen televisions. These growing incomes will also fuel the sale of consumer sports and recreational goods, sporting apparel such as running shoes and gym memberships.

Some segments of the sports industry will have to battle changing habits and interests among younger consumers. The major sports leagues in the U.S. have recently been suffering falling attendance at live games, while TV and cable networks are facing the effects of fewer viewers of broadcasts. It's easy for younger fans, who were raised with advanced technologies, to keep up with scores and game highlights on their smartphones without any significant to attending or viewing entire games.

Technologies will continue to have a very major impact on sporting goods. Consumers already

benefit from advanced fabrics in sporting apparel
(moisture wicking, for example), as well as running
shoes and personal monitors that capture data on their
activities and motion. Data capture technologies are
also showing up in items such as golf clubs.
Advanced materials, such as super-strong carbon-
based nanotechnology, will be incorporated in a wide
range of sports gear. These trends will accelerate
broadly, and may have a profound effect on the way
that people enjoy sports and recreation.

Seniors in rapidly-aging nations such as the U.S.,
Germany and China will be willing to spend on a
wide range of sporting goods and services geared to
their particular needs. The growing popularity of
Pickle Ball, which is a slower, easier-to-play tennis-
style game, is a good example. Gyms and exercise
gear aimed at seniors may become popular.

eSports, that is, the advent of organized play of
electronic games, is growing very quickly. Fans are
clearly excited about the prospects of attending live
game tournaments where they watch highly-skilled
pros play. Fans sit in stadium seats and watch the
action on giant TV monitors. eSports are showing up
in a big way on college campuses. Leagues are
growing, and sponsors are eager to support the eSport
trend. Special eSports stadiums can be found in
several cities, including Las Vegas.

Legalized sports betting is having a significant
impact on the sports industry. Major sports leagues
will benefit from this trend by controlling the data
generated by their teams, players and games.
Smartphone-based betting will enable fans to watch a
game or tournament and bet on it at the same time.
Will that tennis pro win this set? Will this football
team score in this quarter? Technology and
smartphones will enable endless ways to make bets,
large or small. For better or worse, this could
revolutionize the world of sports.

Chapter 2

SPORTS & RECREATION INDUSTRY STATISTICS

Contents:

Sports & Recreation Industry Statistics and Market Size Overview	**36**
Global Sports Industry Revenues, 2020-2022	**37**
Selected U.S. Sports Industry Revenues: 2015-2021	**38**
Sports Industry, Estimated Sources of Revenue & Expenses, U.S.: 2016-2021	**39**
U.S. Spectator Sports, Performing Arts & Related Industries, Breakdown of Expenses: 2018-2021	**40**
Estimated Monthly Sporting Goods Stores Retail Sales, U.S.: 1992- March 2023	**41**
Overview of the Media Contracts of the Four Big Sports Leagues	**42**
Sports Industry Employment by Business Type, U.S.: 2019-2023	**43**

Sports & Recreation Industry Statistics and Market Size Overview

	Amount	Units	Year/Season	Source
Estimated Size of the Sports and Recreation Industry, U.S.[1]	587.7	Bil. US$	2022	PRE
Estimated Size of the Global Sports and Recreation Industry[1]	1.6	Tril. US$	2022	PRE
Major League Baseball (MLB)				
MLB League Revenue	11.0	Bil. US$	2022	PRE
Number of MLB Teams	30	Teams	2023	MLB
Average MLB Game Attendance	27,267	Spectators	2023	ESPN
National Football League (NFL)				
NFL Revenue	16.0	Bil. US$	2022/2023	PRE
Number of NFL Teams	32	Teams	2023	NFL
Average NFL Game Attendance	67,288	Spectators	2021/2022	ESPN
National Basketball Association (NBA)				
NBA League Revenue	10.1	Bil. US$	2021/2022	PRE
Number of NBA Teams	30	Teams	2023	NBA
Average NBA Game Attendance	18,077	Spectators	2020/2021	ESPN
National Hockey League (NHL)				
NHL League Revenue	5.4	Bil. US$	2021/2022	PRE
Number of NHL Teams	32	Teams	2023	NHL
Average NHL Game Attendance	18,371	Spectators	2020/2021	ESPN
Other Sports Industry Data				
Major League Soccer (MLS) Revenue	1	Bil. US$	2022	PRE
NCAA Sports Revenue (Including Div. I, II and III)	1.1	Bil. US$	2021/2022	NCAA
Spectator Sports Revenues[2]	44.1	Bil. US$	2021	Census
Sporting Goods Stores Retail Sales, U.S.	56.3	Bil. US$	2022	Census
Number of Health Clubs, U.S.	32,270	Clubs	2021	IHRSA
Health Club Revenue, Worldwide	78.52	Bil. US$	2022	PRE

PRE = Plunkett Research estimate

IHRSA = International Health, Racquet & Sportsclub Association

1 Includes activities of all types, incl. sporting goods manufacturing and retailing, sports related amusement & recreation, licensing, betting, collectibles, etc.

[2]Includes racetracks, sports teams and other spectator sports.

Source: Plunkett Research,® Ltd.

Global Sports Industry Revenues, 2020-2022

(In Billions of US$)

	2020	2021	2022
Total	**1,354.9**	**1,439.7**	1,497.3
Major Professional Leagues and Teams	80.0	90.0	93.6
College Sports (NCAA)	0.9	1.2	1.2
Other Spectator Sports, Ticket Sales and Misc. Revenues	40.0	60.0	62.4
Sporting Goods at Retail [1]	178.5	175.0	182.0
Sports Apparel at Retail [2]	170.0	160.0	166.4
Amusement and Recreation [3]	152.5	175.5	182.5
Sporting Goods Manufacturing	65.0	63.0	65.5
Other [4]	668.0	715.0	743.6

Note: These figures are estimates. Actual results may vary from those stated here. Details may not add to totals because of rounding.

[1] Specialty and non-specialty stores plus online sales (incl. bicycles, boats, other transport).

[2] Apparel, shoes and activewear at retail, all venues.

[3] Includes Skiing, Golf Courses, Tennis, Marinas, Bowling and Health Club Facilities.

[4] Includes Legal Sports Betting, Illegal Sports Betting, Publishing, Sponsorships, Licensed Merchandise & Collectibles, Video and Online Games, Advertising, Fantasy Sports, Other Goods and Services, Athlete Management and Representation.

Source: Plunkett Research Estimate

Plunkett Research, ® Ltd.

www.plunkettresearch.com

Selected U.S. Sports Industry Revenues: 2015-2021

(In Millions of US$; Latest Year Available)

NAICS Code	Kind of business	2021	2020	2019	2018	2017	2016	2015
Selected sports industry revenues for employer firms								
7112	Spectator sports	44,174	35,806	49,858	48,090	46,202	42,172	39,602
711211	Sports teams and clubs*	32,549	26,170	37,083	35,741	34,249	30,897	28,576
711212	Racetracks*	7,509	5,974	8,827	8,618	8,285	7,580	7,470
711219	Other spectator sports*	4,116	3,662	3,948	3,731	3,668	3,695	3,556
7113	Promoters of performing arts, sports, and similar events	26,130	17,858	33,760	32,105	29,367	26,742	25,473
7114	Agents and managers for artists, athletes, entertainers and other public figures	9,423	6,729	9,298	8,674	7,868	7,728	7,223
7139	Other amusement and recreation industries	91,310	69,621	86,825	82,664	79,505	76,138	71,822
71391	Golf courses and country clubs*	28,315	23,583	24,096	23,744	23,090	22,665	21,993
71392	Skiing facilities*	3,442	3,149	3,357	3,160	2,989	2,698	2,382
71393	Marinas*	NA	5,239	5,174	4,926	4,539	4,326	4,253
71394	Fitness and recreational sports centers*	31,558	24,361	35,889	33,971	33,042	31,223	28,838
71395	Bowling centers*	3,373	2,334	4,109	3,708	3,480	3,461	3,386
71399	All other amusement and recreation industries*	16,969	10,955	14,200	13,155	12,365	11,765	10,970
NAICS Code	**Kind of business**	**2021/20**	**2020/19**	**2019/18**	**2018/17**	**2017/16**	**2016/15**	**2015/14**
Percent change in revenue for selected sports industries' employer firms								
7112	Spectator sports	23.4%	-28.2%	3.7%	4.1%	9.6%	6.5%	6.3%
711211	Sports teams and clubs*	24.4%	-29.4%	3.8%	4.4%	10.8%	8.1%	7.2%
711212	Racetracks*	25.7%	-32.3%	2.4%	4.0%	9.3%	1.5%	3.2%
711219	Other spectator sports*	12.4%	-7.2%	5.8%	1.7%	-0.7%	3.9%	5.9%
7113	Promoters of performing arts, sports, and similar events	46.3%	-47.1%	5.2%	9.3%	9.8%	5.0%	15.7%
7114	Agents and managers for artists, athletes, entertainers and other public figures	40.0%	-27.6%	7.2%	10.2%	1.8%	7.0%	8.2%
7139	Other amusement and recreation industries	31.2%	-19.8%	5.0%	4.0%	4.4%	6.0%	5.9%
71391	Golf courses and country clubs*	20.1%	-2.1%	1.5%	2.8%	1.9%	3.1%	3.6%
71392	Skiing facilities*	9.3%	-6.2%	6.2%	5.7%	10.8%	13.3%	-5.8%
71393	Marinas*	NA	1.3%	5.0%	8.5%	4.9%	1.7%	1.2%
71394	Fitness and recreational sports centers*	29.5%	-32.1%	5.6%	2.8%	5.8%	8.3%	8.1%
71395	Bowling centers*	44.5%	-43.2%	10.8%	6.6%	0.5%	2.2%	-0.5%
71399	All other amusement and recreation industries*	54.9%	-22.9%	7.9%	6.4%	5.1%	7.2%	12.4%

Notes: Dollar volume estimates are published in millions of dollars; consequently, results may not be additive. Estimates cover taxable and tax-exempt firms and are not adjusted for price changes.

Source: U.S. Census Bureau

Plunkett Research, ® Ltd.   www.plunkettresearch.com

Sports Industry,
Estimated Sources of Revenue & Expenses, U.S.: 2016-2021

(In Millions of US$; Latest Year Available)

NAICS Code	Sources of Revenue for Taxable Employer Firms	2021	2020	2019	2018	2017	2016
711211	**Sports Teams & Clubs**						
	Total revenue	32,549	26,552	37,083	35,741	34,249	30,897
	Admissions revenue	7,081	S	S	S	S	S
	All other revenue	25,468	20,881	S	S	S	S
711212	**Racetracks**						
	Total revenue	7,509	6,137	8,827	8,618	8,285	7,580
	Admissions revenue	S	S	S	S	747	637
	All other revenue	6,535	5,382	7,679	7,849	7,538	6,943
711219	**Other Spectator Sports**						
	Total revenue	4,116	3,728	3,948	3,731	3,668	3,695
	Admissions revenue	562	S	S	S	S	177
	All other revenue	3,554	3,517	3,649	3,499	3,477	3,518

NAICS Code	Expenses for Employer Firms	2021	2020	2019	2018	2017	2016
711211	Sports teams & clubs	32,630	28,385	33,167	31,376	29,893	27,385
711212	Racetracks	5,690	4,989	S	S	S	5,948
711219	Other spectator sports	3,441	3,203	3,505	3,525	3,264	3,257
7113	Promoters of performing arts, sports & similar events	24,332	18,629	26,926	25,518	23,472	21,290
7114	Agents & managers for artists, athletes, entertainers & other public figures	6,473	4,930	6,583	6,141	5,826	5,613
71391	Golf courses & country clubs	23,589	20,848	21,853	21,471	20,671	20,177
71392	Skiing facilities	2,686	2,450	2,692	2,589	2,488	2,225
71393	Marinas	3,738	3,495	3,568	3,453	3,262	3,205
71394	Fitness & recreational sports centers	29,604	24,771	31,169	29,787	29,670	28,042
71395	Bowling centers	2,699	2,239	3,115	2,830	2,794	2,770
71399	All other amusement & recreation industries	12,663	9,536	11,508	10,780	10,293	9,579

Notes: Dollar volume estimates are published in millions of dollars; consequently, results may not be additive.

S = Estimate does not meet publication standards because of high sampling variability (coefficient of variation is greater than 30%) or poor response quality (total quantity response rate is less than 50%). Unpublished estimates derived from this table by subtraction are subject to these same limitations and should not be attributed to the U.S. Census Bureau.

Source: U.S. Census Bureau
Plunkett Research, ® Ltd.
www.plunkettresearch.com

U.S. Spectator Sports, Performing Arts & Related Industries, Breakdown of Expenses: 2018-2021

(In Millions of US$; Latest Year Available)

Expenses	2021	2020	2019	2018
Expense	98,361	83,160	108,646	103,587
Gross annual payroll	43,110	38,226	46,780	44,133
Payroll taxes, employer paid insurance premiums (except health), and other employer benefits	4,897	4,725	NA	2,541
Employer's cost for fringe benefits	1,732	S	S	S
Temporary staff and leased employee expense	1,732	S	S	1,886
Expensed purchases of equipment, other materials, parts, and supplies	2,431	1,968	S	S
Expensed purchases of software	350	276	S	S
Depreciation and amortization charges	4,933	4,105	4,507	4,337
Data processing and other purchased computer services	360	294	NA	154
Purchased communication services	1,864	1,623	NA	345
All other operating expenses	27,630	S	S	45,068

Note: Dollar volume estimates are published in millions of dollars; consequently, results may not be additive. Estimates cover taxable and tax-exempt firms and are not adjusted for price changes.

S = Estimate does not meet publication standards because of high variability (coefficient of variation greater than 30%), poor response quality (total quantity response rate is less than 50%) or other concerns about the estimate's quality. NA = Not Available.

Source: U.S. Census Bureau

Plunkett Research, ® Ltd.

www.plunkettresearch.com

Estimated Monthly Sporting Goods Stores Retail Sales, U.S.: 1992-March 2023

(NAICS 45111; In Millions of US$; Not Seasonally Adjusted)

	Jan	Feb	Mar	Apr	May	Jun	Jul	Aug	Sep	Oct	Nov	Dec	Total
1992	972	1,100	1,214	1,267	1,293	1,334	1,340	1,377	1,206	1,120	1,207	2,153	13,430
1993	1,032	984	1,213	1,367	1,387	1,457	1,457	1,531	1,313	1,199	1,377	2,474	14,317
1994	1,168	1,193	1,488	1,551	1,551	1,677	1,584	1,737	1,470	1,324	1,471	2,611	16,214
1995	1,224	1,248	1,599	1,606	1,645	1,750	1,705	1,846	1,569	1,398	1,548	2,731	17,138
1996	1,327	1,309	1,649	1,702	1,773	1,895	1,833	1,992	1,594	1,453	1,608	2,675	18,135
1997	1,337	1,331	1,609	1,726	1,788	1,970	1,838	1,955	1,595	1,521	1,651	2,846	18,321
1998	1,381	1,407	1,754	1,820	1,938	2,120	1,975	2,038	1,701	1,607	1,685	2,858	19,426
1999	1,485	1,469	1,827	1,888	1,993	2,215	2,062	2,143	1,847	1,711	1,832	3,227	20,472
2000	1,591	1,681	2,065	1,991	2,187	2,319	2,237	2,257	2,007	1,725	1,939	3,309	21,999
2001	1,739	1,704	2,111	2,071	2,185	2,352	2,199	2,382	1,984	1,882	2,151	3,398	22,760
2002	1,739	1,763	2,167	2,157	2,141	2,276	2,177	2,384	1,998	1,897	2,133	3,387	22,832
2003	1,761	1,747	2,121	2,135	2,182	2,325	2,293	2,548	2,075	1,970	2,200	3,643	23,357
2004	1,901	1,888	2,287	2,221	2,305	2,514	2,530	2,621	2,216	2,103	2,306	3,748	24,892
2005	1,956	1,976	2,408	2,539	2,493	2,655	2,652	2,788	2,338	2,246	2,492	4,170	26,543
2006	2,100	2,154	2,792	2,713	2,776	3,012	2,872	3,085	2,752	2,447	2,710	4,456	29,413
2007	2,200	2,171	2,969	2,737	3,087	3,380	3,165	3,378	2,712	2,570	2,939	4,496	31,308
2008	2,314	2,413	2,993	2,982	3,273	3,405	3,305	3,539	2,722	2,479	2,794	4,525	32,219
2009	2,442	2,347	2,894	2,959	3,119	3,290	3,209	3,418	2,779	2,571	2,788	4,758	31,816
2010	2,373	2,303	3,118	3,001	3,078	3,413	3,266	3,415	2,828	2,611	3,107	4,894	32,513
2011	2,414	2,456	3,266	3,246	3,169	3,505	3,334	3,623	3,011	2,746	3,227	4,998	33,997
2012	2,505	2,723	3,607	3,304	3,455	3,829	3,551	3,969	3,161	2,959	3,478	5,601	36,541
2013	3,066	3,010	3,822	3,417	3,645	3,939	3,802	4,141	3,212	3,142	3,726	5,479	38,922
2014	2,700	2,779	3,522	3,488	3,647	3,897	3,806	4,345	3,486	3,403	3,865	5,785	38,938
2015	2,839	2,831	3,690	3,573	3,829	4,098	4,102	4,331	3,649	3,422	3,828	6,134	40,192
2016	3,057	3,184	4,009	3,729	3,873	4,554	4,241	4,230	3,527	3,340	3,809	5,746	41,553
2017	2,915	2,990	3,732	3,597	3,750	4,050	3,855	4,156	3,506	3,332	3,910	5,400	39,793
2018	2,721	2,963	3,693	3,446	3,661	3,925	3,711	3,905	3,003	3,061	3,542	4,798	37,631
2019	2,696	2,780	3,571	3,535	3,671	3,994	3,959	4,183	3,276	3,376	3,660	5,107	38,701
2020	2,946	3,054	3,399	2,565	4,307	5,779	5,335	5,047	4,699	4,581	4,527	6,661	46,239
2021	4,060	3,754	6,035	5,760	5,586	5,912	5,721	5,752	4,973	5,011	5,624	7,535	58,188
2022	3,886	4,022	5,271	5,228	5,278	5,949	5,658	5,887	4,953	4,957	5,271	7,385	56,360
2023*	4,061	4,067	5,253	5,219	--	--	--	--	--	--	--	--	18,600

* Preliminary Estimate.

Source: U.S. Census Bureau

Plunkett Research, ® Ltd.

www.plunkettresearch.com

Overview of the Media Contracts of the Four Big Sports Leagues

National Football League (NFL)

Network TV	CBS: Super Bowl in '23, '27 & '31; AFC package, $1.85 billion per year, 2023-33
	FOX: Super Bowl in '24, '28 & '32; NFC package, $2.03 billion per year, 2023-33
	NBC: Super Bowl in '25, '29 & '33; Sun. night games, $1.71 billion per year, 2023-33
	ABC: (w/ESPN & Disney) Super Bowl in '26 & '30; Pro Bowl 2018-33, $2.7 billion per year, 2022-33
Cable TV	ESPN: Monday Night Football 2022-2033 (plus rotating rights to air Super Bowl beginning in 2026) $2.7 bil. yr. (See ABC)
Streaming Services	Amazon Prime Video: Thursday Night Football About $1 bil. yr, 2023-2033; Youtube, Sunday Night, $2 bil yr. 2023-2033
Terrestrial Radio	Sports USA Radio Network; Dial-Global; Compass Media; ESPN Radio; Individual teams
Satellite Radio	Sirius XM: All games, through Super Bowl 2027
Video Games	Electronic Arts, Inc.: Exclusive deal, through May 2026
Internet	NFL.com (operated by NFL)

Major League Baseball (MLB)

Network TV	FOX: $5.1 billion ($510 million annually), 2018-28, 12 Saturday afternoon games, 40 games on Fox Sports 1 (cable), All-Star Game, 2 Division Series, alternate League Championship Series, World Series
Cable TV	ESPN: $5.6 billion total, 2022-28, Mon. & Wed. night, Sun. night (exclusive), tiebreaker games, 1 Wild Card game
	TBS: $2.8 billion ($300 million annually), 2022-28, regular-season Tuesday night games, 1 Nat'l game per week, 1 Wild Card game, 2 Division Series, Alt. League Championship Series
	MLB Network
Satellite TV	DirecTV
Streaming Services:	Apple TV+ Fri. night; Peacock
Terrestrial Radio	ESPN Radio: nat'l broadcast rights, Sunday Night Baseball, playoffs, World Series. Teams also have their own regional networks.
Satellite Radio	Sirius XM
Video Games	Non-exclusive, Sony and MLB Advanced Media
Internet	MLB Advanced Media

National Basketball Association (NBA)

Network TV	ABC: (w/ESPN): $2.6 billion total per year from network and cable TV, through 2024/25
Cable TV	ESPN: (w/ABC): included in ABC Network TV above, through 2024/25
	TNT: included in ABC Network TV above, through 2024/25
Satellite TV	DirecTV: Out-of-market games (exclusive)
Terrestrial Radio	ESPN Radio
Satellite Radio	Sirius XM
Video Games	Non-exclusive, Electronic Arts, Take-Two, Sony Computer Entertainment America
Internet	NBA TV

National Hockey League (NHL)

Network TV	ESPN: ($400M annually) 21-28, 25 regular season per year (+ 75 more on ESPN+/Hulu), 6 playoff games, 1 conf. final, Alt. Stanely Cup finals on ABC (4 finals)	
	Turner: ($225M annually) 21-28, Winter Classic annually, 72 regular-season games per year, 6 playoff games, 1 conf. final, Alt. Stanley Cup finals (3 finals)	
Cable TV	ESPN, TNT, ABC, NHL Network	Canada: Rogers: 12 years, $5.3 bil., 2014/15-2025/26
Satellite TV	DirecTV & Dish: Out-of-market games (non-exclusive)	
Streaming Services	ESPN; Hulu	
Terrestrial Radio	Non-exclusive	
Satellite Radio	Sirius XM	
Video Games	Non-exclusive, Electronic Arts	
Internet	NHL Network	

Source: Plunkett Research,® Ltd.
Plunkett Research, ® Ltd.   www.plunkettresearch.com

Sports Industry Employment by Business Type, U.S.: 2019-2023

(Annual Estimates in Thousands of Employed Workers; Not Seasonally Adjusted)

NAICS Code	Industry Sector	2019	2020	2021	2022	2023[1]
Leisure & Hospitality						
711	Performing arts and spectator sports	518.9	336.3	381.0	513.4	524.2
7112	Spectator sports	254.2	108.2	119.4	135.7	140.2
711211	Sports teams and clubs	102.4	65.7	72.9	78.2	94.2
711212	Racetracks	29.7	22.8	26.2	29.9	28.0
711219	Other spectator sports	22.1	19.7	20.2	23.1	24.1
7113, 4	Arts and sports promoters, agents and managers for public figures	181.0	111.3	129.6	182.0	192.0
7139	Other amusement and recreation industries	1,406.2	1,063.0	1,200.8	1,384.6	1,409.5
71391	Golf courses and country clubs	368.6	332.9	359.8	401.0	410.0
71392	Skiing facilities	45.0	38.6	41.7	50.3	48.8
71393	Marinas	39.0	32.4	37.2	37.6	38.2
71394	Fitness and recreational sports centers	661.1	463.9	513.4	603.5	619.1
71395	Bowling centers	71.8	44.3	56.7	70.6	70.6
71399	All other amusement and recreation industries	220.7	160.9	192.0	215.7	226.0
Wholesale Trade						
42391	Sporting goods	55.3	56.1	60.4	66.7	67.3
Retail Trade						
45111	Sporting goods retailers	273.0	250.3	279.0	308.4	308.4

Occupation Code	May 2022 Data	# Emp-loyed[2]	Median Hourly Wage	Mean Hourly Wage	Mean Annual Wage[3]	Mean Wage RSE[4]
13-1011	Agents and Business Managers of Artists, Performers and Athletes	13.3	$39.68	$57.74	$120,100	4.1%
27-2021	Athletes and Sports Competitors	11.8	[5]	[5]	$358,080	11.4%
27-2022	Coaches and Scouts	218.9	[5]	[5]	$57,450	1.7%
27-2023	Umpires, Referees and Other Sports Officials	12.7	[5]	[5]	$49,030	11.1%

[1] Preliminary estimate.

[2] In thousands of employed workers. Estimates for detailed occupations do not sum to the totals because the totals include occupations not shown separately. Estimates do not include self-employed workers.

[3] Annual wages have been calculated by multiplying the hourly mean wage by a "year-round, full-time" hours figure of 2,080 hours; for those occupations where there is not an hourly mean wage published, the annual wage has been directly calculated from the reported survey data.

[4] The relative standard error (RSE) is a measure of the reliability of a survey statistic. The smaller the relative standard error, the more precise the estimate.

[5] Wages for some occupations that do not generally work year-round or full time are reported either as hourly wages or annual salaries depending on how they are typically paid.

Source: U.S. Bureau of Labor Statistics

Plunkett Research, ® Ltd.

www.plunkettresearch.com

Chapter 3

IMPORTANT SPORTS & RECREATION INDUSTRY CONTACTS

Addresses, Telephone Numbers and Internet Sites

Contents:

1) Advertising/Marketing Associations
2) Automobile Racing Associations
3) Bicycling Associations
4) Broadcasting, Cable, Radio & TV Associations
5) Careers-First Time Jobs/New Grads
6) Careers-General Job Listings
7) Careers-Job Reference Tools
8) Careers-Sports
9) Corporate Information Resources
10) Economic Data & Research
11) Entertainment & Amusement Associations-General
12) Fitness Industry Associations
13) Fitness Resources
14) Games Industry Associations
15) Health Care Business & Professional Associations
16) Industry Research/Market Research
17) Internet Usage Statistics
18) MBA Resources
19) Motorcycle Industry Associations
20) Real Estate Industry Associations
21) Restaurant Industry Associations
22) Spa Industry Associations
23) Sporting Goods Industry Associations
24) Sports Industry Associations
25) Sports Industry Resources
26) Sports Leagues
27) Sports Marketing Associations
28) Technology Transfer Associations
29) Trade Associations-General
30) Trade Associations-Global
31) Trade Resources
32) U.S. Government Agencies
33) Writers, Photographers & Editors Associations

1)	Advertising/Marketing Associations

American Marketing Association (AMA)
130 E. Randolph St., Fl. 22
Chicago, IL 60601 USA
Phone: 312-542-9000
Fax: 312-542-9001
Toll Free: 800-262-1150
Web Address: www.ama.org
The American Marketing Association (AMA) is a massive association for marketing professionals in both business and education and serves all levels of marketing practitioners, educators and students, across all industries.

2) Automobile Racing Associations

Federation Internationale de l'Automobile (FIA)
8 Place de la Concorde
Paris, 75008 France
Phone: 33-1-43-12-4455
Fax: 33-1-43-12-4466
E-mail Address: *admin@fiacommunications.com*
Web Address: www.fia.com
The Federation Internationale de l'Automobile (FIA)
is the governing body for world motor sport and the
federation of one of the world's leading motoring
organizations. Founded in 1904, with headquarters in
Paris, the FIA is a nonprofit association that
combines 227 national motoring and sporting
organizations from 132 countries on five continents.

3) Bicycling Associations

League of American Bicyclists (The)
1612 K St. NW, Ste. 1102
Washington, DC 20006 USA
Phone: 202-822-1333
E-mail Address:
bikeleague@bikeleague.orgcommunications@bikelea
gue.org
Web Address: www.bikeleague.org
The league was formed to promote bicycling for fun,
fitness and transportation and work through advocacy
and education for a bicycle-friendly America. It
represents the interests of the nation's 57 million
cyclists. With a current membership of 300,000
affiliated cyclists, including 25,000 individuals and
700 affiliated organizations.

4) Broadcasting, Cable, Radio & TV Associations

American Sportscasters Association (ASA)
225 Broadway, Ste. 2030
New York, NY 10007 USA
Phone: 212-227-8080
Fax: 212-571-0556
E-mail Address:
inquiry@americansportscastersonline.com
Web Address: www.americansportscastersonline.com
The American Sportscasters Association (ASA) is a
professional organization for the promotion and
support of sports broadcasters. The ASA is also a
resource for those interested in becoming
sportscasters.

5) Careers-First Time Jobs/New Grads

CollegeGrad.com, Inc.
950 Tower Ln., Fl. 6
Foster City, CA 94404 USA
E-mail Address: info@quinstreet.com
Web Address: www.collegegrad.com
CollegeGrad.com, Inc. offers in-depth resources for
college students and recent grads seeking entry-level
jobs.

National Association of Colleges and Employers (NACE)
62 Highland Ave.
Bethlehem, PA 18017-9085 USA
Phone: 610-868-1421
E-mail Address: customerservice@naceweb.org
Web Address: www.naceweb.org
The National Association of Colleges and Employers
(NACE) is a premier U.S. organization representing
college placement offices and corporate recruiters
who focus on hiring new grads.

6) Careers-General Job Listings

CareerBuilder, Inc.
200 N La Salle Dr., Ste. 1100
Chicago, IL 60601 USA
Phone: 773-527-3600
Fax: 773-353-2452
Toll Free: 800-891-8880
Web Address: www.careerbuilder.com
CareerBuilder, Inc. focuses on the needs of
companies and also provides a database of job
openings. The site has over 1 million jobs posted by
300,000 employers and receives an average of 23
million unique visitors monthly. The company also
operates online career centers for 140 newspapers
and 9,000 online partners. Resumes are sent directly
to the company, and applicants can set up a special e-
mail account for job-seeking purposes. CareerBuilder
is primarily a joint venture between three newspaper
giants: The McClatchy Company, Gannett Co., Inc.
and Tribune Company.

CareerOneStop
Toll Free: 877-872-5627
E-mail Address: info@careeronestop.org
Web Address: www.careeronestop.org
CareerOneStop is operated by the employment
commissions of various state agencies. It contains job
listings in both the private and government sectors, as

well as a wide variety of useful career resources and workforce information. CareerOneStop is sponsored by the U.S. Department of Labor.

LaborMarketInfo (LMI)
Employment Development Dept.
P.O. Box 826880, MIC 57
Sacramento, CA 94280-0001 USA
Phone: 916-262-2162
Fax: 916-262-2352
Web Address: www.labormarketinfo.edd.ca.gov
LaborMarketInfo (LMI) provides job seekers and employers a wide range of resources, namely the ability to find, access and use labor market information and services. It provides statistics for employment demographics on both a local and regional level, as well as career searching tools for California residents. The web site is sponsored by California's Employment Development Office.

Recruiters Online Network
E-mail Address: rossi.tony@comcast.net
Web Address: www.recruitersonline.com
The Recruiters Online Network provides job postings from thousands of recruiters, Careers Online Magazine, a resume database, as well as other career resources.

USAJOBS
USAJOBS Program Office
1900 E St. NW, Ste. 6500
Washington, DC 20415-0001 USA
Phone: 818-934-6600
Web Address: www.usajobs.gov
USAJOBS, a program of the U.S. Office of Personnel Management, is the official job site for the U.S. Federal Government. It provides a comprehensive list of U.S. government jobs, allowing users to search for employment by location; agency; type of work; or by senior executive positions. It also has special employment sections for individuals with disabilities, veterans and recent college graduates; an information center, offering resume and interview tips and other information; and allows users to create a profile and post a resume.

7)   Careers-Job Reference Tools

Vault.com, Inc.
132 W. 31st St., Fl. 16
New York, NY 10001 USA
Fax: 212-366-6117
Toll Free: 800-535-2074
E-mail Address: customerservice@vault.com
Web Address: www.vault.com
Vault.com, Inc. is a comprehensive career web site for employers and employees, with job postings and valuable information on a wide variety of industries. Its features and content are largely geared toward MBA degree holders.

8)   Careers-Sports

Jobs in Sports
1719 Penman Rd
Jacksonville Beach, FL 32250 USA
Web Address: www.jobsinsports.com
Jobs in Sports is an employment web site that provides job listings in areas including sports marketing, sports media, sales, health and fitness, computers and administration, as well as other job resources.

Sports Careers
Web Address: www.sportscareers.com
Sports Careers offers a range of services to help individuals and employers in the sports industry, including job listings, a resume bank, industry contacts and salary information.

Sports Job Board
Web Address: www.sportsjobboard.com
The Sports Job Board is an employment web site for the sports industry.

Work in Sports LLC
7010 E. Chauncey Ln., Ste. 115
Phoenix, AZ 85054 USA
Phone: 480-905-7221
Fax: 480-905-7231
Toll Free: 855-220-5627
Web Address: www.workinsports.com
Work in Sports LLC is an online employment resource for the sports industry that posts hundreds of jobs on its web site.

9)   Corporate Information Resources

Business Journals (The)
120 W. Morehead St., Ste. 400
Charlotte, NC 28202 USA
Toll Free: 866-853-3661
E-mail Address: gmurchison@bizjournals.com
Web Address: www.bizjournals.com

Bizjournals.com is the online media division of American City Business Journals, the publisher of dozens of leading city business journals nationwide. It provides access to research into the latest news regarding companies both small and large. The organization maintains 42 websites and 64 print publications and sponsors over 700 annual industry events.

Business Wire
101 California St., Fl. 20
San Francisco, CA 94111 USA
Phone: 415-986-4422
Fax: 415-788-5335
Toll Free: 800-227-0845
E-mail Address: info@businesswire.com
Web Address: www.businesswire.com
Business Wire offers news releases, industry- and company-specific news, top headlines, conference calls, IPOs on the Internet, media services and access to tradeshownews.com and BW Connect On-line through its informative and continuously updated web site.

Edgar Online, Inc.
35 W. Wacker Dr.
Chicago, IL 60601 USA
Phone: 301-287-0300
Fax: 301-287-0390
Toll Free: 800-823-5304
Web Address: www.edgar-online.com
Edgar Online, Inc. is an SEC gateway and search tool for viewing corporate documents, such as annual reports on Form 10-K, filed with the U.S. Securities and Exchange Commission.

PR Newswire Association LLC
200 Vesey St., Fl. 19
New York, NY 10281 USA
Fax: 800-793-9313
Toll Free: 800-776-8090
E-mail Address: mediainquiries@cision.com
Web Address: www.prnewswire.com
PR Newswire Association LLC provides comprehensive communications services for public relations and investor relations professionals, ranging from information distribution and market intelligence to the creation of online multimedia content and investor relations web sites. Users can also view recent corporate press releases from companies across the globe. The Association is owned by United Business Media plc.

10) Economic Data & Research

Centre for European Economic Research (The, ZEW)
L 7, 1
Mannheim, 68161 Germany
Phone: 49-621-1235-01
Fax: 49-621-1235-224
E-mail Address: empfang@zew.de
Web Address: www.zew.de/en
Zentrum fur Europaische Wirtschaftsforschung, The Centre for European Economic Research (ZEW), distinguishes itself in the analysis of internationally comparative data in a European context and in the creation of databases that serve as a basis for scientific research. The institute maintains a special library relevant to economic research and provides external parties with selected data for the purpose of scientific research. ZEW also offers public events and seminars concentrating on banking, business and other economic-political topics.

Economic and Social Research Council (ESRC)
Polaris House
North Star Ave.
Swindon, SN2 1UJ UK
Phone: 44-01793 413000
E-mail Address: esrcenquiries@esrc.ac.uk
Web Address: www.esrc.ac.uk
The Economic and Social Research Council (ESRC) funds research and training in social and economic issues. It is an independent organization, established by Royal Charter. Current research areas include the global economy; social diversity; environment and energy; human behavior; and health and well-being.

Eurostat
5 Rue Alphonse Weicker
Joseph Bech Bldg.
Luxembourg, L-2721 Luxembourg
Phone: 00 800 6789 1011
E-mail Address:
https://ec.europa.eu/eurostat/web/main/home
Web Address: ec.europa.eu/eurostat
Eurostat is the European Union's service that publishes a wide variety of comprehensive statistics on European industries, population, trade, agriculture, technology, environment and other vital business topics.

Federal Statistical Office of Germany
Gustav-Stresemann-Ring 11
Wiesbaden, D-65189 Germany

Phone: 49-611-75-2405
Fax: 49-611-72-4000
Web Address: www.destatis.de
Federal Statistical Office of Germany publishes a
wide variety of nation and regional economic data of
interest to anyone who is studying Germany, one of
the world's leading economies. Data available
includes population, consumer prices, labor markets,
health care, industries and output.

India Brand Equity Foundation (IBEF)
Fl. 20, Jawahar Vyapar Bhawan
Tolstoy Marg
New Delhi, 110001 India
Phone: 91-11-43845500
Fax: 91-11-23701235
E-mail Address: info.brandindia@ibef.org
Web Address: www.ibef.org
India Brand Equity Foundation (IBEF) is a public-
private partnership between the Ministry of
Commerce and Industry, the Government of India
and the Confederation of Indian Industry. The
foundation's primary objective is to build positive
economic perceptions of India globally. It aims to
effectively present the India business perspective and
leverage business partnerships in a globalizing
marketplace.

National Bureau of Statistics (China)
57, Yuetan Nanjie, Sanlihe
Xicheng District
Beijing, 100826 China
Fax: 86-10-6878-2000
E-mail Address: info@gj.stats.cn
Web Address: www.stats.gov.cn/english
The National Bureau of Statistics (China) provides
statistics and economic data regarding China's
economy and society.

**Organization for Economic Co-operation and
Development (OECD)**
2 rue Andre Pascal
Cedex 16
Paris, 75775 France
Phone: 33-1-45-24-82-00
Fax: 33-1-45-24-85-00
E-mail Address: webmaster@oecd.org
Web Address: www.oecd.org
The Organization for Economic Co-operation and
Development (OECD) publishes detailed economic,
government, population, social and trade statistics on
a country-by-country basis for over 30 nations
representing the world's largest economies. Sectors

covered range from industry, labor, technology and
patents, to health care, environment and
globalization.

**Statistics Bureau, Director-General for Policy
Planning (Japan)**
19-1 Wakamatsu-cho
Shinjuku-ku
Tokyo, 162-8668 Japan
Phone: 81-3-5273-2020
E-mail Address: toukeisoudan@soumu.go.jp
Web Address: www.stat.go.jp/english
The Statistics Bureau, Director-General for Policy
Planning (Japan) and Statistical Research and
Training Institute, a part of the Japanese Ministry of
Internal Affairs and Communications, plays the
central role of producing and disseminating basic
official statistics and coordinating statistical work
under the Statistics Act and other legislation.

Statistics Canada
150 Tunney's Pasture Driveway
Ottawa, ON K1A 0T6 Canada
Phone: 514-283-8300
Fax: 514-283-9350
Toll Free: 800-263-1136
E-mail Address: STATCAN.infostats-
infostats.STATCAN@canada.ca
Web Address: www.statcan.gc.ca
Statistics Canada provides a complete portal to
Canadian economic data and statistics. Its conducts
Canada's official census every five years, as well as
hundreds of surveys covering numerous aspects of
Canadian life.

11) Entertainment & Amusement Associations-General

**Information Display and Entertainment
Association (IDEA)**
5901-J Wyoming Blvd. NE
Albuquerque, NM 87109 USA
Phone: 575-405-1977
E-mail Address: info@ideaontheweb.org
Web Address: www.ideaontheweb.org
The Information Display and Entertainment
Association (IDEA) is a worldwide association of
electronic display system and scoreboard operators.

**International Association of Venue Managers
(IAVM)**
635 Fritz Dr., Ste. 100
Coppell, TX 75019-4442 USA

Phone: 972-906-7441
Fax: 972-906-7418
Toll Free: 800-935-4226
E-mail Address: vicki.hawarden@iavm.org
Web Address: www.iavm.org
The International Association of Venue Managers (IAVM), formerly the International Association of Assembly Managers (IAAM), is an international trade organization representing managers and suppliers of public assembly facilities, such as arenas, amphitheaters, auditoriums, convention centers/exhibit halls, performing arts venues, stadiums and university complexes.

International Ticketing Association (INTIX)

5868 E. 71st St., Ste. E 367
Indianapolis, IN 46220 USA
Phone: 212-629-4036
Fax: 212-629-8532
E-mail Address: info@intix.org
Web Address: www.intix.org
International Ticketing Association (INTIX) is a nonprofit professional and trade organization for the admission services industry, representing professionals in the performing arts, theater, entertainment, professional sports and college and university athletics.

National Association of Ticket Brokers (NATB)

401 W St. Charles Rd.
Lombard, IL 60148 USA
Phone: 630-510-4594
Fax: 630-510-4501
E-mail Address: jason@allshows.com
Web Address: www.natb.org
The National Association of Ticket Brokers (NATB) is a nonprofit trade organization representing the ticket broker industry. The association promotes consumer protection and the education of the public concerning the ticket brokers industry.

12) Fitness Industry Associations

Aerobics and Fitness Association of America (AFAA)

355 E. German Rd., Bldg. 6
Gilbert, AZ 85297 USA
Toll Free: 877-446-2322
E-mail Address: customerservice@afaa.com
Web Address: www.afaa.com
The Aerobics and Fitness Association of America (AFAA) provides certification training for personal trainers, group exercise instructors, kickboxing teachers and others in the fitness instruction field. It also offers workshops and answers questions from the public regarding safe and effective exercise programs and practices.

American Fitness Professionals and Associates (AFPA)

1601 Long Beach Blvd.
P.O. Box 214
Ship Bottom, NJ 08008 USA
Phone: 609-978-7583
Fax: 609-978-7582
Toll Free: 800-494-7782
E-mail Address: afpa@afpafitness.com
Web Address: www.afpafitness.com
American Fitness Professionals and Associates (AFPA) offers health and fitness professionals certification programs, continuing education courses, home correspondence courses and regional conventions.

Fitness Industry Council of Canada (FIC)

13543 St. Albert Tr., Fl. 2
Edmonton, AB T5L 5E7 Canada
E-mail Address: info@ficdn.ca
Web Address: ficdn.ca
Fitness Industry Council of Canada (FIC) represents the voice of fitness facility operators across Canada. FIC represents over 5,000 facilities with over 4 million members nationwide.

International Health, Racquet and Sportsclub Association (IHRSA)

70 Fargo St.
Boston, MA 02210 USA
Phone: 617-951-0055
Fax: 617-951-0056
Toll Free: 800-228-4772
E-mail Address: info@ihrsa.org
Web Address: www.ihrsa.org
The International Health, Racquet & Sportsclub Association is the fitness industry's only global trade association. IHRSA represents over 10,000 for profit health and fitness facilities, and over 600 supplier companies in 75 countries.

National Academy of Kinesiology (NAK)

2001 Juniper Dr
Mahomet, IL 61853 USA
Fax: 217-351-1549
E-mail Address:
staff@nationalacademyofkinesiology.org

Web Address:
www.nationalacademyofkinesiology.org
The National Academy of Kinesiology (NAK),
formerly the American Academy of Kinesiology and
Physical Education (AAKPE), promotes research of
human movement and physical activity. NAK's
members transmit knowledge about human
movement and physical activity through yearly
meetings and publications.

**North American Society for the Psychology of
Sport and Physical Activity (NASPSPA)**
E-mail Address: qalmeida@wlu.ca
Web Address: http://naspspa.com
The North American Society for the Psychology of
Sport and Physical Activity (NASPSPA) is an
association of scholars from the behavioral sciences
and related professions that seeks to advance the
scientific study of human behavior in sport and
physical activity.

**SHAPE America-Society of Health and Physical
Educators**
P.O. Box 225
Annapolis Junction, MD 20701 USA
Phone: 703-476-3400
Fax: 703-476-9527
Toll Free: 800-213-7193
Web Address: www.shapeamerica.org
SHAPE America-Society of Health and Physical
Educators, formerly the American Alliance for
Health, Physical Education, Recreation & Dance
(AAHPERD) is an organization of professionals who
support and assist those involved in physical
education, fitness, leisure, dance, health promotion
and education. It works with its 50 state affiliates and
national partners to support initiatives, including the
Presidential Youth Fitness Program and the Jump
Rope For Heart/Hoops For Heart programs.

**Society of Chinese Scholars on Exercise
Physiology and Fitness (SCSEPF)**
Hong Kong Baptist University
Rm. DLB110, David C. Lam Bldg., Shaw Campus
Kowloon Tong, Hong Kong Hong Kong
Phone: 852-3411-5758
Fax: 852-3411-5756
E-mail Address: enquiry@scsepf.org
Web Address: www.scsepf.org
The Society of Chinese Scholars on Exercise
Physiology and Fitness (SCSEPF) is a nonprofit
professional organization committed exclusively to

the advancement and improvement of exercise
physiology and fitness.

13) Fitness Resources

**President's Council on Physical Fitness, Sports
and Nutrition (PCPFSN)**
200 Independence Ave. SW
Washington, DC 20201 USA
Phone: 240-276-9567
Fax: 240-276-9860
Toll Free: 877-696-6775
E-mail Address: fitness@hhs.gov
Web Address: www.hhs.gov/fitness/index.html
The President's Council on Physical Fitness, Sports
and Nutrition (PCPFSN) offers information about
exercise, fitness and nutrition for people of all ages
and works to promote active, healthy lifestyles.

YMCA of the USA
101 N. Wacker Dr.
Chicago, IL 60606 USA
Phone: 312-977-0031
Toll Free: 800-872-9622
E-mail Address: fulfillment@ymca.net
Web Address: www.ymca.net
The YMCA of the USA is the largest nonprofit
community service organization in America, with
over 2,700 YMCA locations in the U.S. These
locations offer youth development and sports
activities, fitness and other community events.

14) Games Industry Associations

**Association for UK Interactive Entertainment
(UKIE)**
24-28 Hatton Wall
London, EC1N 8JH UK
Phone: 44-20-7534-0580
E-mail Address: info@ukie.org.uk
Web Address: www.ukie.org.uk
The Association for UK Interactive Entertainment
(UKIE) is the UK's leading trade body for games and
wider interactive entertainment industry. Membership
includes almost all major companies involved with
the publishing and development of videogames in the
UK.

Entertainment Software Association (ESA)
601 Massachusetts Ave. NW, Ste. 300
Washington, DC 20001 USA
Phone: 202-223-2400

E-mail Address: esa@theesa.com
Web Address: www.theesa.com
The Entertainment Software Association (ESA) is a
U.S. trade association for companies that publish
video and computer games for consoles, personal
computers and the Internet. The ESA owns the E3
Media & Business Summit, a major invitation-only
annual trade show for the video game industry.

Fantasy Sports & Gaming Association (FSGA)
1818 Parmenter St., Ste. 300
Middleton, WI 53562 USA
Phone: 608-310-7540
E-mail Address: marketing@thefsga.org
Web Address: thefsga.org
The Fantasy Sports & Gaming Association (FSGA),
formerly the Fantasy Sports Trade Association, was
founded in 1997 to provide a forum for interaction
between companies in a unique and growing fantasy
sports industry. FSGA represents more than 300
member companies.

Game Manufacturers Association (GAMA)
258 E. Campus View Blvd.
Columbus, OH 43235 USA
Phone: 614-255-4500
Fax: 614-255-4499
E-mail Address: ed@gama.org
Web Address: www.gama.org
The Game Manufacturers Association (GAMA) is an
international non-profit trade association serving the
hobby games industry. It hosts two annual events, the
GAMA Trade Show and Origins Game Fair, and
publishes a quarterly information newsletter,
GAMATimes.

**Independent Game Developers Association
Limited (The, TIGA)**
One London Wall, Fl. 6
London, EC2Y 5EB UK
Phone: 44-845-468-2330
E-mail Address: info@tiga.org
Web Address: www.tiga.org
The Independent Game Developers Association
(TIGA) is the trade association representing the UK's
games industry. Its members include independent
games developers, in-house publisher owned
developers, outsourcing companies, technology
businesses and universities.

**International Game Developers Association
(IGDA)**
1 Eglinton Ave. E., Ste. 705

Toronto, ON M4P 3A1 Canada
Phone: 856-423-2990
E-mail Address: info@igda.org
Web Address: www.igda.org
The International Game Developers Association
(IGDA) represents members involved in the video
game production industry. The firm aims to promote
professional development within the gaming industry
and advocates for issues that affect the game
developer community, including anti-censorship
issues.

**15) Health Care Business & Professional
Associations**

American College of Sports Medicine (ACSM)
401 W. Michigan St.
Indianapolis, IN 46202-3233 USA
Phone: 317-637-9200
Fax: 317-634-7817
Web Address: www.acsm.org
The American College of Sports Medicine (ACSM)
promotes and integrates research, education and
applications of sports medicine and exercise science
to maintain and enhance quality of life. ACSM has
more than 50,000 members and certified
professionals from 90 countries worldwide.

**American Medical Society for Sports Medicine
(AMSSM)**
4000 W. 114th St., Ste. 100
Leawood, KS 66211 USA
Phone: 913-327-1415
Fax: 913-327-1491
E-mail Address: kdewitt@amssm.org
Web Address: www.amssm.org
The mission of the American Medical Society for
Sports Medicine, Inc. (AMSSM) is to offer a forum
that fosters a collegial relationship among dedicated,
competent primary care sports medicine physicians
as they seek to improve their individual expertise and
raise the general level of the sports medicine practice.

**American Orthopedic Society for Sports Medicine
(AOSSM)**
9400 W. Higgins Rd., Ste. 300
Rosemont, IL 60018 USA
Phone: 847-292-4900
Fax: 847-292-4905
Toll Free: 877-321-3500
E-mail Address: mary@aossm.org
Web Address: www.sportsmed.org

The American Orthopedic Society for Sports Medicine (AOSSM) is a trade association for orthopedic doctors and sports medicine practitioners. The AOSSM works to improve the identification, prevention, treatment and rehabilitation of sports injuries.

Association for Applied Sport Psychology (AASP)
8365 Keystone Crossing, Ste. 107
Indianapolis, IN 46240 USA
Phone: 317-205-9225
Fax: 317-205-9481
E-mail Address: info@appliedsportpsych.org
Web Address: appliedsportpsych.org
The Association for Applied Sport Psychology (AASP) provides information about applied sports psychology to coaches, athletes, students, parents, certified consultants and AASP members.

16) Industry Research/Market Research

Forrester Research
60 Acorn Park Dr.
Cambridge, MA 02140 USA
Phone: 617-613-5730
Toll Free: 866-367-7378
E-mail Address: press@forrester.com
Web Address: www.forrester.com
Forrester Research is a publicly traded company that identifies and analyzes emerging trends in technology and their impact on business. Among the firm's specialties are the financial services, retail, health care, entertainment, automotive and information technology industries.

MarketResearch.com
6116 Executive Blvd., Ste. 550
Rockville, MD 20852 USA
Phone: 240-747-3093
Fax: 240-747-3004
Toll Free: 800-298-5699
E-mail Address:
customerservice@marketresearch.com
Web Address: www.marketresearch.com
MarketResearch.com is a leading broker for professional market research and industry analysis. Users are able to search the company's database of research publications including data on global industries, companies, products and trends.

Plunkett Research, Ltd.
P.O. Drawer 541737
Houston, TX 77254-1737 USA

Phone: 713-932-0000
Fax: 713-932-7080
E-mail Address:
customersupport@plunkettresearch.com
Web Address: www.plunkettresearch.com
Plunkett Research, Ltd. is a leading provider of market research, industry trends analysis and business statistics. Since 1985, it has served clients worldwide, including corporations, universities, libraries, consultants and government agencies. At the firm's web site, visitors can view product information and pricing and access a large amount of basic market information on industries such as financial services, InfoTech, ecommerce, health care and biotech.

17) Internet Usage Statistics

Nielsen
85 Broad St.
New York, NY 10004 USA
Toll Free: 800-864-1224
Web Address: www.nielsen.com
Nielsen offers detailed, real-time Internet, retail and media audiences research and analysis.

18) MBA Resources

MBA Depot
Web Address: www.mbadepot.com
MBA Depot is an online community and information portal for MBAs, potential MBA program applicants and business professionals.

19) Motorcycle Industry Associations

Singapore Motor Cycle Trade Association (SMCTA)
9 Jurong Town Hall Rd., #03-13
Singapore, 609431 Singapore
Phone: 65-6297-1991
E-mail Address: mail@smcta.org.sg
Web Address: www.smcta.org.sg
Singapore Motor Cycle Trade Association (SMCTA) represents the motorcycle trade and related industries in Singapore.

20) Real Estate Industry Associations

International Facility Management Association (IFMA)
800 Gessner Rd., Ste. 725

Houston, TX 77034-4257 USA
Phone: 713-623-4362
Fax: 281-974-5650
E-mail Address: ifma@ifma.org
Web Address: www.ifma.org
The International Facility Management Association
(IFMA) is a trade association of facilities managers.
IFMA certifies facility managers, provides
educational programs, conducts research, recognizes
facility management degree and certificate programs
and produces research reports and white papers.

21) Restaurant Industry Associations

National Association of Concessionaires (NAC)
180 N. Michigan Ave., Ste. 2215
Chicago, IL 60601 USA
Phone: 312-236-3858
Fax: 312-236-7809
E-mail Address: info@NAConline.org
Web Address: www.naconline.org
The National Association of Concessionaires (NAC)
is the trade association for owners and operators of
businesses in the recreation and leisure-time food and
beverage concessions industry.

22) Spa Industry Associations

International Spa Association (ISPA)
2365 Harrodsburg Rd., Ste. A325
Lexington, KY 40504 USA
Phone: 859-226-4326
Fax: 859-226-4445
Toll Free: 888-651-4772
E-mail Address: ispa@ispastaff.com
Web Address: www.experienceispa.com
The International Spa Association (ISPA) is a leading
professional organization for the spa industry. It
provides educational and networking opportunities,
promotes the value of the spa experience and fosters
professionalism and growth. ISPA represents health
and wellness facilities and providers in over 70
countries.

23) Sporting Goods Industry Associations

Canadian Sporting Goods Association (CSGA)
Nobleton, ON L7B 0N9 Canada
E-mail Address: info@csga.ca
Web Address: www.csga.ca
The Canadian Sporting Goods Association (CSGA)
represents the sporting goods industry in Canada.

National Bicycle Dealers Association (NBDA)
3972 Barranca Pkwy., Ste. J-423
Irvine, CA 92606 USA
Phone: 949-540-8020
E-mail Address: info@nbda.com
Web Address: www.nbda.com
The NBDA, established in 1946, is a non-profit
association promoting the interests of every specialty
bicycle retailer in the United States. Each dollar
raised goes towards funding member programs, and
every program is approved by an active, elected
volunteer board of directors comprised of specialty
bicycle retailers.

National Ski and Snowboard Retailer Association (NSSRA)
3041 Woodcreek Dr., Ste. 210
Downers Grove, IL 60515 USA
Phone: 224-220-1522
E-mail Address: info@nssra.com
Web Address: www.nssra.com
The National Ski and Snowboard Retailer
Association (NSSRA) provides ski and snowboard
retailers across the U.S. with information and
services. NSSRA also represents ski shops at the
meetings of the American Society for Testing and
Materials (ASTM) committee on snow skiing.

National Sporting Goods Association (NSGA)
3041 Woodcreek Dr., Ste. 210
Downers Grove, IL 60515 USA
Phone: 847-296-6742
E-mail Address: info@nsga.org
Web Address: www.nsga.org
The National Sporting Goods Association (NSGA) is
a trade association designed to help its members
profit in a competitive marketplace. The group
publishes excellent market research in addition to
hosting a major annual conference.

Sports & Fitness Industry Association, The (SFIA)
962 Wayne Ave.
Silver Spring, MD 20910 USA
Phone: 301-495-6321
E-mail Address: info@sfia.org
Web Address: www.sfia.org
The Sports & Fitness Industry Association (SFIA),
formerly the Sporting Goods Manufacturers
Association, is a trade organization representing
manufacturers of sporting goods equipment.

World Federation of the Sporting Goods Industry (WFSGI)
Haus des Sports
Talgut-Zentrum 27
Ittigen, Bern 3063 Switzerland
Phone: 41-31-939-60-61
E-mail Address: info@wfsgi.org
Web Address: www.wfsgi.org
The World Federation of the Sporting Goods Industry (WFSGI) is a global, nonprofit, independent association of sporting goods industry suppliers, national sporting goods organizations and other industry-related businesses.

24) Sports Industry Associations

All-China Sports Federation
8 Tiyuguan Rd.
Dongcheng Dist.
Beijing, 100061 China
Phone: 86-10-6715-8866
E-mail Address: 800@sports.cn
Web Address: www.sport.org.cn
The All-China Sports Federation is a non-governmental organization that promotes sports and fitness in China.

Amateur Athletic Union (AAU)
1910 Hotel Plaza Blvd.
Lake Buena Vista, FL 32830 USA
Phone: 407-934-7200
Fax: 407-934-7242
Toll Free: 800-228-4872
E-mail Address: socialmedia@aausports.org
Web Address: aausports.org
The Amateur Athletic Union (AAU) is a nonprofit, volunteer sports organization dedicated to the promotion and development of amateur sports and physical fitness programs.

American Baseball Coaches Association (ABCA)
4101 Piedmont Pkwy.
Greensboro, NC 27410 USA
Phone: 336-821-3140
Fax: 336-886-0000
E-mail Address: office@abca.org
Web Address: www.abca.org
The American Baseball Coaches Association (ABCA) is a trade organization serving 6,200 baseball coaches from 23 countries. ABCA works with many of the governing bodies represented by its coaches, including the National Collegiate Athletic Association (NCAA), the National Association of

Intercollegiate Athletics (NAIA), the National Junior College Athletic Association (NJCAA) and the National Federation of State High School Associations (NFHS).

American Football Coaches Association (AFCA)
100 Legends Ln.
Waco, TX 76706 USA
Phone: 254-754-9900
Fax: 254-754-7373
E-mail Address: info@afca.com
Web Address: www.afca.com
The American Football Coaches Association (AFCA) is the primary professional association representing all levels of football and the football coaching profession. The organization's 10,000 members include coaches from the U.S., Europe, Canada, Australia, Japan and Mexico.

American Hockey Coaches Association (AHCA)
7 Concord St.
Gloucester, MA 01930 USA
Phone: 978-376-5494
E-mail Address: ahcahockey@comcast.net
Web Address: www.ahcahockey.com
The American Hockey Coaches Association (AHCA) is a trade organization that represents professional, junior, high school and youth coaches. AHCA also represents referees, administrators, sales representatives, journalists and fans.

American Volleyball Coaches Association (AVCA)
2365 Harrodsburg Rd., Ste. A325
Lexington, KY 40504 USA
Phone: 859-226-4315
Fax: 859-317-4212
Toll Free: 866-544-2822
E-mail Address: members@avca.org
Web Address: www.avca.org
The American Volleyball Coaches Association (AVCA) provides professional volleyball coaches with educational programs, recognition opportunities and a forum for information exchange.

American Youth Soccer Organization (AYSO)
19700 S. Vermont Ave., Ste. 103
Torrance, CA 90502 USA
Fax: 310-525-1155
Toll Free: 800-872-2976
E-mail Address: yvonnelara@ayso.org
Web Address: www.ayso.org

The American Youth Soccer Organization (AYSO) is a nonprofit organization engaged in developing and supporting youth soccer programs across the U.S.

Arena Football League Players Union (AFLPU)
6300 Powers Ferry Rd.
Atlanta, GA 30339 USA
Fax: 800-585-0247
Toll Free: 800-585-0248
E-mail Address: info@aflpu.org
Web Address: aflpu.org
The Arena Football League Players Union (AFLPU) is the union for professional arena football players.

Association of Luxury Suite Directors (ALSD)
549 S Fort Thomas Ave.
Fort Thomas, KY 41075 USA
Phone: 513-674-0555
E-mail Address: support@alsd.com
Web Address: www.alsd.com
The Association of Luxury Suite Directors (ALSD) serves and represents businesses in the premium seating industry, especially those offering seating for stadiums and arenas.

Association of Professional Ball Players of America (APBPA)
23623 N Scottsdale Rd., Ste. 290
Scottsdale, AZ 85255 USA
Phone: 602-730-4528
E-mail Address: info@apbpa.org
Web Address: www.apbpa.org
The Association of Professional Ball Players of America (APBPA) provides financial assistance to both major and minor league professional baseball players, coaches, umpires, scouts and clubhouse men in need.

Black Entertainment & Sports Lawyers Association (BESLA)
P.O. Box 351120
Los Angeles, CA 90035 E-mail Address:
info@besla.org
Web Address: www.besla.org
The Black Entertainment & Sports Lawyers Association (BESLA) is an international nonprofit organization of lawyers and other sports industry and entertainment executives, providing its members networking and continuing education programs. BESLA also offers internship opportunities and scholarships for law students.

Black Sports Agents Association (BSAA)
E-mail Address: info@sportsagentsassociation.com
Web Address: www.blacksportsagents.com
The Black Sports Agents Association (BSAA) was founded by the Reverend Jesse Jackson in 1996 to develop the involvement, image and cohesiveness of African Americans in the sports industry.

Black Women in Sport Foundation (BWSF)
4300 Monument Rd.
Philadelphia, PA 19131 USA
Phone: 215-877-1925
E-mail Address: hello@blackwomeninsport.org
Web Address: www.blackwomeninsport.org
The Black Women in Sport Foundation (BWSF) is a nonprofit organization dedicated to facilitating the involvement of black women in U.S. sports, as well as around the world, through grassroots sports outreach programs for young black women and girls.

Canadian Football League Players' Association (CFLPA)
6205 B Airport Rd., Ste. 208
Mississauga, ON L4V 1E3 Canada
Toll Free: 800-616-6865
E-mail Address: admin@cflpa.com
Web Address: cflpa.com
The Canadian Football League Players' Association (CFLPA) is the union for football players in the Canadian Football League (CFL).

Chinese Olympic Committee (COC)
Tiyuguan Rd. 2
Chongwen District
Beijing, 100763 China
Phone: 86-10-6711-6669
Fax: 86-10-6711-5858
E-mail Address: coc@olympic.cn
Web Address: en.olympic.cn
The Chinese Olympic Committee (COC) is a nonprofit organization representing China in international Olympic sports.

College Athletic Business Management Association (CABMA)
Phone: 440-892-4000
E-mail Address: membership@nacda.com
Web Address: nacda.com/sports/cabma
The College Athletic Business Management Association (CABMA) is an organization for those involved in athletics administration, offering educational and networking opportunities. CABMA

is a member of the National Association of Collegiate Directors of Athletics (NACDA).

European Outdoor Group (EOG)
Postfach 7142
Zug, 6302 Switzerland
E-mail Address: info@europeanoutdoorgroup.com
Web Address: www.europeanoutdoorgroup.com
The EOG supports the European outdoor recreation industry with market research, workshops, best practices and other initiatives. It was founded in 2003 by 19 of the largest outdoor industry firms in Europe.

General Administration of Sports (China)
2 Tiyuguan Rd.
Dongcheng District
Beijing, 100763 China
Phone: 86-10-8718-2008
Web Address: www.sport.gov.cn
The General Administration of Sport of China is the national sports development and general administrative association of the Chinese government.

Hong Kong Schools Sports Federation (HKSSF)
7 Carmel Village St., 1/F, Rm. 203
Homantin, Kowloon
Hong Kong, Hong Kong Hong Kong
Phone: 852-2711-9182
Fax: 852-2761-9808
E-mail Address: hkssf@hkssf.org.hk
Web Address: www.hkssf-nt.org.hk
Hong Kong Schools Sports Federation (HKSSF) represents the primary and secondary schools' sports and student athletes, focusing on quality training required for them to achieve higher performance in the All China Secondary School Students Games, inter-city and other international competitions.

Hong Kong Sports Institute
25 Yuen Wo Rd.
Sha Tin, N.T.
Hong Kong, Hong Kong Hong Kong
Phone: 852-2681-6888
Fax: 852-2695-4555
E-mail Address: webmaster@hksi.org.hk
Web Address: www.hksi.org.hk
Hong Kong Sports Institute works closely with national sports associations and other bodies in the identification of talents for elite sports training. It also provides community support for the development of sports training programs and services.

Indian Olympic Association
Olympic Bhawan
B-29 Qutab Institutional Area
New Delhi, 110 016 India
Phone: 91-11-2685-2481
E-mail Address: ioa@olympic.ind.in
Web Address: olympic.ind.in
The Indian Olympic Association web site provides contact information regarding national sports federations, state associations and other recognized sports federations in India.

International Cycling Union (UCI)
Allee Ferdi Kubler 12
Aigle, 1860 Switzerland
Phone: 41-24-468-58-11
E-mail Address: contact@uci.ch
Web Address: www.uci.ch
The International Cycling Union (also known as the Union Cycliste Internationale or UCI) is cycling's International Federation recognized by the International Olympic Committee (IOC). The UCI administers and promotes the development of the eight disciplines of cycling. The UCI's mission is to develop and promote cycling, in close collaboration with National Federations.

International Olympic Committee (IOC)
Maison Olympique
Lausanne, 1007 Switzerland
Phone: 41-21-621-61-11
Fax: 41-21-621-62-16
Web Address: www.olympic.org
The International Olympic Committee (IOC) is the governing body for the Olympic Games.

Major League Baseball Players Alumni Association (MLBPAA)
1631 Mesa Ave., Ste. D
Colorado Springs, CO 80906 USA
Phone: 719-477-1870
E-mail Address: postoffice@mlbpaa.com
Web Address: www.mlb.com/mlbpaa
The Major League Baseball Players Alumni Association (MLBPAA) is a nonprofit organization composed of both current and former major and minor league players, umpires, managers and coaches, as well as baseball fans. It promotes the game of baseball and raises money for charity.

Major League Baseball Players Association (MLBPA)
12 E. 49th St., Fl. 24

New York, NY 10017 USA
Phone: 212-826-0808
Fax: 212-752-4378
E-mail Address: feedback@mlbpa.org
Web Address: www.mlbplayers.com
The Major League Baseball Players Association
(MLBPA), founded in 1968, is the union for
professional baseball players.

National Association of Basketball Coaches (NABC)

1111 Main St., Ste. 1000
Kansas City, MO 64105-2136 USA
Phone: 816-878-6222
E-mail Address: membership@nabc.com
Web Address: www.nabc.org
The National Association of Basketball Coaches
(NABC) is a professional organization representing
college basketball coaches.

National Athletic Trainers' Association (NATA)

1620 Valwood Pkwy., Ste. 115
Carrollton, TX 75006 USA
Phone: 214-637-6282
Fax: 214-637-2206
Toll Free: 800-879-6282
Web Address: www.nata.org
The National Athletic Trainers' Association (NATA)
is a trade association for athletic trainers and those
who support the athletic training profession.

National Basketball Players Association (NBPA)

1133 Avenue of the Americas
New York, NY 10036 USA
Phone: 212-655-0880
Fax: 212-655-0881
Toll Free: 800-955-6272
E-mail Address: info@nbpa.com
Web Address: www.nbpa.com
The National Basketball Players Association (NBPA)
is the union for professional basketball players in the
National Basketball Association (NBA). It works to
protect the rights of players, offering assistance with
professional agreements and negotiations,
educational opportunities and resolving grievances
with a focus on defending their interests and well-
being.

National Collegiate Athletic Association (NCAA)

700 W. Washington St.
P.O. Box 7110
Indianapolis, IN 46206-6222 USA
Phone: 317-917-6222

Fax: 317-917-6888
Web Address: www.ncaa.org
The National Collegiate Athletic Association
(NCAA) is a collegiate sports organization serving
the needs of its college, university and conference
members. It currently includes over 1,121 colleges
and universities and oversees 90 championships in 24
sports across 3 divisions.

National Field Hockey Coaches Association (NFHCA)

P.O. Box 49098
Colorado Springs, CO 80949 E-mail Address:
outreach@nfhca.org
Web Address: www.nfhca.org
The National Field Hockey Coaches Association
(NFHCA) is a nonprofit advocacy organization
serving field hockey coaches across the U.S.

National Football League Players Association (NFLPA)

1133 20th St. NW
Washington, DC 20036 USA
Toll Free: 800-372-2000
E-mail Address: george.atallah@nflpa.com
Web Address: nflpa.com
The National Football League Players Association
(NFLPA) is a non-union trade association
representing professional football players in the
National Football League (NFL). It was decertified as
the NFL labor union following an unresolved labor
dispute in March 2011.

National Golf Foundation (NGF)

501 N Highway A1A
Jupiter, FL 33477-4577 USA
Phone: 561-744-6006
Fax: 561-744-6107
Toll Free: 888-275-4643
E-mail Address: general@ngf.org
Web Address: www.ngf.org
The National Golf Foundation (NGF) provides golf
business research, information and consulting
services to companies and organizations world-wide,
including its 4,000 member companies.

National Hockey League Alumni Association (NHLAA)

400 Kipling Ave.
Toronto, ON M8V 3L1 Canada
Phone: 416-798-2586
E-mail Address: info@nhlalumni.net
Web Address: www.nhlalumni.net

The National Hockey League Alumni Association (NHLAA) is an organization for former NHL players dedicated to the cause of benefitting the lives of retired NHL players and their families.

National Hockey League Players Association (NHLPA)
10 Bay St., Ste. 1200
Toronto, ON M5J 2R8 Canada
Phone: 416-313-2300
E-mail Address: privacy@nhlpa.com
Web Address: www.nhlpa.com
The National Hockey League Players Association (NHLPA) is the union for hockey players in the National Hockey League (NHL). It advocates fairness in terms and conditions of employment for NHL players.

National Lacrosse League Players' Association (NLLPA)
8207 Main St., Ste. 13
Williamsville, NY 14221 Phone: 604-897-5517
Web Address: nllpa.com
The National Lacrosse League Players' Association (NLLPA), formerly the Professional Lacrosse Players' Association (PLPA), is the trade union of players in the National Lacrosse League (NLL). The union was organized to assist with missed work pay for players who miss their regular jobs for games; expanded expense reimbursement; more opportunities for promotional pay on top of their regular game salaries; more time for rookies to assess their initial contracts; game compensation for practice players; free agency; a standard grievance and arbitration process for fines and suspensions.

National Thoroughbred Racing Association (NTRA)
401 W. Main St., Ste. 222
Lexington, KY 40507 USA
Phone: 859-245-6872
Toll Free: 800-792-6872
E-mail Address: info@ntra.com
Web Address: www.ntra.com
The National Thoroughbred Racing Association (NTRA) is the governing body of thoroughbred racing in the U.S.

North American Society for Sport History (NASSH)USA
E-mail Address: m.phillips@uq.edu
Web Address: www.nassh.org

The North American Society for Sport History (NASSH) is a nonprofit organization engaged in the study, research and writing of the history of sport.

North American Society for Sport Management (NASSM)
135 Winterwood Dr.
Butler, PA 16001 USA
Phone: 724-482-6277
E-mail Address: support@nassm.org
Web Address: www.nassm.com
The North American Society for Sport Management (NASSM) supports professionals working in the sport, leisure and recreation fields by encouraging study, research, scholarly writing and professional development in the area of sport management.

North American Society for the Sociology of Sport (NASSS)
E-mail Address: members@nasss.org
Web Address: www.nasss.org
The North American Society for the Sociology of Sport (NASSS) is a nonprofit organization that promotes the sociological study of play, games and sport.

Outdoor Foundation
4909 Pearl E. Cir., Ste. 300
Boulder, CO 80301 USA
Phone: 303-444-3353
Fax: 303-444-3284
E-mail Address: smaez@outdoorfoundation.org
Web Address: outdoorindustry.org/participation/
The Outdoor Foundation, founded by the Outdoor Industry Association in 2000, is a national not-for-profit organization dedicated to inspiring and growing future generations of outdoor leaders and enthusiasts. Through youth engagement, community grant-making and groundbreaking research, the Foundation works with young leaders and partners to mobilize a major cultural shift that leads all Americans to the great outdoors. Each year, the Foundation produces the Outdoor Participation Report, the largest, most comprehensive research report on outdoor recreation participation. The report examines more than 40 outdoor activities in America and provides insights and analysis on geographic and demographic trends, motivations and barriers as well as purchasing behaviors.

Outdoor Industry Association (OIA)
4909 Pearl E. Cir., Ste. 300
Boulder, CO 80301 USA

Phone: 303-444-3353
Fax: 303-444-3284
E-mail Address: info@outdoorindustry.org
Web Address: outdoorindustry.org
Founded in 1989, Outdoor Industry Association (OIA) is a trade association for companies in the outdoor recreation business. OIA provides trade services for over 4,000 manufacturers, distributors, suppliers, sales representatives and retailers in the outdoor industry. Outdoor Industry Association seeks to ensure a healthy and diverse specialty retail and supply chain based on quality, innovation and service. To this end, OIA works diligently to raise the standards of the industry; increase participation in outdoor recreation to strengthen business markets; provide support services to improve member profitability; represent member interests in the legislative/regulatory process; promote professional training and education; support innovation; and offer cost-saving member benefits.

Physical Activity Council (PAC)
Phone: 561-427-0647
E-mail Address: info@sportsmarketingsurveysusa.com
Web Address: www.physicalactivitycouncil.org
The Physical Activity Council (PAC) is made up of the leading sports and manufacturer associations that are dedicated to growing participation in their respective sports and activities. To understand their audiences, these organizations conduct annual studies that provide comprehensive, accurate and actionable data on sports participation. Member associations are the International Health, Racquet & Sports Club Association, Outdoor Industry Foundation, Sports and Fitness Industry Association, United States Tennis Association, National Golf Foundation, Snow Sports Industry Association and Tennis Industry Association.

Professional Hockey Players' Association (PHPA)
3964 Portage Rd.
Niagara Falls, ON L2J 2K9 Canada
Phone: 289-296-5561
Fax: 289-296-4567
E-mail Address: ddionne@phpa.com
Web Address: www.phpa.com
The Professional Hockey Players' Association (PHPA) is the union for professional hockey players in the American Hockey League (AHL), Central Hockey League (CHL) and the Elite Competition Hockey League (ECHL).

SnowSports Industries America (SIA)
1918 Prospector Ave.
Park City, UT 84060 USA
Phone: 435-657-5140
E-mail Address: info@snowsports.org
Web Address: www.snowsports.org
SnowSports Industries America (SIA) is a not-for-profit, North American member-owned trade association representing suppliers of consumer snow sports equipment and services. Members are in the retail, manufacturers' representative and resort communities. Established in 1954, SIA annually produces the SIA Snow Show, the largest snow sports industry trade show and networking environment globally, while delivering research, support, marketing products, government affairs representation, services and programs to the industry.

Special Olympics
2600 Virginia Ave. NW, Fl. 11
Washington, DC 20037 USA
Phone: 202-628-3630
Fax: 202-824-0200
Toll Free: 800-700-8585
E-mail Address: info@specialolympics.org
Web Address: www.specialolympics.org
The Special Olympics is an international organization dedicated to athletes with intellectual disabilities.

Sport Singapore (SportSG)
3 Stadium Dr.
Singapore, 397630 Singapore
Phone: 65-6500-5000
E-mail Address: sport_qsm@sport.gov.sg
Web Address: www.sportsingapore.gov.sg
Sport Singapore (SportSG), formerly Singapore Sports Council, is committed to promoting Singapore as a regional sports hub. SportSG is a statutory board under the Ministry of Community Development, Youth and Sports of Singapore. The site contains a directory of national sports associations, a list of programs, links to sports medicine and training sites and the sports museum.

Sports Field Management Association (SFMA)
805 New Hampshire, Ste. E
Lawrence, KS 66044 USA
Phone: 785-843-2549
Fax: 785-843-2977
Toll Free: 800-323-3875
E-mail Address: sfmainfo@sportsfieldmanagement.org
Web Address: www.sportsfieldmanagement.org

The Sports Field Management Association (SFMA), formerly the Sports Turf Managers Association, provides a network of knowledge sharing and idea exchange between sports turf professionals.

Sports Lawyers Association (SLA)
11130 Sunrise Valley Dr., Ste. 350
Reston, VA 20191 USA
Phone: 703-437-4377
E-mail Address: sla@sportslaw.com
Web Address: www.sportslaw.org
The Sports Lawyers Association (SLA) is an international, nonprofit, professional organization whose purpose is to understand and advance the practice of sports law. SLA has over 1,000 members including law educators, practicing lawyers, law students and other professionals with an interest in professional and amateur sports law.

Stadium Managers Association (SMA)
6919 Vista Dr.
Des Moines, IA 50266 USA
Phone: 515-282-8192
Fax: 515-282-9117
E-mail Address: sma@stadiummanagers.org
Web Address: www.stadiummanagers.org
The Stadium Managers Association (SMA) is a trade organization that promotes the interest of stadium management professionals.

Tennis Industry Association (TIA)
35 E Wacker Dr., Ste. 850
Hilton Head Island, SC 29928 USA
Phone: 312-596-5281
E-mail Address: info@tennisindustry.org
Web Address: www.tennisindustry.org
The TIA's aim is to educate the tennis marketplace, fund research and market intelligence, and supply reliable industry data to its member companies. The TIA produces more than 70 research reports annually including consumer and trade research and quarterly census reports on tennis products. In addition, the TIA's mission is to increase tennis participation through the support of grow the game activities and image campaigns by working closely with the USTA and industry partners.

United States National Soccer Team Players Association (USNSTPA)
680 Maine Ave. SW
Washington, DC 20024 USA
E-mail Address: editor@usnstpa.com
Web Address: www.ussoccerplayers.com

The United States National Soccer Team Players Association (USNSTPA) is the labor organization for current members of the United States Men's National Team, as well as a membership organization for alumni members of the National Team.

United States Olympic Committee (USOC)
27 S. Tejon
Colorado Springs, CO 80903 USA
Phone: 719-632-5551
E-mail Address: newmedia@usoc.org
Web Address: www.teamusa.org
The United States Olympic Committee is a federally chartered nonprofit corporation that preserves Olympic ideals and supports Olympic and Paralympic athletes.

Women in Sports and Events (WISE)
244 Fifth Ave., Ste. 2087
New York, NY 10001 USA
Phone: 212-726-8282
E-mail Address: info@wiseworks.org
Web Address: www.wiseworks.org
Women in Sports and Events (WISE) is a professional networking organization for women in the sports and sports-related events industries.

Women's Basketball Coaches Association (WBCA)
4646 Lawrenceville Hwy.
Lilburn, GA 30047 USA
Phone: 770-279-8027
Fax: 770-279-8473
E-mail Address: membership@wbca.org
Web Address: www.wbca.org
The Women's Basketball Coaches Association (WBCA) promotes women's basketball by providing a network for coaches of professional and amateur women's basketball teams, including those on the college and high school levels.

Women's Golf Coaches Association (WGCA)
11555 Heron Bay Blvd., Ste. 200
Coral Springs, FL 33067 USA
Fax: 800-381-0769
Toll Free: 800-381-0769
Web Address: wgcagolf.com
The Women's Golf Coaches Association (WGCA) is a professional organization for coaches in women's golf. The association has more than 400 coaches from Division I, II, III and NAIA collegiate programs.

25) Sports Industry Resources

American Bar Association (ABA) Forum on the Entertainment & Sports Industries
321 N. Clark St.
Chicago, IL 60654-7598 USA
Phone: 312-988-5580
Fax: 312-988-5677
Toll Free: 800-285-2221
E-mail Address: Service@americanbar.org
Web Address:
www.americanbar.org/groups/entertainment_sports/
The American Bar Association (ABA) Forum on the Entertainment & Sports Industries, formed in 1977, seeks to educate attorneys in the transactional and legal principles of sports and entertainment law. The forum's quarterly newsletter is directed toward lawyers practicing entertainment, sports, arts and intellectual property law.

ESPN, Inc.
ESPN Plz.
Bristol, CT 06010 USA
Toll Free: 888-549-3776
E-mail Address: espnpr@espn.com
Web Address: www.espn.com
ESPN, Inc. is a recognized leader in sports entertainment and information. Launched in 1979, the company broadcasts several television channels; publishes ESPN Magazine; and maintains Internet sites that provide complete coverage of professional sports. The firm is 80% owned by ABC, Inc., which is in turn an indirect subsidiary of The Walt Disney Company. The Hearst Corporation holds the remaining 20%.

FoxSports.com
10201 W. Pico Blvd., Bldg. 101
Los Angeles, CA 90035 USA
Phone: 310-369-1000
Web Address: www.foxsports.com
FoxSports.com is a leader in sports broadcasting, news and information. The site is owned and operated by Fox Sports Interactive Media (FSIM), which is itself a subsidiary of News Corp.

Running USA
5123 W. 98th St., Ste. 1132
Minneapolis, MN 55437 USA
E-mail Address: info@runningusa.org
Web Address: www.runningusa.org
Running USA is a nonprofit organization devoted to promoting the sport of running. It publishes very useful statistics about runners, and it holds an annual industry conference.

Sportcal
John Carpenter St.
Castle Baynard
London, EC4Y 0 UK
Phone: 44-20-7947-2937
E-mail Address: info@sportcal.com
Web Address: www.sportcal.com
GlobalData's Sport Intelligence Center is a world-leading sport market intelligence service, providing unparalleled information, analysis, insights and data on media rights, sponsorship, events and bidding. It is also a source of rich content on sports industry news, with journalists producing daily content that cannot be found anywhere else on the market. â€‹

Sporting News
436 East 36th St
Charlotte, NC 28205 USA
E-mail Address: social@tsn.com
Web Address: www.sportingnews.com
The Sporting News is the oldest sporting publication in the United States. Initially known as the essential source for baseball coverage, in the 1940s it began to cover a wider array of sports, including college sports, the NBA, NFL, NHL, motorsports, golf, tennis, boxing and many others.

Sports Authority of India (SAI)
Lodhi Rd.
Jawaharlal Nehru Stadium Complex (East Gate)
New Delhi, 110 003 India
Phone: 91-11-2436-4243
E-mail Address: itdivisionhq-sai@gov.in
Web Address: sportsauthorityofindia.gov.in/sai/
The Sports Authority of India (SAI) is the field arm of India's Ministry of Youth Affairs & Sports. Its mission is to promote sports at all levels within India.

Sports Business Journal
120 W. Morehead St., Ste. 310
Charlotte, NC 28202 USA
Phone: 704-973-1500
Fax: 704-973-1501
Toll Free: 800-829-9839
E-mail Address: dmoss@sportsbusinessjournal.com
Web Address: www.sportsbusinessjournal.com
Sports Business Journal is a comprehensive weekly magazine for the sports industry, covering teams, players, marketing, labor and facilities.

Sports Illustrated (SI)
200 Vesey St., Fl. 24
New York, NY 10281 USA
E-mail Address: support@si.com
Web Address: www.si.com
Sports Illustrated (SI) is a leading U.S. sports publications company anchored by the Sports Illustrated magazine.

Sports Illustrated for Kids
E-mail Address: service@thearenagroup.net
Web Address: www.sikids.com
Sports Illustrated for Kids, a Time Warner company, offers a magazine and web site devoted to kids who are interested in sports.

Team Marketing Report
1810 N. Rutherford Ave.
Chicago, IL 60707 USA
Phone: 312-725-0645
E-mail Address: help@teammarketing.com
Web Address: www.teammarketing.com
Team Marketing Report provides market research on the sports industry.

USA Today Sports
7950 Jones Branch Dr.
McLean, VA 22108-0605 USA
Phone: 703-854-3400
Toll Free: 800-872-0001
E-mail Address: rpscott@usatoday.com
Web Address: www.usatoday.com/sports/
USA Today Sports provides news and information about the sports industry. It also publishes a weekly magazine, Sports Weekly, that covers football and baseball.

Yahoo! Sports
770 Broadway
New York, NY 1003 USA
Web Address: sports.yahoo.com
Yahoo! Sports, a service of Yahoo! Inc., provides news and information regarding the sports industry.

26) Sports Leagues

American Hockey League (AHL)
1 Monarch Pl., Ste. 2400
Springfield, MA 01144 USA
E-mail Address: ahltv@theahl.com
Web Address: www.theahl.com
The American Hockey League (AHL) is a professional ice hockey league which serves as the main developmental circuit for the National Hockey League (NHL).

Arena Football League (AFL)
Web Address: www.theafl.com
The Arena Football League (AFL) is the governing body for professional arena football in the U.S.

Asian Football Confederation (AFC)
AFC House, Jalan 1/155B
Bukit Jalil
Kuala Lumpur, 57000 Malaysia
Phone: 60-3-8994-3388
Fax: 60-3-8994-2689
E-mail Address: media@the-afc.com
Web Address: www.the-afc.com
The Asian Football Confederation (AFC) is the governing body of football in Asia, including Australia but excluding Israel and Cyprus. The AFC hosts the Asian Cup every four years. It is organized into four regional federations: ASEAN Football Federation, East Asian Football Federation, West Asian Football Federation and the Central and South Asian Football Federation.

Canadian Football League (CFL)
50 Wellington St. E., Fl. 3
Toronto, ON M5E 1C8 Canada
Phone: 416-322-9650
E-mail Address: contact@cfl.ca
Web Address: www.cfl.ca
The Canadian Football League (CFL) is the organizing body for professional football in Canada.

Chinese Basketball Association
4 Tiyuguan Rd., Dongcheng
Beijing, 100062 China
E-mail Address: Dream@cbaleague.com
Web Address: www.cbaleague.com
The Chinese Basketball Association (CBA) is China's top-tier professional basketball league (analogous to the NBA in the U.S.), overseeing some 17 teams across its Northern and Southern Divisions. CBA is associated with China's semi-professional National Basketball League (NBL).

ECHL
830 Broad St., Ste. 3
Shrewsbury, NJ 07702 USA
Phone: 609-452-0770
Fax: 609-452-7147
E-mail Address: echl@echl.com
Web Address: www.echl.com

The ECHL (formerly East Coast Hockey League) is a nationwide developmental league for the American Hockey League (AHL) and the National Hockey League (NHL).

EFL (English Football League)

EFL House
10-12 West Cliff
Preston, PR1 8HU UK
Phone: 44-1772-325800
E-mail Address: enquiries@efl.com
Web Address: www.efl.com
The EFL (English Football League) is the world's original league football competition and is the template for leagues the world over. It is the largest single body of professional Clubs in European football and is responsible for administering and regulating the EFL, the Carabao Cup and the Papa Johns Trophy, as well as reserve and youth football.

Federation International de Football Association (FIFA)

FIFA-Strasse 20
P.O. Box 8044
Zurich, Switzerland
Web Address: www.fifa.com
The Federation International de Football Association (FIFA) is the official governing body for professional soccer worldwide and consists of 209 member associations. Dedicated to the advancement and continuous improvement of the game of soccer, the association organizes both men and women's tournaments at international level.

Football Association of Singapore (FAS)

100 Tyrwhitt Rd.
Jalan Besar Stadium
Singapore, 207542 Singapore
Phone: 65-6880-3199
E-mail Address: info@fas.org.sg
Web Address: www.fas.org.sg
The Football Association of Singapore (FAS) promotes the sport of football and football professionals. FAS provides support to regional football clubs and youth development programs in Singapore.

IFAF (International Federation of American Football)

16 Boulevard Saint Germain
CS 70514 - 75237
Paris, CEDEX 05 France
Phone: 44-7971-497792

E-mail Address: info@americanfootball.sport
Web Address: americanfootball.sport
The IFAF is composed of 64 member nations on six continents (North and South America, Europe, Asia, Africa, and Oceania), all of which possess national federations dedicated solely to American football. The first national American Football federation outside of the United States was founded in Canada in 1896, as Canada already had a long history with Canadian football. Japan was also an early adopter of American football, establishing its national federation in 1936. The first European federation was formed in 1976. Since then, the sport has experienced a significant expansion, especially in Europe, culminating in the founding of the European Federation of American Football in 1993. Five years later (1998), the International Federation of American Football was officially formed. The IFAF became a provisionary member of SportAccord in 2003 and became a full SportAccord member in 2005.

IndyCar

4551 W. 16th St.
Indianapolis, IN 46222 USA
Phone: 317-492-6526
E-mail Address: indycar@indycar.com
Web Address: www.indycar.com
IndyCar, formerly the Indy Racing League (IRL), is the official sanctioning body for Indy auto racing. It operates four racing series, the Verizon IndyCar Series, the Indy Lights, the Pro Mazda and the Cooper Tires USF2000. IndyCar is a subsidiary of Hulman and Co., the owner of the Indianapolis Motor Speedway complex.

International Boxing Federation & United States Boxing Association (IBF/USBA)

899 Mountain Ave., Ste. 2E
Springfield, NJ 07081 USA
Phone: 973-564-8046
Fax: 973-564-8751
E-mail Address: jsalazar@ibfboxing.com
Web Address: www.ibf-usba-boxing.com
The International Boxing Federation & United States Boxing Association (IBF/USBA) is one of many professional boxing organizations that sanctions world championship boxing bouts.

International Professional Rodeo Association (IPRA)

1412 S. Agnew
Oklahoma City, OK 73108 USA
Phone: 405-235-6540

Fax: 405-235-6577
E-mail Address: ipra@iprarodeo.com
Web Address: www.ipra-rodeo.com
The International Professional Rodeo Association
(IPRA) is the premier professional rodeo association
promoting the sport of rodeo by organizing
performance rodeo, western trade show, seminars,
International Finals Youth Rodeo, as well as Miss
Rodeo USA contest.

Ladies Professional Golf Association (LPGA)
100 International Golf Dr.
Daytona Beach, FL 32124-1092 USA
Phone: 386-274-6200
Fax: 386-274-1099
E-mail Address: feedback@lpga.com
Web Address: www.lpga.com
The Ladies Professional Golf Association (LPGA) is
the governing organization for women's professional
golf.

Lega Serie A
Via I. Rosellini 4
Milano, 20124 Italy
Phone: 39-02-699101
E-mail Address: direzione@legaseriea.it
Web Address: www.legaseriea.it
The Serie A Championship is the premier football
division in Italy and is one of the world's elite
football leagues.

Liga Portugal
Rua da Constituicao, No. 2555
Porto, 4250-173 Portugal
Phone: 351-22-834-87-40
E-mail Address: geral@ligaportugal.pt
Web Address: www.ligaportugal.pt/pt/homepage/
Liga Portugal is the football association of Portugal.

Little League International Baseball and Softball
539 U.S. Rte. 15 Hwy
P.O. Box 3485
Williamsport, PA 17701-0485 USA
Phone: 570-326-1921
Fax: 570-326-1074
Web Address: www.littleleague.org
Little League International Baseball and Softball is a
nonprofit organization that supervises and assists
those who participate in Little League Baseball and
Softball across the globe.

Major Arena Soccer League (MASL)
3250 Greyhawk Ct.

Carlsbad, CA 92010 USA
E-mail Address: info@maslsoccer.com
Web Address: www.maslsoccer.com
The Major Arena Soccer League (MASL) is a North
American professional indoor soccer league. The
MASL features teams playing coast-to-coast in the
United States and Mexico.

Major League Baseball (MLB)
1271 Avenue of the Americas
New York, NY 10167 USA
Phone: 315-203-6761
Toll Free: 866-244-2291
Web Address: www.mlb.com
Major League Baseball (MLB) is the governing body
for professional baseball in the U.S.

Major League Soccer (MLS)
420 5th Ave., Fl. 7
New York, NY 10018 USA
Phone: 212-450-1200
Toll Free: 855-657-2245
E-mail Address: feedback@mlssoccer.com
Web Address: www.mlssoccer.com
Major League Soccer (MLS) is the organizing body
for professional soccer in the U.S. MLS was founded
in 1996 after the U.S. hosted the World Cup in 1994.

Minor League Baseball (MiLB)
1271 Avenue of the Americas
New York, NY 100200 USA
Phone: 315-203-6761
Toll Free: 866-244-2291
Web Address: www.milb.com
Minor League Baseball (MiLB), formerly The
National Association of Professional Baseball
Leagues (NAPBL), is the organizing body for U.S.
minor league baseball.

**National Association for Stock Car Auto Racing
(NASCAR)**
International Motorsports Center
One Daytona Blvd.
Daytona Beach, FL 32114 USA
Toll Free: 800-630-0535
E-mail Address: cs_escalations@nascar.com
Web Address: www.nascar.com
The National Association for Stock Car Auto Racing
(NASCAR) is the organizing body for professional
stock car racing. It sanctions over 1,200 races in 30
U.S. states, Canada, Mexico and Europe.

National Basketball Association (NBA)
645 Fifth Ave.
New York, NY 10022 USA
Phone: 212-407-8000
Fax: 212-754-6414
E-mail Address: Accessibility@nba.com
Web Address: www.nba.com
The National Basketball Association (NBA) is the premier professional basketball league in the U.S. It currently has 30 teams.

National Basketball League (China)
Guangqumen St. No. 80, Int'l Bldg.
Dongcheng District
Beijing, 100062 China
Web Address: www.china-nbl.cn
China's National Basketball League (NBL) is the country's primary semi-professional (minor league) basketball association. It is associated with the Chinese Basketball Association, the country's top-tier professional league.

National Football League (NFL)
345 Park Ave.
New York, NY 100154 USA
E-mail Address: enquiries@nfl.com
Web Address: www.nfl.com
The National Football League (NFL) is the organizing body for professional football in the U.S. consisting of 32 teams.

National Hockey League (NHL)
1185 Ave. of the Americas, Fl. 15
New York, NY 10036 USA
Phone: 212-789-2000
Fax: 212-789-2020
Web Address: www.nhl.com
The National Hockey League (NHL) is the organizing body of professional ice hockey and is comprised of 30 member clubs from the U.S. and Canada.

National Lacrosse League (NLL)
1635 Market St., Ste. 1600
Philadelphia, PA 19103 USA
Phone: 267-417-7951
E-mail Address: NLL@NLL.com
Web Address: www.nll.com
The National Lacrosse League (NLL) is the organizing body for professional lacrosse in North America.

NBA G League
645 Fifth Ave.
New York, NY 10022 USA
Phone: 212-407-8000
Web Address: gleague.nba.com
The NBA G League is the development league for the NBA.

NFL FLAG
Toll Free: 844-940-1005
E-mail Address: info@nflflag.com
Web Address: www.nflflag.com
NFL FLAG is a flag football association affiliated with USA Football, the national flag football organization in America. Some of NFL FLAG's teams are loosely associated with major NFL football teams. NFL FLAG teams have the opportunity to earn the right to compete in the NFL FLAG championships at the Superbowl.

NWSL (National Women's Soccer League)
292 Madison Ave., Fl. 3
New York, NY 10017 USA
Phone: 312-549-8900
E-mail Address: info@nwslsoccer.com
Web Address: www.nwslsoccer.com
The National Women's Soccer League (NWSL) is a Division-I women's professional soccer league featuring national team players from Canada, Mexico and the U.S. The clubs include the Boston Breakers, Chicago Red Stars, Houston Dash, FC Kansas City, Portland Thorns FC, Seattle Reign FC, Sky Blue FC, the Washington Spirit and the Western New York Flash. Based in Chicago, the NWSL is supported by the Canadian Soccer Association, Federation of Mexican Football and the United States Soccer Federation.

Premier Lacrosse League (PLL)
530 7th Ave., Ste. 2801
New York, NY 10016 USA
Phone: 310-928-1107
Toll Free: 877-359-1889
E-mail Address: legal@premierlacrosseleague.com
Web Address: premierlacrosseleague.com
Premier Lacrosse League (PLL) is an American professional field lacrosse league, composed of 8 teams.

Professional Bowlers Association (PBA)
222 West 44th St.
New York, NY 10036 USA
Toll Free: 800-342-5263

E-mail Address: GuestService@BowleroCorp.com
Web Address: www.pba.com
The Professional Bowlers Association (PBA) is the governing body of the professional bowling circuit. It has 4,300 members representing 13 countries including Canada, China, Australia, Korea, England, France, Germany, U.S., Sweden, Bermuda, Venezuela and Japan.

Professional Bull Riders, Inc. (PBR)
101 W. Riverwalk
Pueblo, CO 81003 USA
Phone: 719-242-2800
Fax: 719-242-2855
Toll Free: 800-732-1727
E-mail Address: pbrdirect@pbr.com
Web Address: www.pbr.com
The Professional Bull Riders, Inc. (PBR) is the governing body of professional bull riding. Its members include over 600 bull riders from the United States, Australia, Brazil, Canada and Mexico.

Professional Golfers Association (PGA)
1916 PGA Parkway
Frisco, TX 75033 USA
Toll Free: 877 410-7865
Web Address: www.pga.com
The Professional Golfers Association (PGA) is the organizing body for professional golf in the U.S. with membership comprising of over 28,000 men and women golf professionals.

Professional Pickleball Association (PPA)
Phone: 801-543-0324
Web Address: www.ppatour.com
The Professional Pickleball Association (PPA) promotes and oversees a professional tour for the sport of pickleball in the U.S. Tournaments are organized into men's singles, women's singles, men's double, women's doubles and mixed doubles.

Singapore Motor Sports Association
2 Kung Chong Rd.
#05-01 AA Ctr.
Singapore, 159140 Singapore
Phone: 65-6227-7889
Fax: 65-6227-0911
E-mail Address: contactus@mss.org.sg
Web Address: www.mss.org.sg
The Singapore Motor Sports Association is a nonprofit organization representing and promoting the motor sports and racing in Singapore.

U.S. Soccer Federation
303 E Wacker Dr., Ste. 1200
Chicago, IL 60601 USA
Phone: 312-808-1300
E-mail Address: communications@ussoccer.org
Web Address: www.ussoccer.com
The U.S. Soccer Federation is the governing body of soccer in the U.S. Founded in 1913, it was one of the first organizations to be affiliated with FIFA and is dedicated to promote and develop soccer at all recreational and competitive levels.

Union of European Football Associations (UEFA)
Route de Geneve 46
Case postale
Nyon 2, CH-1260 Switzerland
Phone: 41--848-04-2727
E-mail Address: media@uefa.ch
Web Address: www.uefa.com
The Union of European Football Associations (UEFA) is one of the six continental confederations that comprise FIFA, the international governing body of professional soccer. UEFA represents 54 national football associations across Europe.

United Soccer Leagues (USL)
1715 N. Westshore Blvd., Ste. 825
Tampa, FL 33607 USA
Phone: 813-963-3909
Web Address: www.uslsoccer.com
The United Soccer Leagues (USL) is North America's minor soccer league, promoting the growth of the sport within the U.S., Canada and the Caribbean. Among the several leagues it organizes are USL PRO; Major Indoor Soccer League (MISL); USL Premier Development League; and the women's league USL W-League.

United States Figure Skating Association (USFSA)
20 First St.
Colorado Springs, CO 80906 USA
Phone: 719-635-5200
Fax: 719-635-9548
E-mail Address: info@usfigureskating.org
Web Address: www.usfsa.org
The United States Figure Skating Association (USFSA) is the governing body of figure skating in the U.S.

United States Golf Association (USGA)
77 Liberty Corner Rd.
Liberty Corner, NJ 07938 USA
Phone: 908-234-2300

E-mail Address: comments@usga.org
Web Address: www.usga.org
The United States Golf Association (USGA) is the governing body of golf in the U.S. and Mexico. It is a nonprofit organization run by golfers, representing golf courses, clubs and facilities. It also organizes 13 national championships, including the U.S. Open, U.S. Women's Open and U.S. Senior Open.

United States National Teqball Federation
10811 Washington Blvd.
Culver City, CA 90232 USA
E-mail Address: info@teqballus.com
Web Address: www.teqballus.com
The United States National Teqball Federation (USNF) is focused on the growth of the sport of teqball from a grassroots and professional level across the U.S. with its main objectives being the education of amateurs and professionals on the rules of the sport. USNF runs referee webinars and certifications on a national level for all teqball clubs.

United States Tennis Association (USTA)
70 W. Red Oak Ln.
West Harrison, NY 10604 USA
Phone: 914-696-7000
E-mail Address: webresponse@usta.com
Web Address: www.usta.com
The United States Tennis Association (USTA) is the governing body of tennis in the U.S. It currently represents over 700,000 individual members. USTA operates the USTA Billie Jean King National Tennis Center, which plays host to the US Open competition annually.

USA Cycling
210 USA Cycling Pt., Ste. 100
Colorado Springs, CO 80919-2215 USA
Phone: 719-434-4200
E-mail Address: communications@usacycling.org
Web Address: www.usacycling.org
USA Cycling is the official cycling organization responsible for selecting and training cyclists to represent the United States in international competitions. USA Cycling is comprised of the United States Cycling Federation (USCF), National Off-Road Bicycle Association (NORBA), United States Professional Racing Organization (USPRO), the National Collegiate Cycling Association (NCCA) and the BMX Association.

USA Football
45 N. Pennsylvania St., Ste. 800

Indianapolis, IN 46204 USA
Phone: 317-614-7750
Toll Free: 877-536-6822
E-mail Address: support@usafootball.com
Web Address: www.usafootball.com
USA Football is a national governing body, advocating football's development for safe play among youth, high school and other amateur players. USA Football advances coaching education and player skill development for safer play and positive experiences through athletics.

USA Gymnastics
1099 N. Meridian St., Ste. 800
Indianapolis, IN 46204 USA
Phone: 317-237-5050
Fax: 317-732-1791
Toll Free: 800-345-4719
E-mail Address: membership@usagym.org
Web Address: usagym.org
USA Gymnastics is the governing body for gymnastics in the U.S.

USA Hockey, Inc.
1775 Bob Johnson Dr.
Colorado Springs, CO 80906-4090 USA
Phone: 719-576-8724
Fax: 719-538-1160
E-mail Address: usah@usahockey.org
Web Address: www.usahockey.com
USA Hockey, Inc. is the governing body of ice hockey in the U.S. It supports grassroots hockey programs, offers certification programs for coaches and officials, as well as organizes and trains men's and women's teams for international tournaments.

USA Lacrosse
2 Loveton Cir.
Sparks, MD 21152 USA
Phone: 410-235-6882
Fax: 410-472-2168
E-mail Address: info@usalacrosse.com
Web Address: www.usalacrosse.com
USA Lacrosse, with over 63 chapters and nearly 350,000 members, is the national governing body of amateur lacrosse players.

USA Pickleball Association (USAPA)
P.O. Box 7354
Surprise, AZ 85374 USA
E-mail Address: mediarelations@usapickleball.org
Web Address: usapickleball.org

The USA Pickleball Association (USAPA) was organized to promote the growth and development of pickleball, not only on a national but an international level. This organization provides players with official rules, tournaments, rankings and promotional materials.

USA Track & Field (USATF)
132 E. Washington St., Ste. 800
Indianapolis, IN 46204 USA
Phone: 317-261-0500
E-mail Address: membership@usatf.org
Web Address: www.usatf.org
USA Track & Field (USATF) is the governing body for track and field in the U.S.

USFTL (United States Flag & Touch Football League)
9215 Mentor Ave., Ste. 1004
Mentor, OH 44060 USA
Phone: 440-701-6712
E-mail Address: general@usftl.com
Web Address: usftl.sportngin.com
The USFTL offers organized league play, both touch and flag football, for adults across the United States. It also offers a youth league.

Women's National Basketball Association (WNBA)
645 5th Ave.
New York, NY 10022 USA
E-mail Address: leaguepasssupport@wnba.com
Web Address: www.wnba.com
The Women's National Basketball Association (WNBA) is the U.S. professional basketball league for women comprised of 12 teams, six in each conference. The conferences include Eastern Conference and Western Conference.

Women's Tennis Association (WTA)
100 Second Ave. S., Ste. 1100-S
St. Petersburg, FL 33701 USA
Phone: 727-895-5000
Fax: 727-894-1982
E-mail Address: feedback@wtatennis.com
Web Address: www.wtatennis.com
The Women's Tennis Association (WTA) is the governing body of the professional women's tennis tour.

World Boxing Association (WBA)
Av. Aquilino de la Guardia
Calle 47 Ocean Bus. Plaza, Fl. 14, Of. 14-05

Marbella, 0816-01091 Panama
Phone: 507-203-7680
E-mail Address: info@wbanews.com
Web Address: www.wbaboxing.com
The World Boxing Association (WBA) is one of several professional boxing associations that sanction official matches.

World Boxing Council (WBC)
Riobamba 835
Col. Lindavista. Del. Gustavo A. Madero
Mexico City, 07300 Mexico
Phone: 52-55-5119-5273
E-mail Address: contact@wbcboxing.com
Web Address: www.wbcboxing.com
The World Boxing Council (WBC) is one of several professional boxing associations responsible for the sanctioning of official matches.

27) Sports Marketing Associations

National Sports Marketing Network (NSMN)
Phone: 212-227-1300
Web Address: www.sportsmarketingnetwork.com
The National Sports Marketing Network (NSMN) serves as the national organizing body for networking opportunities, education and industry discussion for the sports business industry. Chapters are located in major cities across the U.S., including Atlanta, Boston, Chicago, Denver, Los Angeles, New York City, Philadelphia, San Francisco and Washington, DC.

Sport Marketing Association (SMA)
1972 Clark Ave.
Alliance, OH 44601 USA
Phone: 330-829-8207
E-mail Address:
office@sportmarketingassociation.com
Web Address: www.sportmarketingassociation.com
The Sport Marketing Association (SMA) is a professional association for sport marketing practitioners and academics. The organization seeks to develop beneficial relationships between sport marketing professionals and academicians and expand the field's body of knowledge.

28) Technology Transfer Associations

Licensing Executives Society (USA and Canada), Inc.
11130 Sunrise Valley Dr., Ste. 350

Reston, VA 20191 USA
Phone: 703-234-4058
Fax: 703-435-4390
E-mail Address: info@les.org
Web Address: www.lesusacanada.org
Licensing Executives Society (USA and Canada), Inc., established in 1965, is a professional association composed of about 3,000 members who work in fields related to the development, use, transfer, manufacture and marketing of intellectual property. Members include executives, lawyers, licensing consultants, engineers, academic researchers, scientists and government officials. The society is part of the larger Licensing Executives Society International, Inc. (same headquarters address), with a worldwide membership.

29) Trade Associations-General

BUSINESSEUROPE
168 Ave. de Cortenbergh 168
Brussels, 1000 Belgium
Phone: 32-2-237-65-11
Fax: 32-2-231-14-45
E-mail Address: main@businesseurope.eu
Web Address: www.businesseurope.eu
BUSINESSEUROPE is a major European trade federation that operates in a manner similar to a chamber of commerce. Its members are the central national business federations of the 34 countries throughout Europe from which they come. Companies cannot become direct members of BUSINESSEUROPE, though there is a support group which offers the opportunity for firms to encourage BUSINESSEUROPE objectives in various ways.

United States Council for International Business (USCIB)
1212 Ave. of the Americas
New York, NY 10036 USA
Phone: 212-354-4480
Fax: 212-575-0327
E-mail Address: news@uscib.org
Web Address: www.uscib.org
The United States Council for International Business (USCIB) promotes an open system of world trade and investment through its global network. Standard USCIB members include corporations, law firms, consulting firms and industry associations. Limited membership options are available for chambers of commerce and sole legal practitioners.

VR/AR Association (VRARA)
Palo Alto, CA 94303 USA
Phone: 314-640-1404
E-mail Address: info@thevrara.com
Web Address: www.thevrara.com
The VR/AR Association (VRARA) is an international organization designed to foster collaboration between solution providers and end-users that accelerates growth, fosters research and education, helps develop industry best practices, connects member organizations and promotes the services of member companies.

30) Trade Associations-Global

World Trade Organization (WTO)
Centre William Rappard
Rue de Lausanne 154
Geneva 21, CH-1211 Switzerland
Phone: 41-22-739-51-11
Fax: 41-22-731-42-06
E-mail Address: enquiries@wto.og
Web Address: www.wto.org
The World Trade Organization (WTO) is a global organization dealing with the rules of trade between nations. To become a member, nations must agree to abide by certain guidelines. Membership increases a nation's ability to import and export efficiently.

31) Trade Resources

Made-in-China.com - China Manufacturers Directory
Block A, Software Bldg. No. 9, Xinghuo Rd.
Nanjing New & High Technology Industry Development Zone
Nanjing, Jiangsu 210032 China
Fax: 86-25-6667-0000
Web Address: www.made-in-china.com
Made-in-China.com - China Manufacturers Directory, one of the largest business to business portals in China, helps to connect Chinese manufacturers, suppliers and traders with international buyers. Made-in-China.com contains additional information on trade shows and important laws and regulations about business with China.

32) U.S. Government Agencies

Bureau of Economic Analysis (BEA)
4600 Silver Hill Rd.
Washington, DC 20233 USA

Phone: 301-278-9004
E-mail Address: customerservice@bea.gov
Web Address: www.bea.gov
The Bureau of Economic Analysis (BEA), is an
agency of the U.S. Department of Commerce, is the
nation's economic accountant, preparing estimates
that illuminate key national, international and
regional aspects of the U.S. economy.

Bureau of Labor Statistics (BLS)
2 Massachusetts Ave. NE
Washington, DC 20212-0001 USA
Phone: 202-691-5200
Fax: 202-691-7890
Toll Free: 800-877-8339
E-mail Address: blsdata_staff@bls.gov
Web Address: stats.bls.gov
The Bureau of Labor Statistics (BLS) is the principal
fact-finding agency for the Federal Government in
the field of labor economics and statistics. It is an
independent national statistical agency that collects,
processes, analyzes and disseminates statistical data
to the American public, U.S. Congress, other federal
agencies, state and local governments, business and
labor. The BLS also serves as a statistical resource to
the Department of Labor.

U.S. Census Bureau
4600 Silver Hill Rd.
Washington, DC 20233-8800 USA
Phone: 301-763-4636
Toll Free: 800-923-8282
E-mail Address: pio@census.gov
Web Address: www.census.gov
The U.S. Census Bureau is the official collector of
data about the people and economy of the U.S.
Founded in 1790, it provides official social,
demographic and economic information. In addition
to the Population & Housing Census, which it
conducts every 10 years, the U.S. Census Bureau
conducts numerous other surveys annually.

U.S. Department of Commerce (DOC)
1401 Constitution Ave. NW
Washington, DC 20230 USA
Phone: 202-482-2000
E-mail Address: publicaffairs@doc.gov
Web Address: www.commerce.gov
The U.S. Department of Commerce (DOC) regulates
trade and provides valuable economic analysis of the
economy.

U.S. Department of Labor (DOL)
200 Constitution Ave. NW
Washington, DC 20210 USA
Phone: 202-693-4676
Toll Free: 866-487-2365
E-mail Address: m-DOLPublicAffairs@dol.gov
Web Address: www.dol.gov
The U.S. Department of Labor (DOL) is the
government agency responsible for labor regulations.
The Department of Labor's goal is to foster, promote,
and develop the welfare of the wage earners, job
seekers, and retirees of the United States; improve
working conditions; advance opportunities for
profitable employment; and assure work-related
benefits and rights.

U.S. Securities and Exchange Commission (SEC)
100 F St. NE
Washington, DC 20549 USA
Phone: 202-942-8088
Fax: 202-772-9295
Toll Free: 800-732-0330
E-mail Address: help@sec.gov
Web Address: www.sec.gov
The U.S. Securities and Exchange Commission
(SEC) is a nonpartisan, quasi-judicial regulatory
agency responsible for administering federal
securities laws. These laws are designed to protect
investors in securities markets and ensure that they
have access to disclosure of all material information
concerning publicly traded securities. Visitors to the
web site can access the EDGAR database of
corporate financial and business information.

**33) Writers, Photographers & Editors
Associations**

Associated Press Sports Editors (APSE)
P.O. Box 699
Huntington, NY 11743 USA
E-mail Address: byrne@usatoday.com
Web Address: www.apsportseditors.com
Associated Press Sports Editors (APSE) is a trade
organization for professional sports reporters, editors,
copy editors and designers.

Association for Women in Sports Media (AWSM)
21317 Estero Preserve Run
Estero, FL 33928 USA
E-mail Address: awsmboard@gmail.com
Web Address: www.awsmonline.org
The Association for Women in Sports Media
(AWSM) is a global organization of over 600 people

employed in sports writing, editing, broadcasting and
production, public relations and sports information.
Its mission is to support diversity in sports media
through programs that aid females involved in the
industry.

Football Writers Association of America (FWAA)
18652 Vista del Sol
Dallas, TX 75287 USA
Phone: 972-713-6198
E-mail Address: tiger@fwaa.com
Web Address: www.sportswriters.net/fwaa
The Football Writers Association of America
(FWAA) consists of North American journalists,
broadcasters and publishers that cover college
football. The FWAA also includes executives
involved in various aspects of the game.

**National Collegiate Baseball Writers Association
(NCBWA)**
5201 N. O'Connor Blvd., Ste. 300
Irving, TX 75039 USA
Phone: 214-909-9314
E-mail Address: webmaster@sportswriters.net
Web Address: www.sportswriters.net/ncbwa
The National Collegiate Baseball Writers Association
(NCBWA) consists of writers, broadcasters and
publicists of college baseball in the U.S.

**United States Basketball Writers Association
(USBWA)**
P.O. Box 257
Zionsville, IN 46077 USA
Phone: 814-574-1485
E-mail Address: webmaster@sportswriters.net
Web Address: www.sportswriters.net/usbwa
The United States Basketball Writers Association
(USBWA) is an organization representing college and
high school basketball writers in the U.S.

Chapter 4

THE SPORTS & RECREATION 400: WHO THEY ARE AND HOW THEY WERE CHOSEN

Includes Indexes by Company Name, Industry Code & Location

The companies, organizations, leagues and teams chosen to be listed in PLUNKETT'S SPORTS & RECREATION INDUSTRY ALMANAC comprise a unique list. THE SPORTS & RECREATION 400 were chosen specifically for their dominance in the many facets of the sports, leisure and recreation industry in which they operate. Complete information about each organization can be found in the "Individual Profiles," beginning at the end of this chapter. These profiles are in alphabetical order by organization name.

THE SPORTS & RECREATION 400 teams, leagues and companies are from all parts of the United States, Asia, Canada, Europe and beyond. Essentially, THE SPORTS & RECREATION 400 includes organizations that are deeply involved in the services, teams, leagues and associations that keep the entire industry forging ahead. To be included in our list, the organizations had to meet the following criteria:

1) Generally, these are organizations based in the U.S., however, the headquarters of many are located in other nations.

2) Prominence, or a significant presence, in sports, recreation and supporting fields. (See the following Industry Codes section for a complete list of types of manufacturers, businesses, teams and leagues that are covered).

3) The organizations in THE SPORTS & RECREATION 400 do not have to be exclusively in the sports and recreation industry.

4) Sufficient data and vital statistics must have been available to the editors of this book, either directly from the organization being written about or from outside sources deemed reliable and accurate by the editors. A small number of organizations that we would like to have included are not listed because of a lack of sufficient, objective data.

INDEXES TO THE SPORTS & RECREATION 400, AS FOUND IN THIS CHAPTER AND IN THE BACK OF THE BOOK:

Index of Companies Within Industry Groups	p. 74
Alphabetical Index	p. 84
Index of U.S. Headquarters Location by State	p. 88
Index of Non-U.S. Headquarters Location by Country	p. 91
Index of Firms Noted as "Hot Spots for Advancement" for Women/Minorities	p. 506
Index by Subsidiaries, Brand Names and Selected Affiliations	p. 508

INDEX OF COMPANIES WITHIN INDUSTRY GROUPS

The industry codes shown below are based on the 2012 NAIC code system (NAIC is used by many analysts as a replacement for older SIC codes because NAIC is more specific to today's industry sectors, see www.census.gov/NAICS). Companies are given a primary NAIC code, reflecting the main line of business of each firm.

Industry Group/Company	Industry Code	2022 Sales	2022 Profits
Apparel and Clothing Brands, Designers, Importers and Distributors			
Boardriders Inc	424300	290,000,000	
Columbia Sportswear Company	424300	3,464,152,064	311,440,000
Delta Apparel Inc	424300	484,859,008	19,740,000
Fila USA Inc	424300	346,373,357	-59,883,349
Kellwood Company LLC	424300	480,000,000	
North Face Inc (The)	424300		
Patagonia Inc	424300	1,000,000,000	
Under Armour Inc	424300		
Varsity Brands Holding Co Inc	424300	801,000,000	
VF Corporation	424300	11,841,840,128	1,386,941,056
Apparel Manufacturing, General and Specialty			
Majestic Athletic	315280		
Arts and Sports Promoters and Agents and Managers For Public Figures			
OneTeam Partners LLC	711400		
Automobile (Car) Racing & Motor Sports			
Chip Ganassi Racing With Felix Sabates Inc	711219		
Hendrick Motorsports	711219		
Joe Gibbs Racing	711219		
Legacy Motor Club	711219		
Roush Fenway Keselowski Racing (RFK Racing)	711219		
Team Penske	711219		
Baseball Teams			
Arizona Diamondbacks	711211A	354,250,000	
Atlanta Braves	711211A		
Baltimore Orioles	711211A	329,550,000	
Boston Red Sox	711211A	648,700,000	
Chicago Cubs	711211A	582,400,000	
Chicago White Sox	711211A	352,950,000	
Cincinnati Reds	711211A	352,300,000	
Cleveland Guardians	711211A	362,050,000	
Colorado Rockies	711211A	373,750,000	
Detroit Tigers	711211A	353,600,000	
Houston Astros	711211A	525,200,000	
Kansas City Royals	711211A	334,100,000	
Los Angeles Angels	711211A	460,200,000	
Los Angeles Dodgers	711211A	481,650,000	
Miami Marlins	711211A	300,300,000	
Milwaukee Brewers	711211A	366,600,000	
Minnesota Twins	711211A	367,250,000	

Industry Group/Company	Industry Code	2022 Sales	2022 Profits
New York Mets	711211A	431,600,000	
New York Yankees	711211A	378,300,000	
Oakland Athletics	711211A	281,450,000	
Philadelphia Phillies	711211A	464,750,000	
Pittsburgh Pirates	711211A	345,150,000	
San Diego Padres	711211A	377,650,000	
San Francisco Giants	711211A	543,400,000	
Seattle Mariners	711211A	408,200,000	
St Louis Cardinals	711211A	502,500,000	
Tampa Bay Rays	711211A	250,000,000	
Texas Rangers	711211A	541,500,000	
Toronto Blue Jays	711211A		
Washington Nationals	711211A	519,000,000	
Basketball Teams			
Atlanta Hawks	711211B	273,650,000	
Boston Celtics	711211B	315,250,000	
Brooklyn Nets	711211B	319,800,000	
Charlotte Hornets	711211B	258,700,000	
Chicago Bulls	711211B	333,450,000	
Cleveland Cavaliers	711211B	312,000,000	
Dallas Mavericks	711211B	341,900,000	
Denver Nuggets	711211B	261,950,000	
Detroit Pistons	711211B	272,350,000	
Golden State Warriors	711211B	475,800,000	
Houston Rockets	711211B	345,150,000	
Indiana Pacers	711211B	257,400,000	
Los Angeles Clippers	711211B	312,650,000	
Los Angeles Lakers	711211B	465,400,000	
Memphis Grizzlies	711211B	257,400,000	
Miami HEAT	711211B	314,600,000	
Milwaukee Bucks	711211B	293,150,000	
Minnesota Timberwolves	711211B	268,450,000	
New Orleans Pelicans	711211B	253,500,000	
New York Knickerbockers	711211B	467,300,000	
Oklahoma City Thunder	711211B	272,350,000	
Orlando Magic	711211B	263,900,000	
Philadelphia 76ers	711211B	321,750,000	
Phoenix Suns	711211B	278,200,000	
Portland Trail Blazers	711211B	286,650,000	
Sacramento Kings	711211B	284,050,000	
San Antonio Spurs	711211B	299,000,000	
Toronto Raptors	711211B		
Utah Jazz	711211B	317,200,000	
Washington Wizards	711211B	288,600,000	
Basketball Teams, Women's			
Atlanta Dream	711211E		
Chicago Sky	711211E		
Connecticut Sun	711211E		
Dallas Wings	711211E		

Industry Group/Company	Industry Code	2022 Sales	2022 Profits
Indiana Fever	711211E		
Las Vegas Aces	711211E		
Los Angeles Sparks	711211E		
Minnesota Lynx	711211E		
New York Liberty	711211E		
Phoenix Mercury	711211E		
Seattle Storm	711211E		
Washington Mystics	711211E		
Boat Building			
Marine Products Corporation	336612	380,995,008	40,347,000
Boat Dealers			
MarineMax Inc	441222	2,308,098,048	197,988,992
West Marine Inc	441222		
Bowling Centers			
Bowlero Corp	713950	911,705,024	-29,934,000
Cable TV Programming, Cable Networks and Subscription Video			
DAZN Group Limited	515210		
ESPN Inc	515210	15,500,000,000	
Paramount Global	515210	30,154,000,384	1,104,000,000
Walt Disney Company (The)	515210	82,721,996,800	3,144,999,936
Candy and Chocolate Manufacturing (From Cacao Beans)			
Topps Company Inc (The)	311351		
Casinos (Except Casino Hotels)			
Churchill Downs Incorporated	713210	1,809,799,936	439,400,000
Penn National Gaming Inc	713210	6,401,699,840	222,100,000
Clothing and Apparel Stores			
lululemon athletica inc	448100	6,256,616,960	975,321,984
Computer Peripherals and Accessories, including Printers, Monitors and Terminals Manufacturing			
WHOOP Inc	334118		
Computer Software: Electronic Games, Apps & Entertainment			
eGames.com Holdings LLC (Buzztime)	511210G		
Electronic Arts Inc (EA)	511210G	6,991,000,064	789,000,000
Consulting Services, Administrative and General Management			
Oak View Group	541611		
Diesel, Semidiesel, Locomotive, Marine and Other Non-Automotive or Aircraft Engine Equipment Manufacturing			
Brunswick Corporation	333618	6,812,199,936	677,000,000
Facilities Support Services			
ASM Global	561210		
Fitness Centers, Gyms and Exercise and Fitness Programs			
24 Hour Fitness	713940		
Anytime Fitness LLC	713940		
Canlan Ice Sports Corp	713940	53,777,588	3,450,087
Curves NA	713940		
Equinox Fitness	713940		
Golds Gym International Inc	713940		

Industry Group/Company	Industry Code	2022 Sales	2022 Profits
Grupo Sports World SAB de CV	713940		
HealthFitness Corporation	713940		
LA Fitness (LA Fitness International LLC)	713940		
Life Time Inc	713940		
Little Gym International Inc (The)	713940		
Peloton Interactive Inc	713940	3,582,200,064	-2,827,699,968
Planet Fitness Inc	713940	936,771,968	99,402,000
Snap Fitness Inc	713940		
SoulCycle Inc	713940		
Zumba Fitness LLC	713940		
Food Service Contractors			
Aramark Corporation	722310	16,326,624,256	194,484,000
Delaware North Companies Inc	722310	3,800,000,000	
Sodexo Live!	722310	221,867,100	
Football Teams (American Football)			
Arizona Cardinals	711211C	503,750,000	
Atlanta Falcons	711211C	533,000,000	
Baltimore Ravens	711211C	527,800,000	
Buffalo Bills	711211C	489,450,000	
Carolina Panthers	711211C	518,700,000	
Chicago Bears	711211C	550,550,000	
Cincinnati Bengals	711211C	484,250,000	
Cleveland Browns	711211C	523,900,000	
Dallas Cowboys	711211C	1,170,000,000	
Denver Broncos	711211C	544,700,000	
Detroit Lions	711211C	481,650,000	
Green Bay Packers	711211C	579,000,000	61,600,000
Houston Texans	711211C	602,550,000	
Indianapolis Colts	711211C	504,400,000	
Jacksonville Jaguars	711211C	522,600,000	
Kansas City Chiefs	711211C	519,350,000	
Las Vegas Raiders	711211C	501,800,000	
Los Angeles Chargers	711211C	434,200,000	
Los Angeles Rams	711211C	610,000,000	
Miami Dolphins	711211C	541,450,000	
Minnesota Vikings	711211C	528,450,000	
New England Patriots	711211C	720,200,000	
New Orleans Saints	711211C	550,550,000	
New York Giants	711211C	570,000,000	
New York Jets	711211C	547,300,000	
Philadelphia Eagles	711211C	572,000,000	
Pittsburgh Steelers	711211C	533,650,000	
San Francisco 49ers	711211C	587,600,000	
Seattle Seahawks	711211C	542,100,000	
Tampa Bay Buccaneers	711211C	508,950,000	
Tennessee Titans	711211C	504,400,000	
Washington Commanders	711211C	579,800,000	
Golf Courses and Country Clubs			
Accordia Golf Co Ltd	713910		

Industry Group/Company	Industry Code	2022 Sales	2022 Profits
American Golf Corporation	713910		
ClubCorp Holdings Inc (Invited)	713910		
Hockey Teams			
Anaheim Ducks	711211F	120,250,000	
Arizona Coyotes	711211F	104,650,000	
Boston Bruins	711211F	161,200,000	
Buffalo Sabres	711211F	122,850,000	
Calgary Flames	711211F		
Carolina Hurricanes	711211F	120,250,000	
Chicago Blackhawks	711211F	166,400,000	
Colorado Avalanche	711211F	119,600,000	
Columbus Blue Jackets	711211F	112,450,000	
Dallas Stars	711211F	142,350,000	
Detroit Red Wings	711211F	150,150,000	
Edmonton Oilers	711211F		
Florida Panthers	711211F	148,850,000	
Los Angeles Kings	711211F	168,350,000	
Minnesota Wild	711211F	124,800,000	
Montreal Canadiens	711211F		
Nashville Predators	711211F	124,150,000	
New Jersey Devils	711211F	149,500,000	
New York Islanders	711211F	107,900,000	
New York Rangers	711211F	207,350,000	
Ottawa Senators	711211F		
Philadelphia Flyers	711211F	152,750,000	
Pittsburgh Penguins	711211F	152,750,000	
San Jose Sharks	711211F	118,950,000	
St Louis Blues	711211F	129,350,000	
Tampa Bay Lightning	711211F	133,250,000	
Toronto Maple Leafs	711211F		
Vancouver Canucks	711211F		
Vegas Golden Knights	711211F	150,800,000	
Washington Capitals	711211F	142,350,000	
Winnipeg Jets	711211F		
Internet Search Engines, Online Publishing, Sharing, Gig and Consumer Services, Online Radio, TV and Entertainment Sites and Social Media			
Bleacher Report Inc (B/R)	519130		
DraftKings Inc	519130	2,240,461,056	-1,377,986,944
FanDuel Group	519130	300,000,000	
Major League Baseball Advanced Media LP (MLBAM)	519130		
Score Media Ventures Inc	519130		
Underdog Sports Inc	519130		
Magazine Publishing and Financial Information Publishing			
Sports Illustrated	511120		
Mail Order, Catalogs and Other Direct Marketing, and TV Shopping			
BSN Sports Inc	454113	1,500,000,000	

Industry Group/Company	Industry Code	2022 Sales	2022 Profits
Men's and Boys' Clothing and Furnishings Wholesale Distribution			
ANTA Sports Products Limited	424320	7,791,202,816	1,102,220,416
Motorcycle, Bicycle and Parts Manufacturing			
Cannondale Bicycle Corporation	336991		
Huffy Bicycle Co	336991		
Pacific Cycle Inc	336991		
Specialized Bicycle Components Inc	336991		
Trek Bicycle Corporation	336991		
Online Sales, B2C Ecommerce, Sharing Economy Platforms			
Fanatics Inc	454111	6,300,000,000	
Professional Sports Teams and Clubs			
American Hockey League Inc	711211		
Anschutz Entertainment Group Inc	711211		
Association of Tennis Professionals (ATP Tour Inc)	711211		
Campeonato Nacional de Liga Primera Division (La Liga)	711211		
Canadian Football League	711211		
Celtic PLC	711211	107,538,088	7,128,580
ECHL	711211		
Fenerbahce Spor Kulubu	711211		
FIFA (Federation Internationale de Football Association)	711211		
Formula One Group (F1)	711211		
Fussball Bundesliga	711211		
IndyCar LLC	711211		
International Boxing Federation	711211		
International Olympic Committee (IOC)	711211		
Katz Group Of Companies (The)	711211		
Ladies Professional Golf Association (LPGA)	711211		
Ligue de Football Professionnel	711211		
LIV Golf Inc	711211		
Madison Square Garden Sports Corp	711211	821,353,984	51,131,000
Major League Baseball (MLB)	711211	11,000,000,000	
Major League Soccer (MLS)	711211	990,000,000	
Minor League Baseball	711211		
NASCAR	711211	900,000,000	
National Basketball Association (NBA)	711211	10,100,000,000	
National Football League (NFL)	711211	16,000,000,000	
National Hockey League (NHL)	711211	5,400,000,000	
National Thoroughbred Racing Association	711211		
NBA G League	711211		
PGA European Tour (bda DP World Tour)	711211		
Professional Bowlers Association LLC	711211		
Professional Bull Riders Inc	711211		
Professional Golfers Association of America (PGA)	711211		
Union of European Football Associations (UEFA)	711211		
United Soccer League	711211		
United States Golf Association (USGA)	711211		
United States Olympic & Paralympic Committee (USOPC)	711211	297,000,000	-30,000,000

Industry Group/Company	Industry Code	2022 Sales	2022 Profits
United States Tennis Association (USTA)	711211		
US Figure Skating	711211		
US Soccer Federation	711211		
USA Basketball	711211		
USA Cycling	711211		
USA Gymnastics	711211		
USA Hockey Inc	711211		
USA Swimming	711211		
USA Track & Field Inc	711211		
Womens National Basketball Association (WNBA)	711211		
Womens Tennis Association (WTA)	711211		
World Boxing Association (The)	711211		
World Boxing Council	711211		
Promoters and Producers of Performing Arts, Sports and Other Entertainment Events			
Corporacion Interamericana de Entretenimiento SA	711300		
World Triathlon Corporation (Ironman, WTC)	711300		
Promoters of Performing Arts, Sports and Similar Events with Facilities			
Kroenke Sports & Entertainment LLC	711310		
Maple Leaf Sports & Entertainment Ltd	711310		
Palace Sports & Entertainment Inc	711310		
Racetracks (Including Car and Motorsports)			
Speedway Motorsports LLC	711212		
Radio Networks, Including Commercial Networks Supporting Radio Broadcasting, and Public Radio Networks			
Sirius XM Holdings Inc	515111	9,002,999,808	1,212,999,936
Recreational Goods Rental			
Motivate LLC	532292		
Restaurants, Fast-Food, Pizza Delivery, Takeout and Family			
Ilitch Holdings Inc	722513	3,200,000,000	
Restaurants, Full-Service, Sit Down			
Levy Restaurants	722511	1,200,000,000	
Shoe and Footwear Brands, Designers, Importers and Distributors			
adidas AG	424340	24,039,170,048	653,545,920
AND 1	424340		
ASICS Corp	424340	3,663,337,984	150,335,632
Converse Inc	424340	2,227,000,000	
K-Swiss Inc	424340	145,000,000	-14,465,100
Li Ning Company Limited	424340	3,747,169,536	590,150,336
New Balance Athletic Shoe Inc	424340	5,300,000,000	
Nike Inc	424340	46,710,001,664	6,046,000,128
PUMA SE	424340	9,039,757,312	377,497,536
Reebok International Limited	424340	2,510,000,000	
Small Arms Ammunition Manufacturing			
Vista Outdoor Inc	332992	3,044,621,056	473,225,984

Industry Group/Company	Industry Code	2022 Sales	2022 Profits
Snow Ski Resorts and Skiing Related Facilities			
Alterra Mountain Company	713920		
Aspen Skiing Company	713920		
Booth Creek Ski Holdings Inc	713920		
Boyne Resorts	713920		
Crested Butte Mountain Resort Inc	713920		
Vail Resorts Inc	713920	2,525,912,064	347,923,008
Winter Sports Inc	713920		
Soccer (Futbol/Football) Teams			
AFC Ajax NV	711211D		
Arsenal Football Club Plc	711211D		
AS Roma (Associazione Sportiva Roma)	711211D		
Association Sportive de Saint-Etienne Loire (AS Saint-Etienne)	711211D		
Associazione Calcio Milan spa	711211D		
Aston Villa Football Club	711211D		
Athletic Club (Athletic Bilbao)	711211D		
Atlanta United FC	711211D	107,932,500	
Blackburn Rovers Football Club	711211D		
Borussia Dortmund GmbH & Co KGaA	711211D	375,516,608	-37,439,000
Chelsea Football Club	711211D		
Chicago Fire Soccer Club	711211D	7,426,125	
Club Atletico de Madrid SAD (Atletico Madrid)	711211D		
Club de Foot Montreal (CF Montreal)	711211D		
Club de Futbol America SA de CV (America)	711211D		
Club de Futbol Monterrey	711211D		
Club Deportivo Guadalajara SA de CV (Chivas)	711211D		
Club Universidad Nacional-Asociacion Civil (UNAM/Pumas)	711211D		
Clube de Regatas do Flamengo	711211D		
Colorado Rapids	711211D	5,811,750	
Columbus Crew	711211D	7,389,900	
Cruzeiro Esporte Clube	711211D		
DC United	711211D	13,173,300	
Deportivo Toluca Futbol Club SA de CV	711211D		
Everton Football Club	711211D		
FC Cincinnati	711211D		
FC Dallas	711211D	10,654,875	
Football Club des Girondins de Bordeaux (Bordeaux)	711211D		
Football Club Dynamo Kyiv	711211D		
Football Club Internazionale Milano SpA	711211D		
Football-Club Bayern Munchen eV	711211D		
Football-Club Gelsenkirchen-Schalke 04 eV	711211D		
Fulham Football Club	711211D		
Futbol Club Barcelona	711211D		
Futebol Clube do Porto (FC Porto)	711211D		
Galatasaray Spor Kulubu (Galatasaray SK)	711211D		
Houston Dynamo FC	711211D	7,389,900	
Juventus Football Club SpA	711211D	472,696,768	-271,577,504
Leicester City Football Club	711211D		
Liverpool Football Club	711211D		

Industry Group/Company	Industry Code	2022 Sales	2022 Profits
Los Angeles Football Club	711211D		
Los Angeles Galaxy	711211D	50,673,600	
Manchester City Football Club	711211D		
Manchester United plc	711211D	710,787,392	-140,780,016
Middlesbrough Football Club	711211D		
Minnesota United FC	711211D	7,711,200	
MLS NEXT Pro (Pro Soccer Development LP)	711211D		
New England Revolution	711211D	9,446,220	
New York City FC	711211D	33,736,500	
New York Red Bulls	711211D		
Newcastle United Football Club	711211D		
Norwich City Football Club	711211D		
Olympiacos Football Club	711211D		
Olympique de Marseille	711211D		
Olympique Lyonnais Groupe	711211D	171,368,944	-57,761,928
Orlando City SC	711211D	14,779,800	
Paris Saint-Germain Football Club (PSG)	711211D		
Philadelphia Union	711211D	8,996,400	
Philips Sport Vereniging (PSV Eindhoven)	711211D		
Portland Timbers	711211D	35,235,900	
Real Madrid Club de Futbol	711211D		
Real Salt Lake	711211D	7,426,125	
San Jose Earthquakes	711211D	11,245,500	
Santos Futebol Clube	711211D		
Sao Paulo Futebol Clube	711211D		
Seattle Sounders FC	711211D	15,101,100	
Sociedade Esportiva Palmeiras	711211D		
Societa Sportiva Calcio Napoli (SSC Napoli)	711211D		
Southampton Football Club	711211D		
Sporting Kansas City	711211D	13,883,625	
Sportverein Werder Bremen von 1899 eV	711211D		
St Louis City SC	711211D		
Toronto FC	711211D		
Tottenham Hotspur Football Club	711211D		
USL Championship League (USL Pro LLC)	711211D		
Valencia Club de Futbol (Valencia CF/Valencia)	711211D		
Vancouver Whitecaps FC	711211D		
Verein fur Bewegungsspiele Stuttgart 1893 eV (VfB Stuttgart)	711211D		
West Bromwich Albion Football Club	711211D		
West Ham United Football Club	711211D		
Wolverhampton Wanderers Football Club	711211D		
Sporting Goods Distributors			
Xtep International Holdings Limited	423910	1,877,751,552	133,848,488
Sporting Goods Stores			
Academy Sports & Outdoors Inc	451110	6,773,128,192	671,380,992
Big 5 Sporting Goods Corporation	451110	995,537,984	26,134,000
BPS Direct LLC (Bass Pro Shops)	451110	6,500,000,000	
Cabelas Inc	451110	7,000,000,000	
Dicks Sporting Goods Inc	451110	12,293,367,808	1,519,870,976

Industry Group/Company	Industry Code	2022 Sales	2022 Profits
Eastern Mountain Sports Inc	451110	555,000,000	
Field & Stream	451110		
Golf Galaxy Inc	451110		
Golf Town Limited	451110		
Hibbett Sports Inc	451110	1,691,184,000	174,312,992
Orvis Company Inc (The)	451110	370,000,000	
REI (Recreational Equipment Inc)	451110	3,850,174,000	-164,712,000
Sportsmans Guide Inc (The)	451110		
Sporting Goods, Athletic Products and Recreational Items Manufacturing			
Amer Sports Corporation	339920		
BRG Sports Inc	339920		
CamelBak Products LLC	339920		
Coleman Company Inc (The)	339920		
Everlast Worldwide Inc	339920		
Franklin Sports Inc	339920		
Giant Manufacturing Co Ltd	339920	3,006,194,688	190,864,016
Head Sport GmbH	339920		
Johnson Outdoors Inc	339920	743,355,008	44,491,000
Prince Global Sports LLC	339920		
Rawlings Sporting Goods Company Inc	339920		
Russell Brands LLC	339920	2,900,000,000	
Skis Rossignol SA	339920		
Sport Maska Inc (CCM Hockey)	339920	466,000,000	
Tecnica Group SpA	339920		
Topgolf Callaway Brands Corp	339920	3,995,699,968	157,900,000
Wilson Sporting Goods Co	339920		
Talent Agencies, Agents and Managers for Athletes and Entertainers			
BDA Sports Management	711410		
Endeavor Group Holdings Inc	711410	5,268,136,960	129,133,000
Newport Sports Management Inc	711410		
Octagon Worldwide	711410		
Wasserman Media Group LLC	711410		
Telephone, Internet Access, Cable TV, Broadband, Data Networks, Server Facilities and Telecommunications Services Industry			
Altice USA Inc	517110	9,647,659,008	194,563,008
Comcast Corporation	517110	121,427,001,344	5,369,999,872
Cox Communications Inc	517110	13,800,000,000	
Rogers Communications Inc	517110	11,229,922,304	1,225,400,832
Television Broadcasting			
Disney Media & Entertainment Distribution	515120	52,000,000,000	
Fox Broadcasting Company	515120	7,645,000,000	
Fox Sports (Fox Sports Media Group)	515120		
NBCUniversal Media LLC	515120	36,000,000,000	
Venture Capital, Private Equity Investment and Hedge Funds			
Fenway Sports Group LLC	523910		

ALPHABETICAL INDEX

24 Hour Fitness
Academy Sports & Outdoors Inc
Accordia Golf Co Ltd
adidas AG
AFC Ajax NV
Alterra Mountain Company
Altice USA Inc
Amer Sports Corporation
American Golf Corporation
American Hockey League Inc
Anaheim Ducks
AND 1
Anschutz Entertainment Group Inc
ANTA Sports Products Limited
Anytime Fitness LLC
Aramark Corporation
Arizona Cardinals
Arizona Coyotes
Arizona Diamondbacks
Arsenal Football Club Plc
AS Roma (Associazione Sportiva Roma)
ASICS Corp
ASM Global
Aspen Skiing Company
Association of Tennis Professionals (ATP Tour Inc)
Association Sportive de Saint-Etienne Loire (AS Saint-Etienne)
Associazione Calcio Milan spa
Aston Villa Football Club
Athletic Club (Athletic Bilbao)
Atlanta Braves
Atlanta Dream
Atlanta Falcons
Atlanta Hawks
Atlanta United FC
Baltimore Orioles
Baltimore Ravens
BDA Sports Management
Big 5 Sporting Goods Corporation
Blackburn Rovers Football Club
Bleacher Report Inc (B/R)
Boardriders Inc
Booth Creek Ski Holdings Inc
Borussia Dortmund GmbH & Co KGaA
Boston Bruins
Boston Celtics
Boston Red Sox
Bowlero Corp
Boyne Resorts
BPS Direct LLC (Bass Pro Shops)
BRG Sports Inc
Brooklyn Nets
Brunswick Corporation
BSN Sports Inc
Buffalo Bills

Buffalo Sabres
Cabelas Inc
Calgary Flames
CamelBak Products LLC
Campeonato Nacional de Liga Primera Division (La Liga)
Canadian Football League
Canlan Ice Sports Corp
Cannondale Bicycle Corporation
Carolina Hurricanes
Carolina Panthers
Celtic PLC
Charlotte Hornets
Chelsea Football Club
Chicago Bears
Chicago Blackhawks
Chicago Bulls
Chicago Cubs
Chicago Fire Soccer Club
Chicago Sky
Chicago White Sox
Chip Ganassi Racing With Felix Sabates Inc
Churchill Downs Incorporated
Cincinnati Bengals
Cincinnati Reds
Cleveland Browns
Cleveland Cavaliers
Cleveland Guardians
Club Atletico de Madrid SAD (Atletico Madrid)
Club de Foot Montreal (CF Montreal)
Club de Futbol America SA de CV (America)
Club de Futbol Monterrey
Club Deportivo Guadalajara SA de CV (Chivas)
Club Universidad Nacional-Asociacion Civil (UNAM/Pumas)
ClubCorp Holdings Inc (Invited)
Clube de Regatas do Flamengo
Coleman Company Inc (The)
Colorado Avalanche
Colorado Rapids
Colorado Rockies
Columbia Sportswear Company
Columbus Blue Jackets
Columbus Crew
Comcast Corporation
Connecticut Sun
Converse Inc
Corporacion Interamericana de Entretenimiento SA
Cox Communications Inc
Crested Butte Mountain Resort Inc
Cruzeiro Esporte Clube
Curves NA
Dallas Cowboys
Dallas Mavericks
Dallas Stars
Dallas Wings
DAZN Group Limited
DC United

Delaware North Companies Inc
Delta Apparel Inc
Denver Broncos
Denver Nuggets
Deportivo Toluca Futbol Club SA de CV
Detroit Lions
Detroit Pistons
Detroit Red Wings
Detroit Tigers
Dicks Sporting Goods Inc
Disney Media & Entertainment Distribution
DraftKings Inc
Eastern Mountain Sports Inc
ECHL
Edmonton Oilers
eGames.com Holdings LLC (Buzztime)
Electronic Arts Inc (EA)
Endeavor Group Holdings Inc
Equinox Fitness
ESPN Inc
Everlast Worldwide Inc
Everton Football Club
Fanatics Inc
FanDuel Group
FC Cincinnati
FC Dallas
Fenerbahce Spor Kulubu
Fenway Sports Group LLC
Field & Stream
FIFA (Federation Internationale de Football Association)
Fila USA Inc
Florida Panthers
Football Club des Girondins de Bordeaux (Bordeaux)
Football Club Dynamo Kyiv
Football Club Internazionale Milano SpA
Football-Club Bayern Munchen eV
Football-Club Gelsenkirchen-Schalke 04 eV
Formula One Group (F1)
Fox Broadcasting Company
Fox Sports (Fox Sports Media Group)
Franklin Sports Inc
Fulham Football Club
Fussball Bundesliga
Futbol Club Barcelona
Futebol Clube do Porto (FC Porto)
Galatasaray Spor Kulubu (Galatasaray SK)
Giant Manufacturing Co Ltd
Golden State Warriors
Golds Gym International Inc
Golf Galaxy Inc
Golf Town Limited
Green Bay Packers
Grupo Sports World SAB de CV
Head Sport GmbH
HealthFitness Corporation
Hendrick Motorsports
Hibbett Sports Inc
Houston Astros

Houston Dynamo FC
Houston Rockets
Houston Texans
Huffy Bicycle Co
Ilitch Holdings Inc
Indiana Fever
Indiana Pacers
Indianapolis Colts
IndyCar LLC
International Boxing Federation
International Olympic Committee (IOC)
Jacksonville Jaguars
Joe Gibbs Racing
Johnson Outdoors Inc
Juventus Football Club SpA
Kansas City Chiefs
Kansas City Royals
Katz Group Of Companies (The)
Kellwood Company LLC
Kroenke Sports & Entertainment LLC
K-Swiss Inc
LA Fitness (LA Fitness International LLC)
Ladies Professional Golf Association (LPGA)
Las Vegas Aces
Las Vegas Raiders
Legacy Motor Club
Leicester City Football Club
Levy Restaurants
Li Ning Company Limited
Life Time Inc
Ligue de Football Professionnel
Little Gym International Inc (The)
LIV Golf Inc
Liverpool Football Club
Los Angeles Angels
Los Angeles Chargers
Los Angeles Clippers
Los Angeles Dodgers
Los Angeles Football Club
Los Angeles Galaxy
Los Angeles Kings
Los Angeles Lakers
Los Angeles Rams
Los Angeles Sparks
lululemon athletica inc
Madison Square Garden Sports Corp
Majestic Athletic
Major League Baseball (MLB)
Major League Baseball Advanced Media LP (MLBAM)
Major League Soccer (MLS)
Manchester City Football Club
Manchester United plc
Maple Leaf Sports & Entertainment Ltd
Marine Products Corporation
MarineMax Inc
Memphis Grizzlies
Miami Dolphins
Miami HEAT

Miami Marlins
Middlesbrough Football Club
Milwaukee Brewers
Milwaukee Bucks
Minnesota Lynx
Minnesota Timberwolves
Minnesota Twins
Minnesota United FC
Minnesota Vikings
Minnesota Wild
Minor League Baseball
MLS NEXT Pro (Pro Soccer Development LP)
Montreal Canadiens
Motivate LLC
NASCAR
Nashville Predators
National Basketball Association (NBA)
National Football League (NFL)
National Hockey League (NHL)
National Thoroughbred Racing Association
NBA G League
NBCUniversal Media LLC
New Balance Athletic Shoe Inc
New England Patriots
New England Revolution
New Jersey Devils
New Orleans Pelicans
New Orleans Saints
New York City FC
New York Giants
New York Islanders
New York Jets
New York Knickerbockers
New York Liberty
New York Mets
New York Rangers
New York Red Bulls
New York Yankees
Newcastle United Football Club
Newport Sports Management Inc
Nike Inc
North Face Inc (The)
Norwich City Football Club
Oak View Group
Oakland Athletics
Octagon Worldwide
Oklahoma City Thunder
Olympiacos Football Club
Olympique de Marseille
Olympique Lyonnais Groupe
OneTeam Partners LLC
Orlando City SC
Orlando Magic
Orvis Company Inc (The)
Ottawa Senators
Pacific Cycle Inc
Palace Sports & Entertainment Inc
Paramount Global

Paris Saint-Germain Football Club (PSG)
Patagonia Inc
Peloton Interactive Inc
Penn National Gaming Inc
PGA European Tour (bda DP World Tour)
Philadelphia 76ers
Philadelphia Eagles
Philadelphia Flyers
Philadelphia Phillies
Philadelphia Union
Philips Sport Vereniging (PSV Eindhoven)
Phoenix Mercury
Phoenix Suns
Pittsburgh Penguins
Pittsburgh Pirates
Pittsburgh Steelers
Planet Fitness Inc
Portland Timbers
Portland Trail Blazers
Prince Global Sports LLC
Professional Bowlers Association LLC
Professional Bull Riders Inc
Professional Golfers Association of America (PGA)
PUMA SE
Rawlings Sporting Goods Company Inc
Real Madrid Club de Futbol
Real Salt Lake
Reebok International Limited
REI (Recreational Equipment Inc)
Rogers Communications Inc
Roush Fenway Keselowski Racing (RFK Racing)
Russell Brands LLC
Sacramento Kings
San Antonio Spurs
San Diego Padres
San Francisco 49ers
San Francisco Giants
San Jose Earthquakes
San Jose Sharks
Santos Futebol Clube
Sao Paulo Futebol Clube
Score Media Ventures Inc
Seattle Mariners
Seattle Seahawks
Seattle Sounders FC
Seattle Storm
Sirius XM Holdings Inc
Skis Rossignol SA
Snap Fitness Inc
Sociedade Esportiva Palmeiras
Societa Sportiva Calcio Napoli (SSC Napoli)
Sodexo Live!
SoulCycle Inc
Southampton Football Club
Specialized Bicycle Components Inc
Speedway Motorsports LLC
Sport Maska Inc (CCM Hockey)
Sporting Kansas City

Sports Illustrated
Sportsmans Guide Inc (The)
Sportverein Werder Bremen von 1899 eV
St Louis Blues
St Louis Cardinals
St Louis City SC
Tampa Bay Buccaneers
Tampa Bay Lightning
Tampa Bay Rays
Team Penske
Tecnica Group SpA
Tennessee Titans
Texas Rangers
Topgolf Callaway Brands Corp
Topps Company Inc (The)
Toronto Blue Jays
Toronto FC
Toronto Maple Leafs
Toronto Raptors
Tottenham Hotspur Football Club
Trek Bicycle Corporation
Under Armour Inc
Underdog Sports Inc
Union of European Football Associations (UEFA)
United Soccer League
United States Golf Association (USGA)
United States Olympic & Paralympic Committee (USOPC)
United States Tennis Association (USTA)
US Figure Skating
US Soccer Federation
USA Basketball
USA Cycling
USA Gymnastics
USA Hockey Inc
USA Swimming
USA Track & Field Inc
USL Championship League (USL Pro LLC)
Utah Jazz
Vail Resorts Inc
Valencia Club de Futbol (Valencia CF/Valencia)
Vancouver Canucks
Vancouver Whitecaps FC
Varsity Brands Holding Co Inc
Vegas Golden Knights
Verein fur Bewegungsspiele Stuttgart 1893 eV (VfB Stuttgart)
VF Corporation
Vista Outdoor Inc
Walt Disney Company (The)
Washington Capitals
Washington Commanders
Washington Mystics
Washington Nationals
Washington Wizards
Wasserman Media Group LLC
West Bromwich Albion Football Club
West Ham United Football Club

West Marine Inc
WHOOP Inc
Wilson Sporting Goods Co
Winnipeg Jets
Winter Sports Inc
Wolverhampton Wanderers Football Club
Womens National Basketball Association (WNBA)
Womens Tennis Association (WTA)
World Boxing Association (The)
World Boxing Council
World Triathlon Corporation (Ironman, WTC)
Xtep International Holdings Limited
Zumba Fitness LLC

INDEX OF U.S. HEADQUARTERS LOCATION BY STATE

To help you locate companies geographically, the city and state of the headquarters of each company are in the following index.

ALABAMA
Hibbett Sports Inc; Birmingham

ARIZONA
Arizona Cardinals; Glendale
Arizona Coyotes; Glendale
Arizona Diamondbacks; Phoenix
Little Gym International Inc (The); Scottsdale
Phoenix Mercury; Phoenix
Phoenix Suns; Phoenix

CALIFORNIA
24 Hour Fitness; Carlsbad
American Golf Corporation; El Segundo
Anaheim Ducks; Anaheim
Anschutz Entertainment Group Inc; Los Angeles
ASM Global; Los Angeles
BDA Sports Management; Walnut Creek
Big 5 Sporting Goods Corporation; El Segundo
Bleacher Report Inc (B/R); San Francisco
Boardriders Inc; Huntington Beach
CamelBak Products LLC; Petaluma
Disney Media & Entertainment Distribution; Burbank
eGames.com Holdings LLC (Buzztime); Carlsbad
Electronic Arts Inc (EA); Redwood City
Endeavor Group Holdings Inc; Beverly Hills
Fox Broadcasting Company; Los Angeles
Fox Sports (Fox Sports Media Group); Los Angeles
Golden State Warriors; San Francisco
Kellwood Company LLC; City of Industry
K-Swiss Inc; Westlake Village
LA Fitness (LA Fitness International LLC); Irvine
Los Angeles Angels; Anaheim
Los Angeles Chargers; Cosat Mesa
Los Angeles Clippers; Los Angeles
Los Angeles Dodgers; Los Angeles
Los Angeles Football Club; Los Angeles
Los Angeles Galaxy; Carson
Los Angeles Kings; Los Angeles
Los Angeles Lakers; Los Angeles
Los Angeles Rams; Agoura Hills
Los Angeles Sparks; Los Angeles
Oak View Group; Los Angeles
Oakland Athletics; Oakland
Patagonia Inc; Ventura
Sacramento Kings; Sacramento
San Diego Padres; San Diego
San Francisco 49ers; Santa Clara
San Francisco Giants; San Francisco
San Jose Earthquakes; San Jose
San Jose Sharks; San Jose
Specialized Bicycle Components Inc; Morgan Hill
Topgolf Callaway Brands Corp; Carlsbad
Walt Disney Company (The); Burbank
Wasserman Media Group LLC; Los Angeles
West Marine Inc; Watsonville

COLORADO
Alterra Mountain Company; Denver
Aspen Skiing Company; Aspen
Booth Creek Ski Holdings Inc; Vail
Colorado Avalanche; Denver
Colorado Rapids; Commerce City
Colorado Rockies; Denver
Crested Butte Mountain Resort Inc; Mt. Crested Butte
Denver Broncos; Englewood
Denver Nuggets; Denver
Kroenke Sports & Entertainment LLC; Denver
North Face Inc (The); Denver
Professional Bull Riders Inc; Pueblo
United States Olympic & Paralympic Committee (USOPC); Colorado Springs
US Figure Skating; Colorado Springs
USA Basketball; Colorado Springs
USA Cycling; Colorado Springs
USA Hockey Inc; Colorado Springs
USA Swimming; Colorado Springs
Vail Resorts Inc; Broomfield
VF Corporation; Denver

CONNECTICUT
Cannondale Bicycle Corporation; Wilton
Connecticut Sun; Uncasville
ESPN Inc; Bristol
Octagon Worldwide; Stamford

DISTRICT OF COLUMBIA
DC United; Washington
OneTeam Partners LLC; Washington
Washington Mystics; Washington
Washington Nationals; Washington
Washington Wizards; Washington

FLORIDA
Association of Tennis Professionals (ATP Tour Inc); Ponte Vedra Beach
Fanatics Inc; Jacksonville
Florida Panthers; Sunrise
Jacksonville Jaguars; Jacksonville
Ladies Professional Golf Association (LPGA); Daytona Beach
MarineMax Inc; Clearwater
Miami Dolphins; Miami Gardens
Miami HEAT; Miami
Miami Marlins; Miami
Minor League Baseball; St. Petersburg
NASCAR; Daytona Beach

Orlando City SC; Orlando
Orlando Magic; Orlando
Tampa Bay Buccaneers; Tampa
Tampa Bay Lightning; Tampa
Tampa Bay Rays; St. Petersburg
United Soccer League; Tampa
USL Championship League (USL Pro LLC); Tampa
Womens Tennis Association (WTA); St. Petersburg
World Triathlon Corporation (Ironman, WTC); Tampa
Zumba Fitness LLC; Hallandale

GEORGIA
Atlanta Braves; Atlanta
Atlanta Dream; Atlanta
Atlanta Falcons; Atlanta
Atlanta Hawks; Atlanta
Atlanta United FC; Atlanta
Cox Communications Inc; Atlanta
Marine Products Corporation; Atlanta
Prince Global Sports LLC; Atlanta

ILLINOIS
BRG Sports Inc; Des Plaines
Brunswick Corporation; Mettawa
Chicago Bears; Lake Forrest
Chicago Blackhawks; Chicago
Chicago Bulls; Chicago
Chicago Cubs; Chicago
Chicago Fire Soccer Club; Chicago
Chicago Sky; Chicago
Chicago White Sox; Chicago
Coleman Company Inc (The); Chicago
HealthFitness Corporation; Lake Forest
Levy Restaurants; Chicago
US Soccer Federation; Chicago
Wilson Sporting Goods Co; Chicago

INDIANA
Chip Ganassi Racing With Felix Sabates Inc; Indianapolis
Indiana Fever; Indianapolis
Indiana Pacers; Indianapolis
Indianapolis Colts; Indianapolis
IndyCar LLC; Indianapolis
USA Gymnastics; Indianapolis
USA Track & Field Inc; Indianapolis

KENTUCKY
Churchill Downs Incorporated; Louisville
National Thoroughbred Racing Association; Lexington
Russell Brands LLC; Bowling Green

LOUISIANA
New Orleans Pelicans; Metairie
New Orleans Saints; Metairie

MARYLAND
Baltimore Orioles; Baltimore

Baltimore Ravens; Owings Mills
Fila USA Inc; Sparks
Sodexo Live!; Gaithersburg
Under Armour Inc; Baltimore

MASSACHUSETTS
American Hockey League Inc; Springfield
Boston Bruins; Boston
Boston Celtics; Boston
Boston Red Sox; Boston
Converse Inc; Boston
DraftKings Inc; Boston
Fenway Sports Group LLC; Boston
Franklin Sports Inc; Stoughton
New Balance Athletic Shoe Inc; Boston
New England Patriots; Foxborough
New England Revolution; Foxborough
Reebok International Limited; Canton
WHOOP Inc; Boston

MICHIGAN
Boyne Resorts; Petoskey
Detroit Lions; Allen Park
Detroit Pistons; Auburn Hills
Detroit Red Wings; Detroit
Detroit Tigers; Detroit
Ilitch Holdings Inc; Detroit
Palace Sports & Entertainment Inc; Auburn Hills

MINNESOTA
Anytime Fitness LLC; Woodbury
Life Time Inc; Chanhassen
Minnesota Lynx; Minneapolis
Minnesota Timberwolves; Minneapolis
Minnesota Twins; Minneapolis
Minnesota United FC; Golden Valley
Minnesota Vikings; Eagan
Minnesota Wild; St. Paul
Snap Fitness Inc; Chanhassen
Sportsmans Guide Inc (The); St. Paul
Vista Outdoor Inc; Anoka

MISSOURI
BPS Direct LLC (Bass Pro Shops); Springfield
Everlast Worldwide Inc; Moberly
Kansas City Chiefs; Kansas City
Kansas City Royals; Kansas City
Rawlings Sporting Goods Company Inc; St. Louis
Sporting Kansas City; Kansas City
St Louis Blues; St. Louis
St Louis Cardinals; St. Louis
St Louis City SC; St. Louis

MONTANA
Winter Sports Inc; Whitefish

NEBRASKA
Cabelas Inc; Sidney

NEVADA
Las Vegas Aces; Las Vegas
Las Vegas Raiders; Henderson
Vegas Golden Knights; Las Vegas

NEW HAMPSHIRE
Eastern Mountain Sports Inc; Peterborough
Planet Fitness Inc; Hampton

NEW JERSEY
ECHL; Shrewsbury
International Boxing Federation; Springfield
New Jersey Devils; Newark
New York Giants; East Rutherford
New York Jets; Florham Park
New York Red Bulls; Harrison
United States Golf Association (USGA); Far Hills

NEW YORK
Altice USA Inc; Long Island City
AND 1; New York
Brooklyn Nets; Brooklyn
Buffalo Bills; Orchard Park
Buffalo Sabres; Buffalo
Delaware North Companies Inc; Buffalo
Equinox Fitness; New York
FanDuel Group; New York
Madison Square Garden Sports Corp; New York
Major League Baseball (MLB); New York
Major League Baseball Advanced Media LP (MLBAM); New York
Major League Soccer (MLS); New York
MLS NEXT Pro (Pro Soccer Development LP); New York
Motivate LLC; New York
National Basketball Association (NBA); New York
National Football League (NFL); New York
National Hockey League (NHL); New York
NBA G League; New York
NBCUniversal Media LLC; New York
New York City FC; New York
New York Islanders; Floral Park
New York Knickerbockers; New York
New York Liberty; Brooklyn
New York Mets; Flushing
New York Rangers; New York
New York Yankees; Bronx
Paramount Global; New York
Peloton Interactive Inc; New York
Sirius XM Holdings Inc; New York
SoulCycle Inc; New York
Sports Illustrated; New York
Topps Company Inc (The); New York
Underdog Sports Inc; Brooklyn
United States Tennis Association (USTA); White Plains

Womens National Basketball Association (WNBA); New York

NORTH CAROLINA
Carolina Hurricanes; Raleigh
Carolina Panthers; Charlotte
Charlotte Hornets; Charlotte
Hendrick Motorsports; Charlotte
Joe Gibbs Racing; Huntersville
Legacy Motor Club; Statesville
Roush Fenway Keselowski Racing (RFK Racing); Concord
Speedway Motorsports LLC; Concord
Team Penske; Mooresville

OHIO
Cincinnati Bengals; Cincinnati
Cincinnati Reds; Cincinnati
Cleveland Browns; Berea
Cleveland Cavaliers; Cleveland
Cleveland Guardians; Cleveland
Columbus Blue Jackets; Columbus
Columbus Crew; Columbus
FC Cincinnati; Cincinnati
Huffy Bicycle Co; Centerville

OKLAHOMA
Oklahoma City Thunder; Oklahoma City

OREGON
Columbia Sportswear Company; Portland
Nike Inc; Beaverton
Portland Timbers; Portland
Portland Trail Blazers; Portland

PENNSYLVANIA
Aramark Corporation; Philadelphia
Comcast Corporation; Philadelphia
Dicks Sporting Goods Inc; Coraopolis
Field & Stream; Coraopolis
Golf Galaxy Inc; Coraopolis
Majestic Athletic; Easton
Penn National Gaming Inc; Wyomissing
Philadelphia 76ers; Philadelphia
Philadelphia Eagles; Philadelphia
Philadelphia Flyers; Philadelphia
Philadelphia Phillies; Philadelphia
Philadelphia Union; Chester
Pittsburgh Penguins; Pittsburgh
Pittsburgh Pirates; Pittsburgh
Pittsburgh Steelers; Pittsburgh

SOUTH CAROLINA
Delta Apparel Inc; Greenville

TENNESSEE
Memphis Grizzlies; Memphis

Nashville Predators; Nashville
Tennessee Titans; Nashville

TEXAS
Academy Sports & Outdoors Inc; Katy
BSN Sports Inc; Dallas
ClubCorp Holdings Inc (Invited); Dallas
Curves NA; Woodway
Dallas Cowboys; Frisco
Dallas Mavericks; Dallas
Dallas Stars; Frisco
Dallas Wings; Arlington
FC Dallas; Frisco
Golds Gym International Inc; Dallas
Houston Astros; Houston
Houston Dynamo FC; Houston
Houston Rockets; Houston
Houston Texans; Houston
Professional Golfers Association of America (PGA);
Frisco
San Antonio Spurs; San Antonio
Texas Rangers; Arlington
Varsity Brands Holding Co Inc; Farmers Branch

UTAH
Real Salt Lake; Sandy
Utah Jazz; Salt Lake City

VERMONT
Orvis Company Inc (The); Sunderland

VIRGINIA
Bowlero Corp; Mechanicsville
Professional Bowlers Association LLC; Mechanicsville
Washington Capitals; Arlington
Washington Commanders; Ashburn

WASHINGTON
REI (Recreational Equipment Inc); Kent
Seattle Mariners; Seattle
Seattle Seahawks; Renton
Seattle Sounders FC; Seattle
Seattle Storm; Seattle

WISCONSIN
Green Bay Packers; Green Bay
Johnson Outdoors Inc; Racine
Milwaukee Brewers; Milwaukee
Milwaukee Bucks; Milwaukee
Pacific Cycle Inc; Madison
Trek Bicycle Corporation; Waterloo

INDEX OF NON-U.S. HEADQUARTERS
LOCATION BY COUNTRY

AUSTRIA
Head Sport GmbH; Kennelbach

BRAZIL
Clube de Regatas do Flamengo; Rio de Janeiro
Cruzeiro Esporte Clube; Belo Horizonte
Santos Futebol Clube; Santos
Sao Paulo Futebol Clube; Sao Paulo
Sociedade Esportiva Palmeiras; Sao Paulo

CANADA
Calgary Flames; Calgary
Canadian Football League; Toronto
Canlan Ice Sports Corp; Burnaby
Club de Foot Montreal (CF Montreal); Montreal
Edmonton Oilers; Edmonton
Golf Town Limited; Woodbridge
Katz Group Of Companies (The); Edmonton
lululemon athletica inc; Vancouver
Maple Leaf Sports & Entertainment Ltd; Toronto
Montreal Canadiens; Montreal
Newport Sports Management Inc; Mississauga
Ottawa Senators; Ottawa
Rogers Communications Inc; Toronto
Score Media Ventures Inc; Toronto
Sport Maska Inc (CCM Hockey); Montreal
Toronto Blue Jays; Toronto
Toronto FC; Toronto
Toronto Maple Leafs; Toronto
Toronto Raptors; Toronto
Vancouver Canucks; Vancouver
Vancouver Whitecaps FC; Vancouver
Winnipeg Jets; Winnipeg

CHINA
Li Ning Company Limited; Beijing

FINLAND
Amer Sports Corporation; Helsinki

FRANCE
Association Sportive de Saint-Etienne Loire (AS Saint-
Etienne); Saint-Etienne
Football Club des Girondins de Bordeaux (Bordeaux); Le
Haillan
Ligue de Football Professionnel; Paris
Olympique de Marseille; Marseille
Olympique Lyonnais Groupe; Decines-Charpieu
Paris Saint-Germain Football Club (PSG); Paris
Skis Rossignol SA; Saint-Jean de Moirans

GERMANY
adidas AG; Herzogenaurach

Borussia Dortmund GmbH & Co KGaA; Dortmund
Football-Club Bayern Munchen eV; Munich
Football-Club Gelsenkirchen-Schalke 04 eV;
Gelsenkirchen
Fussball Bundesliga; Frankfurt am Main
PUMA SE; Herzogenaurach
Sportverein Werder Bremen von 1899 eV; Bremen
Verein fur Bewegungsspiele Stuttgart 1893 eV (VfB
Stuttgart); Stuttgart

GREECE
Olympiacos Football Club; Piraeus

HONG KONG
ANTA Sports Products Limited; Hong Kong
Xtep International Holdings Limited; Kowloon Bay,
Kowloon

ITALY
AS Roma (Associazione Sportiva Roma); Roma
Associazione Calcio Milan spa; Milano
Football Club Internazionale Milano SpA; Milan
Juventus Football Club SpA; Turin
Societa Sportiva Calcio Napoli (SSC Napoli); Campania
Tecnica Group SpA; Giavera del Montello

JAPAN
Accordia Golf Co Ltd; Tokyo
ASICS Corp; Kobe

MEXICO
Club de Futbol America SA de CV (America); Mexico
City
Club de Futbol Monterrey; Guadalupe
Club Deportivo Guadalajara SA de CV (Chivas);
Guadalajara
Club Universidad Nacional-Asociacion Civil
(UNAM/Pumas); Mexico City
Corporacion Interamericana de Entretenimiento SA;
Mexico DF
Deportivo Toluca Futbol Club SA de CV; Toluca
Grupo Sports World SAB de CV; Santa Fe
World Boxing Council; Col. Lindavista

PANAMA
World Boxing Association (The); Panama

PORTUGAL
Futebol Clube do Porto (FC Porto); Porto

SPAIN
Athletic Club (Athletic Bilbao); Bilbao
Campeonato Nacional de Liga Primera Division (La Liga);
Madrid
Club Atletico de Madrid SAD (Atletico Madrid); Madrid
Futbol Club Barcelona; Barcelona

Real Madrid Club de Futbol; Madrid
Valencia Club de Futbol (Valencia CF/Valencia); Valencia

SWITZERLAND
FIFA (Federation Internationale de Football Association);
Zurich
International Olympic Committee (IOC); Lausanne
Union of European Football Associations (UEFA); Nyon 2

TAIWAN
Giant Manufacturing Co Ltd; Taichung

THE NETHERLANDS
AFC Ajax NV; Amsterdam
Philips Sport Vereniging (PSV Eindhoven); Eindhoven

TURKEY
Fenerbahce Spor Kulubu; Istanbul
Galatasaray Spor Kulubu (Galatasaray SK); Istanbul

UKRAINE
Football Club Dynamo Kyiv; Kyiv

UNITED KINGDOM
Arsenal Football Club Plc; London
Aston Villa Football Club; Birmingham
Blackburn Rovers Football Club; Blackburn
Celtic PLC; Glasgow
Chelsea Football Club; London
DAZN Group Limited; London
Everton Football Club; Liverpool
Formula One Group (F1); London
Fulham Football Club; Surrey
Leicester City Football Club; Leicester
LIV Golf Inc; London
Liverpool Football Club; Liverpool
Manchester City Football Club; Manchester
Manchester United plc; Manchester
Middlesbrough Football Club; Middlesbrough
Newcastle United Football Club; Newcastle
Norwich City Football Club; Norwich
PGA European Tour (bda DP World Tour); Virginia Water
Southampton Football Club; Southampton
Tottenham Hotspur Football Club; Tottenham
West Bromwich Albion Football Club; West Bromwich
West Ham United Football Club; London
Wolverhampton Wanderers Football Club; Wolverhampton

Individual Profiles
On Each Of
THE SPORTS & RECREATION 400

24 Hour Fitness

NAIC Code: 713940

www.24hourfitness.com

TYPES OF BUSINESS:

Fitness Centers
Mobile Application
Online Fitness
TV Fitness
Virtual Fitness Classes

BRANDS/DIVISIONS/AFFILIATES:

Sculptor Capital Investments LLC
Monarch Alternative Capital LP
Cyrus Capital Partners LP
24GO
24GO Plus
24GO TV
GX24

CONTACTS: *Note: Officers with more than one job title may be intentionally listed here more than once.*

Karl Sanft, CEO
Frank Napolitano, Pres.
Vicki Davis, Corp. Controller
Danny De La Rosa, Pres., Clubs

GROWTH PLANS/SPECIAL FEATURES:

24 Hour Fitness is a leading privately-owned and -operated fitness center chain. The firm has more than 275 clubs in 11 U.S. states, including Washington, Oregon, California, Nevada, Hawaii, Colorado, Texas, Florida, New York, Virginia and Washington DC. 24 Hour Fitness centers are furnished with a variety of strength, cardio and functional training equipment. The company's innovative technology and team of coaches provide personalized support at the clubs and at home via group fitness classes, personal training, virtual training and 24GO digital offerings. 24GO offers an app that enables touch-free club check-in, as well as free on-demand workouts to support fitness at home or in the club. 24GO Plus is a premium digital subscription featuring customizable workouts, audio coaching, access to weekly live-coached virtual group training sessions and more. 24GO Plus is included at no extra cost with 24 Hour Fitness membership. 24GO TV is the company's workout channel, with free streaming content available 24/7 through the 24GO app and on YouTube. GX24 are virtual weekly classes ranging from Zumba and Body Combat to Pilates and signature workouts such as Power24, Core24, HIIT24 and Cycle24. 24 Hour Fitness is privately owned by investment companies Sculptor Capital Investments LLC, Monarch Alternative Capital LP and Cyrus Capital Partners LP.

FINANCIAL DATA: *Note: Data for latest year may not have been available at press time.*

In U.S. $	2022	2021	2020	2019	2018	2017
Revenue	1,200,000,000	911,550,000	885,000,000	1,500,000,000	1,430,000,000	1,430,000,000
R&D Expense						
Operating Income						
Operating Margin %						
SGA Expense						
Net Income						
Operating Cash Flow						
Capital Expenditure						
EBITDA						
Return on Assets %						
Return on Equity %						
Debt to Equity						

CONTACT INFORMATION:

Phone: 303-683-2438   Fax:
Toll-Free:
Address: 12647 Alcosta Blvd., Ste. 500, Carlsbad, CA 94583 United States

STOCK TICKER/OTHER:

Stock Ticker: Private
Employees: 22,000
Parent Company:

Exchange:
Fiscal Year Ends: 12/31

SALARIES/BONUSES:

Top Exec. Salary: $ Bonus: $
Second Exec. Salary: $ Bonus: $

OTHER THOUGHTS:

Estimated Female Officers or Directors: 1
Hot Spot for Advancement for Women/Minorities:

Sales, profits and employees may be estimates. Financial information, benefits and other data can change quickly and may vary from those stated here.

Academy Sports & Outdoors Inc

www.academy.com

NAIC Code: 451110

TYPES OF BUSINESS:

Sporting Goods Stores
Apparel
Footwear
Outdoor Sports Gear
Hunting Licenses

BRANDS/DIVISIONS/AFFILIATES:

GROWTH PLANS/SPECIAL FEATURES:

Academy Sports and Outdoors Inc is engaged in the retail business of sporting goods and outdoor recreation products. The company offers outdoor clothing, backpacks, sunglasses, luggage items, shooting equipment, fishing equipment, boating and water sports equipment, backyard recreation products, outdoor cooking equipment, fitness equipment, electronic items, dog supplies, and other products.

Academy Sports offers its employees comprehensive health benefits, retirement options, life and disability coverage and a variety of employee assistance plans and programs.

CONTACTS: *Note: Officers with more than one job title may be intentionally listed here more than once.*

Kenneth Hicks, CEO
Michael Mullican, CFO
Heather Davis, Chief Accounting Officer
Manish Maini, Chief Information Officer
Samuel Johnson, Executive VP, Divisional
Steven Lawrence, Executive VP
Rene Casares, General Counsel
William Ennis, Other Executive Officer
Jamey Rutherford, Senior VP, Divisional
Sherry Harriman, Senior VP, Divisional

FINANCIAL DATA: *Note: Data for latest year may not have been available at press time.*

In U.S. $	2022	2021	2020	2019	2018	2017
Revenue	6,773,128,000	5,689,233,000	4,829,897,000	4,783,893,000		
R&D Expense						
Operating Income	907,947,000	420,398,000	179,421,000	128,950,000		
Operating Margin %	.13%	.07%	.04%	.03%		
SGA Expense	1,443,148,000	1,313,647,000	1,251,733,000	1,239,002,000		
Net Income	671,381,000	308,764,000	120,043,000	21,442,000		
Operating Cash Flow	673,265,000	1,011,597,000	263,669,000	198,481,000		
Capital Expenditure	76,017,000	41,269,000	62,818,000	107,905,000		
EBITDA	1,013,803,000	531,115,000	341,421,000	264,827,000		
Return on Assets %	.15%	.07%	.03%	.01%		
Return on Equity %	.52%	.29%	.13%	.03%		
Debt to Equity	1.20%	1.74%	2.601	1.816		

CONTACT INFORMATION:

Phone: 281-646-5200   Fax: 281-646-5000
Toll-Free: 888-922-2336
Address: 1800 N. Mason Rd., Katy, TX 77449 United States

STOCK TICKER/OTHER:

Stock Ticker: ASO
Employees: 22,000
Parent Company:

Exchange: NAS
Fiscal Year Ends: 01/30

SALARIES/BONUSES:

Top Exec. Salary: $1,100,000   Bonus: $
Second Exec. Salary: $748,615   Bonus: $

OTHER THOUGHTS:

Estimated Female Officers or Directors: 1
Hot Spot for Advancement for Women/Minorities:

Accordia Golf Co Ltd

www.accordiagolf.co.jp

NAIC Code: 713910

TYPES OF BUSINESS:

Golf Course Operations
Golf Course Renovation
Golf Course Maintenance
Driving Ranges
Golf Course Acquisition
Property Management
Property Leasing

BRANDS/DIVISIONS/AFFILIATES:

Golf Alliance Co Ltd

CONTACTS: *Note: Officers with more than one job title may be intentionally listed here more than once.*

Kan Ishii, CEO
Takabumi Suzuki, Managing Exec. Officer
Takashi Niino, Managing Exec. Officer
Fumio Hattori, Managing Exec. Officer
Motoo Michida, Managing Exec. Officer
Yuko Tashiro, Chmn.

GROWTH PLANS/SPECIAL FEATURES:

Accordia Golf Co., Ltd. is principally engaged in the business of golf course operations in Japan. The firm's guiding strategy is 'It's a new game,' reflecting the intention to foster golf as a fun, casual sport available to everyone. Accordia, marketing its services under the Accordia Golf brand, engages primarily in the acquisition, renovation and maintenance of golf courses; loyalty card services, such as lessons at driving ranges and playing on golf courses; and the sale of golf goods at retail outlets. Additionally, Accordia manages restaurants and hotels, leases and manages real estate properties and operates golf equipment pro shops. The company owns and/or manages approximately 171 golf courses, 22 owned driving ranges and four other driving ranges (as of April 2023). Accordia's golf courses are furnished with restaurant capacities, which the company outsources from a third party. The firm offers golf membership services such as golf equipment repair, membership-only golf competitions, early morning playing times and call center operations for golf course reservations. Golf Alliance Co., Ltd. is a primary subsidiary of Accordia.

FINANCIAL DATA: *Note: Data for latest year may not have been available at press time.*

In U.S. $	2022	2021	2020	2019	2018	2017
Revenue	450,000,000	447,720,000	430,500,000	420,000,000	400,000,000	400,000,000
R&D Expense						
Operating Income						
Operating Margin %						
SGA Expense						
Net Income						
Operating Cash Flow						
Capital Expenditure						
EBITDA						
Return on Assets %						
Return on Equity %						
Debt to Equity						

CONTACT INFORMATION:

Phone: 81 366881500   Fax:
Toll-Free:
Address: 4-12-4 Higashi-shinagawa, Tower 9F, Sinagawa-ku, Tokyo, 140-0002 Japan

STOCK TICKER/OTHER:

Stock Ticker: Private   Exchange:
Employees: 10,520   Fiscal Year Ends:
Parent Company:

SALARIES/BONUSES:

Top Exec. Salary: $ Bonus: $
Second Exec. Salary: $ Bonus: $

OTHER THOUGHTS:

Estimated Female Officers or Directors:
Hot Spot for Advancement for Women/Minorities:

adidas AG

www.adidas.com

NAIC Code: 424340

TYPES OF BUSINESS:

Footwear Distribution
Golf Equipment & Accessories
Street & Sports Apparel
Personal Care Products
Eyewear
Watches

BRANDS/DIVISIONS/AFFILIATES:

adidas
Reebok
adidas Body

GROWTH PLANS/SPECIAL FEATURES:

Adidas designs, develops, produces, and markets athletic and leisure apparel, footwear, accessories, and sports equipment. Under its eponymous brand, it produces apparel for competitive athletics, casual activewear, and casual fashion. Its fashion brands include Ivy Park and Y-3. Adidas sells its products in more than 160 countries through nearly 2,000 owned retail stores, 15,000 mono-branded franchise stores, 150,000 wholesale doors, and owned e-commerce that is available in 65 countries. The company was founded in 1949 in Germany.

CONTACTS: *Note: Officers with more than one job title may be intentionally listed here more than once.*

Kasper Rorsted, CEO
Martin Shankland, Global Oper.
Harm Ohlmeyer, Global Finance
Roland Auschel, Global Sales
Amanda Rajkumar, Human Resources
Brian Grevy, Global Brands
Patrik Nilsson, Pres., Adidas Group North America
Igor Landau, Chmn.

FINANCIAL DATA: *Note: Data for latest year may not have been available at press time.*

In U.S. $	2022	2021	2020	2019	2018	2017
Revenue	24,039,170,000	22,675,480,000	19,686,470,000	25,244,810,000	22,658,400,000	22,658,400,000
R&D Expense						
Operating Income	778,488,500	2,124,024,000	910,906,400	2,854,458,000	2,246,831,000	2,246,831,000
Operating Margin %	.03%	.09%	.05%	.11%	.10%	.10%
SGA Expense	10,694,870,000	9,408,072,000	8,920,048,000	10,348,880,000	9,182,748,000	9,182,748,000
Net Income	653,545,900	2,259,646,000	461,326,500	2,110,142,000	1,171,470,000	1,171,470,000
Operating Cash Flow	-579,861,800	3,408,691,000	1,586,878,000	3,010,369,000	1,759,875,000	1,759,875,000
Capital Expenditure	742,180,400	712,279,600	461,326,500	756,063,000	803,049,900	803,049,900
EBITDA	2,028,983,000	3,323,260,000	2,217,998,000	4,198,926,000	2,743,398,000	2,743,398,000
Return on Assets %	.03%	.10%	.02%	.11%	.08%	.08%
Return on Equity %	.10%	.30%	.07%	.30%	.18%	.18%
Debt to Equity	1.06%	.63%	0.719	0.588	0.163	0.163

CONTACT INFORMATION:

Phone: 49 9132840   Fax: 49 9132842241
Toll-Free:
Address: Adi-Dassler-Strasse 1, Herzogenaurach, BY 91074 Germany

STOCK TICKER/OTHER:

Stock Ticker: ADDDF
Employees: 59,258
Parent Company:

Exchange: PINX
Fiscal Year Ends: 12/31

SALARIES/BONUSES:

Top Exec. Salary: $ Bonus: $
Second Exec. Salary: $ Bonus: $

OTHER THOUGHTS:

Estimated Female Officers or Directors:
Hot Spot for Advancement for Women/Minorities:

AFC Ajax NV
NAIC Code: 711211D

www.ajax.nl

TYPES OF BUSINESS:
Soccer (Futbol/Football) Teams
Team Management and Operations
Professional European Football
Top Tier Soccer

BRANDS/DIVISIONS/AFFILIATES:
Jong Ajax
AFC Ajax Vrouwen

CONTACTS: *Note: Officers with more than one job title may be intentionally listed here more than once.*
Edwin van der Sar, CEO
Susan Lenderink, Dir.-Finance
Menno Geelen, Dir.-Commercial Oper.

GROWTH PLANS/SPECIAL FEATURES:
AFC Ajax NV is a professional football club founded in 1900 and currently plays in the Eredivisie, the top tier in Dutch football. Historically, Ajax is the most successful club in the Netherlands, its home base, with 36 Eredivisie titles and 20 KNVB Cups. The team plays at the Johan Cruyff Arena in Amsterdam, with a seating capacity of 55,865 for games and up to 70,000 capacity for concerts. The average attendance of home games for the AFC Ajax 2022-23 season was 53,861. Within the Eredivisie league there are 18 clubs, each of which play against every other club twice during the season, once at home and once away. Young Ajax (Jong Ajax in Dutch language, is a Dutch association football team, the reserve team of Ajax; and Ajax Women (AFC Ajax Vrouwen) is a Dutch football club in the women's Eredevisie, the top women's league in the Netherlands. Current affiliated clubs of AFC Ajax include Almere City, Barcelona, Cruzeiro, Beijing Guoan, AS Trencin, Guangzhou R&F, Sagan Tosu, Sharjah FC, Sydney FC, Sparta Rotterdam and various HETT clubs. Sponsors and partners of AFC Ajax include adidas, ABN AMRO, Acronis, BLOX, Budweiser, Curacao Tourist Board, Flink, Sandals Resorts, Unibet, BBIN, CSU, Hublot, Mercedes-Benz, PCI Nederland, Replay, and others.

FINANCIAL DATA: *Note: Data for latest year may not have been available at press time.*

In U.S. $	2022	2021	2020	2019	2018	2017
Revenue		122,990,048	172,789,600	222,798,048	127,792,072	127,792,072
R&D Expense						
Operating Income						
Operating Margin %						
SGA Expense						
Net Income		-9,099,123	23,333,372	58,634,400	53,464,416	53,464,416
Operating Cash Flow						
Capital Expenditure						
EBITDA						
Return on Assets %						
Return on Equity %						
Debt to Equity						

CONTACT INFORMATION:
Phone: 31 203111444   Fax: 31 203111480
Toll-Free:
Address: 29 Boulevard Arena, Amsterdam, 1101 AX Netherlands

STOCK TICKER/OTHER:
Stock Ticker: AJAX   Exchange: Amsterdam
Employees: 478   Fiscal Year Ends: 06/30
Parent Company:

SALARIES/BONUSES:
Top Exec. Salary: $ Bonus: $
Second Exec. Salary: $ Bonus: $

OTHER THOUGHTS:
Estimated Female Officers or Directors:
Hot Spot for Advancement for Women/Minorities:

Alterra Mountain Company

www.alterramtnco.com

NAIC Code: 713920

TYPES OF BUSINESS:

Ski Resorts
Real Estate Development
Food and Beverage
Retail
Resort Booking App

BRANDS/DIVISIONS/AFFILIATES:

Big Bear Mountain Resort
Steamboat
Crystal Mountain
Deer Valley Resort
Mammoth Mountain
Sugarbush Resort
Snow Valley
CMH Heli Skiing & Summer Adventures

CONTACTS: *Note: Officers with more than one job title may be intentionally listed here more than once.*

Jared Smith, CEO
Sky Foulkes, COO
Thomas Marano, Director
Wesley Edens, Director
Travis Mayer, Executive VP
Karen Sanford, General Counsel

GROWTH PLANS/SPECIAL FEATURES:

Alterra Mountain Company owns and operates a range of recreation, hospitality, real estate development, food and beverage and retail businesses. Based in Denver, Colorado, Alterra's assets are located throughout the U.S. and Canada, and primarily serve individuals that prefer outdoor adventure. The firm's 15 year-round recreation destinations include: Big Bear Mountain Resort, which comprises two mountains, more than 25 miles of trails and multiple terrain parks for all abilities; Steamboat, offering snow skiing and horseback riding, as well as shopping, dining and off-mountain activities; Stratton, offering ski runs and a village with retail, dining and lodging options; Crystal Mountain, a ski resort situated on the northeast corner of Mt. Rainier National Park; Tremblant, a ski resort with a chalet-style pedestrian village; Deer Valley Resort, offering skiing for all abilities; Mammoth Mountain, comprising 3,500 acres of skiable terrain; June Mountain, a family mountain with a variety of trails; Winter Park Resort, within the Colorado Rockies, full of ski trails; Snowshoe, with various ski trails and a mountain-top village; Blue Mountain, offering skiing, skating, dancing, a village and mountain attractions; Solitude Mountain Resort, offering ski and bike trails; Sugarbush Resort, offering mountain areas of terrain, slopes and backcountry; Snow Valley, a ski resort in southern California near Big Bear Lake; Palisades Tahoe, offers 6,000 acres of progressive terrain, wide-open bowls, 42 lifts and lodges; and CMH Heli Skiing & Summer Adventures, offering skiing and summer activities in Canada. These destinations are located in California, Utah, Virginia, Colorado and Vermont, in the U.S., and in Ontario and Quebec, in Canada. Other holdings include season pass provider Ikon Pass, Westin Mammoth hotel and dining, Ski Butlers ski rental delivery service, Aspenware booking app, and Alpine Aerotech LP helicopter support and maintenance firm.

FINANCIAL DATA: *Note: Data for latest year may not have been available at press time.*

In U.S. $	2022	2021	2020	2019	2018	2017
Revenue	560,000,000	360,809,000	350,300,000	565,000,000	571,000,000	571,000,000
R&D Expense						
Operating Income						
Operating Margin %						
SGA Expense						
Net Income						
Operating Cash Flow						
Capital Expenditure						
EBITDA						
Return on Assets %						
Return on Equity %						
Debt to Equity						

CONTACT INFORMATION:

Phone: 303-749-8200   Fax: 303-749-8340
Toll-Free:
Address: 3501 Wazee St., #400, Denver, CO 80216 United States

STOCK TICKER/OTHER:

Stock Ticker: Private   Exchange:
Employees: 2,900   Fiscal Year Ends: 06/30
Parent Company:

SALARIES/BONUSES:

Top Exec. Salary: $ Bonus: $
Second Exec. Salary: $ Bonus: $

OTHER THOUGHTS:

Estimated Female Officers or Directors: 1
Hot Spot for Advancement for Women/Minorities:

Altice USA Inc

NAIC Code: 517110

TYPES OF BUSINESS:
Cable Television Service
Professional Sports Teams
Television Programming
Communications Services
Movie Theatres
Voice Over Internet Protocol
High-Speed Internet

BRANDS/DIVISIONS/AFFILIATES:
Optimum
Suddenlink
Altice Mobile
News 12 Networks
Cheddar
i24NEWS
a4
New York Interconnect

CONTACTS: Note: Officers with more than one job title may be intentionally listed here more than once.
Dexter Goei, CEO
Michael Grau, CFO
Patrick Drahi, Chairman of the Board
Layth Taki, Chief Accounting Officer
Colleen Schmidt, Executive VP, Divisional
Michael Olsen, Executive VP

GROWTH PLANS/SPECIAL FEATURES:
Altice Europe acquired privately held U.S. cable company Suddenlink in 2015 and Cablevision in 2016. Suddenlink's networks provided television, internet access, and phone services to roughly 3.5 million U.S. homes and businesses located primarily in smaller markets, with major clusters in Texas, West Virginia, Idaho, Arizona, and Louisiana. Cablevision provided comparable services to about 5.5 million homes and business in the New York City metro area. Altice Europe spun off Altice USA, which includes both the Suddenlink and Cablevision operations, to shareholders in 2018. Altice USA also owns News 12 Networks, which broadcasts local 24-hour news networks in New York, i24News, a news operation focused on the Middle East and Israel, and Cheddar, a news upstart.

FINANCIAL DATA: Note: Data for latest year may not have been available at press time.

In U.S. $	2022	2021	2020	2019	2018	2017
Revenue	9,647,659,000	10,090,850,000	9,894,642,000	9,760,859,000	9,306,950,000	9,306,950,000
R&D Expense						
Operating Income	1,932,879,000	2,541,803,000	2,206,362,000	1,896,789,000	993,409,000	993,409,000
Operating Margin %	.20%	.25%	.22%	.19%	.11%	.11%
SGA Expense						
Net Income	194,563,000	990,311,000	436,183,000	138,936,000	1,493,177,000	1,493,177,000
Operating Cash Flow	2,366,901,000	2,854,078,000	2,980,164,000	2,554,169,000	2,018,247,000	2,018,247,000
Capital Expenditure	1,914,282,000	1,231,715,000	1,073,955,000	1,355,350,000	953,056,000	953,056,000
EBITDA	3,622,038,000	4,359,650,000	4,019,127,000	3,986,832,000	3,166,115,000	3,166,115,000
Return on Assets %	.01%	.03%	.01%	.00%	.04%	.04%
Return on Equity %			.77%	.05%	.40%	.40%
Debt to Equity				10.801	3.879	3.879

CONTACT INFORMATION:
Phone: 516 803-2300   Fax: 516 803-2273
Toll-Free:
Address: 1 Court Square West, Long Island City, NY 11101 United States

STOCK TICKER/OTHER:
Stock Ticker: ATUS   Exchange: NYS
Employees: 11,000   Fiscal Year Ends: 12/31
Parent Company: Next Alt Sarl

SALARIES/BONUSES:
Top Exec. Salary: $750,000   Bonus: $
Second Exec. Salary: Bonus: $
$500,000

OTHER THOUGHTS:
Estimated Female Officers or Directors: 4
Hot Spot for Advancement for Women/Minorities: Y

Amer Sports Corporation

www.amersports.com

NAIC Code: 339920

TYPES OF BUSINESS:

Sports Equipment
Sporting Goods
Retail Stores
Ecommerce
Product Development
Product Sales
Apparel
Footwear

BRANDS/DIVISIONS/AFFILIATES:

Anta Sports Products Limited

GROWTH PLANS/SPECIAL FEATURES:

Amer Sports Corporation is a global sporting goods company. The firm sources from suppliers throughout the world and therefore offers many leading brands, and also produces and sells its own sports equipment, apparel, footwear and accessories. Amer's products span a wide range of sports, including tennis, badminton, golf, American football, soccer, baseball, basketball, alpine skiing, snowboarding, cross-country skilling, cycling, running, trail running, hiking and diving. The company has branded sales and retail locations worldwide, as well as approximately 150 ecommerce sites. Amer Sports operates as a subsidiary of Anta Sports Products Limited.

CONTACTS: *Note: Officers with more than one job title may be intentionally listed here more than once.*

James Zheng, CEO
Michael Hauge Sorensen, COO
Andrew Page, CFO
Antti Jaaskelainen, Chief Dev. Officer
Mikko Moilanen, Head -Amer Sports Digital Products & Services
Rob Barker, Pres., Fitness
Michael Dowse, Pres., Ball Sports
Matt Gold, Gen. Mgr.-Asia Pacific
Bernard Millaud, Pres., Cycling & Mavic SAS
Michael White, Gen. Mgr.-Americas
Antti Jaaskelainen, Sr. VP-Supply Chain & Global Oper.

FINANCIAL DATA: *Note: Data for latest year may not have been available at press time.*

In U.S. $	2022	2021	2020	2019	2018	2017
Revenue	3,200,000,000	2,943,220,840	3,424,846,360	3,113,496,691	2,972,984,832	2,972,984,832
R&D Expense						
Operating Income						
Operating Margin %						
SGA Expense						
Net Income						
Operating Cash Flow						
Capital Expenditure						
EBITDA						
Return on Assets %						
Return on Equity %						
Debt to Equity						

CONTACT INFORMATION:

Phone: 358 207870170   Fax:
Toll-Free:
Address: Konepajankuja 6, Helsinki, 00510 Finland

STOCK TICKER/OTHER:

Stock Ticker: Subsidiary   Exchange:
Employees: 9,200   Fiscal Year Ends: 12/31
Parent Company: Anta Sports Products Limited

SALARIES/BONUSES:

Top Exec. Salary: $ Bonus: $
Second Exec. Salary: $ Bonus: $

OTHER THOUGHTS:

Estimated Female Officers or Directors: 2
Hot Spot for Advancement for Women/Minorities:

American Golf Corporation

www.americangolf.com

NAIC Code: 713910

TYPES OF BUSINESS:

Golf Courses
Resorts
Golf Promotion
Weddings & Events

BRANDS/DIVISIONS/AFFILIATES:

Drive Shack Inc
Heartwell Golf Course
Classics Country Club (The)
Bear Creek Country Club
Lakewood Country Club
South Shore Golf Course
Waterview Golf Club
National Golf Club (The)

CONTACTS: *Note: Officers with more than one job title may be intentionally listed here more than once.*

Hana Khouri, CEO
Christine Chong, Sr. VP-Legal Affairs
Christine Chong, Sr. VP-Real Property

GROWTH PLANS/SPECIAL FEATURES:

American Golf Corporation is a premier manager of golf courses and resorts, owning and operating more than 70 private, public and resort golf courses within the U.S. American Golf's portfolio includes courses for golfers of all skill levels. Its properties include Heartwell Golf Course in California, The Classics Country Club in Florida, Bear Creek Country Club in Washington, Lakewood Country Club in California, South Shore Golf Course in New York and Waterview Golf Club in Texas. Over 30 of the firm's golf courses are located within California, with courses near popular destinations such as Los Angeles and San Diego. Additionally, the company operates country clubs featuring spas, tennis, swimming, dining and golf facilities. American Golf offers junior rates for kids who enjoy golfing and has junior camps in operation year around. The firm offers regional golfers clubs throughout the country that provide discount green fees, early twilight access and merchandise discounts. The company also offers the Platinum Club, which enables members to golf at participating American Golf private clubs and public courses all over the country for only a cart fee. Membership also allows golfers to reserve tee times in advance and to bring guests to private clubs for the prevailing guest rate. In addition, the company offers The National Golf Club, which affords members unrestricted access to select private clubs and resort and daily fee courses; a member does not have to pay any fees at the course. The firm's website, AmericanGolf.com, allows users to view the firm's portfolio of courses as well as providing the ability to make golf reservations, access course specials, research wedding and event locations and purchase golf lessons and golf merchandise. The firm is owned by Drive Shack Inc.

FINANCIAL DATA: *Note: Data for latest year may not have been available at press time.*

In U.S. $	2022	2021	2020	2019	2018	2017
Revenue	160,000,000	155,420,280	140,000,000	290,000,000	290,000,000	290,000,000
R&D Expense						
Operating Income						
Operating Margin %						
SGA Expense						
Net Income						
Operating Cash Flow						
Capital Expenditure						
EBITDA						
Return on Assets %						
Return on Equity %						
Debt to Equity						

CONTACT INFORMATION:

Phone: 310-664-4000   Fax: 310-664-4386
Toll-Free:
Address: 909 N. Pacific Coast Hwy., El Segundo, CA 90245 United States

STOCK TICKER/OTHER:

Stock Ticker: Subsidiary   Exchange:
Employees: 16,000   Fiscal Year Ends: 01/31
Parent Company: Drive Shack Inc

SALARIES/BONUSES:

Top Exec. Salary: $ Bonus: $
Second Exec. Salary: $ Bonus: $

OTHER THOUGHTS:

Estimated Female Officers or Directors: 5
Hot Spot for Advancement for Women/Minorities: Y

Sales, profits and employees may be estimates. Financial information, benefits and other data can change quickly and may vary from those stated here.

American Hockey League Inc

www.theahl.com

NAIC Code: 711211

TYPES OF BUSINESS:

Hockey League
AHL Team Merchandising

BRANDS/DIVISIONS/AFFILIATES:

GROWTH PLANS/SPECIAL FEATURES:

American Hockey League, Inc. (AHL) is a minor-league sports organization with 32 teams based in Canada (6) and the U.S. (26). The AHL is generally considered the top-tier minor league hockey organization. The league's teams are divided into four divisions of seven to 10 teams each. These divisions include Atlantic, North, Central and Pacific. At the end of the regular season each year, which runs from October through April, the top AHL team from each division competes for the Calder Cup. The league is the minor affiliation league for the National Hockey League (NHL), and all AHL teams are required to have an affiliation agreement with at least one NHL team. For example, the Grand Rapids Griffins have an affiliation agreement with the NHL Detroit Red Wings. Many teams of the ECHL (the former East Coast Hockey League) and the Central Hockey League (CHL) are also affiliated with AHL teams and act as feeders to the AHL.

CONTACTS: *Note: Officers with more than one job title may be intentionally listed here more than once.*

Scott Howson, CEO
Drew Griffin, Dir.-Finance & Admin.
Sean Lavoine, VP-Mktg. & Bus. Dev.
Drew Griffin, Dir.-Admin.
Rod Pasma, Exec. VP-Hockey Oper.
Chris Nikolis, Exec. VP-Bus. Dev.
Jason Chaimovitch, VP-Comm.
Drew Griffin, Dir.-Finance
Lauren Peterson, Dir.-Hockey Admin. & AHL Central Registry
Maria Lauring, Coordinator-Team Bus. Svcs.
Ashley Grindle, Coordinator-Mktg. Svcs.
Nathan Costa, Mgr.-Team Bus. Svcs.
David Andrews, Chmn.

FINANCIAL DATA: *Note: Data for latest year may not have been available at press time.*

In U.S. $	2022	2021	2020	2019	2018	2017
Revenue		9,080,747	8,816,259	12,357,291	11,769,922	11,769,922
R&D Expense						
Operating Income						
Operating Margin %						
SGA Expense						
Net Income						
Operating Cash Flow						
Capital Expenditure						
EBITDA						
Return on Assets %						
Return on Equity %						
Debt to Equity						

CONTACT INFORMATION:

Phone: 413-781-2030   Fax: 413-733-4767
Toll-Free:
Address: 1 Monarch Place, Ste. 2400, Springfield, MA 01144 United States

STOCK TICKER/OTHER:

Stock Ticker: Private
Employees: 76
Parent Company:

Exchange:
Fiscal Year Ends: 06/30

SALARIES/BONUSES:

Top Exec. Salary: $ Bonus: $
Second Exec. Salary: $ Bonus: $

OTHER THOUGHTS:

Estimated Female Officers or Directors: 4
Hot Spot for Advancement for Women/Minorities: Y

Anaheim Ducks

NAIC Code: 711211F

www.nhl.com/ducks

TYPES OF BUSINESS:

Professional Hockey Team (NHL)
Team Management and Operations

BRANDS/DIVISIONS/AFFILIATES:

Anaheim Arena Management LLC
Honda Center
Mighty Ducks

CONTACTS: *Note: Officers with more than one job title may be intentionally listed here more than once.*

Bill Foltz, CEO
Aaron Teats, Pres.
Bill Pedigo, CCO
Gina Galasso, Chief Human Resources Officer
David McNab, Sr. VP-Hockey Oper.
Doug Heller, VP-Finance
Bruce Boudreau, Head Coach
Bob Murray, Exec. VP
John Viola, VP-Sales
Michael Schulman, Chmn.

GROWTH PLANS/SPECIAL FEATURES:

Anaheim Ducks are a professional ice hockey team in the National Hockey League (NHL). The team was founded in 1993 by The Walt Disney Company and originally named after the Disney film, The Mighty Ducks. It made its first playoff appearance in 1997, losing to the Detroit Red Wings in the semifinals. In 2005, Disney sold the Ducks to Henry Samueli, the co-founder and former chairman of Broadcom Corporation. Samueli also owns Anaheim Arena Management LLC, which operates the Honda Center, the Ducks' home arena. In addition to hosting the Ducks, the Honda Center also serves as a venue for musical artists, traveling circuses and other events. The arena offers three levels of seating and luxury suites, with a total seating capacity for hockey of 17,174. Forbes estimated the Ducks' value at $725 million in December 2022. The Ducks play in the Pacific division of the Western Conference along with the Calgary Flames, Edmonton Oilers, Los Angeles Kings, San Jose Sharks, Seattle Kraken, Vancouver Canucks and Vegas Golden Knights.

FINANCIAL DATA: *Note: Data for latest year may not have been available at press time.*

In U.S. $	2022	2021	2020	2019	2018	2017
Revenue	120,250,000					
R&D Expense						
Operating Income						
Operating Margin %						
SGA Expense						
Net Income						
Operating Cash Flow						
Capital Expenditure						
EBITDA						
Return on Assets %						
Return on Equity %						
Debt to Equity						

CONTACT INFORMATION:

Phone: 714-704-2700   Fax: 714-704-2754
Toll-Free: 877-945-3946
Address: 2695 E. Katella Ave., Anaheim, CA 92806 United States

STOCK TICKER/OTHER:

Stock Ticker: Private   Exchange:
Employees: Fiscal Year Ends: 09/30
Parent Company:

SALARIES/BONUSES:

Top Exec. Salary: $ Bonus: $
Second Exec. Salary: $ Bonus: $

OTHER THOUGHTS:

Estimated Female Officers or Directors:
Hot Spot for Advancement for Women/Minorities: Y

AND 1

www.and1.com

NAIC Code: 424340

TYPES OF BUSINESS:

Footwear Distribution
Street Basketball Tournaments
Basketball Footwear
Basketball Apparel
Apparel and Footwear Manufacturing
Team Uniforms
Basketball Gear
Ecommerce

BRANDS/DIVISIONS/AFFILIATES:

Gainline Capital Partners LP
Galaxy Universal LLC
AND 1 Mix Tape Tour
AND 1 Streetball
Tai Chi

CONTACTS: Note: Officers with more than one job title may be intentionally listed here more than once.

Eddie Esses, CEO-Galaxy Universal
Sue Ehnow, Dir.-Retail Oper.

GROWTH PLANS/SPECIAL FEATURES:

AND 1, often referred to as The Basketball Marketing Company, manufactures shoes, team uniforms and gear, with a strategic focus on hip-hop and non-professional basketball culture. The name AND 1 refers to the free throw that is taken after someone is fouled while scoring a basket. It utilizes its logo as a faceless, raceless basketball player known as The Player. The brand was launched in 1993, initially producing printed t-shirts, and has since expanded into a complete line of basketball apparel including performance shoes, t-shirts, shorts, pants, team duffle bags, hats and other related accessories, as well as basketballs. The company's performance Shooting Shorts line is distinctly designed by players for players. Merchandise is sold internationally through leading sports apparel stores such as Academy Sports & Outdoors, as through the firm's ecommerce website. The company's Tai Chi shoe features a combination of leather and nubuck with overlays to create a form fit, a mesh tongue to promote air flow, a fixed internal EVA footbed to ensure cushion and stability, a low profile design of the outsole yielding court feel and abrasion-resistant herringbone tread pods. AND 1 has gained considerable fame with its AND 1 Mix Tape Tour, a street basketball tournament that emphasizes style, trick moves and showmanship. The Mix Tape Tours basketball team includes a group of 10 young men who promote the AND 1 brand. Additionally, the firm has licensed its brand to video game developers to produce AND 1 Streetball, a streetball video game designed to capture the hip-hop culture surrounding non-professional basketball. AND 1 is owned by Galaxy Universal, LLC, a portfolio company of private equity firm Gainline Capital Partners LP.

FINANCIAL DATA: Note: Data for latest year may not have been available at press time.

In U.S. $	2022	2021	2020	2019	2018	2017
Revenue						
R&D Expense						
Operating Income						
Operating Margin %						
SGA Expense						
Net Income						
Operating Cash Flow						
Capital Expenditure						
EBITDA						
Return on Assets %						
Return on Equity %						
Debt to Equity						

CONTACT INFORMATION:

Phone: 212 425-2999   Fax:
Toll-Free: 800-848-8698
Address: 440 9th Ave., Fl. 9, New York, NY 10001 United States

STOCK TICKER/OTHER:

Stock Ticker: Private   Exchange:
Employees: Fiscal Year Ends: 12/31
Parent Company: Gainline Capital Partners LP

SALARIES/BONUSES:

Top Exec. Salary: $ Bonus: $
Second Exec. Salary: $ Bonus: $

OTHER THOUGHTS:

Estimated Female Officers or Directors: 1
Hot Spot for Advancement for Women/Minorities:

Anschutz Entertainment Group Inc   www.aegworldwide.com

NAIC Code: 711211

TYPES OF BUSINESS:

Stadiums & Sports Teams
Sports and Entertainment
Entertainment Venues
Entertainment Districts
Ticketing Platforms
Marketing Services
Real Estate Development and Management

BRANDS/DIVISIONS/AFFILIATES:

Anschutz Corporation (The)
AEG
AEG Worldwide
AEG 1Source
AEG Real Estate
AEG Global Partners
AEG Community Foundation
AEG 1Earth

CONTACTS: *Note: Officers with more than one job title may be intentionally listed here more than once.*

Dan Beckerman, CEO

GROWTH PLANS/SPECIAL FEATURES:

Anschutz Entertainment Group, Inc. (operating as AEG and also known as AEG Worldwide), a subsidiary of The Anschutz Corporation, is a leading sports and live entertainment company. Through its global network of venues, sports franchises, music brands, integrated entertainment districts, ticketing platforms and sponsorship activations, AEG delivers innovative experiences. The company entertains more than 160 million guests, promotes over 10,000 shows, 22,000+ live events and approximately 25 music festivals each year. AEG 1Source is the firm's supply management shared services business model. AEG Real Estate designs and develops arenas, stadiums, clubs, theaters and entertainment districts worldwide; and its wide range of services include, renovation and leasing of existing buildings, sale of developed land or parcels, land acquisitions and entitlement. AEG Global Partners creates experiences and develops marketing programs for brands, with a focus on reaching audiences in person and online. Based in Los Angeles, California, the firm has offices on five continents. The charitable organization of AEG is AEG Community Foundation. AEG 1Earth is the company's corporate sustainability program.

FINANCIAL DATA: *Note: Data for latest year may not have been available at press time.*

In U.S. $	2022	2021	2020	2019	2018	2017
Revenue						
R&D Expense						
Operating Income						
Operating Margin %						
SGA Expense						
Net Income						
Operating Cash Flow						
Capital Expenditure						
EBITDA						
Return on Assets %						
Return on Equity %						
Debt to Equity						

CONTACT INFORMATION:

Phone: 213-763-7700   Fax: 213-763-5406
Toll-Free:
Address: 800 W. Olympic Blvd., Ste. 305, Los Angeles, CA 90015 United States

STOCK TICKER/OTHER:

Stock Ticker: Subsidiary   Exchange:
Employees: Fiscal Year Ends: 12/31
Parent Company: Anschutz Corporation (The)

SALARIES/BONUSES:

Top Exec. Salary: $ Bonus: $
Second Exec. Salary: $ Bonus: $

OTHER THOUGHTS:

Estimated Female Officers or Directors:
Hot Spot for Advancement for Women/Minorities:

ANTA Sports Products Limited   www.anta.com

NAIC Code: 424320

TYPES OF BUSINESS:
Men's and Boys' Clothing and Furnishings Merchant Wholesalers
Sportswear
Footwear
Apparel
Accessories
Manufacturer

BRANDS/DIVISIONS/AFFILIATES:
ANTA
ANTA Kids
FILA
FILA Kids
DESCENTE
Kolon Sport

GROWTH PLANS/SPECIAL FEATURES:
Anta Sports is the largest Chinese sportswear company, engaging in the design, manufacturing, and marketing of sportswear. Brands under Anta's management include the Anta core brand, Fila, Descente, Sprandi, Kolon, and KingKow. As of the end of 2020, the company had 12,260 stores, of which 9,922 were Anta stores and 2,006 were Fila stores.

CONTACTS: Note: Officers with more than one job title may be intentionally listed here more than once.
Shizhong Ding, Chmn.

FINANCIAL DATA: Note: Data for latest year may not have been available at press time.

In U.S. $	2022	2021	2020	2019	2018	2017
Revenue	7,791,203,000	7,163,417,000	5,157,056,000	4,927,027,000	2,424,085,000	2,424,085,000
R&D Expense						
Operating Income	1,598,147,000	1,581,302,000	1,314,097,000	1,255,282,000	576,545,400	576,545,400
Operating Margin %		.22%	.25%	.25%	.24%	.24%
SGA Expense	3,371,430,000	3,003,297,000	1,871,597,000	1,602,359,000	679,121,000	679,121,000
Net Income	1,102,220,000	1,121,099,000	749,626,000	776,056,100	448,416,800	448,416,800
Operating Cash Flow	1,763,988,000	1,722,455,000	1,083,051,000	1,086,972,000	462,012,500	462,012,500
Capital Expenditure	252,102,100	216,813,600	123,582,300	157,709,000	84,957,960	84,957,960
EBITDA	2,371,444,000	2,170,895,000	1,535,702,000	1,416,767,000	664,581,400	664,581,400
Return on Assets %		.13%	.11%	.16%	.19%	.19%
Return on Equity %		.29%	.23%	.30%	.27%	.27%
Debt to Equity		.50%	0.571	0.373		

CONTACT INFORMATION:
Phone: 86-592-630-5588   Fax: 86-592-630-5678
Toll-Free:
Address: Unite No. 4408, Fl. 44 COSCO Tower, 183 Queen's Rd., Central, Hong Kong, 361008 Hong Kong

STOCK TICKER/OTHER:
Stock Ticker: ANPDY   Exchange: PINX
Employees: 52,000   Fiscal Year Ends: 12/31
Parent Company:

SALARIES/BONUSES:
Top Exec. Salary: $ Bonus: $
Second Exec. Salary: $ Bonus: $

OTHER THOUGHTS:
Estimated Female Officers or Directors:
Hot Spot for Advancement for Women/Minorities:

Anytime Fitness LLC

NAIC Code: 713940

TYPES OF BUSINESS:

Fitness Center
Franchising

BRANDS/DIVISIONS/AFFILIATES:

Self Esteem Brands

GROWTH PLANS/SPECIAL FEATURES:

Anytime Fitness, LLC operates a chain of 24-hour health and fitness clubs, serving members in over 30 countries. The firm's more than 4,700 franchised clubs span seven continents. The gym facilities are open 24 hours a day, every day of the year. The facilities include strength equipment, free weights, cardio machines and functional training equipment such as TRX, kettlebells and BOSU Balance Trainers. Amenities and services offered at the gyms include tanning, personal training, group fitness classes, private restrooms and showers, wellness programs, health plan discounts, HDTVs and 24-hour security. Anytime Fitness also has apps for members, and serves as a platform to download workouts, track food and interact with other uses; and the app is available on Android and iOS. Depending on if the franchisee selects to open a standard or express location, franchise initial investments range anywhere from $381,575 to $783,897. Anytime Fitness is a subsidiary of Self Esteem Brands.

CONTACTS: Note: Officers with more than one job title may be intentionally listed here more than once.

Chuck Runyon, CEO

FINANCIAL DATA: Note: Data for latest year may not have been available at press time.

In U.S. $	2022	2021	2020	2019	2018	2017
Revenue	1,580,000,000	1,215,400,000	1,180,000,000	2,000,000,000	1,450,000,000	1,450,000,000
R&D Expense						
Operating Income						
Operating Margin %						
SGA Expense						
Net Income						
Operating Cash Flow						
Capital Expenditure						
EBITDA						
Return on Assets %						
Return on Equity %						
Debt to Equity						

CONTACT INFORMATION:

Phone: 651-438-5008   Fax:
Toll-Free:
Address: 111 Weir Dr., Woodbury, MN 55125 United States

SALARIES/BONUSES:

Top Exec. Salary: $ Bonus: $
Second Exec. Salary: $ Bonus: $

STOCK TICKER/OTHER:

Stock Ticker: Private   Exchange:
Employees: 6,000   Fiscal Year Ends:
Parent Company: Self Esteem Brands

OTHER THOUGHTS:

Estimated Female Officers or Directors:
Hot Spot for Advancement for Women/Minorities:

Aramark Corporation

NAIC Code: 722310

TYPES OF BUSINESS:

Food Service Contractor
Facilities Management
Uniforms & Career Apparel Rental
Parks & Resorts Concessions & Facilities
Health Care Support Services
Apparel Manufacturing
Clinical Equipment Maintenance

BRANDS/DIVISIONS/AFFILIATES:

GROWTH PLANS/SPECIAL FEATURES:

Aramark provides food, facilities, and uniform services to a variety of clients and institutions. The majority of company revenue comes from its North American food and support services segment. Smaller but substantial segments include food and support services international and uniform and career apparel. The food and support services segments provide food for school districts; colleges; healthcare facilities; correctional institutions; and business, sports, and entertainment venues. The uniform segment rents, delivers, cleans, and maintains work clothes and ancillary items like towels and mats to customers in North America and Japan. The company has hundreds of service locations and distribution centers across the United States and Canada.

Aramark offers medical, dental, vision, life and disability insurance; and pension and employee assistance plans.

CONTACTS: Note: Officers with more than one job title may be intentionally listed here more than once.

John Zillmer, CEO
Thomas Ondrof, CFO
Stephen Sadove, Chairman of the Board
Chris Schilling, Chief Accounting Officer
Marc Bruno, COO, Geographical
Paul Hilal, Director
Lynn McKee, Executive VP, Divisional
Lauren Harrington, General Counsel

FINANCIAL DATA: Note: Data for latest year may not have been available at press time.

In U.S. $	2022	2021	2020	2019	2018	2017
Revenue	16,326,620,000	12,095,970,000	12,829,560,000	16,227,340,000	14,604,410,000	14,604,410,000
R&D Expense						
Operating Income	628,365,000	191,444,000	-66,319,000	734,850,000	801,627,000	801,627,000
Operating Margin %	.04%	.02%	-.01%	.05%	.05%	.05%
SGA Expense	398,362,000	346,749,000	307,016,000	367,256,000	299,170,000	299,170,000
Net Income	194,484,000	-90,833,000	-461,529,000	448,549,000	373,923,000	373,923,000
Operating Cash Flow	694,499,000	657,079,000	176,682,000	984,227,000	1,052,826,000	1,052,826,000
Capital Expenditure	388,397,000	407,818,000	418,508,000	503,090,000	702,965,000	702,965,000
EBITDA	1,169,498,000	831,553,000	336,910,000	1,501,557,000	1,314,849,000	1,314,849,000
Return on Assets %	.01%	-.01%	-.03%	.03%	.03%	.03%
Return on Equity %	.07%	-.03%	-.15%	.14%	.16%	.16%
Debt to Equity	2.53%	2.83%	3.48	1.992	2.111	2.111

CONTACT INFORMATION:

Phone: 215-238-3000   Fax: 415-238-3333
Toll-Free: 800-272-6275
Address: 1101 Market St., Aramark Tower, Philadelphia, PA 19107
United States

STOCK TICKER/OTHER:

Stock Ticker: ARMK
Employees: 273,875
Parent Company:

Exchange: NYS
Fiscal Year Ends: 09/30

SALARIES/BONUSES:

Top Exec. Salary: $1,300,000   Bonus: $
Second Exec. Salary: $800,010   Bonus: $

OTHER THOUGHTS:

Estimated Female Officers or Directors: 1
Hot Spot for Advancement for Women/Minorities:

Arizona Cardinals

www.azcardinals.com

NAIC Code: 711211C

TYPES OF BUSINESS:

Professional Football Team
Team Management and Operations

BRANDS/DIVISIONS/AFFILIATES:

State Farm Stadium

CONTACTS: *Note: Officers with more than one job title may be intentionally listed here more than once.*

Monti Ossenfort, Gen. Mngr.
Greg Lee, CFO
Shaun Mayo, Chief People Officer
David Koeninger, General Counsel
Steve Keim, VP-Football Oper.
Steve Ryan, VP-Bus. Dev.
Mark Dalton, VP-Media Rel.
Teresa Miller, Dir.-Finance
Rick Knight, VP-Security
William V. Bidwill, Jr., VP
John Drum, VP-Stadium Oper.
Ron Campbell, Sr. Dir.-Ticket Sales
William J. Bidwill, Chmn.

GROWTH PLANS/SPECIAL FEATURES:

Arizona Cardinals is a professional football team playing in the National Football League (NFL) and based in Glendale, Arizona. The franchise, founded in 1898, has the distinction of being the oldest continuously run professional football team in the U.S., having won its first NFL championship in 1925. Originally named the Morgan Athletic Club and located in Chicago, the franchise has evolved through several incarnations, including the Normals, the Racine Cardinals, the Chicago Cardinals, the St. Louis Cardinals and the Phoenix Cardinals, before moving to play in the Sun Devil Stadium on the Arizona State University campus in Tempe, Arizona. In September 2018, State Farm acquired the naming rights to the Cardinals Stadium based in Glendale, naming it the State Farm Stadium under an 18-year agreement with the Cardinals. State Farm Stadium has a 63,400-seating capacity, expandable to 72,200 and standing room to at least 78,600. The team places within the National Football Conference (NFC) Western division, and has been owned by the Bidwill family since 1932, when Charles W. Bidwill bought the team for $50,000. Despite several postseason appearances, the team has failed to win a Super Bowl, coming up just short in Super Bowl XLIII in 2009, which it lost to the Pittsburgh Steelers 27-23. Forbes valued the Cardinals at $3.27 during the 2022 season. The team's average home game attendance was 19,817 during the 2022 season.

FINANCIAL DATA: *Note: Data for latest year may not have been available at press time.*

In U.S. $	2022	2021	2020	2019	2018	2017
Revenue	503,750,000					
R&D Expense						
Operating Income						
Operating Margin %						
SGA Expense						
Net Income						
Operating Cash Flow						
Capital Expenditure						
EBITDA						
Return on Assets %						
Return on Equity %						
Debt to Equity						

CONTACT INFORMATION:

Phone: 602-379-0101   Fax: 602-379-1819
Toll-Free: 800-999-1402
Address: 1 Cardinals Dr., Glendale, AZ 85305 United States

STOCK TICKER/OTHER:

Stock Ticker: Private   Exchange:
Employees: 300   Fiscal Year Ends: 01/31
Parent Company:

SALARIES/BONUSES:

Top Exec. Salary: $ Bonus: $
Second Exec. Salary: $ Bonus: $

OTHER THOUGHTS:

Estimated Female Officers or Directors: 3
Hot Spot for Advancement for Women/Minorities: Y

Arizona Coyotes

www.phoenixcoyotes.com

NAIC Code: 711211F

TYPES OF BUSINESS:

Professional Hockey Team (NHL)
Team Management and Operations

BRANDS/DIVISIONS/AFFILIATES:

Mullett Arena
Tucson Roadrunners
Atlanta Gladiators

CONTACTS: *Note: Officers with more than one job title may be intentionally listed here more than once.*

Xavier A. Gutierrez, CEO
Liz Montano, COO
Bill Armstrong, Gen. Mngr.
Chris O' Hearn, Dir.-Hockey Admin.
Brad Treliving, VP-Hockey Oper.
Rich Nairn, Sr. Dir.-Media Rel.
Joe Leibfried, VP-Finance
Dave Tippett, Head Coach
Don Maloney, Gen. Mgr.
Kimberly Trichel, Dir.-Comm. Rel.
Brittany Grant, Dir.-Corp. Partnerships
Alex Meruelo, Chmn.
Robert Neuhauser, Scout-Europe

GROWTH PLANS/SPECIAL FEATURES:

Arizona Coyotes is a National Hockey League (NHL) team based in the Phoenix metropolitan area. The Coyotes entered the NHL in 1979, playing originally as the Jets for the city of Winnipeg in Manitoba, Canada. In 1996, the team moved to its current home in Arizona. The Coyotes have seen some success in its tenure in Phoenix, frequently making the playoffs in the late 1990s but often failing to make it past the first round. The franchise has yet to win a Stanley Cup, conference championship or division championship. From 2005-09, the Coyotes were coached by hockey legend Wayne Gretzky, but were unable to achieve any major success. Gretzky's tenure was cut short by the team's 2009 bankruptcy, during which the NHL took over the team. In the 2011-12 season, the Coyotes earned the Pacific Division Title. Currently, the Coyotes play in the Western Conference, Central Division along with the Chicago Blackhawks, Colorado Avalanche, Dallas Stars, Minnesota Wild, Nashville Predators, St. Louis Blues and Winnipeg Jets. The Coyotes are affiliated with minor league teams the Tucson Roadrunners in the American Hockey League (AHL) and the Atlanta Gladiators in the ECHL. The team's home stadium is the Mullett Arena, located at Arizona State University and having a seating capacity of 5,000. Average attendance for home games was 4,600 during the 2022-23 season. Forbes valued the Arizona Coyotes at $450 million in December 2022. Alex Meruelo and Andrew Barroway own the Coyotes.

FINANCIAL DATA: *Note: Data for latest year may not have been available at press time.*

In U.S. $	2022	2021	2020	2019	2018	2017
Revenue	104,650,000					
R&D Expense						
Operating Income						
Operating Margin %						
SGA Expense						
Net Income						
Operating Cash Flow						
Capital Expenditure						
EBITDA						
Return on Assets %						
Return on Equity %						
Debt to Equity						

CONTACT INFORMATION:

Phone: 623-772-3200   Fax: 623-872-2000
Toll-Free:
Address: 9400 W. Maryland Ave., Glendale, AZ 85305 United States

STOCK TICKER/OTHER:

Stock Ticker: Private
Employees: 216
Parent Company:

Exchange:
Fiscal Year Ends: 06/30

SALARIES/BONUSES:

Top Exec. Salary: $ Bonus: $
Second Exec. Salary: $ Bonus: $

OTHER THOUGHTS:

Estimated Female Officers or Directors: 3
Hot Spot for Advancement for Women/Minorities: Y

Arizona Diamondbacks

www.mlb.com/dbacks

NAIC Code: 711211A

TYPES OF BUSINESS:

Professional Baseball Team
Team Management and Operations

BRANDS/DIVISIONS/AFFILIATES:

CONTACTS: *Note: Officers with more than one job title may be intentionally listed here more than once.*

Derrick Hall, CEO
Cullen Maxey, Exec. VP-Bus. Oper.
Tom Harris, CFO
John Fisher, Sr. VP-Ticket Sales & Mktg.
Joseph Walsh, Sr. VP-People & Culture
Bob Zweig, CTO
Nona Lee, General Counsel
Cullen Maxey, Exec. VP-Bus. Oper.
Kenny Farrell, Sr. Dir.-Bus. Strategy & Oper.
Josh Rawitch, Sr. VP-Comm.
Craig Bradley, VP-Finance
Kevin Towers, Exec. VP
Ken Kendrick, Managing Gen. Partner
Debbie Castaldo, VP-Corp. & Community Impact
Ray Montgomery, Dir.-Scouting
Caleb Jay, General Counsel
Junior Noboa, VP-Latin Oper.

GROWTH PLANS/SPECIAL FEATURES:

The Arizona Diamondbacks joined Major League Baseball (MLB) in 1998 as a National League (NL) expansion team. In just four years, the Diamondbacks (D-Backs) won the World Series, the quickest ascent ever for an MLB expansion team. Baseball was brought to Arizona by Jerry Colangelo, the general manager and minority owner of the NBA's Phoenix Suns, with strong support from baseball owners and MLB Commissioner Bud Selig. The team's venue, Chase Field, seats more than 48,680 and incorporates a massive air-conditioning system, a 136-by-46-foot HD LED board and retractable roof. The seating arrangements provide optimal sight lines and a separate pavilion contains a swimming pool, hot tub and fountains. The park drew as many as 3.6 million fans in its inaugural season, but has since fallen to closer to 2 million per season. Part of this was due to a dismal 2004 season, when the team went 51-111, though attendance numbers had already begun to fall by then. That summer, Jerry Colangelo sold his controlling interest in the team to a group of investors. Colangelo left the team more than $150 million in debt through the payment of deferred contracts to the expensive veterans who helped the D-Backs win the 2001 World Series. Since its formation, the team has won five NL West division titles, most recently in 2011. In 2017, the D-Backs clenched their first wild card berth and went to the playoffs. In the wild card game, they defeated the Colorado Rockies to advance the National League Division Series against the Los Angeles Dodgers, and were swept by the Dodgers three games to none. The D-Backs averaged 19,817 in home game attendance during the 2022 season. Forbes estimated the team's value at approximately $1.38 billion in March 2023.

FINANCIAL DATA: *Note: Data for latest year may not have been available at press time.*

In U.S. $	2022	2021	2020	2019	2018	2017
Revenue	354,250,000					
R&D Expense						
Operating Income						
Operating Margin %						
SGA Expense						
Net Income						
Operating Cash Flow						
Capital Expenditure						
EBITDA						
Return on Assets %						
Return on Equity %						
Debt to Equity						

CONTACT INFORMATION:

Phone: 602-462-6500   Fax: 602-462-6599
Toll-Free:
Address: 401 E. Jefferson St., Phoenix, AZ 85004 United States

STOCK TICKER/OTHER:

Stock Ticker: Private   Exchange:
Employees: 350   Fiscal Year Ends: 10/31
Parent Company:

SALARIES/BONUSES:

Top Exec. Salary: $ Bonus: $
Second Exec. Salary: $ Bonus: $

OTHER THOUGHTS:

Estimated Female Officers or Directors: 6
Hot Spot for Advancement for Women/Minorities: Y

Arsenal Football Club Plc

www.arsenal.com

NAIC Code: 711211D

TYPES OF BUSINESS:
English Premiere Soccer Team
Team Management and Operations

BRANDS/DIVISIONS/AFFILIATES:
Kroenke Sports & Entertainment
Arsenal Holdings Limited
Arsenal Women
Arsenal Academy

CONTACTS: *Note: Officers with more than one job title may be intentionally listed here more than once.*
Vinai Venkatesham, CEO
Stuart Wisely, CFO
Josh Kroenke, Co-Chmn.
Arsene Wenger, Mgr.
Stanley Kroenke, Co-Chmn.

GROWTH PLANS/SPECIAL FEATURES:
Arsenal Football Club is a professional English soccer club based in Holloway, North London. Nicknamed The Gunners, the team plays in the Premier League, and it is one of the most successful clubs in English soccer. The club manages the Arsenal men's, Arsenal Women and Arsenal Academy (youth) soccer teams in London. Arsenal was originally started by the workers at the Woolwich Arsenal Armament Factory, which gave the team its name. The Arsenal men's team has won 13 league championships since its inception, including the 2001-02 and 2003-04 seasons. It has also won 14 FA (Football Association Challenge) Cups (England's national title), most recently in 2020. Arsenal Women FC is a semi-professional women's soccer team, has won 14 FA Women's Cups, five FA WSL Cups, 10 FA Women's Premier League Cups and five FA Women's Community Shield cups, as well as 15 FA Women's Premier League National Division titles (Level 1). The Junior Gunners, the group's youth club, offers Team Junior Gunners Membership for kids 4-11 and Young Guns for children 12-16. Membership gives kids access to discounted tickets, online video streaming, membership merchandise, soccer schools and chances to be a mascot for Young Guns or Ball Squad for Junior Gunners on Match days. Arsenal Academy is the club's youth soccer team for those under 18 years of age. Arsenal operates as a subsidiary of Arsenal Holdings Limited, which itself is privately-owned by Kroenke Sports & Entertainment. Arsenal plays at Emirates Stadium in Holloway, which seats approximately 60,704 fans, with the average home game attendance being 60,191 during the 2022-23 season.

FINANCIAL DATA: *Note: Data for latest year may not have been available at press time.*

In U.S. $	2022	2021	2020	2019	2018	2017
Revenue	475,000,000	465,824,063	428,688,521	451,577,000	542,846,000	542,846,000
R&D Expense						
Operating Income						
Operating Margin %						
SGA Expense						
Net Income		-71,668,623	-14,370,303	-28,876,400	45,322,700	45,322,700
Operating Cash Flow						
Capital Expenditure						
EBITDA						
Return on Assets %						
Return on Equity %						
Debt to Equity						

CONTACT INFORMATION:
Phone: 44-20-7619-5003   Fax: 44-20-7704-4001
Toll-Free:
Address: 75 Drayton Park, Highbury House, London, N5 1BU United Kingdom

STOCK TICKER/OTHER:
Stock Ticker: Private   Exchange:
Employees: 624   Fiscal Year Ends: 05/31
Parent Company: Kroenke Sports & Entertainment

SALARIES/BONUSES:
Top Exec. Salary: $ Bonus: $
Second Exec. Salary: $ Bonus: $

OTHER THOUGHTS:
Estimated Female Officers or Directors:
Hot Spot for Advancement for Women/Minorities:

Sales, profits and employees may be estimates. Financial information, benefits and other data can change quickly and may vary from those stated here.

AS Roma (Associazione Sportiva Roma)

www.asroma.com

NAIC Code: 711211D

TYPES OF BUSINESS:

Soccer Team
Team Management and Operations

BRANDS/DIVISIONS/AFFILIATES:

Friedkin Group (The)
AS Roma Femminile

CONTACTS: *Note: Officers with more than one job title may be intentionally listed here more than once.*

Dan Friedkin, Pres.

GROWTH PLANS/SPECIAL FEATURES:

Associazione Sportiva Roma (A.S. Roma) is a professional football (soccer) club in Rome, Italy, founded in 1927. A.S. Roma plays in the Serie A league, the top tier of Italian football. The team has won the Serie A three times (1941-42, 1982-83 and 2000-01), as well as nine Coppa Italia titles and two Supercoppa Itliana titles. In European competitions, A.S. Roma won the UEFA Europa Conference League in 2021-22 and the Inter-Cities Fairs Cup in 1960-61. The club plays home games in the Stadio Olimpico, Rome's Olympic Stadium built for the 1960 Olympic Games and renovated for the 1990 World Cup. Stadio Olimpico has a seating capacity of 70,634. A.S. Roma is majority-owned (86.6%) by The Friedkin Group, with Dan Friedkin being the president. Jose Mourinho is the team's head coach. New Balance supplies the team's kits and DigitalBits is its shirt sponsor. A.S. Roma Femminile is an Italian women's association football club that also plays in the Serie A, and clenched the Serie A championship during the 2022-23 season. Other titles by the Roma Femminile include the Coppa Italia in 2020-21 and the Supercoppa Italiana in 2022.

FINANCIAL DATA: *Note: Data for latest year may not have been available at press time.*

In U.S. $	2022	2021	2020	2019	2018	2017
Revenue		189,240,464	142,825,968	232,690,528	189,164,640	189,164,640
R&D Expense						
Operating Income						
Operating Margin %						
SGA Expense						
Net Income		-188,979,408	-208,060,208	-24,774,122	-45,451,400	-45,451,400
Operating Cash Flow						
Capital Expenditure						
EBITDA						
Return on Assets %						
Return on Equity %						
Debt to Equity						

CONTACT INFORMATION:

Phone: 39 06501911   Fax: 39 065061736
Toll-Free:
Address: Via di Trigoria, Km 3,600, Roma, RM 00128 Italy

STOCK TICKER/OTHER:

Stock Ticker: ROMA   Exchange: Milan
Employees: 196   Fiscal Year Ends: 06/30
Parent Company: Friedkin Group (The)

SALARIES/BONUSES:

Top Exec. Salary: $ Bonus: $
Second Exec. Salary: $ Bonus: $

OTHER THOUGHTS:

Estimated Female Officers or Directors:
Hot Spot for Advancement for Women/Minorities:

Sales, profits and employees may be estimates. Financial information, benefits and other data can change quickly and may vary from those stated here.

ASICS Corp

NAIC Code: 424340

corp.asics.com/en

TYPES OF BUSINESS:

Footwear Distribution
Sporting Goods
Apparel
Uniforms

BRANDS/DIVISIONS/AFFILIATES:

ASICS America Corp
ASICS Europe BV
Onitsuka Tiger
Impact Guide System
dreamstock inc

GROWTH PLANS/SPECIAL FEATURES:

ASICS Corp is a Japanese manufacturer and distributor of sporting goods. The company organizes itself across three business domains: athletic sports, sports lifestyle, and health/comfort. Athletic sports provide equipment for running, ASICS' core business; training; tennis; and rugby. Sports lifestyle includes fashion and lifestyle apparel and footwear. Health/comfort includes casual leather shoes, safety shoes, and nursing care facilities. The company reports results for three segments: sports shoes, sportswear, and sports equipment. The sports shoes segment contributes to the vast majority of consolidated revenue. Geographically, sales made domestically, across the Americas, and in EMEA contribute significantly to revenue, and collectively constitute the vast majority of sales.

CONTACTS: *Note: Officers with more than one job title may be intentionally listed here more than once.*

Motoi Oyama, CEO
Yasuhito Hirota, Pres.
Toshiyuki Sano, Managing Exec. Officer
Kousuke Hashimoto, Managing Exec. Officer
Masao Hijikata, Exec. Officer
Isao Kato, Exec. Officer
Motoi Oyama, Chmn.

FINANCIAL DATA: *Note: Data for latest year may not have been available at press time.*

In U.S. $	2022	2021	2020	2019	2018	2017
Revenue	3,663,338,000	3,055,003,000	2,486,287,000	2,857,625,000	3,024,175,000	3,024,175,000
R&D Expense						
Operating Income	257,037,900	165,900,600	-29,882,680	80,387,660	147,946,800	147,946,800
Operating Margin %		.05%	-.01%	.03%	.05%	.05%
SGA Expense						
Net Income	150,335,600	71,074,360	-121,904,400	53,649,720	98,046,630	98,046,630
Operating Cash Flow	-161,977,200	371,518,800	146,125,000	111,820,000	280,729,300	280,729,300
Capital Expenditure	86,737,620	72,775,240	69,222,280	86,147,980	107,284,300	107,284,300
EBITDA	361,207,700	228,221,100	-2,857,489	188,745,400	250,453,600	250,453,600
Return on Assets %		.03%	-.05%	.02%	.04%	.04%
Return on Equity %		.07%	-.12%	.04%	.06%	.06%
Debt to Equity		.66%	0.702	0.44	0.277	0.277

CONTACT INFORMATION:

Phone: 81 783032231   Fax: 81 783032241
Toll-Free: 800-678-9435
Address: 1-1, Minatojima-Nakamachi 7-chome, Kobe, 650-8555 Japan

STOCK TICKER/OTHER:

Stock Ticker: ASCCY   Exchange: PINX
Employees: 10,727   Fiscal Year Ends: 12/31
Parent Company:

SALARIES/BONUSES:

Top Exec. Salary: $ Bonus: $
Second Exec. Salary: $ Bonus: $

OTHER THOUGHTS:

Estimated Female Officers or Directors:
Hot Spot for Advancement for Women/Minorities:

ASM Global

NAIC Code: 561210

TYPES OF BUSINESS:

Facilities Management Services
Culinary Services
Engineering and Construction Services
Design and Pre-Opening Solutions
Employee and Professional Training
Security Services

BRANDS/DIVISIONS/AFFILIATES:

Anschutz Entertainment Group Inc
Onex Corporation

CONTACTS: *Note: Officers with more than one job title may be intentionally listed here more than once.*

Ron Bension, CEO
Gary McAneney, VP-Admin.
Gregg Caren, Sr. VP-Strategic Bus. Dev.
Gary McAneney, VP-Finance
Bob McClintock, Sr. VP-SMG Convention Centers
Bob Cavalieri, Sr. VP-Sales & Dev.
Harry Cann, Sr. Regional VP-Arenas
Jim McCue, Sr. VP-Entertainment
John Sutherland, Managing Dir.-SMG Europe

GROWTH PLANS/SPECIAL FEATURES:

ASM Global is a world-leading entertainment facility management company, managing more than 300 facilities on five continents. The company provides operations and management services to stadiums, arenas, convention and exhibition centers, theaters and performing arts centers, recreation and equestrian facilities and other specialized facilities. Services include culinary, sports and entertainment development, partnership networking, design and pre-opening solutions, engineering solutions, employee/professional training, and safety and security services, among others. Affiliated partners include: ABM, a provider of facility solutions such as janitorial, electrical/lighting, energy, HVAC, landscape, parking and more; Honeywell, a technology company service a wide range of industries; The Clorox Company, which produces cleaning, hygiene, cosmetic, aromatic, food and beverage and charcoal products marketed under several brand names, including Pine-Sol, Clorox, Burt's Bees, Glad, Hidden Valley and Kingsford; Infor, a business cloud software firm serving global industries; Marsh McLennan Agency, a provider of business insurance, employee health and benefits, retirement, and private client insurance solutions; Mobilite (soon to be Boldyn Networks), a telecommunications infrastructure company; Sloan, a manufacturer of commercial plumbing systems and restroom solutions; and Wicked Kitchen, a chef-driven firm that provides a range of plant-based foods, meal solutions, ingredients and more, which can be found in more than 10,000 retailers and online. Anschutz Entertainment Group, Inc. and Onex Corporation are equal, co-owners of the firm. Headquartered in the U.S., ASM's global offices are located in Australia, the U.K., the United Arab Emirates and Brazil.

FINANCIAL DATA: *Note: Data for latest year may not have been available at press time.*

In U.S. $	2022	2021	2020	2019	2018	2017
Revenue	62,000,000	60,900,000	58,000,000	290,000,000	275,000,000	275,000,000
R&D Expense						
Operating Income						
Operating Margin %						
SGA Expense						
Net Income						
Operating Cash Flow						
Capital Expenditure						
EBITDA						
Return on Assets %						
Return on Equity %						
Debt to Equity						

CONTACT INFORMATION:

Phone: 610-729-7900   Fax: 610-729-1590
Toll-Free:
Address: 800 West Olympic Blvd., Fl. 3, Los Angeles, CA 90015 United States

STOCK TICKER/OTHER:

Stock Ticker: Private   Exchange:
Employees: 61,000   Fiscal Year Ends:
Parent Company: Onex Corporation

SALARIES/BONUSES:

Top Exec. Salary: $ Bonus: $
Second Exec. Salary: $ Bonus: $

OTHER THOUGHTS:

Estimated Female Officers or Directors: 1
Hot Spot for Advancement for Women/Minorities:

Aspen Skiing Company

www.aspensnowmass.com

NAIC Code: 713920

TYPES OF BUSINESS:

Skiing Facilities
Ski Equipment Rental
Ski Instruction
Resort Operation
Restaurants
Outdoor Activities
Retail Stores
Hotel Management

BRANDS/DIVISIONS/AFFILIATES:

Snowmass Mountain
Aspen Mountain
Aspen Highlands
Buttermilk Mountain
Four Mountain Sports
D&E Retail
Little Nell (The)
Limelight Hotel Aspen

CONTACTS: *Note: Officers with more than one job title may be intentionally listed here more than once.*

Geoff Buchheister, CEO

GROWTH PLANS/SPECIAL FEATURES:

Aspen Skiing Company specializes in ski resort operations. The firm's operations are comprised of four ski areas in the Aspen/Snowmass area: Snowmass Mountain, Aspen Mountain, Aspen Highlands and Buttermilk Mountain. Guests can receive ski and snowboarding lessons at any of the ski areas, ranging from beginner to expert. The ski areas boast multiple snow terrain parks and pipes, as well as tubing facilities, mountain sport rentals and retail stores under names Four Mountain Sports and D&E Retail. During the winter, guests can enjoy snowshoe tours, cross-country skiing, yoga for skiers, powder tours and more. Summer activities range from camping, adaptive programming, ballooning and paragliding, golf, hiking, fishing, horseback riding, rafting and kayaking. Aspen Skiing owns and operates many restaurants in the Aspen and Snowmass Village area, including: Sundeck, Snowcat Dinners at Lynn Britt Cabin, Cloud Nine Alpine Bistro, The Cliffhouse, Elk Camp Restaurant, Sam's, Up 4 Pizza, Two Creeks Cafe, Ullrhof, High Alpine, Ajax Tavern, Bonnie's, Element 47, Merry-Go-Round and Bumps. In addition to ski resort amenities, the company hosts multiple events at its various venues each month, such as bluegrass concerts, mountain biking marathons and farm to table Tuesday. Hotels under management of Aspen Skiing comprise of The Little Nell, the only direct access hotel to the Aspen Mountain; Limelight Hotel Aspen, a hotel bringing luxury and comfort to the outdoors; and Snow Queen Lodge, an economy hotel near downtown Aspen. The company also operates a catering company, ASC Catering.

FINANCIAL DATA: *Note: Data for latest year may not have been available at press time.*

In U.S. $	2022	2021	2020	2019	2018	2017
Revenue						
R&D Expense						
Operating Income						
Operating Margin %						
SGA Expense						
Net Income						
Operating Cash Flow						
Capital Expenditure						
EBITDA						
Return on Assets %						
Return on Equity %						
Debt to Equity						

CONTACT INFORMATION:

Phone: 970-923-1227   Fax:
Toll-Free: 800-525-6200
Address: 117 Aspen Airport Business Cntr., Aspen, CO 81611 United States

STOCK TICKER/OTHER:

Stock Ticker: Private
Employees:
Parent Company:

Exchange:
Fiscal Year Ends:

SALARIES/BONUSES:

Top Exec. Salary: $ Bonus: $
Second Exec. Salary: $ Bonus: $

OTHER THOUGHTS:

Estimated Female Officers or Directors:
Hot Spot for Advancement for Women/Minorities:

Association of Tennis Professionals (ATP Tour Inc)

www.atptour.com

NAIC Code: 711211

TYPES OF BUSINESS:

Tennis Association
Tennis Tournament Organization

BRANDS/DIVISIONS/AFFILIATES:

Emirates ATP Rankings
Emirates ATP Rankings Race to London
ATP Tour
ATP Tour Masters 1000
ATP Tour 500
ATP Tour 250
ATP Challenger Tour
ITF Mens Circuit

CONTACTS: *Note: Officers with more than one job title may be intentionally listed here more than once.*

Massimo Calvelli, CEO
Zehra Mesic, Exec. VP-Finance
Simon Higson, Exec. VP-Communications
Whitney Russ, Exec. VP-People & Culture
Mark Young, Chief Legal Officer
Laurent Delanney, CEO-Europe
Alison Lee, Exec. VP-Int'l Group
Gayle David Bradshaw, Exec. VP-Rules & Competition
Andrea Gaudenzi, Chmn.
Mark Young, CEO-Americas

GROWTH PLANS/SPECIAL FEATURES:

The Association of Tennis Professionals (ATP), based in the U.K., is the governing body for men's professional tennis worldwide. ATP organizes and oversees more than 60 tournaments in 31 countries, including singles and doubles matches. The association also publishes weekly rankings of professional players: Emirates ATP Rankings, known as the world rankings, is a 52-week rolling ranking; and the Emirates ATP Rankings Race to London, a year-to-date ranking. ATP organizes the worldwide tennis tour for men known as the ATP Tour, which comprises ATP Tour Masters 1000, ATP Tour 500 and ATP Tour 250, as well as Grand Slams. ATP also oversees the ATP Challenger Tour, a level below the ATP World Tour; the ITF Men's Circuit; and ATP Champions Tour for seniors. Players and doubles teams with the most ranking points during the calendar year play in the season-ending ATP Tour finals. ATP is affiliated with the International Tennis Hall of Fame, the International Tennis Federation and the Women's Tennis Association. Collectively, these organizations work together to promote the sport of tennis around the world. ATP's Heritage Program incorporates the Emirates ATP Rankings, the ATP World Tour Awards and the ATP Tour Finals. The firm's premier partner is Emirates Airline and its platinum partner is pepperstone, gold partners are Infosys and Nitto, and silver partner is Dunlop.

FINANCIAL DATA: *Note: Data for latest year may not have been available at press time.*

In U.S. $	2022	2021	2020	2019	2018	2017
Revenue		176,800,000	30,000,000	150,000,000	112,000,000	112,000,000
R&D Expense						
Operating Income						
Operating Margin %						
SGA Expense						
Net Income						
Operating Cash Flow						
Capital Expenditure						
EBITDA						
Return on Assets %						
Return on Equity %						
Debt to Equity						

CONTACT INFORMATION:

Phone: 904 285-9886   Fax: 44-20-7381-7895

Toll-Free:

Address: 201 ATP Tour Blvd., Ponte Vedra Beach, FL 32082 United States

STOCK TICKER/OTHER:

Stock Ticker: Private   Exchange:

Employees: Fiscal Year Ends:

Parent Company:

SALARIES/BONUSES:

Top Exec. Salary: $ Bonus: $

Second Exec. Salary: $ Bonus: $

OTHER THOUGHTS:

Estimated Female Officers or Directors: 1

Hot Spot for Advancement for Women/Minorities:

Association Sportive de Saint-Etienne Loire (AS Saint-Etienne)

www.asse.fr

NAIC Code: 711211D

TYPES OF BUSINESS:

Soccer Team
Team Management and Operations

BRANDS/DIVISIONS/AFFILIATES:

Stade Geoffroy-Guichard

GROWTH PLANS/SPECIAL FEATURES:

Association Sportive de Saint-Etienne Loire (AS Saint-Etienne) is a professional football club in France, founded in 1933. AS Saint-Etienne plays in Ligue 2, the second division of French football, with home matches located at the Stade Geoffroy-Guichard stadium, which has a seating capacity of approximately 42,000. The football club achieved 10 league titles between 1956 and 1981. They have won more than 50 European competitions such as the UEFA Champions League, the UEFA Europa League and the UEFA Cup Winners' Cup. During the 2021-22 season, AS Saint-Etienne ranked 18th within Ligue 1. With a total of 18 points at the half of the 2022-23 season, AS Saint-Etienne was in the relegation zone ranked 18th in the table.

CONTACTS: Note: Officers with more than one job title may be intentionally listed here more than once.

Bernard Caiazzo, Pres.

FINANCIAL DATA: Note: Data for latest year may not have been available at press time.

In U.S. $	2022	2021	2020	2019	2018	2017
Revenue	120,000,000	114,817,433	139,025,714	83,288,468	92,465,209	92,465,209
R&D Expense						
Operating Income						
Operating Margin %						
SGA Expense						
Net Income		70,209	498,665	600,245	1,866,266	1,866,266
Operating Cash Flow						
Capital Expenditure						
EBITDA						
Return on Assets %						
Return on Equity %						
Debt to Equity						

CONTACT INFORMATION:

Phone: 33 477 9231   Fax:
Toll-Free:
Address: 11 rue de Verdun, Saint-Etienne, 42580 France

STOCK TICKER/OTHER:

Stock Ticker: Private   Exchange:
Employees: Fiscal Year Ends: 12/31
Parent Company:

SALARIES/BONUSES:

Top Exec. Salary: $ Bonus: $
Second Exec. Salary: $ Bonus: $

OTHER THOUGHTS:

Estimated Female Officers or Directors:
Hot Spot for Advancement for Women/Minorities:

Associazione Calcio Milan spa

www.acmilan.com

NAIC Code: 711211D

TYPES OF BUSINESS:

Professional Soccer Team
Team Management and Operations

BRANDS/DIVISIONS/AFFILIATES:

RedBird Capital Partners
Elliott Management Corporation

CONTACTS: *Note: Officers with more than one job title may be intentionally listed here more than once.*

Silvio Berlusconi, Pres.
Filippo Inzaghi, Head Coach
Barbara Berlusconi, Co-CEO
Paolo Berlusconi, VO
Paolo Scaroni, Chmn.

GROWTH PLANS/SPECIAL FEATURES:

Associazione Calcio Milan s.p.a., commonly referred to as A.C. Milan, is an Italy-based professional soccer club that plays in Serie A, the top of the Italian soccer league system. A.C. Milan was established in 1899 and, in terms of international trophies, is one of the most successful clubs in world soccer, with international trophies recognized by the Union of European Football Associations (UEFA) and the International Federation of Association Football (FIFA). In international play, A.C. Milan has won the UEFA Champions League a total of seven times; the UEFA Winners' Cup twice; the UEFA Super Cup five times; the Intercontinental Cup three times; and the FIFA Club World Cup in 2007. In domestic play, the club has won the top league 19 times, most recently in 2021-22. A.C. Milan plays its home games at the Stadio Giuseppe Meazza, commonly known as San Siro. San Siro is owned by the municipality of Milan and has a capacity of over 80,000. Additionally, AC Milan Football Academies are a network of over 100 affiliated clubs on the Italian territory and in several international countries that offer a technical and educational program based on AC Milan method. Each school is an educational center that, through football, creates and promotes different sport cultures to all children and adults (coaches, directors and parents) involved. RedBird Capital Partners acquired a majority stake (99.93%) in A.C. Milan during 2022, with Elliott Management Corporation holding the remainder.

FINANCIAL DATA: *Note: Data for latest year may not have been available at press time.*

In U.S. $	2022	2021	2020	2019	2018	2017
Revenue	320,000,000	310,809,139	189,640,164	270,019,000	241,991,000	241,991,000
R&D Expense						
Operating Income						
Operating Margin %						
SGA Expense						
Net Income		-112,394,695	-218,888,508	-163,483,000	-37,221,700	-37,221,700
Operating Cash Flow						
Capital Expenditure						
EBITDA						
Return on Assets %						
Return on Equity %						
Debt to Equity						

CONTACT INFORMATION:

Phone: 39-0262281   Fax: 39-026598876
Toll-Free:
Address: Via Also Rossi 8, Milano, 20149 Italy

SALARIES/BONUSES:

Top Exec. Salary: $ Bonus: $
Second Exec. Salary: $ Bonus: $

STOCK TICKER/OTHER:

Stock Ticker: Subsidiary   Exchange:
Employees: 411   Fiscal Year Ends: 06/30
Parent Company: RedBird Capital Partners

OTHER THOUGHTS:

Estimated Female Officers or Directors:
Hot Spot for Advancement for Women/Minorities: Y

Aston Villa Football Club

www.avfc.co.uk

NAIC Code: 711211D

TYPES OF BUSINESS:

Professional Soccer Team
Team Management and Operations

BRANDS/DIVISIONS/AFFILIATES:

NSWE
Villains
Villa Park

CONTACTS: *Note: Officers with more than one job title may be intentionally listed here more than once.*

John Greenfield, Head-Merch.
Sharon Barnhurst, Club Sec.
Brian Doogan, Head-Media
Mark Fairbrother, Head-Finance
Paul Lambert, Mgr.
Terry Gennoe, Coach-First Team Goalkeeping
Gordon Cowans, Coach-Development
Randy Lerner, Owner
Nassef Sawiris, Chmn.

GROWTH PLANS/SPECIAL FEATURES:

Aston Villa Football Club, nicknamed the Claret and Blue after its colors and also known as the Villains, is an English Premier League football (soccer) team based in Aston, Birmingham. Founded in 1874, the team plays at Villa Park, has won the First Division Championship seven times. Other domestic titles include seven FA Cups, five League Cups and one FA Charity Shield. Within Europe, Aston Villa FC won the European Cup in the 1981-82 season, as well as the European Super Cup in 1982 and the Intertoto Cup in 2001. Aston Villa currently holds its training sessions at its own grounds in Warwickshire. Villa Park's soccer-seating capacity is 42,785. The football club's community department runs soccer schools and clinics, educates children about the benefits of a healthy lifestyle and provides coaching to children with special needs. Aston Villa FC averaged approximately 41,680 in game attendance during the 2022-23 season. The club is currently owned by the NSWE group, a company owned by Egyptian Nassef Sawairis and American Wes Edens.

FINANCIAL DATA: *Note: Data for latest year may not have been available at press time.*

In U.S. $	2022	2021	2020	2019	2018	2017
Revenue	250,000,000	249,096,151	132,851,594	68,524,900	94,754,000	94,754,000
R&D Expense						
Operating Income						
Operating Margin %						
SGA Expense						
Net Income		-45,509,601	-112,127,623	-86,949,700	-18,617,000	-18,617,000
Operating Cash Flow						
Capital Expenditure						
EBITDA						
Return on Assets %						
Return on Equity %						
Debt to Equity						

CONTACT INFORMATION:

Phone: 44-121-327-2299   Fax: 44-121-322-2107
Toll-Free:
Address: Trinity Rd., Villa Park, Birmingham, B6 6HE United Kingdom

STOCK TICKER/OTHER:

Stock Ticker: Private
Employees: 663
Parent Company: NSWE

Exchange:
Fiscal Year Ends: 05/31

SALARIES/BONUSES:

Top Exec. Salary: $ Bonus: $
Second Exec. Salary: $ Bonus: $

OTHER THOUGHTS:

Estimated Female Officers or Directors: 5
Hot Spot for Advancement for Women/Minorities: Y

Sales, profits and employees may be estimates. Financial information, benefits and other data can change quickly and may vary from those stated here.

Athletic Club (Athletic Bilbao)

www.athletic-club.eus/en

NAIC Code: 711211D

TYPES OF BUSINESS:
Soccer Team
Team Management and Operations

BRANDS/DIVISIONS/AFFILIATES:
San Mames
Athletic Club Femenino

GROWTH PLANS/SPECIAL FEATURES:
Athletic Club, commonly known as Athletic Bilbao or just Athletic, is a professional football club in Spain, founded in 1898. Athletic Bilbao plays home games at the San Mames stadium, with a seating capacity of more than 53,000. The club is in the La Liga league, the men's top professional football division of the Spanish football league system, which includes the Copa del Rey and Supercopa de Espana domestic cups, and the UEFA Champions League, UEFA Europa League and UEFA Europa Conference League international cups. Athletic Bilbao has clinched eight La Liga titles, with the last being in the 1983-84 season. The club has won 23 Copa del Rey cups. Athletic Club ranked 8th out of 20 in the La Liga 2021-22 season. New Balance is Athletic Bilbao's kit manufacturer and Kutxabank is its shirt sponsor. Athletic Club Femenino is the women's football section of Athletic Bilbao, competing in the Spanish first division.

CONTACTS: Note: Officers with more than one job title may be intentionally listed here more than once.
Jon Uriarte, Pres.

FINANCIAL DATA: Note: Data for latest year may not have been available at press time.

In U.S. $	2022	2021	2020	2019	2018	2017
Revenue	200,000,000	114,938,090	108,638,205			
R&D Expense						
Operating Income						
Operating Margin %						
SGA Expense						
Net Income		-30,262,230	-23,446,630			
Operating Cash Flow						
Capital Expenditure						
EBITDA						
Return on Assets %						
Return on Equity %						
Debt to Equity						

CONTACT INFORMATION:
Phone: 34 944 240877   Fax:
Toll-Free:
Address: Ibaigane Palace, Alameda Mazarredo, 23, Bilbao, 48009 Spain

STOCK TICKER/OTHER:
Stock Ticker: Private   Exchange:
Employees: Fiscal Year Ends: 06/30
Parent Company:

SALARIES/BONUSES:
Top Exec. Salary: $ Bonus: $
Second Exec. Salary: $ Bonus: $

OTHER THOUGHTS:
Estimated Female Officers or Directors:
Hot Spot for Advancement for Women/Minorities:

Atlanta Braves

NAIC Code: 711211A

atlanta.braves.mlb.com

TYPES OF BUSINESS:

Professional Baseball Team
Team Management and Operations

BRANDS/DIVISIONS/AFFILIATES:

Liberty Media Corporation
Gwinnett Stripers
Mississippi Braves
Rome Braves
Augusta GreenJackets
FCL Braves
DSL Braves

CONTACTS: *Note: Officers with more than one job title may be intentionally listed here more than once.*

Derek Schiller, CEO
Jill Robinson, CFO
DeRetta Rhodes, Chief Culture Officer
Robert A. Hope, Dir.-Merch.
John Baxley, Sr. Eng.-Systems
Linda Miller, Mgr.-Admin. Svcs.
Greg Heller, General Counsel
Mike Plant, Exec. VP-Bus. Oper.
Bruce J. Manno, VP
Kimberly Childress, VP
Frank Wren, Exec. VP
Henry Aaron, Sr. VP
Bill Acree, Dir.-Team Travel
Larry Bowman, VP-Stadium Oper. & Security
Terry McGuirk, Chmn.
Johnny Almaraz, Dir.-Int'l Scouting & Oper.

GROWTH PLANS/SPECIAL FEATURES:

The Atlanta Braves is one of the oldest teams in professional baseball. The team began as the Boston Red Stockings in 1871, became the Braves in 1912, moved to Milwaukee during the 1950s and finally relocated to Atlanta in 1966. The team plays its home games at the 41,000-seat Truist Park. A storied franchise, the Braves have won four World Series Championships (2021 most recently), 18 pennants, 22 division titles and two wild card berths. Time Warner subsidiary Turner Broadcasting bought the team from its former owner, media mogul Ted Turner, who owned the team throughout the 1990s when it was the most successful franchise in Major League Baseball (MLB). The Braves' glory days in the 1990s were propelled by its all-star pitching aces Tom Glavine, John Smoltz and Greg Maddux as well as position players such as David Justice and Fred McGriff. The team won its division an unprecedented 14 consecutive times from 1991 to 2005. In 2007, Time Warner sold the team to Liberty Media Corporation. Minor league affiliates of the Braves include the Gwinnett Stripers, Mississippi Braves, Rome Braves, Augusta GreenJackets, FCL Braves and DSL Braves. The team has contributed several players to the National Baseball Hall of Fame, including Hank Aaron, Warren Spahn and Phil Niekro. The Braves averaged 38,641 in home game attendance during the 2022 season, and was averaging 37,726 during the 2023 season (as of May 2023). Forbes estimated the team's value at $2.6 billion in March 2023.

FINANCIAL DATA: *Note: Data for latest year may not have been available at press time.*

In U.S. $	2022	2021	2020	2019	2018	2017
Revenue	600,000,000					
R&D Expense						
Operating Income						
Operating Margin %						
SGA Expense						
Net Income						
Operating Cash Flow						
Capital Expenditure						
EBITDA						
Return on Assets %						
Return on Equity %						
Debt to Equity						

CONTACT INFORMATION:

Phone: 404-522-7630   Fax: 404-614-7391
Toll-Free:
Address: 755 Battery Ave., Atlanta, GA 30339 United States

STOCK TICKER/OTHER:

Stock Ticker: Subsidiary   Exchange:
Employees: 900   Fiscal Year Ends: 12/31
Parent Company: Liberty Media Corporation

SALARIES/BONUSES:

Top Exec. Salary: $ Bonus: $
Second Exec. Salary: $ Bonus: $

OTHER THOUGHTS:

Estimated Female Officers or Directors: 7
Hot Spot for Advancement for Women/Minorities: Y

Sales, profits and employees may be estimates. Financial information, benefits and other data can change quickly and may vary from those stated here.

Atlanta Dream

NAIC Code: 711211E

TYPES OF BUSINESS:

Professional Women's Basketball Team
Team Management and Operations

BRANDS/DIVISIONS/AFFILIATES:

GROWTH PLANS/SPECIAL FEATURES:

The Atlanta Dream is a women's basketball team and a member of the Women's National Basketball Association (WNBA). Established in late 2007, the Dream plays in the WNBA Eastern Conference, along with the Chicago Sky, Connecticut Sun, Indiana Fever, New York Liberty and Washington Mystics. The franchise chose Marynell Meadors as its first coach, whose WNBA experience includes work with the Charlotte Sting (during the WNBA's inaugural 1997 year), Miami Sol and Washington Mystics, in addition to more than 30 years spent coaching at the collegiate level. The Dream franchise has its home court in the Gateway Center Arena, a multi-purpose arena in College Park, Georgia. It holds approximately 3,500 fans for basketball and 5,000 for concerts. The Atlanta Dream have three conference titles, but have yet to win a championship. The team is owned by real estate investors Larry Gottesdiener, Suzanne Abair and former Dream player Renee Montgomery.

CONTACTS:
Note: Officers with more than one job title may be intentionally listed here more than once.

Suzanne Abair, CEO
Morgan Shaw Parker, Pres.
Renee Montgomery, VP
Danielle Browne, Mgr.-Bus. Oper. & Special Projects
Alex Kotz, Mgr.-Mktg. & Social Media
Brad Gust, Mgr.-Media Relations.
Alton Byrd, Chief Revenue Officer
Angela Taylor, Gen. Mgr.
Michael Cooper, Head Coach
Mary Brock, Owner
Kelly Loeffler, Owner

FINANCIAL DATA:
Note: Data for latest year may not have been available at press time.

In U.S. $	2022	2021	2020	2019	2018	2017
Revenue						
R&D Expense						
Operating Income						
Operating Margin %						
SGA Expense						
Net Income						
Operating Cash Flow						
Capital Expenditure						
EBITDA						
Return on Assets %						
Return on Equity %						
Debt to Equity						

CONTACT INFORMATION:

Phone: 877-977-7729   Fax: 404-954-6666
Toll-Free: 877-977-7729
Address: 101 Marietta Street NW, Ste 3550, Atlanta, GA 30303 United States

STOCK TICKER/OTHER:

Stock Ticker: Private
Employees:
Parent Company:

Exchange:
Fiscal Year Ends: 06/30

SALARIES/BONUSES:

Top Exec. Salary: $ Bonus: $
Second Exec. Salary: $ Bonus: $

OTHER THOUGHTS:

Estimated Female Officers or Directors: 15
Hot Spot for Advancement for Women/Minorities: Y

Atlanta Falcons

www.atlantafalcons.com

NAIC Code: 711211C

TYPES OF BUSINESS:

Professional Football Team
Team Management and Operations

BRANDS/DIVISIONS/AFFILIATES:

Atlanta Falcons Youth Foundation

GROWTH PLANS/SPECIAL FEATURES:

The Atlanta Falcons is a professional football team based in Atlanta, Georgia, playing in the National Football Conference (southern) of the National Football League (NFL). The franchise began in 1965, and made its first playoff appearance in 1978. The Falcons team has clenched six division championships (western and southern), and played in the conference championships twice. In total, The Falcons have made 14 playoff appearances. The team's home stadium is the roughly 71,000-seat Mercedes-Benz Stadium, a multi-purpose stadium home also to the Atlanta United Football Club of Major League Soccer. The Falcons' average home game attendance was 69,583 for the 2022 season. The Atlanta Falcons franchise is currently owned by Arthur M. Blank, a co-founder of Home Depot. The organization conducts philanthropy through the Atlanta Falcons Youth Foundation, first established in 1985. Forbes valued the team at $4 billion in 2022.

CONTACTS: Note: Officers with more than one job title may be intentionally listed here more than once.

Rich McKay, CEO
Greg Beadles, Pres.
Terry Fontenot, Gen. Mngr.
Mike Smith, Head Coach
Thomas Dimitroff, Gen. Mgr.
Arthur Blank, Owner
Arthur Blank, Chmn.

FINANCIAL DATA: Note: Data for latest year may not have been available at press time.

In U.S. $	2022	2021	2020	2019	2018	2017
Revenue	533,000,000					
R&D Expense						
Operating Income						
Operating Margin %						
SGA Expense						
Net Income						
Operating Cash Flow						
Capital Expenditure						
EBITDA						
Return on Assets %						
Return on Equity %						
Debt to Equity						

CONTACT INFORMATION:

Phone: 404-223-8444   Fax:
Toll-Free:
Address: 441 Martin Luther King Junior Dr. NW, Atlanta, GA 30313
United States

STOCK TICKER/OTHER:

Stock Ticker: Private
Employees: 490
Parent Company:

Exchange:
Fiscal Year Ends: 02/28

SALARIES/BONUSES:

Top Exec. Salary: $ Bonus: $
Second Exec. Salary: $ Bonus: $

OTHER THOUGHTS:

Estimated Female Officers or Directors:
Hot Spot for Advancement for Women/Minorities: Y

Sales, profits and employees may be estimates. Financial information, benefits and other data can change quickly and may vary from those stated here.

Atlanta Hawks

NAIC Code: 711211B

TYPES OF BUSINESS:

Professional Basketball Team
Team Management and Operations

BRANDS/DIVISIONS/AFFILIATES:

CONTACTS: *Note: Officers with more than one job title may be intentionally listed here more than once.*

Steve Koonin, CEO
Bob Williams, Pres.
Joel Browning, CFO
Melissa Proctor, CMO
Kathy Hakiki, Dir.-Retail Merch.
Caren Cook, Sr. Counsel
Garin Narain, VP-Public Relations.
Michelle Pratt, Sr. Dir.-Acct.
Michael Gearon, Managing Partner
Ed Peskowitz, Partner
Todd Foreman, Partner
Rutherfor Seydel, Partner
Tony Ressler, Chmn.

GROWTH PLANS/SPECIAL FEATURES:

The Atlanta Hawks is a National Basketball Association (NBA) franchise that plays in the Eastern Conference, southeast division. The team was originally formed in 1946 as the Buffalo Bisons, but was relocated the same year to Moline, Illinois and renamed the Tri-Cities Blackhawks. After subsequent moves to Milwaukee (in 1951, when the name was shortened to Hawks) and St. Louis (1955), the team settled in Atlanta in 1968. The Hawks clenched its only championship to date in 1958, but has 12 division titles (2021 most recently). The Hawks' home stadium, State Farm Arena, is a multi-purpose indoor arena in Atlanta, with a seating capacity up to approximately 21,000. Several former Hawks players have been named to the NBA Hall of Fame, including Dominique Wilkins, Bob Pettit and Pistol Pete Maravich. The team averaged 16,408 in home game attendance during the 2022 season, and was averaging 17,555 during the 2023 season as of May 2023. Forbes estimated the Hawks worth approximately $1.975 billion in October 2022. Tony Ressler, co-founder of Ares Management LP, owns the team.

FINANCIAL DATA: *Note: Data for latest year may not have been available at press time.*

In U.S. $	2022	2021	2020	2019	2018	2017
Revenue	273,650,000					
R&D Expense						
Operating Income						
Operating Margin %						
SGA Expense						
Net Income						
Operating Cash Flow						
Capital Expenditure						
EBITDA						
Return on Assets %						
Return on Equity %						
Debt to Equity						

CONTACT INFORMATION:

Phone: 404-878-3800   Fax:
Toll-Free:
Address: 101 Marietta St. NW, Centennial Tower, Ste. 1900, Atlanta, GA 30303 United States

STOCK TICKER/OTHER:

Stock Ticker: Private   Exchange:
Employees: 585   Fiscal Year Ends: 06/30
Parent Company:

SALARIES/BONUSES:

Top Exec. Salary: $ Bonus: $
Second Exec. Salary: $ Bonus: $

OTHER THOUGHTS:

Estimated Female Officers or Directors: 28
Hot Spot for Advancement for Women/Minorities: Y

Atlanta United FC

www.atlutd.com

NAIC Code: 711211D

TYPES OF BUSINESS:

Major League Soccer Team
Team Management and Operations

BRANDS/DIVISIONS/AFFILIATES:

CONTACTS:
Note: Officers with more than one job title may be intentionally listed here more than once.

Garth Lagerwey, CEO
Georgia O'Donoghue, VP-Bus. Oper.
Andy Skorupski, CFO
Carlos Bocanegra, Dir.-IT
Arthur M. Blank, Owner

GROWTH PLANS/SPECIAL FEATURES:

Atlanta United FC is a Major League Soccer (MLS) club based in Atlanta, Georgia. The team is owned by Arthur Blank, co-founder of Home Depot. Atlanta United FC was founded in 2014, and plays as a member of the Eastern Conference. The team placed second overall in the Eastern Conference in 2018, as well as the Supporters Shield. This placement qualified the team for the playoffs for the second year in a row, and they clinched the 2018 MLS Cup championship after beating the Portland Timbers. The win qualified Atlanta United for the 2019 CONCACAF Champions League. The Eastern Conference is also composed of the Chicago Fire FC, Columbus Crew, FC Cincinnati, D.C. United, Inter Miami CF, Charlotte FC, CF Montreal, Nashville SC, New England Revolution, New York City FC, New York Red Bulls, Orlando City SC, Philadelphia Union and Toronto FC. The team plays its home games at Mercedes-Benz Stadium, a multi-purpose stadium comprising approximately 71,000 seats for soccer fans and 73,019 with standing room. Atlanta United has the MLS' highest average home game attendance, averaging 46,552 in the 2022 season.

FINANCIAL DATA: *Note: Data for latest year may not have been available at press time.*

In U.S. $	2022	2021	2020	2019	2018	2017
Revenue	107,932,500					
R&D Expense						
Operating Income						
Operating Margin %						
SGA Expense						
Net Income						
Operating Cash Flow						
Capital Expenditure						
EBITDA						
Return on Assets %						
Return on Equity %						
Debt to Equity						

CONTACT INFORMATION:

Phone: 678-420-7200   Fax:
Toll-Free:
Address: 1 AMB Dr., NW, Atlanta, GA 30313 United States

SALARIES/BONUSES:

Top Exec. Salary: $ Bonus: $
Second Exec. Salary: $ Bonus: $

STOCK TICKER/OTHER:

Stock Ticker: Private   Exchange:
Employees: 165   Fiscal Year Ends:
Parent Company:

OTHER THOUGHTS:

Estimated Female Officers or Directors:
Hot Spot for Advancement for Women/Minorities:

Baltimore Orioles

www.mlb.com/orioles

NAIC Code: 711211A

TYPES OF BUSINESS:

Professional Baseball Team
Team Management and Operations

BRANDS/DIVISIONS/AFFILIATES:

Oriole Park at Camden Yards
Norfolk Tides
Bowie Baysox
Delmarva Shorebirds
Aberdeen IronBirds

CONTACTS: *Note: Officers with more than one job title may be intentionally listed here more than once.*

John Angelos, CEO
Mike Elias, Gen. Mngr.- Exec. VP
Michael D. Hoppes, CFO
Lisa Tolson, Sr. VP-Human Resources
H. Russell Smouse, General Counsel
Janet Marie Smith, VP-Planning & Dev.
Michael D. Hoppes, VP-Finance
Peter C. Angelos, Exec. VP
Buck Showalter, Mgr.
Dan Duquette, Exec. Mgr.
Lou Kousouris, VP
John Angelos, Chmn.
Fred Ferreira, Exec. Dir.-Int'l Recruiting

GROWTH PLANS/SPECIAL FEATURES:

Baltimore Orioles are a Major League Baseball (MLB) franchise based in Baltimore, Maryland. The team was originally founded as the Milwaukee Brewers in 1901, and after a year of play moved to St. Louis and became known as the Browns. Following a string of poor seasons, the club moved to Baltimore and took the name Orioles in 1954, which had been used by other teams in the area since the 19th century. The Orioles held a spot at the top of the MLB rankings from the mid-1960s to the mid-1980s. In its history, the franchise has won three World Series, seven pennants and nine division titles. Cal Ripken, Jr., perhaps the team's most recognized player, broke Lou Gehrig's record for consecutive games played, finishing his streak at 2,632 games, and spent his entire career with the Orioles. Since 1993, the team has been owned by local lawyer Peter Angelos. The Orioles play home games in Oriole Park at Camden Yards, which was constructed in 1992, seats 48,876 and has features inspired by turn-of-the-century ballparks such as Boston's Fenway Park and Chicago's Wrigley Field. During the 2012 season, the club posted its first winning record in 15 years, making the playoffs for the first time since 1997. The Orioles have clenched three wild card berths. Home attendance for the Orioles was 17,543 during the 2022 season. Minor league affiliates of the Orioles include the Norfolk Tides, Bowie Baysox, Aberdeen Ironbirds and Delmarva Shorebirds. Forbes estimated the team's worth at $1.713 billion in March 2023.

FINANCIAL DATA: *Note: Data for latest year may not have been available at press time.*

In U.S. $	2022	2021	2020	2019	2018	2017
Revenue	329,550,000					
R&D Expense						
Operating Income						
Operating Margin %						
SGA Expense						
Net Income						
Operating Cash Flow						
Capital Expenditure						
EBITDA						
Return on Assets %						
Return on Equity %						
Debt to Equity						

CONTACT INFORMATION:

Phone: 410-685-9800   Fax: 410-547-6277
Toll-Free: 888-848-2473
Address: 333 W. Camden St., Baltimore, MD 21201 United States

STOCK TICKER/OTHER:

Stock Ticker: Private   Exchange:
Employees: 615   Fiscal Year Ends: 06/30
Parent Company:

SALARIES/BONUSES:

Top Exec. Salary: $ Bonus: $
Second Exec. Salary: $ Bonus: $

OTHER THOUGHTS:

Estimated Female Officers or Directors: 3
Hot Spot for Advancement for Women/Minorities: Y

Baltimore Ravens

www.baltimoreravens.com

NAIC Code: 711211C

TYPES OF BUSINESS:

Professional Football Team
Team Management and Operations

BRANDS/DIVISIONS/AFFILIATES:

CONTACTS: *Note: Officers with more than one job title may be intentionally listed here more than once.*

Eric DeCosta, Exec. VP
Sashi Brown, Pres.
Jeff Goering, CFO
Brad Downs, VP-Mktg.
Elizabeth Mearman, Sr. VP-People
Asheesh Kinra, VP-IT
Kevin Rochlitz, VP-Corp. Sales & Bus. Dev.
Jim Coller, Controller
John Harbaugh, Head Coach
Ozzie Newsome, Exec. VP
Steve Bisciotti, Owner
Ed Burchell, VP-Regional Partnerships & Sales
Stephen J. Bisciotti, Owner

GROWTH PLANS/SPECIAL FEATURES:

The Baltimore Ravens is a professional football team in the National Football League (NFL) based in Maryland. The team was formed when the Cleveland Browns moved to Baltimore for the 1996 season. Preceded by the Baltimore Colts, who left the city for Indianapolis in the mid-1980s, Baltimore's new NFL franchise was named the Ravens as a tribute to the best-known poem of one of Baltimore's literary figures, Edgar Allan Poe. Although in practice the team has incorporated elements from both its previous life as the Browns and from its Baltimore predecessors, it was technically considered a new expansion franchise when it began play in 1996. The team plays its home games in downtown Baltimore in the M&T Bank Stadium, a 71,008-seat capacity stadium owned by the Maryland Stadium Authority. Average home game attendance was 70,589 for the 2022 season. The Ravens franchise is owned by local businessman Stephen Bisciotti. The team currently plays in the American Football Conference North, and since 1996 has made 14 playoff appearances and has won two Super Bowl championships (2000 and 2012). The Ravens have been the North division champs six times, with the most recent being in 2018 and 2019. Forbes valued the Baltimore Ravens at $3.9 billion in 2022.

FINANCIAL DATA: *Note: Data for latest year may not have been available at press time.*

In U.S. $	2022	2021	2020	2019	2018	2017
Revenue	527,800,000					
R&D Expense						
Operating Income						
Operating Margin %						
SGA Expense						
Net Income						
Operating Cash Flow						
Capital Expenditure						
EBITDA						
Return on Assets %						
Return on Equity %						
Debt to Equity						

CONTACT INFORMATION:

Phone: 410-701-4000   Fax: 410-654-6239
Toll-Free:
Address: 1 Winning Dr., Owings Mills, MD 21117 United States

STOCK TICKER/OTHER:

Stock Ticker: Private
Employees: 490
Parent Company:

Exchange:
Fiscal Year Ends: 01/31

SALARIES/BONUSES:

Top Exec. Salary: $ Bonus: $
Second Exec. Salary: $ Bonus: $

OTHER THOUGHTS:

Estimated Female Officers or Directors: 4
Hot Spot for Advancement for Women/Minorities: Y

Sales, profits and employees may be estimates. Financial information, benefits and other data can change quickly and may vary from those stated here.

BDA Sports Management

www.bdasports.com

NAIC Code: 711410

TYPES OF BUSINESS:

Sports Management
Professional Sport Agency Services
Contract Negotiation
Public Relation Services
Community Relation Services
Social Engagement Services
Brand Building Services

BRANDS/DIVISIONS/AFFILIATES:

Endeavor Group Holdings Inc
WME

GROWTH PLANS/SPECIAL FEATURES:

BDA Sports Management is a global, full-service agency offering services to professional basketball players. The company has represented professional players in the NBA and overseas. BDA specializes in contract negotiations, public relations, community relations, social engagement and brand building. The firm's goal is to support each client for the entirety of their career in all philanthropic efforts and individual brand development. BDA pairs innovative content with its talent to explore projects and expose clients to unique opportunities within the industry. BDA Sports is owned by WME, itself a subsidiary of Endeavor Group Holdings, Inc.

CONTACTS: Note: Officers with more than one job title may be intentionally listed here more than once.

Billy Kuenzinger, Pres.
Billy Kuenzinger, General Counsel
Marlon Harrison, Dir.-Basketball Oper.
Mario Lamont Andrews, Coordinator-Bus. Dev.
Alyson K.F, Dir-Corporate and Client Comm.
Quique Villalobos, Sr. Dir.-Western European Basketball
Olivier Mazet, Sr. Dir.-French Basketball
Ranko Mladjenovic, Sr. Dir.-Eastern European Basketball
Patrick Whitesell, Chmn.-Endeavor

FINANCIAL DATA: Note: Data for latest year may not have been available at press time.

In U.S. $	2022	2021	2020	2019	2018	2017
Revenue						
R&D Expense						
Operating Income						
Operating Margin %						
SGA Expense						
Net Income						
Operating Cash Flow						
Capital Expenditure						
EBITDA						
Return on Assets %						
Return on Equity %						
Debt to Equity						

CONTACT INFORMATION:

Phone: 925-279-1040   Fax: 925-279-1060
Toll-Free:
Address: 700 Ygnacio Valley Rd., Ste. 330, Walnut Creek, CA 94596
United States

STOCK TICKER/OTHER:

Stock Ticker: Subsidiary   Exchange:
Employees: 32   Fiscal Year Ends:
Parent Company: Endeavor Group Holdings Inc

SALARIES/BONUSES:

Top Exec. Salary: $ Bonus: $
Second Exec. Salary: $ Bonus: $

OTHER THOUGHTS:

Estimated Female Officers or Directors: 1
Hot Spot for Advancement for Women/Minorities: Y

Big 5 Sporting Goods Corporation   www.big5sportinggoods.com

NAIC Code: 451110

TYPES OF BUSINESS:

Sporting Goods Stores

BRANDS/DIVISIONS/AFFILIATES:

Golden Bear
Harsh
Pacifica
Rugged Exposure
Big 5 Services Corporation

GROWTH PLANS/SPECIAL FEATURES:

Big 5 Sporting Goods Corp is a specialty retailer company that is principally engaged in the sale of sporting goods in the western United States. Its product mix includes athletic shoes, apparel, and accessories, as well as a broad selection of outdoor and athletic equipment for team sports, fitness, camping, hunting, fishing, tennis, golf, winter and summer recreation and roller sports. The company operates solely as a sporting goods retailer, which includes both retail stores and an e-commerce platform. The company operates a distribution center located in Riverside, California, that services all of its stores and e-commerce platform.

CONTACTS: Note: Officers with more than one job title may be intentionally listed here more than once.

Steven Miller, CEO
Barry Emerson, CFO
Boyd Clark, Executive VP
Jeffrey Fraley, Senior VP, Divisional
Shane Starr, Senior VP, Divisional

FINANCIAL DATA: Note: Data for latest year may not have been available at press time.

In U.S. $	2022	2021	2020	2019	2018	2017
Revenue	995,538,000	1,161,820,000	1,041,212,000	996,495,000	1,009,635,000	1,009,635,000
R&D Expense						
Operating Income	33,515,000	136,017,000	76,265,000	14,829,000	16,342,000	16,342,000
Operating Margin %	.03%	.12%	.07%	.01%	.02%	.02%
SGA Expense	307,700,000	299,812,000	275,406,000	297,193,000	306,990,000	306,990,000
Net Income	26,134,000	102,386,000	55,940,000	8,445,000	1,104,000	1,104,000
Operating Cash Flow	-28,440,000	115,528,000	148,743,000	14,280,000	-4,384,000	-4,384,000
Capital Expenditure	13,193,000	10,864,000	7,347,000	9,363,000	16,462,000	16,462,000
EBITDA	51,988,000	154,292,000	95,079,000	34,637,000	35,718,000	35,718,000
Return on Assets %	.04%	.14%	.08%	.02%	.00%	.00%
Return on Equity %	.10%	.41%	.27%	.05%	.01%	.01%
Debt to Equity	.82%	.79%	0.947	1.542	0.256	0.256

CONTACT INFORMATION:

Phone: 310 536-0611   Fax:
Toll-Free: 800-898-2994
Address: 2525 E. El Segundo Blvd., El Segundo, CA 90245 United States

STOCK TICKER/OTHER:

Stock Ticker: BGFV   Exchange: NAS
Employees: 8,700   Fiscal Year Ends: 12/30
Parent Company:

SALARIES/BONUSES:

Top Exec. Salary: $612,789   Bonus: $750,000
Second Exec. Salary: $357,673   Bonus: $615,000

OTHER THOUGHTS:

Estimated Female Officers or Directors: 2
Hot Spot for Advancement for Women/Minorities:

Blackburn Rovers Football Club

NAIC Code: 711211D

www.rovers.co.uk

TYPES OF BUSINESS:

Professional Soccer Team
Team Management and Operations

BRANDS/DIVISIONS/AFFILIATES:

Venkateshwara Hatcheries Pvt Ltd
Venkys London Limited
Riversiders

CONTACTS: *Note: Officers with more than one job title may be intentionally listed here more than once.*

Steve Waggott, CEO
Karen Silk, Dir.-Finance
Gary Bowyer, Team Mgr.
Craig Short, First Team Coach
John Keeley, Goalkeeping Coach
Tony Grant, First Team Coach

GROWTH PLANS/SPECIAL FEATURES:

Blackburn Rovers Football Club is an English professional football (soccer) club that competes in the EFL Championship, the highest division of the English Football League (EFL). The Rovers have played their home matches at Ewood Park since 1890, though the club was established in 1875 and became a founding member of The Football League in 1888. Ewood Park has a seating capacity of 31,367. The Rovers won five FA Cup finales in the 19th century, and was crowned the English League champions in 1911-12 and 1913-14, then won a sixth FA Cup in 1928. The team was relegated for the first time in 1936. Overall, the Blackburn Rovers (also nicknamed the Riversiders) have won three first division titles in the Premier League, one championship in the Football League's Second Division and one championship in the League's Third Division. As for Cups, the Rovers have clenched six FA Cups, one Football league Cup, a FA Community Shield, a Full Members Cup, and others. The team's kit manufacturer is Macron and its shirt sponsor is Totally Wicked. The Blackburn Rovers are owned by Venkys London Ltd., itself a subsidiary of VH Group.

FINANCIAL DATA: *Note: Data for latest year may not have been available at press time.*

In U.S. $	2022	2021	2020	2019	2018	2017
Revenue	20,000,000	20,081,195	16,635,105	19,542,900	19,319,500	19,319,500
R&D Expense						
Operating Income						
Operating Margin %						
SGA Expense						
Net Income		-9,140,406	-26,985,837	-26,232,100	-6,743,720	-6,743,720
Operating Cash Flow						
Capital Expenditure						
EBITDA						
Return on Assets %						
Return on Equity %						
Debt to Equity						

CONTACT INFORMATION:

Phone: 44 1254 372001   Fax:
Toll-Free:
Address: Ewood Park, Blackburn, Lancashire BB2 4JF United Kingdom

STOCK TICKER/OTHER:

Stock Ticker: Private
Employees: 217
Parent Company: VH Group

Exchange:
Fiscal Year Ends: 06/30

SALARIES/BONUSES:

Top Exec. Salary: $ Bonus: $
Second Exec. Salary: $ Bonus: $

OTHER THOUGHTS:

Estimated Female Officers or Directors:
Hot Spot for Advancement for Women/Minorities:

Bleacher Report Inc (B/R)

bleacherreport.com

NAIC Code: 519130

TYPES OF BUSINESS:

Internet Sports News Sites
Sports Website
Sports News
Sports Analysis Information
Live Scores
Sport Video and Podcast Features
Sport Gaming and eSports

BRANDS/DIVISIONS/AFFILIATES:

Warner Bros Discovery Inc
Shows
B/R Kicks
B/R Gaming
B/R Gridiron

GROWTH PLANS/SPECIAL FEATURES:

Bleacher Report, Inc. (B/R) is a subsidiary of Warner Bros. Discovery, Inc., and operates a website focused on sports and sport culture. The B/R website provides news, analysis, real-time video and live scores of a variety of worldwide sports. B/R website pages click to NBA, NFL, MLB, NHL, WWE, MMA, WNBA, F1, Golf, Tennis, Boxing, among others, which feature information on fantasy games, drafts and archives. The Shows link offers articles, videos and podcasts from around the web, as well as a newsletter related to the user's chosen sport. B/R's videos feature interviews, sport highlights, trending videos, sport episodes, among other video content. B/R Kicks features information, highlights, advertising and interviews related to sport footwear. B/R Gaming features sport gaming for consoles as well as eSports. B/R Gridiron offers football content.

Bleacher Report offers its employees health benefits, a 401(k) and company perks.

CONTACTS: Note: Officers with more than one job title may be intentionally listed here more than once.

Howard Mittman, CEO

FINANCIAL DATA: Note: Data for latest year may not have been available at press time.

In U.S. $	2022	2021	2020	2019	2018	2017
Revenue	235,000,000	220,500,000	210,000,000	175,000,000		
R&D Expense						
Operating Income						
Operating Margin %						
SGA Expense						
Net Income						
Operating Cash Flow						
Capital Expenditure						
EBITDA						
Return on Assets %						
Return on Equity %						
Debt to Equity						

CONTACT INFORMATION:

Phone: 415-777-5505   Fax:
Toll-Free:
Address: 153 Kearny St., Fl. 2, San Francisco, CA 94108 United States

STOCK TICKER/OTHER:

Stock Ticker: Subsidiary   Exchange:
Employees: Fiscal Year Ends:
Parent Company: Warner Bros Discovery Inc

SALARIES/BONUSES:

Top Exec. Salary: $ Bonus: $
Second Exec. Salary: $ Bonus: $

OTHER THOUGHTS:

Estimated Female Officers or Directors:
Hot Spot for Advancement for Women/Minorities:

Sales, profits and employees may be estimates. Financial information, benefits and other data can change quickly and may vary from those stated here.

Boardriders Inc

NAIC Code: 424300

www.boardriders.com

TYPES OF BUSINESS:

Apparel and Clothing Brands, Designers, Importers and Distributors
Snow & Surf Apparel & Equipment
Accessories
Swimwear
Retail Stores
Ecommerce
Sport Apparel Manufacturing
Sport Apparel Design

BRANDS/DIVISIONS/AFFILIATES:

Quicksilver
Baillabong
RCVA
Roxy
Roxy Girl
DC
element
VonZipper

CONTACTS:
Note: Officers with more than one job title may be intentionally listed here more than once.

Arne Arens, CEO
Greg Healy, Global Pres.
John Little, Other Corporate Officer
Francis Roy, Global CFO
Stacy Reece, Chief Digital Officer
Jennifer Marques, Chief Human Resources Officer
David Berry, CIO

GROWTH PLANS/SPECIAL FEATURES:

Boardriders, Inc. is an internationally diversified firm that designs, produces, retails and distributes branded apparel, footwear, accessories and related products. The company's brands are focused on different sports within the outdoor market. The Quicksilver, Billabong, RCVA and Roxy brands are rooted in the sport of surfing and are leading brands representing the board riding lifestyle, which includes surfing, skateboarding and snowboarding. Quicksilver has grown to include shirts, shorts, t-shirts, pants, jackets, fleece, snowboard wear, footwear, hats, backpacks, wetsuits, watches, eyewear and other accessories. In addition, the brand has expanded its target market to include boys, toddlers and infants. The Roxy brand includes sportswear, footwear, backpacks, snowboard wear, swimwear, backpacks, snowboard boots, skis, fragrance, beauty care, bedroom furnishings and other accessories for young women. The brand also includes Roxy Girl for girls and infants. The firm's DC and element brands specialize in technical shoes made for skateboarding and snowboarding as well as sandals and general branded apparel. The company's products are sold in its owned or licensed stores as well as a wide range of other distribution channels, including ecommerce, surf shops, snowboard shops, skate shops and other specialty stores and select department stores. VonZipper is a sunglasses brand. Boardriders is headquartered in California, USA, with international offices in France, Japan, China and Australia.

FINANCIAL DATA:
Note: Data for latest year may not have been available at press time.

In U.S. $	2022	2021	2020	2019	2018	2017
Revenue	290,000,000	392,454,720	381,024,000	396,900,000	360,000,000	360,000,000
R&D Expense						
Operating Income						
Operating Margin %						
SGA Expense						
Net Income						
Operating Cash Flow						
Capital Expenditure						
EBITDA						
Return on Assets %						
Return on Equity %						
Debt to Equity						

CONTACT INFORMATION:

Phone: 714 889-2200   Fax: 714 645-0313
Toll-Free:
Address: 5600 Argasy Cir., Bldg. 100, Huntington Beach, CA 92649 United States

STOCK TICKER/OTHER:

Stock Ticker: Private
Employees: 293
Parent Company:

Exchange:
Fiscal Year Ends: 10/31

SALARIES/BONUSES:

Top Exec. Salary: $ Bonus: $
Second Exec. Salary: $ Bonus: $

OTHER THOUGHTS:

Estimated Female Officers or Directors: 1
Hot Spot for Advancement for Women/Minorities:

Booth Creek Ski Holdings Inc

www.boothcreek.com

NAIC Code: 713920

TYPES OF BUSINESS:

Ski Resorts
Ski Resort Operation
Equipment Rental
Ski Lessons
Weddings and Events
Mountain Tours

BRANDS/DIVISIONS/AFFILIATES:

Booth Creek Ski Group Inc
Sierra-at-Tahoe Resort

GROWTH PLANS/SPECIAL FEATURES:

Booth Creek Ski Holdings, Inc. is a business management company. The firm specializes in ski resort operations and administration as well as the advertising and marketing of those resorts. Booth Creek currently owns Sierra-at-Tahoe Resort in Lake Tahoe, California, which operates under a long-term lease agreement with real estate investment trust (REIT), CNL Lifestyle Properties. Sierra-at-Tahoe is comprised of 2,000 acres and 2,212 vertical feet of skiable terrain, with options for all ski levels. West Bowl, Grandview and Huckleberry Canyon are popular ski runs. The resort offers rentals, lessons, team skiing grouped per age and/or ability level. Other activities include tubing, snow play, mountain tours and snowshoeing. Events also occur at the resort, with a calendar schedule obtainable on its www.sierraattahoe.com website. Weddings can be booked at Sierra-at-Tahoe. Booth Creek is a wholly-owned subsidiary of Booth Creek Ski Group, Inc.

CONTACTS: Note: Officers with more than one job title may be intentionally listed here more than once.

George N. Gillett, Jr., CEO
Jeffrey J. Joyce, Asst. VP-Finance
Christopher P. Ryman, Pres.
Brian Pope, VP-Accounting & Finance
Timothy H. Beck, Exec. VP-Planning
Brian Pope, Principal Acct. Officer

FINANCIAL DATA: Note: Data for latest year may not have been available at press time.

In U.S. $	2022	2021	2020	2019	2018	2017
Revenue	96,500,000	93,809,100	85,281,000	137,550,000	130,000,000	130,000,000
R&D Expense						
Operating Income						
Operating Margin %						
SGA Expense						
Net Income						
Operating Cash Flow						
Capital Expenditure						
EBITDA						
Return on Assets %						
Return on Equity %						
Debt to Equity						

CONTACT INFORMATION:

Phone: 530-550-5100   Fax: 530-550-5116
Toll-Free:
Address: 950 Red Sand Stone Rd., #43, Vail, CO 81657 United States

STOCK TICKER/OTHER:

Stock Ticker: Subsidiary
Employees: 530
Parent Company: Booth Creek Ski Group Inc

Exchange:
Fiscal Year Ends: 10/31

SALARIES/BONUSES:

Top Exec. Salary: $ Bonus: $
Second Exec. Salary: $ Bonus: $

OTHER THOUGHTS:

Estimated Female Officers or Directors: 1
Hot Spot for Advancement for Women/Minorities:

Borussia Dortmund GmbH & Co KGaA

aktie.bvb.de/eng

NAIC Code: 711211D

TYPES OF BUSINESS:

Professional Soccer Team
Team Management and Operations

GROWTH PLANS/SPECIAL FEATURES:

Borussia Dortmund GmbH & Co KGaA operates football club. The company operates its business through the following segments; Borussia Dortmund GmbH & Co KGaA operates a football club including a professional football squad and leverages the associated revenue potential arising from the transfer of players, catering, TV marketing, sponsorship, and ticketing. BVB Merchandising segment consists of the separate merchandising business. BVB Event and Catering Gmbh segment conducts tours, provides and arranges for event staffing services and planning and organizing, catering and steering and conducting events of all types. Besttravel dortmund Gmbh segment comprises arranging travel by air, rail and ship as well. The firm earns the majority of its revenues from Borussia Dortmund GmbH & Co KGaA.

BRANDS/DIVISIONS/AFFILIATES:

BVB
Signal Iduna Park (Westfalenstadion)

CONTACTS: Note: Officers with more than one job title may be intentionally listed here more than once.

Hans-Joachim Watzke, Managing Dir.
Thomas Tress, Dir.-Finance
Josef Schneck, Dir.-Comm.
Christian Hockenjos, Dir.-Organization
Michael Zorc, Dir.-Sports

FINANCIAL DATA: Note: Data for latest year may not have been available at press time.

In U.S. $	2022	2021	2020	2019	2018	2017
Revenue	375,516,600	356,856,400	395,326,900	395,391,000	433,232,600	433,232,600
R&D Expense						
Operating Income	-31,161,970	-76,987,070	-46,066,440	21,198,600	11,381,520	11,381,520
Operating Margin %	-.08%	-.22%	-.12%	.05%	.03%	.03%
SGA Expense	42,401,460	35,790,180	55,894,200	55,395,490	49,606,480	49,606,480
Net Income	-37,439,000	-77,752,740	-46,936,770	18,571,600	8,766,272	8,766,272
Operating Cash Flow	37,451,810	17,029,570	-386,575	30,658,990	117,907,400	117,907,400
Capital Expenditure	86,615,130	97,955,000	169,730,800	148,853,600	111,826,800	111,826,800
EBITDA	87,521,760	41,987,120	67,573,660	124,326,400	78,565,410	78,565,410
Return on Assets %	-.08%	-.15%	-.09%	.04%	.02%	.02%
Return on Equity %	-.14%	-.27%	-.13%	.05%	.03%	.03%
Debt to Equity	.04%	.07%	0.066	0.024	0.027	0.027

CONTACT INFORMATION:

Phone: 49-231-90-202745   Fax: 49-231-902085746
Toll-Free:
Address: Rheinlanddamm 207-209, Dortmund, 44137 Germany

STOCK TICKER/OTHER:

Stock Ticker: BORUF
Employees: 517
Parent Company:

Exchange: PINX
Fiscal Year Ends:

SALARIES/BONUSES:

Top Exec. Salary: $ Bonus: $
Second Exec. Salary: $ Bonus: $

OTHER THOUGHTS:

Estimated Female Officers or Directors:
Hot Spot for Advancement for Women/Minorities:

Boston Bruins

NAIC Code: 711211F

TYPES OF BUSINESS:

Professional Hockey Team (NHL)
Team Management and Operations

BRANDS/DIVISIONS/AFFILIATES:

Delaware North Companies
Providence Bruins
Maine Mariners
Boston Bruins Foundation

CONTACTS: Note: Officers with more than one job title may be intentionally listed here more than once.

Charlie Jacobs, CEO
Cam Neely, Pres.
Glen Thornborough, Chief Revenue Officer
Ryan Nadeau, Dir.-Hockey Admin.
Jen Compton, VP-Mktg
Matthew Chmura, VP-Comm. & Content
Jim Bednarek, VP-Finance
Peter Chiarelli, Gen. Mgr.
Don Sweeney, Assistant Gen. Mgr.
Claude Julien, Head Coach
Chris Johnson, VP- Corporate Partnerships
Jeremy M. Jacobs, Chmn.

GROWTH PLANS/SPECIAL FEATURES:

The Boston Bruins, formed in 1924, is the third-oldest surviving franchise within the National Hockey League (NHL). The Bruins is based in Massachusetts and administered by the Boston Professional Hockey Association, Inc. The franchise is owned by Jeremy Jacobs and his company, Delaware North Companies. The Bruins plays at the TD Garden arena, featuring 19,600-seats, 90 executive suites, 1,100 club seats and complete 360-degree LED technology. The stadium is also home to the NBA's Boston Celtics. The Bruins' 2022-23 home game attendance averaged 18,372. The Boston Bruins reached the Stanley Cup playoffs every year from 1968 to 1996, a record setting 28 years, and has made approximately 20 trips to the Stanley Cup finals, winning six championship titles, the last one in 2011. In total, the franchise has clinched 27 division championships (2022-23 most recently), four President's trophies and five conference championships. Over its long history, the team has enrolled such well-known players as Edward Shore, Lionel Hitchman, Bobby Orr and Cameron Neely. The team operates the Boston Bruins Foundation, which is designed to fund charitable organizations that aid children in the Boston area. Guests can plan birthday parties during Bruins games, which include discounted tickets and an autographed puck as well as a happy birthday message on the video scoreboard. The Bruins' primary minor league affiliates are the American Hockey League's Providence Bruins and the Maine Mariners in the ECHL. Per a recent Forbes estimate (December 2022), the team is valued at $1.4 billion.

FINANCIAL DATA: Note: Data for latest year may not have been available at press time.

In U.S. $	2022	2021	2020	2019	2018	2017
Revenue	161,200,000					
R&D Expense						
Operating Income						
Operating Margin %						
SGA Expense						
Net Income						
Operating Cash Flow						
Capital Expenditure						
EBITDA						
Return on Assets %						
Return on Equity %						
Debt to Equity						

CONTACT INFORMATION:

Phone: 617-624-1900   Fax: 617-523-7184
Toll-Free:
Address: 100 Legends Way, Boston, MA 02114 United States

STOCK TICKER/OTHER:

Stock Ticker: Private
Employees: 315
Parent Company:

Exchange:
Fiscal Year Ends: 06/30

SALARIES/BONUSES:

Top Exec. Salary: $ Bonus: $
Second Exec. Salary: $ Bonus: $

OTHER THOUGHTS:

Estimated Female Officers or Directors: 1
Hot Spot for Advancement for Women/Minorities:

Boston Celtics

NAIC Code: 711211B

TYPES OF BUSINESS:

Professional Basketball Team
Team Management and Operations

BRANDS/DIVISIONS/AFFILIATES:

Boston Basketball Partners LLC

CONTACTS: *Note: Officers with more than one job title may be intentionally listed here more than once.*

Wyc Grousbeck, CEO
Peter Fayette, Dir.-Oper.
Rich Gotham, Pres.
Bill Reissfelder, CFO
Shawn Sullivan, CMO
Barbara Reed, VP-Human Resources
Jay Wessland, CTO
Patrick Lynch, Sr. Dir.-Oper.
Ted Dalton, VP-Bus. Dev. & Corp. Partnerships
Peter Stringer, Sr. Dir.-Digital Media
Jeffrey Twiss, VP-Media & Alumni Rel.
Barbara Reed, Sr. Dir.-Investor Svcs.
Patrick Lynch, Sr. Dir.-Acct.
Danny Ainge, Pres., Basketball Oper.
Brad Stevens, Head Coach
Tim Rath, VP. & Controller
Heather Walker, Sr. Dir.-Public Rel.

GROWTH PLANS/SPECIAL FEATURES:

Boston Celtics, owned and operated by Boston Basketball Partners, LLC, is a professional basketball team playing in the Atlantic division of the Eastern conference of the National Basketball Association (NBA). The team was a charter member of the Basketball Association of America, which evolved into the NBA, and its green colors and winking leprechaun have been recognized symbols for over 50 years. The Celtics have won a record 17 NBA championships including a record eight in a row from 1959-66, as well as 10 conference and 33 division titles, most recently in 2022 and 2023. Such NBA greats as Bill Russell, Tommy Heinsohn, Red Auerbach, Bob Cousy, Dave Cowens, Jon Havlicek, Kevin McHale, Robert Parish and Larry Bird have played for the Celtics. The team is owned by Boston Basketball Partners, LLC, which consists of Wycliffe Grousbeck, Stephen Pagliuca, H. Irving Grousbeck and The Abbey Group. The Celtics play home games at TD Garden, which holds nearly 20,000 spectators and is owned by Delaware North Companies. The Celtics averaged 19,156 in home game attendance during the 2022-23 season. Forbes estimated the team to be worth $4 billion, the 5th most valuable team in the NBA (as of October 2022).

FINANCIAL DATA: *Note: Data for latest year may not have been available at press time.*

In U.S. $	2022	2021	2020	2019	2018	2017
Revenue	315,250,000					
R&D Expense						
Operating Income						
Operating Margin %						
SGA Expense						
Net Income						
Operating Cash Flow						
Capital Expenditure						
EBITDA						
Return on Assets %						
Return on Equity %						
Debt to Equity						

CONTACT INFORMATION:

Phone: 617-854-8000   Fax: 617-367-4286
Toll-Free:
Address: 226 Causeway St., Fl. 8, Boston, MA 02114 United States

STOCK TICKER/OTHER:

Stock Ticker: Private   Exchange:
Employees: 180   Fiscal Year Ends: 06/30
Parent Company:

SALARIES/BONUSES:

Top Exec. Salary: $ Bonus: $
Second Exec. Salary: $ Bonus: $

OTHER THOUGHTS:

Estimated Female Officers or Directors: 33
Hot Spot for Advancement for Women/Minorities: Y

Boston Red Sox

boston.redsox.mlb.com

NAIC Code: 711211A

TYPES OF BUSINESS:

Professional Baseball Team
Team Management and Operations

BRANDS/DIVISIONS/AFFILIATES:

Fenway Sports Group LLC
New England Sports Network

CONTACTS: *Note: Officers with more than one job title may be intentionally listed here more than once.*

Sam Kennedy, CEO
Jonathan Gilula, COO
Tim Zue, CFO
Adam Grossman, CMO
Amy Waryas, Chief People & Culture Officer
Brian Shield, CTO
Ed Weiss, General Counsel
Ben Cherington, Exec. VP-Baseball Oper.
Tim Zue, VP-Bus. Dev.
Zineb Curran, Dir.-Corp. Comm.
Mark Solitro, Controller
John W. Henry, Owner
David Ginsberg, Vice Chmn.
Phillip H. Morse, Vice Chmn.
Pete Nesbit, Sr. Dir.-Ballpark Oper.
Thomas C. Werner, Chmn.
Eddie Romero, Dir.-Int'l Scouting

GROWTH PLANS/SPECIAL FEATURES:

The Boston Red Sox is an organization in Major League Baseball (MLB). Formerly the Boston Somersets and later the Pilgrims, the team became known as the Red Sox in 1912. One of the most recognizable teams in the world, the Red Sox are especially well-known for their rivalry with the New York Yankees, which was exacerbated by the sale of Babe Ruth to New York in 1919. Many other legends have played for the Red Sox, including Cy Young, Ted Williams, Carl Yastrzemski, Wade Boggs and Roger Clemens. The team is owned by Fenway Sports Group, LLC (FSG), a group owned by Tom Werner, Sam Kennedy and former Marlins owner John Henry. Fenway Park, home to the Red Sox since 1912, is the oldest major league ballpark still in operation and has a seating capacity of over 37,300. Notable features of the ballpark include the 36-foot-tall left field wall, dubbed the Green Monster. The team sells out many home games, and averaged 32,408 fans per game during the 2022 season, and was averaging 31,111 during the 2023 season (as of May 2023). The Red Sox plays in the East Division of the American League. The franchise has won the World Series nine times, with the first being in the 2003-04 season and the last being the 2017-18 season. The Red Sox have 14 AL pennants, 10 east division titles and eight wild card berths. In March 2023, Forbes placed the Red Sox third on its annual list of the most valuable MLB teams, with an estimated value of $4.5 billion.

FINANCIAL DATA: *Note: Data for latest year may not have been available at press time.*

In U.S. $	2022	2021	2020	2019	2018	2017
Revenue	648,700,000					
R&D Expense						
Operating Income						
Operating Margin %						
SGA Expense						
Net Income						
Operating Cash Flow						
Capital Expenditure						
EBITDA						
Return on Assets %						
Return on Equity %						
Debt to Equity						

CONTACT INFORMATION:

Phone: 617-226-6000   Fax:
Toll-Free:
Address: 4 Jersey St., Boston, MA 02215 United States

STOCK TICKER/OTHER:

Stock Ticker: Private   Exchange:
Employees: 1,020   Fiscal Year Ends: 12/31
Parent Company:

SALARIES/BONUSES:

Top Exec. Salary: $ Bonus: $
Second Exec. Salary: $ Bonus: $

OTHER THOUGHTS:

Estimated Female Officers or Directors: 11
Hot Spot for Advancement for Women/Minorities: Y

Sales, profits and employees may be estimates. Financial information, benefits and other data can change quickly and may vary from those stated here.

Bowlero Corp

www.bowlerocorp.com

NAIC Code: 713950

TYPES OF BUSINESS:

Bowling Centers
Bowling Equipment
Bowling Software
Bowling Apparel
Bowling Centers
Professional Bowling League
Video Games
Food and Beverages

BRANDS/DIVISIONS/AFFILIATES:

Bowlmor Lanes
Bowlero
AMF
Professional Bowlers Association (PBA)

GROWTH PLANS/SPECIAL FEATURES:

Bowlero Corp is a operator of bowling entertainment centers. It operate traditional bowling centers and more upscale entertainment concepts with lounge seating, arcades, enhanced food and beverage offerings, and more robust customer service for individuals and group events, as well as hosting and overseeing professional and non-professional bowling tournaments and related broadcasting.

Bowlero offers its employees comprehensive benefits and company perks.

CONTACTS: Note: Officers with more than one job title may be intentionally listed here more than once.

Tom Shannon, CEO
Brett Parker, Pres.

FINANCIAL DATA: Note: Data for latest year may not have been available at press time.

In U.S. $	2022	2021	2020	2019	2018	2017
Revenue	911,705,000	395,234,000	520,431,000			
R&D Expense						
Operating Income	114,064,000	-58,487,000	-7,372,000			
Operating Margin %	.13%	-.15%				
SGA Expense	180,702,000	78,335,000	84,103,000			
Net Income	-29,934,000	-126,461,000	-90,892,000			
Operating Cash Flow	177,670,000	58,232,000	18,822,000			
Capital Expenditure	164,798,000	43,197,000	119,711,000			
EBITDA	170,793,000	53,212,000	87,247,000			
Return on Assets %	-.02%	-.08%				
Return on Equity %	-.46%	-.54%				
Debt to Equity		6.59%				

CONTACT INFORMATION:

Phone: 804-417-2000   Fax:
Toll-Free:
Address: 7313 Bell Creek Rd., Mechanicsville, VA 23111 United States

STOCK TICKER/OTHER:

Stock Ticker: BOWL   Exchange: NYS
Employees: 9,390   Fiscal Year Ends: 06/30
Parent Company:

SALARIES/BONUSES:

Top Exec. Salary: $ Bonus: $
Second Exec. Salary: $ Bonus: $

OTHER THOUGHTS:

Estimated Female Officers or Directors:
Hot Spot for Advancement for Women/Minorities:

Boyne Resorts

www.boyneresorts.com

NAIC Code: 713920

TYPES OF BUSINESS:

Ski Resorts
Golf Courses
Real Estate Development
Retail Operations
Indoor Waterpark
Spas
Restaurants

BRANDS/DIVISIONS/AFFILIATES:

Big Sky Resort
Sugarloaf
Sunday River Resort
Avalanche Bay Indoor Waterpark
Boyne Country Sports
Loon Mountain Resort
Gatlinburg SkyLift Park
Cypress Mountain

CONTACTS: Note: Officers with more than one job title may be intentionally listed here more than once.

Stephen Kircher, CEO
Ed Grice, Pres., Boyne Mountain Resort
Brad Keen, Pres., Boyne Highlands Resort
Kathrynn Kircher, Principal - Boyne Design Group

GROWTH PLANS/SPECIAL FEATURES:

Boyne Resorts is a Michigan-based corporation that owns and operates mountain resorts, golf courses and attractions throughout the U.S. and Canada. The company also comprises an outdoor lifestyle equipment/apparel retail division with stores in cities throughout Michigan. Boyne locations include: Big Sky Resort in Montana; Sugarloaf, Sunday River Resort and Pleasant Mountain in Maine; The Highlands, Boyne Mountain Resort, Avalanche Bay Indoor Waterpark, Inn at Bay Harbor-Autograph Collection, and Boyne Country Sports in Michigan; Loon Mountain Resort in New Hampshire; Gatlinburg SkyLift Park in Tennessee; Brighton Resort in Utah; The Summit at Snoqualmie in Washington; and Cypress Mountain in Vancouver, British Columbia. Boyne has meeting planners to help those who want to host meetings, with a choice of destinations that comprise meeting venues, hotel rooms and suites, and a variety of activities. Boyne also offers destinations for weddings and receptions, which include Big Sky Resort, The Highlands, Boyne Mountain Resort, Inn at Bay Harbor, Loon Mountain, Sugarloaf and Sunday River, as well as Brighton's Millicent Chalet and Snoqualmie Pass' The Summit at Snoqualmie.

FINANCIAL DATA: Note: Data for latest year may not have been available at press time.

In U.S. $	2022	2021	2020	2019	2018	2017
Revenue	380,000,000	234,000,000	225,000,000	400,000,000	355,000,000	355,000,000
R&D Expense						
Operating Income						
Operating Margin %						
SGA Expense						
Net Income						
Operating Cash Flow						
Capital Expenditure						
EBITDA						
Return on Assets %						
Return on Equity %						
Debt to Equity						

CONTACT INFORMATION:

Phone: 231-439-4750   Fax: 231-439-4786
Toll-Free:
Address: 3951 Charlevoix Ave., Petoskey, MI 49770 United States

SALARIES/BONUSES:

Top Exec. Salary: $ Bonus: $
Second Exec. Salary: $ Bonus: $

STOCK TICKER/OTHER:

Stock Ticker: Private   Exchange:
Employees: 11,000   Fiscal Year Ends: 12/31
Parent Company:

OTHER THOUGHTS:

Estimated Female Officers or Directors: 2
Hot Spot for Advancement for Women/Minorities:

BPS Direct LLC (Bass Pro Shops)

www.basspro.com

NAIC Code: 451110

TYPES OF BUSINESS:

Sporting Goods, Retail
Sport Boats
Hunting & Fishing Equipment
Catalog & Online Sales
Outdoor Apparel
Resort Operations
Television Production

BRANDS/DIVISIONS/AFFILIATES:

Bass Pro Shops
Cabelas
RedHead
Offshore Angler
White River Fly Shops
American Rod & Gun
Wonders of Wildlife
Big Cedar Lodge

CONTACTS: *Note: Officers with more than one job title may be intentionally listed here more than once.*

John L. Morris, CEO
Martin G. MacDonald, Dir.-Conservation

GROWTH PLANS/SPECIAL FEATURES:

BPS Direct, LLC does business as Bass Pro Shops, a leader in sporting goods retail. The company markets its products through 170 Bass Pro Shops and Cabela's retail stores in the U.S. and Canada, as well as through mail-order catalog and ecommerce sites. The firm provides outdoor recreational products, including specialty apparel, and also aims to inspire environmental conservation among its customers. Products include boats and campers as well as fishing, hunting, camping, automobile and marine supplies. Many of these stores have a variety of unique features and attractions to draw more customers, including restaurants, snack bars, archery ranges, aquariums, waterfalls and video arcades. Aside from its stores, the company sells goods over the internet and through catalogs/sales flyers under the Bass Pro Shops, RedHead, Offshore Angler and White River Fly Shops brand names. Its wholesale operations consist of Tracker Marine Group, a leader in sport boat manufacturing, and American Rod & Gun, one of the largest wholesale hunting and fishing distributors in the country. In addition to offering a variety of hunting and fishing trips and contests, Bass Pro runs the Wonders of Wildlife facility, a museum and conservation education center near its corporate headquarters, and Big Cedar Lodge, an outdoors-themed vacation spot in Missouri located near the company's own nature park, Dogwood Canyon Adventure Park. The company also produces a weekly television program on The Outdoor Channel and an international radio show. In May 2023, Bass Pro Shops announced plans for a new mega Outdoor World destination retail store in St. Johns County, Florida, which would be the 13th Bass Pro Shop location in that state.

FINANCIAL DATA: *Note: Data for latest year may not have been available at press time.*

In U.S. $	2022	2021	2020	2019	2018	2017
Revenue	6,500,000,000	6,072,966,900	5,675,670,000	5,159,700,000	4,680,000,000	4,680,000,000
R&D Expense						
Operating Income						
Operating Margin %						
SGA Expense						
Net Income						
Operating Cash Flow						
Capital Expenditure						
EBITDA						
Return on Assets %						
Return on Equity %						
Debt to Equity						

CONTACT INFORMATION:

Phone: 417-873-5000   Fax: 417-873-5060
Toll-Free: 800-227-7776
Address: 2500 E. Kearney St., Springfield, MO 65898 United States

STOCK TICKER/OTHER:

Stock Ticker: Private
Employees: 40,000
Parent Company:

Exchange:
Fiscal Year Ends: 12/31

SALARIES/BONUSES:

Top Exec. Salary: $ Bonus: $
Second Exec. Salary: $ Bonus: $

OTHER THOUGHTS:

Estimated Female Officers or Directors:
Hot Spot for Advancement for Women/Minorities:

BRG Sports Inc

www.brgsports.com

NAIC Code: 339920

TYPES OF BUSINESS:
Manufacturing-Sporting Goods
Team Sports Equipment
Action Sports Equipment
Accessories
Helmets
Apparel

BRANDS/DIVISIONS/AFFILIATES:
Fenway Partners LLC
Riddell
Helmet Technology Center
MIPS

CONTACTS: Note: Officers with more than one job title may be intentionally listed here more than once.
Dan Arment, CEO
Jackelyn E. Werblo, Sr. VP-Corp. Comm.
Daniel J. Arment, Pres., Riddell Sports
Mike Zlakmet, Pres., Easton Sports
Jessica Klodnicki, Exec. VP

GROWTH PLANS/SPECIAL FEATURES:
BRG Sports, Inc. is a corporate holding company of leading brands that design, develop and market innovative sports equipment, smart helmet technology, team apparel and accessories. The firm's core brand is Riddell, an industry leader in football helmet technology. Riddell developed the first football helmet to achieve the highest protective 5-star rating by Virginia Tech University. The company's Helmet Technology Center, known as The DOME, is a cutting-edge research and design facility dedicated to helmet technology located in Scotts Valley, with a sister facility in Hong Kong. BRG Sports also has an investment in the patented head protection system, MIPS. BRG has offices and facilities worldwide, and is owned by private equity firm Fenway Partners, LLC.

BRG Sports offers its employees medical, dental, life, accidental death and disability insurance; an employee assistance program; 401(k); and flexible spending accounts.

FINANCIAL DATA: Note: Data for latest year may not have been available at press time.

In U.S. $	2022	2021	2020	2019	2018	2017
Revenue	550,000,000	483,600,000	465,000,000	620,000,000	590,000,000	590,000,000
R&D Expense						
Operating Income						
Operating Margin %						
SGA Expense						
Net Income						
Operating Cash Flow						
Capital Expenditure						
EBITDA						
Return on Assets %						
Return on Equity %						
Debt to Equity						

CONTACT INFORMATION:
Phone: 224-585-5200 Fax:
Toll-Free:
Address: 1700 W. Higgins Rd., Ste. 500, Des Plaines, IL 60018 United States

STOCK TICKER/OTHER:
Stock Ticker: Private
Employees: 1,400
Parent Company: Fenway Partners LLC
Exchange:
Fiscal Year Ends: 12/31

SALARIES/BONUSES:
Top Exec. Salary: $ Bonus: $
Second Exec. Salary: $ Bonus: $

OTHER THOUGHTS:
Estimated Female Officers or Directors: 2
Hot Spot for Advancement for Women/Minorities: Y

Sales, profits and employees may be estimates. Financial information, benefits and other data can change quickly and may vary from those stated here.

Brooklyn Nets

NAIC Code: 711211B

www.nba.com/nets

TYPES OF BUSINESS:

Professional Basketball Team
Team Management and Operations

BRANDS/DIVISIONS/AFFILIATES:

Long Island Nets

CONTACTS: *Note: Officers with more than one job title may be intentionally listed here more than once.*

Sam Zussman, CEO
Jeff Gewirtz, Exec. VP-Business Affairs
Irina Pavlova, Pres., Onexim Sports and Entertainment
Peter Stern, CFO
Andrew Karson, Sr. VP-Brand Marketing & Strategy
Maribeth Gainard, Chief Human Resources Officer
Keia Cole, Chief Digital Officer
Leo Ehrline, Chief Admin. & Rel. Officer
Jeff Gewirtz, Business Affairs & Chief Legal Officer
Billy King, Gen. Mgr.-Basketball Oper.
Charlie Mierswa, Exec. VP-Bus. Oper.
Gary Sussman, VP-Public Rel.
Paul Koehler, Controller
Mikhail Prokhorov, Principal Owner
Barry Baum, Exec. VP-Bus. & Chief Comm. Officer
Sam Altman, Chief Corporate Dev. Officer

GROWTH PLANS/SPECIAL FEATURES:

The Brooklyn Nets joined the American Basketball Association (ABA) in 1967 as the New Jersey Americans. The team was renamed the New York Nets after its move to Long Island. Following the merger of the ABA with the National Basketball Association (NBA), the Nets officially joined the NBA, and the club was later renamed the New Jersey Nets for the 1977-78 season. In 2011, the team was renamed the Brooklyn Nets after moving to the 17,732-seat capacity Barclays Center arena. The franchise managed to win two ABA championships prior to the merger, but since joining the NBA, the team has been without a championship, despite winning four division titles and two conference titles. The Nets play in the Atlantic division of the Eastern Conference, along with the Toronto Raptors, Boston Celtics, New York Knicks and Philadelphia 76ers. The team owns D-League affiliate, Long Island Nets, which played their home games during the 2016-17 season at the Barclays Center, and then at the Nassau Coliseum when renovations were completed for the 2017-18 season. The Nets organization is currently majority-owned by Joseph Tsai, who also acquired the Barclays Center in 2019. The team's home attendance averaged 17,669 per game in the 2022-23 season. Forbes estimated the Brooklyn Nets to be worth $3.5 billion in October 2022.

FINANCIAL DATA: *Note: Data for latest year may not have been available at press time.*

In U.S. $	2022	2021	2020	2019	2018	2017
Revenue	319,800,000					
R&D Expense						
Operating Income						
Operating Margin %						
SGA Expense						
Net Income						
Operating Cash Flow						
Capital Expenditure						
EBITDA						
Return on Assets %						
Return on Equity %						
Debt to Equity						

CONTACT INFORMATION:

Phone: 718-933-3000   Fax: 718-942-9595
Toll-Free:
Address: 168 39th St., Fl. 7, Brooklyn, NY 11232 United States

STOCK TICKER/OTHER:

Stock Ticker: Private   Exchange:
Employees: 325   Fiscal Year Ends: 06/30
Parent Company:

SALARIES/BONUSES:

Top Exec. Salary: $ Bonus: $
Second Exec. Salary: $ Bonus: $

OTHER THOUGHTS:

Estimated Female Officers or Directors: 55
Hot Spot for Advancement for Women/Minorities: Y

Brunswick Corporation

www.brunswick.com

NAIC Code: 333618

TYPES OF BUSINESS:

Marine Engines Manufacturing
Boat Manufacturing
Engine Manufacturing
Engine Procurement
Engine Parts
Boat Parts
Accessories

BRANDS/DIVISIONS/AFFILIATES:

Sea Ray
Bayliner
Boston Whaler
Lund
Heyday
Crestliner
Cypress Cay
Fanautic Club

CONTACTS: *Note: Officers with more than one job title may be intentionally listed here more than once.*

David Foulkes, CEO
Ryan Gwillim, CFO
Nancy Cooper, Chairman of the Board
Randall Altman, Chief Accounting Officer
Brenna Preisser, Chief Strategy Officer
Christopher Dekker, General Counsel
Brett Dibkey, President, Divisional
Aine Denari, President, Divisional
Christopher Drees, President, Subsidiary

GROWTH PLANS/SPECIAL FEATURES:

Brunswick Corp is the leader in several recreational sectors. The firm is the leading boat manufacturer, and its brands include Mercury and Mariner outboard engines; Mercury MerCruiser inboard engines; Boston Whaler, and Bayliner boats. It is also the leading manufacturer of fitness equipment, under the Life Fitness and Hammer Strength brands. The firm also manufactures billiards equipment under the Brunswick and Contender brands. The company has three reportable segments Propulsion, Parts & Accessories, and Boat. It derives a majority of its revenue from the United States.

FINANCIAL DATA: *Note: Data for latest year may not have been available at press time.*

In U.S. $	2022	2021	2020	2019	2018	2017
Revenue	6,812,200,000	5,846,200,000	4,347,500,000	4,108,400,000	3,802,200,000	3,802,200,000
R&D Expense	202,900,000	154,500,000	125,900,000	121,600,000	111,600,000	111,600,000
Operating Income	972,900,000	813,700,000	543,400,000	489,800,000	378,900,000	378,900,000
Operating Margin %	.14%	.14%	.12%	.12%	.10%	.10%
SGA Expense	771,400,000	697,800,000	543,700,000	509,600,000	458,100,000	458,100,000
Net Income	677,000,000	593,300,000	372,700,000	-131,000,000	146,400,000	146,400,000
Operating Cash Flow	586,100,000	574,000,000	798,300,000	434,200,000	400,300,000	400,300,000
Capital Expenditure	388,300,000	267,100,000	182,400,000	232,600,000	178,000,000	178,000,000
EBITDA	1,182,900,000	980,400,000	693,400,000	325,400,000	326,400,000	326,400,000
Return on Assets %	.12%	.13%	.10%	-.03%	.04%	.04%
Return on Equity %	.34%	.35%	.27%	-.09%	.10%	.10%
Debt to Equity	1.23%	.97%	0.648	0.875	0.291	0.291

CONTACT INFORMATION:

Phone: 847 735-4700   Fax: 847 735-4765
Toll-Free:
Address: 26125 N. Riverwoods Blvd., Ste 500, Mettawa, IL 60045-3420
United States

STOCK TICKER/OTHER:

Stock Ticker: BC
Employees: 19,800
Parent Company:

Exchange: NYS
Fiscal Year Ends: 12/31

SALARIES/BONUSES:

Top Exec. Salary: $1,118,423   Bonus: $
Second Exec. Salary: $586,539   Bonus: $

OTHER THOUGHTS:

Estimated Female Officers or Directors: 4
Hot Spot for Advancement for Women/Minorities: Y

Sales, profits and employees may be estimates. Financial information, benefits and other data can change quickly and may vary from those stated here.

BSN Sports Inc

NAIC Code: 454113

TYPES OF BUSINESS:

Sporting Goods, Direct Sales
Ecommerce
Sports Catalogs
Sport Apparel and Goods Manufacture
Physical Education Products
Sporting Good Distribution
Customized Sport Apparel
Sport Marketing Services

BRANDS/DIVISIONS/AFFILIATES:

Varsity Brands Inc
Herff Jones Inc
BSN Sports
BSN Sports Direct
BSNSPORTS Equipment
Donnelley Sports
Unique Image LLC

CONTACTS: *Note: Officers with more than one job title may be intentionally listed here more than once.*

Adam Blumenfeld, CEO
Terry Babilla, Pres.
Terrence M. Babilla, General Counsel

GROWTH PLANS/SPECIAL FEATURES:

BSN Sports, Inc. manufactures, distributes and markets sport-related goods. The firm's primary products include sporting goods equipment, soft good athletic apparel, recreational and leisure products, physical education products and footwear. BSN primarily sells its products through direct catalogs, ecommerce sites, telemarketers and direct sales teams. The company offers brand name and private-label products, including Nike and Under Armour, among others. Catalogs include BSN Sports, BSN Sports Direct and BSNSPORTS Equipment. The company's website, BSNSports.com, enables consumers to place orders, access account information, track orders and perform routine customer service inquiries. Customized services include screen printing, embroidery, numbering, sublimation, logos, lettering, laser engraving and digital fusion. In addition, the company has licenses and marketing alliances with national organizations such as YMCA, YWCA, Little League Baseball and American Youth Football. BSN Sports markets over 50,000 products to the U.S. institutional market, comprised of schools, colleges, universities, government agencies, military facilities, athletic clubs, athletic teams and dealers, youth sports leagues and recreational organizations. BSN is a subsidiary of Herff Jones, Inc., which itself is a subsidiary of Varsity Brands, Inc. In late-2022, BSN Sports acquired Donnelley Sports, which services the team sports market in the state of Idaho; and acquired Unique Image LLC, which offers customized promotional, corporate and team athletic products and apparel since its 1979 founding.

FINANCIAL DATA: *Note: Data for latest year may not have been available at press time.*

In U.S. $	2022	2021	2020	2019	2018	2017
Revenue	1,500,000,000	1,200,000,000	1,000,000,000	875,000,000	575,000,000	575,000,000
R&D Expense						
Operating Income						
Operating Margin %						
SGA Expense						
Net Income						
Operating Cash Flow						
Capital Expenditure						
EBITDA						
Return on Assets %						
Return on Equity %						
Debt to Equity						

CONTACT INFORMATION:

Phone: 972 484-9484   Fax: 972 484-0497
Toll-Free: 800-856-3488
Address: 14460 Varsity Brands Way, Dallas, TX 75244 United States

STOCK TICKER/OTHER:

Stock Ticker: Private   Exchange:
Employees: 1,200   Fiscal Year Ends: 03/31
Parent Company: Varsity Brands Inc

SALARIES/BONUSES:

Top Exec. Salary: $ Bonus: $
Second Exec. Salary: $ Bonus: $

OTHER THOUGHTS:

Estimated Female Officers or Directors:
Hot Spot for Advancement for Women/Minorities:

Buffalo Bills

www.buffalobills.com

NAIC Code: 711211C

TYPES OF BUSINESS:

Professional Football Team
Team Management and Operations

BRANDS/DIVISIONS/AFFILIATES:

CONTACTS: Note: Officers with more than one job title may be intentionally listed here more than once.

Terry Pegula, CEO
Kim Pegula, Pres.
Josh Dziurlikowski, VP-Finance
Jordan McCarren, VP-Mktg.
Dan Evans, VP-IT
Jim Overdorf, Sr. VP-Football Admin.
Mary Owen, Exec. VP-Strategic Planning
Gregg Pastore, Sr. Dir.-Digital Media
Scott Berchtold, Sr. VP-Comm.
Josh Dziurlikowski, Controller
Doug Marrone, Head Coach
Jim Monos, Dir.-Player Personnel
Bill Munson, Sr. VP-Gov't Rel. & External Affairs
Bruce Popko, Chief Revenue Officer
Ron Raccuia, COO

GROWTH PLANS/SPECIAL FEATURES:

The Buffalo Bills is a National Football League (NFL) team that plays in the eastern division of the American Football Conference (AFC). The Bills are based in Orchard Park, New York, and play at Highmark Stadium. The stadium is owned by Erie County, New York, and the team's home game attendance averaged 68,431 in 2022. The Bills were a charter member of the American Football League (AFL), and won the AFL championship in both 1964 and 1965. The team entered the NFL when the AFL was absorbed in the league merger of 1970. The Bills reached the Super Bowl in four consecutive years (from 1990-1993, the only NFL team to do so) only to lose the championship game each time. In total, the franchise has won four conference championships, 13 division championships and gained 22 playoff berths since its inception. While the team achieved a relatively high amount of success in the 1990s, it has just recently made it back to the playoffs, in 2017, 2019, 2020, 2021 and 2022. The team's Hall of Fame players include O.J. Simpson, Thurman Thomas, Bruce Smith, Jim Kelly Andre Reed and Bill Polian. Forbes valued the Buffalo Bills at $3.4 billion in August 2022.

FINANCIAL DATA: Note: Data for latest year may not have been available at press time.

In U.S. $	2022	2021	2020	2019	2018	2017
Revenue	489,450,000					
R&D Expense						
Operating Income						
Operating Margin %						
SGA Expense						
Net Income						
Operating Cash Flow						
Capital Expenditure						
EBITDA						
Return on Assets %						
Return on Equity %						
Debt to Equity						

CONTACT INFORMATION:

Phone: 716-648-1800   Fax: 716-649-6446
Toll-Free:
Address: 1 Bills Dr., Orchard Park, NY 14127 United States

STOCK TICKER/OTHER:

Stock Ticker: Private   Exchange:
Employees: 480   Fiscal Year Ends: 12/31
Parent Company:

SALARIES/BONUSES:

Top Exec. Salary: $ Bonus: $
Second Exec. Salary: $ Bonus: $

OTHER THOUGHTS:

Estimated Female Officers or Directors: 32
Hot Spot for Advancement for Women/Minorities: Y

Sales, profits and employees may be estimates. Financial information, benefits and other data can change quickly and may vary from those stated here.

Buffalo Sabres
NAIC Code: 711211F

www.nhl.com/sabres

TYPES OF BUSINESS:
Professional Hockey Team (NHL)
Team Management and Operations

BRANDS/DIVISIONS/AFFILIATES:
French Connection
Rochester Americans
Cincinnati Cyclones

CONTACTS: *Note: Officers with more than one job title may be intentionally listed here more than once.*
Terry Pegula, CEO
Kim Pegula, Pres.
Mike McFarlane, Sr. VP-Finance & Admin.
John Durbin, Sr. VP-Mktg. & Bus. Strategy
Christie Joseph, Sr. VP-Human Resources
Todd Henzler, Dir.-IT
Mike Kaminska, Dir.-Merch.
Dave Zygaj, VP-Admin. Affairs
Dave Zygaj, VP-Legal Affairs
Chuck LaMattina, VP-Bus. Oper. & Finance
Cliff Benson, Chief Dev. Officer
Michael Gilbert, VP-Public & Community Rel.
Kristin Zirnheld, Corp. Controller
Terrence M. Pegula, Owner
Tim Murray, Gen. Mgr.
Ted Nolan, Head Coach
Chrisanne Bellas, VP-Broadcasting
Kevyn Adams, General Manager

GROWTH PLANS/SPECIAL FEATURES:
The Buffalo Sabres are a National Hockey League (NHL) team based in Buffalo, New York, playing in the Atlantic division of the Eastern conference. Founded in 1969, the team quickly rose to prominence behind its line of Rick Martin, Hall of Famer Gilbert Perreault and Rene Robert, together known as the French Connection, finishing the 1974-75 season with a 49-16-15 record. Despite the Sabres having only been in the league for five years, the team went on to its first appearance in the Stanley Cup Finals that season, losing to the Philadelphia Flyers. One of the most notable events of the team's early history came in 1976 when the Sabres played the Soviet Wings in an exhibition game, with Cold War tension running high, defeating the Wings 12-6 in what then ranked as the worst ever loss by a Soviet team in international competition. The Sabres' rosters have included such greats as Dominick Hasek (who won four consecutive Vezina trophies and two consecutive Hart Trophies, becoming the only goaltender to do so); Pat LaFontaine; Miroslav Satan; Donald Audette; and Rob Ray, who holds the team's record for penalty minutes. The team has won six division championships and three conference championships. The Sabres play in the KeyBank Center, which seats over 19,070 spectators. The team's average attendance was 15,567 for the 2022-23 season. Minor league affiliates include the Rochester Americans, of the American Hockey League (AHL), and the Cincinnati Cyclones of the ECHL. Forbes estimated the team's value to be $610 million in December 2022.

FINANCIAL DATA: *Note: Data for latest year may not have been available at press time.*

In U.S. $	2022	2021	2020	2019	2018	2017
Revenue	122,850,000					
R&D Expense						
Operating Income						
Operating Margin %						
SGA Expense						
Net Income						
Operating Cash Flow						
Capital Expenditure						
EBITDA						
Return on Assets %						
Return on Equity %						
Debt to Equity						

CONTACT INFORMATION:
Phone: 716-855-4100   Fax: 716-855-4122
Toll-Free: 888-467-2273
Address: One Seymour H. Knox III Plz., Buffalo, NY 14203-4122 United States

STOCK TICKER/OTHER:
Stock Ticker: Private   Exchange:
Employees: 280   Fiscal Year Ends: 08/31
Parent Company:

SALARIES/BONUSES:
Top Exec. Salary: $ Bonus: $
Second Exec. Salary: $ Bonus: $

OTHER THOUGHTS:
Estimated Female Officers or Directors: 22
Hot Spot for Advancement for Women/Minorities: Y

Cabelas Inc

www.cabelas.com

NAIC Code: 451110

TYPES OF BUSINESS:

Sporting Goods Stores
Hunting & Fishing Supplies
Camping Equipment
Outdoor Apparel
Catalog & Online Sales
Custom Embroidery and Design Services

BRANDS/DIVISIONS/AFFILIATES:

BPS Direct LLC (Bass Pro Shops)
Cabelas.com
Cabelas.ca

GROWTH PLANS/SPECIAL FEATURES:

Cabela's, Inc., a subsidiary of BPS Direct, LLC (dba Bass Pro Shops), is a leading retailer of outdoor and hunting supply merchandise. The company's products include merchandise and equipment for hunting, fishing, marine use, camping and recreational sport shooting, as well as casual and outdoor apparel, footwear, optics, vehicle accessories and gifts and home furnishings comprising an outdoor theme. Retail stores range in size from 40,000 to 246,000 square feet, which either comprise the company's standard format or its large/tourist format. Cabela's also offers its products via ecommerce websites (Cabelas.com and Cabelas.ca), mobile apps, in-bound telemarketing and print catalog distributions. The websites provide information regarding custom embroidery and design services for clubs, companies, associations and teams.

CONTACTS: *Note: Officers with more than one job title may be intentionally listed here more than once.*

Johnny Morris, CEO-BPS
Thomas Millner, CEO
Douglas Means, Executive VP
Scott Williams, President
Brent LaSure, Secretary

FINANCIAL DATA: *Note: Data for latest year may not have been available at press time.*

In U.S. $	2022	2021	2020	2019	2018	2017
Revenue	7,000,000,000	6,621,615,000	5,093,550,000	4,630,500,000	4,200,000,000	4,200,000,000
R&D Expense						
Operating Income						
Operating Margin %						
SGA Expense						
Net Income						
Operating Cash Flow						
Capital Expenditure						
EBITDA						
Return on Assets %						
Return on Equity %						
Debt to Equity						

CONTACT INFORMATION:

Phone: 308 254-5505   Fax: 308 254-4800
Toll-Free: 800-237-4444
Address: One Cabela Dr., Sidney, NE 69160 United States

STOCK TICKER/OTHER:

Stock Ticker: Private   Exchange:
Employees: 19,100   Fiscal Year Ends: 12/31
Parent Company: BPS Direct LLC (Bass Pro Shops)

SALARIES/BONUSES:

Top Exec. Salary: $ Bonus: $
Second Exec. Salary: $ Bonus: $

OTHER THOUGHTS:

Estimated Female Officers or Directors: 2
Hot Spot for Advancement for Women/Minorities:

Calgary Flames

NAIC Code: 711211F

TYPES OF BUSINESS:

Professional Hockey Team (NHL)
Team Management and Operations

BRANDS/DIVISIONS/AFFILIATES:

Calgary Sports and Entertainment Corporation
Calgary Wranglers
Rapit City Rush

CONTACTS: *Note: Officers with more than one job title may be intentionally listed here more than once.*

Don Maloney, Interim Gen. Mngr.
Don Maloney, Sr. VP-Hockey Oper.
Mike Burke, Dir.-Admin.
Brad Treliving, Gen. Mgr.-Hockey Oper.
Peter Hanlon, VP-Comm.
Chris Snow, Dir.-Video Analysis

GROWTH PLANS/SPECIAL FEATURES:

The Calgary Flames is an NHL (National Hockey League) club owned by the Calgary Sports and Entertainment Corporation, and plays in the Pacific division of the Western conference. Based in Calgary, Alberta, the Flames play at the Scotiabank Saddledome, which is owned by the City of Calgary. The arena seats 19,289 fans, and the team averaged 17,956 per home game attendance during the 2022-23 season. The franchise was started in Atlanta, Georgia in 1972 as the Atlanta Flames. The team became the Calgary Flames when it moved to Canada in 1980 and has made three Stanley Cup appearances since then. Lanny McDonald, a Hockey Hall of Fame member, played forward and was the team captain that led the Flames to their only Stanley Cup victory, in the 1988-89 season. The Flames have won two Presidents Trophies for first overall in 1988 and 1989; three conference titles in 1986, 1989 and 2004; and seven division championships, with the most recent being 2018-19 and 2021-22. The team maintains two minor league affiliations: the Calgary Wranglers in the American Hockey League (AHL) and the Rapid City Rush in the ECHL. Forbes valued the Calgary Flames at $855 million in December 2022.

FINANCIAL DATA: *Note: Data for latest year may not have been available at press time.*

In U.S. $	2022	2021	2020	2019	2018	2017
Revenue	100,000,000	71,000,000	120,000,000	138,000,000	129,000,000	129,000,000
R&D Expense						
Operating Income						
Operating Margin %						
SGA Expense						
Net Income		-39,000,000	400,000	3,600,000	5,400,000	5,400,000
Operating Cash Flow						
Capital Expenditure						
EBITDA						
Return on Assets %						
Return on Equity %						
Debt to Equity						

CONTACT INFORMATION:

Phone: 403-777-2177   Fax: 403-777-2171
Toll-Free:
Address: P.O. Box 1540, Stn. M, Calgary, AB T2P 3B9 Canada

STOCK TICKER/OTHER:

Stock Ticker: Private   Exchange:
Employees: 350   Fiscal Year Ends: 06/30
Parent Company: Calgary Sports Entertainment Corporation

SALARIES/BONUSES:

Top Exec. Salary: $ Bonus: $
Second Exec. Salary: $ Bonus: $

OTHER THOUGHTS:

Estimated Female Officers or Directors: 2
Hot Spot for Advancement for Women/Minorities: Y

CamelBak Products LLC

www.camelbak.com

NAIC Code: 339920

TYPES OF BUSINESS:

Hydration Products
Outdoor Sports Backpacks
Military & Law Enforcement Equipment
Hydration Packs
Hydration Accessories

BRANDS/DIVISIONS/AFFILIATES:

Vista Outdoor Inc

CONTACTS: Note: Officers with more than one job title may be intentionally listed here more than once.

Greg Williamson, Pres.

GROWTH PLANS/SPECIAL FEATURES:

CamelBak Products, LLC manufactures, designs and distributes specialized hydration equipment and other gear, including gloves, tactical packs and electrolyte tablets. The firm markets its products primarily to skiers, snowboarders, motocross riders, runners, cyclists, hikers, soldiers, construction workers, airport tarmac personnel and law enforcement staff. Many of CamelBak's systems offer special features designed for specific activities such as insulated tubes and mouthpieces for winter sports, bite valves for bicyclists and camouflaged exteriors for hunting. The company also offers a line of spill-proof water bottles; and hands-free hydration products, which are water containers worn as backpacks, with over-the-shoulder drinking tubes that enable users to drink water without using their hands. For military and law enforcement customers, CamelBak has introduced products with additional features such as accommodations for concealed weapons, antenna ports, low infrared reflectivity for concealment purposes, built-in microfilters and drinking tubes compatible with chem/bio protection equipment such as gas masks. Accessories offered by CamelBak include adapters, caps, carriers, cleaning supplies, tubes, valves and more. CamelBak operates as a subsidiary of Vista Outdoor, Inc.

FINANCIAL DATA: Note: Data for latest year may not have been available at press time.

In U.S. $	2022	2021	2020	2019	2018	2017
Revenue	160,000,000	156,436,800	150,420,000	138,000,000	130,000,000	130,000,000
R&D Expense						
Operating Income						
Operating Margin %						
SGA Expense						
Net Income						
Operating Cash Flow						
Capital Expenditure						
EBITDA						
Return on Assets %						
Return on Equity %						
Debt to Equity						

CONTACT INFORMATION:

Phone: 707-792-9700   Fax: 707-665-9231
Toll-Free: 800-767-8725
Address: 2000 S. McDowell Blvd., Ste 200, Petaluma, CA 94954 United States

STOCK TICKER/OTHER:

Stock Ticker: Subsidiary
Employees: 500
Parent Company: Vista Outdoor Inc

Exchange:
Fiscal Year Ends: 12/31

SALARIES/BONUSES:

Top Exec. Salary: $ Bonus: $
Second Exec. Salary: $ Bonus: $

OTHER THOUGHTS:

Estimated Female Officers or Directors: 1
Hot Spot for Advancement for Women/Minorities:

Campeonato Nacional de Liga Primera Division (La Liga)

www.laliga.com/en-US

NAIC Code: 711211

TYPES OF BUSINESS:

Professional Soccer League
Professional Spanish Football

BRANDS/DIVISIONS/AFFILIATES:

Loarre Investments Sarl
Union of European Football Association
Copa del Rey
Supercopa de Espana
UEFA Champions League
UEFA Europa League
UEFA Europa Conference League

CONTACTS: *Note: Officers with more than one job title may be intentionally listed here more than once.*

Javier Tebas Medrano, CEO
Jose Luis Astiazaran, Pres.

GROWTH PLANS/SPECIAL FEATURES:

Campeonato Nacional de Liga de Primera Division (La Liga) is the premier division of men's professional football in Spain, according to the Union of European Football Associations (UEFA). La Liga comprises 20 teams, with the three lowest-placed teams at the end of each season being relegated to the second division and replaced by the top two teams as well as a playoff winner in that division. The 2022-23 season was won by Barcelona with four games to spare. Since its 1929 inception, a total of 62 teams have competed in La Liga (as of the end of the 2023 season). Seasons last from August to May, and each club plays every other club twice, once at home and once away. Competition-wise, domestic cups include the Copa del Rey and the Supercopa de Espana; and international cups include the UEFA Champions League, the UEFA Europa League and the UEFA Europa Conference League. La Liga has a partnership with Loarre Investments S.a.r.l. to enhance the development of the teams and to improve their infrastructure, digital development, internationalization and sporting projects, among other purposes.

FINANCIAL DATA: *Note: Data for latest year may not have been available at press time.*

In U.S. $	2022	2021	2020	2019	2018	2017
Revenue	2,320,000,000	2,254,961,418	2,139,613,341	2,203,945,160		
R&D Expense						
Operating Income						
Operating Margin %						
SGA Expense						
Net Income		14,285		15,913		
Operating Cash Flow						
Capital Expenditure						
EBITDA						
Return on Assets %						
Return on Equity %						
Debt to Equity						

CONTACT INFORMATION:

Phone: 34-91-205-5000   Fax: 34-91-408-0828
Toll-Free:
Address: Calle Torrelaguna 60, Madrid, 28043 Spain

STOCK TICKER/OTHER:

Stock Ticker: Private   Exchange:
Employees: 498   Fiscal Year Ends: 06/30
Parent Company:

SALARIES/BONUSES:

Top Exec. Salary: $ Bonus: $
Second Exec. Salary: $ Bonus: $

OTHER THOUGHTS:

Estimated Female Officers or Directors:
Hot Spot for Advancement for Women/Minorities:

Canadian Football League

www.cfl.ca

NAIC Code: 711211

TYPES OF BUSINESS:

Professional Football League

BRANDS/DIVISIONS/AFFILIATES:

CONTACTS: *Note: Officers with more than one job title may be intentionally listed here more than once.*

Randy Ambrosie, Commissioner
Doug Allison, VP-Bus. Oper.
Matt Maychak, Dir.-Comm. & Broadcasting
Doug Allison, VP-Finance
Adrian Sciarra, VP-Commercial Assets
Tom Higgins, Dir.-Officiating
Kevin McDonald, VP-Football Oper.

GROWTH PLANS/SPECIAL FEATURES:

The Canadian Football League (CFL) is a nine-team professional league that plays a variation of U.S. football throughout Canada. The major differences between Canadian and American football are that the CFL uses a longer field, an additional player on the field and a three-down rule. CFL teams are divided into two divisions: East (Hamilton Tiger-Cats, Montreal Alouettes, Toronto Argonauts and Ottawa Redblacks) and West (British Columbia Lions, Calgary Stampeders, Edmonton Elks, Saskatchewan Roughriders and Winnipeg Blue Bombers). The organization has a limit on the number of non-Canadian born players on its teams. The league's season includes an 18-game, 21-week regular season that runs from mid-June to early-November; and a three-week division playoff in the Grey Cup championship game in late-November, which is regularly one of Canada's highest-rated televised sports events. The CFL has boasted several legendary players, including Herb Trawick, Granville Liggins, Tommy Joe Coffey, Tobin Rote, Matt Dunigan and Tony Gabriel.

FINANCIAL DATA: *Note: Data for latest year may not have been available at press time.*

In U.S. $	2022	2021	2020	2019	2018	2017
Revenue	110,000,000	92,400,000	66,000,000	230,000,000	220,000,000	220,000,000
R&D Expense						
Operating Income						
Operating Margin %						
SGA Expense						
Net Income						
Operating Cash Flow						
Capital Expenditure						
EBITDA						
Return on Assets %						
Return on Equity %						
Debt to Equity						

CONTACT INFORMATION:

Phone: 416-322-9650   Fax: 416-322-9651
Toll-Free:
Address: 50 Wellington St. E., Fl. 3, Toronto, ON M5E 1C8 Canada

STOCK TICKER/OTHER:

Stock Ticker: Private
Employees: 165
Parent Company:

Exchange:
Fiscal Year Ends: 06/30

SALARIES/BONUSES:

Top Exec. Salary: $ Bonus: $
Second Exec. Salary: $ Bonus: $

OTHER THOUGHTS:

Estimated Female Officers or Directors: 6
Hot Spot for Advancement for Women/Minorities: Y

Canlan Ice Sports Corp

NAIC Code: 713940

www.canlansports.com/corporate

TYPES OF BUSINESS:

Fitness and Recreational Sports Centers
Recreation Facilities
Operations and Management
Sports Facility Investment
Sports Programs
Ice Skating
Soccer
Court Sports

BRANDS/DIVISIONS/AFFILIATES:

Play Forward Pathway
Canlan Youth Hockey League
Adult Safe Hockey League
Canlan Classic Tournaments

GROWTH PLANS/SPECIAL FEATURES:

Canlan Ice Sports Corp is focused on the development, lease, acquisition, and operation of multi-purpose recreation and entertainment facilities in North America.

CONTACTS: *Note: Officers with more than one job title may be intentionally listed here more than once.*

Joey St-Aubin, CEO
Mark Faubert, COO
Ivan Wu, CFO
Liana Guiry, VP-Mktg. & Sales
Rita Price, VP-Human Resources
Costa Kladianos, VP-Technology & Innovation
Michael Gellard, Executive VP
Mark Reynolds, Vice President, Divisional
Ken Male, Vice President, Divisional
Hailey Clark, Vice President, Divisional
Greg Porcellato, Vice President, Divisional
Victor D'Souza, Chmn.

FINANCIAL DATA: *Note: Data for latest year may not have been available at press time.*

In U.S. $	2022	2021	2020	2019	2018	2017
Revenue	53,777,590	29,462,870	28,635,720	64,436,390	62,299,230	62,299,230
R&D Expense						
Operating Income	1,652,103	-1,460,999	-5,116,778	4,082,481	4,259,727	4,259,727
Operating Margin %		-.05%	-.18%	.06%	.07%	.07%
SGA Expense	36,861,950	25,219,190	26,552,540	42,250,070	42,965,620	42,965,620
Net Income	3,450,087	-796,511	-4,641,206	1,785,584	2,594,495	2,594,495
Operating Cash Flow	7,714,919	8,852,062	-6,412,202	6,490,977	7,978,235	7,978,235
Capital Expenditure	2,669,623	382,938	1,059,826	15,957,930	3,520,839	3,520,839
EBITDA	11,775,520	5,747,713	1,703,891	10,690,160	10,156,970	10,156,970
Return on Assets %		-.01%	-.05%	.02%	.03%	.03%
Return on Equity %		-.03%	-.14%	.05%	.08%	.08%
Debt to Equity		1.22%	1.378	1.25	1.10	1.10

CONTACT INFORMATION:

Phone: 604 736-9152   Fax: 604 736-9170
Toll-Free: 888 422-6526
Address: 6501 Sprott St., Burnaby, BC V6B 3B8 Canada

STOCK TICKER/OTHER:

Stock Ticker: CNLFF   Exchange: PINX
Employees: 1,100   Fiscal Year Ends: 12/31
Parent Company:

SALARIES/BONUSES:

Top Exec. Salary: $ Bonus: $
Second Exec. Salary: $ Bonus: $

OTHER THOUGHTS:

Estimated Female Officers or Directors:
Hot Spot for Advancement for Women/Minorities:

Cannondale Bicycle Corporation

www.cannondale.com

NAIC Code: 336991

TYPES OF BUSINESS:

Bicycle Manufacturing
Bike Development
Bike Production
Electric Bikes
Mountain Bikes
Fitness Bikes
Accessories
Gear

BRANDS/DIVISIONS/AFFILIATES:

Dorel Industries Inc

GROWTH PLANS/SPECIAL FEATURES:

Cannondale Bicycle Corporation is an American division of Canadian giant Dorel Industries, Inc., and a designer, developer and producer of bicycles. The firm's bike varieties include mountain, road, active and electric. Mountain bikes are rugged and capable of handling off-road terrain and include over-mountain bikes, full suspension light bikes, hardtail bikes, trail bikes, sport bikes and fat bikes. Cannondale's road bikes include race bikes, endurance bikes, all-road bikes, cyclocross bikes and triathlon bikes. Active bikes are compatible for transport, comfort, fitness and fun. Electric bikes are offered for road, fitness, mountain, urban and tour riding. Cannondale engineers bike models for men, women and children; and sells cycling-related gear such as bicycle shocks and suspension, grips, rear racks, water bottles, gloves, apparel, locks, pumps, bicycle-mounted computers, tire patches and repair tools.

CONTACTS: Note: Officers with more than one job title may be intentionally listed here more than once.

Peter Woods, CEO
Michael De Leon, Mgr.-Public Rel. & Advocacy

FINANCIAL DATA: Note: Data for latest year may not have been available at press time.

In U.S. $	2022	2021	2020	2019	2018	2017
Revenue						
R&D Expense						
Operating Income						
Operating Margin %						
SGA Expense						
Net Income						
Operating Cash Flow						
Capital Expenditure						
EBITDA						
Return on Assets %						
Return on Equity %						
Debt to Equity						

CONTACT INFORMATION:

Phone: 203-845-8300   Fax:
Toll-Free:
Address: 1 Cannondale Way, Wilton, CT 06897 United States

STOCK TICKER/OTHER:

Stock Ticker: Subsidiary   Exchange:
Employees: 175   Fiscal Year Ends: 06/30
Parent Company: Dorel Industries Inc

SALARIES/BONUSES:

Top Exec. Salary: $ Bonus: $
Second Exec. Salary: $ Bonus: $

OTHER THOUGHTS:

Estimated Female Officers or Directors:
Hot Spot for Advancement for Women/Minorities:

Sales, profits and employees may be estimates. Financial information, benefits and other data can change quickly and may vary from those stated here.

Carolina Hurricanes

www.nhl.com/hurricanes

NAIC Code: 711211F

TYPES OF BUSINESS:

Professional Hockey Team (NHL)
Team Management and Operations

BRANDS/DIVISIONS/AFFILIATES:

Canes (The)
Chicago Wolves
Norfolk Admirals

CONTACTS: *Note: Officers with more than one job title may be intentionally listed here more than once.*

Tom Dundon, Governor
Don Waddell, Pres.
Shaun Nicholson, CFO
Mike Forman, CMO
Keitha Stanley, VP-Human Resources
Glenn Johnson, CIO
Bill Peters, Head Coach
Mike Vellucci, Dir.-Hockey Oper.
Mike Sundheim, Sr. Dir.-Comm.
Ron Francis, Exec. VP
Davin Olsen, Exec. VP
Aaron Schwartz, Dir.-Hockey Oper.

GROWTH PLANS/SPECIAL FEATURES:

The Carolina Hurricanes (also known as The Canes) is a National Hockey League (NHL) team based in Raleigh, North Carolina that plays in the Metropolitan division of the Eastern conference. The franchise was started in 1972 as part of the World Hockey Association (WHA). The team was known as the New England Whalers, being later changed to the Hartford Whalers. The franchise joined the NHL in 1979 when the WHA ceased operations. Today's team was created when Peter Karmanos, the founder and chairman of Compuware, acquired the Whalers in 1994 and moved the team to its current location in 1997. In 2002, the Hurricanes made it to the Stanley Cup finals for the first time in franchise history, but lost to the Detroit Red Wings. They clenched the Stanley Cup in the 2005-06 season. The Hurricanes have six division championships (most recently in 2020-21, 2021-22 and 2022-23). The Hurricanes play in the PNC Arena, which offers 19,722 seats for basketball, and 18,680 for ice hockey. The team's average home attendance was 19,526 during the 2022-23 season. Notable past players include Ron Francis, Paul Coffey and Mark Recchi. Minor League affiliates include the Chicago Wolves of the American Hockey League (AHL) and the Norfolk Admirals of the ECHL. Forbes estimated the team's value to be $640 million in December 2022.

FINANCIAL DATA: *Note: Data for latest year may not have been available at press time.*

In U.S. $	2022	2021	2020	2019	2018	2017
Revenue	120,250,000					
R&D Expense						
Operating Income						
Operating Margin %						
SGA Expense						
Net Income						
Operating Cash Flow						
Capital Expenditure						
EBITDA						
Return on Assets %						
Return on Equity %						
Debt to Equity						

CONTACT INFORMATION:

Phone: 919-467-7825   Fax: 919-462-7030
Toll-Free:
Address: 1400 Edwards Mill Rd., RBC Center, Raleigh, NC 27607
United States

STOCK TICKER/OTHER:

Stock Ticker: Private
Employees: 300
Parent Company:

Exchange:
Fiscal Year Ends: 06/30

SALARIES/BONUSES:

Top Exec. Salary: $ Bonus: $
Second Exec. Salary: $ Bonus: $

OTHER THOUGHTS:

Estimated Female Officers or Directors: 26
Hot Spot for Advancement for Women/Minorities: Y

Carolina Panthers

www.panthers.com

NAIC Code: 711211C

TYPES OF BUSINESS:

Professional Football Team
Team Management and Operations

BRANDS/DIVISIONS/AFFILIATES:

CONTACTS: *Note: Officers with more than one job title may be intentionally listed here more than once.*

Scott Fitterer, General Mngr.
Mike Anderson, Dir.-Football Oper.
Kristi Coleman, Pres.
Kalen Karahalios, Dir.-Mktg.
Kisha Smith, Chief People Officer
Jake Burns, Chief Commercial Officer
Rob Rogers, Dir.-Team Admin.
Richard M. Thigpen, General Counsel
Brandon Beane, Dir.-Football Oper.
Charlie Dayton, Dir.-Comm.
Ron Rivera, Head Coach
Marty Hurney, Gen. Mgr.-Football Oper.
Dave Gettleman, Gen. Mgr.
Tina Becker, Dir.-Entertainment
Mike Whitehead, CFO

GROWTH PLANS/SPECIAL FEATURES:

The Carolina Panthers is a professional football team based in Charlotte, North Carolina, and plays in the southern conference of the National Football Conference (NFC) of the National Football League (NFL). The team was formed in 1993 as the 29th franchise in the league and the first NFL expansion team since 1976, when former Baltimore Colts receiver Jerry Richardson, the second former player to own an NFL team, bought the franchise for $140 million. Though winning the NFC conference title in 2003 and 2015, the team has yet to clinch a Super Bowl Championship. In total, the Panthers have won six division championships and have made eight playoff appearances. Home games are played in the Bank of America Stadium, an approximately 75,523-seat, privately financed, open-air and natural grass athletic field owned by the city of Charlotte. The team's average home game attendance was 71,351 during the 2022 season. Forbes valued the team at $3.6 billion in August 2022. David A. Tepper has owned the Panthers since 2018.

FINANCIAL DATA: *Note: Data for latest year may not have been available at press time.*

In U.S. $	2022	2021	2020	2019	2018	2017
Revenue	518,700,000					
R&D Expense						
Operating Income						
Operating Margin %						
SGA Expense						
Net Income						
Operating Cash Flow						
Capital Expenditure						
EBITDA						
Return on Assets %						
Return on Equity %						
Debt to Equity						

CONTACT INFORMATION:

Phone: 704-358-7000   Fax: 714-358-7618
Toll-Free:
Address: 800 S. Mint St., Charlotte, NC 28202 United States

STOCK TICKER/OTHER:

Stock Ticker: Private   Exchange:
Employees: 490   Fiscal Year Ends: 12/31
Parent Company:

SALARIES/BONUSES:

Top Exec. Salary: $ Bonus: $
Second Exec. Salary: $ Bonus: $

OTHER THOUGHTS:

Estimated Female Officers or Directors: 3
Hot Spot for Advancement for Women/Minorities: Y

Celtic PLC

NAIC Code: 711211

TYPES OF BUSINESS:
Sports Teams and Clubs

GROWTH PLANS/SPECIAL FEATURES:
Celtic PLC through its subsidiary is engaged in the operation of a professional football club. Business activity of the company includes Football and Stadium Operations, Merchandising, and Multimedia and Other Commercial Activities. The group operates only in the United Kingdom and the majority of revenue for the company is generated from Merchandising and Football and Stadium Operations.

BRANDS/DIVISIONS/AFFILIATES:

CONTACTS: Note: Officers with more than one job title may be intentionally listed here more than once.
Ian Bankier, Chmn.

FINANCIAL DATA: Note: Data for latest year may not have been available at press time.

In U.S. $	2022	2021	2020	2019	2018	2017
Revenue	107,538,100	74,078,000	85,597,810	101,657,500	110,468,000	110,468,000
R&D Expense						
Operating Income	-20,156,000	-24,854,360	-27,495,430	-5,372,334	8,243,754	8,243,754
Operating Margin %	-.19%	-.34%	-.32%	-.05%	.07%	.07%
SGA Expense						
Net Income	7,128,581	-15,357,710	-448,507	10,649,600	8,405,850	8,405,850
Operating Cash Flow	12,709,320	-14,461,910	-4,894,577	-6,252,286	19,496,650	19,496,650
Capital Expenditure	26,325,410	17,199,270	30,082,880	19,412,550	15,388,180	15,388,180
EBITDA	27,199,270	4,034,126	18,848,260	29,067,640	19,954,910	19,954,910
Return on Assets %	.04%	-.09%	.00%	.06%	.07%	.07%
Return on Equity %	.12%	-.22%	-.01%	.15%	.20%	.20%
Debt to Equity	.01%	.04%	0.056	0.066	0.171	0.171

CONTACT INFORMATION:
Phone: 44 8712261888   Fax:
Toll-Free:
Address: Celtic Park, Glasgow, G40 3RE United Kingdom

STOCK TICKER/OTHER:
Stock Ticker: CLTFF   Exchange: PINX
Employees: 841   Fiscal Year Ends: 06/30
Parent Company:

SALARIES/BONUSES:
Top Exec. Salary: $374,725   Bonus: $38,848
Second Exec. Salary: Bonus: $37,706
$261,527

OTHER THOUGHTS:
Estimated Female Officers or Directors:
Hot Spot for Advancement for Women/Minorities:

Charlotte Hornets

NAIC Code: 711211B

www.nba.com/hornets

TYPES OF BUSINESS:

Professional Basketball Team
Team Management and Operations

BRANDS/DIVISIONS/AFFILIATES:

Michael Jordan
Charlotte Bobcats
Hugo the Hornet
Charlotte Honey Bees
Greensboro Swarm

CONTACTS: *Note: Officers with more than one job title may be intentionally listed here more than once.*

Mitch Kupchak, Pres.-Operations & Gen. Mngr.
James R. Jordan, COO
Fred Whitfield, Pres.
Fred Whitfield, Pres.
Seth Bennett, CMO
Curtis Polk, Managing Partner
Jacob Gallagher, Chief Revenue Officer
Bill Duffy, Chief Admin. Officer
Andre Walters, VP-Legal Affairs
Rod Higgins, Pres., Basketball Oper.
B. J. Evans, VP-Comm.
Rich Cho, Gen. Mgr.
Steve Cliforrod, Head Coach
Seth Bennett, Sr. VP-Mktg.
Flavil Hampsten, VP-Ticket Sales & Database Mktg.
Michael Jordan, Chmn.

GROWTH PLANS/SPECIAL FEATURES:

The Charlotte Hornets, which were the Charlotte Bobcats from 2004-2014, are an American professional basketball team that plays in the Southeast division of the Eastern conference within the National Basketball Association (NBA). The franchise was formed in 2003 after former Charlotte franchise, the Charlotte Hornets, relocated to New Orleans for the 2002-03 season. On-court struggles have plagued the club since its establishment, earning only one winning season and posting the worst winning percentage in the NBA during the strike-shortened 2011-12 season. As of the 2014-2015 season, the Charlotte Bobcats became Charlotte Hornets, with Hugo the Hornet being the team's mascot. The team is currently owned by former NBA star Michael Jordan, who became the first former player to own a majority stake in an NBA franchise when he purchased the club for $175 million in 2010. The team plays its home games at the Spectrum Center, an indoor arena in uptown Charlotte, with a seating capacity of 19,077 for NBA games, expandable to 20,200 for college basketball games. Average home game attendance was 17,123 during the 2022-23 season. The Hornets have an official cheerleading squad, the Charlotte Honey Bees, who perform sideline dances as well as center-court dances during games; and maintain an affiliate D-League team, the Greensboro Swarm, which play their home games at the Greensboro Coliseum Fieldhouse. Forbes estimated the Hornets value worth $1.7 billion in October 2022.

FINANCIAL DATA: *Note: Data for latest year may not have been available at press time.*

In U.S. $	2022	2021	2020	2019	2018	2017
Revenue	258,700,000					
R&D Expense						
Operating Income						
Operating Margin %						
SGA Expense						
Net Income						
Operating Cash Flow						
Capital Expenditure						
EBITDA						
Return on Assets %						
Return on Equity %						
Debt to Equity						

CONTACT INFORMATION:

Phone: 704-688-8600   Fax: 704-688-8727
Toll-Free:
Address: 333 E. Trade St., Charlotte, NC 28202 United States

STOCK TICKER/OTHER:

Stock Ticker: Private
Employees: 525
Parent Company:

Exchange:
Fiscal Year Ends: 06/30

SALARIES/BONUSES:

Top Exec. Salary: $ Bonus: $
Second Exec. Salary: $ Bonus: $

OTHER THOUGHTS:

Estimated Female Officers or Directors: 3
Hot Spot for Advancement for Women/Minorities: Y

Chelsea Football Club
NAIC Code: 711211D

www.chelseafc.com

TYPES OF BUSINESS:
Professional Soccer Team
Team Management and Operations

BRANDS/DIVISIONS/AFFILIATES:
Blues Partners Limited

CONTACTS: *Note: Officers with more than one job title may be intentionally listed here more than once.*
Tom Glick, Pres.
David Barnard, Club Sec.
Chris Alexander, Dir.-Oper.
Chris Alexander, Dir.-Finance
Mike Forde, Dir.-Football Oper.
Michael Emenalo, Technical Dir.
Todd Boehly, Chmn.

GROWTH PLANS/SPECIAL FEATURES:
Chelsea Football Club is an English professional soccer club based in west London. Founded in 1905, the team plays in the Premier League, the highest level of the English football league system consisting of 20 clubs. Chelsea is considered one of the best teams in the league, finishing in the top tier for more than a decade. Home games are played at the Stamford Bridge football stadium in Fulham, which holds 40,343 spectators and is owned by Chelsea Pitch Owners plc, a nonprofit organization. Home game attendance averaged 36,424 during the 2022 season. Nationally, Chelsea FC has won six league titles (the latest in 2016-17), eight FA Cups, five League Cups, four FA Community Shields and two Full Members Cup. Abroad, the team has taken home two UEFA (Union of European Football Associations) Cup Winners' Cups, two UEFA Super Cups (most recently in 2021), two UEFA Europa League titles and two UEFA Champions League (most recently in 2020-21). In 2021, Chelsea clenched its first FIFA Club World Cup. Nike is Chelsea's kit manufacturer and Three is its shirt sponsor. Forbes valued Chelsea FC at $3.1 billion in 2022. During 2022, Chelsea Football Club was acquired by Blues Partners Limited.

FINANCIAL DATA: *Note: Data for latest year may not have been available at press time.*

In U.S. $	2022	2021	2020	2019	2018	2017
Revenue	595,000,000	577,206,945	477,894,000	585,894,000	468,570,000	468,570,000
R&D Expense						
Operating Income						
Operating Margin %						
SGA Expense						
Net Income		-15,193,848	44,848,400	-126,701,000	19,791,500	19,791,500
Operating Cash Flow						
Capital Expenditure						
EBITDA						
Return on Assets %						
Return on Equity %						
Debt to Equity						

CONTACT INFORMATION:
Phone: 44-207-915-2900   Fax: 44-20-7381-4831
Toll-Free:
Address: Fulham Rd., Stamford Bridge, London, SW6 1HS United Kingdom

STOCK TICKER/OTHER:
Stock Ticker: Private   Exchange:
Employees: 417   Fiscal Year Ends: 06/30
Parent Company: Blues Partners Limited

SALARIES/BONUSES:
Top Exec. Salary: $ Bonus: $
Second Exec. Salary: $ Bonus: $

OTHER THOUGHTS:
Estimated Female Officers or Directors:
Hot Spot for Advancement for Women/Minorities:

Chicago Bears

www.chicagobears.com

NAIC Code: 711211C

TYPES OF BUSINESS:

Professional Football Team
Team Management and Operations

BRANDS/DIVISIONS/AFFILIATES:

CONTACTS: *Note: Officers with more than one job title may be intentionally listed here more than once.*

Kevin Warren, CEO
Ryan Poles, Gen. Mgr.
Karen Murphy, CFO
Elaine Delos Reyes, Dir.-Fan Research & Mktg.
John Bostrom, VP-Bus. Admin.
Cliff Stein, General Counsel
Geoff Bunzol, Dir.-Team & Building Oper.
Brian J. McCaskey, Sr. Dir.-Bus. Dev.
Scott Hagel, VP-Comm.
Jake Jones, Dir.-Finance
Marc Trestman, Head Coach
Phil Emery, Gen. Mgr.
Caroline Schrenker, Dir.-Community Rel.
George H. McCaskey, Chmn.

GROWTH PLANS/SPECIAL FEATURES:

The Chicago Bears is a team in the National Football League's (NFL) Northern division of its National Football Conference (NFC). In 1919, the A.E. Staley Company of Decatur, Illinois established a football team called the Decatur Staleys. The next year, Staley gave the reigns to George Halas who relocated the team to Chicago, where it became a charter member of the NFL. Halas purchased the rights of the team for $100. By 1922, the team was known as the Chicago Bears. The team has won nine league titles, including Super Bowl XX in 1985. In total, the organization has accrued 28 playoff appearances and 19 division championships. The Bears play home games at historic Soldier Field, located at the edge of Chicago's lakefront. The stadium, owned by the Chicago Park District, was originally completed in 1920 and underwent major renovations in 2003. It now seats approximately 61,500 spectators, and the Bears averaged 59,823per home game attendance during the 2022 season. The Bears have 30 members enshrined in the Pro Football Hall of Fame (an NFL record). Among the franchise's legendary Hall of Fame inductees are Dick Butkus, Walter Payton, Mike Singletary, Dan Hampton, Wilber Marshall and former coach Mike Ditka. Forbes valued the Bears at $5.8 billion in August 2022.

FINANCIAL DATA: *Note: Data for latest year may not have been available at press time.*

In U.S. $	2022	2021	2020	2019	2018	2017
Revenue	550,550,000					
R&D Expense						
Operating Income						
Operating Margin %						
SGA Expense						
Net Income						
Operating Cash Flow						
Capital Expenditure						
EBITDA						
Return on Assets %						
Return on Equity %						
Debt to Equity						

CONTACT INFORMATION:

Phone: 847-295-6600   Fax: 847-295-8986
Toll-Free:
Address: 1920 Football Dr., Lake Forrest, IL 60045 United States

STOCK TICKER/OTHER:

Stock Ticker: Private
Employees: 500
Parent Company:

Exchange:
Fiscal Year Ends: 02/28

SALARIES/BONUSES:

Top Exec. Salary: $ Bonus: $
Second Exec. Salary: $ Bonus: $

OTHER THOUGHTS:

Estimated Female Officers or Directors: 3
Hot Spot for Advancement for Women/Minorities: Y

Sales, profits and employees may be estimates. Financial information, benefits and other data can change quickly and may vary from those stated here.

Chicago Blackhawks

NAIC Code: 711211F

www.nhl.com/blackhawks

TYPES OF BUSINESS:

Professional Hockey Team (NHL)
Team Management and Operations

BRANDS/DIVISIONS/AFFILIATES:

Wirtz Corporation
United Center JV
United Center
Rockford IceHogs
Indy Fuel

CONTACTS: *Note: Officers with more than one job title may be intentionally listed here more than once.*

Danny Wirtz, CEO
Jaime Faulkner, Pres.-Bus. Oper.
Joel Quenneville, Head Coach
Al MacIsaac, VP-Hockey Oper.
W. Rockwell (Rocky) Wirtz, Chmn.

GROWTH PLANS/SPECIAL FEATURES:

The Chicago Blackhawks, founded in 1926, is one of the six original teams to begin playing in the National Hockey League (NHL). The Blackhawks achieved a measure of early success, winning two championships in the 1930s and another title in 1961. The club saw only modest levels of success in subsequent decades, and was unable to make deep runs into the playoffs. The team has since seen a resurgence as new owner Rocky Wirtz took control of the team from his father, Bill Wirtz, and instituted highly successful changes that led to a Stanley Cup victory in the 2009-10 season. Altogether, the team has won six Stanley Cups, four conference championships and 16 division championships. The Blackhawks have some of the best attendance numbers in the league. Currently, United Center JV owns the stadium in which the Blackhawks and the Chicago Bulls play their home games, and each team owns a 50% share in United Center. The Blackhawks averaged 17,167 fans per home game during the 2022-23 season. The team plays in the Central division of the Western conference. The team's roster has featured such famous players as Stan Mikita, Bobby Hull and the Esposito brothers. Blackhawk minor league affiliations include the Rockford IceHogs, an American Hockey League (AHL) team, and the Indy Fuel, an ECHL team. Forbes valued the team at approximately $1.5 billion in December 2022, ranking fourth in the NHL.

FINANCIAL DATA: *Note: Data for latest year may not have been available at press time.*

In U.S. $	2022	2021	2020	2019	2018	2017
Revenue	166,400,000					
R&D Expense						
Operating Income						
Operating Margin %						
SGA Expense						
Net Income						
Operating Cash Flow						
Capital Expenditure						
EBITDA						
Return on Assets %						
Return on Equity %						
Debt to Equity						

CONTACT INFORMATION:

Phone: 312-455-7000   Fax: 312-455-7041
Toll-Free:
Address: 1901 W. Madison St., Chicago, IL 60612 United States

STOCK TICKER/OTHER:

Stock Ticker: Private   Exchange:
Employees: 350   Fiscal Year Ends: 06/30
Parent Company:

SALARIES/BONUSES:

Top Exec. Salary: $ Bonus: $
Second Exec. Salary: $ Bonus: $

OTHER THOUGHTS:

Estimated Female Officers or Directors: 6
Hot Spot for Advancement for Women/Minorities: Y

Chicago Bulls

www.nba.com/bulls

NAIC Code: 711211B

TYPES OF BUSINESS:

Professional Basketball Team
Team Management and Operations

BRANDS/DIVISIONS/AFFILIATES:

United Center JV
United Center
Windy City Bulls

CONTACTS: Note: Officers with more than one job title may be intentionally listed here more than once.

Marc Eversley, Gen. Manager
Michael Reinsdorf, Pres.
Kieran Kelliher, VP-Finance
Susan Goodenow, Exec. VP-Mktg. & Communications
Arturas Karnisovas, Exec. VP-Basketball Oper.
Matt Kobe, Exec. VP-Revenue & Strategy
Irwin Mandel, Sr. VP-Legal
Steve Schanwald, Exec. VP-Bus. Oper.
Jeremy Thum, Dir.-Interactive Mktg.
Susan Goodenow, VP-Comm. & Branding
Irwin Mandel, Sr. VP-Finance
John Paxson, Exec. VP-Basketball Oper.
Stu Bookman, Controller
Tom Thibodeau, Head Coach
Gar Forman, Gen. Mgr.
Jerry Reinsdorf, Chmn.

GROWTH PLANS/SPECIAL FEATURES:

The Chicago Bulls is a professional basketball team playing in the Central division of the Eastern conference of the National Basketball Association (NBA). The Bulls joined the NBA during the 1966-67 season. The team struggled for more than two decades until it signed Michael Jordan, who led the Bulls to six championship titles in eight years, from 1990 to 1993 and from 1995 to 1998. The team became the third franchise in history to garner three consecutive titles. In total, the Bulls have clenched six conference titles and nine division titles (the latest in 2012). Following the departures of Jordan and Scottie Pippen and the losses of Dennis Rodman and former coach Phil Jackson, the Bulls have struggled to return to their former glory. The club's home games are played in the United Center, which seats approximately 20,917 spectators. Currently, United Center JV owns the stadium, and the Chicago Bulls and the Chicago Blackhawks are the joint venture entities that each hold a 50% share. The Bulls' home attendance average during the 2022-23 season was 20,527, the highest in the league. Windy City Bulls is an American professional basketball affiliate of the Chicago Bulls, playing in the NBA G League. Forbes estimated the Chicago Bulls to be worth $4.1 billion in October 2022.

FINANCIAL DATA: Note: Data for latest year may not have been available at press time.

In U.S. $	2022	2021	2020	2019	2018	2017
Revenue	333,450,000					
R&D Expense						
Operating Income						
Operating Margin %						
SGA Expense						
Net Income						
Operating Cash Flow						
Capital Expenditure						
EBITDA						
Return on Assets %						
Return on Equity %						
Debt to Equity						

CONTACT INFORMATION:

Phone: 312-455-4000   Fax: 312-455-4189
Toll-Free:
Address: 1901 W. Madison St., United Center, Chicago, IL 60612-2459
United States

STOCK TICKER/OTHER:

Stock Ticker: Private   Exchange:
Employees: 500   Fiscal Year Ends:
Parent Company:

SALARIES/BONUSES:

Top Exec. Salary: $ Bonus: $
Second Exec. Salary: $ Bonus: $

OTHER THOUGHTS:

Estimated Female Officers or Directors: 38
Hot Spot for Advancement for Women/Minorities: Y

Sales, profits and employees may be estimates. Financial information, benefits and other data can change quickly and may vary from those stated here.

Chicago Cubs

NAIC Code: 711211A

TYPES OF BUSINESS:

Professional Baseball Team
Team Management and Operations

BRANDS/DIVISIONS/AFFILIATES:

Chicago White Stockings
Iowa Cubs
Tennessee Smokies
South Bend Cubs
Myrtle Beach Pelicans

CONTACTS: *Note: Officers with more than one job title may be intentionally listed here more than once.*

Jed Hoyer, Pres.
Jon Greifenkamp, CFO
Colin Faulkner, Exec. VP-Sales & Mktg.
Sara Schultz, Sr. VP-Human Resources
Steve Inman, VP-Technology
Michael Lufrano, General Counsel
Crane Kenney, Pres., Bus. Oper.
Alex Sugarman, Sr. VP-Strategy & Dev.
Julian Green, VP-Comm. & Community Affairs
Theo Epstein, Pres., Baseball Oper.
Jed Hoyer, Exec. VP
Colin Faulkner, VP-Ticket Sales & Partnerships
Jason McLeod, Sr. VP-Scouting & Player Dev.
Tom Ricketts, Chmn.
Patrick Meenan, Dir.-Sourcing & Procurement

GROWTH PLANS/SPECIAL FEATURES:

The Chicago Cubs is one of the oldest franchises within Major League Baseball (MLB). Originally founded in 1871 as the Chicago White Stockings, one of eight charter members of the National League, the club was renamed the Cubs in 1902 by the Chicago Daily Tribune. The Cubs have played home games at famed Wrigley Field since 1916. The ballpark, nicknamed the Friendly Confines, has hosted many unforgettable baseball moments, including Babe Ruth's called shot in the 1932 World Series. In its heyday, the team won the World Series in two consecutive years, in 1907 and 1908, becoming the first team in baseball history to do so. However, the Cubs did not win another World Series since until 2016, when they beat the Cleveland Indians 8-7 in the final game. Other titles encompass 17 national league pennants, six central division titles, two east division titles and three wild card berths. The Chicago Cubs have included such greats as Rogers Hornsby, Ferguson Jenkins, Hack Wilson, Ernie Banks, Mordecai Brown, Ryne Sandberg, Jackie Robinson and Sammy Sosa. The franchise, which was owned by the Wrigley Company from 1921 to 1981, was sold in 1981 to the Tribune Company, publishers of the Chicago Tribune newspaper. In 2009, the club was sold to the family trust of the Ricketts family, including J. Joseph Ricketts, founder of TD Ameritrade, for $900 million. The Cubs averaged 32,305 fans per home game for the 2022 season. In March 2023, Forbes placed the Cubs fourth on its annual list of most valuable MLB teams, with an estimated value of $4.1 billion.

FINANCIAL DATA: *Note: Data for latest year may not have been available at press time.*

In U.S. $	2022	2021	2020	2019	2018	2017
Revenue	582,400,000					
R&D Expense						
Operating Income						
Operating Margin %						
SGA Expense						
Net Income						
Operating Cash Flow						
Capital Expenditure						
EBITDA						
Return on Assets %						
Return on Equity %						
Debt to Equity						

CONTACT INFORMATION:

Phone: 773-404-2827   Fax: 773-404-4129
Toll-Free:
Address: 1060 W. Addison St., Chicago, IL 60613-4397 United States

STOCK TICKER/OTHER:

Stock Ticker: Private   Exchange:
Employees: 585   Fiscal Year Ends: 12/31
Parent Company:

SALARIES/BONUSES:

Top Exec. Salary: $ Bonus: $
Second Exec. Salary: $ Bonus: $

OTHER THOUGHTS:

Estimated Female Officers or Directors: 11
Hot Spot for Advancement for Women/Minorities: Y

Chicago Fire Soccer Club

www.chicagofirefc.com

NAIC Code: 711211D

TYPES OF BUSINESS:

Major League Soccer Team
Team Management and Operations

BRANDS/DIVISIONS/AFFILIATES:

GROWTH PLANS/SPECIAL FEATURES:

Chicago Fire Soccer Club is an American professional soccer club that competes in Major League Soccer, within the Eastern Conference. Other teams in the eastern division include Atlanta United FC, Columbus Crew, FC Cincinnati, D.C. United, Inter Miami CF, Charlotte FC, CF Montreal, New England Revolution, New York City FC, New York Red Bulls, Orlando City SC, Philadelphia Union and Toronto FC. The franchise is named after the Great Chicago Fire of 1871, and was founded in 1997, the event's 126th anniversary. Chicago Fire began playing in 1998, and won the MLS Cup and the U.S. Open Cup that first season. Additional U.S. Open Cups were clinched by Chicago Fire in 2000, 2003 and 2006, as well as the MLS Supporters Shield in 2003. Chicago Fire plays in the Soldier Field in Chicago, Illinois, which has a seating capacity of 61,500, and the team nearly sold out every home game during the 2021-22 season with a 16,947 average. The franchise is owned by Joe Mansueto, who purchased the club in 2019.

CONTACTS:
Note: *Officers with more than one job title may be intentionally listed here more than once.*

Dave Baldwin, Pres.-Bus. Oper.
Pawel Szynalik, CFO
Emily Wondergem, Dir.-Mktg.
Jillian Kozlowski, Human Resources
Gina Fremouw, Dir.-IT
Pawel Szynalik, VP-Admin.
Javier Leon, Pres., Team Oper.
Emigdio Gamboa, VP-Comm.
Pawel Szynalik, VP-Finance
Frank Klopas, Head Coach
Mike Ernst, VP-Ticket Sales & Svcs.
Joe Mansueto, Chmn.

FINANCIAL DATA:
Note: *Data for latest year may not have been available at press time.*

In U.S. $	2022	2021	2020	2019	2018	2017
Revenue	7,426,125					
R&D Expense						
Operating Income						
Operating Margin %						
SGA Expense						
Net Income						
Operating Cash Flow						
Capital Expenditure						
EBITDA						
Return on Assets %						
Return on Equity %						
Debt to Equity						

CONTACT INFORMATION:

Phone: 708-594-7200   Fax: 708-496-6050
Toll-Free:
Address: 1 N. Dearborn St., Ste. 1300, Chicago, IL 60602 United States

STOCK TICKER/OTHER:

Stock Ticker: Private   Exchange:
Employees: Fiscal Year Ends:
Parent Company:

SALARIES/BONUSES:

Top Exec. Salary: $ Bonus: $
Second Exec. Salary: $ Bonus: $

OTHER THOUGHTS:

Estimated Female Officers or Directors: 13
Hot Spot for Advancement for Women/Minorities: Y

Chicago Sky
NAIC Code: 711211E

sky.wnba.com

TYPES OF BUSINESS:
Professional Women's Basketball Team
Team Management and Operations

BRANDS/DIVISIONS/AFFILIATES:

GROWTH PLANS/SPECIAL FEATURES:
Chicago Sky is an American professional basketball team based in Illinois, playing in the Eastern Conference of the Women's National Basketball Association (WNBA). The team is relatively young being founded in 2005. Chicago Sky plays its home games in the Wintrust Arena, which has a seating capacity of more than 10,300. Chicago Sky averaged approximately 7,180 fans in home game attendance during the 2022 season. Other teams within the Eastern Conference include Atlanta Dream, Connecticut Sun, Indiana Fever, New York Liberty and Washington Mystics. Chicago Sky won their first WNBA Championship in 2021 after defeating the Phoenix Mercury 3-1 in the finals. Previously, the team won their first conference title in 2014, but were swept by the Phoenix Mercury in three games. Chicago Sky's team colors are sky blue, yellow, black and white.

CONTACTS: *Note: Officers with more than one job title may be intentionally listed here more than once.*
Adam Fox, CEO
James Wade, Gen. Mngr.
Stephanie Hedrick, CFO
Margaret Stender, Chmn.

FINANCIAL DATA: *Note: Data for latest year may not have been available at press time.*

In U.S. $	2022	2021	2020	2019	2018	2017
Revenue						
R&D Expense						
Operating Income						
Operating Margin %						
SGA Expense						
Net Income						
Operating Cash Flow						
Capital Expenditure						
EBITDA						
Return on Assets %						
Return on Equity %						
Debt to Equity						

CONTACT INFORMATION:
Phone: 312-828-9550   Fax:
Toll-Free: 866-759-9622
Address: 2301 S. Lake Shore Dr., Lakeside Cntr. East Bldg., Chicago, IL 60616 United States

STOCK TICKER/OTHER:
Stock Ticker: Private
Employees:
Parent Company:

Exchange:
Fiscal Year Ends:

SALARIES/BONUSES:
Top Exec. Salary: $ Bonus: $
Second Exec. Salary: $ Bonus: $

OTHER THOUGHTS:
Estimated Female Officers or Directors:
Hot Spot for Advancement for Women/Minorities:

Chicago White Sox

www.mlb.com/whitesox

NAIC Code: 711211A

TYPES OF BUSINESS:
Professional Baseball Team
Team Management and Operations

BRANDS/DIVISIONS/AFFILIATES:
Charlotte Knights
Birmingham Barons
Winston-Salem Dash
Kannapolis Cannon Ballers

CONTACTS: Note: Officers with more than one job title may be intentionally listed here more than once.
Rick Hahn, Gen. Mngr.
Howard Pizer, Sr. Exec. VP
Bill Waters, VP-Finance
Brooks Boyer, CMO
Moira Foy, VP-Human Resources & Risk Mgmt.
Scott Reifert, Sr. VP-Communications
Don Esposito, Sr. Dir.-Construction & Maintenance
Tim Buzard, Sr. VP-Admin.
Allan Muchin, Corp. Counsel
Dan Fabian, Dir.-Baseball Oper.
Bob Grim, Sr. Dir.-Bus. Dev. & Broadcasting
Scott Reifert, Sr. VP-Comm.
Bill Waters, Sr. Dir.-Finance
Howard Pizer, Sr. Exec. VP
Ken Williams, Exec. VP
Rick Hahn, Sr. VP
Terry Savarise, Sr. VP-Stadium Oper.
Jerry Reinsdorf, Chmn.
Don Esposito, Sr. Dir.-Purchasing

GROWTH PLANS/SPECIAL FEATURES:
The Chicago White Sox is a Major League Baseball (MLB) franchise that plays in the American League, Central Division. The team's ballpark is located on the south side of Chicago at Guaranteed Rate Field, a stadium with a 40,615-seat capacity. Home game attendance was 24,704 during the 2022 season. As a charter member of the American League, the White Sox organization was strong during the early part of the 20th century. The ballclub won its first World Series in 1906 over its intra-city rival, the Chicago Cubs. The White Sox also won a World Series in 1917 led by baseball legend Shoeless Joe Jackson. Two years later, the outcome of the World Series was allegedly fixed by gamblers, and the White Sox lost to the Cincinnati Reds. The next year, because of a different game-fixing event, details of the White Sox scandal came to light. Eventually, eight players, including Jackson, were banned from baseball. In the decades following this indignity, the White Sox were a relatively mediocre team, playing in the World Series only once, in 1959. Finally, in 2005, the White Sox won another World Series, its third in 105 years. In total, the franchise has three World Championships, six pennants and six division titles (most recently in 2021). They clenched their first wild card berth in 2020. The team has contributed several players to the National Baseball Hall of Fame, including Luis Aparicio, Luke Appling, Eddie Collins, Charles Comiskey, George Davis, Red Faber, Nellie Fox, Ted Lyons, Ray Schalk, Bill Veeck and Ed Walsh. Forbes valued the White Sox at $2.05 billion in March 2023. Minor league affiliates of the Sox include the Charlotte Knights, Birmingham Barons, Winston-Salem Dash and Kannapolis Cannon Ballers.

FINANCIAL DATA: Note: Data for latest year may not have been available at press time.

In U.S. $	2022	2021	2020	2019	2018	2017
Revenue	352,950,000					
R&D Expense						
Operating Income						
Operating Margin %						
SGA Expense						
Net Income						
Operating Cash Flow						
Capital Expenditure						
EBITDA						
Return on Assets %						
Return on Equity %						
Debt to Equity						

CONTACT INFORMATION:
Phone: 312-674-1000   Fax: 312-924-3296
Toll-Free: 886-769-4263
Address: 333 W. 35th St., Chicago, IL 60616 United States

STOCK TICKER/OTHER:
Stock Ticker: Private
Employees: 585
Parent Company:
Exchange:
Fiscal Year Ends: 10/31

SALARIES/BONUSES:
Top Exec. Salary: $ Bonus: $
Second Exec. Salary: $ Bonus: $

OTHER THOUGHTS:
Estimated Female Officers or Directors: 10
Hot Spot for Advancement for Women/Minorities: Y

Chip Ganassi Racing With Felix Sabates Inc
www.chipganassiracing.com
NAIC Code: 711219

TYPES OF BUSINESS:
Stock Car Racing
Racing Teams
Race Car Operations and Maintenance

BRANDS/DIVISIONS/AFFILIATES:
Chip Ganassi Racing

CONTACTS: *Note: Officers with more than one job title may be intentionally listed here more than once.*
Chip Ganassi, CEO
Felix Sabates, Co-Owner

GROWTH PLANS/SPECIAL FEATURES:
Chip Ganassi Racing With Felix Sabates, Inc. does business as Chip Ganassi Racing (CGR), a leading auto racing operation. Chip Ganassi founded the business in 1990, and purchased a majority stake in Felix Sabates' Team SABCO NASCAR team and merged the operations in 2009. Rob Kauffman purchased a stake in CGR in 2015. Sabates retired from his ownership role after the 2020 season. CGR's teams have clinched 19 total drivers' championships and more than 245 race victories. Driver IndyCar and Indianapolis 500 champions include Jimmy Vasser, Alex Zanardi, Juan Pablo Montoya, Scott Dixon, Dario Franchitti, Alex Palou and Marcus Ericsson (most recent, 2022). Currently, CGR participates in the IndyCar Series, WeatherTech SportsCar Championship, World Endurance Championship and Extreme E. IndyCar race drivers include Marcus Ericsson, Scott Dixon, Alex Palou, Marcus Armstrong (road/street) and Takuma Sato (ovals). WeatherTech drivers include Sebastien Bourdais, Scott Dixon, Renger van der Zande, Earl Bamber, Alex Lynn and Richard Westbrook. FIA World Endurance drivers include Earl Bamber, Alex Lynn, Richard Westbrook, Sebastien Bourdais, Renger van der Zande and Jack Aitken. Extreme E drivers include Amanda Sorensen and R.J. Anderson. CGR's state-of-the-art race shop facility and corporate office are located in Indianapolis, Indiana.

FINANCIAL DATA: *Note: Data for latest year may not have been available at press time.*

In U.S. $	2022	2021	2020	2019	2018	2017
Revenue		9,603,000	9,900,000	45,000,000	49,000,000	49,000,000
R&D Expense						
Operating Income						
Operating Margin %						
SGA Expense						
Net Income				2,000,000	4,000,000	4,000,000
Operating Cash Flow						
Capital Expenditure						
EBITDA						
Return on Assets %						
Return on Equity %						
Debt to Equity						

CONTACT INFORMATION:
Phone: 317-802-0000   Fax:
Toll-Free:
Address: 7777 Woodland Dr., Indianapolis, IN 46278 United States

STOCK TICKER/OTHER:
Stock Ticker: Private   Exchange:
Employees: 80   Fiscal Year Ends:
Parent Company:

SALARIES/BONUSES:
Top Exec. Salary: $ Bonus: $
Second Exec. Salary: $ Bonus: $

OTHER THOUGHTS:
Estimated Female Officers or Directors: 1
Hot Spot for Advancement for Women/Minorities:

Churchill Downs Incorporated

www.churchilldownsincorporated.com

NAIC Code: 713210

TYPES OF BUSINESS:

Horse Racing
Pari-mutuel Wagering
Simulcasting
Live Racing and Wagering
Online Racing and Wagering
Casino Properties
Slot Machines

BRANDS/DIVISIONS/AFFILIATES:

Churchill Downs Racetrack
Derby City Gaming
Oak Grove
Turfway Park
Newport
TwinSpires
Calder Casino and Racing
Lady Luck Casino Nemacolin

CONTACTS: Note: Officers with more than one job title may be intentionally listed here more than once.

William Carstanjen, CEO
Marcia Dall, CFO
R. Rankin, Chairman of the Board
William Mudd, COO
Austin Miller, Senior VP, Divisional

GROWTH PLANS/SPECIAL FEATURES:

Churchill Downs Inc is a gaming entertainment, online wagering, and racing company. It operates through three business segments: Live and Historical Racing, TwinSpires, and Gaming. The Live and Historical Racing segment includes live and historical pari-mutuel racing. The TwinSpires segment includes the revenue and expenses for online horse racing and the online and retail sports betting and iGaming wagering business. The company generates more than half of its revenue from the Gaming segment includes revenue from casino properties and associated racetrack or jai alai facilities which support the casino license as applicable.

FINANCIAL DATA: Note: Data for latest year may not have been available at press time.

In U.S. $	2022	2021	2020	2019	2018	2017
Revenue	1,809,800,000	1,597,200,000	1,054,000,000	1,329,700,000	882,600,000	882,600,000
R&D Expense						
Operating Income	402,200,000	328,000,000	78,700,000	221,000,000	169,700,000	169,700,000
Operating Margin %	.22%	.21%	.07%	.17%	.19%	.19%
SGA Expense	164,200,000	138,500,000	114,800,000	122,000,000	83,500,000	83,500,000
Net Income	439,400,000	249,100,000	-81,900,000	137,500,000	140,500,000	140,500,000
Operating Cash Flow	536,800,000	335,500,000	141,900,000	289,600,000	215,100,000	215,100,000
Capital Expenditure	456,800,000	91,800,000	234,200,000	163,300,000	116,900,000	116,900,000
EBITDA	875,100,000	536,800,000	185,900,000	368,300,000	266,400,000	266,400,000
Return on Assets %	.10%	.09%	-.03%	.06%	.06%	.06%
Return on Equity %	1.02%	.74%	-.19%	.28%	.21%	.21%
Debt to Equity	8.27%	6.39%	4.408	2.892	1.757	1.757

CONTACT INFORMATION:

Phone: 502 636-4400   Fax: 502 636-4560
Toll-Free:
Address: 600 N. Hurstbourne Pkwy., Ste. 400, Louisville, KY 40222 United States

STOCK TICKER/OTHER:

Stock Ticker: CHDN   Exchange: NAS
Employees: 7,000   Fiscal Year Ends: 12/31
Parent Company:

SALARIES/BONUSES:

Top Exec. Salary: $1,500,000   Bonus: $
Second Exec. Salary: Bonus: $
$1,100,000

OTHER THOUGHTS:

Estimated Female Officers or Directors: 1
Hot Spot for Advancement for Women/Minorities:

Cincinnati Bengals

NAIC Code: 711211C

www.bengals.com

TYPES OF BUSINESS:

Professional Football Team
Team Management and Operations

BRANDS/DIVISIONS/AFFILIATES:

CONTACTS: *Note: Officers with more than one job title may be intentionally listed here more than once.*

Steve Johnson, Managing Dir.
Mike Brown, Pres.
Johanna Kappner, CFO
Brian Sells, Chief Business Officer
Emily Parker, Dir.-Communications
Jake Kiser, Sr. Dir.-Technology
Bob Bedinghaus, Dir.-Bus. Dev.
Jack Brennan, Dir.-Public Rel.
Johanna Kappner, Controller
Troy Blackburn, VP
Marvin Lewis, Head Coach
Katie Blackburn, Exec. VP
John Sawyer, VP
Andrew Maxwell, Mngr.-Digital Mktg.

GROWTH PLANS/SPECIAL FEATURES:

The Cincinnati Bengals is a professional football team playing in the American Football Conference (North) of the National Football League (NFL). The Bengals came out of the 1970s with a mediocre 74 wins to 70 losses record. During the 1980s, the team went to the Super Bowl twice, but lost both times to the era's dominant San Francisco 49ers. However, from 1991 to 2004, the team failed to post a winning season. The Bengals held the NFL's worst record throughout the 1990s, ending the decade with an overall record of 52-108. The franchise has won five Northern division titles, 2005, 2009, 2013, 2015 and 2021, and won three Conference championships, with the most recent being in 2021. The Bengals have made a total of 16 playoff appearances (AFC Central and North divisions), with the most recent occurring in 2021 and 2022. During the 2022 season, the Cincinnati Bengals beat the Kansas City Chiefs 34-31 to clench the division, won the playoff game against the Las Vegas Raiders 26-19 in the Wild Card round, advanced to the Super Bowl when Evan McPherson kicked a 33-yard field goal in overtime, but lost in a close game against the Los Angeles Rams in Super Bowl LVI, 23-20. The team plays its home games at Paycor Stadium, is owned by Hamilton County, Ohio, and has a seating capacity of over 65,500. During the 2022 season, the Bengals averaged 66,247 in home game attendance. Paul Brown's son, Mike, currently owns the Bengals. Forbes valued the team at $3 billion in August 2022.

FINANCIAL DATA: *Note: Data for latest year may not have been available at press time.*

In U.S. $	2022	2021	2020	2019	2018	2017
Revenue	484,250,000					
R&D Expense						
Operating Income						
Operating Margin %						
SGA Expense						
Net Income						
Operating Cash Flow						
Capital Expenditure						
EBITDA						
Return on Assets %						
Return on Equity %						
Debt to Equity						

CONTACT INFORMATION:

Phone: 513-621-3550   Fax: 513-621-3570
Toll-Free:
Address: One Paul Brown Stadium, Cincinnati, OH 45202-3418 United States

STOCK TICKER/OTHER:

Stock Ticker: Private   Exchange:
Employees: 160   Fiscal Year Ends: 02/28
Parent Company:

SALARIES/BONUSES:

Top Exec. Salary: $ Bonus: $
Second Exec. Salary: $ Bonus: $

OTHER THOUGHTS:

Estimated Female Officers or Directors: 3
Hot Spot for Advancement for Women/Minorities: Y

Cincinnati Reds

www.mlb.com/reds

NAIC Code: 711211A

TYPES OF BUSINESS:

Professional Baseball Team
Team Management and Operations

BRANDS/DIVISIONS/AFFILIATES:

Louisville Bats
Chattanooga Lookouts
Daytona Dragons
Dayton Tortugas

CONTACTS: *Note: Officers with more than one job title may be intentionally listed here more than once.*

Robert H. Castellini, CEO
Phillip J. Castellini, Pres.
Doug Healy, CFO
Ralph Mitchell, VP-Mktg. & Comm.
Victor Livisay, VP-People & Culture
Brian Keys, Sr. VP-Technology
Lauren Werner, VP-Merch. & Event Svcs.
James A. Marx, General Counsel
Walt Jocketty, Pres., Baseball Oper.
Karen Forgus, Sr. VP-Bus. Oper.
Lisa Braun, Dir.-Digital Media
Rob Butcher, Dir.-Media Rel.
Thomas L. Williams, Treas.
Dick Williams, VP-Baseball Oper.
Bentley Viator, Controller
Sean Brown, Dir.-Ballpark Oper.
Christopher L. Fister, Sec.
W. Joseph Williams, Jr., Chmn.
Bill Bavasi, VP-Scouting, Player Dev. & Int'l Oper.

GROWTH PLANS/SPECIAL FEATURES:

The Cincinnati Reds is a Major League Baseball (MLB) team playing in the Central Division of the National League. Baseball in Cincinnati dates to 1882 with the Cincinnati Red Stockings. The first openly all-professional baseball team, the Red Stockings first game was a 12-3 victory over the St. Louis club. The current Reds franchise is the third Red Stockings incarnation, which began in the American Association in 1882. The club later joined the National League and won its first World Series in 1919, though the Chicago White Sox infamously threw the series. The team rose to some prominence in the 1970s, with a lineup that featured future Hall of Famers Johnny Bench, Joe Morgan and Tony Perez as well as Pete Rose, with a MLB record of 4,256 hits. In all, the franchise has won five World Series (its most recent championship was 1990), nine pennants and 10 division titles (seven western and three central). The Reds clenched a wild card berth in 2013 and 2020. The team has played at the modern, 42,300-seat Great American Ball Park since 2003, and averaged 17,447 fans per home game during the 2022 season. The club's affiliated minor league teams include the Louisville Bats, Chattanooga Lookouts, Daytona Dragons and Daytona Tortugas. In March 2023, Forbes estimated the value of the team at $1.19 billion.

FINANCIAL DATA: *Note: Data for latest year may not have been available at press time.*

In U.S. $	2022	2021	2020	2019	2018	2017
Revenue	352,300,000					
R&D Expense						
Operating Income						
Operating Margin %						
SGA Expense						
Net Income						
Operating Cash Flow						
Capital Expenditure						
EBITDA						
Return on Assets %						
Return on Equity %						
Debt to Equity						

CONTACT INFORMATION:

Phone: 513-765-7000   Fax: 513-765-7048
Toll-Free:
Address: 100 Joe Nuxhall Way, Cincinnati, OH 45202 United States

STOCK TICKER/OTHER:

Stock Ticker: Private   Exchange:
Employees: 570   Fiscal Year Ends: 10/31
Parent Company:

SALARIES/BONUSES:

Top Exec. Salary: $ Bonus: $
Second Exec. Salary: $ Bonus: $

OTHER THOUGHTS:

Estimated Female Officers or Directors: 11
Hot Spot for Advancement for Women/Minorities: Y

Cleveland Browns

NAIC Code: 711211C

www.clevelandbrowns.com

TYPES OF BUSINESS:
Professional Football Team
Team Management and Operations

BRANDS/DIVISIONS/AFFILIATES:

CONTACTS: *Note: Officers with more than one job title may be intentionally listed here more than once.*
Andrew Berry, Gen. Mgr.
David A. Jenkins, COO
Gregory Rush, CFO
Brent Rossi, Sr. VP-Mktg. & Media
Mike Nikolaus, Chief Human Resources Officer
Brandon Covert, VP-IT
Kevin Griffin, VP-Fan Experience & Mktg.
Todd Argust, Dir.-Stadium Oper.
Mike Nikolaus, Dir.-Admin.
Sashi Brown, General Counsel
Phil Dangerfield, Dir.-Oper.
Bryan Wiedmeier, Exec. VP-Strategic Initiatives
Neal Gulkis, VP-Media Rel.
Gregory Rush, Dir.-Finance
Brent Stehlik, Chief Revenue Officer
Michael Lombardi, Gen. Mgr.
Rob Chudzinski, Head Coach
Matt Goodman, VP-Corp. Partnerships
Paul De Podesta, Chief Strategy Officer

GROWTH PLANS/SPECIAL FEATURES:
The Cleveland Browns is a professional football team based in Cleveland, Ohio that plays in the American Football Conference (North) of the National Football League (NFL). The team joined the NFL in 1949, after five years in the short-lived All-American Football Conference. Controversial figure Art Modell purchased the team in 1961 for $4 million. In 1996, Modell announced that he had signed a deal to relocate the Browns to Baltimore for the 1996 season. Over 100 lawsuits were filed by fans, the city of Cleveland and others, and Congress held hearings on the matter. Eventually a settlement was reached that called for Modell's starting a new franchise in Baltimore, and Cleveland retaining the Browns' name, colors, history, awards and archives. The Browns ceased activities from 1996 until 1999. The team plays its home games at the Cleveland Browns Stadium, owned by the City of Cleveland, and averaged 67,431 in home game attendance during the 2022 season, selling out the stadium. In 1998, ownership of the team was sold to Al Lerner for $530 million. When Lerner died in 2002, his 90% stake went to his family. In 2012, the team was sold to Jimmy and Dee Haslam for $1 billion. Over the years, the Browns have sent several players to the Pro Football Hall of Fame, including Jim Brown, Leroy Kelly, Bobby Mitchell, Ozzie Newsome, Paul Warfield and Gene Hickerson. Though the team has made 29 playoff appearances, won 12 division championships and clinched 11 conference championships, it has never reached the Super Bowl. Forbes valued the Cleveland Browns at $3.85 billion in August 2022.

FINANCIAL DATA: *Note: Data for latest year may not have been available at press time.*

In U.S. $	2022	2021	2020	2019	2018	2017
Revenue	523,900,000					
R&D Expense						
Operating Income						
Operating Margin %						
SGA Expense						
Net Income						
Operating Cash Flow						
Capital Expenditure						
EBITDA						
Return on Assets %						
Return on Equity %						
Debt to Equity						

CONTACT INFORMATION:
Phone: 440-891-5000   Fax: 440-891-5009
Toll-Free:
Address: 76 Lou Groza Blvd., Berea, OH 44017 United States

STOCK TICKER/OTHER:
Stock Ticker: Private   Exchange:
Employees: 575   Fiscal Year Ends: 12/31
Parent Company:

SALARIES/BONUSES:
Top Exec. Salary: $ Bonus: $
Second Exec. Salary: $ Bonus: $

OTHER THOUGHTS:
Estimated Female Officers or Directors: 6
Hot Spot for Advancement for Women/Minorities: Y

Cleveland Cavaliers

www.nba.com/cavaliers

NAIC Code: 711211B

TYPES OF BUSINESS:

Professional Basketball Team
Team Management and Operations

BRANDS/DIVISIONS/AFFILIATES:

CONTACTS: *Note: Officers with more than one job title may be intentionally listed here more than once.*

Nic Barlage, CEO
Kolby Altman, Pres.-Bus. Oper.
Len Komoroski, Pres.
Jason Hillman, General Counsel
David Griffin, VP-Basketball Oper.
Tad Carper, Sr. VP-Comm.
Sue Owca, Controller
Byron Scott, Head Coach
Chris Grant, Gen. Mgr.
Antony Bonavita, VP-Facility Oper.
Ron Velazquez, Dir.-Ticket Oper.
Dan Gilbert, Chmn.

GROWTH PLANS/SPECIAL FEATURES:

The Cleveland Cavaliers entered the National Basketball Association (NBA) in 1970 and plays in the Central Division of the Eastern Conference. Although the team has had little success throughout its history, the arrival of Lebron James in 2003 significantly improved franchise records and helped earn the Cavaliers five straight playoff appearances. This was only the second time in the Cavaliers' history that it could make the playoffs for five consecutive seasons, with 1992-96 being the first. However, the loss of James to free agency following the 2009-10 season proved to be a major blow to the franchise, finishing the 2010-11 season with a 19-63 record, including a record 26 game losing streak. In 2014, James opted out of his contract with the Miami Heat, returning to the Cavaliers via a two-year, $42.1 million contract with an option to become a free agent again in 2015. In 2015, the team made the NBA Playoffs, reaching the NBA Championship, but were defeated by the Golden State Warriors 2-4. The following year (2016), the Cavaliers won their first NBA Championship, tackling the Golden State Warriors once again in a tight 4-3 game. The Cavaliers made it to the 2022-23 playoffs with a 108-91 win over the Houston Rockets; but lost in their first playoff round to the New York Knicks four games to one. Home games are played in the Rocket Mortgage FieldHouse, offering a 19,432-basketball-seating capacity; with attendance averaging 19,432 during the 2022-23 season. Former Cavaliers Nate Thurmond, Walt Frazier, Lenny Wilkens, Ben Wallace and Shaquille O'Neal have earned spots in the Basketball Hall of Fame, as well as coach Chuck Daly, Lenny Wilkens and Bill Fitch. Forbes estimated the Cavaliers' value at $2.05 billion in October 2022.

FINANCIAL DATA: *Note: Data for latest year may not have been available at press time.*

In U.S. $	2022	2021	2020	2019	2018	2017
Revenue	312,000,000					
R&D Expense						
Operating Income						
Operating Margin %						
SGA Expense						
Net Income						
Operating Cash Flow						
Capital Expenditure						
EBITDA						
Return on Assets %						
Return on Equity %						
Debt to Equity						

CONTACT INFORMATION:

Phone: 216-420-2000   Fax:
Toll-Free: 888-894-9424
Address: 1 Center Court, Cleveland, OH 44115 United States

STOCK TICKER/OTHER:

Stock Ticker: Private
Employees: 140
Parent Company:

Exchange:
Fiscal Year Ends: 10/31

SALARIES/BONUSES:

Top Exec. Salary: $ Bonus: $
Second Exec. Salary: $ Bonus: $

OTHER THOUGHTS:

Estimated Female Officers or Directors: 14
Hot Spot for Advancement for Women/Minorities: Y

Cleveland Guardians

www.mlb.com/guardians

NAIC Code: 711211A

TYPES OF BUSINESS:

Professional Baseball Team
Team Management and Operations

BRANDS/DIVISIONS/AFFILIATES:

Cleveland Forest Citys
Bluebirds
Cleveland Indians
Columbus Clippers
Akron RubberDucks
Lake County Captains
Lynchburg Hillcats

CONTACTS: *Note: Officers with more than one job title may be intentionally listed here more than once.*

Paul J. Dolan, CEO
Chris Antonetti, Pres.-Baseball Operations
Rich Dorffer, CFO
Alex King, Sr. VP-Mktg. & Brand Strategy
Sara Lehrke, Sr. VP-Human Resources
Keith Woolner, Dir.-Baseball Analytics
Neil Weiss, CIO
Neil Weiss, Sr. VP-Tech.
Karen Fox, Dir.-Merch.
Joe Znidarsic, General Counsel
Jim Folk, VP-Ballpark Oper.
Victor Gregovits, Sr. VP-Bus. Dev. & Sales
Bob DiBiasio, Sr. VP-Public Affairs
Sarah Taylor, Controller
Chris Antonetti, Exec. VP
Andrew Miller, Sr. VP-Strategy & Bus. Analytics
Dennis Lehman, Exec. VP-Bus.
Ross Atkins, VP-Player Dev.
Paul J. Dolan, Chmn.
Ramon Pena, Dir.-Latin American Oper.

GROWTH PLANS/SPECIAL FEATURES:

The Cleveland Guardians are a professional Major League Baseball (MLB) franchise based in Cleveland, Ohio, playing in the Central Division of the American League. The city of Cleveland has been home to professional baseball since 1869, when the team was known as the Cleveland Forest City. In 1901, the club, then known as the Bluebirds, was a charter member of the newly established American League (AL). Over the next several years, the team played under various monikers, but became the Indians following the 1914 season. The team ceased using the name Indians following the 2021 season, and were renamed the Cleveland Guardians for 2022, due to Native American controversy. The franchise was one of the first to play with an integrated team. Before current owner Lawrence Dolan bought the team in 2000, the then Indians were the first publicly traded team in the MLB. The ball club has played in six World Series, winning two (1920 and 1948), and most recently losing to the Chicago Cubs 7-8 in the final game of the 2016 World Series. The Guardians hold ten Central division titles, including 2016, 2017 and 2018. It clenched two wild card berths, in 2013 and 2020. The organization's minor league affiliates include the Columbus Clippers, Akron RubberDucks, Lake County Captains and Lynchburg Hillcats. Progressive Field, home to the Guardians since 1994, is located in downtown Cleveland and features a seating capacity of over 35,000. The team averaged 17,050 in home game attendance during the 2022 season. Forbes estimated the franchise value at $1.3 billion in March 2023.

FINANCIAL DATA: *Note: Data for latest year may not have been available at press time.*

In U.S. $	2022	2021	2020	2019	2018	2017
Revenue	362,050,000					
R&D Expense						
Operating Income						
Operating Margin %						
SGA Expense						
Net Income						
Operating Cash Flow						
Capital Expenditure						
EBITDA						
Return on Assets %						
Return on Equity %						
Debt to Equity						

CONTACT INFORMATION:

Phone: 216-420-4487   Fax: 216-420-4430
Toll-Free:
Address: 2401 Ontario St., Progressive Field, Cleveland, OH 44115 United States

STOCK TICKER/OTHER:

Stock Ticker: Private
Employees: 500
Parent Company:

Exchange:
Fiscal Year Ends: 12/31

SALARIES/BONUSES:

Top Exec. Salary: $ Bonus: $
Second Exec. Salary: $ Bonus: $

OTHER THOUGHTS:

Estimated Female Officers or Directors: 6
Hot Spot for Advancement for Women/Minorities: Y

Club Atletico de Madrid SAD (Atletico Madrid)

en.atleticodemadrid.com
NAIC Code: 711211D

TYPES OF BUSINESS:

Soccer Team
Team Management and Operations

BRANDS/DIVISIONS/AFFILIATES:

GROWTH PLANS/SPECIAL FEATURES:

Club Atletico de Madrid S.A.D. (Atletico Madrid) is a professional football club founded in 1903 and based in Spain, currently playing in the La Liga league. Home games are played at the Estadio Metropolitano stadium, which has a seating capacity of more than 68,000. Domestically, Atletico Madrid has won 11 La Liga titles, 10 Copa del Rey titles, and two Supercopa de Espana titles. Internationally, the club has won one European Cup Winners' Cup, three EUFA Europa League titles, three UEFA Super Cups and one Intercontinental Cup. The team's kit manufacturer is Nike. The club is majority-owned (65.98%) by Atletico HoldCo, with Idan Ofer owning the remainder.

CONTACTS: *Note: Officers with more than one job title may be intentionally listed here more than once.*

Miguel Angel Gil Marin, CEO
Enrique Cerezo, Pres.

FINANCIAL DATA: *Note: Data for latest year may not have been available at press time.*

In U.S. $	2022	2021	2020	2019	2018	2017
Revenue		396,000,000	368,000,000	363,000,000		
R&D Expense						
Operating Income						
Operating Margin %						
SGA Expense						
Net Income		45,000,000	62,000,000	38,000,000		
Operating Cash Flow						
Capital Expenditure						
EBITDA						
Return on Assets %						
Return on Equity %						
Debt to Equity						

CONTACT INFORMATION:

Phone: 34 91 726 0403   Fax:
Toll-Free:
Address: Av. de Luis Aragones 4, Madrid, 28022 Spain

STOCK TICKER/OTHER:

Stock Ticker: Joint Venture   Exchange:
Employees: Fiscal Year Ends:
Parent Company: Atletico HoldCo

SALARIES/BONUSES:

Top Exec. Salary: $ Bonus: $
Second Exec. Salary: $ Bonus: $

OTHER THOUGHTS:

Estimated Female Officers or Directors:
Hot Spot for Advancement for Women/Minorities:

Club de Foot Montreal (CF Montreal)   www.cfmontreal.com

NAIC Code: 711211D

TYPES OF BUSINESS:

Professional Soccer Team
Team Management and Operations

BRANDS/DIVISIONS/AFFILIATES:

GROWTH PLANS/SPECIAL FEATURES:

Club de Foot Montreal, also referred to as CF Montreal is a professional soccer team based in Montreal, Canada. The club played as a member of the North American Soccer League but joined Major League Soccer (MLS) in the 2012 season. CF Montreal competes in the Eastern Conference of the MLS, and were the runners-up in the CONCACAF Champions League in 2014-15, and the champions in the Walt Disney World Pro Soccer Classes in 2013. Nationally, the club has won the Voyageurs Cup 11 times, most recently occurring in 2019 and 2021. The Montreal Impact plays its home games at the Saputo Stadium, which has a 19,619-seating capacity. The soccer club averaged 15,905 in attendance per home game during the 2022 season. A recent Forbes estimate values the team at $168 million.

CONTACTS: *Note: Officers with more than one job title may be intentionally listed here more than once.*

Gabriel Gervais, Pres.
Veronique Fortin, Dir.-Game Day Oper.
John Di Terlizzi, VP-Dev.
Patrick Vallee, Dir.-Comm.
John Papadakis, Controller
Richard Legendre, Exec. VP
Brian Weightman, Dir.-Sales & Service
Stefanie Bureau, Dir.-Mktg.
Joey Saputo, Chmn.

FINANCIAL DATA: *Note: Data for latest year may not have been available at press time.*

In U.S. $	2022	2021	2020	2019	2018	2017
Revenue	66,000,000	6,520,500	5,670,000	27,000,000	26,000,000	26,000,000
R&D Expense						
Operating Income						
Operating Margin %						
SGA Expense						
Net Income				-5,000,000		
Operating Cash Flow						
Capital Expenditure						
EBITDA						
Return on Assets %						
Return on Equity %						
Debt to Equity						

CONTACT INFORMATION:

Phone: 514-328-3668   Fax: 514-328-1287
Toll-Free:
Address: 4750 Sherbrooke Est., Montreal, QC H1V 3S8 Canada

STOCK TICKER/OTHER:

Stock Ticker: Private   Exchange:
Employees: Fiscal Year Ends:
Parent Company:

SALARIES/BONUSES:

Top Exec. Salary: $ Bonus: $
Second Exec. Salary: $ Bonus: $

OTHER THOUGHTS:

Estimated Female Officers or Directors: 2
Hot Spot for Advancement for Women/Minorities:

Club de Futbol America SA de CV (America)

www.clubamerica.com.mx
NAIC Code: 711211D

TYPES OF BUSINESS:

Soccer Team
Team Management and Operations

BRANDS/DIVISIONS/AFFILIATES:

Grupo Televisa SAB
Estadio Azteca

GROWTH PLANS/SPECIAL FEATURES:

Club de Futbol America SA de CV (America) is a professional football club in Mexico, playing in the Liga MX league, the top division of the Mexican football league system. America plays its home games at the Estadio Azteca stadium in Mexico City, with a seating capacity of more than 87,500. Domestically, the club has won 13 Primera Division/Liga MX titles, six Copa Mexico cups and six Campeon de Campeones cups. Internationally, America has won seven CONCACAF Champions' Cups, two Copa Interamericana titles and one CONCACAF Giants Cup. Nike is the team's kit supplier and AT&T is their shirt sponsor. America is owned by Grupo Televisa SAB.

CONTACTS: Note: Officers with more than one job title may be intentionally listed here more than once.

Emilio Azcarraga Jean, Chmn.

FINANCIAL DATA: Note: Data for latest year may not have been available at press time.

In U.S. $	2022	2021	2020	2019	2018	2017
Revenue						
R&D Expense						
Operating Income						
Operating Margin %						
SGA Expense						
Net Income						
Operating Cash Flow						
Capital Expenditure						
EBITDA						
Return on Assets %						
Return on Equity %						
Debt to Equity						

CONTACT INFORMATION:

Phone: 52 55 5015 3700   Fax:
Toll-Free:
Address: Prol. Division del Nte. 3901, Coapa, Ex-Hacienda C, Mexico City, CMX 04850 Mexico

STOCK TICKER/OTHER:

Stock Ticker: Subsidiary
Employees:
Parent Company: Grupo Televisa SAB

Exchange:
Fiscal Year Ends:

SALARIES/BONUSES:

Top Exec. Salary: $ Bonus: $
Second Exec. Salary: $ Bonus: $

OTHER THOUGHTS:

Estimated Female Officers or Directors:
Hot Spot for Advancement for Women/Minorities:

Sales, profits and employees may be estimates. Financial information, benefits and other data can change quickly and may vary from those stated here.

Club de Futbol Monterrey

NAIC Code: 711211D

www.rayados.com

TYPES OF BUSINESS:

Soccer Team
Team Management and Operations

BRANDS/DIVISIONS/AFFILIATES:

Fomento Economico Mexicano SAB de CV
Rayados

GROWTH PLANS/SPECIAL FEATURES:

Club de Futbol Monterrey, nicknamed as Rayados, is a professional football club in Mexico that plays in the Liga MX league, the top tier of Mexican football. Founded in 1945, the team is owned by Fomento Economico Mexicano SAB de CV (FEMSA). Monterey's home games are played at the Estadio BBVA stadium, which comprises a seating capacity of 53,500. Domestically, Monterey has won five Liga MX titles and three Copa MX titles. Internationally, the club has won five CONCACAF Champions League titles (most recently in 2021) and one CONCACAF Cup Winners' Cup. Puma is Monterey's kit manufacturer and Codere is its shirt sponsor.

CONTACTS: Note: Officers with more than one job title may be intentionally listed here more than once.

Manuel Filizola Flores, Chmn.

FINANCIAL DATA: Note: Data for latest year may not have been available at press time.

In U.S. $	2022	2021	2020	2019	2018	2017
Revenue						
R&D Expense						
Operating Income						
Operating Margin %						
SGA Expense						
Net Income						
Operating Cash Flow						
Capital Expenditure						
EBITDA						
Return on Assets %						
Return on Equity %						
Debt to Equity						

CONTACT INFORMATION:

Phone: 81271500   Fax: 81 83879514
Toll-Free:
Address: Av Pablo Livas 2011, Col. LA Pastora, Guadalupe, NL 63820 Mexico

STOCK TICKER/OTHER:

Stock Ticker: Subsidiary   Exchange:
Employees: Fiscal Year Ends:
Parent Company: Fomento Economico Mexicano SAB de CV (FEMSA)

SALARIES/BONUSES:

Top Exec. Salary: $ Bonus: $
Second Exec. Salary: $ Bonus: $

OTHER THOUGHTS:

Estimated Female Officers or Directors:
Hot Spot for Advancement for Women/Minorities:

Club Deportivo Guadalajara SA de CV (Chivas)

www.chivasdecorazon.com.mx/en
NAIC Code: 711211D

TYPES OF BUSINESS:

Soccer Team
Team Management and Operations

BRANDS/DIVISIONS/AFFILIATES:

Grupo Omnilife
Chivas

GROWTH PLANS/SPECIAL FEATURES:

Club Deportivo Guadalajara SA de CV (Chivas) is a professional football club in Mexico, playing in the Liga MX league, the top tier of the Mexican football league system. Founded in 1905, Chivas plays its home games in the Estadio Akron stadium, which has a seating capacity of more than 48,000. Domestically, Chivas has won 12 Primera Division/Liga MX titles, four Copa Mexico cups, seven Campeon de Campeones titles and one SuperCopa MX title. Internationally, the club has won two CONCACAF Champions Cups. Puma is the team's kit provider. Chivas is owned by Grupo Omnilife, a Guadalajara-based multi-level marketing company.

CONTACTS: Note: Officers with more than one job title may be intentionally listed here more than once.

Amaury Vergara, Pres.

FINANCIAL DATA: Note: Data for latest year may not have been available at press time.

In U.S. $	2022	2021	2020	2019	2018	2017
Revenue						
R&D Expense						
Operating Income						
Operating Margin %						
SGA Expense						
Net Income						
Operating Cash Flow						
Capital Expenditure						
EBITDA						
Return on Assets %						
Return on Equity %						
Debt to Equity						

CONTACT INFORMATION:

Phone: 0133 3540 2100   Fax:
Toll-Free:
Address: Inglaterra 3089 Vallarta Poniente, Chapalita, Guadalajara, JAL 44500 Mexico

STOCK TICKER/OTHER:

Stock Ticker: Subsidiary
Employees:
Parent Company: Grupo Omnilife
Exchange:
Fiscal Year Ends:

SALARIES/BONUSES:

Top Exec. Salary: $ Bonus: $
Second Exec. Salary: $ Bonus: $

OTHER THOUGHTS:

Estimated Female Officers or Directors:
Hot Spot for Advancement for Women/Minorities:

Sales, profits and employees may be estimates. Financial information, benefits and other data can change quickly and may vary from those stated here.

Club Universidad Nacional-Asociacion Civil (UNAM/Pumas)

www.pumas.mx
NAIC Code: 711211D

TYPES OF BUSINESS:
Soccer Team
Team Management and Operations

BRANDS/DIVISIONS/AFFILIATES:
Universidad Nacional Autonoma de Mexico
Estadio Olimpico Universitario

GROWTH PLANS/SPECIAL FEATURES:
Club Universidad Nacional-Asociacion Civil (UNAM/Pumas) is a professional football club in Mexico, playing in the Liga MX league, the top tier of the Mexican football league system. Founded in 1954, UNAM/Pumas plays its home games in the Estadio Olimpico Universitario stadium, which has a seating capacity of more than 58,000. Domestically, UNAM/Pumas has won seven Liga MX titles, one Copa MX titles and two Campeon de Campeones titles, Internationally, the club has one three CONCACAF Champions League titles and one Copa Interamericana title.

CONTACTS: *Note: Officers with more than one job title may be intentionally listed here more than once.*
Leopoldo Silva Gutierrez, Pres.
Manuel Jacobo Cadena Lau, Dir.-Oper.
Jose Genaro Montiel Rangel, Dir.-Admin & Finance
Jose Francisco de Dios Gomez, Dir.-Mktg.
Luis Eduardo de Buen Rodriguez, Dir.-Human Resources
Pablo Macedo Angle, Dir.-Social Communication
Miguel Mejia Baron, VP-Sports

FINANCIAL DATA: *Note: Data for latest year may not have been available at press time.*

In U.S. $	2022	2021	2020	2019	2018	2017
Revenue						
R&D Expense						
Operating Income						
Operating Margin %						
SGA Expense						
Net Income						
Operating Cash Flow						
Capital Expenditure						
EBITDA						
Return on Assets %						
Return on Equity %						
Debt to Equity						

CONTACT INFORMATION:
Phone: 0155 55289800   Fax: 0155 55289831
Toll-Free:
Address: Totonacas No. 560, Delegacion Coyoacan, Mexico City, 04300 Mexico

STOCK TICKER/OTHER:
Stock Ticker: Subsidiary   Exchange:
Employees: Fiscal Year Ends:
Parent Company: Universidad Nacional Autonoma de Mexico

SALARIES/BONUSES:
Top Exec. Salary: $ Bonus: $
Second Exec. Salary: $ Bonus: $

OTHER THOUGHTS:
Estimated Female Officers or Directors:
Hot Spot for Advancement for Women/Minorities:

ClubCorp Holdings Inc (Invited)

www.invitedclubs.com

NAIC Code: 713910

TYPES OF BUSINESS:

Golf Courses & Country Clubs
Golf and Country Club Ownership
Golf and Country Club Operations
City Clubs
Stadium Clubs
Virtual Golf Activities
Tennis and Swimming
Food and Beverages

BRANDS/DIVISIONS/AFFILIATES:

Invited
BigShots

CONTACTS: *Note: Officers with more than one job title may be intentionally listed here more than once.*

David Pillsbury, CEO
Robert Morse, Pres.
Andrew Lacko, CFO
Jim Berra, CMO
Sherry Vidal-Brown, Chief People Officer
Brian Koch, CIO
John Beckert, Director
Patrick Droesch, Executive VP, Divisional
Charles Feddersen, Executive VP, Divisional
Andrew Miller, Executive VP, Divisional
Ingrid Keiser, Executive VP, Divisional
Tom Bennison, Chief Development Officer

GROWTH PLANS/SPECIAL FEATURES:

ClubCorp Holdings, Inc. operates under the Invited brand name, and is the owner and operator of golf and country clubs, city clubs and stadium clubs, as well as BigShots Golf virtual entertainment establishments. Invited's golf and country clubs are located in major cities and residential areas and feature private, semi-private and public golf courses and private tennis courts, as well as fitness facilities, swimming pools, splash pads and miniature golf for children at many of the golf and country clubs. They also feature dining experiences with crafted menus and a wide selection of wine and beer. Invited's city clubs are located in influential business districts across the U.S., and typically placed on the top of prominent buildings, where active professionals from diverse backgrounds can connect, share ideas and pursue passions at hosted events. Casual workspaces are also available at the city clubs, as well as private boardrooms equipped for collaborating and offering presentations. Invited's stadium clubs are located on university campuses, and designed to bring alumni, faculty, fans and community to host, connect, work, play and celebrate in a private club setting. Stadium clubs are available on game days as well as throughout the year. BigShots Golf establishments offer a golf entertainment experience via state-of-the-art virtual games and courses, full-service food, sports bars, outdoor patios, miniature golf, private event spaces and climate-controlled tee boxes for every level of player. In addition, Invited specializes in offering entertainment and events at its country club, city and stadium locations, and provides planning and services in regards to entertainment, food and beverages, weddings and more. In late-2022, Invited acquired The Haven Country Club, located in Boylston, Massachusetts.

FINANCIAL DATA: *Note: Data for latest year may not have been available at press time.*

In U.S. $	2022	2021	2020	2019	2018	2017
Revenue	1,100,000,000	892,500,000	850,000,000	1,207,500,000	1,100,000,000	1,100,000,000
R&D Expense						
Operating Income						
Operating Margin %						
SGA Expense						
Net Income						
Operating Cash Flow						
Capital Expenditure						
EBITDA						
Return on Assets %						
Return on Equity %						
Debt to Equity						

CONTACT INFORMATION:

Phone: 972-243-6191   Fax: 972-406-7856
Toll-Free:
Address: 3030 LBJ Freeway, Ste. 500, Dallas, TX 75234 United States

STOCK TICKER/OTHER:

Stock Ticker: Private   Exchange:
Employees: 20,000   Fiscal Year Ends: 12/27
Parent Company: Apollo Global Management LLC

SALARIES/BONUSES:

Top Exec. Salary: $ Bonus: $
Second Exec. Salary: $ Bonus: $

OTHER THOUGHTS:

Estimated Female Officers or Directors: 1
Hot Spot for Advancement for Women/Minorities:

Clube de Regatas do Flamengo

NAIC Code: 711211D

TYPES OF BUSINESS:

Soccer Team
Team Management and Operations

BRANDS/DIVISIONS/AFFILIATES:

CONTACTS: *Note: Officers with more than one job title may be intentionally listed here more than once.*

Rodolfo Landim, Pres.
Rodrigo Tostes Solon de Pontes, VP-Finance
Gustavo Carvalho de Oliveira, VP-Communications & Mktg.
Ricardo Campelo Trevia de Almeida, VP-Admin.

GROWTH PLANS/SPECIAL FEATURES:

Clube de Regatas do Flamengo is a sports club in Brazil, primarily known for their professional football team. Founded in 1895, Flamengo played in the Campeonato Brasileiro Serie A Championship, a top level Brazilian professional league for men's football. Flamengo's home games are played in Estadio Jornalista Mario Filho stadium (Maracana), which comprises a seating capacity of nearly 80,000. Average home game attendance was 54,599 during the 2022 season. The football team has won two FIFA Club World Cups, one Intercontinental Cup, two Copa de Oros, 21 Supercopa Libertadores, 18 Copa Mercosurs, two Recopa Sudamericanas, 10 Copa Sudamericanas, and 94 Copa Libertadores. Adidas is the club's uniform supplier. Flamengo also plays in the Campeonato Carioca, Rio de Janiero's state league, having clenched seven Campeonato Brasileiro Serie A, the 1987 Cpoa Uniao, four Copa do Brasil and 37 Campeonato Carioca. Other types of sports within Club de Regatas do Flamengo have included men's basketball, women's football, women's basketball, rowing, water polo, American football, tennis, esports and more.

FINANCIAL DATA: *Note: Data for latest year may not have been available at press time.*

In U.S. $	2022	2021	2020	2019	2018	2017
Revenue	200,000,000	181,604,324	123,829,456			
R&D Expense						
Operating Income						
Operating Margin %						
SGA Expense						
Net Income		31,461,284	-20,556,182			
Operating Cash Flow						
Capital Expenditure						
EBITDA						
Return on Assets %						
Return on Equity %						
Debt to Equity						

CONTACT INFORMATION:

Phone: 55 21 2159-0100   Fax:
Toll-Free:
Address: Av. Borges de Medeiros, 997, Lagoa, Rio de Janeiro, RJ 22430-041 Brazil

STOCK TICKER/OTHER:

Stock Ticker: Private   Exchange:
Employees: Fiscal Year Ends: 12/31
Parent Company:

SALARIES/BONUSES:

Top Exec. Salary: $ Bonus: $
Second Exec. Salary: $ Bonus: $

OTHER THOUGHTS:

Estimated Female Officers or Directors:
Hot Spot for Advancement for Women/Minorities:

Coleman Company Inc (The)

www.coleman.com

NAIC Code: 339920

TYPES OF BUSINESS:

Camping Equipment
Outdoor Cookware
Lanterns
Fishing & Hunting Apparel
Flotation Equipment
ATV Accessories
Product Design and Manufacturing
Product Marketing and Ecommerce

BRANDS/DIVISIONS/AFFILIATES:

Newell Brands Inc
Coleman
Hyperflame

CONTACTS: *Note: Officers with more than one job title may be intentionally listed here more than once.*

Lori Becker, VP
Robert F. Marcovitch, Pres.
Martin E. Franklin, Chmn.

GROWTH PLANS/SPECIAL FEATURES:

The Coleman Company, Inc., a subsidiary of Newell Brands, Inc., manufactures and markets equipment for outdoor recreational use. Founded in 1905, the firm operates factory outlet stores in select states throughout the U.S., as well as international operations. The Coleman brand offers travel trailers, heating/cooling systems, cameras, binoculars, solar products, apparel, outdoor motors/boats/ATVs/UTVs, luggage, ice chests, grills, stoves, drinkware, cookware, tents, sleeping bags, air beds, cots, lanterns, camping furniture, backpacks, hot water systems, canopies and screen houses, emergency gear, hunting apparel, pet products, insect repellants, sump pumps, watches and more. The firm sells its products online, through Coleman factory outlet stores and through independent retailers to customers in the hiking and tailgating, backyard recreation and family and extreme camping markets. Coleman's patent-pending Hyperflame technology reduces wind exposure to grill flames, eliminating the need for side panels so that larger pots and pans can be used on Coleman-branded stoves. Through Coleman.com, the company offers customers free advice on topics such as selecting the correct gear for their needs, camping, recipes, packing and preparing for a trip and conservation.

FINANCIAL DATA: *Note: Data for latest year may not have been available at press time.*

In U.S. $	2022	2021	2020	2019	2018	2017
Revenue	1,750,000,000	1,716,750,000	1,635,000,000	1,500,000,000	1,300,000,000	1,300,000,000
R&D Expense						
Operating Income						
Operating Margin %						
SGA Expense						
Net Income						
Operating Cash Flow						
Capital Expenditure						
EBITDA						
Return on Assets %						
Return on Equity %						
Debt to Equity						

CONTACT INFORMATION:

Phone: 770-418-7000   Fax:
Toll-Free:
Address: 180 N. Lasalle St., Ste. 700, Chicago, IL 60601-2503 United States

STOCK TICKER/OTHER:

Stock Ticker: Subsidiary
Employees: 3,600
Parent Company: Newell Brands Inc

Exchange:
Fiscal Year Ends: 12/31

SALARIES/BONUSES:

Top Exec. Salary: $ Bonus: $
Second Exec. Salary: $ Bonus: $

OTHER THOUGHTS:

Estimated Female Officers or Directors:
Hot Spot for Advancement for Women/Minorities:

Sales, profits and employees may be estimates. Financial information, benefits and other data can change quickly and may vary from those stated here.

Colorado Avalanche

www.nhl.com/avalanche

NAIC Code: 711211F

TYPES OF BUSINESS:
Professional Hockey Team (NHL)
Team Management and Operations

BRANDS/DIVISIONS/AFFILIATES:
Kroenke Sports & Entertainment
Colorado Avalanche LLC
Quebec Nordiques
Colorado Eagles
Utah Grizzlies

CONTACTS: *Note: Officers with more than one job title may be intentionally listed here more than once.*
Josh Kroenke, Pres.
Charlotte Grahame, VP-Hockey Admin.
Joe Sakic, Exec. VP-Hockey Oper.
E. Stanley Kroenke, Owner

GROWTH PLANS/SPECIAL FEATURES:
The Colorado Avalanche is a Denver, Colorado-based National Hockey League (NHL) hockey team administered by Colorado Avalanche, LLC and owned by Kroenke Sports & Entertainment (KSE). The Avalanche currently plays in the Central division of the Western conference of the NHL. The team originally played as the Quebec Nordiques before it was sold and moved to Denver in 1995. The Avalanche plays its home games at the Ball Arena in Denver, which has a seating capacity of approximately 18,000. The hockey team averaged 17,991 in home game attendance during the 2022 season. In 1996, the Avalanche was the first Colorado sports franchise to ever win a championship; they clenched another Stanley Cup in 2001, and again in 2021-22 when they defeated the Tampa Bay Lightning in six games. Overall, the team has won 12 division titles (most recently in 2020-21 and 2021-22) and three President's Trophies. The Avalanche retired the jersey number of its legendary goalie, Patrick Roy, who played with the team from its inception until 2003. The Avalanche is affiliated with the Colorado Eagles of the American Hockey League (AHL) and the Utah Grizzlies of the ECHL. Forbes estimated the team's value at $860 million in December 2022.

FINANCIAL DATA: *Note: Data for latest year may not have been available at press time.*

In U.S. $	2022	2021	2020	2019	2018	2017
Revenue	119,600,000					
R&D Expense						
Operating Income						
Operating Margin %						
SGA Expense						
Net Income						
Operating Cash Flow						
Capital Expenditure						
EBITDA						
Return on Assets %						
Return on Equity %						
Debt to Equity						

CONTACT INFORMATION:
Phone: 303-405-1100   Fax: 303-575-1920
Toll-Free:
Address: 1000 Chopper Cir., Denver, CO 80204 United States

STOCK TICKER/OTHER:
Stock Ticker: Private   Exchange:
Employees: Fiscal Year Ends: 06/30
Parent Company: Kroenke Sports & Entertainment

SALARIES/BONUSES:
Top Exec. Salary: $ Bonus: $
Second Exec. Salary: $ Bonus: $

OTHER THOUGHTS:
Estimated Female Officers or Directors: 1
Hot Spot for Advancement for Women/Minorities:

Colorado Rapids

www.coloradorapids.com

NAIC Code: 711211D

TYPES OF BUSINESS:

Major League Soccer Team
Team Management and Operations

GROWTH PLANS/SPECIAL FEATURES:

The Colorado Rapids is a professional soccer team based in Denver, Colorado, playing in the Western Conference of the Major League Soccer (MLS) league. E. Stanley Kroenke owns the Rapids through his management team, Kroenke Sports & Entertainment (KSE). Other teams in the western conference include Austin FC, FC Dallas, Houston Dynamo FC, LA Galaxy, Los Angeles FC, Minnesota United FC, Portland Timbers, Real Salt Lake, San Jose Earthquakes, Seattle Sounders FC, Sporting Kansas City, St. Louis City SC and Vancouver Whitecaps FC. The Rapids won their first and only MLS Cup in 2010, defeating FC Dallas 2-1. Home games are played in Dick's Sporting Goods Park, which is owned by the city of Commerce City in Colorado, and is equipped with about 18,060 seats for soccer games and 27,000 for concerts. The Rapids averaged 14,473 in home game attendance during the 2022 season. Forbes valued the Rapids at $350 million in February 2023.

BRANDS/DIVISIONS/AFFILIATES:

Kroenke Sports & Entertainment

CONTACTS: *Note: Officers with more than one job title may be intentionally listed here more than once.*

Padraig Smith, Pres.
Matt Hutchings, COO
Josh Kroenke, Alternate Governor
Jeff Jacobsen, VP-Commercial Oper.
German Sferra, Dir.-Digital Media
David Lindholm, Dir.-Media Rel.
David Burke, Chief Revenue Officer
E. Stanley Kroenke, Owner
Michael Benson, Treas.
Oscar Pareja, Head Coach
Wilmer Cabrera, Asst. Coach
Wayne Brant, Chief Business Officer

FINANCIAL DATA: *Note: Data for latest year may not have been available at press time.*

In U.S. $	2022	2021	2020	2019	2018	2017
Revenue	5,811,750					
R&D Expense						
Operating Income						
Operating Margin %						
SGA Expense						
Net Income						
Operating Cash Flow						
Capital Expenditure						
EBITDA						
Return on Assets %						
Return on Equity %						
Debt to Equity						

CONTACT INFORMATION:

Phone: 303-727-3500   Fax: 303-727-3536
Toll-Free:
Address: 6000 Victory Way, Commerce City, CO 80022 United States

STOCK TICKER/OTHER:

Stock Ticker: Private   Exchange:
Employees: 240   Fiscal Year Ends:
Parent Company: Kroenke Sports & Entertainment

SALARIES/BONUSES:

Top Exec. Salary: $ Bonus: $
Second Exec. Salary: $ Bonus: $

OTHER THOUGHTS:

Estimated Female Officers or Directors: 6
Hot Spot for Advancement for Women/Minorities: Y

Colorado Rockies

NAIC Code: 711211A

www.mlb.com/rockies

TYPES OF BUSINESS:

Professional Baseball Team
Team Management and Operations

BRANDS/DIVISIONS/AFFILIATES:

Albuquerque Isotopes
Hartford Yard Goats
Spokane Indians
Fresno Grizzlies

CONTACTS: *Note: Officers with more than one job title may be intentionally listed here more than once.*

Richard L. Monfort, CEO
Gregory D. Feasel, Pres.
Michael Kent, CFO
Alyssa Bruno, VP-Communications & Mktg.
Kimberly Molina, VP-Human Resources
Mike Bush, Sr. Dir.-Info. Systems
Aaron Heinrich, Dir.-Retail Oper.
James Wiener, Sr. Dir.-Eng. & Facilities
Harold R. Roth, General Counsel
Kevin H. Kahn, VP-Ballpark Oper.
Jay E. Alves, VP-Comm.
Michael J. Kent, VP-Finance
William P. Geivett, Sr. VP-Major League Oper.
Sue Ann McClaren, VP-Ticket Sales, Oper. & Svcs.
Daniel J. O'Dowd, Exec. VP
James P. Kellogg, VP-Community & Retail Oper.
Richard L. Monfort, Chmn.
Gary Lawrence, Sr. Dir.-Purchasing

GROWTH PLANS/SPECIAL FEATURES:

The Colorado Rockies is a Major League Baseball (MLB) team that plays in the West Division of the National League (NL). Established as an expansion franchise in 1993, brothers Charles and Richard Monfort are the current owners of the club. The Rockies play home games at Coors Field located in Denver; an open-air field that seats approximately 47,000 spectators (50,100 standing), the highest altitude stadium in the MLB. The team averaged 32,467 in home game attendance during the 2022 season. Throughout the 1990s, the Rockies set attendance records within the NL, with its 1993 season record of 4,483,350 among the highest in the history of the MLB. Before 2007, the Rockies had only reached the postseason once, in 1995. Some analysts have speculated that this was due to the disparity of playing in a high-altitude, offense-friendly stadium where pitches do not break as much, outfielders have more ground to cover and the ball travels farther. Since 2002, the team has stored game baseballs in a humidor; consequently, offensive production has decreased. In total, the team has clenched five wild card berths in 1995, 2007, 2009, 2017 and 2018. Forbes estimated the Colorado Rockies' value at $1.475 billion in March 2023. Minor league affiliates of the organization include the Albuquerque Isotopes, Hartford Yard Goats, Spokane Indians and Fresno Grizzlies.

FINANCIAL DATA: *Note: Data for latest year may not have been available at press time.*

In U.S. $	2022	2021	2020	2019	2018	2017
Revenue	373,750,000					
R&D Expense						
Operating Income						
Operating Margin %						
SGA Expense						
Net Income						
Operating Cash Flow						
Capital Expenditure						
EBITDA						
Return on Assets %						
Return on Equity %						
Debt to Equity						

CONTACT INFORMATION:

Phone: 303-292-0200   Fax: 303-312-2116
Toll-Free:
Address: 2001 Blake St., Denver, CO 80205-2000 United States

STOCK TICKER/OTHER:

Stock Ticker: Private   Exchange:
Employees: 500   Fiscal Year Ends: 12/31
Parent Company:

SALARIES/BONUSES:

Top Exec. Salary: $ Bonus: $
Second Exec. Salary: $ Bonus: $

OTHER THOUGHTS:

Estimated Female Officers or Directors: 4
Hot Spot for Advancement for Women/Minorities: Y

Columbia Sportswear Company

www.columbia.com

NAIC Code: 424300

TYPES OF BUSINESS:

Apparel and Clothing Brands, Designers, Importers and Distributors
Sports Accessories & Equipment
Footwear
Retail Sales
Bicycles

BRANDS/DIVISIONS/AFFILIATES:

Columbia
Mountain Hardwear
Sorel
prAna
OutDry

GROWTH PLANS/SPECIAL FEATURES:

Columbia Sportswear Co makes outdoor and active-lifestyle apparel, footwear, equipment, and accessories that it sells under four primary brands: Columbia, Sorel, Mountain Hardwear, and prAna. The majority of sales are in the United States, but the company also has significantÂ sales in its three other geographic segments: Latin American and Asia-Pacific; Europe, Middle East, and Africa; and Canada. The majority ofÂ sales are through wholesale channels, including sporting goods and department stores, but the company also operates its own branded stores in each of its geographic segments. Columbia sources products from around the world and uses contract manufacturers outside the United States, predominantly in Asia, to manufacture its products.

Columbia offers its employees comprehensive health benefits, retirement option, disability coverage and employee assistance programs.

CONTACTS: Note: Officers with more than one job title may be intentionally listed here more than once.

Timothy Boyle, CEO
Jim Swanson, CFO
Peter Bragdon, Chief Administrative Officer
Joseph Boyle, Executive VP, Divisional
Franco Fogliato, Executive VP, Divisional
Lisa Kulok, Executive VP
Douglas Morse, Senior VP, Divisional

FINANCIAL DATA: Note: Data for latest year may not have been available at press time.

In U.S. $	2022	2021	2020	2019	2018	2017
Revenue	3,464,152,000	3,126,402,000	2,501,554,000	3,042,478,000	2,466,105,000	2,466,105,000
R&D Expense						
Operating Income	428,704,000	450,504,000	137,049,000	394,971,000	262,969,000	262,969,000
Operating Margin %	.12%	.14%	.05%	.13%	.11%	.11%
SGA Expense	1,304,394,000	1,180,323,000	1,098,948,000	1,136,186,000	910,894,000	910,894,000
Net Income	311,440,000	354,108,000	108,013,000	330,489,000	105,123,000	105,123,000
Operating Cash Flow	-25,241,000	354,406,000	276,077,000	285,452,000	341,128,000	341,128,000
Capital Expenditure	58,467,000	34,744,000	28,758,000	123,516,000	53,352,000	53,352,000
EBITDA	546,103,000	566,075,000	283,650,000	516,696,000	327,108,000	327,108,000
Return on Assets %	.10%	.12%	.04%	.12%	.05%	.05%
Return on Equity %	.16%	.19%	.06%	.19%	.07%	.07%
Debt to Equity	.16%	.16%	0.193	0.201		

CONTACT INFORMATION:

Phone: 503 985-4000   Fax:
Toll-Free: 800-622-6953
Address: 14375 NW Science Park Dr., Portland, OR 97229 United States

STOCK TICKER/OTHER:

Stock Ticker: COLM
Employees: 9,450
Parent Company:

Exchange: NAS
Fiscal Year Ends: 12/31

SALARIES/BONUSES:

Top Exec. Salary: $1,000,169   Bonus: $
Second Exec. Salary: $465,231   Bonus: $100,000

OTHER THOUGHTS:

Estimated Female Officers or Directors: 5
Hot Spot for Advancement for Women/Minorities: Y

Sales, profits and employees may be estimates. Financial information, benefits and other data can change quickly and may vary from those stated here.

Columbus Blue Jackets

NAIC Code: 711211F

www.nhl.com/bluejackets

TYPES OF BUSINESS:

Professional Hockey Team (NHL)
Team Management and Operations

BRANDS/DIVISIONS/AFFILIATES:

Cleveland Monsters
Kalamazoo Wings

CONTACTS: *Note: Officers with more than one job title may be intentionally listed here more than once.*

John P. McConnell, Governor
Mike Priest, Pres.
T. J. LaMendola, CFO
Kathryn Dobbs, CMO
Becky Magaw, VP-Human Resources
Jim Connolly, Dir.-IT
Todd Richards, Head Coach
Cameron Scholvin, COO

GROWTH PLANS/SPECIAL FEATURES:

The Columbus Blue Jackets is a National Hockey League (NHL) team that entered the league as an expansion team in 2000. John P. McConnell owns the Blue Jackets via JMAC Hockey, LLC. The Columbus Blue Jackets play in the Metropolitan division of the Eastern conference, alongside the Carolina Hurricanes, New Jersey Devils, New York Islanders, New York Rangers, Philadelphia Flyers, Pittsburgh Penguins and Washington Capitals. The team has yet to win a championship, including a division championship. Home games are played in the Nationwide Arena, which is also home to Arena Football League's Columbus Destroyers, with a seating capacity of 18,500 for hockey games, 19,500 for basketball games and 20,000 for concerts. The Blue Jackets' average attendance was 16,860 during the 2023 season. Nationwide is one of the very few arenas in the NHL that has an ice rink (Ice Haus) used for practice, which is attached to the arena where the team plays home games. Ice Haus also offers ice time for figure skating, youth hockey and public skating. Minor league affiliates include the Cleveland Monsters, an American Hockey League (AHL) team; and Kalamazoo Wings of the ECHL. In December 2022, Forbes estimated the Blue Jackets' value at $620 million.

FINANCIAL DATA: *Note: Data for latest year may not have been available at press time.*

In U.S. $	2022	2021	2020	2019	2018	2017
Revenue	112,450,000					
R&D Expense						
Operating Income						
Operating Margin %						
SGA Expense						
Net Income						
Operating Cash Flow						
Capital Expenditure						
EBITDA						
Return on Assets %						
Return on Equity %						
Debt to Equity						

CONTACT INFORMATION:

Phone: 614-246-4625   Fax: 614-246-4007
Toll-Free:
Address: 200 W. Nationwide Blvd., Suite Level, Columbus, OH 43215
United States

STOCK TICKER/OTHER:

Stock Ticker: Private
Employees:
Parent Company:

Exchange:
Fiscal Year Ends: 06/30

SALARIES/BONUSES:

Top Exec. Salary: $ Bonus: $
Second Exec. Salary: $ Bonus: $

OTHER THOUGHTS:

Estimated Female Officers or Directors: 29
Hot Spot for Advancement for Women/Minorities: Y

Columbus Crew

www.columbuscrew.com

NAIC Code: 711211D

TYPES OF BUSINESS:

Major League Soccer Team
Team Management and Operations

BRANDS/DIVISIONS/AFFILIATES:

GROWTH PLANS/SPECIAL FEATURES:

The Columbus Crew is a founding member of North America's Major League Soccer (MLS). The team is currently owned by Dee and Jimmy Haslam, JW and Whitney Johnson and Dr. Pete Edwards. Columbus Crew plays in the Eastern Conference of the MLS, along with Atlanta United FC, Charlotte FC, Chicago Fire FC, FC Cincinnati, DC United, Inter Miami CF, CF Montreal, Nashville SC, New England Revolution, New York City FC, New York Red Bulls, Orlando City SC, Philadelphia Union and Toronto FC. Home games are played at Lower.com Field, with has a seating capacity of over 20,300. Columbus Crew averaged 19,237 in attendance per home game in the 2022-23 season. The team has won the MLS Cup twice, in 2008 and 2020, and has won three Supporters' Shield titles and one U.S. Open Cup title.

CONTACTS: Note: Officers with more than one job title may be intentionally listed here more than once.

Tim Bezbatchenko, Pres.
Kristin Bernert, Pres.-Bus. Oper.
Molly Zaluski, Sr. Dir.-Mktg. & Events
Tom Patton, VP-Admin.
Andrew Arthurs, VP-Soccer Bus. Dev.
Alex Caulfield, Sr. Dir.-Comm.
Tom Patton, VP-Finance
John Wagner, Pres., Hunt Sports
Tucker Walther, Dir.-Team Oper.
Robert Warzycha, Head Coach
Chris Previte, VP-Corp. Partnerships
Clark Beacom, VP-Ticket Sales

FINANCIAL DATA: Note: Data for latest year may not have been available at press time.

In U.S. $	2022	2021	2020	2019	2018	2017
Revenue	7,389,900					
R&D Expense						
Operating Income						
Operating Margin %						
SGA Expense						
Net Income						
Operating Cash Flow						
Capital Expenditure						
EBITDA						
Return on Assets %						
Return on Equity %						
Debt to Equity						

CONTACT INFORMATION:

Phone: 614-447-2739   Fax: 614-447-4109
Toll-Free:
Address: 1 Black & Gold Blvd., Columbus, OH 43211 United States

STOCK TICKER/OTHER:

Stock Ticker: Private   Exchange:
Employees: 230   Fiscal Year Ends:
Parent Company:

SALARIES/BONUSES:

Top Exec. Salary: $ Bonus: $
Second Exec. Salary: $ Bonus: $

OTHER THOUGHTS:

Estimated Female Officers or Directors: 4
Hot Spot for Advancement for Women/Minorities: Y

Comcast Corporation

corporate.comcast.com

NAIC Code: 517110

TYPES OF BUSINESS:

Cable Television
VoIP Service
Cable Network Programming
High-Speed Internet Service
Video-on-Demand
Advertising Services
Streaming TV Programming
Wireless Services

BRANDS/DIVISIONS/AFFILIATES:

Sky Limited
XFINITY
Universal Pictures
Sky News
Sky Sports
Philadelphia Flyers
Universal Studios
Peacock

CONTACTS: *Note: Officers with more than one job title may be intentionally listed here more than once.*

Jeffrey Shell, CEO, Subsidiary
David Watson, CEO, Subsidiary
Brian Roberts, CEO
Michael Cavanagh, CFO
Daniel Murdock, Chief Accounting Officer
Adam Miller, Chief Administrative Officer
Thomas Reid, Chief Legal Officer
Sheldon Bonovitz, Director Emeritus

GROWTH PLANS/SPECIAL FEATURES:

Comcast is made up of three parts. The core cable business owns networks capable of providing television, internet access, and phone services to roughly 61 million U.S. homes and businesses, or nearly half of the country. About 55% of the homes in this territory subscribe to at least one Comcast service. Comcast acquired NBCUniversal from General Electric in 2011. NBCU owns several cable networks, including CNBC, MSNBC, and USA, the NBC broadcast network, several local NBC affiliates, Universal Studios, and several theme parks. Sky, acquired in 2018, is the dominant television provider in the U.K. and has invested heavily in exclusive and proprietary content to build this position. Sky is also the largest pay-television provider in Italy and has a presence in Germany and Austria.

FINANCIAL DATA: *Note: Data for latest year may not have been available at press time.*

In U.S. $	2022	2021	2020	2019	2018	2017
Revenue	121,427,000,000	116,385,000,000	103,564,000,000	108,942,000,000	85,029,000,000	85,029,000,000
R&D Expense						
Operating Income	22,624,000,000	20,817,000,000	17,493,000,000	21,125,000,000	18,018,000,000	18,018,000,000
Operating Margin %	.19%	.18%	.17%	.19%	.21%	.21%
SGA Expense	8,506,000,000	7,695,000,000	6,741,000,000	7,617,000,000	6,519,000,000	6,519,000,000
Net Income	5,370,000,000	14,159,000,000	10,534,000,000	13,057,000,000	22,735,000,000	22,735,000,000
Operating Cash Flow	26,413,000,000	29,146,000,000	24,737,000,000	25,697,000,000	21,261,000,000	21,261,000,000
Capital Expenditure	13,767,000,000	12,057,000,000	11,634,000,000	12,428,000,000	11,155,000,000	11,155,000,000
EBITDA	27,001,000,000	37,178,000,000	31,753,000,000	34,516,000,000	28,569,000,000	28,569,000,000
Return on Assets %	.02%	.05%	.04%	.05%	.12%	.12%
Return on Equity %	.06%	.15%	.12%	.17%	.37%	.37%
Debt to Equity	1.15%	.96%	1.114	1.182	0.866	0.866

CONTACT INFORMATION:

Phone: 215 286-1700   Fax:
Toll-Free: 800-266-2278
Address: One Comcast Center, Philadelphia, PA 19103 United States

STOCK TICKER/OTHER:

Stock Ticker: CMCSA   Exchange: NAS
Employees: 186,000   Fiscal Year Ends: 12/31
Parent Company:

SALARIES/BONUSES:

Top Exec. Salary: $3,249,415   Bonus: $
Second Exec. Salary: Bonus: $
$2,500,000

OTHER THOUGHTS:

Estimated Female Officers or Directors: 16
Hot Spot for Advancement for Women/Minorities: Y

Connecticut Sun

sun.wnba.com

NAIC Code: 711211E

TYPES OF BUSINESS:

Women's Basketball Team
Team Management and Operations

BRANDS/DIVISIONS/AFFILIATES:

Mohegan Tribal Gaming Authority
Mohegan Sun Casino
Mohegan Sun Arena

CONTACTS: Note: Officers with more than one job title may be intentionally listed here more than once.

Jennifer Rizzotti, Pres.
Krista May, Dir.-Mktg.
April Paris, Dir.-Box Office Oper.
Bill Tavares, Mgr.-Media Rel. & Community Rel.
Anne Donovan, Head Coach
Chris Sienko, VP
Brennan Galloway, Mgr.-Game Oper.
Lisa White, Strength & Conditioning Coach
Darius Taylor, Gen. Mngr.

GROWTH PLANS/SPECIAL FEATURES:

The Connecticut Sun is a Women's National Basketball Association (WNBA) team. After joining the WNBA in 2002, the team came to Connecticut from Florida as the result of a 2003 buy-out by the Mohegan Tribal Gaming Authority, well-known for operating one of the world's largest gaming facilities, the Mohegan Sun Casino. Thus, Connecticut Sun is named after the casino, along with its home stadium, the Mohegan Sun Arena, a 9,323-seat facility located on the casino grounds. During the 2022 season, the Sun averaged 5,712 in home game attendance. The franchise does not share its market with an NBA (National Basketball Association) team and is not owned by an NBA team owner. The Connecticut Sun plays in the WNBA's Eastern Conference, alongside the Atlanta Dream, Chicago Sky, Indiana Fever, New York Liberty and Washington Mystics. The team has won three Conference Finals (2004, 2005 and 2022), but have yet to win a championship title in the WNBA Finals. The Sun's jersey sponsor is Frontier Communications.

FINANCIAL DATA: Note: Data for latest year may not have been available at press time.

In U.S. $	2022	2021	2020	2019	2018	2017
Revenue						
R&D Expense						
Operating Income						
Operating Margin %						
SGA Expense						
Net Income						
Operating Cash Flow						
Capital Expenditure						
EBITDA						
Return on Assets %						
Return on Equity %						
Debt to Equity						

CONTACT INFORMATION:

Phone: 860-862-4000   Fax: 860-862-4010
Toll-Free: 877-786-8499
Address: 1 Mohegan Sun Blvd., Uncasville, CT 06382-1355 United States

STOCK TICKER/OTHER:

Stock Ticker: Private   Exchange:
Employees: Fiscal Year Ends: 09/30
Parent Company: Mohegan Tribal Gaming Authority

SALARIES/BONUSES:

Top Exec. Salary: $ Bonus: $
Second Exec. Salary: $ Bonus: $

OTHER THOUGHTS:

Estimated Female Officers or Directors: 8
Hot Spot for Advancement for Women/Minorities: Y

Converse Inc

NAIC Code: 424340

www.converse.com

TYPES OF BUSINESS:
Footwear Distribution
Athletic Apparel
Retail Stores
Manufacturing
Ecommerce

BRANDS/DIVISIONS/AFFILIATES:
Nike Inc
Chuck Taylor All Star Classic

CONTACTS: *Note: Officers with more than one job title may be intentionally listed here more than once.*
G. Scott Uzzell, CEO
Keith Gulla, Mgr.-Communications

GROWTH PLANS/SPECIAL FEATURES:
Converse, Inc., a wholly owned subsidiary of Nike, Inc., is a leading designer and producer of casual shoes and sports apparel. The company, headquartered in Massachusetts, is most famous for its iconic Chuck Taylor All Star canvas basketball shoes. The company has sold nearly a billion pairs of this model of shoe alone. The shoe was introduced in 1917, and was the only high-performance basketball shoe mass-produced for over 50 years. Currently, Converse manufactures footwear, apparel and accessories for men, women and children. Footwear include high top, low top, mid top, platform, slip on and boot styles. The Chuck Taylor All Star Classic is among the company's best-selling footwear. Clothing consists of tops, tees, hoodies, sweatshirts, pants, shorts and jackets; and accessories include various bags, backpacks, sunglasses, socks, hats and shoelaces. Through the Converse website, customers can create custom shoes, such as choosing colors, materials and patterns, as well as details such as patches, laces and text. Aside from direct product sales, the firm also generates revenues by licensing its name to third-party sports apparel manufacturers. Converse has retail stores located throughout the U.S., as well as internationally.

Converse offers its employees life and health insurance packages, and financial health/savings plans.

FINANCIAL DATA: *Note: Data for latest year may not have been available at press time.*

In U.S. $	2022	2021	2020	2019	2018	2017
Revenue	2,227,000,000	2,205,000,000	1,846,000,000	1,906,000,000	2,042,000,000	2,042,000,000
R&D Expense						
Operating Income						
Operating Margin %						
SGA Expense						
Net Income						
Operating Cash Flow						
Capital Expenditure						
EBITDA						
Return on Assets %						
Return on Equity %						
Debt to Equity						

CONTACT INFORMATION:
Phone: 617-248-9530   Fax:
Toll-Free:
Address: 1 Lovejoy Wharf, Boston, MA 02114 United States

STOCK TICKER/OTHER:
Stock Ticker: Subsidiary   Exchange:
Employees: 2,531   Fiscal Year Ends: 05/31
Parent Company: Nike Inc

SALARIES/BONUSES:
Top Exec. Salary: $ Bonus: $
Second Exec. Salary: $ Bonus: $

OTHER THOUGHTS:
Estimated Female Officers or Directors:
Hot Spot for Advancement for Women/Minorities:

Corporacion Interamericana de Entretenimiento SA

www.cie.com.mx
NAIC Code: 711300

TYPES OF BUSINESS:

Live Events
Gambling

BRANDS/DIVISIONS/AFFILIATES:

GROWTH PLANS/SPECIAL FEATURES:

Corporacion Interamericana de Entretenimiento SAB de CV is a Mexico-based company engaged in the business of providing entertainment services in Latin America and worldwide. It offers a wide Range of entertainment options to a variety of audiences and budgets in large- and medium-sized cities. Its services include concerts, theatrical productions, sporting events, family events and cultural events, among others. In addition, it operates an amusement park in Colombia.

CONTACTS:
Note: Officers with more than one job title may be intentionally listed here more than once.

Luis Alejandro Soberon Kuri, CEO
Luis Alejandro Soberon Kuri, Chmn.

FINANCIAL DATA:
Note: Data for latest year may not have been available at press time.

In U.S. $	2022	2021	2020	2019	2018	2017
Revenue		240,292,000	80,341,140	621,387,600	528,259,900	528,259,900
R&D Expense						
Operating Income		14,373,880	-53,192,780	76,038,640	53,172,940	53,172,940
Operating Margin %		.06%	-.66%	.12%	.10%	.10%
SGA Expense		25,554,120	14,173,280	16,389,280	16,467,020	16,467,020
Net Income		306,204,800	-82,810,820	-13,770,430	-6,397,671	-6,397,671
Operating Cash Flow		-75,720,540	25,044,290	64,586,150	134,092,400	134,092,400
Capital Expenditure				31,196,250	28,404,180	28,404,180
EBITDA		34,132,290	-38,532,440	123,923,500	75,538,570	75,538,570
Return on Assets %		.49%	-.14%	-.02%	-.01%	-.01%
Return on Equity %		1.49%	-.89%	-.10%	-.04%	-.04%
Debt to Equity		.02%	3.066	1.222	0.795	0.795

CONTACT INFORMATION:

Phone: 52 552019000   Fax: 52 552019384
Toll-Free:
Address: Av. Industria Militar S/N, Mexico DF, 11600 Mexico

STOCK TICKER/OTHER:

Stock Ticker: CIEB   Exchange: MEX
Employees: 5,152   Fiscal Year Ends: 12/31
Parent Company:

SALARIES/BONUSES:

Top Exec. Salary: $ Bonus: $
Second Exec. Salary: $ Bonus: $

OTHER THOUGHTS:

Estimated Female Officers or Directors:
Hot Spot for Advancement for Women/Minorities:

Cox Communications Inc

NAIC Code: 517110

www.cox.com/aboutus/home.html

TYPES OF BUSINESS:

Cable TV Service and Internet Access
Broadband
Internet
TV
Streaming
Smart Home
Security
Telephone Service

BRANDS/DIVISIONS/AFFILIATES:

Cox Enterprises Inc

GROWTH PLANS/SPECIAL FEATURES:

Cox Communications, Inc., a subsidiary of Cox Enterprises, Inc., is a broadband communications and entertainment company, serving millions of customers throughout the U.S. Cox Communications' products and services include internet, TV, streaming, smart home, security, home phone and bundled deals. The company serves both residential and business customers, with business solutions also including security systems, networking, collaboration and cloud services. Cox Business solutions primarily serve the education, healthcare, government, hospitality and wireless carrier industries.

Cox offers its employees comprehensive health care, a 401(k), continuing education and professional development funds and other benefits.

CONTACTS: Note: Officers with more than one job title may be intentionally listed here more than once.

Mark Greatrex, Pres.
Colleen Langner, COO
Perley McBride, CFO
Sujata Gosalia, Chief Strategy Officer
Karen Bennett, Chief People Officer
Len Barlik, CTO
Len Barlik, Exec. VP-Prod. Mgmt. & Dev.
Asheesh Saksena, Chief Strategy Officer
Joseph J. Rooney, Sr. VP-Social Media, Advertising & Brand Mktg.
William (Bill) J. Fitzsimmons, Chief Acct. Officer
Philip G. Meeks, Sr. VP-Cox Bus.
Jennifer W. Hightower, Sr. VP-Law & Policy
David Pugliese, Sr. VP-Product Mktg.
Mark A. Kaish, Sr. VP-Tech. Oper.
George Richter, VP-Supply Chain Mgmt.

FINANCIAL DATA: Note: Data for latest year may not have been available at press time.

In U.S. $	2022	2021	2020	2019	2018	2017
Revenue	13,800,000,000	13,104,000,000	12,600,000,000	12,300,000,000	11,550,000,000	11,550,000,000
R&D Expense						
Operating Income						
Operating Margin %						
SGA Expense						
Net Income						
Operating Cash Flow						
Capital Expenditure						
EBITDA						
Return on Assets %						
Return on Equity %						
Debt to Equity						

CONTACT INFORMATION:

Phone: 404-843-5000   Fax: 404-843-5939
Toll-Free: 888-566-7751
Address: 6205-B Peachtree Dunwoody Rd. NE, Atlanta, GA 30328 United States

STOCK TICKER/OTHER:

Stock Ticker: Subsidiary   Exchange:
Employees: 18,000   Fiscal Year Ends: 12/31
Parent Company: Cox Enterprises Inc

SALARIES/BONUSES:

Top Exec. Salary: $ Bonus: $
Second Exec. Salary: $ Bonus: $

OTHER THOUGHTS:

Estimated Female Officers or Directors: 3
Hot Spot for Advancement for Women/Minorities: Y

Crested Butte Mountain Resort Inc

www.skicb.com

NAIC Code: 713920

TYPES OF BUSINESS:

Ski Resort
Real Estate
Restaurants
Year-Round Activities
Zipline
Hiking

BRANDS/DIVISIONS/AFFILIATES:

Vail Resorts Inc
Evolution Bike Park
Plaza (The)
Lodge at Mountaineer Square (The)
Grand Lodge Crested Butte Hotel & Suites (The)

CONTACTS: *Note: Officers with more than one job title may be intentionally listed here more than once.*

Bill Rock, Corp. Pres.-Mountain Division
Tim Mueller, Pres.

GROWTH PLANS/SPECIAL FEATURES:

Crested Butte Mountain Resort, Inc. is a ski resort located at Mount Crested Butte in Gunnison County, Colorado. The resort is open year-round with amenities and terrain for activities such as skiing, snowboarding, mountain biking and hiking. During winter, Crested Butte offers runs for every type of skier. During summer, downhill and cross-country mountain bikers enjoy Evolution Bike Park, a network of lift-served riding for all levels of mountain bikers. Crested Butte offers bike lessons, providing customized beginner, intermediate and advanced lessons so that riders can either improve riding skills or improve time on the hill. The company also offers lift-served hiking, chairlift rides, zipline tours, archery courses, disc golf, fishing, 4WD tours, horseback riding rafting and backcountry adventure tours. Lodging establishments include The Plaza, a condominium just 100 yards from the main Silver Queen quad lift, with elevators, restaurant, bar, daily housekeeping, covered parking and two hot tubs; The Lodge at Mountaineer Square, located in the base area and steps away from the ski lifts, hiking and biking as well as shopping and restaurants; and The Grand Lodge Crested Butte Hotel & Suites, featuring oversized hotel rooms and suites to accommodate all types of travelers. Crested Butte Mountain Resort is owned by Vail Resorts, Inc.

FINANCIAL DATA: *Note: Data for latest year may not have been available at press time.*

In U.S. $	2022	2021	2020	2019	2018	2017
Revenue						
R&D Expense						
Operating Income						
Operating Margin %						
SGA Expense						
Net Income						
Operating Cash Flow						
Capital Expenditure						
EBITDA						
Return on Assets %						
Return on Equity %						
Debt to Equity						

CONTACT INFORMATION:

Phone: 877-547-5143   Fax: 970-349-2250
Toll-Free: 800-810-7669
Address: 12 Snowmass Rd., Mt. Crested Butte, CO 81225 United States

STOCK TICKER/OTHER:

Stock Ticker: Subsidiary   Exchange:
Employees: 200   Fiscal Year Ends:
Parent Company: Vail Resorts Inc

SALARIES/BONUSES:

Top Exec. Salary: $ Bonus: $
Second Exec. Salary: $ Bonus: $

OTHER THOUGHTS:

Estimated Female Officers or Directors:
Hot Spot for Advancement for Women/Minorities:

Cruzeiro Esporte Clube

www.cruzeiro.com.br

NAIC Code: 711211D

TYPES OF BUSINESS:

Soccer Team
Team Management and Operations

BRANDS/DIVISIONS/AFFILIATES:

Estadio Governador Magalhaes Pinto

CONTACTS: *Note: Officers with more than one job title may be intentionally listed here more than once.*

Sergio Santos Rodrigues, Pres.

GROWTH PLANS/SPECIAL FEATURES:

Cruzeiro Esporte Clube is a sports club in Brazil that competes in various sports, but is primarily known for its association football team. Cruzeiro plays in the Campeonato Brasileiro Serie A, the first tier of the Brazilian football league system, as well as in the Campeonato Mineiro, the state of Minas Gerais' premier state league. The club was founded in 1921 by a combination of sportsmen from Italy, some were members of Yale Atletico Clube and some were Italian immigrant workers. Home games are played in the Mineirao (officially Estadio Governador Magalhaes Pinto), which has a seating capacity of nearly 62,000. Cruzeiro won the Campeonato Brasileiro Serie B championship in 2022, moving the team up into the Serie A league again for the 2023 season. Regionally, Cruzeiro has won two Copa Sul-Minas titles, one Copa Centro-Oeste title, a Supercampeonato Mineiuro title and more than 35 Campeonato Mineiro titles, among others. Nationally, the club has won four Campeonato Brasileiro Serie A titles and six Copa do Brasil titles. Internationally, Cruzeiro has won two Copa Libertadores de America titles, two Supercopa Sudamerica titles, and one each of Copa Ouro, Recopa Sul-Americana and Copa Master de Supercopa championships. The team's kit supplier is Adidas, and its sponsor is Betfair. Other sports Cruzeiro Esporte Clube is engaged in includes basketball, volleyball and eSports.

FINANCIAL DATA: *Note: Data for latest year may not have been available at press time.*

In U.S. $	2022	2021	2020	2019	2018	2017
Revenue						
R&D Expense						
Operating Income						
Operating Margin %						
SGA Expense						
Net Income						
Operating Cash Flow						
Capital Expenditure						
EBITDA						
Return on Assets %						
Return on Equity %						
Debt to Equity						

CONTACT INFORMATION:

Phone: 5531 3195 6946　　　　Fax:
Toll-Free:
Address: Av. Dos Andradas, 3000 Santa Efigenia, Belo Horizonte, MG 30260-070 Brazil

STOCK TICKER/OTHER:

Stock Ticker: Private　　　　　　　　Exchange:
Employees:　　　　　　　　　　　　Fiscal Year Ends:
Parent Company:

SALARIES/BONUSES:

Top Exec. Salary: $　　　　Bonus: $
Second Exec. Salary: $　　　Bonus: $

OTHER THOUGHTS:

Estimated Female Officers or Directors:
Hot Spot for Advancement for Women/Minorities:

Curves NA

NAIC Code: 713940

TYPES OF BUSINESS:

Fitness Centers
Circuit Training
Franchise
Nutrition
Fitness Coaching
Online Fitness
Mobile App

BRANDS/DIVISIONS/AFFILIATES:

MyCurves On Demand
Cuves On the Go

CONTACTS: *Note: Officers with more than one job title may be intentionally listed here more than once.*

Krishea Holloway, Pres.
Jeff Burchfield, VP-Legal
Diane Heavin, Publisher-DIANE Magazine

GROWTH PLANS/SPECIAL FEATURES:

Curves NA operates a leading chain of fitness centers for women, with more than 200 franchise locations throughout the U.S., as well as locations in Canada, Australia and New Zealand. Curves is famous for its 30-minute circuit that works every major muscle group with strength training, cardio and stretching, and there is always a coach on hand to help members with proper form, to answer questions and to offer encouragement. Founded in 1992, each Curves fitness and weight-loss facility is designed specifically for women. Curves offers personalized weight loss and weight management solutions that includes the Curves fitness program, a customizable meal plan and one-on-one coaching and support. Higher intensity programs include cardio and boxing, and lower intensity programs cover body basics and balance for creating a strong core. MyCurves On Demand is a 30-minute total body online platform for working out at home or while traveling, etc. Curves On the Go is a mobile, pop-up style workout program for all fitness levels, combining low and high intensity moves in circuit style format.

FINANCIAL DATA: *Note: Data for latest year may not have been available at press time.*

In U.S. $	2022	2021	2020	2019	2018	2017
Revenue		24,211,200	40,352,000	41,600,000	43,000,000	43,000,000
R&D Expense						
Operating Income						
Operating Margin %						
SGA Expense						
Net Income						
Operating Cash Flow						
Capital Expenditure						
EBITDA						
Return on Assets %						
Return on Equity %						
Debt to Equity						

CONTACT INFORMATION:

Phone: 254-399-9285   Fax:
Toll-Free:
Address: 100 Ritchie Rd., Woodway, TX 76712 United States

STOCK TICKER/OTHER:

Stock Ticker: Private   Exchange:
Employees: 2,100   Fiscal Year Ends: 12/31
Parent Company:

SALARIES/BONUSES:

Top Exec. Salary: $ Bonus: $
Second Exec. Salary: $ Bonus: $

OTHER THOUGHTS:

Estimated Female Officers or Directors:
Hot Spot for Advancement for Women/Minorities:

Dallas Cowboys

www.dallascowboys.com

NAIC Code: 711211C

TYPES OF BUSINESS:

Professional Football Team
Team Management and Operations

BRANDS/DIVISIONS/AFFILIATES:

CONTACTS: *Note: Officers with more than one job title may be intentionally listed here more than once.*

Jerry Jones, Pres.
Stephen Jones, COO
Charlotte Jones, Chief Brand Officer
Jerry Jones, Jr., Chief Sales & Mktg. Officer
Jason Garrett, Head Coach
Charlotte Jones Anderson, Exec. VP-Brand Mgmt.

GROWTH PLANS/SPECIAL FEATURES:

The Dallas Cowboys, owned by businessman Jerry Jones, is a professional football team that plays in the National Football Conference (East) of the National Football League (NFL). Based in Texas, the franchise was started in 1960. Legendary Cowboys quarterback Roger Staubach, after throwing a desperation touchdown pass in the fourth quarter with only seconds left to wide receiver Drew Pearson in 1975, introduced the term Hail Mary pass, describing the play at a press conference. Along with Staubach, the Cowboys bench has included other Hall of Famers, such as running back Tony Dorsett; quarterback Troy Aikman, one of only a handful of players in NFL history to have led a team to three Super Bowl victories; the team's first head coach Tom Landry, who had the third most wins in NFL history; and the first president and general manager, Tex Schramm, from 1959 to 1989. The Cowboys have gone to 10 Super Bowls and won five, including three in four years: back-to-back in 1992 and 1993, and again in 1995. The team has 24 division championships, with 2021 being the most recent. Since 2009, the Cowboys have played their home games in AT&T Stadium, which is owned by the city of Arlington, Texas. The stadium is designed to fit up to 105,000 for larger events. During the 2022-23 season, average home game attendance for the Dallas Cowboys was 93,465. In August 2022, Forbes valued the Cowboys franchise at $8 billion, ranking first in the NFL.

FINANCIAL DATA: *Note: Data for latest year may not have been available at press time.*

In U.S. $	2022	2021	2020	2019	2018	2017
Revenue	1,170,000,000					
R&D Expense						
Operating Income						
Operating Margin %						
SGA Expense						
Net Income						
Operating Cash Flow						
Capital Expenditure						
EBITDA						
Return on Assets %						
Return on Equity %						
Debt to Equity						

CONTACT INFORMATION:

Phone: 972-556-9900   Fax: 972-556-9304
Toll-Free:
Address: 1 Cowboys Way, Frisco, TX 75034 United States

STOCK TICKER/OTHER:

Stock Ticker: Private   Exchange:
Employees: 1,000   Fiscal Year Ends: 02/28
Parent Company:

SALARIES/BONUSES:

Top Exec. Salary: $ Bonus: $
Second Exec. Salary: $ Bonus: $

OTHER THOUGHTS:

Estimated Female Officers or Directors: 1
Hot Spot for Advancement for Women/Minorities:

Dallas Mavericks

www.mavs.com

NAIC Code: 711211B

TYPES OF BUSINESS:

Professional Basketball Team
Team Management and Operations

BRANDS/DIVISIONS/AFFILIATES:

CONTACTS: *Note: Officers with more than one job title may be intentionally listed here more than once.*

Cynthia Marshal, CEO
Floyd Jahner, COO
Terdema Ussery, II, Pres.
Matt Wojciechowski, CFO
Iris Diaz, CMO
Tarsha LaCour, Sr. VP-Human Resources
David Herr, CTO
Steve Letson, VP-Oper. & Arena Dev.
Sarah Melton, Dir.-Basketball Comm.
Ronnie Fauss, Controller
George Killebrew, Sr. VP-Corp. Sponsorships
Donn Nelson, Pres., Basketball Oper.
Rick Carlisle, Head Coach

GROWTH PLANS/SPECIAL FEATURES:

The Dallas Mavericks, a National Basketball Association (NBA) team, was formed in 1980 following the departure of the Dallas Chaparrals to San Antonio, Texas. The Mavericks play in the American Airlines Center, which is owned by the city of Dallas and has a capacity of over 21,140 with standing room. The team averaged 20, 177 in home game attendance during the 2022-23 season. The Mavericks are part of the Southwest division of the Western conference, and has one NBA Finals championship (2010-11 season), two conference championships, four division titles and several playoff appearances. The organization is unique in that it is probably as well known for the flamboyant antics of billionaire owner Mark Cuban as for the team's players. Cuban bought the team from Ross Perot, Jr. in 2000 for $280 million and has been a highly visible member of the franchise ever since, sitting in the bleachers with fans and repeatedly racking up enormous fines for fighting with referees, NBA officials and opposing team members (he is also known for matching many of his fines with charitable contributions). Dallas Mavericks Basketball Hall of Famers include Alex English, Adrian Dantley and Dennis Rodman, and more recently Jason Kidd (inducted in 2018), Steve Nash (2018), Tim Hardaway (2022) and Dirk Nowitzki (2023). Forbes estimated the team to be worth $23.3 billion in October 2022.

FINANCIAL DATA: *Note: Data for latest year may not have been available at press time.*

In U.S. $	2022	2021	2020	2019	2018	2017
Revenue	341,900,000					
R&D Expense						
Operating Income						
Operating Margin %						
SGA Expense						
Net Income						
Operating Cash Flow						
Capital Expenditure						
EBITDA						
Return on Assets %						
Return on Equity %						
Debt to Equity						

CONTACT INFORMATION:

Phone: 214-747-6287   Fax: 214-752-3860
Toll-Free:
Address: 2909 Taylor St., The Pavilion, Dallas, TX 75226 United States

STOCK TICKER/OTHER:

Stock Ticker: Private   Exchange:
Employees: 400   Fiscal Year Ends: 06/30
Parent Company:

SALARIES/BONUSES:

Top Exec. Salary: $ Bonus: $
Second Exec. Salary: $ Bonus: $

OTHER THOUGHTS:

Estimated Female Officers or Directors: 25
Hot Spot for Advancement for Women/Minorities: Y

Dallas Stars

NAIC Code: 711211F

www.nhl.com/stars

TYPES OF BUSINESS:

Professional Hockey Team (NHL)
Team Management and Operations

BRANDS/DIVISIONS/AFFILIATES:

Texas Stars
Idaho Steelheads

CONTACTS: *Note: Officers with more than one job title may be intentionally listed here more than once.*

Brad Alberts, CEO
Tom Gaglardi, Governor
Therese Baird, CFO
Joanne Lovato, VP-Mktg.
Lindsay Dowdy, Sr. VP-Human Resources
Matthew Keller, VP-Technology
Toni May, VP-Admin.
Lindy Ruff, Head Coach
James R. Lites, Chmn.

GROWTH PLANS/SPECIAL FEATURES:

The Dallas Stars are a Dallas, Texas-based National Hockey League (NHL) team. The team plays at the American Airlines Center, which offers 19,200 basketball seats; and averaged 18,371 in attendance per home game during the 2022-23 season. The Stars play in the Central division of the Western conference along with the Arizona Coyotes, Chicago Blackhawks, Colorado Avalanche, Minnesota Wild, Nashville Predators, St. Louis Blues and Winnipeg Jets. The franchise was founded in 1967 as the Minnesota North Stars, was relocated to Dallas in 1993 and renamed the Dallas Stars by then-owner Norm Green. Today, the Stars are owned by Canadian businessman Tom Gaglardi. The team clenched its first and only Stanley Cup in the 1998-99 season; and has three conference championships, two President's Trophies and eight division championships. The team maintains minor league affiliations Texas Stars in the American Hockey League (AHL), and the Idaho Steelheads in the ECHL. In December 2022, Forbes listed the club's value at $925 million.

FINANCIAL DATA: *Note: Data for latest year may not have been available at press time.*

In U.S. $	2022	2021	2020	2019	2018	2017
Revenue	142,350,000					
R&D Expense						
Operating Income						
Operating Margin %						
SGA Expense						
Net Income						
Operating Cash Flow						
Capital Expenditure						
EBITDA						
Return on Assets %						
Return on Equity %						
Debt to Equity						

CONTACT INFORMATION:

Phone: 214-387-5500   Fax: 214-387-5610
Toll-Free:
Address: 2601 Ave. of the Stars, Frisco, TX 75034 United States

STOCK TICKER/OTHER:

Stock Ticker: Private   Exchange:
Employees: 275   Fiscal Year Ends: 06/30
Parent Company:

SALARIES/BONUSES:

Top Exec. Salary: $ Bonus: $
Second Exec. Salary: $ Bonus: $

OTHER THOUGHTS:

Estimated Female Officers or Directors: 4
Hot Spot for Advancement for Women/Minorities: Y

Dallas Wings

wings.wnba.com

NAIC Code: 711211E

TYPES OF BUSINESS:
Women's Professional Basketball Team
Team Management and Operations

BRANDS/DIVISIONS/AFFILIATES:

GROWTH PLANS/SPECIAL FEATURES:
The Dallas Wings is a Women's National Basketball Association (WNBA) team. The team, originally named the Detroit Shock (1998) and based in Detroit, Michigan, was moved to Tulsa, Oklahoma at the end of the 2009 season. In October 2015, the Shock moved to Arlington, Texas for the 2016 season and changed its named to the Dallas Wings. The team plays in the WNBA's Western conference alongside the Los Angeles Sparks, Las Vegas Aces, Minnesota Lynx, Phoenix Mercury and Seattle Storm. Dallas Wings' home court is the College Park Center located at The University of Texas at Arlington, which seats up to 7,000 spectators. The team averaged 3,788 in attendance during the 2022 season. The Dallas Wings won Conference titles in 2003, 2006, 2007 and 2008, and three WNBA Championship titles (2003, 2006 & 2008).

CONTACTS:
Note: Officers with more than one job title may be intentionally listed here more than once.

Greg Bibb, CEO
Amber Cox, COO
Christal Mallard, VP-Finance & Accounting
Andy Esworthy, VP-Broadcasting & Communications
Leah Babbitt, VP-Human Resources
Travis Charles, VP-Basketball Oper.
Aimee Cooper, Manager-Public Rel. & Comm. Rel.
Gary Kloppenburg, Head Coach
Emily Fergason, Manager-Game Entertainment & Social Media
Marlene Livaudais, Dir.-Partnerships
Carrie Kmetzo, Dir.-Ticket Sales & Services
Bill Cameron, Chmn.

FINANCIAL DATA:
Note: Data for latest year may not have been available at press time.

In U.S. $	2022	2021	2020	2019	2018	2017
Revenue						
R&D Expense						
Operating Income						
Operating Margin %						
SGA Expense						
Net Income						
Operating Cash Flow						
Capital Expenditure						
EBITDA						
Return on Assets %						
Return on Equity %						
Debt to Equity						

CONTACT INFORMATION:
Phone: 817-469-9464   Fax:
Toll-Free:
Address: 500 E. Border St., Ste. 250, Arlington, TX 76010 United States

STOCK TICKER/OTHER:
Stock Ticker: Private
Employees: 51
Parent Company:

Exchange:
Fiscal Year Ends: 12/31

SALARIES/BONUSES:
Top Exec. Salary: $ Bonus: $
Second Exec. Salary: $ Bonus: $

OTHER THOUGHTS:
Estimated Female Officers or Directors: 7
Hot Spot for Advancement for Women/Minorities: Y

DAZN Group Limited

davzngroup.com

NAIC Code: 515210

TYPES OF BUSINESS:

Sports Streaming Service
Sports Streaming Platform
Subscription Services
Live and On-Demand Streaming
Pay-Per-View Services
Sports Betting
Ecommerce

BRANDS/DIVISIONS/AFFILIATES:

Access Industries Inc
DAZN
DAZN Boxing.io
DAZN Moments
DAZN Store
DAZN Pay-Per-View
DAZN Bet
Eleven Group

CONTACTS: *Note: Officers with more than one job title may be intentionally listed here more than once.*

Shay Segev, CEO
Darren Waterman, CFO
Pete Oliver Jones, CMO
Sandeep Tiku, CTO
Kevin Mayer, Chmn.

GROWTH PLANS/SPECIAL FEATURES:

DAZN Group Limited is a British sports media company that operates DAZN, a global sports subscription streaming platform. Created by fans, for fans, the platform offers affordable access to sports content 24/7, with both live and on-demand programming covering more than 25,000 events per year. DAZN is available on most internet-connected devices, including smart TVs, smartphones, tablets, PCs, game consoles, streaming sticks and set-top boxes. The service is available across more than 200 countries and territories worldwide. DAZN Group acquires rights to sporting events via multi-year global relationships. DAZN offers BAZN Boxing.io (beta) and DAZN Moments, each of which are NFT marketplaces; DAZN Store, which first launched in Germany in 2022 and scheduled to expand to all markets, offering related merchandise; DAZN Pay-Per-View, allowing customers to access and pay for single blockbuster events without being a monthly subscriber; and DAZN Bet, a partnership with Pragmatic Group to create recreational betting product. DAZN Group is owned by Access Industries, Inc. In early-2023, DAZN Group acquired Eleven Group and social media creative agency Team Whistle. Eleven enhances DAZN's local services and sports rights in several territories, including Belgium, Portugal and Taiwan. Team Whistle is part of Eleven, and gives DAZN access to 700 million followers across social channels and access to new online audiences.

FINANCIAL DATA: *Note: Data for latest year may not have been available at press time.*

In U.S. $	2022	2021	2020	2019	2018	2017
Revenue	1,000,000,000	906,709,440	871,836,000	819,055,000	591,681,000	591,681,000
R&D Expense						
Operating Income						
Operating Margin %						
SGA Expense						
Net Income			-1,304,939,000	-1,435,108,000	-499,525,000	-499,525,000
Operating Cash Flow						
Capital Expenditure						
EBITDA						
Return on Assets %						
Return on Equity %						
Debt to Equity						

CONTACT INFORMATION:

Phone: 44 7970 169 554   Fax:
Toll-Free:
Address: 12 Hammersmith Grove, London, W6 7AP United Kingdom

STOCK TICKER/OTHER:

Stock Ticker: Subsidiary   Exchange:
Employees: Fiscal Year Ends: 12/31
Parent Company: Access Industries Inc

SALARIES/BONUSES:

Top Exec. Salary: $ Bonus: $
Second Exec. Salary: $ Bonus: $

OTHER THOUGHTS:

Estimated Female Officers or Directors:
Hot Spot for Advancement for Women/Minorities:

DC United

www.dcunited.com

NAIC Code: 711211D

TYPES OF BUSINESS:
Major League Soccer Team
Team Management and Operations

BRANDS/DIVISIONS/AFFILIATES:
DC United Holdings
Black-and-Red

CONTACTS: Note: Officers with more than one job title may be intentionally listed here more than once.

Danita Johnson, Pres.-Bus. Oper.
Dan Franceschini, Sr. VP-Finance
Lisa Franklin, CMO
Sara Lee, Head-People & Culture
Zach Abaie, VP-Communications & Content
Nathan Fry, Dir.-Merch.
Azhar Zaky, Team Admin. Coordinator
Jason Amaguana, Dir.-Oper.
Mike Achoenbrun, VP-Bus. Dev. & Partnerships
Rebecca Payne, Mgr.-Advertising & Digital Comm.
Aprile Pritchet, Dir.-Community Rel.
Andy Skorupski, Sr. Accountant
Dave Kasper, Gen. Mgr.
Ben Olsen, Head Coach
Drew Bentley, VP-Bus. Strategy & Analytics

GROWTH PLANS/SPECIAL FEATURES:

D.C. United is a Major League Soccer (MLS) team based in Washington, D.C. Nicknamed the Black-and-Red, the team is owned and operated by D.C. United Holdings and plays its home games at the soccer-specific, 20,000-seat Audi Field. Average home game attendance was 16,256 for the 2022 season. D.C. United is a member of the Eastern Conference along with Atlanta United FC, Charlotte FC, Chicago Fire FC, FC Cincinnati, Columbus Crew, Inter Miami CF, CF Montreal, Nashville SC, New England Revolution, New York City FC, New York Red Bulls, Orlando City SC, Philadelphia Union and Toronto FC. Since the MLS's inception in 1996, the team has been a dominant force, winning domestic and international championships, including four MLS Cups, four Supporters Shields and three US Open Cup titles. It started this run by winning the 1996 MLS Cup after which the team won the 1996 U.S. Open Cup, the first-ever double in U.S. soccer history. D.C. United then went on to win the 1997 MLS Cup; 1998 CONCACAF Champions Cup, their first international tournament win and the first time an American club team had won a continental championship; the 1998 Inter-American Cup against Brazil, who was the current South American champion; and the 1999 MLS Cup. After its 1999 win, the team struggled through a string of poor seasons during which it changed head coaches and dealt with national team call-ups of key players. In 2004, the team defeated the Kansas City Wizards (now Sporting Kansas City) to capture its fourth MLS Cup. Statista estimated the value of the team at $700 million in early-2023.

FINANCIAL DATA: Note: Data for latest year may not have been available at press time.

In U.S. $	2022	2021	2020	2019	2018	2017
Revenue	13,173,300					
R&D Expense						
Operating Income						
Operating Margin %						
SGA Expense						
Net Income						
Operating Cash Flow						
Capital Expenditure						
EBITDA						
Return on Assets %						
Return on Equity %						
Debt to Equity						

CONTACT INFORMATION:
Phone: 202-655-2842   Fax:
Toll-Free:
Address: 100 Potomac Ave. SW, Washington, DC 20024 United States

STOCK TICKER/OTHER:
Stock Ticker: Private   Exchange:
Employees: 340   Fiscal Year Ends:
Parent Company:

SALARIES/BONUSES:
Top Exec. Salary: $ Bonus: $
Second Exec. Salary: $ Bonus: $

OTHER THOUGHTS:
Estimated Female Officers or Directors: 6
Hot Spot for Advancement for Women/Minorities: Y

Delaware North Companies Inc

www.delawarenorth.com

NAIC Code: 722310

TYPES OF BUSINESS:

Food Service Contractors
Hospitality Services
Entertainment Venue and Airport Concessions
Restaurant and Catering Services
Retail Stores
Casino and Gaming Concessions
Sport Stadium, Ballpark and Arena Hospitality Services
Airport Restaurants and Retail Stores

BRANDS/DIVISIONS/AFFILIATES:

Boston Holdings
TD Garden
Patina Restaurant Group

CONTACTS: *Note: Officers with more than one job title may be intentionally listed here more than once.*

Jerry Jacobs Jr., Co-CEO
Lou Jacobs, Co-CEO
Charlie Jacobs, Co-CEO
Todd Merry, CMO
Heather Jacobs, Chief Human Resources Officer
Jeff Wilkinson, CIO
Rajat Shah, General Counsel
Nate Brunner, VP-Financial Planning & Analysis
Wendy A. Watkins, VP-Corp. Comm.
Scott Socha, Treas.
John Wentzell, Pres., DNC Sportservice
Paula Halligan, VP-Retail
Simon Dobson, Managing Dir.-U.K.
William J. Bissett, Pres., DNC Gaming & Entertainment
Jeremy M. Jacobs, Chmn.
Gary Brown, Managing Dir.-Australia & New Zealand
Michael Reinert, VP-Supply Mgmt. Svcs.

GROWTH PLANS/SPECIAL FEATURES:

Delaware North Companies, Inc. is a hospitality company that manages and provides food and beverage concessions, premium dining, entertainment, lodging and retail at many large venues and other establishments. Delaware North operates through seven divisions. The Boston Holdings division owns and operates TD Garden, home of the National Hockey League's Boston Bruins and the National Basketball Association's Boston Celtics. Delaware North Chairman Jeremy Jacobs owns the Boston Bruins. TD Garden also hosts entertainment such as live concerts, and features restaurants, stores, residences, offices and a hotel. The gaming division specializes in regional gaming venues throughout the U.S., with slots and video gaming machines, table games, poker rooms, restaurants and hotels. The parks and resorts division offers a range of services, including lodging, food and beverage, retail and recreation at many national and state parks and attractions (Yellowstone and Grand Canyon, and Kennedy Space Center Visitor Complex), as well as at destination resorts. The Patina Restaurant Group division operates in the premium restaurant and catering industry, with more than 50 restaurants and managing catering and food service operations at locations in high-profile cultural and entertainment venues such as Metropolitan Opera, Lincoln Center, Anaheim's Downtown Disney, Epcot World Showcase and the Empire State Building. The specialty retail division operates more than 300 stores and shops in stadiums, ballparks, arenas, national and state parks, resorts, cultural attractions, airports, toll plazas, open-air marketplaces and regional destination casinos. The sports service division provides hospitality services at more than 50 stadiums, ballparks and arenas in the U.S., such as concessions, dining, event catering and retail. Last, the travel division operates in more than 30 airports and travel hubs worldwide, and manages 200+ brands in restaurants and retail stores, with airports including Los Angeles International Airport, London Heathrow Airport and Melbourne International Airport.

FINANCIAL DATA: *Note: Data for latest year may not have been available at press time.*

In U.S. $	2022	2021	2020	2019	2018	2017
Revenue	3,800,000,000	2,693,600,000	2,072,000,000	3,700,000,000	3,310,000,000	3,310,000,000
R&D Expense						
Operating Income						
Operating Margin %						
SGA Expense						
Net Income						
Operating Cash Flow						
Capital Expenditure						
EBITDA						
Return on Assets %						
Return on Equity %						
Debt to Equity						

CONTACT INFORMATION:

Phone: 716-858-5000   Fax: 716-858-5479
Toll-Free:
Address: 250 Delaware Ave., Buffalo, NY 14202 United States

STOCK TICKER/OTHER:

Stock Ticker: Private   Exchange:
Employees: 40,000   Fiscal Year Ends: 12/31
Parent Company:

SALARIES/BONUSES:

Top Exec. Salary: $ Bonus: $
Second Exec. Salary: $ Bonus: $

OTHER THOUGHTS:

Estimated Female Officers or Directors: 5
Hot Spot for Advancement for Women/Minorities: Y

Sales, profits and employees may be estimates. Financial information, benefits and other data can change quickly and may vary from those stated here.

Delta Apparel Inc

www.deltaapparelinc.com

NAIC Code: 424300

TYPES OF BUSINESS:

Apparel and Clothing Brands, Designers, Importers and Distributors

GROWTH PLANS/SPECIAL FEATURES:

Delta Apparel Inc together with its subsidiaries is an international apparel design, marketing, manufacturing, and sourcing company. It operates its business in two distinct segments: Delta Group and Salt Life Group. The company offers a diverse portfolio of lifestyle basics and branded activewear apparel, headwear, and related accessory products. It specializes in selling casual and athletic products through distribution channels and distribution tiers, including specialty stores, boutiques, department stores, mid and mass channels, e-retailers, and the U.S. military. It also offers its products direct-to-consumer on its websites and in its retail stores. The company derives the maximum revenue from the wholesale of goods through the Delta Group in the United States.

BRANDS/DIVISIONS/AFFILIATES:

MJ Soffe LLC
DTG2Go LLC
Salt Life LLC
Delta
Coast

CONTACTS: Note: Officers with more than one job title may be intentionally listed here more than once.

Robert Humphreys, CEO
Deborah Merrill, CFO
Jeffery Stillwell, President, Subsidiary
Arjona Encalada, Vice President, Divisional

FINANCIAL DATA: Note: Data for latest year may not have been available at press time.

In U.S. $	2022	2021	2020	2019	2018	2017
Revenue	484,859,000	436,750,000	381,035,000	431,730,000	385,082,000	385,082,000
R&D Expense						
Operating Income	31,781,000	32,711,000	-7,075,000	15,895,000	16,179,000	16,179,000
Operating Margin %	.07%	.07%	-.02%	.04%	.04%	.04%
SGA Expense	79,455,000	70,743,000	68,383,000	70,220,000	67,408,000	67,408,000
Net Income	19,740,000	20,296,000	-10,577,000	8,242,000	10,511,000	10,511,000
Operating Cash Flow	-20,115,000	25,467,000	31,795,000	9,428,000	13,938,000	13,938,000
Capital Expenditure	12,509,000	12,153,000	8,990,000	6,063,000	7,085,000	7,085,000
EBITDA	46,813,000	46,465,000	5,681,000	27,659,000	25,788,000	25,788,000
Return on Assets %	.04%	.05%	-.03%	.02%	.03%	.03%
Return on Equity %	.11%	.13%	-.07%	.05%	.07%	.07%
Debt to Equity	1.07%	.95%	1.192	0.792	0.563	0.563

CONTACT INFORMATION:

Phone: 864 232-5200   Fax: 864-232-5199
Toll-Free:
Address: 322 S. Main St., Greenville, SC 29601 United States

SALARIES/BONUSES:

Top Exec. Salary: $832,500   Bonus: $
Second Exec. Salary: Bonus: $250,000
$187,500

STOCK TICKER/OTHER:

Stock Ticker: DLA   Exchange: ASE
Employees: 8,600   Fiscal Year Ends: 06/30
Parent Company:

OTHER THOUGHTS:

Estimated Female Officers or Directors: 5
Hot Spot for Advancement for Women/Minorities: Y

Denver Broncos

NAIC Code: 711211C

www.denverbroncos.com

TYPES OF BUSINESS:

Professional Football Team
Team Management and Operations

BRANDS/DIVISIONS/AFFILIATES:

Walton-Penner Family Ownership Group

CONTACTS: *Note: Officers with more than one job title may be intentionally listed here more than once.*

Greg Penner, CEO
Damani Leech, Pres.
Justin Webster, CFO
Halley Sullivan, CMO
Aracely Gomez, VP-Human Resources
Patrick Smuth, Chief Communications Officer
Mike Sullivan, Dir.-Football Admin.
Rich Slivka, General Counsel
John Elway, Exec. VP-Football Oper.
Mac Freeman, Sr. VP-Bus. Dev.
Jim Saccomano, VP-Corp. Comm.
John Fox, Head Coach
Chip Conway, VP-Oper.
Cindy Kellogg, VP-Corp. Partnerships
Andy Gorchiv, Gen. Mgr.
George Paton, Gen. Mngr.

GROWTH PLANS/SPECIAL FEATURES:

The Denver Broncos is a professional football team playing in the National Football League (NFL). Founded in 1960, the team is an original franchise of the American Football League (AFL), and currently plays in the AFC western division. The Broncos saw a great deal of success in the 1980s and early 90s, making a total of 10 playoff appearances between 1983 and 1998. After four unsuccessful appearances in the championship game, the team won back-to-back Super Bowls in the 1997 and 1998 seasons. During this era, the organization's success was largely due to Hall of Fame quarterback John Elway and notable running back Terrell Davis. Elway retired in 1999, Davis in 2001. In total, the Broncos have clenched three Super Bowl championships, eight Conference championships, 15 Division championships and 22 Playoff appearances. Other notable Bronco Hall of Famers include Gary Zimmerman, Floyd Little, Shannon Sharpe, Champ Bailey and Steve Atwater, as well as coach Pat Bowlen. The Broncos play their games at the Empower Field at Mile High, with a football seating capacity of over 76,000. Average home attendance was 75,980 for the 2022-23 season. Forbes valued the team at $4.65 billion in August 2022. During 2022, the Denver Broncos was acquired by Walton-Penner Family Ownership Group.

FINANCIAL DATA: *Note: Data for latest year may not have been available at press time.*

In U.S. $	2022	2021	2020	2019	2018	2017
Revenue	544,700,000					
R&D Expense						
Operating Income						
Operating Margin %						
SGA Expense						
Net Income						
Operating Cash Flow						
Capital Expenditure						
EBITDA						
Return on Assets %						
Return on Equity %						
Debt to Equity						

CONTACT INFORMATION:

Phone: 303-649-9000   Fax: 303-649-0562
Toll-Free:
Address: 13655 Broncos Pkwy., Englewood, CO 80112 United States

STOCK TICKER/OTHER:

Stock Ticker: Private   Exchange:
Employees: 118   Fiscal Year Ends: 03/31
Parent Company:

SALARIES/BONUSES:

Top Exec. Salary: $ Bonus: $
Second Exec. Salary: $ Bonus: $

OTHER THOUGHTS:

Estimated Female Officers or Directors: 6
Hot Spot for Advancement for Women/Minorities: Y

Denver Nuggets

www.nba.com/nuggets

NAIC Code: 711211B

TYPES OF BUSINESS:

Professional Basketball Team
Team Management and Operations

BRANDS/DIVISIONS/AFFILIATES:

Ball Arena

CONTACTS: *Note: Officers with more than one job title may be intentionally listed here more than once.*

E. Stanley Kroenk, Governor
Calvin Booth, Gen. Mngr.
Lisa Johnson, Exec. Dir.-Basketball Admin.
Stephen Stieneker, General Counsel
Masai Ujiri, Exec. VP-Basketball Oper.
Tim Gelt, Dir.-Media Rel.
Mark Waggoner, Sr. VP-Finance-Kronke Sports Enterprises LLC
E. Stanley Kroenke, Owner
George Karl, Head Coach
Pete D'Alessandro, VP-Basketball Oper.
Tim Dixon, Dir.-Team Svcs.

GROWTH PLANS/SPECIAL FEATURES:

The Denver Nuggets are a professional basketball team in the NBA (National Basketball Association). The team dates to 1967, when it was founded as the Denver Larks (later Rockets), a charter member of the ABA (American Basketball Association). Upon the ABA's merger with the NBA in 1976, the organization became the Nuggets. Since its founding, the franchise that plays in the northwest division of the western conference has earned 12 division championships (two in ABA and 10 in NBA), with its most recent being in 2023 when it won the division and conference titles, making it to the NBA Finals for the first time ever. The Nuggets defeated the Miami Heat 4-1, capturing the 2023 NBA Championship. Home games are played at the Ball Arena, a multi-purpose arena in Denver, with a seating capacity of 18,000. Hall of Fame players include Dan Issel, David Thompson, Alex English, Sarunas Marciulionis, Spencer Haywood, Dikembe Mutombo, Allen Iverson, George McGinnis, Charlie Scott, Bobby Jones and Tim Hardaway. Forbes estimated (October 2022) the franchise to be worth $1.93 billion. The team's home attendance average was 19,235 per game during the 2022-23 season.

FINANCIAL DATA: *Note: Data for latest year may not have been available at press time.*

In U.S. $	2022	2021	2020	2019	2018	2017
Revenue	261,950,000					
R&D Expense						
Operating Income						
Operating Margin %						
SGA Expense						
Net Income						
Operating Cash Flow						
Capital Expenditure						
EBITDA						
Return on Assets %						
Return on Equity %						
Debt to Equity						

CONTACT INFORMATION:

Phone: 303-405-1100   Fax: 303-575-1920
Toll-Free:
Address: 1000 Chopper Cir., Denver, CO 80204 United States

STOCK TICKER/OTHER:

Stock Ticker: Private   Exchange:
Employees: Fiscal Year Ends: 06/30
Parent Company: Kroenke Sports & Entertainment

SALARIES/BONUSES:

Top Exec. Salary: $ Bonus: $
Second Exec. Salary: $ Bonus: $

OTHER THOUGHTS:

Estimated Female Officers or Directors: 1
Hot Spot for Advancement for Women/Minorities:

Deportivo Toluca Futbol Club SA de CV

www.tolucafc.com

NAIC Code: 711211D

TYPES OF BUSINESS:

Soccer Team
Team Management and Operations

BRANDS/DIVISIONS/AFFILIATES:

Estadio Nemesio Diez

GROWTH PLANS/SPECIAL FEATURES:

Deportivo Toluca Futbol Club SA de CV is a professional football club in Mexico, playing in the Liga MX, the top-tier of the Mexican football league system. Founded in 1917, Deportivo Toluca FC plays its home games at the Estadio Nemesio Diez in Toluca, which has a seating capacity of approximately 30,000. Domestically, the club has won 10 Primera Division titles, one Segunda Division de Mexico titles, two Copa Mexico titles and four Campeon de Campeones titles. Internationally, Deportivo Toluca FC has won two CONCACAF Champions' Cups. New Balance is the team's kit manufacturer and Roshfrans is its shirt sponsor.

CONTACTS: *Note: Officers with more than one job title may be intentionally listed here more than once.*

Francisco Suinaga Conde, Chmn.

FINANCIAL DATA: *Note: Data for latest year may not have been available at press time.*

In U.S. $	2022	2021	2020	2019	2018	2017
Revenue						
R&D Expense						
Operating Income						
Operating Margin %						
SGA Expense						
Net Income						
Operating Cash Flow						
Capital Expenditure						
EBITDA						
Return on Assets %						
Return on Equity %						
Debt to Equity						

CONTACT INFORMATION:

Phone: 52 722 214 5709   Fax:
Toll-Free:
Address: Constituent Av. Pte. # 1000, Colonia La Merced, Toluca, MEX 50080 Mexico

STOCK TICKER/OTHER:

Stock Ticker: Private   Exchange:
Employees: Fiscal Year Ends:
Parent Company:

SALARIES/BONUSES:

Top Exec. Salary: $ Bonus: $
Second Exec. Salary: $ Bonus: $

OTHER THOUGHTS:

Estimated Female Officers or Directors:
Hot Spot for Advancement for Women/Minorities:

Detroit Lions

www.detroitlions.com

NAIC Code: 711211C

TYPES OF BUSINESS:

Professional Football Team
Team Management and Operations

BRANDS/DIVISIONS/AFFILIATES:

Ford Field

CONTACTS: *Note: Officers with more than one job title may be intentionally listed here more than once.*

Rod Wood, CEO
Mike Disner, COO
Allison Maki, CFO
Emily Griffin, Sr. VP-Mktg. & Brand
Lindsay Verstegen, Chief People Officer
Steve Lancaster, VP-IT
Allison Maki, VP-Admin.
Martin Mayhew, Exec. VP-Football Oper.
Kevin Currie, Dir.-Digital Strategy & Partnerships
Bill Keenist, Sr. VP-Comm.
Allison Maki, VP-Finance
Jim Schwartz, Head Coach
Cedric Saunders, VP-Football Oper.
Matt Barnhart, Dir.-Media Rel.
Iain Nelson, Dir.-Football Admin.
Sheila Ford Hamp, Chmn.

GROWTH PLANS/SPECIAL FEATURES:

The Detroit Lions is a professional football team playing in the National Football League (NFL) and based in Detroit, Michigan. The team was founded in 1930 as the Portsmouth Spartans (based in Ohio) and moved to Detroit four years later. The team's golden years were in the 1950s, when it reached the NFL championships four times and won three titles (in 1952, 1953 and 1957), led by quarterback Bobby Layne. Later, led by superstar running back Barry Sanders, the Lions made a solid run though the 1990s, making six post-season appearances. The franchise reached its all-time nadir in 2008 when it became only the second team in NFL history to have a winless season. The team bounced back and entered the playoffs in 2011, 2014 and 2016, for a total of 21 playoff appearances. The Lions' current owner is Sheila Ford Hamp, a descendant of both the Ford and Firestone families, of which the Ford family purchased the team in 1964. The Lions play at the indoor, 65,000-seat Ford Field, owned by the City of Detroit and with naming rights claimed by Ford Motor Company until approximately 2022. Ford Motors has further tied the life of the team with its hometown's automobile industry by furnishing the field with a special blend of FieldTurf incorporating recycled Firestone tires. Several former Lions have been inducted into the Pro Football Hall of Fame over the course of the team's history, including Layne and Sanders, Lem Barney, Jack Christiansen, Dick (Night Train) Lane, Yale Lary, Doak Walker, Dick Stanfel, Curley Culp and Alex Wojciechowicz. Forbes Magazine valued the team at $3.05 billion in August 2022. The team's average home game attendance was 63,423 during the 2022

FINANCIAL DATA: *Note: Data for latest year may not have been available at press time.*

In U.S. $	2022	2021	2020	2019	2018	2017
Revenue	481,650,000					
R&D Expense						
Operating Income						
Operating Margin %						
SGA Expense						
Net Income						
Operating Cash Flow						
Capital Expenditure						
EBITDA						
Return on Assets %						
Return on Equity %						
Debt to Equity						

CONTACT INFORMATION:

Phone: 313-216-4000   Fax: 313-216-4226
Toll-Free:
Address: 222 Republic Dr., Allen Park, MI 48101 United States

STOCK TICKER/OTHER:

Stock Ticker: Private
Employees: 390
Parent Company:

Exchange:
Fiscal Year Ends: 02/28

SALARIES/BONUSES:

Top Exec. Salary: $ Bonus: $
Second Exec. Salary: $ Bonus: $

OTHER THOUGHTS:

Estimated Female Officers or Directors: 5
Hot Spot for Advancement for Women/Minorities: Y

Detroit Pistons

www.nba.com/pistons

NAIC Code: 711211B

TYPES OF BUSINESS:

Professional Basketball Team
Team Management and Operations

BRANDS/DIVISIONS/AFFILIATES:

Motor City Cruise

CONTACTS: *Note: Officers with more than one job title may be intentionally listed here more than once.*

Troy Weaver, Gen. Mngr.
Mario Etemad, Exec. VP-Oper.
Lucinda Treat, Exec. VP-Bus. Oper. & Strategy
Kevin Grigg, VP-Public Rel.
Dan Lincoln, VP-Finance
Joe Dumars, Pres., Basketball Oper.
Tom Gores, Owner

GROWTH PLANS/SPECIAL FEATURES:

The Detroit Pistons joined the National Basketball Association (NBA) in 1949 as the Fort Wayne Pistons. The franchise officially became known as the Detroit Pistons after it moved to Detroit in 1957. The team struggled to find success until the late 1980s, when the team reached but failed to win the Eastern Division championship in the 1986-87 season. The Pistons followed up with a trip (and loss) to the 1987-88 finals, but finally attained a championship win in the 1988-89 season under the guidance of Joe Dumars, Isiah Thomas and Dennis Rodman. The team repeated this feat with another championship win in the 1989-90 season. Despite a decade-long drought after these wins, the Pistons again clinched the NBA title in the 2003-04 season. In addition, the franchise has clenched five conference titles and 11 division titles. The Pistons maintain a development league affiliation with the Motor City Cruise. The Little Caesars Arena, the home stadium of the Pistons, is one of the largest sports arenas in the NBA and features a basketball capacity of 20,000+ seats. The team's home attendance average was 16,184 for the 2022 season. Hall of Fame members who played as Pistons range from Andy Phillip, inducted in 1961 to Grant Hill (2018) and Ben Wallace (2021), respectively. Forbes estimated the team to be worth $1.9 billion in October 2022. Billionaire Tom Gores owns the team.

FINANCIAL DATA: *Note: Data for latest year may not have been available at press time.*

In U.S. $	2022	2021	2020	2019	2018	2017
Revenue	272,350,000					
R&D Expense						
Operating Income						
Operating Margin %						
SGA Expense						
Net Income						
Operating Cash Flow						
Capital Expenditure						
EBITDA						
Return on Assets %						
Return on Equity %						
Debt to Equity						

CONTACT INFORMATION:

Phone: 248-377-0100   Fax: 248-377-3260
Toll-Free:
Address: 6 Championship Dr., Auburn Hills, MI 48236 United States

STOCK TICKER/OTHER:

Stock Ticker: Private   Exchange:
Employees: 320   Fiscal Year Ends: 06/30
Parent Company:

SALARIES/BONUSES:

Top Exec. Salary: $ Bonus: $
Second Exec. Salary: $ Bonus: $

OTHER THOUGHTS:

Estimated Female Officers or Directors: 1
Hot Spot for Advancement for Women/Minorities: Y

Detroit Red Wings

www.nhl.com/redwings

NAIC Code: 711211F

TYPES OF BUSINESS:

Professional Hockey Team (NHL)
Team Management and Operations

BRANDS/DIVISIONS/AFFILIATES:

Grand Rapids Griffins
Toledo Walleye
Little Caesars Arena

CONTACTS: *Note: Officers with more than one job title may be intentionally listed here more than once.*

Christopher Ilitch, CEO
Nicklas Lidstrom, VP-Hockey Oper.
Paul Macdonald, VP-Finance
Robert E. Carr, Sr. VP-Legal Affairs
Robert E. Carr, Sr. VP-Oper.
Russ Gregory, Dir.-Corp. Dev.
Craig Turnbull, Sr. VP-Comm. & Mktg.
Paul MacDonald, VP-Finance
Mike Babcock, Head Coach
Mike Ilitch, Co-Owner
Marian Ilitch, Co-Owner

GROWTH PLANS/SPECIAL FEATURES:

The Detroit Red Wings is a National Hockey League (NHL) team based in Detroit, Michigan, playing in the Atlantic division of the Eastern conference. The team was founded in 1926 when the roster of the Victoria Cougars was sold to a group from Detroit that had recently been awarded an NHL franchise. This initial team played as the Detroit Cougars until 1930 and then for one year as the Detroit Falcons. In 1932, grain and shipping magnate James Norris, Sr. acquired the team and changed the name to the Detroit Red Wings. The moniker was a reference to the amateur hockey team Norris played on in Montreal, the Winged Wheelers. The Red Wings won its first Stanley Cup in 1936, a second in 1937 and five more over the next 18 years. In total, the team has clenched 11 Stanley Cups, six Conference championships, six Presidents' Trophies and 19 division championships. In 1982, the Ilitch family, founders of Little Caesar's Pizza, purchased the Red Wings. The team plays in the Detroit-based Little Caesars Arena, which offers up to 22,000 in total seating capacity and over 19,500 for hockey games. The Red Wings averaged 18,819 fans per home game attendance during the 2022-23 season. The Red Wings are affiliated with the Grand Rapids Griffins of the American Hockey League (AHL) and the Toledo Walleye of the ECHL. Forbes valued the Red Wings at $1.03 billion in December 2022.

FINANCIAL DATA: *Note: Data for latest year may not have been available at press time.*

In U.S. $	2022	2021	2020	2019	2018	2017
Revenue	150,150,000					
R&D Expense						
Operating Income						
Operating Margin %						
SGA Expense						
Net Income						
Operating Cash Flow						
Capital Expenditure						
EBITDA						
Return on Assets %						
Return on Equity %						
Debt to Equity						

CONTACT INFORMATION:

Phone: 313-396-7544   Fax: 313-567-0296
Toll-Free:
Address: 2645 Woodward Ave., Detroit, MI 48201 United States

STOCK TICKER/OTHER:

Stock Ticker: Private   Exchange:
Employees: 135   Fiscal Year Ends: 06/30
Parent Company:

SALARIES/BONUSES:

Top Exec. Salary: $ Bonus: $
Second Exec. Salary: $ Bonus: $

OTHER THOUGHTS:

Estimated Female Officers or Directors: 23
Hot Spot for Advancement for Women/Minorities: Y

Sales, profits and employees may be estimates. Financial information, benefits and other data can change quickly and may vary from those stated here.

Detroit Tigers

www.mlb.com/tigers

NAIC Code: 711211A

TYPES OF BUSINESS:

Professional Baseball Team
Team Management and Operations

BRANDS/DIVISIONS/AFFILIATES:

Ilitch Holdings Inc
Toledo Mud Hens
Erie SeaWolves
West Michigan Whitecaps
Lakeland Flying Tigers

CONTACTS: *Note: Officers with more than one job title may be intentionally listed here more than once.*

Christopher Ilitch, CEO
Ryan Gustafson, COO
Russ Borrows, Sr. VP-Finance
Alexis Lee, CMO
Michele Bartos, Sr. VP-Human Resources
Ron Colangelo, Sr. VP-Communications & Broadcasting
Stephen Quinn, VP-Admin.
John Westhoff, VP-Baseball Legal Counsel
Duane McLean, Exec. VP-Bus. Oper.
Ron Colangelo, VP-Comm.
Kelli Kollman, Sr. Dir.-Finance
Michael Ilitch, Owner
Jim Devellano, Sr. VP
Elaine Lewis, VP-Community & Public Affairs
Steve Harms, VP-Corp. Partnerships
Christopher Ilitch, Chmn.
Tom Moore, Dir.-Int'l Oper.
DeAndre Berry, Dir.-Purchasing & Supplier Diversity

GROWTH PLANS/SPECIAL FEATURES:

The Detroit Tigers is a Major League Baseball (MLB) team based in Detroit, Michigan, playing in the Central Division of the American League. The team was established in 1894 and was an inaugural member of the American League. In all, the Tigers have won four World Series titles, 11 pennants, seven division titles (most recently in 2014) and one wild card berth. Notable Tigers include Al Kaline, Ty Cobb, Hank Greenberg, Lou Whitaker, Charlie Gehringer and Willie Horton. In the past two decades, the team has been rather poor, posting 12 consecutive losing seasons from 1994-2005, including 119 losses in 2003, the most since the New York Mets' inaugural 1962 campaign. However, in 2006, the Tigers made the playoffs for the first time in 19 years, converting a Wild Card berth into the American League pennant before losing to the St. Louis Cardinals in the World Series. In 2012, the club posted a record of 88-74 and won its second consecutive AL Central division title. After advancing to the World Series, the Tigers were defeated in four games by the San Francisco Giants. The team has been owned by Ilitch Holdings, Inc., the parent company of the Detroit Red Wings and Little Caesars Pizza, since 1992. In 2000, the club began playing home games in the 41,083-seat capacity Comerica Park. Average home game attendance was 19,634 for the 2022 season. Minor league affiliate teams include the Toledo Mud Hens, the Erie SeaWolves, West Michigan Whitecaps and the Lakeland Flying Tigers. Forbes estimated the team to be worth $1.45 billion in March 2023.

FINANCIAL DATA: *Note: Data for latest year may not have been available at press time.*

In U.S. $	2022	2021	2020	2019	2018	2017
Revenue	353,600,000					
R&D Expense						
Operating Income						
Operating Margin %						
SGA Expense						
Net Income						
Operating Cash Flow						
Capital Expenditure						
EBITDA						
Return on Assets %						
Return on Equity %						
Debt to Equity						

CONTACT INFORMATION:

Phone: 313-471-2000   Fax: 313-471-2138
Toll-Free:
Address: 2100 Woodward Ave., Comerica Park, Detroit, MI 48201 United States

STOCK TICKER/OTHER:

Stock Ticker: Private
Employees: 475
Parent Company:

Exchange:
Fiscal Year Ends: 12/31

SALARIES/BONUSES:

Top Exec. Salary: $ Bonus: $
Second Exec. Salary: $ Bonus: $

OTHER THOUGHTS:

Estimated Female Officers or Directors: 8
Hot Spot for Advancement for Women/Minorities: Y

Dicks Sporting Goods Inc

www.dickssportinggoods.com

NAIC Code: 451110

TYPES OF BUSINESS:

Sporting Goods Stores
Outdoor Apparel
Footwear
Hunting & Fishing Supplies
Golf Supplies
Bicycles
Online Sales

BRANDS/DIVISIONS/AFFILIATES:

Dicks Sporting Goods
Golf Galaxy
Field & Stream
Public Lands
GameChanger
Alpine Design
CALIA
DSG

GROWTH PLANS/SPECIAL FEATURES:

Dick's Sporting Goods retails athletic apparel, footwear, and equipment for sports. Dick's operates digital platforms, about 740 stores under its namesake brand (including outlet stores), and about 130 specialty stores under the Golf Galaxy and Public Lands nameplates. Dick's carries private-label merchandise and national brands such as Nike, The North Face, Under Armour, Callaway Golf, and TaylorMade. Based in the Pittsburgh area, Dick's was founded in 1948 by the father of current executive chairman and controlling shareholder Edward Stack.

CONTACTS: *Note: Officers with more than one job title may be intentionally listed here more than once.*

Lauren Hobart, CEO
Lee Belitsky, CFO
Edward Stack, Chairman of the Board
Navdeep Gupta, Chief Accounting Officer
Vlad Rak, Chief Technology Officer
William Colombo, Director
Donald Germano, Executive VP, Divisional
John Hayes, General Counsel
Julie Lodge-Jarrett, Other Executive Officer

FINANCIAL DATA: *Note: Data for latest year may not have been available at press time.*

In U.S. $	2022	2021	2020	2019	2018	2017
Revenue	12,293,370,000	9,584,019,000	8,750,743,000	8,436,570,000		
R&D Expense						
Operating Income	2,034,503,000	741,477,000	375,613,000	444,733,000		
Operating Margin %	.17%	.08%	.04%	.05%		
SGA Expense	2,664,083,000	2,298,534,000	2,173,677,000	1,986,576,000		
Net Income	1,519,871,000	530,251,000	297,462,000	319,864,000		
Operating Cash Flow	1,616,872,000	1,552,769,000	404,612,000	712,755,000		
Capital Expenditure	308,261,000	224,027,000	217,461,000	198,219,000		
EBITDA	2,374,828,000	1,086,561,000	760,462,000	749,495,000		
Return on Assets %	.18%	.07%	.06%	.08%		
Return on Equity %	.68%	.26%	.16%	.17%		
Debt to Equity	1.92%	1.14%	1.546	0.027		

CONTACT INFORMATION:

Phone: 724 273-3400   Fax:
Toll-Free: 877-846-9997
Address: 345 Court St., Coraopolis, PA 15108 United States

STOCK TICKER/OTHER:

Stock Ticker: DKS   Exchange: NYS
Employees: 50,800   Fiscal Year Ends: 02/02
Parent Company:

SALARIES/BONUSES:

Top Exec. Salary: $1,100,000   Bonus: $
Second Exec. Salary: $1,100,000   Bonus: $

OTHER THOUGHTS:

Estimated Female Officers or Directors: 4
Hot Spot for Advancement for Women/Minorities: Y

Disney Media & Entertainment Distribution dmedmedia.disney.com
NAIC Code: 515120

TYPES OF BUSINESS:
Broadcast TV
Media and Entertainment
Media Technology
Content Commercialization
Content Distribution
Media Advertising and Sales
Streaming Management Services
Broadcast and Cable Television Networks

BRANDS/DIVISIONS/AFFILIATES:
Walt Disney Company (The)

GROWTH PLANS/SPECIAL FEATURES:
Disney Media & Entertainment Distribution (DMED) is one of five major businesses within The Walt Disney Company. DMED is responsible for media and entertainment products, technology and commercialization, including profit and loss management and all distribution, network and engineering operations. It provides sales, advertising, data and certain key technology functions worldwide for Disney's content engines. DMED also manages operations of Disney's streaming services, including Disney+, Hulu, ESPN+ and Disney+ Hoststar, as well as domestic broadcast and cable television networks.

CONTACTS:
Note: Officers with more than one job title may be intentionally listed here more than once.

Peter DiCecco, Sr. VP-Bus. & Legal Affairs, Music
Vince Roberts, Exec. VP-Global Oper.
Albert Cheng, Exec. VP
Kevin Brockman, Exec. VP-Global Comm.
Ben Sherwood, Co-Pres., Disney
James Goldston, Pres., ABC News
Paul Lee, Pres., ABC Entertainment Group
Gary Marsh, Pres.
Kareem Daniel, Chmn.

FINANCIAL DATA:
Note: Data for latest year may not have been available at press time.

In U.S. $	2022	2021	2020	2019	2018	2017
Revenue	52,000,000,000	50,866,000,000	48,350,000,000	34,213,000,000	21,299,000,000	21,299,000,000
R&D Expense						
Operating Income						
Operating Margin %						
SGA Expense						
Net Income		7,295,000,000	7,653,000,000	5,644,000,000	7,196,000,000	7,196,000,000
Operating Cash Flow						
Capital Expenditure						
EBITDA						
Return on Assets %						
Return on Equity %						
Debt to Equity						

CONTACT INFORMATION:
Phone: 818-560-1000   Fax:
Toll-Free:
Address: 500 S. Buena Vista St., Burbank, CA 91521 United States

STOCK TICKER/OTHER:
Stock Ticker: Subsidiary   Exchange:
Employees: 21,000   Fiscal Year Ends: 09/30
Parent Company: Walt Disney Company (The)

SALARIES/BONUSES:
Top Exec. Salary: $ Bonus: $
Second Exec. Salary: $ Bonus: $

OTHER THOUGHTS:
Estimated Female Officers or Directors: 3
Hot Spot for Advancement for Women/Minorities: Y

DraftKings Inc

www.draftkings.com

NAIC Code: 519130

TYPES OF BUSINESS:

Fantasy Sports Leagues
Online Sports Betting
Mobile Spots Betting
Regulated Gaming
Fantasy Sports
Sports Betting Solutions
Management Solutions

BRANDS/DIVISIONS/AFFILIATES:

Daily Fantasy Sports
Sportsbook
SBTech Malta Limited

GROWTH PLANS/SPECIAL FEATURES:

DraftKings Inc is a digital sports entertainment and gaming company. The company provides users with daily fantasy sports (DFS), sports betting, and iGaming opportunities and is also involved in the design & development of sports betting and casino gaming platform software for online and retail sportsbook and casino gaming products. It operates in two segments: Business-to-consumer(B2C) and Business-to-Business(B2B), of which the vast majority of its revenue comes from the B2C segment. Geographically, it derives most of its revenue from the United States.

CONTACTS: Note: Officers with more than one job title may be intentionally listed here more than once.

Jason Robins, CEO
Jason Park, CFO
Erik Bradbury, Chief Accounting Officer
R. Dodge, Chief Legal Officer
Paul Liberman, Co-Founder
Matthew Kalish, Co-Founder
Harry Sloan, Director

FINANCIAL DATA: Note: Data for latest year may not have been available at press time.

In U.S. $	2022	2021	2020	2019	2018	2017
Revenue	2,240,461,000	1,296,025,000	614,532,000	323,410,000	191,844,000	191,844,000
R&D Expense	318,247,000	253,655,000	168,633,000	55,929,000	20,212,000	20,212,000
Operating Income	-1,511,756,000	-1,561,617,000	-843,256,000	-146,545,000	-73,198,000	-73,198,000
Operating Margin %	-.67%	-1.20%	-1.37%	-.45%		
SGA Expense	1,949,697,000	1,809,825,000	942,566,000	310,137,000	213,080,000	213,080,000
Net Income	-1,377,987,000	-1,523,195,000	-1,231,835,000	-142,734,000	-75,556,000	-75,556,000
Operating Cash Flow	-625,519,000	-419,508,000	-194,157,000	-46,578,000	-88,437,000	-88,437,000
Capital Expenditure	103,645,000	98,276,000	46,071,000	42,271,000	7,715,000	7,715,000
EBITDA	-1,342,504,000	-1,440,479,000	-765,846,000	-132,909,000	-66,897,000	-66,897,000
Return on Assets %	-.34%	-.41%	-.65%	-.45%		
Return on Equity %	-.92%	-.71%	-.95%			
Debt to Equity	1.00%	.78%	0.026			

CONTACT INFORMATION:

Phone: 617-986-6744   Fax:
Toll-Free:
Address: 222 Berkeley St., Fl. 5, Boston, MA 02116 United States

STOCK TICKER/OTHER:

Stock Ticker: DKNG   Exchange: NAS
Employees: 4,200   Fiscal Year Ends: 12/31
Parent Company:

SALARIES/BONUSES:

Top Exec. Salary: $425,000   Bonus: $500,000
Second Exec. Salary: Bonus: $
$500,000

OTHER THOUGHTS:

Estimated Female Officers or Directors:
Hot Spot for Advancement for Women/Minorities:

Sales, profits and employees may be estimates. Financial information, benefits and other data can change quickly and may vary from those stated here.

Eastern Mountain Sports Inc

NAIC Code: 451110

www.ems.com

TYPES OF BUSINESS:

Sporting Goods Stores
Outdoor Apparel
Outdoor Gear
Outdoor Sports Instruction
Retail Stores
Ecommerce

BRANDS/DIVISIONS/AFFILIATES:

GoDigital Media Group
EMS
EMS Rewards
Eastern Mountain Sports Schools

CONTACTS: *Note: Officers with more than one job title may be intentionally listed here more than once.*

Dave Barton, CEO
Ralph Lucarelli, Dir.-Visual Merch.
Ralph Lucarelli, Dir.-Store Planning
Joe Lentini, Dir.-Climbing & Adventure School

GROWTH PLANS/SPECIAL FEATURES:

Eastern Mountain Sports, Inc. (EMS) operates outdoor specialty retail stores in the northeast region of the U.S. The stores provide an extensive selection of clothing and gear for activities such as rock and ice climbing, mountaineering, kayaking and canoeing, camping, cycling and fitness. EMS stocks popular outdoor brand names such as Eastern Mountain Sports, Kuhl, Marmot, Merrell, prAna, Osprey, Salomon, Smartwool, Teva, The North Face, Thule, Yeti and more. In addition, the company designs and offers its own line of outdoor gear and clothing under the EMS name. The firm utilizes a large store format that includes comprehensive product offerings, allowing it to provide lower prices than those offered by local specialty outdoor retailers. EMS has a liberal return policy that allows customers to exchange, return or repair any item with a web invoice or original store receipt, even if the item has been damaged from use. EMS Rewards is a loyalty program for consumers. Many of the company's products are tested and demonstrated at its outdoor skills training schools. Eastern Mountain Sports Schools help people try new things and learn new skills, offering climbing, kayaking, paddleboarding and skiing programs for people of all ages at locations throughout the northeast. During 2022, EMS was acquired by GoDigital Media Group, a diversified multi-national company.

EMS offers its employees comprehensive health benefits, 401(k), life insurance, short/long-term disability coverage and an employee assistance program.

FINANCIAL DATA: *Note: Data for latest year may not have been available at press time.*

In U.S. $	2022	2021	2020	2019	2018	2017
Revenue	555,000,000	543,400,000	522,500,000	475,000,000	450,000,000	450,000,000
R&D Expense						
Operating Income						
Operating Margin %						
SGA Expense						
Net Income						
Operating Cash Flow						
Capital Expenditure						
EBITDA						
Return on Assets %						
Return on Equity %						
Debt to Equity						

CONTACT INFORMATION:

Phone: 603-924-9571   Fax: 603-924-9138
Toll-Free: 888-463-6367
Address: 1 Vose Farm Rd., Peterborough, NH 03458 United States

STOCK TICKER/OTHER:

Stock Ticker: Subsidiary
Employees: 1,130
Parent Company: GoDigital Media Group

Exchange:
Fiscal Year Ends: 04/30

SALARIES/BONUSES:

Top Exec. Salary: $ Bonus: $
Second Exec. Salary: $ Bonus: $

OTHER THOUGHTS:

Estimated Female Officers or Directors:
Hot Spot for Advancement for Women/Minorities:

ECHL

NAIC Code: 711211

www.echl.com

TYPES OF BUSINESS:

Minor Hockey League

BRANDS/DIVISIONS/AFFILIATES:

CONTACTS: *Note: Officers with more than one job title may be intentionally listed here more than once.*

Ryan Crelin, Commissioner
Ryan Crelin, VP-Bus. Oper.
Rich Bello, Dir.-Team Bus. Dev.
Joe Babik, Dir.-Comm.
Todd Corliss, Dir.-Finance
Joe Ernst, VP-Hockey Oper.
Jeff Zavatsky, Dir.-Hockey Oper.
Kristin Kellner, Assistant-Mktg.

GROWTH PLANS/SPECIAL FEATURES:

ECHL, established in 1988, operates a class I-AA minor hockey league of 28 teams dispersed across the U.S. and one franchises in Canada. ECHL stands for East Coast Hockey League and is one tier below the American Hockey League. The league operates in two conferences: Eastern and Western. The Eastern Conference contains the North and South divisions, while the Western Conference is comprised of the Central and Mountain divisions. The winners of each conference play each other in the annual Kelly Cup. ECHL's teams act as feeder teams for several American Hockey League (AHL) and National Hockey League (NHL) teams. As for the 2022-23 season, all but four National Hockey League teams had affiliations with an ECHL team (Nashville Predators, St. Louis Blues, Vancouver Canucks and Winnipeg Jets). The Savannah Ghost Pirates became the newest team of the ECHL (2022-23 season), is based in Savannah, Georgia and plays at the Enmarket Arena. An Athens ECHL team, based in Athens, Georgia is scheduled to join in 2024, and will play at the Classic Center Arena.

FINANCIAL DATA: *Note: Data for latest year may not have been available at press time.*

In U.S. $	2022	2021	2020	2019	2018	2017
Revenue						
R&D Expense						
Operating Income						
Operating Margin %						
SGA Expense						
Net Income						
Operating Cash Flow						
Capital Expenditure						
EBITDA						
Return on Assets %						
Return on Equity %						
Debt to Equity						

CONTACT INFORMATION:

Phone: 609-452-0770   Fax: 609-452-7147
Toll-Free:
Address: 830 Broad St., Ste. 3, Shrewsbury, NJ 07702 United States

STOCK TICKER/OTHER:

Stock Ticker: Private   Exchange:
Employees: 225   Fiscal Year Ends: 12/31
Parent Company:

SALARIES/BONUSES:

Top Exec. Salary: $ Bonus: $
Second Exec. Salary: $ Bonus: $

OTHER THOUGHTS:

Estimated Female Officers or Directors: 1
Hot Spot for Advancement for Women/Minorities: Y

Edmonton Oilers

NAIC Code: 711211F

TYPES OF BUSINESS:
Professional Hockey Team (NHL)
Team Management and Operations

BRANDS/DIVISIONS/AFFILIATES:
Bakersfield Condors
Fort Wayne Komets

CONTACTS: Note: Officers with more than one job title may be intentionally listed here more than once.
Jurgen Schreiber, CEO
Stuart Ballantyne, Pres.
Jason Quilley, Exec. VP-Finance
Daryl Katz, Governor
Stew MacDonald, Pres.
Rick Olczyk, Dir.-Legal Affairs & Hockey Oper.
Kevin Lowe, Pres., Hockey Oper.
Allan Watt, VP-Comm. & Broadcasting
Darryl Boessenkool, VP-Finance
Scott Howson, Sr. VP-Hockey Oper.
Ralph Krueger, Head Coach
Craig MacTavish, Gen. Mgr.
Stew MacDonald, Chief Revenue Officer
Bob Nicholson, Chmn.

GROWTH PLANS/SPECIAL FEATURES:

The Edmonton Oilers is a National Hockey League (NHL) team that plays in the Pacific division of the Western conference. The franchise was founded in the early 1970s as a member of the World Hockey Association (WHA), and joined the NHL when the WHA collapsed in 1973. The Oilers' first Stanley Cup Final appearance in 1983 ended in a loss. The team soon developed under the lead of Wayne Gretzky, dominating the NHL throughout the 1980s with four Stanley Cup titles in five appearances. The franchise won its fifth Stanley Cup in 1990 after trading Gretzky to the Los Angeles Kings. In 1993, the team missed the playoffs for the first time since its inaugural season, ushering in a period of mediocrity. The Oilers later returned to the NHL Finals in the 2005-06 season but lost to the Carolina Hurricanes. Though Wayne Gretzky finished his NHL career with the New York Rangers, he is best known for his achievements while playing with the Oilers. Gretzky is a Hockey Hall of Fame member and so widely respected that when he retired in 1999, the NHL retired his sweater number (99) across the entire league. The Oilers play in Rogers Place, a multi-use indoor arena in Edmonton, Alberta, with a hockey seating capacity of 18,347, of which the club fills to capacity during home games. The Edmonton Oilers averaged 17,838 in home game attendance during the 2022-23 season. The team maintains minor league affiliations with the Bakersfield Condors in the American Hockey League (AHL) and the Fort Wayne Komets in the ECHL. Forbes valued the Oilers at $1.275 billion in December 2022.

FINANCIAL DATA: Note: Data for latest year may not have been available at press time.

In U.S. $	2022	2021	2020	2019	2018	2017
Revenue	140,000,000	89,000,000	137,000,000	154,000,000	151,000,000	151,000,000
R&D Expense						
Operating Income						
Operating Margin %						
SGA Expense						
Net Income		-23,000,000	17,000,000	16,000,000	24,000,000	24,000,000
Operating Cash Flow						
Capital Expenditure						
EBITDA						
Return on Assets %						
Return on Equity %						
Debt to Equity						

CONTACT INFORMATION:
Phone: 780-414-4625   Fax:
Toll-Free:
Address: 300, 10214 104 Ave. NW, Edmonton, AB T5J 0H6 Canada

STOCK TICKER/OTHER:
Stock Ticker: Private   Exchange:
Employees: 240   Fiscal Year Ends: 07/31
Parent Company:

SALARIES/BONUSES:
Top Exec. Salary: $ Bonus: $
Second Exec. Salary: $ Bonus: $

OTHER THOUGHTS:
Estimated Female Officers or Directors:
Hot Spot for Advancement for Women/Minorities:

eGames.com Holdings LLC (Buzztime)

www.buzztime.com

NAIC Code: 511210G

TYPES OF BUSINESS:

Computer Software, Electronic Games, Apps & Entertainment
Video Game Development
Video Game Publishing
Online and Mobile App Gaming
Video Game Tablets
Trivia Games
Business Marketing Solutions
Massively Multiplayer Video Games

BRANDS/DIVISIONS/AFFILIATES:

Buzztime Bar

GROWTH PLANS/SPECIAL FEATURES:

eGames.com Holdings LLC, doing business as Buzztime, and is a video game developer and publisher that offers games online and via mobile app, as well as for businesses who want to provide the games for free to their customers. Buzztime's online games are grouped into the following categories, trivia, tablet-only games and Playmaker-only games. The company offers interactive game content so that players and/or patrons can engage with one another. Competition games are provided between various venues, including massively multiplayer gaming. Types of competition games are announced on the Buzztime platform, which are categorized within Pacific, Mountain, Central and Eastern time zones. Buzztime also offers gaming tablets and its Buzztime app. For businesses in the restaurant/hospitality industry, Buzztime Bar Trivia offer video games specifically designed to turn customers into bar buddies, making business more profitable and fun.

CONTACTS: *Note: Officers with more than one job title may be intentionally listed here more than once.*

Thomas Pulley, CFO

FINANCIAL DATA: *Note: Data for latest year may not have been available at press time.*

In U.S. $	2022	2021	2020	2019	2018	2017
Revenue		15,894,315	14,854,500	19,806,000	21,274,000	21,274,000
R&D Expense						
Operating Income						
Operating Margin %						
SGA Expense						
Net Income				-2,047,000	-1,077,000	-1,077,000
Operating Cash Flow						
Capital Expenditure						
EBITDA						
Return on Assets %						
Return on Equity %						
Debt to Equity						

CONTACT INFORMATION:

Phone: 760 438-7400   Fax: 760 438-7470
Toll-Free:
Address: 6965 El Camino Real, Ste. 105-517, Carlsbad, CA 92009
United States

STOCK TICKER/OTHER:

Stock Ticker: Private
Employees: 40
Parent Company:

Exchange:
Fiscal Year Ends: 12/31

SALARIES/BONUSES:

Top Exec. Salary: $ Bonus: $
Second Exec. Salary: $ Bonus: $

OTHER THOUGHTS:

Estimated Female Officers or Directors: 2
Hot Spot for Advancement for Women/Minorities:

Electronic Arts Inc (EA)

www.ea.com

NAIC Code: 511210G

TYPES OF BUSINESS:
Computer Software, Electronic Games, Apps & Entertainment
Online Interactive Games
E-Commerce Sales
Mobile Games
Apps

BRANDS/DIVISIONS/AFFILIATES:
Battlefield
Sims (The)
Apex Legends
Need for Speed
Plants vs Zombies

GROWTH PLANS/SPECIAL FEATURES:
EA is one of the world's largest third-party video game publishers and has transitioned from a console-based video game publisher to the one of the largest publishers on consoles, PC, and mobile. The firm owns number of large franchises, including Madden, FIFA, Battlefield, Apex Legends, Mass Effect, Dragon's Age, and Need for Speed.

EA offers its employees health care coverage, retirement and financial plans, and company perks.

CONTACTS: Note: Officers with more than one job title may be intentionally listed here more than once.
Andrew Wilson, CEO
Blake Jorgensen, CFO
Eric Kelly, Chief Accounting Officer
Jacob Schatz, Chief Legal Officer
Kenneth Moss, Chief Technology Officer
Christopher Bruzzo, Other Executive Officer
Laura Miele, Other Executive Officer
Vijayanthimala Singh, Other Executive Officer
Kenneth Barker, Senior VP, Divisional

FINANCIAL DATA: Note: Data for latest year may not have been available at press time.

In U.S. $	2022	2021	2020	2019	2018	2017
Revenue	6,991,000,000	5,629,000,000	5,537,000,000	4,950,000,000	4,845,000,000	4,845,000,000
R&D Expense	2,186,000,000	1,778,000,000	1,559,000,000	1,433,000,000	1,205,000,000	1,205,000,000
Operating Income	1,129,000,000	1,046,000,000	1,450,000,000	1,010,000,000	1,224,000,000	1,224,000,000
Operating Margin %	.16%	.19%	.26%	.20%	.25%	.25%
SGA Expense	1,634,000,000	1,281,000,000	1,137,000,000	1,162,000,000	1,112,000,000	1,112,000,000
Net Income	789,000,000	837,000,000	3,039,000,000	1,019,000,000	967,000,000	967,000,000
Operating Cash Flow	1,899,000,000	1,934,000,000	1,797,000,000	1,547,000,000	1,578,000,000	1,578,000,000
Capital Expenditure	188,000,000	124,000,000	140,000,000	119,000,000	123,000,000	123,000,000
EBITDA	1,625,000,000	1,243,000,000	1,702,000,000	1,267,000,000	1,427,000,000	1,427,000,000
Return on Assets %	.06%	.07%	.30%	.12%	.13%	.13%
Return on Equity %	.10%	.11%	.48%	.21%	.26%	.26%
Debt to Equity	.25%	.24%	0.053	0.186	0.244	0.244

CONTACT INFORMATION:
Phone: 650 628-1500   Fax: 650 628-1414
Toll-Free:
Address: 209 Redwood Shores Pkwy., Redwood City, CA 94065 United States

STOCK TICKER/OTHER:
Stock Ticker: EA   Exchange: NAS
Employees: 12,900   Fiscal Year Ends: 03/31
Parent Company:

SALARIES/BONUSES:
Top Exec. Salary: $51,154   Bonus: $4,000,000
Second Exec. Salary: Bonus: $
$1,292,923

OTHER THOUGHTS:
Estimated Female Officers or Directors: 2
Hot Spot for Advancement for Women/Minorities:

Endeavor Group Holdings Inc

www.endeavorco.com

NAIC Code: 711410

TYPES OF BUSINESS:

Talent Agency
Literary Agency
Sports Marketing & Agents
Media Consulting

GROWTH PLANS/SPECIAL FEATURES:

Endeavor Group Holdings Inc is an entertainment, sports and content company. It offers services through its integrated capabilities of talent representation, content development, content distribution and sales, event management, marketing and licensing, and direct-to-consumer offerings. It operates its business in three segments: Owned Sports Properties; Events, Experiences & Rights; and Representation.

BRANDS/DIVISIONS/AFFILIATES:

art+commerce
dixon talent inc
Endeavor
Endeavor Streaming
Turkish Airlines EuroLeague
IMG
PBR
sntv

CONTACTS: *Note: Officers with more than one job title may be intentionally listed here more than once.*

Ariel Emanuel, CEO
Mark Shapiro, Pres.
Jason Lublin, CFO
Patrick Whitesell, Chmn.

FINANCIAL DATA: *Note: Data for latest year may not have been available at press time.*

In U.S. $	2022	2021	2020	2019	2018	2017
Revenue	5,268,137,000	5,077,713,000	3,478,743,000			
R&D Expense						
Operating Income	576,623,000	-85,906,000	-19,731,000			
Operating Margin %	.11%	-.02%	-.01%			
SGA Expense	2,358,962,000	2,283,558,000	1,442,316,000			
Net Income	129,133,000	-328,311,000	-654,934,000			
Operating Cash Flow	502,934,000	333,599,000	161,218,000			
Capital Expenditure	147,964,000	99,802,000	71,651,000			
EBITDA	445,795,000	134,537,000	238,752,000			
Return on Assets %	.01%	-.03%				
Return on Equity %	.08%	-.39%				
Debt to Equity	2.88%	4.81%	21.984			

CONTACT INFORMATION:

Phone: 310 285-9000   Fax:
Toll-Free:
Address: 9601 Wilshire Blvd., Fl. 3, Beverly Hills, CA 90210 United States

STOCK TICKER/OTHER:

Stock Ticker: EDR
Employees: 11,000
Parent Company:

Exchange: NYS
Fiscal Year Ends: 12/31

SALARIES/BONUSES:

Top Exec. Salary: $4,000,000   Bonus: $10,000,000
Second Exec. Salary: $3,000,000   Bonus: $7,768,797

OTHER THOUGHTS:

Estimated Female Officers or Directors:
Hot Spot for Advancement for Women/Minorities:

Equinox Fitness
NAIC Code: 713940

www.equinox.com

TYPES OF BUSINESS:
Fitness Centers
Fitness Clubs
Retail Fitness Centers
Hotels
Fitness Apparel
Ecommerce
Stationary Bikes
Spa Services

BRANDS/DIVISIONS/AFFILIATES:
Related Companies LP (The)
Furthermore From Equinox
Eqx
Equinox Hotel

CONTACTS: *Note: Officers with more than one job title may be intentionally listed here more than once.*
Harvey Spevak, Chmn.

GROWTH PLANS/SPECIAL FEATURES:
Equinox Fitness is a luxury fitness company with national headquarters in New York. The firm operates more than 105 upscale, full-service clubs throughout the U.S., as well as in Canada and the U.K. Equinox clubs typically feature yoga studios, a Pilates studio, a competitive cycling classes and many more signature fitness classes. Equinox offers an integrated selection of Equinox-branded programs, services and products, personal training, spa services and products, apparel and food/juice bars. The firm's website also contains a shopping link that includes apparel labels such as Lululemon, Spiritual Gangster and Monrow, and also sells at-home stationary bikes under the SoulCycle brand name. Furthermore, From Equinox is the company's online magazine featuring blogs about the body, food and life. The firm's Eqx app assists users with personalizing workout plans and features performance tracking tools. In addition, Equinox began constructing upscale, health-focused hotels, with its first location having opened in New York City's Hudson Yards. The hotel encompasses a workout studio, spa, pools, fresh/locally-sourced foods and dining options and more. Equinox is owned by The Related Companies LP.

FINANCIAL DATA: *Note: Data for latest year may not have been available at press time.*

In U.S. $	2022	2021	2020	2019	2018	2017
Revenue	1,200,000,000	885,885,000	843,700,000	1,430,000,000	1,090,000,000	1,090,000,000
R&D Expense						
Operating Income						
Operating Margin %						
SGA Expense						
Net Income						
Operating Cash Flow						
Capital Expenditure						
EBITDA						
Return on Assets %						
Return on Equity %						
Debt to Equity						

CONTACT INFORMATION:
Phone: 212-677-0180   Fax:
Toll-Free:
Address: 31 Hudson Yards, New York, NY 10001 United States

STOCK TICKER/OTHER:
Stock Ticker: Private   Exchange:
Employees: Fiscal Year Ends:
Parent Company: Related Companies LP (The)

SALARIES/BONUSES:
Top Exec. Salary: $ Bonus: $
Second Exec. Salary: $ Bonus: $

OTHER THOUGHTS:
Estimated Female Officers or Directors:
Hot Spot for Advancement for Women/Minorities:

ESPN Inc

espn.com

NAIC Code: 515210

TYPES OF BUSINESS:

Sports Television-Cable
Sports Radio Broadcasting
Online Sports Information
Magazine & Book Publishing
Sports Websites and Apps
Sports Podcasts
Sports Event Management
Direct-to-Consumer Video Service

BRANDS/DIVISIONS/AFFILIATES:

Walt Disney Company (The)
ABC Inc
Hearst Corporation
ESPN
SportsCenter
ESPN+
ESPN Radio
ESPN.com

CONTACTS: *Note: Officers with more than one job title may be intentionally listed here more than once.*

James Pitaro, CEO
Patrick Stiegman, Editor-in-Chief

GROWTH PLANS/SPECIAL FEATURES:

ESPN, Inc. is a multinational, multi-media sports entertainment company with a portfolio of related assets. The firm's headquarters in Bristol, the ESPN Plaza, comprises more than 1.3 million square feet in 19 buildings on 120 acres. ESPN's primary business divisions include: U.S. television networks, direct-to-consumer, audio, digital, overseas and event management. The U.S. television networks division operates ESPN on ABC's broadcasting network, as well as eight domestic cable networks, with five offering high-definition simulcast services. Key programming by this division includes: SportsCenter, offering breaking news, highlights, sports features and in-depth sports analysis via journalists; NFL's Monday Night Football, which also offers programming across MLB, NBA, WNBA, NHL, college football, men's and women's college basketball, tennis, golf, Little League World Series and more; daily and weekly sport-specific studio shows for NFL, MLB, NBA and college football/basketball; and documentaries and original programming, including 30 for 30 films. The direct-to-consumer division operates the ESPN+ multi-sport, direct-to-consumer video service from The Walt Disney Company's Direct-to-Consumer and International (DTCI) segment and ESPN. The audio division operates: ESPN Radio, which provides talk and event content across 500 stations, and its programming is also available on Sirius XM, ESPNRadio.com and through various distributors; and the ESPN Audio podcast, which focuses on sports passions, storytelling and interviews. The digital division operates ESPN.com, the ESPN app, ESPN Fantasy Sports and related interactive games. The overseas division operates through affiliated networks and businesses, reaching sports fans worldwide via 44 networks across more than 70 countries and territories in several languages. Last, the event management division owns and operates 35 events, including college bowl games and college basketball events, as well as ESPYS, X Games and Winter X Games. ESPN is 80%-owned by ABC, Inc., an indirect subsidiary of The Walt Disney Company; and 20%-owned by Hearst Corporation.

FINANCIAL DATA: *Note: Data for latest year may not have been available at press time.*

In U.S. $	2022	2021	2020	2019	2018	2017
Revenue	15,500,000,000	13,292,370,000	11,076,975,000	11,361,000,000	10,750,000,000	10,750,000,000
R&D Expense						
Operating Income						
Operating Margin %						
SGA Expense						
Net Income						
Operating Cash Flow						
Capital Expenditure						
EBITDA						
Return on Assets %						
Return on Equity %						
Debt to Equity						

CONTACT INFORMATION:

Phone: 860-766-2000   Fax: 860-766-2213
Toll-Free:
Address: 545 Middle St., Bristol, CT 06010 United States

SALARIES/BONUSES:

Top Exec. Salary: $ Bonus: $
Second Exec. Salary: $ Bonus: $

STOCK TICKER/OTHER:

Stock Ticker: Subsidiary   Exchange:
Employees: 7,500   Fiscal Year Ends: 09/30
Parent Company: Walt Disney Company (The)

OTHER THOUGHTS:

Estimated Female Officers or Directors: 1
Hot Spot for Advancement for Women/Minorities: Y

Everlast Worldwide Inc

www.everlast.com

NAIC Code: 339920

TYPES OF BUSINESS:

Sporting Goods Manufacturing--Boxing
Apparel
Work Boots & Safety Footwear
Boxing Equipment
Product Licensing
Ecommerce
Manufacturing
Global Production and Distribution

BRANDS/DIVISIONS/AFFILIATES:

Frasers Group plcs
Everlast

CONTACTS: *Note: Officers with more than one job title may be intentionally listed here more than once.*

Michael Murray, Chief Executive-Frasers Group
Gerard J. Delisser, Chief Merch. Officer
Angelo V. Giusti, Sec.
Angelo V. Giusti, Pres., Sporting Equipment Bus.

GROWTH PLANS/SPECIAL FEATURES:

Everlast Worldwide, Inc., a subsidiary of Frasers Group plc, designs, manufactures, markets, licenses and sells active wear, sportswear and outerwear, with a particular focus on boxing related products, such as gloves, heavy bags, speed bags, trunks and gym equipment. The company is a leading brand for boxing and mixed martial arts enthusiasts, selling everything from training equipment to heavy duty competition cages. The firm also licenses the Everlast trademark to companies that produce women's and children's apparel, underwear, footwear, eyewear, hats, fragrances, batteries, jewelry, nutritional products, fitness toys, heart rate monitors and other products. Everlast products are sold across more than 75 countries and six continents. The firm's graphic arts department develops advertising campaigns and provide brand management, packaging solutions, retail advertising and catalogs for all of the company's product lines. Everlast has received continued exposure in print, television and movie media as well as product placement on the Academy Award winning movie Million Dollar Baby, the reality TV drama The Contender, the movie Cinderella Man and the EA Sports Fight Night videogame. Everlast Worldwide has partnered with several health and fitness businesses, including 24 Hour Fitness, Crunch, Lifetime Fitness, Xtreme Couture MMA, Title Boxing, Gleason's Gym, Five Points Academy and Everlast Sports Nutrition.

FINANCIAL DATA: *Note: Data for latest year may not have been available at press time.*

In U.S. $	2022	2021	2020	2019	2018	2017
Revenue						
R&D Expense						
Operating Income						
Operating Margin %						
SGA Expense						
Net Income						
Operating Cash Flow						
Capital Expenditure						
EBITDA						
Return on Assets %						
Return on Equity %						
Debt to Equity						

CONTACT INFORMATION:

Phone: 660-263-4381   Fax:
Toll-Free: 800-821-7930
Address: 1900 Highway DD, Moberly, MO 65270 United States

SALARIES/BONUSES:

Top Exec. Salary: $ Bonus: $
Second Exec. Salary: $ Bonus: $

STOCK TICKER/OTHER:

Stock Ticker: Subsidiary   Exchange:
Employees: 350   Fiscal Year Ends: 12/31
Parent Company: Frasers Group plc

OTHER THOUGHTS:

Estimated Female Officers or Directors:
Hot Spot for Advancement for Women/Minorities:

Everton Football Club

www.evertonfc.com

NAIC Code: 711211D

TYPES OF BUSINESS:
English Premiere Soccer Team
Team Management and Operations

BRANDS/DIVISIONS/AFFILIATES:

GROWTH PLANS/SPECIAL FEATURES:
Everton Football Club is one of the oldest and most successful soccer teams in the English Premier League. The club has two nicknames, the Toffees and the Blues. Domestically, Everton FC has won the League Championship nine times, the FA Cup five times, the FA Charity Shield nine times, and won the European Cup internationally in its 1984-85 season. The team plays in the Goodison Park located in Walton, Liverpool, England, which provides approximately a 39,570-seating capacity. The club has competed in the top division the majority of the time, missing only four times since its 1888 creation. Key players over the years range from Jack Sharp who played from 1899 through 1909 to Gary Stevens and Pat van den Hauwe, who were inducted as key FC players in 2020. Team revenue is generated largely from payments related to premiership broadcasting rights and home game ticket sales as well as program sales and concessions.

CONTACTS: *Note: Officers with more than one job title may be intentionally listed here more than once.*
Denise Barrett-Baxendale, CEO
Philip Carter, Pres.
Grant Ingles, Dir.-Finance
Grant Ingles, Company Sec.
David Harrison, Head-Football Oper.
Mark Rowan, Head-Media & Comm.
Grant Ingles, Head-Finance
Dave Biggar, Dir.-Commercial
Alan Bowen, Head-Stadium Oper.
Paul Tyrrell, Dir.-Comm.
Bill Kenwright, Chmn.

FINANCIAL DATA: *Note: Data for latest year may not have been available at press time.*

In U.S. $	2022	2021	2020	2019	2018	2017
Revenue	272,000,000	267,485,672	229,049,377	246,582,000	219,937,000	219,937,000
R&D Expense						
Operating Income						
Operating Margin %						
SGA Expense						
Net Income		-167,482,706	-172,350,778	-160,016,000	38,517,900	38,517,900
Operating Cash Flow						
Capital Expenditure						
EBITDA						
Return on Assets %						
Return on Equity %						
Debt to Equity						

CONTACT INFORMATION:
Phone: 44 151-556-1878   Fax:
Toll-Free:
Address: Goodison Rd., Goodison Park, Liverpool, L4 4EL United Kingdom

STOCK TICKER/OTHER:
Stock Ticker: Private
Employees: 450
Parent Company:

Exchange:
Fiscal Year Ends: 06/30

SALARIES/BONUSES:
Top Exec. Salary: $ Bonus: $
Second Exec. Salary: $ Bonus: $

OTHER THOUGHTS:
Estimated Female Officers or Directors:
Hot Spot for Advancement for Women/Minorities:

Fanatics Inc

NAIC Code: 454111

TYPES OF BUSINESS:

Electronic Shopping of Licensed Sports Merchandise
Ecommerce
Vertical Commerce
Licensed Sports Merchandise
Digital Sports Platform
Sports Product Design and Manufacturing
Ecommerce Supply Chain and Logistics
Betting and Gaming Databases

BRANDS/DIVISIONS/AFFILIATES:

Fanatics Commerce
Fanatics Collectibles
Fanatics Betting & Gaming

CONTACTS: *Note: Officers with more than one job title may be intentionally listed here more than once.*

Michael Rubin, CEO
Tucker Kain, Chief Strategy Officer
Jamie Davis, Pres.
Glenn H. Schiffman, CFO
Meier Raivich, Exec. VP-Global Communications
Robin Eletto, Chief People Officer
Larry Dolan, Chief Information Security Officer
Jack Boyle, Pres., Merch.
Mitch Trager, Chief Strategy Officer
Meier Raivich, VP-Branding
Gary Gertzog, Exec. VP-Bus. Affairs
Orlando Ashford, Chmn.

GROWTH PLANS/SPECIAL FEATURES:

Fanatics, Inc. is an online retailer of licensed sports merchandise. The firm's global digital sports platform also features NFTs/digital collectibles, sports betting and iGaming, trading cards and more. Fanatics has relationships with over 900 properties and includes many prominent brands. Subsidiary Fanatics Commerce comprises an innovative vertical commerce business strategy that allows the company to swiftly design, manufacture and distribute high-quality fan gear, jerseys, lifestyle and streetwear products, as well as headwear and hardgoods. This division offers a broad assortment of first and third-party fan merchandise and memorabilia, whether manufactured in-house, sourced from fan apparel brands or available via drop-ship. Fanatics Collectibles implements a vertical commerce model, an innovative technology platform and an agile supply chain to offer a mobile-first consumer brand. Its operations encompass technology, on-demand manufacturing and logistics. Fanatics Betting & Gaming combines global databases of sports fans, creative marketing, social strategies, technology and brand recognition. Fanatics, Inc. is headquartered in Florida, with international headquarter locations in the U.K. and Japan.

FINANCIAL DATA: *Note: Data for latest year may not have been available at press time.*

In U.S. $	2022	2021	2020	2019	2018	2017
Revenue	6,300,000,000	4,000,000,000	2,887,500,000	2,500,000,000	2,415,000,000	2,415,000,000
R&D Expense						
Operating Income						
Operating Margin %						
SGA Expense						
Net Income						
Operating Cash Flow						
Capital Expenditure						
EBITDA						
Return on Assets %						
Return on Equity %						
Debt to Equity						

CONTACT INFORMATION:

Phone: 904-421-1897   Fax:
Toll-Free: 877-833-7397
Address: 8100 Nations Way, Jacksonville, FL 32256 United States

STOCK TICKER/OTHER:

Stock Ticker: Private   Exchange:
Employees: 18,000   Fiscal Year Ends: 12/31
Parent Company:

SALARIES/BONUSES:

Top Exec. Salary: $ Bonus: $
Second Exec. Salary: $ Bonus: $

OTHER THOUGHTS:

Estimated Female Officers or Directors:
Hot Spot for Advancement for Women/Minorities:

FanDuel Group

www.fanduel.com

NAIC Code: 519130

TYPES OF BUSINESS:

Fantasy Sports
Online Fantasy Sports
Sports Betting Platforms
Sportsbook
Sports Betting Leagues
Online Casino Games
Online Racing Games

BRANDS/DIVISIONS/AFFILIATES:

Flutter Entertainment plc
FanDuel

CONTACTS: Note: Officers with more than one job title may be intentionally listed here more than once.

Amy Howe, CEO
Christian Genetski, Pres.
David Jennings, CFO
Mike Raffensperger, CCO
Tricia Alcamo, Chief People Officer
Andrew Sheh, CTO
Andy Giancamilli, COO

GROWTH PLANS/SPECIAL FEATURES:

FanDuel Group operates an online fantasy sports platform that enables users to play fantasy games and win cash prizes. The platform is comprised of season-long fantasy sports leagues which are compressed into a free and/or paid daily game of skill. Players can enter one-day leagues without having to commit to season-long gaming via downloadable and mobile devices. FanDuel has over 12 million registered players. With thousands of leagues to choose from, contests include NFL, NBA, WNBA, MLB, NHL and PGA, as well as European football leagues (EPL and UCL). FanDuel pays out millions in cash prizes every week, with instant payouts as soon as contests end. While FanDuel group has a presence across all 50 states, as of late-2022, FanDuel sportsbook betting was available in the U.S. states of Arizona, Colorado, Connecticut, Iowa, Illinois, Indiana, Louisiana, Michigan, New Jersey, Pennsylvania, Tennessee, Virginia and West Virginia. FanDuel Group also offers online casino games, including slots, roulette, live dealer, blackjack and other online table games, as well as online racing. FanDuel Group operates as a subsidiary of Flutter Entertainment plc, which owns approximately 95% of FanDuel. FanDuel offers its employees health insurance, flexible work hours and employee development opportunities.

FINANCIAL DATA: Note: Data for latest year may not have been available at press time.

In U.S. $	2022	2021	2020	2019	2018	2017
Revenue	300,000,000	176,379,301	150,150,000	143,000,000	124,000,000	124,000,000
R&D Expense						
Operating Income						
Operating Margin %						
SGA Expense						
Net Income						
Operating Cash Flow						
Capital Expenditure						
EBITDA						
Return on Assets %						
Return on Equity %						
Debt to Equity						

CONTACT INFORMATION:

Phone: 415-237-2774   Fax:
Toll-Free: 800-475-2250
Address: 1375 Broadway, New York, NY 10018 United States

STOCK TICKER/OTHER:

Stock Ticker: Subsidiary   Exchange:
Employees: 1,500   Fiscal Year Ends: 12/31
Parent Company: Flutter Entertainment plc

SALARIES/BONUSES:

Top Exec. Salary: $ Bonus: $
Second Exec. Salary: $ Bonus: $

OTHER THOUGHTS:

Estimated Female Officers or Directors:
Hot Spot for Advancement for Women/Minorities:

FC Cincinnati

NAIC Code: 711211D

www.fccincinnati.com

TYPES OF BUSINESS:

Major League Soccer
Team Management and Operations

BRANDS/DIVISIONS/AFFILIATES:

GROWTH PLANS/SPECIAL FEATURES:

FC Cincinnati is an American soccer team playing in Major League Soccer (MLS) and is based in Cincinnati, Ohio. The team is an expansion team that joined the MLS, playing its inaugural match in Mach 2019. FC Cincinnati succeeded the USL Championship, the second-tier of American soccer, of the same name. The team currently plays at TQL Stadium (also known as West End Stadium), which has a capacity of 26,000 and is a soccer-specific facility in Cincinnati. FC Cincinnati averaged 22,487 in attendance during the 2022 season.

CONTACTS: *Note: Officers with more than one job title may be intentionally listed here more than once.*

Carl H. Lindner III, Managing Owner and CEO Managing Owner and CEO
Jeff Berding, Co-CEO
Dennis Carroll, COO
John Durbin, Chief Commercial Officer
Kimberly Eppert, Sr. Dir.-Human Resources
Lindsey Braun, VP-Bus. Strategy & Innovation
Paula Boggs Muething, Chief Legal & Admin. Officer

FINANCIAL DATA: *Note: Data for latest year may not have been available at press time.*

In U.S. $	2022	2021	2020	2019	2018	2017
Revenue						
R&D Expense						
Operating Income						
Operating Margin %						
SGA Expense						
Net Income						
Operating Cash Flow						
Capital Expenditure						
EBITDA						
Return on Assets %						
Return on Equity %						
Debt to Equity						

CONTACT INFORMATION:

Phone: 513-977-5435   Fax:
Toll-Free:
Address: 14 E. 4th St., Ste. 300, Cincinnati, OH 45202 United States

STOCK TICKER/OTHER:

Stock Ticker: Private   Exchange:
Employees: 570   Fiscal Year Ends:
Parent Company:

SALARIES/BONUSES:

Top Exec. Salary: $ Bonus: $
Second Exec. Salary: $ Bonus: $

OTHER THOUGHTS:

Estimated Female Officers or Directors:
Hot Spot for Advancement for Women/Minorities:

FC Dallas

www.fcdallas.com

NAIC Code: 711211D

TYPES OF BUSINESS:

Major League Soccer Team
Team Management and Operations

BRANDS/DIVISIONS/AFFILIATES:

Dallas Burn
Hunt Sports Group

CONTACTS: Note: Officers with more than one job title may be intentionally listed here more than once.

Clark Hunt, CEO
Dan Hunt, Pres.
Jimmy Smith, CFO
Jerome Elenez, VP-Mktg.
Eliud Jimenez, Dir.-Human Resources
Michael McGrory, Dir.-Media & Communications
Tim Henning, Dir.-Merch.
Evie Baker, Sr. Dir.-Admin.
Nick Shafer, VP-Stadium Oper.
Kelly Weller, VP-Strategic Planning
Kelly Weller, VP-Corp. Comm.
Schellas Hyndman, Head Coach
James C. Walter, II, Dir.-Medical
Luiz Muzzi, Dir.-Soccer Oper.
Erik Davila, Dir.-Creative
Clark Hunt, Chmn.
Cesar Velasco, Sr. Dir.-Int'l Mktg. & Comm.

GROWTH PLANS/SPECIAL FEATURES:

FC Dallas is a Major League Soccer (MLS) team based in Dallas, Texas, playing in the Western Conference. The team is the latest incarnation of professional soccer in Dallas, whose soccer history began shortly after the 1966 World Cup. That first team, the Dallas Tornados, played in the North American Soccer League until 1981. Dallas also hosted a professional indoor soccer team, the Dallas Sidekicks, until operations were suspended following the 2004 season. FC Dallas, a charter member of the MLS, began life in 1995 as the Dallas Burn. The team qualified for the playoffs the first seven years of its existence, from 1995 to 2002, and made it to the finals on two occasions. The Burn also won the Lamar Hunt U.S. Open Cup in 1997. In early 2005, the Burn changed their name to FC Dallas when they moved into their Pizza Hut Park stadium a 20,500-seat soccer-specific stadium located in Frisco, Texas. In 2013, Toyota acquired the naming rights of the stadium, changing it to Toyota Stadium. FC Dallas' average home game attendance was 16,469 during the 2022 season. FC Dallas won the Western Conference regular season in 2006, 2015 and 2016, as well as the U.S. Open Cup, again, in 2016. The team is owned and operated by the Hunt Sports Group.

FINANCIAL DATA: Note: Data for latest year may not have been available at press time.

In U.S. $	2022	2021	2020	2019	2018	2017
Revenue	10,654,875					
R&D Expense						
Operating Income						
Operating Margin %						
SGA Expense						
Net Income						
Operating Cash Flow						
Capital Expenditure						
EBITDA						
Return on Assets %						
Return on Equity %						
Debt to Equity						

CONTACT INFORMATION:

Phone: 469-365-0000   Fax: 214-705-0099
Toll-Free:
Address: 9200 World Cup Way, Ste. 202, Frisco, TX 75034 United States

STOCK TICKER/OTHER:

Stock Ticker: Private   Exchange:
Employees: 350   Fiscal Year Ends:
Parent Company:

SALARIES/BONUSES:

Top Exec. Salary: $ Bonus: $
Second Exec. Salary: $ Bonus: $

OTHER THOUGHTS:

Estimated Female Officers or Directors: 12
Hot Spot for Advancement for Women/Minorities: Y

Fenerbahce Spor Kulubu

www.fenerbahce.org

NAIC Code: 711211

TYPES OF BUSINESS:

Sports Management
Turkish Sports Club

BRANDS/DIVISIONS/AFFILIATES:

Fenerbahce SA
Fenerbahce Futbol AS
Fenerbahce Sukru Saracoolu Stadium

CONTACTS: *Note: Officers with more than one job title may be intentionally listed here more than once.*

Ali Koc, Pres.
Vedat Olcay, Gen. Sec.
Nihat Ozdemir, Contact-Media
Mahmut Nedim Uslu, VP-Amateur Departments
Serhat Cecen, VP-Formal Association Rel.
Mithat Yenigun, VP-Social Organizations & Associations
Nihat Ozbagi, VP-Investment & Projects

GROWTH PLANS/SPECIAL FEATURES:

Fenerbahce Spor Kulubu, founded in 1907, is a sports club that features teams who compete in soccer, swimming, boxing, rowing, volleyball, sailing and table tennis. Soccer is its most prominent sport and Fenerbahce's team is the most successful in the Turkish Super League, having won 17 times. They made it to the playoffs in the 2021-22 season, but were eliminated by Slavia Prague 2-3 in Istanbul. The Fenerbahce Sukru Saracoolu Stadium is the club's premier stadium with a capacity of 62,000 and features a VIP section, dining facilities, work areas and a social venue. Additionally, the club has a training complex for its athletes, camp facilities, a youth football center, museum, sports hall and a swimming pool. The club's subsidiary, Fenerbahce Futbol AS, manages the professional soccer team's sporting, educational, legal and economic activities. These activities include the management and marketing of the Fenerbahce brand name and rights, broadcasting rights, stadium and advertising activities and the generation of income from sponsorship agreements.

FINANCIAL DATA: *Note: Data for latest year may not have been available at press time.*

In U.S. $	2022	2021	2020	2019	2018	2017
Revenue		80,267,427	79,451,456	119,134,170	85,128,408	85,128,408
R&D Expense						
Operating Income						
Operating Margin %						
SGA Expense						
Net Income		-23,519,923	-22,595,758	-34,673,486	-27,103,060	-27,103,060
Operating Cash Flow						
Capital Expenditure						
EBITDA						
Return on Assets %						
Return on Equity %						
Debt to Equity						

CONTACT INFORMATION:

Phone: 90-216-542-1907   Fax: 90-216-542-1960
Toll-Free:
Address: Arayicibasi Sokak 5, Istanbul, 34724 Turkey

STOCK TICKER/OTHER:

Stock Ticker: FENER   Exchange: Istanbul
Employees: 544   Fiscal Year Ends: 05/31
Parent Company: Fenerbahce SA

SALARIES/BONUSES:

Top Exec. Salary: $ Bonus: $
Second Exec. Salary: $ Bonus: $

OTHER THOUGHTS:

Estimated Female Officers or Directors:
Hot Spot for Advancement for Women/Minorities:

Fenway Sports Group LLC

fenwaysportsgroup.com

NAIC Code: 523910

TYPES OF BUSINESS:

Venture Capital/Private Equity Investment/Hedge Funds
Management of Business & Enterprises
Business Investments
Holding Company
Sports Team Investments
Real Estate Development
Sports Branding
Sports Arenas

BRANDS/DIVISIONS/AFFILIATES:

Boston Red Sox
Liverpool FC
Pittsburgh Penguins
Fenway Park
Anfield
Fenway Sports Management
Fenway Sports Group Real Estate
New England Sports Network

CONTACTS:
Note: Officers with more than one job title may be intentionally listed here more than once.

John W. Henry, CEO
Michael Gordon, Pres.
Sam Kennedy, Pres., Fenway Sports Management
Lawrence (Larry) Lucchino, CEO
Thomas C. Werner, Chmn.

GROWTH PLANS/SPECIAL FEATURES:

Fenway Sports Group, LLC (FSG) is a sports investment company whose holdings include Major League Baseball (MLB) team Boston Red Sox, Liverpool Football Club of the English Premier League (EPL) and the Pittsburgh Penguins of the National Hockey League (NHL). FSG also owns Fenway Park, the Red Sox's home stadium, and Anfield, home of Liverpool FC. The group is vertically- and horizontally-integrated across the disciplines of sports management and team ownership. Subsidiary Fenway Sports Management (FSM) specializes in global sponsorship sales and brand management consulting. Fenway Sports Group Real Estate (FSGRE) oversees the assets, acquisitions and development of FSG's properties. Additional ownerships by FSG include: a 50% stake in RFK Racing, one of NASCAR's largest premier racing teams, with Roush Racing owning the other half; an 80% stake in the New England Sports Network (NESN), with Delaware North Companies owning the remaining 20%.; and a minority interest in The SpringHill Company, an entertainment business founded by LeBron James and Maverick Carter designed to empower athletes, artists and brands.

FINANCIAL DATA:
Note: Data for latest year may not have been available at press time.

In U.S. $	2022	2021	2020	2019	2018	2017
Revenue						
R&D Expense						
Operating Income						
Operating Margin %						
SGA Expense						
Net Income						
Operating Cash Flow						
Capital Expenditure						
EBITDA						
Return on Assets %						
Return on Equity %						
Debt to Equity						

CONTACT INFORMATION:

Phone: 617-226-6300   Fax: 617-226-6484
Toll-Free:
Address: 82 Brookline Ave., Boston, MA 02215 United States

STOCK TICKER/OTHER:

Stock Ticker: Private   Exchange:
Employees: 2,700   Fiscal Year Ends:
Parent Company:

SALARIES/BONUSES:

Top Exec. Salary: $ Bonus: $
Second Exec. Salary: $ Bonus: $

OTHER THOUGHTS:

Estimated Female Officers or Directors:
Hot Spot for Advancement for Women/Minorities:

Field & Stream

NAIC Code: 451110

TYPES OF BUSINESS:

Sporting Goods, Retail
Footwear
Ecommerce
Hunting and Fishing Products
Boating and Camping Products
Outdoor Recreation Products
Outdoor Recreation Apparel

BRANDS/DIVISIONS/AFFILIATES:

Dicks Sporting Goods Inc
Field & Stream

CONTACTS: *Note: Officers with more than one job title may be intentionally listed here more than once.*

Edward W. Stack, Chmn.-Dicks Sporting Goods

GROWTH PLANS/SPECIAL FEATURES:

Field & Stream is a retailer of hunting, fishing, boating, camping and related outdoor recreation apparel and merchandise. The firm is a subsidiary of Dick's Sporting Goods, Inc., a leading sporting goods retailer in the U.S. There four Field & Stream brick-and-mortar retail locations in the U.S.; therefore, the company sells its merchandise and gift cards online. Hunting and shooting products include guns, archery, decoys, tree stands, calls, apparel, optics, knives and multi-tools, boots, tail cameras and more. Fishing products include baits and lures, rods and reals, tackle line, tackle boxes and bags, fishing electronics, apparel, waders, wading boots, fly fishing, saltwater fishing, ice fishing and bowfishing. Boating products include kayaks, canoes, paddleboards, paddles, trolling, boat safety items, life jackets and vests, racks, carts, boating electronics and accessories. Camping products include tents, sleeping bags and bedding, camp furniture, backpacks and bags, cookware, stoves, coolers, hydration supplies, lighting, knives and tools, first aid and survival products and kits, camping electronics and accessories. Field & Stream's wide range of apparel is offered for men, women and kids, as well as accessories such as hats/visors, gloves, socks, sunglasses, neck gaiters, face masks, belts, wallets and watches. Footwear is also available for men, women and children. Other items span outdoor grills, firepits, heaters, coolers, chairs, canopies/shelter, hammocks, games and toys, as well as automotive accessories.

FINANCIAL DATA: *Note: Data for latest year may not have been available at press time.*

In U.S. $	2022	2021	2020	2019	2018	2017
Revenue						
R&D Expense						
Operating Income						
Operating Margin %						
SGA Expense						
Net Income						
Operating Cash Flow						
Capital Expenditure						
EBITDA						
Return on Assets %						
Return on Equity %						
Debt to Equity						

CONTACT INFORMATION:

Phone: 724-273-3400   Fax:
Toll-Free: 877 846-9997
Address: 345 Court St., Coraopolis, PA 15108 United States

STOCK TICKER/OTHER:

Stock Ticker: Subsidiary   Exchange:
Employees: Fiscal Year Ends:
Parent Company: Dicks Sporting Goods Inc

SALARIES/BONUSES:

Top Exec. Salary: $ Bonus: $
Second Exec. Salary: $ Bonus: $

OTHER THOUGHTS:

Estimated Female Officers or Directors:
Hot Spot for Advancement for Women/Minorities:

FIFA (Federation Internationale de Football Association)
www.fifa.com
NAIC Code: 711211

TYPES OF BUSINESS:
International Soccer Association
International Football Association

BRANDS/DIVISIONS/AFFILIATES:
FIFA Council
FIFA Statutes
FIFA Museum
FIFA World Cup

CONTACTS: *Note: Officers with more than one job title may be intentionally listed here more than once.*
Gianni Infantino, Pres.
Julio H. Grondona, Sr. VP
Angel Maria Villar Llona, VP
Issa Hayatou, VP
Michel Platini, VP
David Chung, VP
Jim Boyce, VP
Ali Bin Al Hussein, VP

GROWTH PLANS/SPECIAL FEATURES:
FIFA (Federation Internationale de Football Association) is the international governing body of soccer, with over 210 associations worldwide, including men's and women's teams. FIFA supports the affiliated associations financially and logistically through various programs. The associations represent FIFA in their respective countries, have obligations to adhere to FIFA rules and governing bodies and to promote and manage the sport accordingly. The FIFA Council is a bureau that deals with all matters requiring immediate settlement between two meetings of the FIFA Council. FIFA Statutes provide a separation between strategic oversight and executive, operational and administrative functions. FIFA's member associations and the regional confederations meet once per year to agree on ways to promote and develop football worldwide. The FIFA Museum covers all aspects of international football heritage and showcases the history of the FIFA World Cup. Current (mid-2023) FIFA partners include Adidas, Coca-Cola and Wanda.

FINANCIAL DATA: *Note: Data for latest year may not have been available at press time.*

In U.S. $	2022	2021	2020	2019	2018	2017
Revenue	789,000,000	766,488,000	266,541,000	776,000,000	734,202,000	734,202,000
R&D Expense						
Operating Income						
Operating Margin %						
SGA Expense						
Net Income		-312,212,000	-682,994,000	-185,287,000	-191,522,000	-191,522,000
Operating Cash Flow						
Capital Expenditure						
EBITDA						
Return on Assets %						
Return on Equity %						
Debt to Equity						

CONTACT INFORMATION:
Phone: 41-43-222-7777   Fax: 41-43-222-7878
Toll-Free:
Address: FIFA-Strasse 20, Zurich, 8044 Switzerland

STOCK TICKER/OTHER:
Stock Ticker: Private
Employees: 815
Parent Company:

Exchange:
Fiscal Year Ends: 12/31

SALARIES/BONUSES:
Top Exec. Salary: $ Bonus: $
Second Exec. Salary: $ Bonus: $

OTHER THOUGHTS:
Estimated Female Officers or Directors:
Hot Spot for Advancement for Women/Minorities:

Fila USA Inc

NAIC Code: 424300

www.fila.com

TYPES OF BUSINESS:

Apparel and Clothing Brands, Designers, Importers and Distributors
Footwear
Casual Wear
Workwear
Active Wear
Athletic Shoes
Accessories

BRANDS/DIVISIONS/AFFILIATES:

Fila Holdings Corp

CONTACTS: Note: Officers with more than one job title may be intentionally listed here more than once.

Todd Klein, Pres.
Jarita Bridges, Mgr.-Prod. Placement & Entertainment Mktg.
Kelly Macmanus Funke, Sr. Mgr.-e-commerce
Jarita Bridges, Head-Investor Rel.
Gene Yoon, CEO
Rob Baker, Dir.-Sportstyle Mktg.

GROWTH PLANS/SPECIAL FEATURES:

Fila USA, Inc., a subsidiary of Fila Holdings Corp. based in South Korea, produces athletic footwear, apparel and accessories for men, women and children. The company's original focus revolved around the textiles business before going on to specialize in knitwear production. Fila entered the sports industry in 1973, and eventually established itself within the tennis apparel industry through its innovative tubular manufacturing process that, until then, was only used for other products. Fila also challenged the white-only tradition on tennis courts by creating a line of colored tennis apparel. The firm continues to be committed to using cutting-edge technology and innovative materials. Footwear products by Fila primarily include sneakers and athletic shoes, as well as sandals, slip-ons, boots and work shoes such as steel toe, slip resistant and composite toe. Apparel items include tops, shirts, hoodies, sweats, shorts, pants, sweaters, outerwear, swimsuits, tracksuits, workwear, socks and a wide range of accessories.

Fila USA offers its employees comprehensive health and retirement benefits.

FINANCIAL DATA: Note: Data for latest year may not have been available at press time.

In U.S. $	2022	2021	2020	2019	2018	2017
Revenue	346,373,357	478,117,576	468,525,000	540,154,000	304,665,000	304,665,000
R&D Expense						
Operating Income						
Operating Margin %						
SGA Expense						
Net Income	-59,883,349	8,711,071	3,970,160	24,998,532	1,136,000	1,136,000
Operating Cash Flow						
Capital Expenditure						
EBITDA						
Return on Assets %						
Return on Equity %						
Debt to Equity						

CONTACT INFORMATION:

Phone: 410-773-3236   Fax: 410-773-4989
Toll-Free:
Address: 930 Ridgebrook Rd., Ste. 200, Sparks, MD 21152 United States

STOCK TICKER/OTHER:

Stock Ticker: Subsidiary   Exchange:
Employees: 415   Fiscal Year Ends: 12/31
Parent Company: Fila Holdings Corp

SALARIES/BONUSES:

Top Exec. Salary: $ Bonus: $
Second Exec. Salary: $ Bonus: $

OTHER THOUGHTS:

Estimated Female Officers or Directors: 3
Hot Spot for Advancement for Women/Minorities: Y

Florida Panthers

www.nhl.com/panthers

NAIC Code: 711211F

TYPES OF BUSINESS:

Professional Hockey Team (NHL)
Team Management and Operations

BRANDS/DIVISIONS/AFFILIATES:

Sunrise Sports & Entertainment
Charlotte Checkers
Greenville Swamp Rabbits

CONTACTS: *Note: Officers with more than one job title may be intentionally listed here more than once.*

Matthew Caldwell, CEO
Bryce Hollweg, COO
James Suh, CFO
Lauren Cochran, CMO
Rob Stevenson, Exec. VP-People & Facilities
Mark Zarthar, Chief Strategy Officer
Dale Tallon, Exec. VP-Oper.
Bill Zito, Gen. Mngr.

GROWTH PLANS/SPECIAL FEATURES:

The Florida Panthers, owned by Sunrise Sports & Entertainment, is a professional hockey team founded in 1993 that plays in the Atlantic division of the Eastern conference within the National Hockey League (NHL). The franchise entered the NHL as an expansion team, and clenched the conference championship in the 1995-96 season, but lost in the finals to the Colorado Avalanche. To date, the Panthers have won three division championships and two conference championships (with the most recent being 2022-23). The team lost the 2023 Stanley Cup to the Vegas Golden Knights in five games. The team has yet to win a Stanley Cup; but, clenched its first President's Trophy in 2021-22 after defeating the Ottawa Senators 4-0. The Florida Panthers play home games at the FLA Live Arena, which has a seating capacity of about 19,250 for ice hockey. Average attendance for the team was 16,682 during the 2022-23 season. Minor league affiliates include the Charlotte Checkers in the American Hockey League (AHL), and the Florida Everblades in the ECHL. Forbes valued the Panthers at $550 million in December 2023, 31st in the league.

FINANCIAL DATA: *Note: Data for latest year may not have been available at press time.*

In U.S. $	2022	2021	2020	2019	2018	2017
Revenue	148,850,000					
R&D Expense						
Operating Income						
Operating Margin %						
SGA Expense						
Net Income						
Operating Cash Flow						
Capital Expenditure						
EBITDA						
Return on Assets %						
Return on Equity %						
Debt to Equity						

CONTACT INFORMATION:

Phone: 954-835-7000   Fax: 954-835-7600
Toll-Free:
Address: 1 Panther Pkwy., Sunrise, FL 33323 United States

SALARIES/BONUSES:

Top Exec. Salary: $ Bonus: $
Second Exec. Salary: $ Bonus: $

STOCK TICKER/OTHER:

Stock Ticker: Private   Exchange:
Employees: 340   Fiscal Year Ends: 06/30
Parent Company: Sunrise Sports & Entertainment

OTHER THOUGHTS:

Estimated Female Officers or Directors: 9
Hot Spot for Advancement for Women/Minorities: Y

Sales, profits and employees may be estimates. Financial information, benefits and other data can change quickly and may vary from those stated here.

Football Club des Girondins de Bordeaux (Bordeaux)

www.girondins.com/fr

NAIC Code: 711211D

TYPES OF BUSINESS:

Soccer Team
Team Management and Operations

BRANDS/DIVISIONS/AFFILIATES:

Matmut Atlantique

GROWTH PLANS/SPECIAL FEATURES:

Football Club des Girondins de Bordeaux (Bordeaux) is a professional football club in France that was relegated to Ligue 2 for the first time since the 1990-91 season, due to financial difficulties. Ligue 2 is the second division of the French professional football league. Founded in 1881, Bordeaux plays its home games at the Matmut Atlantique stadium, which has a seating capacity of over 42,000. The team averaged 20,712 in home game attendance during the 2022-23 season. Domestically, Bordeaux has won six Ligue 1 titles, four Ligue 2 titles, four Coupe de France titles, three Coupe de la Ligue titles, three Trophee des Champions titles and two Coupe Gambardella titles. Internationally, the club has one UEFA Intertoto Cup title. Adidas is the teams' equipment manufacturer, and its primary sponsors include the Bistro Regent restaurant chain, the Betclic online betting company, and the SEAT Cupra car dealership.

CONTACTS: *Note: Officers with more than one job title may be intentionally listed here more than once.*

Gerard Lopez, Pres.

FINANCIAL DATA: *Note: Data for latest year may not have been available at press time.*

In U.S. $	2022	2021	2020	2019	2018	2017
Revenue	80,000,000	46,290,247	66,367,948	79,838,179	79,576,236	79,576,236
R&D Expense						
Operating Income						
Operating Margin %						
SGA Expense						
Net Income		-75,890,051	-42,906,108	-28,782,642	17,349,804	17,349,804
Operating Cash Flow						
Capital Expenditure						
EBITDA						
Return on Assets %						
Return on Equity %						
Debt to Equity						

CONTACT INFORMATION:

Phone: 0892 683433   Fax: 330 556 575446
Toll-Free:
Address: Rue Joliot Curie, Le Haillan, 33187 France

STOCK TICKER/OTHER:

Stock Ticker: Private   Exchange:
Employees: Fiscal Year Ends: 12/31
Parent Company:

SALARIES/BONUSES:

Top Exec. Salary: $ Bonus: $
Second Exec. Salary: $ Bonus: $

OTHER THOUGHTS:

Estimated Female Officers or Directors:
Hot Spot for Advancement for Women/Minorities:

Football Club Dynamo Kyiv

www.fcdynamo.kiev.ua/en

NAIC Code: 711211D

TYPES OF BUSINESS:

Soccer Team
Team Management and Operations

BRANDS/DIVISIONS/AFFILIATES:

Olimpiyskiy National Sports Complex

GROWTH PLANS/SPECIAL FEATURES:

Football Club Dynamo Kyiv is a professional football club in Ukraine, playing in the Ukrainian Premier League, the highest division of Ukrainian annual football championships. Founded in 1927, Dynamo Kyiv plays its home games in the Olimpiyskiy National Sports Complex, which has a seating capacity of 70,050. The club has won 16 Ukrainian Premier League titles, with the most recent being the 2020-21 season. They placed second in the 2021-22 season. Other Urkainian competition titles include 13 Ukrainian Cups and nine Ukrainian Super Cups. Dynamo Kyiv has also won 13 Soviet Top League competitions, nine Soviet Cups, three Soviet Super Cups, two UEFA Cups, one UEFA Super Cups, four Commonwealth of Independent States Cups, among others. New Balance is the club's kit manufacturer and A-Bank is its shirt sponsor.

CONTACTS: *Note: Officers with more than one job title may be intentionally listed here more than once.*

Ihor Surkis, Pres.

FINANCIAL DATA: *Note: Data for latest year may not have been available at press time.*

In U.S. $	2022	2021	2020	2019	2018	2017
Revenue						
R&D Expense						
Operating Income						
Operating Margin %						
SGA Expense						
Net Income						
Operating Cash Flow						
Capital Expenditure						
EBITDA						
Return on Assets %						
Return on Equity %						
Debt to Equity						

CONTACT INFORMATION:

Phone: 38 044 597 0008   Fax: 38 044 278 41 35
Toll-Free:
Address: 3, Hrushevskyy St., Kyiv, 01001 Ukraine

STOCK TICKER/OTHER:

Stock Ticker: Private   Exchange:
Employees: Fiscal Year Ends:
Parent Company:

SALARIES/BONUSES:

Top Exec. Salary: $ Bonus: $
Second Exec. Salary: $ Bonus: $

OTHER THOUGHTS:

Estimated Female Officers or Directors:
Hot Spot for Advancement for Women/Minorities:

Football Club Internazionale Milano SpA

www.inter.it/en/hp

NAIC Code: 711211D

TYPES OF BUSINESS:

Professional Soccer Team
Team Management and Operations

BRANDS/DIVISIONS/AFFILIATES:

Suning Holdings GroupCo Ltd
LionRock Capital
Pirelli & C SpA
Inter Milan

CONTACTS: *Note: Officers with more than one job title may be intentionally listed here more than once.*

Kangyang (Steven) Zhang, Pres.
Franco Combi, Chief Medical Staff
Umberto Marino, General Sec.
Susanna Wermelinger, Head-Corp. Comm.
Walter Mazzarri, Head Coach
Angelomario Moratti, VP
Rinaldo Ghelfi, VP
Francesca Muttini, Chief Legal Officer

GROWTH PLANS/SPECIAL FEATURES:

Football Club Internazionale Milano SpA, commonly referred to as Inter Milan, is an Italian soccer team based in Milan and playing in Serie A, the top level of the Italian soccer league system. Inter Milan was founded in 1908 and plays its home games at Stadio Giuseppe Meazza, commonly referred to as San Siro. San Siro has a seating capacity of over 80,000 and is owned by the municipality of Milan. Inter Milan shares its home stadium with its local rival A.C. Milan. In international play, the club has won the European Cup/Union of European Football Associations (UEFA) Champions League three times, most recently in 2009-10; the UEFA Cup three times; the Intercontinental Cup twice; and the International Federation of Association Football (FIFA) Club World Cup in 2010. In domestic play, Inter Milan has been very successful over the course of its history, having won Serie A 19 times, most recently in 2020-21; the Coppa Italia nine times, most recently in 2021-22 and 2022-23; and the Supercoppa Italiana seven times, most recently in 2022. The club's kit is manufactured by Nikie and its shirt sponsors include DigitalBits, eBay and Lenovo. Inter Milan is majority-owned by Suning Holdings Group Co. Ltd., and minority-owned by LionRock Capital, Pirelli & C SpA and other shareholders. Inter Milan was valued at $1 billion by Forbes in 2023.

FINANCIAL DATA: *Note: Data for latest year may not have been available at press time.*

In U.S. $	2022	2021	2020	2019	2018	2017
Revenue	460,000,000	434,160,721	418,812,111	466,982,000	363,044,000	363,044,000
R&D Expense						
Operating Income						
Operating Margin %						
SGA Expense						
Net Income		-292,342,467	-115,164,342	-54,201,300	-28,066,900	-28,066,900
Operating Cash Flow						
Capital Expenditure						
EBITDA						
Return on Assets %						
Return on Equity %						
Debt to Equity						

CONTACT INFORMATION:

Phone: 39 02 82719080   Fax:
Toll-Free:
Address: Viale dell Liberazione 16/18, Milan, 20124 Italy

SALARIES/BONUSES:

Top Exec. Salary: $ Bonus: $
Second Exec. Salary: $ Bonus: $

STOCK TICKER/OTHER:

Stock Ticker: Private   Exchange:
Employees: 520   Fiscal Year Ends: 06/30
Parent Company: Suning.com Co Ltd

OTHER THOUGHTS:

Estimated Female Officers or Directors: 2
Hot Spot for Advancement for Women/Minorities:

Football-Club Bayern Munchen eV   www.fcbayern.telekom.de/en

NAIC Code: 711211D

TYPES OF BUSINESS:

Professional Soccer Team
Team Management and Operations

BRANDS/DIVISIONS/AFFILIATES:

FC Bayern
Bayern Munich

CONTACTS: *Note: Officers with more than one job title may be intentionally listed here more than once.*

Oliver Kahn, CEO

GROWTH PLANS/SPECIAL FEATURES:

Football-Club Bayern Munchen e.V., commonly referred to as FC Bayern or Bayern Munich, is a Munich, Germany-based professional soccer team playing in the Bundesliga, the top tier of the German soccer league system. The club was founded in 1900 and plays its home games at Allianz Arena in Munich, which is owned by Allianz Arena Munchen Stadion GmbH, has a league standing and seating capacity of over 75,000 and an international contest seating capacity of over 70,000. FC Bayern is Germany's most successful soccer club in terms of national titles and cups. Domestically, the club has won the German Championship 32 times, with consecutive wins from 2012-13 to 2021-22; the DFB-Pokal 20 times; the DFB-Ligapokal six times; and the DFB/DFL-Supercup 10 times (most recent in 2022). In international play, FC Bayern has won the Union of European Football Associations (UEFA) Champions League/European Cup six times; the UEFA Cup Winners' Cup in 1967; the UEFA Europa League/UEFA Cup in 1996; the UEFA Super Cup in 2013 and 2020; the FIFA Club World Cup in 2013 and 2020; and the Intercontinental Cup in 1976 and 2001. The club is well known for its charitable ventures. Forbes ranked FC Bayern with a value of $4.275 billion in 2022.

FINANCIAL DATA: *Note: Data for latest year may not have been available at press time.*

In U.S. $	2022	2021	2020	2019	2018	2017
Revenue	800,000,000	766,511,438	785,057,000	782,070,000	766,633,000	766,633,000
R&D Expense						
Operating Income						
Operating Margin %						
SGA Expense						
Net Income		2,261,798	11,022,300	181,596,000	79,298,600	79,298,600
Operating Cash Flow						
Capital Expenditure						
EBITDA						
Return on Assets %						
Return on Equity %						
Debt to Equity						

CONTACT INFORMATION:

Phone: 49-89-699-31-0   Fax: 49-89-64-41-65
Toll-Free:
Address: Sabener Strasse 51-57, Munich, D-81547 Germany

STOCK TICKER/OTHER:

Stock Ticker: Private   Exchange:
Employees: 293   Fiscal Year Ends: 06/30
Parent Company:

SALARIES/BONUSES:

Top Exec. Salary: $ Bonus: $
Second Exec. Salary: $ Bonus: $

OTHER THOUGHTS:

Estimated Female Officers or Directors:
Hot Spot for Advancement for Women/Minorities:

Football-Club Gelsenkirchen-Schalke 04 eV www.schalke04.de/en
NAIC Code: 711211D

TYPES OF BUSINESS:
Professional Soccer Team
Team Management and Operations

BRANDS/DIVISIONS/AFFILIATES:
Schalke 04

CONTACTS: *Note: Officers with more than one job title may be intentionally listed here more than once.*
Jens Keller, Head Coach
Axel Hefer, Chmn.

GROWTH PLANS/SPECIAL FEATURES:
Football-Club Gelsenkirchen-Schalke 04 eV, commonly referred to as Schalke 04, is a Gelsenkirchen, Germany-based soccer team playing in the 2. Bundesliga, the second tier of the German soccer league system. The club was established in 1904 and plays its home games at its wholly-owned stadium, Veltins-Arena. The stadium has a seating and standing league capacity of over 54,700 and an international match seating capacity of over 62,000. In international play, the club has won one major European trophy, the Union of European Football Associations (UEFA) Cup in 1997, as well as the lesser UEFA Inertoto Cup in 2003 and 2004. In domestic play, Schalke 04 has won the German Championship seven times, with the most recent occurring in 1958; the DFB-Pokal five times, the most recent in 2011; the DFB-Ligapokal in 2005; and the DFL-Supercup in 2011. As for the 2. Bundesliga, Schalke 04 has clenched the domestic title three times, in 1981-12, 1990-91 and 2021-22. In its earlier years, the club won the Oberliga West in 1951 and 1958, the Gauliga Westfalen eleven times and the West German football championship four times. Notable players of Schalke 04 have included the likes of Klaus Fichtel, Norbert Nigbur, Klaus Fischer and Rudiger Abramczik.

FINANCIAL DATA: *Note: Data for latest year may not have been available at press time.*

In U.S. $	2022	2021	2020	2019	2018	2017
Revenue	200,000,000	189,174,836	214,525,339	279,965,000	287,487,000	287,487,000
R&D Expense						
Operating Income						
Operating Margin %						
SGA Expense						
Net Income		-21,181,584	-65,186,682	-11,198,600	-14,374,400	-14,374,400
Operating Cash Flow						
Capital Expenditure						
EBITDA						
Return on Assets %						
Return on Equity %						
Debt to Equity						

CONTACT INFORMATION:
Phone: 49-209-3618-0   Fax: 49-209-3618-109
Toll-Free:
Address: Ernst-Kuzorra-Weg 1, Gelsenkirchen, 45891 Germany

STOCK TICKER/OTHER:
Stock Ticker: Private   Exchange:
Employees: 404   Fiscal Year Ends: 12/31
Parent Company:

SALARIES/BONUSES:
Top Exec. Salary: $ Bonus: $
Second Exec. Salary: $ Bonus: $

OTHER THOUGHTS:
Estimated Female Officers or Directors:
Hot Spot for Advancement for Women/Minorities:

Formula One Group (F1)

www.formula1.com

NAIC Code: 711211

TYPES OF BUSINESS:

Car Racing
Single-Seat Car Racing
Sponsorships and Advertising Packages
International Racing

BRANDS/DIVISIONS/AFFILIATES:

Formula One Management
Formula One Licensing BV
Formula One Promotions and Administration
Formula One Paddock Club
Liberty Media Corporation

CONTACTS: *Note: Officers with more than one job title may be intentionally listed here more than once.*

Stefano Domenicali, CEO
Chase Carey, Chmn.

GROWTH PLANS/SPECIAL FEATURES:

Formula One Group (F1) is a conglomerate of companies involved in the promotion of the Formula One World Championship, a single seater auto racing championship. Through its numerous subsidiaries, including Formula One Management (FOM), Formula One Licensing BV and Formula One Promotions and Administration, the company maintains the various rights, licensing and management operations of the championship. FOM, the main operating firm of the group, is in charge of the broadcasting, promotional rights and organization of Formula One. FOM is also in charge of maintaining all of the televised broadcasts of Grand Prix events, which are then aired through the Eurovision satellite network to broadcasters who subsequently provide the commentary and distribution of the broadcasts to regional networks. Formula One holds Grand Prix races in locations across the world, such as Australia, Bahrain, China, Hungary, Japan, Mexico, Spain and the U.S. In addition to its main operating subsidiaries, the firm includes Formula One Paddock Club, a VIP service offering clients exclusive seating and dining, and host to numerous film stars, models, sports stars, politicians, pop music groups and business moguls. Formula One Group is owned by Liberty Media Corporation.

FINANCIAL DATA: *Note: Data for latest year may not have been available at press time.*

In U.S. $	2022	2021	2020	2019	2018	2017
Revenue	2,200,000,000	2,136,000,000	1,145,000,000	2,022,000,000	1,783,000,000	1,783,000,000
R&D Expense						
Operating Income						
Operating Margin %						
SGA Expense						
Net Income		92,000,000	-386,000,000	17,000,000	-37,000,000	-37,000,000
Operating Cash Flow						
Capital Expenditure						
EBITDA						
Return on Assets %						
Return on Equity %						
Debt to Equity						

CONTACT INFORMATION:

Phone: 44-203-027-5063   Fax:
Toll-Free:
Address: No. 2 St. James' Market, London, SW1Y 4AH United Kingdom

STOCK TICKER/OTHER:

Stock Ticker: Subsidiary
Employees:
Parent Company: Liberty Media Corporation

Exchange:
Fiscal Year Ends: 12/31

SALARIES/BONUSES:

Top Exec. Salary: $ Bonus: $
Second Exec. Salary: $ Bonus: $

OTHER THOUGHTS:

Estimated Female Officers or Directors:
Hot Spot for Advancement for Women/Minorities:

Fox Broadcasting Company

www.fox.com

NAIC Code: 515120

TYPES OF BUSINESS:

Television Broadcasting
Television Stations
Television Broadcast
Television Stations
Primetime Entertainment
News
Sports Evens
Streaming

BRANDS/DIVISIONS/AFFILIATES:

Fox Corporation
Fox Television Stations Inc
MyNetworkTV
FOX Sports
FOX Business
FOX News
FOX NOW

CONTACTS: *Note: Officers with more than one job title may be intentionally listed here more than once.*

Rob Wade, CEO
Ira Kurgan, Chief-Network Bus. Oper.
Preston Beckman, Sr. Strategist
David Wertheimer, Pres., Digital
Shannon Ryan, Exec. VP-Mktg. & Comm.
Simon Andrae, Exec. VP-Alternative Entertainment
Jean Rossi, Exec. VP-Sales
Dan Harrison, Exec. VP-Scheduling
Laurel Bernard, Exec. VP-Mktg.
Jon Hookstratten, Exec. VP-Network Distribution

GROWTH PLANS/SPECIAL FEATURES:

Fox Broadcasting Company (FOX) operates as an American commercial broadcast television network within the Fox Corporation, specifically Fox Entertainment. The network consists of over 15 owned-and-operated, full-power stations, as well as affiliate agreements with additional television stations through its Fox Television Stations, Inc. subsidiary. The stations reach approximately 99.9% of all households in the U.S. FOX also oversees the MyNetworkTV commercial broadcast television syndication service. The company's target audience consists of adults aged 18-49, with the median age of the FOX viewer around 51. The firm broadcasts primetime entertainment, sports events and news content, with networks including FOX Sports, FOX Business and FOX News. FOX NOW offers television streaming services of FOX shows live or on-demand, including primetime shows. FOX principally derives its revenues from the sale of advertising time sold to national advertisers.

FOX offers its employees comprehensive health and retirement benefits, as well as employee assistance plans and programs.

FINANCIAL DATA: *Note: Data for latest year may not have been available at press time.*

In U.S. $	2022	2021	2020	2019	2018	2017
Revenue	7,645,000,000	7,048,000,000	6,661,000,000	5,979,000,000	7,065,000,000	7,065,000,000
R&D Expense						
Operating Income						
Operating Margin %						
SGA Expense						
Net Income						
Operating Cash Flow						
Capital Expenditure						
EBITDA						
Return on Assets %						
Return on Equity %						
Debt to Equity						

CONTACT INFORMATION:

Phone: 310-369-3553   Fax: 310-369-1283
Toll-Free:
Address: 10201 W. Pico Blvd., Los Angeles, CA 90035 United States

STOCK TICKER/OTHER:

Stock Ticker: Subsidiary   Exchange:
Employees: Fiscal Year Ends: 06/30
Parent Company: Fox Corporation

SALARIES/BONUSES:

Top Exec. Salary: $ Bonus: $
Second Exec. Salary: $ Bonus: $

OTHER THOUGHTS:

Estimated Female Officers or Directors: 6
Hot Spot for Advancement for Women/Minorities: Y

Sales, profits and employees may be estimates. Financial information, benefits and other data can change quickly and may vary from those stated here.

Fox Sports (Fox Sports Media Group)   www.foxsports.com

NAIC Code: 515120

TYPES OF BUSINESS:

Television Production-Sports
Film & TV Production & Distribution
Online Sports Broadcasting
Television Sport Networks
Broadcast Agreements
Language Rights
Sport Asset Operation and Management
Sport Digital Properties and Applications

BRANDS/DIVISIONS/AFFILIATES:

Fox Corporation
Fox Sports 1 (FS1)
Fox Sports 2 (FS2)
Fox Sports Racing
Fox Soccer Plus
Fox Deportes
FoxSports.com
Big Ten Network

CONTACTS: Note: Officers with more than one job title may be intentionally listed here more than once.

Eric Shanks, CEO
George Greenberg, Exec. VP-Prod. & Programming
Pete Vlastelica, Sr. VP-Digital
Lou D'Ermilio, Sr. VP-Comm.
Robert Thompson, Pres., Fox National Cable Sports Networks
Randy Freer, Co-Pres., Fox Sports Media

GROWTH PLANS/SPECIAL FEATURES:

The Fox Sports Media Group (Fox Sports), a business unit within Fox Corporation, operates the wide array of multi-platform sports assets of Fox Corporation. Assets controlled by Fox Sports consist of ownership and interests in linear television networks, digital and mobile programming, broadband platforms, multiple websites, joint venture businesses and licensing relationships. Primary assets of Fox Sports include Fox Sports 1 (FS1), Fox Sports 2 (FS2), Fox Sports Racing, Fox Soccer Plus and Fox Deportes. Digital properties include FoxSports.com and the Fox Sports App, which provides live streaming video and Fox Sports content, instant scores, stats and alerts to iOS and Android devices. Other ownership interests include Big Ten Network and BTN 2Go, as well as Fox Sports Radio Network. Moreover, Fox Sports has a six-year broadcast agreement (from 2022 to 2028) with the Union of European Football Associations (UEFA), owning English-language rights to UEFA national team matches and airing tournaments such as the UEFA Euro 2024 and UEFA Euro 2028.

FINANCIAL DATA: Note: Data for latest year may not have been available at press time.

In U.S. $	2022	2021	2020	2019	2018	2017
Revenue						
R&D Expense						
Operating Income						
Operating Margin %						
SGA Expense						
Net Income						
Operating Cash Flow						
Capital Expenditure						
EBITDA						
Return on Assets %						
Return on Equity %						
Debt to Equity						

CONTACT INFORMATION:

Phone: 310 369-1000   Fax: 310 369-1049
Toll-Free:
Address: 10201 W. Pico Blvd., Bldg. 88, Fl. 3, Los Angeles, CA 90064
United States

STOCK TICKER/OTHER:

Stock Ticker: Subsidiary
Employees: 2,200
Parent Company: Fox Corporation

Exchange:
Fiscal Year Ends: 06/30

SALARIES/BONUSES:

Top Exec. Salary: $ Bonus: $
Second Exec. Salary: $ Bonus: $

OTHER THOUGHTS:

Estimated Female Officers or Directors:
Hot Spot for Advancement for Women/Minorities:

Sales, profits and employees may be estimates. Financial information, benefits and other data can change quickly and may vary from those stated here.

Franklin Sports Inc

www.franklinsports.com

NAIC Code: 339920

TYPES OF BUSINESS:

Sports Equipment
Sports Apparel
Sport Games
Specialty Gloves
Specialty Eyewear

BRANDS/DIVISIONS/AFFILIATES:

GROWTH PLANS/SPECIAL FEATURES:

Franklin Sports, Inc., founded in 1946, manufactures and markets sports equipment and apparel for baseball, hockey, football and soccer, as well as fan products and youth sports, indoor and outdoor game products. Franklin's baseball products include batting and fielding gloves, batting tees, balls, base sets, protective gear and pitch return trainers; hockey products are for ice and field, and include sticks, pucks, goals and protective gear; inflatable products include a variety of balls; football products include gloves and flags; and soccer products consist of goals, nets/bungees, guards and related accessories. Other sports products include golf gloves, pickleballs and paddles. The company also sells replacement parts for pitching machines and other sports equipment. Franklin's clothing line include hats, t-shirts, hoodies and sweatshirts.

CONTACTS: Note: Officers with more than one job title may be intentionally listed here more than once.

Larry J. Franklin, CEO
Joe Murphy, VP-Sales, US

FINANCIAL DATA: Note: Data for latest year may not have been available at press time.

In U.S. $	2022	2021	2020	2019	2018	2017
Revenue						
R&D Expense						
Operating Income						
Operating Margin %						
SGA Expense						
Net Income						
Operating Cash Flow						
Capital Expenditure						
EBITDA						
Return on Assets %						
Return on Equity %						
Debt to Equity						

CONTACT INFORMATION:

Phone: 781-344-1111   Fax: 781-341-0333
Toll-Free: 877-377-6787
Address: 17 Campanelli Pkwy., Stoughton, MA 02072 United States

STOCK TICKER/OTHER:

Stock Ticker: Private   Exchange:
Employees: 140   Fiscal Year Ends:
Parent Company:

SALARIES/BONUSES:

Top Exec. Salary: $ Bonus: $
Second Exec. Salary: $ Bonus: $

OTHER THOUGHTS:

Estimated Female Officers or Directors:
Hot Spot for Advancement for Women/Minorities:

Fulham Football Club

www.fulhamfc.com

NAIC Code: 711211D

TYPES OF BUSINESS:

English Premier Soccer Team
Team Management and Operations
Youth & Community Programs

BRANDS/DIVISIONS/AFFILIATES:

CONTACTS: *Note: Officers with more than one job title may be intentionally listed here more than once.*

Sean O'Loughlin, Dir.-Finance
Karim Fayed, Vice Chmn.
Shahid Khan, Chmn.

GROWTH PLANS/SPECIAL FEATURES:

Fulham Football Club is a professional soccer team based in London, founded in 1879 as the St. Andrews Cricket & Football Club. Fulham played in the Premier League (2020-21 season), and relegated to the EFL Championship league. The English Football League (EFL) Championship is the highest division of the EFL and second-highest overall in the English football league system after the Premier League. Fulham subsequently clenched the 2021-22 EFL Championship. Fulham plays its home games at Craven Cottage on the banks of the Thames and is owned by Shahid Khan, who acquired the team from Al Fayed in 2013. It was Al Fayed, a wealthy businessman, who took control of the club in 1997, when it had hit rock bottom and desperately needed a boost to move it up out of division two. He began by signing well-recognized manager Kevin Keegan and offering million-pound contracts to obtain Canadian striker Paul Peschisolido and Chris Coleman, who were playing with the competitive Blackburn Rovers. The club facilities were upgraded and, with added media and fan interest, the club won division II, then division I titles to be promoted to the Premiership in 2001. Title-wise, Fulham FC clenched the UEFA Intertoto Cup in 2002. In both the 2018 and 2020 seasons, Fulham were the EFL play-off champions. Gambling firm W88 became Fulham FC's kit sponsor for the 2022-23 season, and World Mobile is an official partner of the team.

FINANCIAL DATA: *Note: Data for latest year may not have been available at press time.*

In U.S. $	2022	2021	2020	2019	2018	2017
Revenue	170,000,000	160,803,285	71,534,648	174,799,457	45,313,900	45,313,900
R&D Expense						
Operating Income						
Operating Margin %						
SGA Expense						
Net Income		-130,669,028	-60,352,161	-25,932,875	-27,645,400	-27,645,400
Operating Cash Flow						
Capital Expenditure						
EBITDA						
Return on Assets %						
Return on Equity %						
Debt to Equity						

CONTACT INFORMATION:

Phone: 44-0870-442-1222   Fax: 44-0870-442-0236
Toll-Free:
Address: Motspur Park, New Malden, Surrey, KT3 6PT United Kingdom

STOCK TICKER/OTHER:

Stock Ticker: Private
Employees: 275
Parent Company:

Exchange:
Fiscal Year Ends: 06/30

SALARIES/BONUSES:

Top Exec. Salary: $ Bonus: $
Second Exec. Salary: $ Bonus: $

OTHER THOUGHTS:

Estimated Female Officers or Directors:
Hot Spot for Advancement for Women/Minorities:

Fussball Bundesliga

www.bundesliga.de

NAIC Code: 711211

TYPES OF BUSINESS:

Professional Soccer League

BRANDS/DIVISIONS/AFFILIATES:

CONTACTS: *Note: Officers with more than one job title may be intentionally listed here more than once.*

Donata Hopfen, CEO
Reinhard Rauball, Pres.
Christian Pfennig, VP-Comm.
Peter Peters, VP
Harald Strutz, VP
Holger Hieronymus, Deputy CEO
Tom Bender, Gen. Mgr.

GROWTH PLANS/SPECIAL FEATURES:

Fussball Bundesliga is responsible for organizing and supervising professional soccer in Germany. The professional German league, like many of its European counterparts, is divided into two divisions: a first tier division, known simply as Bundesliga, and a second tier division referred to as 2. Bundesliga. There are currently 36 professional teams playing in Fussball Bundesliga's two divisions, spilt equally among both. Each year, the two worst performing teams in the top tier are relegated to the 2. Bundesliga, while the two best teams from the lower division are promoted to the first tier. In recent decades, the league has been dominated by FC Bayern Munich, which has won the league title 31 times, including the 2021-22 season. Other standout teams in the Bundesliga include Borussia Dortmund, Werder Bremen and VfB Stuttgart. Average attendance at German football games continues to exceed other European leagues, with an average of over 42,600 fans per Bundesliga games, which is more than twice the average of the 2. Bundesliga. The Bundesliga is operated by DFL Deutsche Fuball Liga GmbH, a wholly-owned subsidiary of Die Liga Fuballverband e.V. (Ligaverband). Ligaverband is an association of the 36 German professional football clubs, or their companies, that partake in the Bundesliga and 2. Bundesliga, which represents their interests.

FINANCIAL DATA: *Note: Data for latest year may not have been available at press time.*

In U.S. $	2022	2021	2020	2019	2018	2017
Revenue						
R&D Expense						
Operating Income						
Operating Margin %						
SGA Expense						
Net Income						
Operating Cash Flow						
Capital Expenditure						
EBITDA						
Return on Assets %						
Return on Equity %						
Debt to Equity						

CONTACT INFORMATION:

Phone: 49-69-65005-0   Fax: 49-69-65005-557
Toll-Free:
Address: Otto-Fleck-Schneise 6a, Frankfurt am Main, 60528 Germany

STOCK TICKER/OTHER:

Stock Ticker: Private   Exchange:
Employees: Fiscal Year Ends:
Parent Company: Die Liga Fuballverband eV

SALARIES/BONUSES:

Top Exec. Salary: $ Bonus: $
Second Exec. Salary: $ Bonus: $

OTHER THOUGHTS:

Estimated Female Officers or Directors:
Hot Spot for Advancement for Women/Minorities:

Futbol Club Barcelona

www.fcbarcelona.com

NAIC Code: 711211D

TYPES OF BUSINESS:

Professional Soccer Team
Team Management and Operations

BRANDS/DIVISIONS/AFFILIATES:

Barca
Camp Nou

CONTACTS: *Note: Officers with more than one job title may be intentionally listed here more than once.*

Joan Laporta, Pres.
Emili Sabadell, Dir.-Oper.
Lluis Alsina, Dir.-Online Dept.
Xavi Martin, Dir.-Comm.
Nestor Amela, Dir.-Economics & Finance
Josep Cortada, Dir.-FC Barcelona Foundation
Antoni Rossich, Gen. Dir.
Andoni Zubizarreta, Dir.-Football Sports Area
Raul Sanllehi, Dir.-Football Mgmt. Area

GROWTH PLANS/SPECIAL FEATURES:

Futbol Club Barcelona, commonly referred to as Barca, is a Barcelona, Spain-based professional soccer club playing in La Liga, the top tier of the Spanish soccer league system. The club is one of three founding member teams to never have been relegated from La Liga. Barca was established in 1899 and currently plays in its wholly-owned stadium Camp Nou. Camp Nou has been the club's home field since 1957. The stadium is the third largest association football stadium in the world and has a league seating capacity of over 99,354. In 2014, Barcelona's board of directors agreed to remodel Camp Nou to bring the capacity up to 105,000, with work beginning in 2018 and ending early 2021. Barca is considered one of the most successful clubs in the world, having won, on the international side, the European Cup/UEFA Champions League five times, most recently in 2014-15; the European Cup Winners' Cup/UEFA Winners' Cup four times; the European Super Cup/UEFA Super Cup five times; and the FIFA Club World Cup three times. Domestically, the club has won La Liga 27 times, most recently in 2022-23; the Copa del Rey 31 times (most recently in 2020-21); Supercopa de Espania 14 times, most recently in 2022-23; Copa Eva Duarte three times; and the Copa de la Liga twice. Sponsors of the team include kit manufacturer Nike, and shirt sponsors Spotify and UNHCR. Forbes ranked Barca at $5 billion in 2022.

FINANCIAL DATA: *Note: Data for latest year may not have been available at press time.*

In U.S. $	2022	2021	2020	2019	2018	2017
Revenue		685,023,618	962,122,000	1,089,000,000	848,087,000	848,087,000
R&D Expense						
Operating Income						
Operating Margin %						
SGA Expense						
Net Income		-572,970,574	-109,479,000	12,100,000	21,561,500	21,561,500
Operating Cash Flow						
Capital Expenditure						
EBITDA						
Return on Assets %						
Return on Equity %						
Debt to Equity						

CONTACT INFORMATION:

Phone: 34-93-902-189900   Fax:
Toll-Free:
Address: Aristides Maillol s/n, Barcelona, 08028 Spain

STOCK TICKER/OTHER:

Stock Ticker: Cooperative
Employees: 1,289
Parent Company:

Exchange:
Fiscal Year Ends: 06/30

SALARIES/BONUSES:

Top Exec. Salary: $ Bonus: $
Second Exec. Salary: $ Bonus: $

OTHER THOUGHTS:

Estimated Female Officers or Directors:
Hot Spot for Advancement for Women/Minorities:

Sales, profits and employees may be estimates. Financial information, benefits and other data can change quickly and may vary from those stated here.

Futebol Clube do Porto (FC Porto)

NAIC Code: 711211D

www.fcporto.pt/pt

TYPES OF BUSINESS:

Soccer Team
Team Management and Operations

BRANDS/DIVISIONS/AFFILIATES:

GROWTH PLANS/SPECIAL FEATURES:

Futebol Clube do Porto (FC Porto) is a professional sports club in Portugal, primarily known for its professional football team playing in the Primeira Liga, the top-tier of Portuguese football. Founded in 1893, FC Porto plays home games in the Estado do Dragao stadium, which has a seating capacity of over 50,000. Domestically, FC Porto has won 30 Primeira Liga titles (most recently in 2019-20 and 2021-22), 18 Taca de Portugal titles, 23 Supertaca Candido de Oliveira titles and four Campeonato de Portugal titles. The club has also won two European Cups (UEFA Champions League), two UEFA Cups (UEFA Europa League), one UEFA Super Cup, and two Intercontinental Cups. New Balance is FC Porto's kit manufacturer and Betano is its shirt sponsor. Other sports within FC Porto include basketball, billiards, boxing, cycling, handball, roller hockey and swimming, among others.

CONTACTS: *Note: Officers with more than one job title may be intentionally listed here more than once.*

Jorge Nuno Pinto da Costa, Pres.

FINANCIAL DATA: *Note: Data for latest year may not have been available at press time.*

In U.S. $	2022	2021	2020	2019	2018	2017
Revenue						
R&D Expense						
Operating Income						
Operating Margin %						
SGA Expense						
Net Income						
Operating Cash Flow						
Capital Expenditure						
EBITDA						
Return on Assets %						
Return on Equity %						
Debt to Equity						

CONTACT INFORMATION:

Phone: 351-225-570-400   Fax:
Toll-Free:
Address: Futebol Clube do Porto, East Entrance, Fl. 3, Porto, 4350-415 Portugal

STOCK TICKER/OTHER:

Stock Ticker: Subsidiary   Exchange:
Employees: Fiscal Year Ends: 06/30
Parent Company: Futebol Clube do Porto Futebol SAD

SALARIES/BONUSES:

Top Exec. Salary: $ Bonus: $
Second Exec. Salary: $ Bonus: $

OTHER THOUGHTS:

Estimated Female Officers or Directors:
Hot Spot for Advancement for Women/Minorities:

Galatasaray Spor Kulubu (Galatasaray SK)

www.galatasaray.org/en/Homepage
NAIC Code: 711211D

TYPES OF BUSINESS:

Soccer Team
Team Management and Operations

BRANDS/DIVISIONS/AFFILIATES:

GROWTH PLANS/SPECIAL FEATURES:

Galatasaray Spor Kulubu (Galatasaray SK) is a professional football club in Turkey, playing in the Super Lig, the top-tier Turkish league for association football clubs. Founded in 1905, Galatasaray SK plays its home games in the Nef Stadium, which has a seating capacity of over 52,000. Domestically, the club has won 22 Super Lig titles, 18 Turkish Cups, 16 Turkish Super Cups, among others. Internationally, Galatasaray SK has won one UEFA Cup and one UEFA Super Cup. Nike is the club's kit manufacturer, and Sixt SE (domestic matches) and Turkish Airlines (international matches) are its shirt sponsors.

CONTACTS: Note: Officers with more than one job title may be intentionally listed here more than once.

Dursun Aydin Ozbek, Chmn.

FINANCIAL DATA: Note: Data for latest year may not have been available at press time.

In U.S. $	2022	2021	2020	2019	2018	2017
Revenue						
R&D Expense						
Operating Income						
Operating Margin %						
SGA Expense						
Net Income						
Operating Cash Flow						
Capital Expenditure						
EBITDA						
Return on Assets %						
Return on Equity %						
Debt to Equity						

CONTACT INFORMATION:

Phone: 90 212 273 2850   Fax: 90 212 251 1212
Toll-Free:
Address: Akinci Bayiri Sokak 8, Mecidiyekoy, Istanbul, 34394 Turkey

STOCK TICKER/OTHER:

Stock Ticker: Private
Employees:
Parent Company:

Exchange:
Fiscal Year Ends:

SALARIES/BONUSES:

Top Exec. Salary: $ Bonus: $
Second Exec. Salary: $ Bonus: $

OTHER THOUGHTS:

Estimated Female Officers or Directors:
Hot Spot for Advancement for Women/Minorities:

Giant Manufacturing Co Ltd

www.giant-bicycles.com

NAIC Code: 339920

TYPES OF BUSINESS:

Bicycle Manufacturing
Bicycle Parts & Care Products
Apparel & Accessories
Fitness Equipment

GROWTH PLANS/SPECIAL FEATURES:

Giant Manufacturing Co Ltd is a manufacturer and distributor of bicycles and bicycle-related components, domiciled in Taiwan. The company produces bicycles for both recreational and professional use. Products include mountain bicycles, road and racing bicycles, bicycle motocross, or BMX, folding bicycles, children and youth bicycles, electric bicycles, helmets, components, and related parts and accessories. Giant distributes bicycles and components both domestically and internationally, and largely sells products under the Giant brand name.

BRANDS/DIVISIONS/AFFILIATES:

CONTACTS: Note: Officers with more than one job title may be intentionally listed here more than once.

Young Liu, CEO
Biyu Wang, CFO
Bonnie Tu, Chmn.

FINANCIAL DATA: Note: Data for latest year may not have been available at press time.

In U.S. $	2022	2021	2020	2019	2018	2017
Revenue	3,006,195,000	2,672,933,000	2,286,591,000	2,072,295,000	1,803,245,000	1,803,245,000
R&D Expense	50,029,690	34,003,950	30,697,500	28,534,030	25,850,710	25,850,710
Operating Income	277,345,900	284,773,900	224,761,100	158,617,800	96,346,000	96,346,000
Operating Margin %		.11%	.10%	.08%	.05%	.05%
SGA Expense	352,747,900	326,729,300	272,621,200	258,891,100	238,332,700	238,332,700
Net Income	190,864,000	193,679,300	161,635,600	110,217,300	67,093,510	67,093,510
Operating Cash Flow	16,708,240	-161,985,700	372,260,000	63,275,060	89,266,020	89,266,020
Capital Expenditure	88,184,330	77,643,280	93,427,720	111,896,200	54,111,830	54,111,830
EBITDA	369,379,800	355,737,800	288,753,400	221,135,600	140,968,400	140,968,400
Return on Assets %		.08%	.08%	.06%	.04%	.04%
Return on Equity %		.23%	.21%	.16%	.10%	.10%
Debt to Equity		.15%	0.197	0.122	0.03	0.03

CONTACT INFORMATION:

Phone: 886 426814771   Fax: 886 426810280
Toll-Free:
Address: 19, Shun-Farn Rd., Dajia District, Taichung, 43774 Taiwan

STOCK TICKER/OTHER:

Stock Ticker: GTMUF   Exchange: PINX
Employees: Fiscal Year Ends: 12/31
Parent Company:

SALARIES/BONUSES:

Top Exec. Salary: $ Bonus: $
Second Exec. Salary: $ Bonus: $

OTHER THOUGHTS:

Estimated Female Officers or Directors:
Hot Spot for Advancement for Women/Minorities:

Golden State Warriors

www.nba.com/warriors

NAIC Code: 711211B

TYPES OF BUSINESS:

Professional Basketball Team
Team Management and Operations

BRANDS/DIVISIONS/AFFILIATES:

GROWTH PLANS/SPECIAL FEATURES:

The Golden State Warriors joined the American Basketball Association (ABA) as the Philadelphia Warriors in 1946. The team moved to Oakland in 1971 and became known as the Golden State Warriors in the National Basketball Association (NBA). Warrior home games are played in the Chase Center in the Mission Bay area of San Francisco, with a basketball seating capacity of 18,064 and an expanded capacity to 19,500 for other purposes. The team sold out its home games during the 2022-23 season. Since its inception, the franchise has obtained seven NBA championships in 1947, 1956, 1975, 2015, 2017, 2018 and 2022. The Warriors beat the Boston Celtics in the 2022 finals 4-2, becoming the NBA champions. The team also has seven conference titles, having obtained consecutive wins in the conference and division from 2015 through 2019. Noteworthy Warrior players include Wilt Chamberlain, Nate Thurmond, Al Attles, Tim Hardaway, Rick Barry, Mitch Richmond, Chris Mullin, Jo Jo White and Stephen Curry. Forbes Magazine estimated the team to be worth $7 billion in October 2022.

CONTACTS:
Note: Officers with more than one job title may be intentionally listed here more than once.

Bob Myers, Gen. Mngr.
Bob Myers, Pres.-Basketball Oper.
Jennifer Cabalquinto, CFO
Chip Bowers, CMO
Erin Dangerfield, VP-Human Resources
Kenny Lauer, VP-Digital & Mktg.
David Kelly, General Counsel
Ellen Warner, VP-Dev.
Jim Weyermann, VP-New Franchise Dev.
Raymond Riddler, VP-Comm.
Gail Hunter, VP-Public Affairs & Event Mgmt.
Alvin Huggins, Controller
Mark Jackson, Head Coach
Peter Guber, Co-Chmn.
Brett Yamaguchi, Dir.-Game Oper.
Brandon Schneider, VP-Ticket Sales & Services
Brandon Schneider, COO

FINANCIAL DATA:
Note: Data for latest year may not have been available at press time.

In U.S. $	2022	2021	2020	2019	2018	2017
Revenue	475,800,000					
R&D Expense						
Operating Income						
Operating Margin %						
SGA Expense						
Net Income						
Operating Cash Flow						
Capital Expenditure						
EBITDA						
Return on Assets %						
Return on Equity %						
Debt to Equity						

CONTACT INFORMATION:

Phone: 415-388-0100   Fax:
Toll-Free:
Address: 1 Warriors Way, San Francisco, CA 94158 United States

STOCK TICKER/OTHER:

Stock Ticker: Private   Exchange:
Employees: 875   Fiscal Year Ends:
Parent Company:

SALARIES/BONUSES:

Top Exec. Salary: $ Bonus: $
Second Exec. Salary: $ Bonus: $

OTHER THOUGHTS:

Estimated Female Officers or Directors: 3
Hot Spot for Advancement for Women/Minorities: Y

Golds Gym International Inc

www.goldsgym.com

NAIC Code: 713940

TYPES OF BUSINESS:

Fitness Centers
Franchising
Digital Personal Exercise and Training

BRANDS/DIVISIONS/AFFILIATES:

RSG Group GmbH
Golds Gym
BOOTCAMP
GOLDS FIT
GOLDS BURN
GOLDS CYCLE
GOLDS AMP

GROWTH PLANS/SPECIAL FEATURES:

Gold's Gym International, Inc. maintains a chain of over 600 co-ed gyms worldwide. Company-owned and franchised Gold's Gym locations measure between 10,000 and 25,000 square feet in size. Personalized transformation plans are offered, and each location features state-of-the-art equipment, certified personal trainers, a variety of group exercise programs. Its BOOTCAMP group training offers members access to boutique-style classes such as GOLD'S FIT, GOLD'S BURN and GOLD'S CYCLE. GOLD'S AMP is a digital personal training app that can be used at GOLD'S brick-and-mortar gyms. Gold's Gym International is owned by RSG Group GmbH, a global leader in the fitness and lifestyle sector.

CONTACTS: Note: Officers with more than one job title may be intentionally listed here more than once.

Danny Waggoner, Co-CEO
Brian Warne, Co-CEO
Tim Keightley, VP-Fitness

FINANCIAL DATA: Note: Data for latest year may not have been available at press time.

In U.S. $	2022	2021	2020	2019	2018	2017
Revenue	775,000,000	552,240,000	531,000,000	900,000,000	850,000,000	850,000,000
R&D Expense						
Operating Income						
Operating Margin %						
SGA Expense						
Net Income						
Operating Cash Flow						
Capital Expenditure						
EBITDA						
Return on Assets %						
Return on Equity %						
Debt to Equity						

CONTACT INFORMATION:

Phone: 214-265-0053   Fax: 214-296-5000
Toll-Free: 800-994-6537
Address: 5420 Lyndon B. Johnson Fwy., Ste. 610, Dallas, TX 75240
United States

STOCK TICKER/OTHER:

Stock Ticker: Private   Exchange:
Employees: 30,000   Fiscal Year Ends: 02/28
Parent Company: RSG Group GmbH

SALARIES/BONUSES:

Top Exec. Salary: $ Bonus: $
Second Exec. Salary: $ Bonus: $

OTHER THOUGHTS:

Estimated Female Officers or Directors: 2
Hot Spot for Advancement for Women/Minorities:

Golf Galaxy Inc

www.golfgalaxy.com

NAIC Code: 451110

TYPES OF BUSINESS:

Golf Equipment-Retail
Ecommerce
Golf Consultation & Instruction
Repair & Maintenance Services
Retail Stores
Specialty Retail

BRANDS/DIVISIONS/AFFILIATES:

Dicks Sporting Goods Inc
Advantage Club
GolfGalaxy.com

CONTACTS: Note: Officers with more than one job title may be intentionally listed here more than once.

Edward W. Stack, CEO-Dick's Sporting Goods
Edward W. Stack, Chmn.-Dicks

GROWTH PLANS/SPECIAL FEATURES:

Golf Galaxy, Inc., a subsidiary of Dick's Sporting Goods Inc., is a leading golf specialty retailer selling national brand golf merchandise throughout the U.S. The company's stores average 15,000 square feet and contain numerous interactive selling features such as artificial putting greens and golf simulators. Golf Galaxy's product offerings include clubs, bags, balls, gloves, accessories, apparel and footwear from leading sports equipment brands such as Callaway Golf, TaylorMade, Cobra, Cleveland, PING, Titleist, Nike Golf, adidas and FootJoy. Service offerings include lessons, club technician workshops, fitting bays, club trade-ins, custom putter fitting and full-service club repair. Golf Galaxy staffs its stores with full-time PGA professionals who offer customers a consultative selling approach, as well as pro-shop services and golf lessons featuring digital video swing analysis. The firm's store-within-a-store concept consists of golf clubroom components; club making tools and supplies; technical information; and services such as club repair, regripping and club upgrade. In addition to its superstores, the firm maintains an eCommerce site at GolfGalaxy.com. The Advantage Club loyalty program offers members in-store events, email bargains and direct mail promotions. Golf Galaxy also purchases pre-owned equipment in exchange for in-store credit.

FINANCIAL DATA: Note: Data for latest year may not have been available at press time.

In U.S. $	2022	2021	2020	2019	2018	2017
Revenue						
R&D Expense						
Operating Income						
Operating Margin %						
SGA Expense						
Net Income						
Operating Cash Flow						
Capital Expenditure						
EBITDA						
Return on Assets %						
Return on Equity %						
Debt to Equity						

CONTACT INFORMATION:

Phone: 724-273-3400   Fax:
Toll-Free: 800-287-9060
Address: 345 Court St., Coraopolis, PA 15108 United States

STOCK TICKER/OTHER:

Stock Ticker: Subsidiary
Employees: 20,500
Parent Company: Dicks Sporting Goods Inc

Exchange:
Fiscal Year Ends: 02/28

SALARIES/BONUSES:

Top Exec. Salary: $ Bonus: $
Second Exec. Salary: $ Bonus: $

OTHER THOUGHTS:

Estimated Female Officers or Directors:
Hot Spot for Advancement for Women/Minorities:

Golf Town Limited

NAIC Code: 451110

www.golftown.com

TYPES OF BUSINESS:

Golf Equipment-Retail
Golf Retail Sales
Golf Retail Stores
Ecommerce
Golf Clubs
Golf Accessories
Golf Carts
Golf Equipment Services

BRANDS/DIVISIONS/AFFILIATES:

Sporting Life Group Limited

CONTACTS: *Note: Officers with more than one job title may be intentionally listed here more than once.*

Chad McKinnon, Pres.
Marc Roy, Exec. VP-Corp. Merch.
Paul Renaud, CEO

GROWTH PLANS/SPECIAL FEATURES:

Golf Town Limited is a leading Canadian golf merchandise retailer, with approximately 50 stores located in Ontario, British Columbia, Alberta, Manitoba, Quebec, Saskatchewan and Nova Scotia. The company is owned by Sporting Life Group Limited. The firm's stores average approximately 18,000 square feet in size, and merchandise is also available through its ecommerce platforms. Golf Town's products are grouped into several categories, including: clubs, such as drivers, iron sets, fairway woods, hybrids, wedges, putters, package sets, grips and shafts, tools and supplies, pre-owned clubs and clubs for juniors, men and women; balls, including practice golf balls, premium golf balls, colored golf balls and balls for men and women; shoes, including golf shoes, casual shoes, sandals and golf shoe accessories; clothing, including shirts, polos, pants, shorts, sweaters, vests, dresses, skirts, skorts, outerwear, hats and gloves, socks and underwear, belts and sunglasses; bags and carts, including stand bags, cart bags, staff bags, Sunday bags, travel covers, luggage and totes, push and pull carts, electric carts and related accessories; golf technology, including handheld global positioning systems (GPS), GPS watches, rangefinders, launch monitors, speakers, training technology and related accessories; and accessories, including golf gloves, headcovers, ball retrievers, cleaning and repair tools, divot tools, ball markers, tees, towels, umbrellas, coolers and water bottles, sun care, swing aids, putting aids and much more. Services offered by Golf Town include custom fitting, club trade-in, pro shop services, tournament planning and other services.

FINANCIAL DATA: *Note: Data for latest year may not have been available at press time.*

In U.S. $	2022	2021	2020	2019	2018	2017
Revenue						
R&D Expense						
Operating Income						
Operating Margin %						
SGA Expense						
Net Income						
Operating Cash Flow						
Capital Expenditure						
EBITDA						
Return on Assets %						
Return on Equity %						
Debt to Equity						

CONTACT INFORMATION:

Phone: 905-479-6978   Fax: 905-479-7125
Toll-Free:
Address: 7777 Weston Rd., Ste. 900, Woodbridge, ON L4L OG9 Canada

SALARIES/BONUSES:

Top Exec. Salary: $ Bonus: $
Second Exec. Salary: $ Bonus: $

STOCK TICKER/OTHER:

Stock Ticker: Private   Exchange:
Employees: Fiscal Year Ends: 12/31
Parent Company: Sporting Life Group Limited

OTHER THOUGHTS:

Estimated Female Officers or Directors:
Hot Spot for Advancement for Women/Minorities:

Green Bay Packers

www.packers.com

NAIC Code: 711211C

TYPES OF BUSINESS:

Professional Football Team
Team Management and Operations

BRANDS/DIVISIONS/AFFILIATES:

Green Bay Packers Inc

CONTACTS: *Note: Officers with more than one job title may be intentionally listed here more than once.*

Mark Murphy, CEO
Ed Policy, COO
Paul Baniel, VP-Finance & Admin.
Gabrielle Valdez Dow, VP-Mktg. & Fan Engagement
Nicole Ledvina, VP-Human Resources
Mike Eayrs, Dir.-R&D
Craig Benzel, VP-Sales & Bus. Dev.
Paul Baniel, VP-Admin.
Ed Policy, General Counsel
Mark Wagner, Dir.-Ticket Oper.
Marisa Kornowski, Mgr.-Retail Oper. e-commerce Mktg.
Jason Wahlers, Dir.-Public Rel.
Paul Baniel, VP-Finance
Mike McCarthy, Head Coach
Ted Thompson, Exec. VP
Kate Hogan, Dir.-Retail Oper.
Rob Davis, Dir.-Player Dev.
Bob Harlan, Chmn.

GROWTH PLANS/SPECIAL FEATURES:

The Green Bay Packers is a professional football team playing in the North Division of the National Football Conference in the National Football League (NFL). The team's ownership structure is notable because its owner, Green Bay Packers, Inc., is a nonprofit organization. The Packers is the NFL's only community-owned franchise, with approximately 361,000 shareholders. The team's shares include voting rights, but do not increase in value or pay dividends and can only be sold back to the team. No individual can own more than 200,000 shares, in order that no one person becomes a majority owner of the club. Green Bay was founded in 1919 and became a part of the NFL in 1921. The Packers is the longest-standing team name in NFL history. The franchise counts numerous players and coaches who spent most their careers with the team in the Pro Football Hall of Fame. These individuals include Earl L. Lambeau, the franchise's founder, player, head coach and vice president from 1919-49; Don Hutson, a wide receiver, kicker and safety from 1935-1945; Bart Starr, a quarterback from 1956-71; and Vince Lombardi, the legendary head coach who led the team throughout the 1960s. The franchise has won 11 NFL championships, four Super Bowl championships, nine conference championships and 21 division championships (the latest in 2021 of the NFC North division). The team's most recent Super Bowl win came in 2010. The Packers play at Lambeau Field, the longest continually-occupied stadium in the NFL. The stadium is owned by the City of Green Bay, with the Packers averaging 76,180 fans in home game attendance during the 2022 season. Forbes estimated the team at about $4.25 billion in 2022.

FINANCIAL DATA: *Note: Data for latest year may not have been available at press time.*

In U.S. $	2022	2021	2020	2019	2018	2017
Revenue	579,000,000	371,055,000	506,885,000	477,943,000	441,402,000	441,402,000
R&D Expense						
Operating Income						
Operating Margin %						
SGA Expense						
Net Income	61,600,000	60,700,000			72,772,000	72,772,000
Operating Cash Flow						
Capital Expenditure						
EBITDA						
Return on Assets %						
Return on Equity %						
Debt to Equity						

CONTACT INFORMATION:

Phone: 920-569-7500   Fax: 920-569-7301
Toll-Free:
Address: 1265 Lombardi Ave., Green Bay, WI 54304 United States

STOCK TICKER/OTHER:

Stock Ticker: WBAY
Employees: 570
Parent Company: Green Bay Packers Inc

Exchange:
Fiscal Year Ends: 03/31

SALARIES/BONUSES:

Top Exec. Salary: $ Bonus: $
Second Exec. Salary: $ Bonus: $

OTHER THOUGHTS:

Estimated Female Officers or Directors: 5
Hot Spot for Advancement for Women/Minorities: Y

Grupo Sports World SAB de CV

www.sportsworld.com.mx

NAIC Code: 713940

TYPES OF BUSINESS:

Fitness and Recreational Sports Centers
Facility Management

GROWTH PLANS/SPECIAL FEATURES:

Grupo Sports World SAB de CV is an operator of family sports clubs in Mexico and the only public company in the Wellness industry in Latin America. The company offers a wide range of activities and sports programs focused on the specific needs and demands of clients, as well as training, health and nutrition services in accordance with the latest international trends in the industry.

BRANDS/DIVISIONS/AFFILIATES:

Sports World Club
SW Gym Plus
Fitkidz
In Shape
Sports World Fit
SW Gym

CONTACTS: Note: Officers with more than one job title may be intentionally listed here more than once.

Fabian Bifaretti Zanetto, CEO
Cynthia Ulloa Ayon, Dir.-Oper. & Customer Experience
Roberto Cayetano Jimenez Celorio, CFO
Fernando Guzman Lopez, Dir.-Commercial
Noelia Aguirre, Dir.-Human Resources
Fabian Gosselin Castro, Chmn.

FINANCIAL DATA: Note: Data for latest year may not have been available at press time.

In U.S. $	2022	2021	2020	2019	2018	2017
Revenue		34,433,560	48,139,980	106,932,300	88,404,440	88,404,440
R&D Expense						
Operating Income		-10,331,880	-26,684,490	13,792,670	5,931,036	5,931,036
Operating Margin %		- .30%	- .55%	.13%	.07%	.07%
SGA Expense		3,209,502	4,085,723	5,598,453	5,231,322	5,231,322
Net Income		-31,678,170	-32,243,720	-3,696,144	2,799,226	2,799,226
Operating Cash Flow		10,325,830	3,526,908	37,993,100	13,333,990	13,333,990
Capital Expenditure		1,295,306	5,317,135	14,609,130	19,753,000	19,753,000
EBITDA		784,465	4,411,407	41,924,020	15,858,160	15,858,160
Return on Assets %		- .11%	- .12%	- .02%	.03%	.03%
Return on Equity %		-3.93%	- .94%	- .07%	.06%	.06%
Debt to Equity			7.123	2.927	0.48	0.48

CONTACT INFORMATION:

Phone: 52 54817777   Fax: 52 54817778
Toll-Free:
Address: Vasco de Quiroga No 3880, Santa Fe, DF 05300 Mexico

STOCK TICKER/OTHER:

Stock Ticker: SPORTS   Exchange: MEX
Employees: 2,710   Fiscal Year Ends: 12/31
Parent Company:

SALARIES/BONUSES:

Top Exec. Salary: $ Bonus: $
Second Exec. Salary: $ Bonus: $

OTHER THOUGHTS:

Estimated Female Officers or Directors:
Hot Spot for Advancement for Women/Minorities:

Head Sport GmbH

www.head.com

NAIC Code: 339920

TYPES OF BUSINESS:

Sporting Goods
Racquet Sports Equipment
Ski & Snowboard Equipment
Diving Equipment & Accessories
Licensing
Retail
Ecommerce

BRANDS/DIVISIONS/AFFILIATES:

Tyrolia
Mares
Penn
SSI
rEvo

CONTACTS: *Note: Officers with more than one job title may be intentionally listed here more than once.*

Clare Vincent, Dir.-Investor Rel.
Georg Kroell, Exec. VP-Licensing Div.
Ottmar Barbian, Exec. VP-Racquets Sports Div.
Klaus Hotter, Exec. VP-Winter Sports Div.
Klaus Thurner, Exec. VP-Sportswear Div.
Johan Eliasch, Chmn.
Kevin Kempin, CEO

GROWTH PLANS/SPECIAL FEATURES:

Head Sport GmbH is a global manufacturer and marketer of branded sports equipment and apparel. Founded in 1950 by Howard Head, an engineer and the inventor credited with developing the first laminated metal skis, the company later expanded into other sporting goods through the acquisition of the Tyrolia bindings and Mares diving brands in the 1970s. It further expanded into the sports equipment market through the acquisitions of the Penn racquet and tennis ball, and SSI and rEvo diving brands. Head's products are sold by more than 31,000 dealers in more than 80 countries worldwide, including specialty retailers, mass merchants and pro shops. Head's operations are organized under five divisions: winter sports, racquet sports, water sports, sportswear and licensing. Under its winter sports division, Head designs and manufactures several various lines of ski equipment, including skis, ski boots, snowboards and various accessories such as helmets, goggles, bags and poles. Head's racquet sports division manufactures equipment for tennis, squash, badminton and racquetball. The company's water sports division encompasses products such as water-related technologies and instruments, swimwear (open water, multi-sport and free-swimming), swim caps, vests, diving suits, masks, snorkels, water shoes and other swimming and diving accessories. The sportswear division includes additional clothing offerings such as sport and casual socks, gloves and underwear. Head's licensing division grants rights to the Head brand for product categories such as apparel, footwear, luggage, eyewear, watches, bikes, toiletries, skates, bags and golf clubs.

FINANCIAL DATA: *Note: Data for latest year may not have been available at press time.*

In U.S. $	2022	2021	2020	2019	2018	2017
Revenue	540,000,000	538,125,000	550,000,000	500,000,000	475,000,000	475,000,000
R&D Expense						
Operating Income						
Operating Margin %						
SGA Expense						
Net Income						
Operating Cash Flow						
Capital Expenditure						
EBITDA						
Return on Assets %						
Return on Equity %						
Debt to Equity						

CONTACT INFORMATION:

Phone: 43 5574 6080   Fax: 43 5574-608130
Toll-Free: 800-289-7366
Address: Wuhrkopfweg 1, Kennelbach, 6921 Austria

STOCK TICKER/OTHER:

Stock Ticker: Private
Employees: 2,400
Parent Company: Head Austria GmbH

Exchange:
Fiscal Year Ends: 12/31

SALARIES/BONUSES:

Top Exec. Salary: $ Bonus: $
Second Exec. Salary: $ Bonus: $

OTHER THOUGHTS:

Estimated Female Officers or Directors: 1
Hot Spot for Advancement for Women/Minorities:

HealthFitness Corporation

healthfitness.com

NAIC Code: 713940

TYPES OF BUSINESS:

Fitness Center Management
Consulting Services
Corporate & Hospital-Based Fitness Centers
Fitness Center Design
Wellness Programs
Health & Fitness Assessment
On-Site Physical Therapy Services

BRANDS/DIVISIONS/AFFILIATES:

Trustmark
FitReserve

CONTACTS: *Note: Officers with more than one job title may be intentionally listed here more than once.*

Sean McManamy, Pres.
Mark Totts, VP-Prod. Dev.
Bob George, VP-Oper.
Sean McManamy, Sr. VP-Corp. Dev.
Dennis Richling, Chief Medical & Wellness Officer
Kelly Merriman, VP-Service Delivery
Katherine Meacham, VP-Account Mgmt.
Debra Marshall, VP-Mktg.

GROWTH PLANS/SPECIAL FEATURES:

HealthFitness Corporation, a Trustmark company, provides fitness, health and condition management services to employees, college students and community residents. The company's services include onsite, web-based and telephonic workplace population programs intended to promote employee health and fitness, and to prevent injury. The health and fitness division creates personalized health experiences by evaluating lifestyle behaviors, health measures and motivation. Coaching services are provided, as well as education resources, employee engagement opportunities, 24/7 nurse support, health screenings and wellness/fitness challenges. Injury prevention and treatment programs are provided to create and sustain a healthy work environment, and include work conditioning programs that prepare employees for job demands, ergonomic services, movement efficiency solutions, post-offer employment testing, early intervention programs and physical/occupational therapy for recovery and stress-reduction purposes. During 2022, parent Trustmark acquired FitReserve, which offers a multi-studio fitness subscription that allows member to mix and match in-person, live stream and on-demand workouts from top studios and instructors. FitReserve will help more employees working from home or in a mix of in-office and virtual work environments to access health and fitness care.

FINANCIAL DATA: *Note: Data for latest year may not have been available at press time.*

In U.S. $	2022	2021	2020	2019	2018	2017
Revenue	107,500,000	102,039,600	98,115,000	105,500,000	106,000,000	106,000,000
R&D Expense						
Operating Income						
Operating Margin %						
SGA Expense						
Net Income						
Operating Cash Flow						
Capital Expenditure						
EBITDA						
Return on Assets %						
Return on Equity %						
Debt to Equity						

CONTACT INFORMATION:

Phone: 847 615-1500   Fax:
Toll-Free: 800-639-7913
Address: 400 Field Dr., Lake Forest, IL 60045 United States

STOCK TICKER/OTHER:

Stock Ticker: Subsidiary   Exchange:
Employees: 4,000   Fiscal Year Ends: 12/31
Parent Company: Trustmark

SALARIES/BONUSES:

Top Exec. Salary: $ Bonus: $
Second Exec. Salary: $ Bonus: $

OTHER THOUGHTS:

Estimated Female Officers or Directors: 6
Hot Spot for Advancement for Women/Minorities: Y

Hendrick Motorsports

www.hendrickmotorsports.com

NAIC Code: 711219

TYPES OF BUSINESS:

Stock Car Racing Teams
Automotive Engineering
Racing Merchandise
Professional Auto Racing Organization
Automotive Dealerships
Automotive Collision Centers

BRANDS/DIVISIONS/AFFILIATES:

Hendrick Automotive Group

GROWTH PLANS/SPECIAL FEATURES:

Hendrick Motorsports is a professional auto racing organization established in 1984, clenching 14 car owner championships in NASCAR's premier division. The organization fields four full-time Chevrolet teams on the NASCAR Cup Series circuit, with drivers including Kyle Larson, Chase Elliot, William Byron and Alex Bowman. In 1984, the team was founded as All Star Racing by Rick Hendrick, and formerly fielded teams in the now-NASCAR Xfinity Series before merging with JR Motorsports. Overall, Hendrick Motorsports has won 14 Cup Series championships, with the most recent occurring in 2020 and 2021; one Xfinity Series championship, and three Truck series championships. Hendrick Motorsports also owns Hendrick Automotive Group, which represents 130 automobile dealership franchises and 25 manufacturer nameplates, as well as collision centers and accessory distributors throughout the U.S.

CONTACTS: *Note: Officers with more than one job title may be intentionally listed here more than once.*

Marshall Carlson, Pres.
Jeff Gordon, Vice Chmn.
Doug Duchardt, VP-Dev.
Alan Gustafson, Crew Chief-Team 24
Chad Knaus, Crew Chief-Team 48
Steve Letarte, Crew Chief-Team 88
Kenny Francis, Crew Chief-Team 5
Rick Hendrick, Chmn.

FINANCIAL DATA: *Note: Data for latest year may not have been available at press time.*

In U.S. $	2022	2021	2020	2019	2018	2017
Revenue		36,704,800	37,840,000			
R&D Expense						
Operating Income						
Operating Margin %						
SGA Expense						
Net Income				7,000,000	21,000,000	21,000,000
Operating Cash Flow						
Capital Expenditure						
EBITDA						
Return on Assets %						
Return on Equity %						
Debt to Equity						

CONTACT INFORMATION:

Phone: 704-455-3400   Fax: 704-455-0346
Toll-Free: 877-467-4890
Address: 4400 Papa Joe Hendrick Blvd., Charlotte, NC 28262 United States

STOCK TICKER/OTHER:

Stock Ticker: Private
Employees: 5
Parent Company:

Exchange:
Fiscal Year Ends: 12/31

SALARIES/BONUSES:

Top Exec. Salary: $ Bonus: $
Second Exec. Salary: $ Bonus: $

OTHER THOUGHTS:

Estimated Female Officers or Directors:
Hot Spot for Advancement for Women/Minorities:

Sales, profits and employees may be estimates. Financial information, benefits and other data can change quickly and may vary from those stated here.

Hibbett Sports Inc

www.hibbett.com

NAIC Code: 451110

TYPES OF BUSINESS:

Sporting Goods Stores
Sports Apparel
Athletic Shoes
Training Equipment
Footwear

GROWTH PLANS/SPECIAL FEATURES:

Hibbett Inc is engaged in the retail of sports goods. The company operates small to midsize stores and focuses its business on the South, Southwest, mid-Atlantic, and Midwest areas of the country. It offers a broad range of sporting goods, including apparel, footwear, accessories, and equipment needed for team sports, with brands such as Nike, Under Armour, Adidas, The North Face, Jordan, Costa, and others. The company consists of three kinds of stores: Hibbett Sports, the company's primary retail format stores, accounting for most of the company's total stores, City Gear, and Sports Additions, smaller-format stores primarily offering athletic footwear with a fashion-based style.

Hibbett Sports offers its employees comprehensive health benefits, life and disability insurance, retirement options and employee assistance plans and programs.

BRANDS/DIVISIONS/AFFILIATES:

Hibbett Sports
Sports Additions
City Gear

CONTACTS: *Note: Officers with more than one job title may be intentionally listed here more than once.*

Michael Longo, CEO
Robert Volke, CFO
Anthony Crudele, Chairman of the Board
Ronald Blahnik, Chief Information Officer
David Benck, General Counsel
Jared Briskin, Other Corporate Officer
William Quinn, Senior VP, Divisional
Benjamin Knighten, Senior VP, Divisional

FINANCIAL DATA: *Note: Data for latest year may not have been available at press time.*

In U.S. $	2022	2021	2020	2019	2018	2017
Revenue	1,691,184,000	1,419,657,000	1,184,234,000	1,008,682,000		
R&D Expense						
Operating Income	228,166,000	118,049,000	36,117,000	37,541,000		
Operating Margin %	.13%	.08%	.03%	.04%		
SGA Expense	382,414,000	356,856,000	318,011,000	264,142,000		
Net Income	174,313,000	74,266,000	27,344,000	28,421,000		
Operating Cash Flow	159,488,000	197,716,000	92,289,000	73,417,000		
Capital Expenditure	71,153,000	34,760,000	17,326,000	17,696,000		
EBITDA	264,036,000	128,098,000	66,665,000	65,324,000		
Return on Assets %	.23%	.09%	.04%	.06%		
Return on Equity %	.51%	.21%	.08%	.09%		
Debt to Equity	.73%	.48%	0.585	0.006		

CONTACT INFORMATION:

Phone: 205 942-4292   Fax: 205 912-7290
Toll-Free:
Address: 2700 Milan Ct., Birmingham, AL 35211 United States

STOCK TICKER/OTHER:

Stock Ticker: HIBB   Exchange: NAS
Employees: 11,000   Fiscal Year Ends: 01/31
Parent Company:

SALARIES/BONUSES:

Top Exec. Salary: $700,000   Bonus: $
Second Exec. Salary: Bonus: $
$485,000

OTHER THOUGHTS:

Estimated Female Officers or Directors: 3
Hot Spot for Advancement for Women/Minorities: Y

Houston Astros

NAIC Code: 711211A

www.mlb.com/astros

TYPES OF BUSINESS:

Professional Baseball Team
Team Management and Operations

BRANDS/DIVISIONS/AFFILIATES:

CONTACTS: *Note: Officers with more than one job title may be intentionally listed here more than once.*

Jared Crane, Sr. VP-Exec. Oper.
Marcel Braithwaite, Sr. VP-Bus. Oper
Michael Slaughter, CFO
Anita Sehgal, Sr. VP-Mktg. & Communications
Jennifer Springs, VP-Human Resources
Chris Hanz, VP-IT
Tom Jennings, Dir.-Merch. & Retail
Jeff Luhnow, Gen. Mgr.-Baseball Oper.
Gene Dias, Sr. Dir.-Media Rel.
Doug Seckel, VP-Finance
Jason Howard, VP-Ticket Sales & Service
Jamie Hildreth, Sr. VP-Premium Sponsorships
Jonathan Germer, Controller
Brooke Ellenberger, Sr. Dir.-Ticket Oper. & Strategy
Jim Crane, Chmn.
Oz Ocampo, Dir.-Int'l

GROWTH PLANS/SPECIAL FEATURES:

The Houston Astros is an organization within Major League Baseball (MLB). Founded in 1962, the team was originally called the Colt .45s. The club was renamed the Astros in 1965 and played for many years in the Astrodome, the world's first domed ballpark. In 2005, the team capitalized on its Wild Card playoff berth to win the League Championship, but was swept in the World Series. In 2011, Texas businessman Drayton McLane, who had owned the club since 1993, sold the franchise to Jim Crane for $610 million. As part of the transaction, Crane moved the club from the NL Central division to the AL West in 2013. During McLane's tenure, which was characterized by periodic team success, a group of hitting stars known as the Killer Bs came to prominence. Craig Biggio, Jeff Bagwell, Derek Bell and Sean Berry were the initial group; it later included Lance Berkman. Today, the Astros play at Minute Maid Park, a $250-million stadium with a retractable roof situated in downtown Houston. In the 2015 season, the Astros made the playoffs for the first time since 2005. In 2017, the Astros became the first franchise in MLB history to have won a pennant in both the NL and the AL, when they defeated the New York Yankees in the ALCS. They subsequently won the 2017 World Series against the Los Angeles Dodgers, 4-3, its first World Series title. In 2022, the Astros clenched their second World Series title against the Philadelphia Phillies. Other titles include four AL Pennants, one NL Pennant, five AL West Division titles, four NL Central Division titles, three NL West Division titles and four Wild Card berths. The ball club's average home attendance was 33,197 for the 2022 season. Forbes valued the franchise at $2.25 billion in March 2023.

FINANCIAL DATA: *Note: Data for latest year may not have been available at press time.*

In U.S. $	2022	2021	2020	2019	2018	2017
Revenue	525,200,000					
R&D Expense						
Operating Income						
Operating Margin %						
SGA Expense						
Net Income						
Operating Cash Flow						
Capital Expenditure						
EBITDA						
Return on Assets %						
Return on Equity %						
Debt to Equity						

CONTACT INFORMATION:

Phone: 713-259-8000   Fax: 713-259-8025
Toll-Free:
Address: 501 Crawford St., Houston, TX 77002 United States

STOCK TICKER/OTHER:

Stock Ticker: Private   Exchange:
Employees: 550   Fiscal Year Ends: 12/31
Parent Company:

SALARIES/BONUSES:

Top Exec. Salary: $ Bonus: $
Second Exec. Salary: $ Bonus: $

OTHER THOUGHTS:

Estimated Female Officers or Directors: 3
Hot Spot for Advancement for Women/Minorities: Y

Sales, profits and employees may be estimates. Financial information, benefits and other data can change quickly and may vary from those stated here.

Houston Dynamo FC

www.houstondynamo.com

NAIC Code: 711211D

TYPES OF BUSINESS:

Major League Soccer Team
Team Management and Operations

BRANDS/DIVISIONS/AFFILIATES:

CONTACTS: *Note: Officers with more than one job title may be intentionally listed here more than once.*

Pat Onstad, Gen. Mngr.
Jessica O'Neill, COO
Nicolas Somoano, CFO
S. J. Luedtke, CMO
Jasmine James, Chief of Staff
Lyle Ayes, Vice Chmn.
Frank Arnold, Dir.-Oper.
Chris Canetti, Pres., Bus. Oper.
Lester Gretsch, Sr. Dir.-Comm. & Broadcasting
Dominic Kinnear, Head Coach
Maria Duran, Sr. Mgr.-Dynamo Charities
Travis Watkins, Sr. Dir.-Ticket & Premium Svcs.
Ted Segal, Chmn.

GROWTH PLANS/SPECIAL FEATURES:

The Houston Dynamo FC is a Major League Soccer (MLS) club based in Houston, Texas. The team changed its name from the San Jose Earthquakes and relocated to Houston in December 2005 in time for the start of the 2006 season. Most of the team's members in the inaugural season were players from the former Earthquakes team, with the addition of players from the 2006 and 2007 MLS draft. The Dynamo's stadium, Shell Energy Stadium, is an open-air arena featuring a 22,039-seating capacity. The arena is the first soccer-specific stadium in MLS history to be in a city's downtown sector. The club plays in the MLS Western Conference along with the Austin FC, Colorado Rapids, FC Dallas, LA Galaxy, Los Angeles FC, Minnesota United FC, Portland Timbers, Real Salt Lake, San Jose Earthquakes, Seattle Sounders FC, Sporting Kansas City, St. Louis City SC and Vancouver Whitecaps FC. The Houston team is one of the few clubs to win back-to-back league championships, including its inaugural 2006 season and its 2007 season. The Dynamo won the U.S. Open Cup in 2018. Notable players have included Brian Ching, Dwayne de Rosario and Ryan Cochrane. Average attendance at home games was 16,426 during the 2022 season. The Houston Dynamo and the Houston Dash professional men's and women's soccer teams are majority-owned by Ted Segal, with minority owners including Lyle Ayes and James Harden.

FINANCIAL DATA: *Note: Data for latest year may not have been available at press time.*

In U.S. $	2022	2021	2020	2019	2018	2017
Revenue	7,389,900					
R&D Expense						
Operating Income						
Operating Margin %						
SGA Expense						
Net Income						
Operating Cash Flow						
Capital Expenditure						
EBITDA						
Return on Assets %						
Return on Equity %						
Debt to Equity						

CONTACT INFORMATION:

Phone: 713-276-7500   Fax: 713-276-7572
Toll-Free:
Address: 1001 Avenida de las Americas, Ste. 200, Houston, TX 77010
United States

STOCK TICKER/OTHER:

Stock Ticker: Private   Exchange:
Employees: 275   Fiscal Year Ends:
Parent Company:

SALARIES/BONUSES:

Top Exec. Salary: $ Bonus: $
Second Exec. Salary: $ Bonus: $

OTHER THOUGHTS:

Estimated Female Officers or Directors: 8
Hot Spot for Advancement for Women/Minorities: Y

Houston Rockets

www.nba.com/rockets

NAIC Code: 711211B

TYPES OF BUSINESS:

Professional Basketball Team
Team Management and Operations

BRANDS/DIVISIONS/AFFILIATES:

CONTACTS: *Note: Officers with more than one job title may be intentionally listed here more than once.*

Gretchen Sheirr, Pres.-Bus. Oper.
Larry Kaiser, CFO
Rafael Stone, General Counsel
Daryl Morey, Managing Dir.-Basketball Oper.
Scott Andrews, Chief Strategy Officer
Paul Suarez, Mgr.-e-Mktg.
Nelson Luis, Dir.-Media Rel.
Larry Kaiser, Sr. Dir.-Finance
Kevin McHale, Head Coach
Ken Sheirr, Sr. Dir.-Mktg. Oper.
Tilman J. Fertitta, Owner

GROWTH PLANS/SPECIAL FEATURES:

The Houston Rockets originally entered the National Basketball Association (NBA) as the San Diego Rockets in 1967, and was relocated to Houston in 1971. All home games are played at the Toyota Center, which opened in 2003. The arena occupies 750,000 square feet of downtown Houston and features an 18,500-seating capacity for basketball fans. The team's home attendance average was 16,313 in the 2022-23 season. The Rockets won consecutive NBA championships in 1994 and 1995 under center Hakeem Olajuwon and Coach Rudy Tomjanovich. Though the club has made several return trips to the NBA postseason, it has failed to win a third championship. Nonetheless, the Rockets have clenched four conference titles and eight division titles (with consecutive wins from 2018 to 2020). Notable former players include Elvin Hayes, Robert Reid, Moses Malone, Ralph Sampson, Clyde Drexler, Charles Barkley, Rodney McCray, Yao Ming and James Harden. Forbes estimated the Rockets' value at $3.2 billion in October 2022.

FINANCIAL DATA: *Note: Data for latest year may not have been available at press time.*

In U.S. $	2022	2021	2020	2019	2018	2017
Revenue	345,150,000					
R&D Expense						
Operating Income						
Operating Margin %						
SGA Expense						
Net Income						
Operating Cash Flow						
Capital Expenditure						
EBITDA						
Return on Assets %						
Return on Equity %						
Debt to Equity						

CONTACT INFORMATION:

Phone: 713-758-7200   Fax: 713-758-7315
Toll-Free:
Address: 1510 Polk St., Houston, TX 77002 United States

SALARIES/BONUSES:

Top Exec. Salary: $ Bonus: $
Second Exec. Salary: $ Bonus: $

STOCK TICKER/OTHER:

Stock Ticker: Private   Exchange:
Employees: 340   Fiscal Year Ends: 06/30
Parent Company:

OTHER THOUGHTS:

Estimated Female Officers or Directors: 13
Hot Spot for Advancement for Women/Minorities: Y

Houston Texans

NAIC Code: 711211C

www.houstontexans.com

TYPES OF BUSINESS:

Professional Football Team
Team Management and Operations

GROWTH PLANS/SPECIAL FEATURES:

The Houston Texans is a professional football team in the southern American Football Conference (AFC) of the National Football League (NFL), and based in Houston, Texas. The franchise was founded as an expansion team in 1999 and played its first game in 2002. Even though the Texans were only the NFL's second expansion team to win its first game, its performance on the field since then has been decidedly mixed. The team is owned by Robert McNair, who is founder of Cogen Technologies and responsible for bringing the Texans to Houston. The team's home, NRG Stadium, is owned by Harris County, Texas and seats nearly 72,000 fans. It was the first NFL stadium to feature a retractable roof. The Texan's average home game attendance was 67,911 during 2022-23 season. In the 2011 season, the franchise won the AFC South division championship and made its first playoff appearance. The 2012 season showed the Texans repeating as the AFC South division champions, thus earning a second playoff berth; and winning the division again in 2015, 2016, 2018 and 2019. Forbes estimated the Houston Texans to be worth $4.7 billion in 2022.

BRANDS/DIVISIONS/AFFILIATES:

NRG Stadium

CONTACTS: *Note: Officers with more than one job title may be intentionally listed here more than once.*

D. Cal McNair, CEO
Greg Grissom, Pres.
Marilan Logan, CFO
Jeff Schmitz, CIO
Anita Martin, VP-Human Resources
Tim Brog, Dir.-Football Tech & Decision Science
Suzie Thomas, Chief Admin. Officer
Suzie Thomas, General Counsel
Rick Smith, Gen. Mgr.
Greg Grissom, VP-Corp. Dev.
Kevin Cooper, Sr. Dir.-Comm.
Marilan Logan, Chief Acct. Officer
Greg Watson, VP-Finance
Gary Kubiak, Head Coach
John Schriever, Sr. VP-Ticketing & Event Mgmt.
Jan Kelly, Sr. Dir.-Risk Mgmt. & Controller
Juan Rodriguez, Sr. VP-Oper.

FINANCIAL DATA: *Note: Data for latest year may not have been available at press time.*

In U.S. $	2022	2021	2020	2019	2018	2017
Revenue	602,550,000					
R&D Expense						
Operating Income						
Operating Margin %						
SGA Expense						
Net Income						
Operating Cash Flow						
Capital Expenditure						
EBITDA						
Return on Assets %						
Return on Equity %						
Debt to Equity						

CONTACT INFORMATION:

Phone: 832-667-2002   Fax: 832-667-2188
Toll-Free:
Address: Two NRG Park, Houston, TX 77054 United States

STOCK TICKER/OTHER:

Stock Ticker: Private   Exchange:
Employees: 425   Fiscal Year Ends:
Parent Company:

SALARIES/BONUSES:

Top Exec. Salary: $ Bonus: $
Second Exec. Salary: $ Bonus: $

OTHER THOUGHTS:

Estimated Female Officers or Directors: 7
Hot Spot for Advancement for Women/Minorities: Y

Sales, profits and employees may be estimates. Financial information, benefits and other data can change quickly and may vary from those stated here.

Huffy Bicycle Co

www.huffybikes.com

NAIC Code: 336991

TYPES OF BUSINESS:

Bicycles and Parts Manufacturing
Bike Manufacturing
Electric Bikes
Mountain Bikes
Cruiser Bikes
Scooters
Bike Gears and Parts
Ecommerce

BRANDS/DIVISIONS/AFFILIATES:

Huffy Corporation
Perfect Fit Frame

CONTACTS: *Note: Officers with more than one job title may be intentionally listed here more than once.*

Claude Jordan, CEO
Bill Smith, Pres.
Robert L. Diekman, Sr. VP-Oper.
Robert L. Diekman, Sr. VP-Logistics

GROWTH PLANS/SPECIAL FEATURES:

Huffy Bicycle Co., founded in 1892 and a subsidiary of Huffy Corporation, designs and sells Huffy brand products, primarily bicycles and scooters. The wheeled products are manufactured in Southeast Asian locations including Taiwan and China and are sold by retailers throughout the U.S., including Walmart, Ace, Target, TrueValue, Meijer, Academy Sports + Outdoors, Dunham's Sports, Hardware Hank, Bigg's, Amazon.com and others. Huffy offers several categories of wheeled products, including tricycles for children four years and younger, scooters and kids bikes for those ages ten and up. Popular children's products available include the Green Machine and branded bicycles such as Disney, Marvel, Panama Jack and Star Wars. The firm also offers BMX bikes, mountain bikes, cruiser bikes, electric bikes and hybrids, which are designed more toward teens and adults. Huffy's Perfect Fit Frame is designed to enable riders to put both feet flat on the ground when stopped, offering enhanced control and comfort. Gears and parts are also sold by Huffy.

FINANCIAL DATA: *Note: Data for latest year may not have been available at press time.*

In U.S. $	2022	2021	2020	2019	2018	2017
Revenue						
R&D Expense						
Operating Income						
Operating Margin %						
SGA Expense						
Net Income						
Operating Cash Flow						
Capital Expenditure						
EBITDA						
Return on Assets %						
Return on Equity %						
Debt to Equity						

CONTACT INFORMATION:

Phone: 937-865-2800   Fax: 937-865-5470
Toll-Free: 800-872-2453
Address: 6551 Centerville Business Pkwy., Centerville, OH 45459 United States

STOCK TICKER/OTHER:

Stock Ticker: Subsidiary
Employees: 130
Parent Company: Huffy Corporation

Exchange:
Fiscal Year Ends: 12/31

SALARIES/BONUSES:

Top Exec. Salary: $ Bonus: $
Second Exec. Salary: $ Bonus: $

OTHER THOUGHTS:

Estimated Female Officers or Directors:
Hot Spot for Advancement for Women/Minorities:

Sales, profits and employees may be estimates. Financial information, benefits and other data can change quickly and may vary from those stated here.

Ilitch Holdings Inc

NAIC Code: 722513

TYPES OF BUSINESS:

Pizza Restaurants
Investment Company
Pizza Stores
Sports Teams
Food Services
Sport and Entertainment Venue Operations
Food Manufacturer
Event Booking Services

BRANDS/DIVISIONS/AFFILIATES:

Little Caesars Pizza
Detroit Red Wings
Olympia Development of Michigan
Ilitch Sports + Entertainment
Detroit Tigers
Motor City Casino and Hotel
313 Presents

CONTACTS: *Note: Officers with more than one job title may be intentionally listed here more than once.*

Christopher Ilitch, CEO
Scott Fisher, CFO
Marian Ilitch, Vice Chmn.
Mike McLauchlan, VP-Gov't Rel.
John Kotlar, VP-Tax Affairs
Marian Ilitch, Chmn.

GROWTH PLANS/SPECIAL FEATURES:

Ilitch Holdings, Inc. is a holding company engaged in the sports, entertainment and food segments throughout North America. Ilitch provides professional services as well as technical services to all the companies owned by the Ilitch family. These companies include: Little Caesars Pizza, a leading pizza chain with stores in all 50 U.S. states and over 20 international markets; the Detroit Red Wings, an NHL hockey league; the Detroit Tigers, a major league baseball team; Olympia Development of Michigan, a real estate developer and investment firm; Ilitch Sports + Entertainment, which operates sport and entertainment venues, arenas, parks and theaters; Motor City Casino and Hotel, offering gaming, a luxury hotel and spa, a theater, restaurants and meeting/conference facilities; and 313 Presents, a joint venture between Ilitch Sports + Entertainment and Pistons Sports & Entertainment, offering event bookings, production, accounting, marketing and public relations for entertainment events, concerts, family shows and community functions.

FINANCIAL DATA: *Note: Data for latest year may not have been available at press time.*

In U.S. $	2022	2021	2020	2019	2018	2017
Revenue	3,200,000,000	3,100,000,000	2,546,000,000	3,800,000,000	3,600,000,000	3,600,000,000
R&D Expense						
Operating Income						
Operating Margin %						
SGA Expense						
Net Income						
Operating Cash Flow						
Capital Expenditure						
EBITDA						
Return on Assets %						
Return on Equity %						
Debt to Equity						

CONTACT INFORMATION:

Phone: 313-471-6600   Fax: 313-471-6094
Toll-Free:
Address: 2211 Woodward Ave., Fox Office Cntr., Detroit, MI 48201
United States

STOCK TICKER/OTHER:

Stock Ticker: Private
Employees: 24,000
Parent Company:

Exchange:
Fiscal Year Ends: 12/31

SALARIES/BONUSES:

Top Exec. Salary: $ Bonus: $
Second Exec. Salary: $ Bonus: $

OTHER THOUGHTS:

Estimated Female Officers or Directors: 2
Hot Spot for Advancement for Women/Minorities: Y

Indiana Fever

NAIC Code: 711211E

www.wnba.com/fever

TYPES OF BUSINESS:

Women's National Basketball Association Team
Team Management and Operations

BRANDS/DIVISIONS/AFFILIATES:

Freddy Fever
Inferno Dance Team

CONTACTS: *Note: Officers with more than one job title may be intentionally listed here more than once.*

Kelly Krauskopf, Pres.
Julie Graue, VP-Bus. Oper.
Quinn Buckner, VP-Corp. Comm.
Matt Albrecht, Controller
Herbert Simon, Owner
Lin Dunn, Head Coach
Julie Graue, VP-Sales
Herbert Simon, Chmn.

GROWTH PLANS/SPECIAL FEATURES:

The Indiana Fever is a Women's National Basketball Association (WNBA) team that gained league entry in 2000. It plays in the Eastern Conference along with the Atlanta Dream, Chicago Sky, Connecticut Sun, New York Liberty and Washington Mystics. The Fever played its home games in the Indiana Farmers Coliseum and Gainbridge Fieldhouse arena in the 2021 season, which offer 6,500 and nearly 18,000 seats, respectively. Home game attendance averaged 1,776 for the Fever's 2022 season. The team is owned by Herb Simon and has seen some success, including the 2009 season in which it won a conference championship but ultimately fell to the Phoenix Mercury in the final game. In 2012, the Fever won the WNBA Championship for its first and only time. In 2015, the Fever won its third conference title, and advanced to WNBA final, but lost to the Minnesota Lynx, 2-3. Game night entertainment includes Freddy Fever, the team mascot, and the Inferno Dance Team, which is comprised of high school and college students. The team's roster has included players such as Tamika Catchings, a 7-time WNBA All-Star and an Olympic gold medalist.

FINANCIAL DATA: *Note: Data for latest year may not have been available at press time.*

In U.S. $	2022	2021	2020	2019	2018	2017
Revenue						
R&D Expense						
Operating Income						
Operating Margin %						
SGA Expense						
Net Income						
Operating Cash Flow						
Capital Expenditure						
EBITDA						
Return on Assets %						
Return on Equity %						
Debt to Equity						

CONTACT INFORMATION:

Phone: 317-917-2500   Fax: 317-917-2599
Toll-Free:
Address: 125 S. Pennsylvania St., Indianapolis, IN 46204 United States

STOCK TICKER/OTHER:

Stock Ticker: Private   Exchange:
Employees: 140   Fiscal Year Ends: 06/30
Parent Company:

SALARIES/BONUSES:

Top Exec. Salary: $ Bonus: $
Second Exec. Salary: $ Bonus: $

OTHER THOUGHTS:

Estimated Female Officers or Directors: 45
Hot Spot for Advancement for Women/Minorities: Y

Indiana Pacers

NAIC Code: 711211B

TYPES OF BUSINESS:

Professional Basketball Team
Team Management and Operations

BRANDS/DIVISIONS/AFFILIATES:

Pacers Sports & Entertainment
Gainbridge Fieldhouse
Indiana Fever
Reading Time-Outs
Read to Achieve
Pacers Learning Center
Get Pacers Fit

CONTACTS: *Note: Officers with more than one job title may be intentionally listed here more than once.*

Chad Buchanan, Gen. Mngr.
Kevin Pritchard, Pres.-Basketball Oper.
Larry Bird, Pres., Basketball Oper.
Greg Schenkel, VP-Corp., Public & Community Rel.
Matt Albrecht, VP-Finance
Frank Vogel, Head Coach
Barry Gibson, VP-Ticket Sales Dev.
Terry Tiernon, VP-Corp. Partnerships
Herbert Simon, Chmn.

GROWTH PLANS/SPECIAL FEATURES:

The Indiana Pacers entered the American Basketball Association (ABA) in the 1967-68 season and entered the National Basketball Association (NBA) in 1976, the year the ABA and NBA merged. The team arena is located in Indianapolis at the Gainbridge Fieldhouse, seating nearly 18,000 basketball fans. Home game attendance averaged 15,647 for the Pacers in its 2022-23 season. Notable former players of the Pacers include George McGinnis, Mel Daniels, Reggie Miller and Roger Brown. Since its founding, the franchise has won three league championships (all within the ABA), one conference title and nine division titles (six since joining the NBA, and the most recent wins being in 2013 and 2014). The team has established the Pacers Foundation, Inc. in order to provide support to children through community activities and education. Additional community outreach programs include education initiatives such as Reading Time-Outs, Read to Achieve and the Pacers Learning Center; and health programs, including Get Pacers Fit and the Riley Hospital for Children Basketball Buddies Pacers Youth Basketball. Forbes estimated the Indiana Pacers value at $1.8 billion in October 2022.

FINANCIAL DATA: *Note: Data for latest year may not have been available at press time.*

In U.S. $	2022	2021	2020	2019	2018	2017
Revenue	257,400,000					
R&D Expense						
Operating Income						
Operating Margin %						
SGA Expense						
Net Income						
Operating Cash Flow						
Capital Expenditure						
EBITDA						
Return on Assets %						
Return on Equity %						
Debt to Equity						

CONTACT INFORMATION:

Phone: 317-917-2500   Fax: 317-917-2599
Toll-Free:
Address: 125 S. Pennsylvania St., Indianapolis, IN 46204 United States

STOCK TICKER/OTHER:

Stock Ticker: Private   Exchange:
Employees: 300   Fiscal Year Ends: 06/30
Parent Company:

SALARIES/BONUSES:

Top Exec. Salary: $ Bonus: $
Second Exec. Salary: $ Bonus: $

OTHER THOUGHTS:

Estimated Female Officers or Directors: 8
Hot Spot for Advancement for Women/Minorities: Y

Indianapolis Colts

www.colts.com

NAIC Code: 711211C

TYPES OF BUSINESS:

Professional Football Team
Team Management and Operations

BRANDS/DIVISIONS/AFFILIATES:

CONTACTS: *Note: Officers with more than one job title may be intentionally listed here more than once.*

James Irsay, CEO
Pete Ward, COO
E. J. Tolentino, CFO
Roger VanDerSnick, Chief Sales & Mktg. Officer
Jon Scott, VP-Equipment Oper.
Larry Hall, VP-Ticket Oper. & Guest Svcs.
Mike Bluem, Dir.-Football Admin.
Dan Emerson, General Counsel
Jimmy Raye, VP-Football Oper.
Dan Plumlee, Dir.-Digital Media
Avis Roper, Sr. Dir.-Comm.
Kurt Humphrey, VP-Finance
Chuck Pagano, Head Coach
Carlie Irsay-Gordon, Vice Chmn.
Casey Irsay Foyt, Vice Chmn.
Ryan Grigson, Gen. Mgr.
Chris Ballard, Gen. Mngr.

GROWTH PLANS/SPECIAL FEATURES:

The Indianapolis Colts is a professional football team in the National Football League's (NFL) Southern Division of the American Football Conference (AFC). The franchise was founded in 1953 when Carroll Rosenbloom won the rights to a new team in Baltimore; thus, the Baltimore Colts was founded. In 1972, Rosenbloom traded the Colts to Robert Isray for the Los Angeles Rams. The two teams, however, stayed in their respective cities. The Baltimore Colts won four NFL league championships (1958, 1959, 1968 and 1970), the first two coached by Hall of Famer Weeb Ewbank. In March 1984, Isray controversially moved the Baltimore Colts to Indianapolis over a dispute with the city of Baltimore. Football legend Johnny Unitas, a Baltimore Colt, asked the NFL Hall of Fame to remove his museum display unless it made clear reference to his being a Baltimore Colt. In the recent past, the Colts, led by quarterback Peyton Manning, saw a great deal of regular season success, winning the AFC South division title nine times since 2003. However, the team was only able to capture one Super Bowl title in this span (XLI in the 2006 season). Overall, the Colts have made 29 NFL playoff appearances, with the most recent being in 2020. The team plays at the 63,000-seat capacity Lucas Oil Stadium in downtown Indianapolis, and average home game attendance was 65,559 during the 2022-23 season. Forbes estimated the Colts to be worth $3.8 billion in 2022.

FINANCIAL DATA: *Note: Data for latest year may not have been available at press time.*

In U.S. $	2022	2021	2020	2019	2018	2017
Revenue	504,400,000					
R&D Expense						
Operating Income						
Operating Margin %						
SGA Expense						
Net Income						
Operating Cash Flow						
Capital Expenditure						
EBITDA						
Return on Assets %						
Return on Equity %						
Debt to Equity						

CONTACT INFORMATION:

Phone: 317-297-2658   Fax: 317-297-8971
Toll-Free: 800-805-2658
Address: 7001 W. 56th St., Indianapolis, IN 46254 United States

STOCK TICKER/OTHER:

Stock Ticker: Private
Employees: 380
Parent Company:

Exchange:
Fiscal Year Ends: 01/31

SALARIES/BONUSES:

Top Exec. Salary: $ Bonus: $
Second Exec. Salary: $ Bonus: $

OTHER THOUGHTS:

Estimated Female Officers or Directors: 4
Hot Spot for Advancement for Women/Minorities: Y

IndyCar LLC
NAIC Code: 711211

www.indycar.com

TYPES OF BUSINESS:
Automobile Racing League
Racing Circuit Operations
Single-Seat Open Cockpit Racecars

BRANDS/DIVISIONS/AFFILIATES:
Penske Corporation
Penske Entertainment Corp
Indianapolis Motor Speedway
NTT IndyCar Series
Indy NXT
Indy Pro 2000 Championship
US F2000 National Championship
IndyCar Radio

CONTACTS: *Note: Officers with more than one job title may be intentionally listed here more than once.*
Jay Frye, Pres.
John Griffin, Contact-Public Rel.
Beaux Barfield, Pres.-Competition

GROWTH PLANS/SPECIAL FEATURES:
IndyCar, LLC is an American-based auto racing sanctioning body for Indy car racing and other types of open wheel car racing. The league is owned by Roger Penske via Penske Entertainment Corp., a subsidiary of Penske Corporation. Penske acquired IndyCar and the Indianapolis Motor Speedway from Hulman & Co. in late-2019. IndyCar sanctions five racing series: the premier IndyCar Series, the developmental series Indy NXT, the Indy Pro 2000 Championship and the U.S. F2000 National Championship. These racing series are all a part of the Road to Indy and the Global Mazda MX-5 Cup. The famous Indianapolis 500 race is part of the IndyCar Series. IndyCar is recognized as a member organization of the Federation Internationale de l'Automobile (FIA) through Automobile Competition Committee for the United States (ACCUS). IndyCar Radio comprises a broadcast network that offers information on races, teams, drivers and more via radio and on-demand podcasts. IndyCar Nation offers weekly e-newsletters and insider information on races, drivers and teams, as well as discounts on official merchandise, race tickets, special events and more. IndyCar App is powered by NTT Data, and features live audio, exclusive content, live in-car cameras, live timing and score, play fantasy racing, and favorite drivers and teams. IndyCar LIVE is supplied in collaboration between IndyCar Live and StayLive, and enables viewers live access for watching the NTT IndyCar Series.

FINANCIAL DATA: *Note: Data for latest year may not have been available at press time.*

In U.S. $	2022	2021	2020	2019	2018	2017
Revenue						
R&D Expense						
Operating Income						
Operating Margin %						
SGA Expense						
Net Income						
Operating Cash Flow						
Capital Expenditure						
EBITDA						
Return on Assets %						
Return on Equity %						
Debt to Equity						

CONTACT INFORMATION:
Phone: 317-492-6526   Fax: 317-492-6525
Toll-Free:
Address: 4551 W. 16th St., Indianapolis, IN 46222 United States

STOCK TICKER/OTHER:
Stock Ticker: Subsidiary   Exchange:
Employees: 128   Fiscal Year Ends:
Parent Company: Penske Corporation

SALARIES/BONUSES:
Top Exec. Salary: $ Bonus: $
Second Exec. Salary: $ Bonus: $

OTHER THOUGHTS:
Estimated Female Officers or Directors:
Hot Spot for Advancement for Women/Minorities:

International Boxing Federation

www.ibf-usba-boxing.com

NAIC Code: 711211

TYPES OF BUSINESS:

Boxing Association
Professional Boxing Supervisory Organization

BRANDS/DIVISIONS/AFFILIATES:

United States Boxing Association (USBA)
www.ibf.usba-boxing.com

CONTACTS: *Note: Officers with more than one job title may be intentionally listed here more than once.*

Daryl J. Peoples, Pres.
Louis Priluker, Corp. Sec.
Lindsey E. Tucker, Chmn.-Championship
William James, Chmn.-Ratings

GROWTH PLANS/SPECIAL FEATURES:

The International Boxing Federation (IBF) is a voluntary membership non-profit corporation engaged in the supervision of professional boxing. IBF promulgates rules, suggests standards for boxing guidance, sanctions title fights to establish champions and prepares monthly ratings of the outstanding contenders in 17 weight classes for men and 15 weight classes for women. Weight classes span Mini Flyweight, Junior Flyweight, Flyweight, Junior Bantamweight, Bantamweight, Junior Featherweight, Featherweight, Junior Lightweight, Lightweight, Junior Welterweight, Welterweight, Junior Middleweight, Middleweight, Super Middleweight, Light Heavyweight, Cruiserweight and Heavyweight. Women's Light Heavyweight and Heavyweight have yet to be inaugurated by IBF. Regional and cross-regional competitions enable professional boxers the opportunity to work their way up through the organization's ratings and aim for the world championship title. Each year, IBF holds an IBF/USBA (United States Boxing Association) convention with a full day dedicated to professional seminars, including a judge's seminar and a referee's seminar. Seminar goals is to achieve uniformity in judging and refereeing of professional boxing matches. A medical seminar is also held during the annual convention with the purpose of enlightening individuals close to the boxers (such as family members) of the signs of possible serious injury and how to potentially avoid such a situation. Rules, ratings, memberships, boxing schedules and more can be retrieved from IBF's website, www.ibf.usba-boxing.com.

FINANCIAL DATA: *Note: Data for latest year may not have been available at press time.*

In U.S. $	2022	2021	2020	2019	2018	2017
Revenue		4,576,000	1,336,505	2,560,659	1,996,552	1,996,552
R&D Expense						
Operating Income						
Operating Margin %						
SGA Expense						
Net Income			149,382			
Operating Cash Flow						
Capital Expenditure						
EBITDA						
Return on Assets %						
Return on Equity %						
Debt to Equity						

CONTACT INFORMATION:

Phone: 973-564-8046   Fax: 973-564-8751
Toll-Free:
Address: 899 Mountain Ave., Ste. 2E, Springfield, NJ 07081 United States

STOCK TICKER/OTHER:

Stock Ticker: Private
Employees: 90
Parent Company:

Exchange:
Fiscal Year Ends: 12/31

SALARIES/BONUSES:

Top Exec. Salary: $ Bonus: $
Second Exec. Salary: $ Bonus: $

OTHER THOUGHTS:

Estimated Female Officers or Directors: 1
Hot Spot for Advancement for Women/Minorities:

International Olympic Committee (IOC)
NAIC Code: 711211

www.olympic.org

TYPES OF BUSINESS:
Sports Association
Licensing & Broadcast Rights
Global Sport Competition

BRANDS/DIVISIONS/AFFILIATES:
Olympic Games
International Paralympic Committee
Paralympic Games

CONTACTS: *Note: Officers with more than one job title may be intentionally listed here more than once.*
Thomas Bach, Pres.
Ser Miang Ng, VP
Thomas Bach, VP
Nawal El Moutawakel, VP
Craig Reedle, VP

GROWTH PLANS/SPECIAL FEATURES:
International Olympic Committee (IOC) organizes the Olympic Games, in which approximately 200 countries participate. The IOC was established in 1894 to organize an international revival of the ancient Greek Olympic Games. The first modern Olympic competition organized by the IOC was held in 1896 in Athens, Greece and featured athletes from 14 countries. Since then, the Olympics have been held every four years, excluding the 1916, 1940 and 1944 games due to WWI and II. From a modest 43 events at the 1896 Athens games, the international competition has expanded to include over 300 events and 28 sports. The summer and winter Olympics alternate on a two-year schedule, with the most recent events being the 2020 Tokyo Summer Olympics and the 2022 Beijing Winter Olympics. The 2024 Summer Olympics will be held in Paris, France and the 2026 Winter Olympics will be held in Milano Cortina, Italy. To qualify as an Olympic sport, a game must have an international governing organization, 50 countries on three continents with men participating in the sport and/or 35 countries on three continents with women participating in the sport. IOC officially recognizes a sport for a three-year examination period after which it becomes an official Olympic sport or is no longer recognized. IOC's revenue comes from selling broadcast rights for the Olympics, corporate sponsorship, ticketing and licensing the Olympic symbol. About 90% of its revenue is distributed to national Olympic committees, international sports federations and the host city's organizing committee of the Olympic Games, while IOC retains 10%. The International Paralympic Committee is the international non-profit organization and global governing body for the Paralympic Games, promoting sport opportunities for all persons with a disability, from beginner to elite level.

FINANCIAL DATA: *Note: Data for latest year may not have been available at press time.*

In U.S. $	2022	2021	2020	2019	2018	2017
Revenue		4,161,660,000	623,803,000	694,538,000	661,407,000	661,407,000
R&D Expense						
Operating Income						
Operating Margin %						
SGA Expense						
Net Income		843,757,000	-55,022,000	73,895,000	8,725,000	8,725,000
Operating Cash Flow						
Capital Expenditure						
EBITDA						
Return on Assets %						
Return on Equity %						
Debt to Equity						

CONTACT INFORMATION:
Phone: 41-21-621-61-11   Fax: 41-21-621-62-16
Toll-Free:
Address: Chateau de Vidy, Lausanne, 1001 Switzerland

STOCK TICKER/OTHER:
Stock Ticker: Private   Exchange:
Employees: 759   Fiscal Year Ends: 12/31
Parent Company:

SALARIES/BONUSES:
Top Exec. Salary: $ Bonus: $
Second Exec. Salary: $ Bonus: $

OTHER THOUGHTS:
Estimated Female Officers or Directors: 1
Hot Spot for Advancement for Women/Minorities:

Jacksonville Jaguars

www.jaguars.com

NAIC Code: 711211C

TYPES OF BUSINESS:

Professional Football Team
Team Management and Operations

BRANDS/DIVISIONS/AFFILIATES:

TIAA Bank Field

CONTACTS: Note: Officers with more than one job title may be intentionally listed here more than once.

Mark Lamping, Pres.
Chad Johnson, COO
Mark Sirota, CFO
Chris Gargani, VP-Mktg. & Sales
John Dever, Chief Communications Officer
Megha Parekh, General Counsel
Kelly Flanagan, VP-Planning
Dan Edwards, Sr. VP-Comm. & Media
Kelly Flanagan, VP-Finance
Gus Bradley, Head Coach
Hussain Naqi, Sr. VP-Fan Engagement
Scott Massey, Sr. VP-Corp. Partnership
Peter Racine, Pres., Jaguars Foundation
Shahd Khan, Owner

GROWTH PLANS/SPECIAL FEATURES:

The Jacksonville Jaguars is a professional football team in the National Football League (NFL) based in Jacksonville, Florida. The franchise began in 1995 as the NFL's 30th team. In 1997, its second year of play, the team not only made it to the playoffs, it reached the American Football Conference (AFC) Championship. However, the team lost the championship game to the New England Patriots. In 1998, the Jaguars won the AFC Central Division title and became the first NFL expansion team to make the playoffs three times in its first four seasons of play. The franchise hosted its first Super Bowl, Super Bowl XXXIX in 2005. The team reached the playoffs four times since 1999, in 2005, 2007, 2017 and 2022. The Jaguars were also the southern division champions in 2017 and 2022. The team plays its home games at TIAA Bank Field, which is owned by the City of Jacksonville and holds over 67,900 football spectators and is expandable to approximately 82,000 seats for other events. The Jaguar's average home game attendance was 66,459 during the 2022-23 season. Forbes estimated the Jaguars to be worth $3.475 billion in 2022.

FINANCIAL DATA: Note: Data for latest year may not have been available at press time.

In U.S. $	2022	2021	2020	2019	2018	2017
Revenue	522,600,000					
R&D Expense						
Operating Income						
Operating Margin %						
SGA Expense						
Net Income						
Operating Cash Flow						
Capital Expenditure						
EBITDA						
Return on Assets %						
Return on Equity %						
Debt to Equity						

CONTACT INFORMATION:

Phone: 904-633-6000   Fax: 904-633-6050
Toll-Free:
Address: 1 TIAA Bank Field Dr., Jacksonville, FL 32202 United States

STOCK TICKER/OTHER:

Stock Ticker: Private
Employees: 360
Parent Company:

Exchange:
Fiscal Year Ends: 03/31

SALARIES/BONUSES:

Top Exec. Salary: $ Bonus: $
Second Exec. Salary: $ Bonus: $

OTHER THOUGHTS:

Estimated Female Officers or Directors: 3
Hot Spot for Advancement for Women/Minorities: Y

Joe Gibbs Racing

NAIC Code: 711219

www.joegibbsracing.com

TYPES OF BUSINESS:

Racing Team
Retail Merchandise
Motor Oil
Racing Teams
Race Cars

BRANDS/DIVISIONS/AFFILIATES:

GROWTH PLANS/SPECIAL FEATURES:

Joe Gibbs Racing (JGR) is a NASCAR racing team, which fields four cars in the Cup Series and three cars in the Xfinity Series. The company is headquartered in a 225,000-square-foot, state-of-the-art race shop in Huntersville, North Carolina. Drivers for the company include Denny Hamlin, Martin Truex Jr., Christopher Bell, Ty Gibbs, Sammy Smith, John Hunter Nemechek, Ryan Truex and William Sawalich. JGR drivers have won five Cup Series championships: 2000, 2002, 2005, 2015 and 2019; four Xfinity Series: 2009, 2016, 2021 and 2022; and one ARCA Menards Series: 2021. Race victories for JGR include 203 Cup Series, 197 Xfinity Series and 23 ARCA Menards Series. Toyota manufactures the race cars for JGR, and sponsors include (but are not limited to) FedEx, Interstate Batteries, Sport clips, Coca-Cola, Bass Pro Shops, Auto-Owners Insurance, DeWalt, Rheem, SiriusXM, Monster Energy, Pilot Flying J and Starkey. JGR has a race shop that opens for public viewing, and the adjacent JGR Souvenir Store retails NASCAR and Joe Gibbs team merchandise. In addition to the company's racing efforts, JGR sells Joe Gibbs synthetic racing oil.

CONTACTS: *Note: Officers with more than one job title may be intentionally listed here more than once.*

Dave Alpern, Pres.
Michael Guttilla, COO
Tim Carmichael, CFO
Eric Schaffer, CCO
Toni Rogers, Chief People Officer
Bryan (Boris) Cook, Chief Digital Officer
Todd Meredith, VP-Oper.
Dean Noble, VP-Bus. Affairs
Don Meredith, Exec. VP
Jimmy Makar, Sr. VP-Racing Oper.
Steve deSouza, VP-Nationwide Series Oper.
Joe Gibbs, Owner

FINANCIAL DATA: *Note: Data for latest year may not have been available at press time.*

In U.S. $	2022	2021	2020	2019	2018	2017
Revenue		28,512,000	29,700,000	135,000,000	131,000,000	131,000,000
R&D Expense						
Operating Income						
Operating Margin %						
SGA Expense						
Net Income				5,000,000	6,000,000	6,000,000
Operating Cash Flow						
Capital Expenditure						
EBITDA						
Return on Assets %						
Return on Equity %						
Debt to Equity						

CONTACT INFORMATION:

Phone: 704-944-5000   Fax: 704-944-5059
Toll-Free:
Address: 13415 Reese Blvd. W., Huntersville, NC 28078 United States

STOCK TICKER/OTHER:

Stock Ticker: Private   Exchange:
Employees: 450   Fiscal Year Ends:
Parent Company:

SALARIES/BONUSES:

Top Exec. Salary: $ Bonus: $
Second Exec. Salary: $ Bonus: $

OTHER THOUGHTS:

Estimated Female Officers or Directors:
Hot Spot for Advancement for Women/Minorities:

Johnson Outdoors Inc

www.johnsonoutdoors.com

NAIC Code: 339920

TYPES OF BUSINESS:

Outdoor Recreation Products
Tents & Backpacks
Marine Electronics
Watercraft
Diving Equipment
Field Compasses

GROWTH PLANS/SPECIAL FEATURES:

Johnson Outdoors Inc is a global manufacturer and marketer of branded seasonal, outdoor recreation products used Â for fishing from a boat, diving, paddling, hiking and camping. The company has four operating segment: Fishing, Camping, Watercraft Recreation, and Diving. It generates maximum revenue from the Fishing segment. Geographically, it derives a majority of revenue from the United States and also has a presence in Europe, Canada, and Other Countries. Its Fishing brands include Minn Kota; Humminbird and Cannon.

BRANDS/DIVISIONS/AFFILIATES:

Minn Kota
Hummingbird
Eureka!
Jetboil
SCUBAPRO
Ocean Kayak
Old Town

CONTACTS: Note: Officers with more than one job title may be intentionally listed here more than once.

Helen Johnson-Leipold, CEO
David Johnson, CFO
Thomas Pyle, Director

FINANCIAL DATA: Note: Data for latest year may not have been available at press time.

In U.S. $	2022	2021	2020	2019	2018	2017
Revenue	743,355,000	751,651,000	594,209,000	562,419,000	490,565,000	490,565,000
R&D Expense	27,712,000	25,700,000	24,621,000	21,926,000	19,166,000	19,166,000
Operating Income	66,310,000	111,283,000	71,070,000	63,774,000	45,591,000	45,591,000
Operating Margin %	.09%	.15%	.12%	.11%	.09%	.09%
SGA Expense	177,310,000	197,142,000	169,302,000	164,056,000	146,183,000	146,183,000
Net Income	44,491,000	83,381,000	55,233,000	51,413,000	35,157,000	35,157,000
Operating Cash Flow	-62,144,000	58,318,000	61,493,000	45,844,000	46,350,000	46,350,000
Capital Expenditure	31,690,000	21,409,000	15,600,000	16,786,000	11,613,000	11,613,000
EBITDA	73,275,000	126,468,000	88,771,000	80,643,000	62,047,000	62,047,000
Return on Assets %	.07%	.14%	.11%	.12%	.11%	.11%
Return on Equity %	.09%	.20%	.16%	.17%	.16%	.16%
Debt to Equity	.10%	.10%	0.092			

CONTACT INFORMATION:

Phone: 262 631-6600   Fax: 262 631-6601
Toll-Free:
Address: 555 Main St., Racine, WI 53403 United States

STOCK TICKER/OTHER:

Stock Ticker: JOUT   Exchange: NAS
Employees: 1,500   Fiscal Year Ends: 09/30
Parent Company:

SALARIES/BONUSES:

Top Exec. Salary: $829,511   Bonus: $95,186
Second Exec. Salary: Bonus: $32,067
$441,692

OTHER THOUGHTS:

Estimated Female Officers or Directors: 4
Hot Spot for Advancement for Women/Minorities: Y

Juventus Football Club SpA

www.juventus.com/juve/en/welcome

NAIC Code: 711211D

TYPES OF BUSINESS:

Professional Soccer Team
Team Management and Operations

GROWTH PLANS/SPECIAL FEATURES:

Juventus Football Club SpA operates as a professional football club in Italy. It generates revenue from the sale of tickets, sponsorship activities, sale of advertising space, licensing of television and media rights. The company's main segment is participation in national and international competitions and the organization of matches. The greater part of the Company's business activity is carried out in Italy.

BRANDS/DIVISIONS/AFFILIATES:

Juventus
Exor SpA
Juventus Stadium
J Medical

CONTACTS: Note: Officers with more than one job title may be intentionally listed here more than once.

Fabio Paratici, Chief Football Officer
Andrea Agnelli, Pres.
Marco Re, Dir.-Finance
Fabio Tucci, Head of Legal and Human Resources
Claudio Leonardi, IT
Antonio Conte, Mgr.
Andrea Agnelli, Chmn.

FINANCIAL DATA: Note: Data for latest year may not have been available at press time.

In U.S. $	2022	2021	2020	2019	2018	2017
Revenue	472,696,800	511,064,700	611,281,300	663,644,500	600,911,000	600,911,000
R&D Expense						
Operating Income	-248,890,700	-191,278,700	-42,839,490	3,122,141	75,794,820	75,794,820
Operating Margin %	-.53%	-.37%	-.07%	.00%	.13%	.13%
SGA Expense	62,988,160	54,325,470	61,147,120	69,172,290	52,771,700	52,771,700
Net Income	-271,577,500	-224,133,600	-95,770,220	-42,604,140	45,457,670	45,457,670
Operating Cash Flow	-34,315,720	44,875,990	-62,632,090	-3,868,633	59,426,750	59,426,750
Capital Expenditure	249,583,500	211,887,700	511,015,700	416,469,300	307,695,400	307,695,400
EBITDA	-49,777,020	27,593,490	151,383,600	158,875,900	174,245,400	174,245,400
Return on Assets %	-.28%	-.20%	-.08%	-.05%	.06%	.06%
Return on Equity %	-2.57%	-1.57%	-.66%	-.77%	.58%	.58%
Debt to Equity	1.18%	12.06%	1.094	13.808	2.068	2.068

CONTACT INFORMATION:

Phone: 39-899-999-897   Fax: 39-11-5119214
Toll-Free:
Address: 32 Corso Galileo Ferraris, Turin, 10128 Italy

STOCK TICKER/OTHER:

Stock Ticker: JVTSF   Exchange: PINX
Employees: 906   Fiscal Year Ends:
Parent Company: Exor SpA

SALARIES/BONUSES:

Top Exec. Salary: $ Bonus: $
Second Exec. Salary: $ Bonus: $

OTHER THOUGHTS:

Estimated Female Officers or Directors: 2
Hot Spot for Advancement for Women/Minorities:

Kansas City Chiefs

www.kcchiefs.com

NAIC Code: 711211C

TYPES OF BUSINESS:

Professional Football Team
Team Management and Operations

BRANDS/DIVISIONS/AFFILIATES:

Arrowhead Stadium

CONTACTS: *Note: Officers with more than one job title may be intentionally listed here more than once.*

Clark Hunt, CEO
Mark Donovan, Pres.
Dan Crumb, CFO
Lara Krug, CMO
Carolyn Messick, Mngr.-Human Resources
Kevin Higgins, VP-IT
Kirsten Krug, VP-Admin.
Bill Chapin, Sr. VP-Bus. Oper.
Ted Crews, VP-Comm.
Brian Dunn, Controller
Andy Reid, Head Coach
John Dorsey, Gen. Mgr.
Trip MacCracken, Dir.-Football Admin.
Chris Ballard, Dir.-Player Personnel
Brett Veach, Gen. Mngr.

GROWTH PLANS/SPECIAL FEATURES:

The Kansas City Chiefs is a professional football team playing in the Western Division of the American Football Conference of the National Football League (NFL). The team was founded in 1959 by Texas oilman Lamar Hunt. He was also a founding member and key originator of the American Football League (AFL). The team, a member of the AFL, was formerly known as the Dallas Texans. As part of the AFL, the franchise won three AFL League Championships (1962, 1966 and 1969). In 1963, the team moved to Kansas City, Missouri and became the Kansas City Chiefs. In 1964, the Chiefs played in the first game between AFL and NFL teams, beating the Chicago Bears 66-24. In 1967, the team played in but lost the first title match between the AFL and the NFL, which would later be called Super Bowl I. In 1970, the franchise joined the NFL when the AFL and NFL merged. The team also won Super Bowl IV that year. Since then, the franchise has won 15 AFC West Championships (with recent consecutive wins from 2016 through 2022), and three conference championships (2019, 2020 and 2022). The team defeated the Philadelphia Eagles to win Super Bowl LVII in the 2022-23 season. The Chiefs is owned and operated by the Hunt family and is run by Clark Hunt, son of founder Lamar Hunt and founding investor-owner in Major League Soccer. The team plays at the Arrowhead Stadium, which is owned by Jackson County and accommodates about 76,600 spectators. The Chiefs' average home attendance was 73,499 for the 2022-23 season. Forbes estimated the Chiefs to be worth $3.7 billion in 2022.

FINANCIAL DATA: *Note: Data for latest year may not have been available at press time.*

In U.S. $	2022	2021	2020	2019	2018	2017
Revenue	519,350,000					
R&D Expense						
Operating Income						
Operating Margin %						
SGA Expense						
Net Income						
Operating Cash Flow						
Capital Expenditure						
EBITDA						
Return on Assets %						
Return on Equity %						
Debt to Equity						

CONTACT INFORMATION:

Phone: 816-920-9300   Fax: 816-923-4719
Toll-Free:
Address: 1 Arrowhead Dr., Kansas City, MO 64129 United States

STOCK TICKER/OTHER:

Stock Ticker: Private   Exchange:
Employees: 450   Fiscal Year Ends: 01/31
Parent Company:

SALARIES/BONUSES:

Top Exec. Salary: $ Bonus: $
Second Exec. Salary: $ Bonus: $

OTHER THOUGHTS:

Estimated Female Officers or Directors: 3
Hot Spot for Advancement for Women/Minorities: Y

Sales, profits and employees may be estimates. Financial information, benefits and other data can change quickly and may vary from those stated here.

Kansas City Royals

NAIC Code: 711211A

www.mlb.com/royals

TYPES OF BUSINESS:

Professional Baseball Team
Team Management and Operations

BRANDS/DIVISIONS/AFFILIATES:

Kauffman Stadium
Omaha Storm Chasers
Northwest Arkansas Naturals
Quad cities River Bandits
Columbia Fireflies
Royal Charities

CONTACTS: *Note: Officers with more than one job title may be intentionally listed here more than once.*

John Sherman, CEO
Brooks Sherman, Pres.-Bus. Oper.
Whitney Beaver, CFO
Sarah Tourville, CCO
Iris Edelen, VP-People & Culture
Mike Groopman, Dir.-Baseball Analytics
Brian Himstedt, VP-Tech. & Bus. Analytics
David Laverentz, VP-Admin.
Dan Crabtree, General Counsel
Kevin Uhlich, Sr. VP-Bus. Oper.
Michael Bucek, VP-Bus. Dev.
Erin Sleddens, Dir.-Digital & Social Media
Michael Swanson, VP-Comm. & Broadcasting
David Laverentz, VP-Finance
Dayton Moore, Sr. VP-Baseball Oper.
Dean Taylor, VP-Baseball Oper.
Toby Cook, VP-Community Affairs & Publicity
Bob Rice, VP-Ballpark Oper. & Dev.
J. J. Picollo, Exec. VP

GROWTH PLANS/SPECIAL FEATURES:

The Kansas City Royals are a Major League Baseball (MLB) team playing in the Central Division of the American League (AL). An expansion team in 1969, the team was born following the relocation of the Kansas City Athletics to Oakland, California. The Royals got off to a fast start, with an early roster that included 1969 Rookie of the Year winner Lou Piniella. The team won three straight division championships from 1976 to 1978 and made its first World Series appearance in 1980. It developed several young talents throughout the '80s, including George Brett, Bret Saberhagen and Bo Jackson. The team won the World Series in 1985, defeating their intra-state rivals, the St. Louis Cardinals. In the mid-90s, the team has seen very little success, posting a winning record in only two of 20 seasons. Since 2000, the team has been owned by David Glass, former president and CEO of Wal-Mart. The franchise has played at the 37,903-seat Kauffman Stadium since 1973, and averaged 15,974 fans in attendance per home game during the 2022-23 season. In 2015, the Royals not only won the Central Division title, but the AL Pennant and their second World Series. Its minor league affiliations include the Omaha Storm Chasers, Northwest Arkansas Naturals, Quad Cities River Bandits, and Columbia Fireflies, as well as rookie teams. The Royals sponsors the Royals Charities program, which provides financial support for new programs, scholarships for area youth and grants for major renovations for youth softball and baseball fields in the Midwest region. Forbes estimated the value of the club at $1.2 billion in March 2023.

FINANCIAL DATA: *Note: Data for latest year may not have been available at press time.*

In U.S. $	2022	2021	2020	2019	2018	2017
Revenue	334,100,000					
R&D Expense						
Operating Income						
Operating Margin %						
SGA Expense						
Net Income						
Operating Cash Flow						
Capital Expenditure						
EBITDA						
Return on Assets %						
Return on Equity %						
Debt to Equity						

CONTACT INFORMATION:

Phone: 816-921-8000   Fax: 816-921-1366
Toll-Free:
Address: 1 Royal Way, Kansas City, MO 64129 United States

STOCK TICKER/OTHER:

Stock Ticker: Private   Exchange:
Employees: 515   Fiscal Year Ends:
Parent Company:

SALARIES/BONUSES:

Top Exec. Salary: $ Bonus: $
Second Exec. Salary: $ Bonus: $

OTHER THOUGHTS:

Estimated Female Officers or Directors: 3
Hot Spot for Advancement for Women/Minorities: Y

Katz Group Of Companies (The)

www.katzgroup.ca

NAIC Code: 711211

TYPES OF BUSINESS:

Sports Teams and Clubs
Business Investments
Sports and Entertainment
Retail Cannabis
Hospitality
Film Production
Real Estate Development
Commercial and Residential Asset Management

BRANDS/DIVISIONS/AFFILIATES:

DAK Capital
OEG Inc
Katz Group Real Estate
Edmonton Oilers
Tokyo Smoke
Dark Castle Entertainment
Oliver and Bonacini and Concorde Group

CONTACTS: *Note: Officers with more than one job title may be intentionally listed here more than once.*

Brad Gilewich, Pres.
Daryl Katz, Chmn.

GROWTH PLANS/SPECIAL FEATURES:

The Katz Group Of Companies is a privately-owned Canadian enterprise that comprises businesses that are overseen by subsidiary DAK Capital. OEG, Inc. is active across a range of industries, including sports/entertainment, retail cannabis and hospitality, with a focus on executing a lifestyle and experience strategy across the three divisions. OEG's major assets include: the Edmonton Oilers of the National Hockey League franchise; a portfolio of Canadian retail cannabis locations led by flagship brand Tokyo Smoke; film production by Dark Castle Entertainment; and Oliver and Bonacini and Concorde Group, which operates restaurants, bars and event venues in Canada. Katz Group Real Estate is a private real estate developer and operator in Canada, responsible for Edmonton's ICE District, a 25-acre mixed-use development with commercial, residential, retail and public spaces. The firm's real estate capabilities include asset management, leasing, property redevelopment/repositioning and financing. Katz Group Real Estate is also the asset manager for a variety of properties in Edmonton's ICE District through a collaboration with OEG's sports and entertainment division.

FINANCIAL DATA: *Note: Data for latest year may not have been available at press time.*

In U.S. $	2022	2021	2020	2019	2018	2017
Revenue						
R&D Expense						
Operating Income						
Operating Margin %						
SGA Expense						
Net Income						
Operating Cash Flow						
Capital Expenditure						
EBITDA						
Return on Assets %						
Return on Equity %						
Debt to Equity						

CONTACT INFORMATION:

Phone: 780 990-0505   Fax:
Toll-Free:
Address: 2700, 10111-104 Ave., Edmonton, AB T5J 0J4 Canada

STOCK TICKER/OTHER:

Stock Ticker: Private   Exchange:
Employees: Fiscal Year Ends:
Parent Company:

SALARIES/BONUSES:

Top Exec. Salary: $ Bonus: $
Second Exec. Salary: $ Bonus: $

OTHER THOUGHTS:

Estimated Female Officers or Directors:
Hot Spot for Advancement for Women/Minorities:

Kellwood Company LLC

www.kellwood.com

NAIC Code: 424300

TYPES OF BUSINESS:

Apparel and Clothing Brands, Designers, Importers and Distributors
Women's Sportswear
Intimate Apparel
Infant Apparel
Childrens Apparel
Apparel Sourcing and Production

BRANDS/DIVISIONS/AFFILIATES:

Jolt
Rewind
Missy
reCreation
Wit & Wisdom
Democracy
Briggs New York

CONTACTS: *Note: Officers with more than one job title may be intentionally listed here more than once.*

David Falwell, CEO

GROWTH PLANS/SPECIAL FEATURES:

Kellwood Company, LLC is an apparel manufacturer in the U.S., and has provided female fashion since 1961. The company develops, builds and manages brands, with a portfolio of women's, junior's and girls' apparel covering a wide range of demographics. Kellwood's portfolio of brands includes Jolt, Rewind, Missy, reCreation, Wit & Wisdom, Democracy and Briggs New York. Kellwood's locations include: Kellwood West, within the City of Industry near Los Angeles, which houses a state-of-the-art pattern and sample making room, corporate product development units, showrooms, sales and design teams and shipping capabilities; and Kellwood East, within New York City's garment center, comprising multiple showrooms and sales teams. An additional office is located in St. Louis, Missouri, as well as sourcing and production offices in China, Vietnam and Guatemala. Kellwood partners with key retailers in both private label and brand segments, including Target, Nordstrom, Dillard's, Kohl's, Costco, Buckle, Stitch Fix, Boot Barn, Amazon, Walmart Canada, FredMeyer, HSN, and many others. Kellwood is privately-owned by an unnamed Hong Kong investor group.

FINANCIAL DATA: *Note: Data for latest year may not have been available at press time.*

In U.S. $	2022	2021	2020	2019	2018	2017
Revenue	480,000,000	460,166,960	418,333,600	1,000,000,000	945,000,000	945,000,000
R&D Expense						
Operating Income						
Operating Margin %						
SGA Expense						
Net Income						
Operating Cash Flow						
Capital Expenditure						
EBITDA						
Return on Assets %						
Return on Equity %						
Debt to Equity						

CONTACT INFORMATION:

Phone: 626-934-4122   Fax:
Toll-Free:
Address: 13071 E. Temple Ave., City of Industry, CA 91746 United States

STOCK TICKER/OTHER:

Stock Ticker: Private
Employees: 3,000
Parent Company:

Exchange:
Fiscal Year Ends: 01/31

SALARIES/BONUSES:

Top Exec. Salary: $ Bonus: $
Second Exec. Salary: $ Bonus: $

OTHER THOUGHTS:

Estimated Female Officers or Directors: 2
Hot Spot for Advancement for Women/Minorities: Y

Kroenke Sports & Entertainment LLC

www.pepsicenter.com

NAIC Code: 711310

TYPES OF BUSINESS:

Sports Stadium Operator
Property Ownership and Development
Entertainment
Professional Sports Teams
Property Management
Sport Team Management
Venues
Theaters

BRANDS/DIVISIONS/AFFILIATES:

Los Angeles Rams
Denver Nuggets
Colorado Avalanche
Colorado Rapids
Colorado Mammoth
SoFi Stadium
Ball Arena
Dicks Sporting Goods Park

GROWTH PLANS/SPECIAL FEATURES:

Kroenke Sports & Entertainment LLC (KSE) is a world-leading ownership, entertainment and management group. KSE's portfolio of professional sports teams and venues include the Los Angeles Rams (NFL), Denver Nuggets (NBA), Colorado Avalanche (NHL), Colorado Rapids (MLS), Colorado Mammoth (NLL), SoFi Stadium, Ball Arena, Dick's Sporting Goods Park and Paramount Theatre. Ball Arena is a partnership between KSE and Ball Corporation, with Ball acquiring the naming rights to the venue and changed its name from Pepsi Center to Ball Arena in 2020. The arena has a seating capacity that ranges from 17,809 to 21,000, and it is where the Colorado Avalanche, Denver Nuggets and Colorado Mammoth play their home games. Additional properties under KSE's umbrella include Altitude Sports & Entertainment, a 24-hour regional television network; and Altitude Authentics, a retail provider.

CONTACTS:

Note: Officers with more than one job title may be intentionally listed here more than once.

Jim Martin, Pres.
Stephen Stieneker, General Counsel
Dave Jolette, VP-Venue Oper.
Deb Dowling, VP-Community Rel.
Mark Waggoner, Sr. VP-Finance
Michael Benson, Sr. VP-Bus. Affairs
Doug Ackerman, Sr. VP-Venues
Che Vialpando, VP-Ticket Sales & Team Mktg.
Josh Kroenke, Pres.
E Stanley Kroenke, Owner

FINANCIAL DATA:

Note: Data for latest year may not have been available at press time.

In U.S. $	2022	2021	2020	2019	2018	2017
Revenue						
R&D Expense						
Operating Income						
Operating Margin %						
SGA Expense						
Net Income						
Operating Cash Flow						
Capital Expenditure						
EBITDA						
Return on Assets %						
Return on Equity %						
Debt to Equity						

CONTACT INFORMATION:

Phone: 303-405-1100   Fax: 303-575-1920
Toll-Free:
Address: 1000 Chopper Cir., Denver, CO 80204 United States

STOCK TICKER/OTHER:

Stock Ticker: Private   Exchange:
Employees: Fiscal Year Ends: 06/30
Parent Company:

SALARIES/BONUSES:

Top Exec. Salary: $ Bonus: $
Second Exec. Salary: $ Bonus: $

OTHER THOUGHTS:

Estimated Female Officers or Directors: 2
Hot Spot for Advancement for Women/Minorities:

K-Swiss Inc

NAIC Code: 424340

www.kswiss.com

TYPES OF BUSINESS:

Footwear Distribution
Athletic Footwear & Apparel
Online Sales
Manufacturing
Product Distribution
Ecommerce

BRANDS/DIVISIONS/AFFILIATES:

Xtep International Holdings Limited
K-Swiss

CONTACTS: *Note: Officers with more than one job title may be intentionally listed here more than once.*

Larry Remington, CEO
George Powlick, Chief Admin. Officer
Lee Green, Corp. Counsel
Kimberly Scully, Corp. Controller
Brian Sullivan, VP-National Accounts
David Nichols, Exec. VP

GROWTH PLANS/SPECIAL FEATURES:

K-Swiss, Inc. designs, develops and markets an array of athletic footwear for high-performance sports use, fitness activities and casual wear under the K-Swiss brand. The firm is best known for its original K-Swiss Classic shoe, an all-white, all-weather, all-leather tennis shoe, which has undergone only slight modifications since its introduction in 1966. In addition to footwear, the K-Swiss brand is used to market a line of branded apparel and accessories, including high-tech tennis apparel that consists of skirts, shorts, tops, polos, dresses and warm-ups for both men and women. The firm's apparel is targeted to a variety of markets, from consumers wanting performance apparel and accessories to casual athleisure consumers. The company's products are manufactured by independent suppliers in China, Thailand, Vietnam and Indonesia, and are sold in department and specialty retail stores as well as directly through the firm's website. As a marketing strategy, the firm endeavors to use classic styling instead of fashion-oriented footwear in order to reduce the impact of changes in consumer taste and prolong the life cycle of its products. K-Swiss is a wholly-owned subsidiary of Xtep International Holdings Limited.

FINANCIAL DATA: *Note: Data for latest year may not have been available at press time.*

In U.S. $	2022	2021	2020	2019	2018	2017
Revenue	145,000,000	141,345,750	108,727,500	114,450,000	95,920,000	95,920,000
R&D Expense						
Operating Income						
Operating Margin %						
SGA Expense						
Net Income	-14,465,100					
Operating Cash Flow						
Capital Expenditure						
EBITDA						
Return on Assets %						
Return on Equity %						
Debt to Equity						

CONTACT INFORMATION:

Phone: 818 706-5100   Fax: 818 706-5390
Toll-Free: 844-284-1292
Address: 31248 Oak Crest Dr., Westlake Village, CA 91361 United States

STOCK TICKER/OTHER:

Stock Ticker: Subsidiary   Exchange:
Employees: 500   Fiscal Year Ends: 12/31
Parent Company: Xtep International Holdings Limited

SALARIES/BONUSES:

Top Exec. Salary: $ Bonus: $
Second Exec. Salary: $ Bonus: $

OTHER THOUGHTS:

Estimated Female Officers or Directors: 1
Hot Spot for Advancement for Women/Minorities:

LA Fitness (LA Fitness International LLC)   www.lafitness.com

NAIC Code: 713940

TYPES OF BUSINESS:

Fitness Clubs
Franchising

BRANDS/DIVISIONS/AFFILIATES:

LA Fitness
Esporta Fitness
City Sports Club
Kids Klub
My LAFitness
MYZone

CONTACTS: *Note: Officers with more than one job title may be intentionally listed here more than once.*

Louis Welch, Pres.
Todd Von Sprecken, Chief Dev. Officer

GROWTH PLANS/SPECIAL FEATURES:

LA Fitness, the trade name of Fitness International LLC, owns and operates a franchise of fitness clubs across the U.S. and Canada. The firm has more than 700 locations operating under the brand names LA Fitness, Esporta Fitness, City Sports Club and Club Studio. Gyms may be equipped with facilities for basketball, free weights, racquetball, swimming, steam rooms and saunas, indoor cycling, cardio training and personal training. They also offer classes such as cardio kickboxing, cycling, water fitness, aerobics, Pilates, tai chi, boxing fitness, hip hop, step workouts, total body conditioning, hot yoga, Zumba, yoga high-intensity interval training (HIIT) and belly dancing. Most properties offer league play and tournaments for sports such as basketball and racquetball, as well as private lessons. The firm's website offers customers an online account access page, where they can update address and billing information, pay bills, manage memberships, book personal training sessions and access workout and class schedules at their home club. In addition to sports and training facilities, many of the company's gyms feature Nrgize Lifestyle Cafe branded juice bars. LA Fitness offers a turnkey corporate wellness program for employers; and Kids Klub, a babysitting service on premises for members. The company also gives members resources including: My LAFitness, where members can manage their accounts; MyZone, a specialized heart rate monitor; and the Living Healthy Podcast for both members and listeners.

FINANCIAL DATA: *Note: Data for latest year may not have been available at press time.*

In U.S. $	2022	2021	2020	2019	2018	2017
Revenue	1,850,000,000	1,349,920,000	1,298,000,000	2,200,000,000	2,100,000,000	2,100,000,000
R&D Expense						
Operating Income						
Operating Margin %						
SGA Expense						
Net Income						
Operating Cash Flow						
Capital Expenditure						
EBITDA						
Return on Assets %						
Return on Equity %						
Debt to Equity						

CONTACT INFORMATION:

Phone: 949-502-2043   Fax: 888-601-5870
Toll-Free:
Address: 6400 Irvine Blvd, Irvine, CA 92620 United States

STOCK TICKER/OTHER:

Stock Ticker: Private   Exchange:
Employees: 8,000   Fiscal Year Ends:
Parent Company:

SALARIES/BONUSES:

Top Exec. Salary: $ Bonus: $
Second Exec. Salary: $ Bonus: $

OTHER THOUGHTS:

Estimated Female Officers or Directors: 1
Hot Spot for Advancement for Women/Minorities:

Ladies Professional Golf Association (LPGA)   www.lpga.com

NAIC Code: 711211

TYPES OF BUSINESS:

Golf Association
Professional Women's Golf
Golf Tournaments

BRANDS/DIVISIONS/AFFILIATES:

LPGA Tour
LPGA Professionals
LPGA Foundation
Epson Tour

CONTACTS: *Note: Officers with more than one job title may be intentionally listed here more than once.*

Mollie Marcoux Samaan, Commissioner
Edward Willett, VP-Bus. Dev.
Brian Carroll, VP-Television & Emerging Markets

GROWTH PLANS/SPECIAL FEATURES:

The Ladies Professional Golf Association (LPGA) is one of the longest-running women's sports associations in the world, founded in 1950. Though the firm initially operated as a playing tour, the LPGA has evolved into a nonprofit organization involved in every facet of golf. The LPGA is organized into two segments: LPGA Tour and LPGA Professionals. The 2022 LPGA Tour will host 33 official events, with members competing for a record-setting $101.4 million in official purses. LPGA Professionals, founded in 1959, has the largest membership of women golf professionals in the country, with more than 1,800 members. Programs include teaching, coaching, nutrition, employment services, online education, junior golf programs, business management and leadership training programs and conferences. The LPGA Foundation, established in 1991, maintains a strong focus on charity through tournaments, its grassroots junior and women's programs and its affiliation with Susan G. Komen for the Cure. The golf association also administers several scholarships for men and women. The LPGA additionally sponsors an official developmental tour called the Epson Tour, the second-tier professional golf tour in the U.S. The Epson Tour 2023 expanded from 21 to 22 tournaments, and is held from March through October. The LPGA is based in Daytona Beach, Florida. The firm's headquarters, known as LPGA International, feature two 18-hole golf courses called the Champions and the Legends.

FINANCIAL DATA: *Note: Data for latest year may not have been available at press time.*

In U.S. $	2022	2021	2020	2019	2018	2017
Revenue						
R&D Expense						
Operating Income						
Operating Margin %						
SGA Expense						
Net Income						
Operating Cash Flow						
Capital Expenditure						
EBITDA						
Return on Assets %						
Return on Equity %						
Debt to Equity						

CONTACT INFORMATION:

Phone: 386-274-6200   Fax: 386-274-1099
Toll-Free:
Address: 100 International Golf Dr., Daytona Beach, FL 32124-1092
United States

STOCK TICKER/OTHER:

Stock Ticker: Private   Exchange:
Employees: 335   Fiscal Year Ends:
Parent Company:

SALARIES/BONUSES:

Top Exec. Salary: $ Bonus: $
Second Exec. Salary: $ Bonus: $

OTHER THOUGHTS:

Estimated Female Officers or Directors:
Hot Spot for Advancement for Women/Minorities: Y

Las Vegas Aces

NAIC Code: 711211E

TYPES OF BUSINESS:

Women's Professional Basketball Team
Team Management and Operations

BRANDS/DIVISIONS/AFFILIATES:

Utah Starzz
San Antonio Stars
San Antonio Silver Stars

CONTACTS: Note: Officers with more than one job title may be intentionally listed here more than once.

Larry Delsen, CEO
Nikki Fargas, Pres.
Matt Delsen, CFO
Blair Hardiek, CMO
Jennifer Azzi, Chief Bus. Dev. Officer
Lori Warren, Sr. VP-Corp. Admin.
Rick Pych, Pres., Bus. Oper.
Rick Pych, Exec. VP-Corp. Dev.
Lindsey Campbell, Mgr.-Public Rel.
Lori Warren, Sr. VP-Finance
Dan Hughes, Gen. Mgr.
R.C. Buford, Pres., Sport Franchises
Lawrence Panye, Exec. VP-Corp. Partnership & Broadcasting
Joe Clark, VP-Ticket Sales & Svcs.

GROWTH PLANS/SPECIAL FEATURES:

The Las Vegas Aces, formerly the Utah Starzz and San Antonio Stars, are one of the eight original Women's National Basketball Association (WNBA) teams founded in 1997. The franchise moved to Las Vegas for the 2018 season, prior to which they were the San Antonio Stars and the San Antonio Silver Stars. The Aces play in the WNBA's Western Conference, alongside the Dallas Wings, Los Angeles Sparks, Minnesota Lynx, Phoenix Mercury and Seattle Storm. The franchise is one of a few WNBA teams that is not affiliated with a National Basketball Association (NBA) franchise. The Aces is owned by Mark Davis. The team plays their home games at the Michelob Ultra Arena, a 12,000-seat indoor arena at the Mandalay Bay Resort and Casino, on the Las Vegas Strip, in Paradise, Nevada. Average attendance for the Aces was 5,607 during the 2022 season. The Aces previously had two conference titles (2008 and 2020) until they clenched their first WNBA Championship in 2022 after defeating the third-seeded Connecticut Sun in four games.

FINANCIAL DATA: Note: Data for latest year may not have been available at press time.

In U.S. $	2022	2021	2020	2019	2018	2017
Revenue						
R&D Expense						
Operating Income						
Operating Margin %						
SGA Expense						
Net Income						
Operating Cash Flow						
Capital Expenditure						
EBITDA						
Return on Assets %						
Return on Equity %						
Debt to Equity						

CONTACT INFORMATION:

Phone: 702-632-7777   Fax:
Toll-Free: 877-632-7400
Address: 3950 S Las Vegas Blvd., Las Vegas, NV 89119 United States

STOCK TICKER/OTHER:

Stock Ticker: Private   Exchange:
Employees: Fiscal Year Ends:
Parent Company: MGM Resorts International

SALARIES/BONUSES:

Top Exec. Salary: $ Bonus: $
Second Exec. Salary: $ Bonus: $

OTHER THOUGHTS:

Estimated Female Officers or Directors: 3
Hot Spot for Advancement for Women/Minorities: Y

Las Vegas Raiders

NAIC Code: 711211C

www.raiders.com

TYPES OF BUSINESS:

Professional Football Team
Team Management and Operations

BRANDS/DIVISIONS/AFFILIATES:

CONTACTS: *Note: Officers with more than one job title may be intentionally listed here more than once.*

Dave Ziegler, Gen. Mngr.
Sandra Douglass Morgan, Pres.
Tom Delaney, Dir.-Football Admin.
Mark Davis, Owner
Dennis Allen, Head Coach
Reggie McKenzie, Gen. Mgr.
Shaun Herock, Dir.-College Scouting

GROWTH PLANS/SPECIAL FEATURES:

The Las Vegas Raiders, formerly the Oakland Raiders, is a National Football League (NFL) team founded in 1960 as part of the American Football League (AFL), and joined the NFL in 1970. The franchise resided in Los Angeles between 1982 and 1994. The Raiders have won the Super Bowl three times, in 1976, 1980 and 1983. Most recently, the team advanced to the Super Bowl in the 2002 season, but lost to the Tampa Bay Buccaneers. Former coach John Madden helped make the Raiders one of the most successful franchises in NFL history. In 2016, the team reached the playoffs for the first time since the 2002 season. The Raiders also made the playoffs in 2021. The team has been home to many Hall of Fame members and other star players, including Marcus Allen, Jim Otto, Art Shell, Billy Cannon, multi-sport star Bo Jackson, Ken Stabler, Charles Woodson and Cliff Branch. Longtime owner and manager Al Davis passed away during the 2011 season, with current majority ownership held by his wife Carol Davis and son Mark Davis. The Raiders currently play at the Allegiant Stadium, which can hold about 65,000 football spectators and expandable to nearly 72,000 seats. The team averaged approximately 62,045 fans in attendance per home game for the 2022-23 season. Forbes valued the Raiders at $5.1 billion in 2022.

FINANCIAL DATA: *Note: Data for latest year may not have been available at press time.*

In U.S. $	2022	2021	2020	2019	2018	2017
Revenue	501,800,000					
R&D Expense						
Operating Income						
Operating Margin %						
SGA Expense						
Net Income						
Operating Cash Flow						
Capital Expenditure						
EBITDA						
Return on Assets %						
Return on Equity %						
Debt to Equity						

CONTACT INFORMATION:

Phone: 702-520-2020   Fax:
Toll-Free:
Address: 1475 Raiders Way, Henderson, NV 89052 United States

STOCK TICKER/OTHER:

Stock Ticker: Private   Exchange:
Employees: 550   Fiscal Year Ends: 06/30
Parent Company:

SALARIES/BONUSES:

Top Exec. Salary: $ Bonus: $
Second Exec. Salary: $ Bonus: $

OTHER THOUGHTS:

Estimated Female Officers or Directors:
Hot Spot for Advancement for Women/Minorities: Y

Legacy Motor Club

legacymotorclub.com

NAIC Code: 711219

TYPES OF BUSINESS:

Racing Teams
Auto Racing Club
Professional Racing
Truck Racing Club

BRANDS/DIVISIONS/AFFILIATES:

GMS Racing
Petty GMS Motorsports

GROWTH PLANS/SPECIAL FEATURES:

Legacy Motor Club (formerly Petty GMS Motorsports) is a professional auto racing club owned by businessman and entrepreneur Maurice J. Gallagher and seven-time NASCAR Cup Series (NCS) champion Jimmie Johnson. The club competes full-time in the NCS via Chevrolet Camazro ZL1 vehicles No. 42 and No. 43, driven by Noah Gragson and Erik Jones. No. 84 is a part-time entry for Johnson to race in the 2023 series. Richard Petty serves as team ambassador. The Legacy Motor Club moniker signifies a nod to car clubs of past eras. The company operates alongside GMS Racing, which fields three full-time entries in the NASCAR Truck Series. In January 2023, Petty GMS Motorsports announced the rebranding of the organization to Legacy Motor Club.

CONTACTS: *Note: Officers with more than one job title may be intentionally listed here more than once.*

Mike Beam, Team Pres.
Maury Gallagher, Co-Owner
Richard Petty, Co-Owner
Jim Hannigan, VP-Merch.
Sammy Johns, Dir.-Oper.
Richard Petty, Team Owner
Andrew Murstein, Team Owner
Doug Bergeron, Team Owner
Jim Hannigan, VP-Licensing
Richard Petty, Team Ambassador

FINANCIAL DATA: *Note: Data for latest year may not have been available at press time.*

In U.S. $	2022	2021	2020	2019	2018	2017
Revenue		4,620,000	4,400,000	20,000,000	43,000,000	43,000,000
R&D Expense						
Operating Income						
Operating Margin %						
SGA Expense						
Net Income				3,000,000	2,400,000	2,400,000
Operating Cash Flow						
Capital Expenditure						
EBITDA						
Return on Assets %						
Return on Equity %						
Debt to Equity						

CONTACT INFORMATION:

Phone: 704 658-2305   Fax:
Toll-Free:
Address: 310 West Aviation Dr., Statesville, NC 28677 United States

STOCK TICKER/OTHER:

Stock Ticker: Private   Exchange:
Employees: 75   Fiscal Year Ends:
Parent Company:

SALARIES/BONUSES:

Top Exec. Salary: $ Bonus: $
Second Exec. Salary: $ Bonus: $

OTHER THOUGHTS:

Estimated Female Officers or Directors:
Hot Spot for Advancement for Women/Minorities:

Sales, profits and employees may be estimates. Financial information, benefits and other data can change quickly and may vary from those stated here.

Leicester City Football Club

www.lcfc.com

NAIC Code: 711211D

TYPES OF BUSINESS:

English Premiere Soccer Team
Team Management and Operations

BRANDS/DIVISIONS/AFFILIATES:

King Power International Group
King Power Stadium
Foxes (The)
Leicester City FC Academy
LCFC Women

CONTACTS: *Note: Officers with more than one job title may be intentionally listed here more than once.*

Dean Smith, Manager
Aiyawatt Srivaddhanaprabha, Chmn.

GROWTH PLANS/SPECIAL FEATURES:

Leicester City Football Club, owned by King Power International Group, is a professional English soccer team based in Leicester, England. Leicester City plays in the Premier League, the highest level of England's football league system. The club was founded in 1884 as Leicester Fosse F.C. and adopted the name Leicester City in 1919. The team plays at King Power Stadium, named after the owners of the club. Leicester City F.C. operates a men's team and a women's soccer team (LCFC Women). The men's first team is a recently-established Premier League participant, having won the League Title during the 2015-2016 season, after finishing 14th the season before. Leicester clenched their first FA Cup in the 2020-21 season, and also has three League Cups and two FA Charity Shield/FA Community Shield cups. The Foxes is the most common nickname for Leicester City FC, with the team's motto being Foxes Never Quit and the words placed above the tunnel inside the stadium. The Leicester City FC Academy is a youth team of Leicester City that has held Category 1 status under the Elite Player Performance Plan since mid-2013. LCFC Women compete in the FA Women's Super League (also known as Barclays Women's Super League), the highest league of women's football in England.

FINANCIAL DATA: *Note: Data for latest year may not have been available at press time.*

In U.S. $	2022	2021	2020	2019	2018	2017
Revenue	330,000,000	320,827,395	185,090,783	227,900,000	299,156,000	299,156,000
R&D Expense						
Operating Income						
Operating Margin %						
SGA Expense						
Net Income		-44,258,364	-74,139,998	-25,900,000	118,764,000	118,764,000
Operating Cash Flow						
Capital Expenditure						
EBITDA						
Return on Assets %						
Return on Equity %						
Debt to Equity						

CONTACT INFORMATION:

Phone: 0344 815 5000   Fax: 0116 291 5278
Toll-Free:
Address: King Power Stadium, Filbert Way, Leicester, LE2 7FL United Kingdom

STOCK TICKER/OTHER:

Stock Ticker: Subsidiary   Exchange:
Employees: 435   Fiscal Year Ends: 05/31
Parent Company: King Power International Group

SALARIES/BONUSES:

Top Exec. Salary: $ Bonus: $
Second Exec. Salary: $ Bonus: $

OTHER THOUGHTS:

Estimated Female Officers or Directors:
Hot Spot for Advancement for Women/Minorities:

Levy Restaurants

www.levyrestaurants.com

NAIC Code: 722511

TYPES OF BUSINESS:

Restaurants
Merchandise Retailing
Professional Dining and Catering Services
Restaurant Management and Operation
Sport and Event Venue Food Services
Integrated Technologies
Guest and Employee Experience Management

BRANDS/DIVISIONS/AFFILIATES:

Compass Group plc
Abernethys
Jake Melnicks Corner Tap
Line & Lure Seafood Kitchen and Tap
Michael Jordans Steak House
DBA Studio
E15
Rank + Rally

CONTACTS: *Note: Officers with more than one job title may be intentionally listed here more than once.*

Andrew J. Lansing, CEO
Rob Ellis, Pres.
Elizabeth Shakespeare, CFO
Alison Weber, Chief Creative Officer
Shauna Gilhooly, Chief People Officer
Robert Nicklin, Sr. VP-Bus. Dev.
Michael Perlberg, General Counsel
Alison Weber, Chief Innovation Officer
Jeff Wineman, Exec. VP-Bus. Dev.

GROWTH PLANS/SPECIAL FEATURES:

Levy Restaurants owns, manages and operates restaurants, serving a range of venues and event locations throughout the U.S. and Canada. The firm markets its wide range of signature food and hospitality services to sport and entertainment venues and convention centers. Levy provides general concessions, private event catering, services to private clubs and luxury suites, mini restaurants, maintaining affiliations with numerous professional and collegiate sports leagues, as well as other major establishments. Levy pioneered fine dining at sporting venues in 1982 at Comiskey Park, home of the Chicago White Sox. The company's restaurants include rotating and emerging chefs concept Abernethy's, neighborhood bar and restaurant concept Jake Melnick's Corner Tap, classic French concept Kendall's, Pacific Northwest seafood concept Line & Lure Seafood Kitchen and Tap, classic steakhouse celebrity concept Michael Jordan's Steak House, Harley-Davidson museum riverfront dining concept MOTOR Bar & Restaurant, steamboat dining concept Paddlefish, Lincoln Park Zoo al fresco restaurant and bar concept Patio at CafÃ© Brauer, among many others. Venue and Events dining and professional catering services are provided by Levy Restaurants at nearly 200 locations, including arenas, ballparks, colleges, convention centers, entertainment venues, racing venues, stadiums, golf courses, and special event locations. In addition, DBA Studio is Levy's innovation hub that partners with startups and emerging technology companies to pilot and scale technologies across its entire portfolio, to enhance operations and guest/employee experiences. Subsidiary E15 provides advanced analytics services to sports, entertainment, hospitality and retail organizations; and Rank + Rally designs merchandise across the retail experience, from sports teams to cultural institutions. Levy Restaurants itself operates as a subsidiary of Compass Group plc.

Levy offers its employees comprehensive health and retirement benefits.

FINANCIAL DATA: *Note: Data for latest year may not have been available at press time.*

In U.S. $	2022	2021	2020	2019	2018	2017
Revenue	1,200,000,000	1,185,408,000	987,840,000	1,764,000,000	1,600,000,000	1,600,000,000
R&D Expense						
Operating Income						
Operating Margin %						
SGA Expense						
Net Income						
Operating Cash Flow						
Capital Expenditure						
EBITDA						
Return on Assets %						
Return on Equity %						
Debt to Equity						

CONTACT INFORMATION:

Phone: 312-664-8200   Fax: 312-280-2739
Toll-Free:
Address: 980 N. Michigan Ave., Chicago, IL 60611-4501 United States

STOCK TICKER/OTHER:

Stock Ticker: Private   Exchange:
Employees: Fiscal Year Ends: 12/31
Parent Company: Compass Group plc

SALARIES/BONUSES:

Top Exec. Salary: $ Bonus: $
Second Exec. Salary: $ Bonus: $

OTHER THOUGHTS:

Estimated Female Officers or Directors: 2
Hot Spot for Advancement for Women/Minorities: Y

Sales, profits and employees may be estimates. Financial information, benefits and other data can change quickly and may vary from those stated here.

Li Ning Company Limited

NAIC Code: 424340

TYPES OF BUSINESS:

Footwear Distribution
Sports Apparel

BRANDS/DIVISIONS/AFFILIATES:

AIGLE
Kason
LI-NING

GROWTH PLANS/SPECIAL FEATURES:

Established in 1989, Li Ning is one of the largest sportswear companies in China. Headquartered in Beijing, Li Ning mainly sells professional and leisure footwear and apparel under the Li Ning brand. Despite having a single-brand strategy, Li Ning launched multiple sub-brands (such as China Li Ning and Li Ning 1990) to appeal to different demographics. As of the end of 2021, the company had 7,137 stores in China, of which 1,232 were directly operated, and 5,905 were franchised.

CONTACTS: *Note: Officers with more than one job title may be intentionally listed here more than once.*

Li Ning, CEO
Wah-Fung (Terence) Tsang, CFO
Liao Bin, Dir. HR
Edwin Alexander Jonkers, Chief Prod. & Merch. Officer
Zhang Zhi Yong, Exec. Dir.
Jin-Goon Kim, Exec. Vice. Chmn.
Deng Hongbing, Chief Supply Chain Officer

FINANCIAL DATA: *Note: Data for latest year may not have been available at press time.*

In U.S. $	2022	2021	2020	2019	2018	2017
Revenue	3,747,170,000	3,277,949,000	2,099,443,000	2,014,149,000	1,288,670,000	1,288,670,000
R&D Expense						
Operating Income	650,948,200	714,573,200	304,127,500	211,443,500	61,427,520	61,427,520
Operating Margin %		.22%	.14%	.10%	.05%	.05%
SGA Expense	1,223,845,000	1,052,664,000	759,468,500	786,124,800	549,719,900	549,719,900
Net Income	590,150,300	582,460,500	246,654,000	217,705,100	74,810,860	74,810,860
Operating Cash Flow	568,334,000	947,609,700	401,291,900	508,774,100	168,330,800	168,330,800
Capital Expenditure	265,814,500	149,250,500	108,281,000	99,592,660	62,098,000	62,098,000
EBITDA	1,012,376,000	948,744,300	481,354,200	395,422,300	133,373,200	133,373,200
Return on Assets %		.18%	.13%	.14%	.07%	.07%
Return on Equity %		.27%	.21%	.23%	.11%	.11%
Debt to Equity		.05%	0.079	0.078		

CONTACT INFORMATION:

Phone: 8610-8080-0808   Fax: 8610-8080-0000
Toll-Free:
Address: 8 Xing Guang, 5th St., Opto-Mechanics Industrial P, Beijing, Beijing 101111 China

STOCK TICKER/OTHER:

Stock Ticker: LNNGY   Exchange: PINX
Employees: 4,019   Fiscal Year Ends: 12/31
Parent Company:

SALARIES/BONUSES:

Top Exec. Salary: $ Bonus: $
Second Exec. Salary: $ Bonus: $

OTHER THOUGHTS:

Estimated Female Officers or Directors: 2
Hot Spot for Advancement for Women/Minorities: Y

Life Time Inc

www.lifetime.life

NAIC Code: 713940

TYPES OF BUSINESS:

Fitness Centers
Fitness Resorts
Fitness Center Design and Construction
Fitness Operations
Spa Services
Coaching Services
Sports Events

BRANDS/DIVISIONS/AFFILIATES:

Life Time Group Holdings Inc

CONTACTS: *Note: Officers with more than one job title may be intentionally listed here more than once.*

Bahram Akradi, CEO
Jeff Zwiefel, Pres.
John Hugo, Chief Accounting Officer
Robert Houghton, CFO
Eric Buss, Chief Admin. Officer
Parham Javaheri, Chief Property Dev. Officer
R.J. Singh, Chief Digital Officer
Jess Elmquist, Executive VP, Divisional
Eric Buss, Executive VP
Erik Lindseth, General Counsel
James Spolar, Other Corporate Officer
Bahram Akradi, Chmn.

GROWTH PLANS/SPECIAL FEATURES:

Life Time, Inc., a wholly-owned subsidiary of Life Time Group Holdings, Inc., provides premium health, fitness and wellness experiences at its more than 160 athletic resort destinations and through its digital platform and athletic events. Life Time designs, builds and operates large, multi-use sports and athletic resort destinations to offer professional fitness, family recreation and spa services in resort-style environments. The firm specializes in areas such as healthy living, health aging and healthy entertainment. Resort amenities span indoor/outdoor pools, group fitness studios, cycle studios, yoga and pilates studios, indoor/outdoor tennis courts, poolside cafe services, free weights and resistance equipment, cardiovascular equipment, steam room and sauna, racquetball and squash spaces, locker rooms, child center, kid's center, basketball courts, volleyball courts and pickleball courts. Fitness clubs average 100,000 square feet in size. Activities may include athletic leagues and tournaments, summer/vacation camps for kids, sports training camps, athletic events, social events, outdoor group runs, outdoor group cycle rides, swim meets and more. Services include group trainings, weight loss coaching, nutrition coaching, spa services, physical therapy, chiropractic services, lab assessment/testing, sport-specific coaching, endurance coaching, swim lessons, swim team coaching, and towel and locker services. Life Time resorts are located in the U.S. and Canada.

FINANCIAL DATA: *Note: Data for latest year may not have been available at press time.*

In U.S. $	2022	2021	2020	2019	2018	2017
Revenue	1,044,000,000	995,625,000	737,500,000	1,250,000,000	1,500,000,000	1,500,000,000
R&D Expense						
Operating Income						
Operating Margin %						
SGA Expense						
Net Income						
Operating Cash Flow						
Capital Expenditure						
EBITDA						
Return on Assets %						
Return on Equity %						
Debt to Equity						

CONTACT INFORMATION:

Phone: 952 947-0000　Fax: 952 947-9137
Toll-Free:
Address: 2902 Corporate Pl., Chanhassen, MN 55317 United States

STOCK TICKER/OTHER:

Stock Ticker: Subsidiary　Exchange:
Employees: 27,000　Fiscal Year Ends: 12/31
Parent Company: Life Time Group Holdings Inc

SALARIES/BONUSES:

Top Exec. Salary: $　Bonus: $
Second Exec. Salary: $　Bonus: $

OTHER THOUGHTS:

Estimated Female Officers or Directors: 3
Hot Spot for Advancement for Women/Minorities: Y

Ligue de Football Professionnel

NAIC Code: 711211

www.lfp.fr

TYPES OF BUSINESS:

Professional Soccer League
European Football

BRANDS/DIVISIONS/AFFILIATES:

Ligue 1
Ligue 2
Championnat National

CONTACTS: *Note: Officers with more than one job title may be intentionally listed here more than once.*

Arnaud Rouger, CEO
Frederic Thiriez, Pres.
Pascal Urano, Sec.
Jean-Pierre Denis, Treas.
Jean-Michel Aulas, VP
Henri Legarda, VP
Joel Muller, VP
Philippe Piat, VP

GROWTH PLANS/SPECIAL FEATURES:

The Ligue de Football Professionnel (LFP) is the official governing body of professional soccer in France. LFP is responsible for overseeing play between 44 professional clubs in France (20 in Ligue 1, 20 in Ligue 2 and four in the Championnat National). The league is also responsible for setting and enforcing various rules and mandates for league play and oversees the Direction Nationale du Controle de Gestion (DNCG), an administrative body charged with monitoring the financial condition of the professional teams in France. Average attendance levels for league matches are slightly lower than in surrounding countries such as Germany, England, Spain and Italy, with approximately 23,800 fans in attendance per game for Ligue 1 competition during the 2022 season. Attendance levels remain higher for the league's elite teams, with Olympique de Marseille, Paris Saint-Germain and Olympique Lyon averaging 62,571, 46,127 and 46,058 spectators per game, respectively.

FINANCIAL DATA: *Note: Data for latest year may not have been available at press time.*

In U.S. $	2022	2021	2020	2019	2018	2017
Revenue						
R&D Expense						
Operating Income						
Operating Margin %						
SGA Expense						
Net Income						
Operating Cash Flow						
Capital Expenditure						
EBITDA						
Return on Assets %						
Return on Equity %						
Debt to Equity						

CONTACT INFORMATION:

Phone: 33-1-5365-3800   Fax: 33-1-5365-3804
Toll-Free:
Address: 6 rue Leo Delibes, Paris, 75116 France

STOCK TICKER/OTHER:

Stock Ticker: Private   Exchange:
Employees: Fiscal Year Ends:
Parent Company:

SALARIES/BONUSES:

Top Exec. Salary: $ Bonus: $
Second Exec. Salary: $ Bonus: $

OTHER THOUGHTS:

Estimated Female Officers or Directors:
Hot Spot for Advancement for Women/Minorities:

Sales, profits and employees may be estimates. Financial information, benefits and other data can change quickly and may vary from those stated here.

Little Gym International Inc (The)

www.thelittlegym.com

NAIC Code: 713940

TYPES OF BUSINESS:

Children's Gymnasiums
Childrens Exercise Programs
Summer & Holiday Camps
Gymnastics Franchising
Child Development Activities

BRANDS/DIVISIONS/AFFILIATES:

Unleashed Brands Group
Little Gym Camps
Build & Play

CONTACTS: *Note: Officers with more than one job title may be intentionally listed here more than once.*

Nancy Bigley, CEO
Alex Bingham, Sr. VP-Oper.
Gerald Moore, VP-Real Estate Dev.
Robert Hicks, Sr. VP-Franchise Service & Support

GROWTH PLANS/SPECIAL FEATURES:

The Little Gym International, Inc. provides various exercise programs for children aged four months through 12 years. Programs are offered through more than 300 franchised locations worldwide. Classes offered by The Little Gym are grouped into categories such as parent/child, Pre-K gymnastics, grade school gymnastics, dance and enrichment programs that balance physical activities with cognitive development for school preparedness purposes. The Little Gym also offers birthday parties, providing access to the whole facility, instructor-led games, music and LEGO building activities created especially for the birthday boy or girl. The Little Gym Camps combine physical activity, gymnastics, games and arts & crafts for when kids are out of school during the summer or other school breaks. Practice Time is a structured and supervised period to practice the essential gymnastics skills they are learning in class each week. Build & Play enables parents to bond and play together in monthly, complimentary events. Each The Little Gym is independently owned and operated, which occurs in an eight-step process: an overview of goals, brand review, request for consideration, funding and territory analysis, review of franchise disclosure and document, launch day, final franchise and financial validation, and signing the franchise agreement. Estimated start-up costs range from $465,250 to $637,000, and the initial franchise fee is $59,500 (as of June 2023). The Little Gym International is an Unleashed Brands Group company.

FINANCIAL DATA: *Note: Data for latest year may not have been available at press time.*

In U.S. $	2022	2021	2020	2019	2018	2017
Revenue						
R&D Expense						
Operating Income						
Operating Margin %						
SGA Expense						
Net Income						
Operating Cash Flow						
Capital Expenditure						
EBITDA						
Return on Assets %						
Return on Equity %						
Debt to Equity						

CONTACT INFORMATION:

Phone: 480-948-2878   Fax: 480-948-2765
Toll-Free: 888-228-2878
Address: 7500 N. Dobson Rd., Ste. 220, Scottsdale, AZ 85256 United States

STOCK TICKER/OTHER:

Stock Ticker: Private
Employees: 460
Parent Company: Unleashed Brands Group

Exchange:
Fiscal Year Ends:

SALARIES/BONUSES:

Top Exec. Salary: $ Bonus: $
Second Exec. Salary: $ Bonus: $

OTHER THOUGHTS:

Estimated Female Officers or Directors:
Hot Spot for Advancement for Women/Minorities:

LIV Golf Inc

www.livgolf.com

NAIC Code: 711211

TYPES OF BUSINESS:

Professional Golf Association
Professional Golf Tournaments

BRANDS/DIVISIONS/AFFILIATES:

Public Investment Fund
LIV Golf League
Individual Champion
Team Champion

CONTACTS: *Note: Officers with more than one job title may be intentionally listed here more than once.*

Greg Norman, CEO
Yasir al-Rumayyan, Chmn.

GROWTH PLANS/SPECIAL FEATURES:

LIV Golf, Inc. is a professional golf tour owned by the Public Investment Fund, which is based in Saudi Arabia. LIV Golf was founded in 2021 and inaugurated its first season in 2022. Its LIV name refers to the Roman numerals for 54, the score of every hole on a par-72 course and the number of holes to be played at LIV events. As for the 2023 season, the LIV Golf League consists of 14 54-hole tournaments featuring 48 players and no cut, and a team championship event at the end of the season. Twelve teams and 48 individuals compete for prize money ($405 million total in 2023). The LIV Golf teams include 4 Aces GC, Cleeks GC, Crushers GC, Fireballs GC, HyFlyers GC, Iron Heads GC, Majesticks GC, RangeGoats GC, Ripper GC, Smash GC, Stinger GC and Torque GC. Official events begin in February and end in November. At the end of the events, an individual champion is crowned based on points accumulated throughout the season. For individual events, every stroke counts and the individual winner is the one with the lowest 54-hole stroke play total. The player with the most ranking points after league events, is named the Individual Champion. The Team Championship is a seeded four-day, four-round, match play knockout tournament. For the 2022 season, Dustin Johnson was the individual champion and the 4 Aces GC was the championship team. In early-2023, The CW signed a multi-year deal with LIV Golf to broadcast and stream the tournaments in the U.S. In mid-2023, the firm agreed to merge with the U.S.-based PGA Tour. The deal is subject to review by anti-trust authorities.

FINANCIAL DATA: *Note: Data for latest year may not have been available at press time.*

In U.S. $	2022	2021	2020	2019	2018	2017
Revenue						
R&D Expense						
Operating Income						
Operating Margin %						
SGA Expense						
Net Income						
Operating Cash Flow						
Capital Expenditure						
EBITDA						
Return on Assets %						
Return on Equity %						
Debt to Equity						

CONTACT INFORMATION:

Phone: 44 808-258-3912   Fax:
Toll-Free:
Address: Fl. 11, 1 Lyric Sq., London, W6 0NB United Kingdom

STOCK TICKER/OTHER:

Stock Ticker: Private   Exchange:
Employees: Fiscal Year Ends:
Parent Company: Public Investment Fund

SALARIES/BONUSES:

Top Exec. Salary: $ Bonus: $
Second Exec. Salary: $ Bonus: $

OTHER THOUGHTS:

Estimated Female Officers or Directors:
Hot Spot for Advancement for Women/Minorities:

Liverpool Football Club

www.liverpoolfc.com

NAIC Code: 711211D

TYPES OF BUSINESS:

Professional Soccer Team
Team Management and Operations

BRANDS/DIVISIONS/AFFILIATES:

Fenway Sports Group Holdings LLC
Anfield

CONTACTS: Note: Officers with more than one job title may be intentionally listed here more than once.

Matt Parish, CEO
Holly Chan, Dir.-Finance
Brendan Rodgers, Manager
Tom Werner, Chmn.

GROWTH PLANS/SPECIAL FEATURES:

The Liverpool Football Club, owned by Fenway Sports Group Holdings LLC, is a professional English football club based in Liverpool. The club plays in the English Premier League, and has historically enjoyed tremendous winning success. Liverpool FC was founded in 1892 by John Houlding. In its long history, the club has won 19 First Division titles, four Second Division titles, eight FA Cups (most recently in 2021-22), nine Football League Cups (most recently in 2021-22), 16 FA Charity/Community Shield titles (2022) and one Football League Super Cup. Internationally, Liverpool FC has won the European Cup/UEFA Champions League six times, the UEFA Cup three times and the European Super Cup/UEFA Super Cup four times. Liverpool FC plays at Anfield, a football stadium in the district of Anfield in Liverpool. The team has played at Anfield since its inception in 1892. The stadium holds 53,394 seats and is owned by Liverpool FC. Home game attendance averages approximately 53,000 for Liverpool FC. Forbes valued the club at $4.45 billion in 2022.

FINANCIAL DATA: Note: Data for latest year may not have been available at press time.

In U.S. $	2022	2021	2020	2019	2018	2017
Revenue	710,000,000	691,234,653	604,658,691	725,317,000	467,351,000	467,351,000
R&D Expense						
Operating Income						
Operating Margin %						
SGA Expense						
Net Income		-13,523,586	-48,697,576	55,087,400	50,577,900	50,577,900
Operating Cash Flow						
Capital Expenditure						
EBITDA						
Return on Assets %						
Return on Equity %						
Debt to Equity						

CONTACT INFORMATION:

Phone: 44-151-263-2361   Fax: 44-151-260-8813
Toll-Free:
Address: Anfield Rd., Liverpool, L4 OTH United Kingdom

SALARIES/BONUSES:

Top Exec. Salary: $ Bonus: $
Second Exec. Salary: $ Bonus: $

STOCK TICKER/OTHER:

Stock Ticker: Private   Exchange:
Employees: 1,000   Fiscal Year Ends: 05/31
Parent Company: Fenway Sports Group Holdings LLC

OTHER THOUGHTS:

Estimated Female Officers or Directors:
Hot Spot for Advancement for Women/Minorities:

Sales, profits and employees may be estimates. Financial information, benefits and other data can change quickly and may vary from those stated here.

Los Angeles Angels

www.mlb.com/angels

NAIC Code: 711211A

TYPES OF BUSINESS:

Professional Baseball Team
Team Management and Operations

BRANDS/DIVISIONS/AFFILIATES:

CONTACTS: *Note: Officers with more than one job title may be intentionally listed here more than once.*

Perry Minasian, Gen. Mngr.
John Carpino, Pres.
Molly Jolly, Sr. VP-Finance & Admin.
Dana Wells, Exec. VP
Deborah Jonston, VP-Human Resources
Brian Sanders, VP-Ballpark Oper.
Molly Taylor Jolly, Sr. VP-Admin.
Alex Winsberg, Dir.-Legal Affairs & Risk Mgmt.
Justin Hollander, Dir.-Baseball Oper.
Mike Fach, Sr. Dir.-Bus. Dev.
Tim Mead, VP-Comm.
Molly Taylor Jolly, Sr. VP-Finance
Jerry Dipoto, Gen. Mgr.
Mike Scioscia, Mgr.
Jenny Price, Sr. Dir.-Community Rel.
Brian Sanders, Sr. Dir.-Ballpark Oper.
Dennis Kuhl, Chmn.
Carlos Gomez, Dir.-Int'l Scouting

GROWTH PLANS/SPECIAL FEATURES:

The Los Angeles Angels is a Major League Baseball (MLB) franchise that plays in the Western Division of the American League. Originally owned by singer and actor Gene Autry, the team began playing in the American League in 1961. In 1966, the Angels moved into a new ballpark in Anaheim and became the California Angels. The 1970s were kind to the Angels, as they acquired legendary pitcher Nolan Ryan from the New York Mets in 1972. In California, Ryan pitched four no-hitters, and in 1973, set a single season record by striking out 383 batters. However, in 1979, general manager Buzzie Bavasi ignominiously let Ryan become a free agent. Throughout the 1970s and 1980s, the Angels would come close to playing in the World Series yet would continually fall short. In 1996, the team was acquired by the Disney Corporation, which renamed the club the Anaheim Angels. In 2002, the Angels at last won a World Series, defeating intra-state rivals the San Francisco Giants. Additionally, the ball club has won one American League pennant and nine Western division titles, with the latest being 2014. In 2003, the Angels were sold to Angels Baseball LP, a group headed by advertising entrepreneur Arturo Moreno; Moreno thereby became the first Hispanic baseball team owner. In 2005, the Angels changed their name yet again, this time to their current moniker, the Los Angeles Angels of Anaheim. The team plays at Angel Stadium of Anaheim, which has a capacity of nearly 46,000. The team averaged 30, 339 fans in attendance per home game during the 2022-23 season. Forbes valued the Angels franchise at approximately $2.7 billion in March 2023, seventh out of the MLB clubs.

FINANCIAL DATA: *Note: Data for latest year may not have been available at press time.*

In U.S. $	2022	2021	2020	2019	2018	2017
Revenue	460,200,000					
R&D Expense						
Operating Income						
Operating Margin %						
SGA Expense						
Net Income						
Operating Cash Flow						
Capital Expenditure						
EBITDA						
Return on Assets %						
Return on Equity %						
Debt to Equity						

CONTACT INFORMATION:

Phone: 714-940-2000   Fax: 714-940-2001
Toll-Free:
Address: 2000 Gene Autrey Way, Anaheim, CA 92806 United States

STOCK TICKER/OTHER:

Stock Ticker: Private   Exchange:
Employees: 520   Fiscal Year Ends: 12/31
Parent Company:

SALARIES/BONUSES:

Top Exec. Salary: $ Bonus: $
Second Exec. Salary: $ Bonus: $

OTHER THOUGHTS:

Estimated Female Officers or Directors: 5
Hot Spot for Advancement for Women/Minorities: Y

Los Angeles Chargers

www.chargers.com

NAIC Code: 711211C

TYPES OF BUSINESS:

Professional Football Team
Team Management and Operations

BRANDS/DIVISIONS/AFFILIATES:

San Diego Chargers

CONTACTS: *Note: Officers with more than one job title may be intentionally listed here more than once.*

A.G. Spanos, Pres.-Bus. Oper.
Dennis Abraham, Dir.-Pro Scouting
Michael A. Spanos, Vice. Chmn.
John Spanos, Exec. VP-Football Oper.
Ed McGuire, Exec. VP-Football Admin. & Player Finance
Jeremiah T. Murphy, Exec. VP-Admin.
John Hinek, Dir.-Bus. Oper.
Nicoletta Ruhl, Dir.-Digital Media
Kimberley Layton, Dir.-Public Affairs & Corp. Rel.
Marsha Wells, Controller
Norv Turner, Head Coach
Tom Telesco, Gen. Mgr.
Michael A. Spanos, Exec. VP
Alex Spanos, Owner
Dean A. Spanos, Chmn.

GROWTH PLANS/SPECIAL FEATURES:

The Los Angeles Chargers is a National Football League (NFL) team playing in the Western Division of the American Football Conference (AFC). The club was originally known as the Los Angeles Chargers when it began play in 1960 as a charter member of the American Football League (AFL). The Chargers only spent one season in Los Angeles before moving to San Diego and taking on the San Diego Chargers name. In 1963, the team won their first and only AFL championship. After the league merger in 1970, the Chargers enjoyed some small successes, but failed to advance very far during the postseason. In 1995, the Chargers made their first and only Super Bowl appearance but lost to the San Francisco 49ers. The franchise has achieved some recent success, winning five AFL West Division championships and 10 AFC Western Division championships. Its last playoff appearance was in 2022, with a total of 20 playoff appearances across the AFL and NFL. The team is currently owned by Dean Spanos. The Los Angeles Chargers play their home games at SoFi Stadium in Inglewood, which has a seating capacity ranging from 70,240 to 100,240, depending on the event. Average home game attendance was 72,734 during the 2022-23 season. Several well-known Hall of Fame inductees have played for the Chargers, including Dan Fouts, Lance Alworth, Fred Dean, Charlie Joiner, Ron Mix, Kellen Winslow, Junior Seau and LaDainian Tomlinson. Forbes estimated the team worth $3.875 billion in 2022.

FINANCIAL DATA: *Note: Data for latest year may not have been available at press time.*

In U.S. $	2022	2021	2020	2019	2018	2017
Revenue	434,200,000					
R&D Expense						
Operating Income						
Operating Margin %						
SGA Expense						
Net Income						
Operating Cash Flow						
Capital Expenditure						
EBITDA						
Return on Assets %						
Return on Equity %						
Debt to Equity						

CONTACT INFORMATION:

Phone: 877-242-7437   Fax:
Toll-Free:
Address: 3333 Susan St., Cosat Mesa, CA 92626 United States

STOCK TICKER/OTHER:

Stock Ticker: Private
Employees: 335
Parent Company:

Exchange:
Fiscal Year Ends: 12/31

SALARIES/BONUSES:

Top Exec. Salary: $ Bonus: $
Second Exec. Salary: $ Bonus: $

OTHER THOUGHTS:

Estimated Female Officers or Directors: 5
Hot Spot for Advancement for Women/Minorities: Y

Sales, profits and employees may be estimates. Financial information, benefits and other data can change quickly and may vary from those stated here.

Los Angeles Clippers

NAIC Code: 711211B

www.nba.com/clippers

TYPES OF BUSINESS:

Professional Basketball Team
Team Management and Operations

BRANDS/DIVISIONS/AFFILIATES:

Ontario Clippers

CONTACTS: *Note: Officers with more than one job title may be intentionally listed here more than once.*

Lawrence Frank, Pres.-Basketball Oper.
Andy Roeser, Pres.
Dennis Wong, Vice Chmn.
Bob Platt, General Counsel
Gary Sacks, VP-Basketball Oper.
Joe Safety, VP-Corp. Comm.
Vinny Del Negro, Head Coach
Chuck Loth, Dir.-Ticket Oper.
Christian Howard, VP-Mktg. & Broadcasting
Chris Beyer, Sr. Dir.-Sponsorship Sales
Steve Ballmer, Chmn.

GROWTH PLANS/SPECIAL FEATURES:

The Los Angeles Clippers originally joined the National Basketball Association (NBA) in 1970 as the Buffalo Braves and changed its name to the San Diego Clippers in 1978 after its subsequent relocation to California. In 1984, the Clippers moved to Los Angeles and officially became known as the Los Angeles Clippers. Since its founding, the team has been a perennial contender for the bottom of the standings, with two division titles in 2013 and 2014. The franchise is owned by Steve Ballmer and plays all its home games at the Crypto.com Arena in downtown Los Angeles, with a basketball seating capacity of over 19,000. The team's home attendance averaged 17,574 during the 2022-23 season. The Clippers play in the Pacific division of the Western Conference. The team has two division titles (2013 and 2014). The Ontario Clippers are the affiliates for the LA Clippers, playing in the NBA G League and based in Ontario, California. Forbes estimated the Los Angeles Clippers' value at $3.9 billion in October 2022.

FINANCIAL DATA: *Note: Data for latest year may not have been available at press time.*

In U.S. $	2022	2021	2020	2019	2018	2017
Revenue	312,650,000					
R&D Expense						
Operating Income						
Operating Margin %						
SGA Expense						
Net Income						
Operating Cash Flow						
Capital Expenditure						
EBITDA						
Return on Assets %						
Return on Equity %						
Debt to Equity						

CONTACT INFORMATION:

Phone: 213-204-2800   Fax:
Toll-Free:
Address: 1212 S. Flower St., Fl. 5, Los Angeles, CA 90015 United States

STOCK TICKER/OTHER:

Stock Ticker: Private   Exchange:
Employees: 420   Fiscal Year Ends: 07/31
Parent Company:

SALARIES/BONUSES:

Top Exec. Salary: $ Bonus: $
Second Exec. Salary: $ Bonus: $

OTHER THOUGHTS:

Estimated Female Officers or Directors: 28
Hot Spot for Advancement for Women/Minorities: Y

Los Angeles Dodgers

www.mlb.com/dodgers

NAIC Code: 711211A

TYPES OF BUSINESS:

Professional Baseball Team
Team Management and Operations

BRANDS/DIVISIONS/AFFILIATES:

Dodgers Stadium
Guggenheim Baseball

CONTACTS: *Note: Officers with more than one job title may be intentionally listed here more than once.*

Stan Kasten, CEO
Bob Wolfe, COO
Lon Rosen, CMO
Allister Annear, Dir.-Merch. & Retail
Sam Fernandez, General Counsel
Francine Hughes, VP-Stadium Oper.
Janet Marie Smith, Sr. VP-Planning & Dev.
Renata Simril, Sr. VP-External Affairs
Paige Bobbitt, Dir.-Finance
Ned Colletti, Gen. Mgr.
Michael Young, Sr. VP-Corp. Partnerships
Erik Braverman, Sr. Dir.-Mktg. & Broadcasting
Joe Jareck, Dir.-Public Rel.
Mark Walter, Chmn.
Bob Engle, VP-Intl Scouting

GROWTH PLANS/SPECIAL FEATURES:

The Los Angeles Dodgers is a baseball team playing in the Western Division of the National League (NL) of Major League Baseball (MLB). The franchise was founded in 1884 in Brooklyn and had several other names before settling on Dodgers in 1932. The team moved west in 1957, becoming the Los Angeles Dodgers. The franchise made baseball and civil rights history while still in Brooklyn, becoming the first MLB team to invite a black player, Jackie Robinson, to join its roster. Other famous Dodgers include Roy Campanella, Pee Wee Reese, Don Drysdale, Sandy Koufax, Orel Hershiser, Ralph Branca and manager Tommy Lasorda, who led the team to its 1981 and 1988 World Series wins. One of baseball's most venerable franchises, the Dodgers have made several post-season appearances, winning seven World Series titles (most recent in 2020), 24 National League pennants, one AA Pennant and 20 division titles (most recent in 2022). After falling into bankruptcy due to the financial difficulties of owner Frank McCourt, the team was purchased in 2012 by Guggenheim Baseball, a group of investors that includes former NBA star Magic Johnson, and financed largely by Guggenheim Partners, for approximately $2 billion. The Dodgers play home games at the 56,000-seat capacity Dodgers Stadium, built for roughly $23 million in 1962. The franchise sees some of the highest home game attendance figures in the league, averaging 47,671 in the 2022 season. Forbes estimated the team at $4.8 billion in March 2023, second in MLB.

FINANCIAL DATA: *Note: Data for latest year may not have been available at press time.*

In U.S. $	2022	2021	2020	2019	2018	2017
Revenue	481,650,000					
R&D Expense						
Operating Income						
Operating Margin %						
SGA Expense						
Net Income						
Operating Cash Flow						
Capital Expenditure						
EBITDA						
Return on Assets %						
Return on Equity %						
Debt to Equity						

CONTACT INFORMATION:

Phone: 323-224-1500   Fax: 323-224-1269
Toll-Free:
Address: 1000 Elysian Park Ave., Los Angeles, CA 90012 United States

STOCK TICKER/OTHER:

Stock Ticker: Private   Exchange:
Employees: 735   Fiscal Year Ends: 10/31
Parent Company:

SALARIES/BONUSES:

Top Exec. Salary: $ Bonus: $
Second Exec. Salary: $ Bonus: $

OTHER THOUGHTS:

Estimated Female Officers or Directors: 7
Hot Spot for Advancement for Women/Minorities: Y

Los Angeles Football Club

www.lafc.com

NAIC Code: 711211D

TYPES OF BUSINESS:

Major League Soccer
Team Management and Operations

BRANDS/DIVISIONS/AFFILIATES:

LAFC
LAFC Academy

CONTACTS: *Note: Officers with more than one job title may be intentionally listed here more than once.*

Larry Freedman, Chief Business Officer
Stacy Johns, CFO
Sandy Lim, Exec. VP-People
Christian Lau, CTO
Benny Tran, Exec. VP-Corp. Strategy & Dev.

GROWTH PLANS/SPECIAL FEATURES:

Los Angeles Football Club, known as LAFC, is a Major League Soccer (MLS) team based in Los Angeles, California playing in the Western Conference. The team is an expansion team, awarded to Los Angeles in 2014 and began playing in March 2018. The team plays at BMO Stadium, which has a capacity of 22,000 and sells out at most home games. LAFC averaged 22,090 in home game attendance during the 2022 season. In its 2018 inaugural season, the club made the MLS Playoffs, losing to Real Salt Lake in the Knockout Round. LAFC clenched the Supporters' Shield title in 2019, and then again in 2022. It captured the Western Conference title in 2019 and 2022, made the playoffs in 2022 and won the MLS in 2022, defeating the Philadelphia Union in a penalty shootout following a 3-3 draw via extra time. Adidas is the kit manufacturer for the LAFC, FLEX is the shirt sponsor and Ford is the sleeve sponsor. The club runs the LAFC Academy which opened in February 2016 and gives the community in Los Angeles greater access to the game and a pathway to professionalism for elite athletes. Forbes estimated that the club is worth $1 billion in late-2022, the first MLS team to cross the $1 billion mark in the history of the league.

FINANCIAL DATA: *Note: Data for latest year may not have been available at press time.*

In U.S. $	2022	2021	2020	2019	2018	2017
Revenue						
R&D Expense						
Operating Income						
Operating Margin %						
SGA Expense						
Net Income						
Operating Cash Flow						
Capital Expenditure						
EBITDA						
Return on Assets %						
Return on Equity %						
Debt to Equity						

CONTACT INFORMATION:

Phone: 213-519-9900   Fax:
Toll-Free:
Address: 818 W. 7 St., #1200, Los Angeles, CA 90017 United States

STOCK TICKER/OTHER:

Stock Ticker: Private   Exchange:
Employees: Fiscal Year Ends:
Parent Company:

SALARIES/BONUSES:

Top Exec. Salary: $ Bonus: $
Second Exec. Salary: $ Bonus: $

OTHER THOUGHTS:

Estimated Female Officers or Directors:
Hot Spot for Advancement for Women/Minorities:

Los Angeles Galaxy

www.lagalaxy.com

NAIC Code: 711211D

TYPES OF BUSINESS:

Major League Soccer Team
Team Management and Operations

BRANDS/DIVISIONS/AFFILIATES:

Anschutz Entertainment Group
Cozmo

CONTACTS: *Note: Officers with more than one job title may be intentionally listed here more than once.*

Chris Klein, Pres.
Lisa Rollins, Sr. Mgr.-Database & Analytics
Martha Romero, Dir.-Team Admin.
David Kammarman, Dir.-Soccer Oper.
Lisa Bergman, Mgr.-Digital & Social Media
Justin Pearson, Sr. Mgr.-Comm.
Bruce Arena, Head Coach
Sabrina Higdon, Dir.-Partnership Sales
Lauren Nowinski, Mgr.-Community Rel. & LA Galaxy Foundation

GROWTH PLANS/SPECIAL FEATURES:

The Los Angeles Galaxy is a founding member of Major League Soccer (MLS). The team is owned by Anschutz Entertainment Group, a leading sports and entertainment presenter. The Galaxy plays in MLS's Western Conference, alongside Austin FC, Colorado Rapids, FC Dallas, Houston Dynamo FC, Los Angeles FC, Minnesota United FC, Portland Timbers, Real Salt Lake, San Jose Earthquakes, Seattle Sounders FC, Sporting Kansas City, St. Louis City SC and Vancouver Whitecaps FC. The Galaxy plays its home games at the Dignity Health Sports Park which has a capacity of 27,000, and the team averaged 22,841 fans per home game attendance during the 2022 season. LA Galaxy has won the MLS Cup five times, the MLS Supporter's Shield four times, and the U.S. Open Cup twice. The Galaxy won the MLS Western Conference playoffs nine times. The team has hosted several MLS's star players, including forward Landon Donovan, defender Alexi Lalas, midfielder Paul Caligiuri and international superstar David Beckham. Cozmo is the team's mascot, an extraterrestrial frog. Forbes estimated the Galaxy to be worth $98 million in 2022.

FINANCIAL DATA: *Note: Data for latest year may not have been available at press time.*

In U.S. $	2022	2021	2020	2019	2018	2017
Revenue	50,673,600					
R&D Expense						
Operating Income						
Operating Margin %						
SGA Expense						
Net Income						
Operating Cash Flow						
Capital Expenditure						
EBITDA						
Return on Assets %						
Return on Equity %						
Debt to Equity						

CONTACT INFORMATION:

Phone: 310-630-2200   Fax: 310-630-2250
Toll-Free: 877-342-5299
Address: 18400 Avalon Blvd., Ste. 200, Carson, CA 90746 United States

STOCK TICKER/OTHER:

Stock Ticker: Private   Exchange:
Employees: 300   Fiscal Year Ends:
Parent Company: Anschutz Entertainment Group

SALARIES/BONUSES:

Top Exec. Salary: $ Bonus: $
Second Exec. Salary: $ Bonus: $

OTHER THOUGHTS:

Estimated Female Officers or Directors: 12
Hot Spot for Advancement for Women/Minorities: Y

Los Angeles Kings

NAIC Code: 711211F

TYPES OF BUSINESS:

Professional Hockey Team (NHL)
Team Management and Operations

BRANDS/DIVISIONS/AFFILIATES:

Anshutz Entertainment Group
Ontario Reign

CONTACTS: *Note: Officers with more than one job title may be intentionally listed here more than once.*

Dan Beckerman, CEO
Luc Robitaille, Pres
Scott Sangrey, VP-Finance
Michael Altieri, Sr. VP-Mktg. & Communications
Jennifer Zelaya, Dir.-Human Resources
Darshan Parikh, Sr. Dir.-IT
Jeff Solomon, VP-Legal Affairs & Hockey Oper.
Luc Robitaille, Pres., Bus. Oper.
Dewayne Hankins, Dir.-Digital Media
Michael Altieri, VP-Comm. & Content
Peter Mazur, VP-Finance
Philip F. Anschutz, Co-Owner
Edward P. Roski, Jr., Co-Owner
Darryl Sutter, Head Coach
Bill Pedigo, Sr. VP-Corp. Partnership
Kelly Cheeseman, COO

GROWTH PLANS/SPECIAL FEATURES:

The Los Angeles Kings is a professional hockey team playing in the Pacific division of the Western conference within the National Hockey League (NHL). The team was founded as an expansion franchise in 1967. The most famous King in club history is Wayne Gretzky, who led the team to a 1993 Championship game. Unfortunately, the Kings lost that game to the Montreal Canadians. However, their performance led to spreading enthusiasm for hockey throughout Southern California. Other team heroes have included Marcel Dionne and Luc Robitaille. The Kings play home games at the Crypto.com Arena owned by Denver billionaire Philip Anschutz and his Anschutz Entertainment Group (AEG). The venue seats 18,230 hockey fans, and the Los Angeles Kings averaged 17,067 in home game attendance during the 2022-23 season. In 2011-12, the team clenched its first Stanley Cup, and then won again the following year in 2013-14. The Kings have won three Conference Championships and one Division Championship. The team's minor league affiliates include the Ontario Reign of the American Hockey League (AHL), and the Greenville Swamp Rabbits in the East Coast Hockey League (ECHL). Forbes estimated the team's value at $1.3 billion in December 2022.

FINANCIAL DATA: *Note: Data for latest year may not have been available at press time.*

In U.S. $	2022	2021	2020	2019	2018	2017
Revenue	168,350,000					
R&D Expense						
Operating Income						
Operating Margin %						
SGA Expense						
Net Income						
Operating Cash Flow						
Capital Expenditure						
EBITDA						
Return on Assets %						
Return on Equity %						
Debt to Equity						

CONTACT INFORMATION:

Phone: 213-742-7100   Fax: 213-742-7296
Toll-Free:
Address: 1111 S. Figueroa St., Ste. 3100, Los Angeles, CA 90015 United States

STOCK TICKER/OTHER:

Stock Ticker: Private   Exchange:
Employees: 160   Fiscal Year Ends: 07/31
Parent Company: Anschutz Entertainment Group

SALARIES/BONUSES:

Top Exec. Salary: $ Bonus: $
Second Exec. Salary: $ Bonus: $

OTHER THOUGHTS:

Estimated Female Officers or Directors: 5
Hot Spot for Advancement for Women/Minorities: Y

Los Angeles Lakers

www.nba.com/lakers

NAIC Code: 711211B

TYPES OF BUSINESS:

Professional Basketball Team
Team Management and Operations

BRANDS/DIVISIONS/AFFILIATES:

Los Angeles Lakers Inc
Lakers Read to Achieve
Los Angeles Lakers Youth Foundation

CONTACTS: *Note: Officers with more than one job title may be intentionally listed here more than once.*

Jeanie Buss, CEO
Jerry Buss, Pres.
Joe McCormack, CFO
Terree Sholl, Dir.-Corp. Admin. & Legal
Jim Perzik, General Counsel
Jeanie Buss, Exec. VP-Bus. Oper.
Johnny Buss, Exec. VP-Strategic Dev.
Ty Nowell, Mgr.-New Media
John Black, VP-Public Rel.
Susan Matson, Controller
Mike D'Antoni, Head Coach
Mitch Kupchak, Gen. Mgr.-Basketball Oper.
Eva Campbell, Exec. Dir.-Corp. Sponsorships
Eugene Chow, Dir.-Community Rel.

GROWTH PLANS/SPECIAL FEATURES:

The Los Angeles Lakers basketball team, founded in 1946, is one of the most successful franchises within the National Basketball Association (NBA). The organization holds several NBA records, with having 17 championships, 19 conference titles and 33 division titles, with the most recent for each being in 2020. The franchise originally joined the National Basketball League (NBL) as the Minneapolis Lakers and was later renamed the Los Angeles Lakers after moving to California in 1960. The Lakers have had a long history of Hall of Fame players, including Wilt 'The Stilt' Chamberlain, Earvin 'Magic' Johnson, Kareem Abdul-Jabbar and Jerry West, as well as Shaquille O'Neal, Steve Nash and Kobe Bryant. The Lakers play at the Crypto-com Arena, offering a 19,079 basketball seating capacity, with home-game attendance averaging 18,613 during the 2022-23 season. The franchise hosts a variety of community outreach programs such as Lakers Read to Achieve and the Los Angeles Lakers Youth Foundation, which assists nonprofit communities in the use of athletics to promote education. Bibigo is the Lakers' main sponsor. According to a Forbes estimate (October 2022), the franchise is the third most valuable team in the NBA, with a value of $5.9 billion.

FINANCIAL DATA: *Note: Data for latest year may not have been available at press time.*

In U.S. $	2022	2021	2020	2019	2018	2017
Revenue	465,400,000					
R&D Expense						
Operating Income						
Operating Margin %						
SGA Expense						
Net Income						
Operating Cash Flow						
Capital Expenditure						
EBITDA						
Return on Assets %						
Return on Equity %						
Debt to Equity						

CONTACT INFORMATION:

Phone: 310-426-6000   Fax: 310-426-6115
Toll-Free:
Address: 1111 S. Figueroa St., Los Angeles, CA 90015 United States

STOCK TICKER/OTHER:

Stock Ticker: Private   Exchange:
Employees: 240   Fiscal Year Ends: 07/31
Parent Company:

SALARIES/BONUSES:

Top Exec. Salary: $ Bonus: $
Second Exec. Salary: $ Bonus: $

OTHER THOUGHTS:

Estimated Female Officers or Directors: 8
Hot Spot for Advancement for Women/Minorities: Y

Los Angeles Rams

NAIC Code: 711211C

TYPES OF BUSINESS:

Professional Football Team
Team Management and Operations

BRANDS/DIVISIONS/AFFILIATES:

Cleveland Rams
St Lous Rams

CONTACTS: *Note: Officers with more than one job title may be intentionally listed here more than once.*

Les Snead, Gen. Manager
Kevin Demoff, COO
Todd Davis, General Counsel
Kevin Demoff, Exec. VP-Football Oper.
Brian Killingsworth, VP-Brand Strategy & Mktg.
Keith Harris, Dir.-Internet Svcs. & Bus. Dev.
Molly Higgins, VP-Corp. Comm. & Civic Affairs
Michael T. Naughton, VP-Finance
Jeff Fisher, Head Coach
Les Snead, Gen. Mgr.
Mike O'Keefe, VP-Sales
Jeff Brewer, Treas.
E. Stanley Kroenke, Chmn.

GROWTH PLANS/SPECIAL FEATURES:

The Los Angeles Rams is a professional football team playing in the NFC western division of the National Football League (NFL). The team began its history in 1936, playing in Cleveland, Ohio as a second version of the previous Cleveland Rams team, a charter member of the American Football League (AFL). The franchise then became known as the Los Angeles Rams after moving to Los Angeles, California in 1946. In 1995, the team moved to St. Louis, playing as the St. Louis Rams through to the 2015 season, and then returned to California in 2016 as the Los Angeles Rams. The Rams have won two Super Bowl championships (1999 and 2021), eight conference championships and 18 division titles. The team has contributed several players and coaches to the Pro Football Hall of Fame, including Merlin Olsen, Marshall Faulk, George Allen and Jack Youngblood. Stan Kroenke, who also owns several other sports franchises including English football club Arsenal, bought the team in 2010 for $750 million. The Rams play at the SoFi Stadium in Inglewood, with a seating capacity that ranges from 70,240 to over 100,000, depending on the event. The team's average home game attendance was 72,734 during the 2022-23 season. Forbes estimated the team at $6.2 billion in August 2022.

FINANCIAL DATA: *Note: Data for latest year may not have been available at press time.*

In U.S. $	2022	2021	2020	2019	2018	2017
Revenue	610,000,000					
R&D Expense						
Operating Income						
Operating Margin %						
SGA Expense						
Net Income						
Operating Cash Flow						
Capital Expenditure						
EBITDA						
Return on Assets %						
Return on Equity %						
Debt to Equity						

CONTACT INFORMATION:

Phone: 818-338-0011   Fax:
Toll-Free:
Address: 29899 Agoura Rd., Agoura Hills, CA 91301 United States

STOCK TICKER/OTHER:

Stock Ticker: Private   Exchange:
Employees: 260   Fiscal Year Ends: 12/31
Parent Company:

SALARIES/BONUSES:

Top Exec. Salary: $ Bonus: $
Second Exec. Salary: $ Bonus: $

OTHER THOUGHTS:

Estimated Female Officers or Directors: 5
Hot Spot for Advancement for Women/Minorities: Y

Los Angeles Sparks

www.wnba.com/sparks

NAIC Code: 711211E

TYPES OF BUSINESS:

Women's National Basketball Association Team
Team Management and Operations

BRANDS/DIVISIONS/AFFILIATES:

Sparks LA Sports LLC

CONTACTS: *Note: Officers with more than one job title may be intentionally listed here more than once.*

Karen Bryant, Chief Admin. Officer
Antoinette Brown, VP-Bus. Oper.
Melissa Korc, Mgr.-Ticket Oper.
Stacey Mitch, Dir.-Comm.
Ali Zaidi, Dir.-Finance
Penny Toler, Gen. Mgr.
Tiffany Fan, Mgr.-Mktg. & Sponsorship
Carol Ross, Head Coach

GROWTH PLANS/SPECIAL FEATURES:

The Los Angeles Sparks is one of the eight original Women's National Basketball Association (WNBA) teams founded in 1997. The team is owned by Sparks LA Sports, LLC, which was formed by famed NBA player, Earvin "Magic" Johnson and Stan Kasten. Today, Sparks LA Sports' ownership members also include Mark Walter, Todd Boehly and Bobby Patton. The Los Angeles Sparks played in the WNBA's inaugural game against the New York Liberty. The Sparks made the playoffs eight years in a row, from 1999-2006, and have clenched the WNBA Championship in 2001, 2002 and 2016. Former long-time Sparks captain and WNBA icon Lisa Leslie helped the U.S. women's basketball team take the gold medal in the 1996, 2000, 2004 and 2008 Olympics. The team plays its home games at the Cyrpto.com Arena, offering a 19,079 basketball seating capacity, with the Sparks averaging 5,653 in attendance during the 2022 season. The Spark's community initiatives include WNBA FIT and WNBA Cares programs. The team plays in the Western Conference of the WBNA, with teams including the Dallas Wings, Las Vegas Aces, Minnesota Lynx, Phoenix Mercury and Seattle Storm.

FINANCIAL DATA: *Note: Data for latest year may not have been available at press time.*

In U.S. $	2022	2021	2020	2019	2018	2017
Revenue						
R&D Expense						
Operating Income						
Operating Margin %						
SGA Expense						
Net Income						
Operating Cash Flow						
Capital Expenditure						
EBITDA						
Return on Assets %						
Return on Equity %						
Debt to Equity						

CONTACT INFORMATION:

Phone: 213-929-1300 Fax: 213-929-1325
Toll-Free:
Address: 5120 Goldleaf Cir., #130, Los Angeles, CA 90017 United States

STOCK TICKER/OTHER:

Stock Ticker: Private Exchange:
Employees: 78 Fiscal Year Ends:
Parent Company: Sparks LA Sports LLC

SALARIES/BONUSES:

Top Exec. Salary: $ Bonus: $
Second Exec. Salary: $ Bonus: $

OTHER THOUGHTS:

Estimated Female Officers or Directors: 20
Hot Spot for Advancement for Women/Minorities: Y

lululemon athletica inc

shop.lululemon.com

NAIC Code: 448100

TYPES OF BUSINESS:

Athletic Apparel
Organic Products
Accessories
Online Exercise Classes and Devices

BRANDS/DIVISIONS/AFFILIATES:

lululemon
MIRROR
Curiouser Products Inc

GROWTH PLANS/SPECIAL FEATURES:

Lululemon Athletica Inc. designs, distributes, and markets athletic apparel, footwear, and accessories for women, men, and girls. Lululemon offers pants, shorts, tops, and jackets for both leisure and athletic activities such as yoga and running. The company also sells fitness accessories, such as bags, yoga mats, and equipment. Lululemon sells its products through more than 600 company-owned stores in 18 countries, e-commerce, outlets, and wholesale accounts. The company was founded in 1998 and is based in Vancouver, Canada.

CONTACTS: *Note: Officers with more than one job title may be intentionally listed here more than once.*

Calvin McDonald, CEO
Meghan Frank, CFO
Glenn Murphy, Chairman of the Board
Andre Maestrini, Executive VP, Divisional
Nicole Neuberger, Other Executive Officer
Sun Choe, Other Executive Officer
Celeste Burgoyne, President, Divisional

FINANCIAL DATA: *Note: Data for latest year may not have been available at press time.*

In U.S. $	2022	2021	2020	2019	2018	2017
Revenue	6,256,617,000	4,401,879,000	3,979,296,000	3,288,319,000		
R&D Expense						
Operating Income	1,374,749,000	849,828,000	889,110,000	705,836,000		
Operating Margin %	.22%	.19%	.22%	.21%		
SGA Expense	2,225,034,000	1,609,003,000	1,334,247,000	1,110,379,000		
Net Income	975,322,000	588,913,000	645,596,000	483,801,000		
Operating Cash Flow	1,389,108,000	803,336,000	669,316,000	742,779,000		
Capital Expenditure	394,502,000	229,226,000	283,048,000	225,807,000		
EBITDA	1,598,955,000	1,035,306,000	1,051,043,000	828,320,000		
Return on Assets %	.21%	.16%	.24%	.24%		
Return on Equity %	.37%	.26%	.38%	.32%		
Debt to Equity	.25%	.25%	0.313			

CONTACT INFORMATION:

Phone: 604 732-6124   Fax: 604 874-6124
Toll-Free: 877-263-9300
Address: 1818 Cornwall Ave., Vancouver, BC V6J 1C7 Canada

STOCK TICKER/OTHER:

Stock Ticker: LULU   Exchange: NAS
Employees: 29,000   Fiscal Year Ends: 01/31
Parent Company:

SALARIES/BONUSES:

Top Exec. Salary: $1,250,000   Bonus: $
Second Exec. Salary: $687,500   Bonus: $126,042

OTHER THOUGHTS:

Estimated Female Officers or Directors: 5
Hot Spot for Advancement for Women/Minorities: Y

Madison Square Garden Sports Corp

www.themadisonsquaregardencompany.com
NAIC Code: 711211

TYPES OF BUSINESS:

Sports Teams
Theaters
Live Entertainment
Arenas

GROWTH PLANS/SPECIAL FEATURES:

Madison Square Garden Sports Corp is engaged in live sports and entertainment business. The Company's reportable segment: MSG Entertainment consists of live entertainment events, including concerts and other live events, such as family shows, performing arts and special events.

BRANDS/DIVISIONS/AFFILIATES:

MSG Sports & Entertainment LLC
Madison Square Garden
Hulu Theater at Madison Square Garden
Radio City Music Hall
New York KNicks
New York Rangers
New York LIberty
Hartford Wolf Pack

CONTACTS: Note: Officers with more than one job title may be intentionally listed here more than once.

Andrew Lustgarten, CEO
Victoria Mink, CFO
James Dolan, Chairman of the Board
Alexander Shvartsman, Chief Accounting Officer
Lawrence Burian, Executive VP, Divisional

FINANCIAL DATA: Note: Data for latest year may not have been available at press time.

In U.S. $	2022	2021	2020	2019	2018	2017
Revenue	821,354,000	415,721,000	603,319,000	729,404,000	1,318,452,000	1,318,452,000
R&D Expense						
Operating Income	86,080,000	-78,443,000	-93,866,000	-58,195,000	-56,310,000	-56,310,000
Operating Margin %	.10%	-.19%	-.16%	-.08%	-.04%	-.04%
SGA Expense	229,668,000	206,700,000	319,675,000	327,441,000	406,951,000	406,951,000
Net Income	51,131,000	-13,954,000	-182,388,000	11,427,000	-72,723,000	-72,723,000
Operating Cash Flow	178,056,000	-35,326,000	3,568,000	161,253,000	223,532,000	223,532,000
Capital Expenditure	932,000	466,000	362,475,000	188,834,000	44,224,000	44,224,000
EBITDA	90,709,000	-73,183,000	-225,000	63,522,000	30,384,000	30,384,000
Return on Assets %	.04%	-.01%	-.07%	.00%	-.02%	-.02%
Return on Equity %			-.15%	.00%	-.03%	-.03%
Debt to Equity					0.044	0.044

CONTACT INFORMATION:

Phone: 212 465-6000   Fax:
Toll-Free:
Address: Two Penn Plaza, New York, NY 10121-0091 United States

STOCK TICKER/OTHER:

Stock Ticker: MSGS   Exchange: NYS
Employees: 892   Fiscal Year Ends: 06/30
Parent Company:

SALARIES/BONUSES:

Top Exec. Salary: $900,000   Bonus: $
Second Exec. Salary: Bonus: $
$840,000

OTHER THOUGHTS:

Estimated Female Officers or Directors:
Hot Spot for Advancement for Women/Minorities:

Majestic Athletic

www.majesticathletic.com

NAIC Code: 315280

TYPES OF BUSINESS:

Professional Sports Uniforms
Apparel & Outerwear

BRANDS/DIVISIONS/AFFILIATES:

Fanatics Inc
MajesticAthletic.com
FanZones

CONTACTS: *Note: Officers with more than one job title may be intentionally listed here more than once.*

Michael Rubin, CEO-Fanatics

GROWTH PLANS/SPECIAL FEATURES:

Majestic Athletic, a subsidiary of Fanatics, Inc., is one of the largest designers, marketers and manufacturers of athletic team uniforms, performance apparel and outerwear in the U.S. The company is the official, exclusive provider of apparel for Major League Baseball (MLB), and manufactures sports apparel under license of other professional leagues such as the National Basketball Association (NBA), the National Football League (NFL), the National Hockey League (NHL), Major League Soccer (MLS) and the Australian Football League (AFL). Majestic Athletic also manufactures apparel representing more than 500 national college teams, and international professional football/soccer teams. Uniform apparel includes jackets, jerseys, outerwear, turtlenecks, t-shirts and fleece, as well as championship gear and jerseys. All decorations and embroidery on Majestic products are done by hand. Majestic sporting gear can be found in retail stores such as Foot Locker, Champs and Academy as well as at concession stands and sporting events. In addition, Majestic's FanZones is an in-stadium on-the-spot micro factory with the ability to customize licensed sport jerseys and team apparel on-demand. The firm's website, MajesticAthletic.com, features apparel available for purchase online. Size charts, shipping rates and order tracking are solutions offered on the ecommerce site.

FINANCIAL DATA: *Note: Data for latest year may not have been available at press time.*

In U.S. $	2022	2021	2020	2019	2018	2017
Revenue						
R&D Expense						
Operating Income						
Operating Margin %						
SGA Expense						
Net Income						
Operating Cash Flow						
Capital Expenditure						
EBITDA						
Return on Assets %						
Return on Equity %						
Debt to Equity						

CONTACT INFORMATION:

Phone: 610-746-6800   Fax: 610-746-7728
Toll-Free:
Address: 2320 Newlins Mill Rd., Easton, PA 18045 United States

STOCK TICKER/OTHER:

Stock Ticker: Subsidiary   Exchange:
Employees: Fiscal Year Ends: 06/30
Parent Company: Fanatics Inc

SALARIES/BONUSES:

Top Exec. Salary: $ Bonus: $
Second Exec. Salary: $ Bonus: $

OTHER THOUGHTS:

Estimated Female Officers or Directors:
Hot Spot for Advancement for Women/Minorities:

Major League Baseball (MLB)

www.mlb.com

NAIC Code: 711211

TYPES OF BUSINESS:

Professional Baseball League
Professional Baseball League Regulator
Umpire Crew Management
Contract Negotiation
Labor Negotiation
National Broadcasting Right Marketing

BRANDS/DIVISIONS/AFFILIATES:

National League
American League
All-Star Game
World Series
MLB Advanced Media LP
MLB Productions
Major League Baseball Players Association
MLB.com

CONTACTS: *Note: Officers with more than one job title may be intentionally listed here more than once.*

Rob Manfred, Commissioner
Chris Marinak, Chief Operations & Strategy Officer
Bob Starkey, CFO
Karin Timpone, CMO
Tony Reagins, Chief Baseball Dev. Officer
Pat Courtney, CCO
John McHale, Jr., Exec. VP-Admin.
Joe Torre, Exec. VP-Baseball Oper.
Frank Robinson, Exec. VP-Baseball Dev.
Thomas C. Brasuell, VP-Community Affairs
Timothy J. Brosnan, Exec. VP-Bus.
Robert D. Manfred, Jr., Exec. VP-Economics & League Affairs
Noah Garden, Chief Revenue Officer

GROWTH PLANS/SPECIAL FEATURES:

Major League Baseball (MLB), created through the mergers of the National League (NL) and the American League (AL), is the men's professional baseball league in the U.S., with 29 teams in the U.S. and one in Canada. Both the NL and AL teams are divided into three regional divisions: Central, West and East. Each league team operates as a separate business, while the league sets official rules, regulates team ownership; collects licensing fees for merchandise, hires and maintains umpiring crews and negotiates marketing and labor contracts. It also sells national broadcasting rights and distributes broadcasting fees to the teams. Regional broadcasting rights are held by each franchise. MLB's regular season consists of 162 games per team, running from April through the beginning of October. The postseason consists of one winner-takes-all wild card game per league and two elimination rounds in the AL and NL, culminating in the World Series, a best-of-seven series played between the league champions. The organization also holds the All-Star Game, an exhibition game in mid-July. MLB players are represented by the powerful Major League Baseball Players Association (MLBPA), which called work stoppages in 1981 and 1994. Unlike other major U.S. professional sports leagues, MLB does not maintain a player salary cap. However, the league does impose a revenue sharing program that seeks to level income disparity between large-market teams (such as the New York Yankees and Boston Red Sox) and small-market teams (including the Pittsburgh Pirates, Kansas City Royals and Tampa Bay Rays). The league's production and multimedia subsidiary, MLB Advanced Media LP, maintains MLB.com and all 30 of the individual team websites. MLB Productions handles video and broadcast operations. In 2022, league-wide attendance was more than 64.5 million spectators.

FINANCIAL DATA: *Note: Data for latest year may not have been available at press time.*

In U.S. $	2022	2021	2020	2019	2018	2017
Revenue	11,000,000,000	10,000,000,000	6,500,000,000	10,700,000,000	10,000,000,000	10,000,000,000
R&D Expense						
Operating Income						
Operating Margin %						
SGA Expense						
Net Income						
Operating Cash Flow						
Capital Expenditure						
EBITDA						
Return on Assets %						
Return on Equity %						
Debt to Equity						

CONTACT INFORMATION:

Phone: 212-931-7800   Fax: 212-949-8636
Toll-Free:
Address: 1271 Avenue of the Americas, New York, NY 10020 United States

STOCK TICKER/OTHER:

Stock Ticker: Private   Exchange:
Employees: 12,000   Fiscal Year Ends: 10/31
Parent Company:

SALARIES/BONUSES:

Top Exec. Salary: $ Bonus: $
Second Exec. Salary: $ Bonus: $

OTHER THOUGHTS:

Estimated Female Officers or Directors:
Hot Spot for Advancement for Women/Minorities:

Sales, profits and employees may be estimates. Financial information, benefits and other data can change quickly and may vary from those stated here.

Major League Baseball Advanced Media LP (MLBAM)
www.mlb.com
NAIC Code: 519130

TYPES OF BUSINESS:
Online Delivery of Sporting Events
Streaming Sports Media
Digital Baseball Content
Web Applications
Mobile Applications
Content Strategy
User Experience and Product Design
Proprietary Software

BRANDS/DIVISIONS/AFFILIATES:
MLB.com
MLB Network
MLB Productions
At Bat

CONTACTS: *Note: Officers with more than one job title may be intentionally listed here more than once.*
Lisa Pitaro Wisch, Exec. VP
Chris Marinak, COO
Bob Starkey, CFO
Karin Timpone, CMO
Tony Reagins, Chief Baseball Dev. Officer
Pat Courtney, CCO
Rob Manfred, Commissioner

GROWTH PLANS/SPECIAL FEATURES:
Major League Baseball Advanced Media LP (MLBAM) is a full-service solutions provider that delivers digital content through all forms of interactive media. Its capabilities are designed for web, mobile applications and connected devices while integrating live and on-demand multimedia. MLB.com, MLB Network and MLB Productions are all under MLBAM. The company's services include business and content strategy, delivering back-end infrastructure, as well as development and operational management of custom multi-platform applications; UX (user experience) and product design, providing solutions for all forms of digital presence such as websites, mobile web applications, connected devices, marketing campaigns and social media; social media and marketing, a suite of marketing solutions that are fully customizable and able to develop, integrate and manage initiatives; ticketing, which supports digital ticketing strategies such as print-at-home, mobile, season and package plans, secondary market, dynamic pricing and interactive seating; sponsorship and advertising; eCommerce and paid content, a subscription platform that supports digital products such as live and on-demand multimedia, fantasy games, gamecast applications and fan clubs with password-protected login; multimedia and live streaming, which operates and distributes live events and daily streams; mobile web and applications; and statistics and data applications, which deploys proprietary software to chronicle every pitch of every game throughout the season, in-game highlights, box scores and player stats. The firm's At Bat offering is a subscription-based application that provides live scores, statistics, pitch tracking, player cards, notifications and news via online and mobile devices.

FINANCIAL DATA: *Note: Data for latest year may not have been available at press time.*

In U.S. $	2022	2021	2020	2019	2018	2017
Revenue	105,000,000	99,225,000	94,500,000	135,000,000	110,000,000	110,000,000
R&D Expense						
Operating Income						
Operating Margin %						
SGA Expense						
Net Income						
Operating Cash Flow						
Capital Expenditure						
EBITDA						
Return on Assets %						
Return on Equity %						
Debt to Equity						

CONTACT INFORMATION:
Phone: 212-931-7800   Fax:
Toll-Free:
Address: 1271 Avenue of the Americas, New York, NY 10020 United States

STOCK TICKER/OTHER:
Stock Ticker: Subsidiary
Employees:
Parent Company: Major League Baseball
Exchange:
Fiscal Year Ends:

SALARIES/BONUSES:
Top Exec. Salary: $ Bonus: $
Second Exec. Salary: $ Bonus: $

OTHER THOUGHTS:
Estimated Female Officers or Directors:
Hot Spot for Advancement for Women/Minorities:

Major League Soccer (MLS)

www.mlssoccer.com

NAIC Code: 711211

TYPES OF BUSINESS:

Professional Soccer League

BRANDS/DIVISIONS/AFFILIATES:

MLS Cup
Eastern Conference
Western Conference

CONTACTS: Note: Officers with more than one job title may be intentionally listed here more than once.

Gary Stevenson, Pres.
JoAnn Neale, Pres.
Sean Prendergast, CFO
Miarisabel Munoz, Sr. VP-Communications
Jennifer Carroll, Sr. VP-Talent & Culture
John Sullivan, Sr. VP-IT
Maribeth Towers, Sr. VP-Consumer Products
JoAnn Neale, VP-Admin.
Bill Ordower, General Counsel
Nelson Rodriguez, Exec. VP-Game Oper.
Dan Courtemanche, Exec. VP-Corp. Comm.
J. Todd Durbin, Exec. VP-Player Rel. & Comm.
Don Garber, Commissioner
Kathy Carter, Pres., Soccer United Mktg.
Don Garber, Commissioner
David Wright, Sr. VP-Global Sponsorship

GROWTH PLANS/SPECIAL FEATURES:

Major League Soccer LLC (MLS) is a professional soccer league that represents the sport's highest level in both the U.S. and Canada. The league consists of 29 teams, 26 in the U.S. and three in Canada. League teams compete from March to October with 34 regular season games per team (17 home and 17 away) and its championship game, the MLS Cup. The playoffs for the Cup start in late October until the final championship match in November. The league is organized into a two-conference format. The Eastern Conference includes the Atlanta United FC, Charlotte FC, Chicago Fire FC, FC Cincinnati, Columbus Crew, DC United, Inter Miami CF, CF Montreal, Nashville SC, New England Revolution, New York City FC, New York Red Bulls, Orlando City SC, Philadelphia Union and Toronto FC. The Western Conference includes Austin FC, Colorado Rapids, FC Dallas, Houston Dynamo FC, LA Galaxy, Los Angeles FC, Minnesota United FC, Portland Timbers, Real Salt Lake, San Jose Earthquakes, Seattle Sounders FC, Sporting Kansas City, St. Louis City SC and Vancouver Whitecaps FC. Each MLS team's roster is composed of up to 30 players on its first team roster, and all 30 players are eligible for selection to each 18-player game-day squad during the regular season and playoffs. MLS operates under a single-entity structure in which teams and player contracts are centrally owned by the league. To control costs, MLS shares revenues and holds players contracts instead of players contracting with individual teams. MLS average game attendance for the 2022 season was 752,286 total. The majority of league games can be viewed on live television.

FINANCIAL DATA: Note: Data for latest year may not have been available at press time.

In U.S. $	2022	2021	2020	2019	2018	2017
Revenue	990,000,000	900,000,000	580,000,000	700,000,000	478,000,000	478,000,000
R&D Expense						
Operating Income						
Operating Margin %						
SGA Expense						
Net Income						
Operating Cash Flow						
Capital Expenditure						
EBITDA						
Return on Assets %						
Return on Equity %						
Debt to Equity						

CONTACT INFORMATION:

Phone: 212-450-1200   Fax: 212-450-1300
Toll-Free:
Address: 420 Fifth Ave., Fl. 7, New York, NY 10018 United States

STOCK TICKER/OTHER:

Stock Ticker: Private   Exchange:
Employees: 310   Fiscal Year Ends: 12/31
Parent Company:

SALARIES/BONUSES:

Top Exec. Salary: $ Bonus: $
Second Exec. Salary: $ Bonus: $

OTHER THOUGHTS:

Estimated Female Officers or Directors: 3
Hot Spot for Advancement for Women/Minorities: Y

Manchester City Football Club

NAIC Code: 711211D

TYPES OF BUSINESS:

Professional Soccer Team
Team Management and Operations

BRANDS/DIVISIONS/AFFILIATES:

City Football Group Limited
Abu Dhabi United Group
Silver Lake
CITIC Group Corporation Ltd
Manchester City Womens Football Club

CONTACTS: *Note: Officers with more than one job title may be intentionally listed here more than once.*

Pep Guardioloa, Manager
Mike Rigg, Dir.-Tech.
Vicky Kloss, Chief Comm. Officer
Brian Marwood, Football Admin. Officer
Khaldoon Al Mubarak, Chmn.

GROWTH PLANS/SPECIAL FEATURES:

Manchester City Football Club is an English Premiership Soccer team based in Manchester, England. The team plays its home games at the Etihad Stadium, with a soccer seating capacity of 53,400 and up to 60,000 seats for other events. Affiliate Manchester City Women's Football Club plays in the Academy Stadium in Manchester. Domestically, Manchester City FC has clenched nine first division titles in the Premier League, including seasons 1936-37, 1967-68, 2011-12, 2013-14, 2017-18, 2018-19, 2020-21, 2021-22 and 2022-23; six FA Cups, most recently in 2018-19; eight Football League Cups/EFL Cups, most recently in 2017-18, 2018-19, 2019-20 and 2020-21; and six FA Community Shield titles, most recently in 2019. Internationally, the club clenched the European Cup Winners' Cup in 1969-70. The team is one of the most valuable soccer franchises in the world, worth $4.25 billion in 2022 according to a Forbes estimate. Manchester FC is owned by City Football Group Limited, a holding company owned by three organizations: Abu Dhabi United Group (81%), Silver Lake (18%) and CITIC Group Corporation Ltd. (1%).

FINANCIAL DATA: *Note: Data for latest year may not have been available at press time.*

In U.S. $	2022	2021	2020	2019	2018	2017
Revenue	800,000,000	789,189,579	589,448,311	707,971,000	613,906,000	613,906,000
R&D Expense						
Operating Income						
Operating Margin %						
SGA Expense						
Net Income		110,126,658	-155,278,231	14,000,000	1,410,990	1,410,990
Operating Cash Flow						
Capital Expenditure						
EBITDA						
Return on Assets %						
Return on Equity %						
Debt to Equity						

CONTACT INFORMATION:

Phone: 44-870-062-1894   Fax: 44-161-438-7999
Toll-Free:
Address: City of Manchester Stadium, Etihad Campus, Manchester, M11 3FF United Kingdom

STOCK TICKER/OTHER:

Stock Ticker: Private   Exchange:
Employees: 509   Fiscal Year Ends: 06/30
Parent Company: City Football Group Limited

SALARIES/BONUSES:

Top Exec. Salary: $ Bonus: $
Second Exec. Salary: $ Bonus: $

OTHER THOUGHTS:

Estimated Female Officers or Directors: 2
Hot Spot for Advancement for Women/Minorities:

Manchester United plc

www.manutd.com

NAIC Code: 711211D

TYPES OF BUSINESS:

English Premiership Soccer Club
Team Management and Operations

BRANDS/DIVISIONS/AFFILIATES:

Manchester United Football Club
MUTV

GROWTH PLANS/SPECIAL FEATURES:

Manchester United PLC operates a professional football club together with related and ancillary activities. The company manages the soccer team and all affiliated club activities of the Manchester United Football Club, which includes the media network, foundation, fan zone, news, and sports features, and team merchandise. Manchester United is based in England. The company has three principal sectors from which the majority of the revenue is generated including Commercial, Broadcasting, and Matchday.

CONTACTS: Note: Officers with more than one job title may be intentionally listed here more than once.

Joel Glazer, Co-Chmn. & Dir.
Avram Glazer, Co-Chmn. & Dir.
Cliff Baty, CFO
Ed Woodward, Chief of Staff
Patrick Stewart, Dir.-Legal & Bus. Affairs
Phil Townsend, Dir.-Comm.
Steve Deaville, Dir.-Finance
Malcolm Glazer, Owner
Alex Ferguson, Team Mgr.
John Alexander, Club Sec.
Sameer Pabari, Dir.-Media
Richard Arnold, Group Managing Dir.

FINANCIAL DATA: Note: Data for latest year may not have been available at press time.

In U.S. $	2022	2021	2020	2019	2018	2017
Revenue	710,787,400	602,214,500	620,403,400	764,316,900	708,414,400	708,414,400
R&D Expense						
Operating Income	-103,079,800	-52,934,800	-12,421,690	54,641,070	82,723,950	82,723,950
Operating Margin %	- .15%	- .09%	- .02%	.07%	.12%	.12%
SGA Expense	490,753,200	408,050,000	372,749,500	436,494,800	360,295,000	360,295,000
Net Income	-140,780,000	-112,390,000	-28,315,660	23,011,580	47,786,720	47,786,720
Operating Cash Flow	117,454,000	137,822,100	-4,655,698	298,335,200	277,465,000	277,465,000
Capital Expenditure	150,808,000	176,026,800	294,781,200	233,896,400	246,432,700	246,432,700
EBITDA	50,756,860	165,198,000	174,108,500	231,747,700	260,739,800	260,739,800
Return on Assets %	- .09%	- .07%	- .02%	.01%	.03%	.03%
Return on Equity %	- .58%	- .30%	- .06%	.04%	.08%	.08%
Debt to Equity	4.18%	1.72%	1.49	1.218	1.037	1.037

CONTACT INFORMATION:

Phone: 44 1618688000   Fax:
Toll-Free:
Address: Sir Matt Busby Way, Old Trafford, Manchester, M16 0RA United Kingdom

STOCK TICKER/OTHER:

Stock Ticker: MANU
Employees: 1,035
Parent Company:

Exchange: NYS
Fiscal Year Ends: 06/30

SALARIES/BONUSES:

Top Exec. Salary: $ Bonus: $
Second Exec. Salary: $ Bonus: $

OTHER THOUGHTS:

Estimated Female Officers or Directors:
Hot Spot for Advancement for Women/Minorities:

Sales, profits and employees may be estimates. Financial information, benefits and other data can change quickly and may vary from those stated here.

Maple Leaf Sports & Entertainment Ltd

www.mlse.com

NAIC Code: 711310

TYPES OF BUSINESS:
Sports Stadium Operator
Sports Team Ownership
Sport Venue Ownership and Management
Professional Sports

BRANDS/DIVISIONS/AFFILIATES:
Toronto Maple Leafs
Toronto Raptors
Toronto Football Club
Toronto Argonauts
Toronto Marlies
Raptors 905
Toronto FC II
Scotiabank Arena

CONTACTS: *Note: Officers with more than one job title may be intentionally listed here more than once.*
Cynthia Devine, Interim CEO
Nick Eaves, COO
Tom Anselmi, Pres.
Sabina Rizvi, CFO
Shannon Hosford, CMO
Teri Dennis-Davies, Chief People Officer
Humza Teherany, CTO
Robert Hunter, Exec. VP-Venues & Entertainment
Peter Miller, General Counsel
Ian Clarke, Exec. VP-Bus. Dev.
Chris Hebb, Sr. VP-Content & Comm.
Kevin Nonomura, Sr. VP-Finance
Bryan Colangelo, Pres., Toronto Raptors
David Nonis, Gen. Mgr.-Toronto Maple Leafs
Kevin Payne, Gen. Mgr.-Toronto FC
Beth Robertson, Sr. VP-Ticket Sales & Svcs.
Lawrence M. (Larry) Tanenbaum, Chmn.

GROWTH PLANS/SPECIAL FEATURES:
Maple Leaf Sports & Entertainment Ltd. (MLSE) is a Canadian sports and entertainment firm. MLSE owns the National Hockey League's Toronto Maple Leafs, the National Basketball Association's Toronto Raptors, Major League Soccer's Toronto FC, the Canadian Football League's Toronto Argonauts and development teams with the Toronto Marlies (American Hockey League), Raptors 905 (NBA G League) and Toronto FC II (United Soccer League). MLSE owns or operates all of the venues its teams play and train in, including Scotiabank Arena, BMO Field, Coca-Cola Coliseum, Ford Performance Centre, BMO Training Ground and the OVO Athletic Centre. These assets cause MLSE to rank among the largest sports and entertainment companies in Canada, as well as one of the largest in North America. MLSE was founded by Conn Smythe in 1931 as Maple Leaf Gardens Limited (MLGL), to act as a holding company for the Toronto Maple Leafs and their planned new arena Maple Leaf Gardens. Smythe transferred his ownership of the Leafs to the company in exchange for shares in MLGL. From that point the company began to extend its ownership and operations.

FINANCIAL DATA: *Note: Data for latest year may not have been available at press time.*

In U.S. $	2022	2021	2020	2019	2018	2017
Revenue						
R&D Expense						
Operating Income						
Operating Margin %						
SGA Expense						
Net Income						
Operating Cash Flow						
Capital Expenditure						
EBITDA						
Return on Assets %						
Return on Equity %						
Debt to Equity						

CONTACT INFORMATION:
Phone: 416-815-5400   Fax: 416-815-6050
Toll-Free:
Address: 50 Bay St., Ste. 500, Toronto, ON M5J 2L2 Canada

STOCK TICKER/OTHER:
Stock Ticker: Private   Exchange:
Employees: 1,700   Fiscal Year Ends:
Parent Company:

SALARIES/BONUSES:
Top Exec. Salary: $ Bonus: $
Second Exec. Salary: $ Bonus: $

OTHER THOUGHTS:
Estimated Female Officers or Directors: 4
Hot Spot for Advancement for Women/Minorities: Y

Marine Products Corporation   www.marineproductscorp.com

NAIC Code: 336612

TYPES OF BUSINESS:
Boat Building

GROWTH PLANS/SPECIAL FEATURES:
Marine Products Corp is a manufacturer of fiberglass motorized boats distributed and marketed through its independent dealer network. It operates in the Powerboat Manufacturing business segment through Nashville, Georgia, Valdosta, and Georgia. Its product offerings include Chaparral sterndrive, outboard, and jet pleasure boats and Robalo outboard sport fishing boats. The company offers its products to the family recreational and cruiser markets through its Chaparral brand and to the sportfishing market through its Robalo brand.

BRANDS/DIVISIONS/AFFILIATES:
Chaparral Boats Inc
Robalo Acquisition Company LLC
Chaparral
Robalo
SSi
SSX
Sunesta
Signature

CONTACTS: Note: Officers with more than one job title may be intentionally listed here more than once.
Richard Hubbell, CEO
Ben Palmer, CFO
Gary Rollins, Chairman of the Board

FINANCIAL DATA: Note: Data for latest year may not have been available at press time.

In U.S. $	2022	2021	2020	2019	2018	2017
Revenue	380,995,000	298,014,000	239,825,000	292,136,000	267,316,000	267,316,000
R&D Expense						
Operating Income	51,796,000	36,392,000	24,361,000	34,135,000	29,759,000	29,759,000
Operating Margin %	.14%	.12%	.10%	.12%	.11%	.11%
SGA Expense	41,921,000	31,880,000	29,244,000	31,259,000	29,261,000	29,261,000
Net Income	40,347,000	29,026,000	19,444,000	28,239,000	19,300,000	19,300,000
Operating Cash Flow	49,348,000	457,000	29,874,000	33,917,000	29,639,000	29,639,000
Capital Expenditure	2,500,000	1,248,000	2,099,000	2,334,000	2,410,000	2,410,000
EBITDA	53,701,000	38,208,000	26,315,000	36,225,000	31,285,000	31,285,000
Return on Assets %	.27%	.23%	.17%	.27%	.20%	.20%
Return on Equity %	.35%	.31%	.24%	.36%	.28%	.28%
Debt to Equity						

CONTACT INFORMATION:
Phone: 404 321-7910   Fax: 404 321-5483
Toll-Free:
Address: 2801 Buford Highway NE, Ste. 520, Atlanta, GA 30329 United States

STOCK TICKER/OTHER:
Stock Ticker: MPX
Employees: 935
Parent Company:

Exchange: NYS
Fiscal Year Ends: 12/31

SALARIES/BONUSES:
Top Exec. Salary: $431,058   Bonus: $
Second Exec. Salary: $394,711   Bonus: $

OTHER THOUGHTS:
Estimated Female Officers or Directors:
Hot Spot for Advancement for Women/Minorities:

MarineMax Inc

www.marinemax.com

NAIC Code: 441222

TYPES OF BUSINESS:

Recreational Boats, Retail
Boat Parts & Accessories
Boat Repair & Maintenance
Boat Financing & Insurance
Slip & Storage Accommodations
Yacht Charter Services

BRANDS/DIVISIONS/AFFILIATES:

MarineMax Vacations
Fraser Yachts Group
Cruisers Yachts
Intrepid

GROWTH PLANS/SPECIAL FEATURES:

MarineMax Inc is a United-States-based company that sells new and used recreational boats under premium brands, and related marine products, like engines, parts, and accessories. The company is also engaged in other businesses, including providing services of repair, maintenance and storage; managing related boat financing, insurance, and others; offering brokerage sales of boats and yachts; and operating a yacht charter business. The sale of new and used boats account for the majority of the company's total revenue. It serves customers across the U.S.

CONTACTS: Note: Officers with more than one job title may be intentionally listed here more than once.

William McGill, CEO
Michael Mclamb, CFO
William Mcgill, Chairman of the Board
Anthony Cassella, Chief Accounting Officer
Charles Cashman, Executive VP

FINANCIAL DATA: Note: Data for latest year may not have been available at press time.

In U.S. $	2022	2021	2020	2019	2018	2017
Revenue	2,308,098,000	2,063,257,000	1,509,713,000	1,237,153,000	1,052,320,000	1,052,320,000
R&D Expense						
Operating Income	265,204,000	209,459,000	106,715,000	60,532,000	45,289,000	45,289,000
Operating Margin %	.11%	.10%	.07%	.05%	.04%	.04%
SGA Expense	540,550,000	449,974,000	291,998,000	262,300,000	220,026,000	220,026,000
Net Income	197,989,000	154,979,000	74,634,000	35,985,000	23,547,000	23,547,000
Operating Cash Flow	76,595,000	373,881,000	304,675,000	-12,426,000	4,745,000	4,745,000
Capital Expenditure	58,456,000	26,125,000	12,807,000	17,061,000	14,367,000	14,367,000
EBITDA	284,622,000	225,065,000	119,487,000	72,129,000	54,653,000	54,653,000
Return on Assets %	.17%	.17%	.10%	.05%	.04%	.04%
Return on Equity %	.29%	.30%	.18%	.10%	.08%	.08%
Debt to Equity	.17%	.24%	0.09			

CONTACT INFORMATION:

Phone: 727 531-1700   Fax: 727 524-3954
Toll-Free:
Address: 2600 McCormick Dr., Ste. 200, Clearwater, FL 33759 United States

STOCK TICKER/OTHER:

Stock Ticker: HZO   Exchange: NYS
Employees: 3,410   Fiscal Year Ends: 09/30
Parent Company:

SALARIES/BONUSES:

Top Exec. Salary: $815,000   Bonus: $
Second Exec. Salary: $630,000   Bonus: $

OTHER THOUGHTS:

Estimated Female Officers or Directors: 1
Hot Spot for Advancement for Women/Minorities:

Memphis Grizzlies

www.nba.com/grizzlies

NAIC Code: 711211B

TYPES OF BUSINESS:

Professional Basketball Team
Team Management and Operations

BRANDS/DIVISIONS/AFFILIATES:

Memphis Basketball LLC
FedExForum
Grizzlies Read to Achieve Program
Stay in School Challenge
Grizzlies Hoops Camp Series

GROWTH PLANS/SPECIAL FEATURES:

The Memphis Grizzlies is a professional basketball franchise playing in the National Basketball Association (NBA). The team was established in 1995 as one of two Canadian expansion teams. Originally based in Vancouver, the organization relocated to Memphis, Tennessee in 2001. The Grizzlies is owned and operated by Memphis Basketball, LLC, and currently plays home games in the FedExForum, an 18,119-basketball-seat facility located in downtown Memphis. The team's home attendance average was 17,264 for the 2022-23 season. While the Grizzlies have yet to achieve any championship success, they have shown steady improvement and clenched division titles in 2022 and 2023. The team's community programs include the Grizzlies' Read to Achieve Program, the Stay in School Challenge and the Grizzlies Hoops Camp Series. The Grizzlies' main sponsor is FedEx. Forbes estimated the team to be worth $1.65 billion in October 2022.

CONTACTS:

Note: Officers with more than one job title may be intentionally listed here more than once.

Joe Abadi, Exec. Dir.
Jason Wexler, Pres.-Bus. Oper.
Nancy Alyea, VP-Finance
Rolanda Gregory, VP-Mktg.
Arnetria Knowles, VP-Human Resources
Darrell DeRosia, Sr. Dir.-IT
John Pugliese, VP-Mktg. Comm. & Broadcast
Michael Behrman, VP-Finance
Chris Wallace, Gen. Mgr.
Lionel Hollins, Head Coach
Chad Bolen, VP-Corp. Partnership
Robert J. Pera, Owner
Roberet J. Pera, Chmn.

FINANCIAL DATA: *Note: Data for latest year may not have been available at press time.*

In U.S. $	2022	2021	2020	2019	2018	2017
Revenue	257,400,000					
R&D Expense						
Operating Income						
Operating Margin %						
SGA Expense						
Net Income						
Operating Cash Flow						
Capital Expenditure						
EBITDA						
Return on Assets %						
Return on Equity %						
Debt to Equity						

CONTACT INFORMATION:

Phone: 901-888-4667   Fax: 901-205-1235
Toll-Free:
Address: 191 Beale St., Memphis, TN 38103 United States

STOCK TICKER/OTHER:

Stock Ticker: Private   Exchange:
Employees: 280   Fiscal Year Ends:
Parent Company:

SALARIES/BONUSES:

Top Exec. Salary: $ Bonus: $
Second Exec. Salary: $ Bonus: $

OTHER THOUGHTS:

Estimated Female Officers or Directors:
Hot Spot for Advancement for Women/Minorities: Y

Miami Dolphins

NAIC Code: 711211C

www.miamidolphins.com

TYPES OF BUSINESS:

Professional Football Team
Team Management and Operations

BRANDS/DIVISIONS/AFFILIATES:

CONTACTS: *Note: Officers with more than one job title may be intentionally listed here more than once.*

Tom Garfinkel, CEO
Chris Grier, Gen. Mngr.
Chris Clements, CFO
Ben Roller, VP-Mktg. & Analytics
Jeremy Campos, Sr. Dir.-Human Resources
Kim Rometo, CIO
Mark Brockelman, Chief Admin. Officer
Dawn Aponte, Sr. VP-Football Oper.
Scott Stone, Sr. Dir.-Digital & Print Media
Harvey Greene, Sr. VP-Media Rel.
Betsy Christy, Sr. Dir.-Finance
Joe Philbin, Head Coach
Jeff Ireland, Gen. Mgr.
Jim Rushton, Chief Revenue Officer
Brett Annis, Dir.-Ticket Oper. & Acct.
Stephen M. Ross, Chmn.

GROWTH PLANS/SPECIAL FEATURES:

The Miami Dolphins is a professional football team in the National Football League (NFL), playing in the Eastern Division of the American Football Conference (AFC). The Dolphins began play as a 1966 expansion team in the AFL and joined the NFL as part of the league merger. In 1972, the Dolphins completed a perfect season, winning every regular season game, all its playoff appearances and Super Bowl VII. It is the only NFL team to have ever been undefeated throughout an entire season and post-season. The Dolphins won Super Bowl VIII the next year, making it the first NFL team to appear in three consecutive Super Bowls (1971-73). Throughout these years, the team was coached by Don Shula, the head coach with the most wins in NFL history, and led by quarterback Bob Griese. During the 1980s and 1990s, the Dolphins continued their winning ways led by quarterback Dan Marino. He led the team to multiple playoff appearances and Super Bowl XIX, which it lost to the San Francisco 49ers. In total, the Dolphins have made it to the playoffs 24 times, most recently in 2022. Real estate developer Stephen M. Ross holds an approximate 95% ownership stake in the team and its stadium. The team plays in the Hard Rock Stadium, with a seating capacity of nearly 65,000. The Dolphins averaged 66,230 fans in attendance per home game for the 2022-23 season. Forbes estimated the value of the Dolphins franchise at $4.6 billion in 2022.

FINANCIAL DATA: *Note: Data for latest year may not have been available at press time.*

In U.S. $	2022	2021	2020	2019	2018	2017
Revenue	541,450,000					
R&D Expense						
Operating Income						
Operating Margin %						
SGA Expense						
Net Income						
Operating Cash Flow						
Capital Expenditure						
EBITDA						
Return on Assets %						
Return on Equity %						
Debt to Equity						

CONTACT INFORMATION:

Phone: 954-452-7000   Fax: 954-452-7027
Toll-Free:
Address: 347 Don Shula Dr., Miami Gardens, FL 33056 United States

STOCK TICKER/OTHER:

Stock Ticker: Private   Exchange:
Employees: 335   Fiscal Year Ends: 12/31
Parent Company:

SALARIES/BONUSES:

Top Exec. Salary: $ Bonus: $
Second Exec. Salary: $ Bonus: $

OTHER THOUGHTS:

Estimated Female Officers or Directors: 8
Hot Spot for Advancement for Women/Minorities: Y

Miami HEAT

www.nba.com/heat

NAIC Code: 711211B

TYPES OF BUSINESS:

Professional Basketball Team
Team Management and Operations

BRANDS/DIVISIONS/AFFILIATES:

HEAT Academy
Miami Heat Learn & Play Center
HEAT Youth Basketball League

CONTACTS: *Note: Officers with more than one job title may be intentionally listed here more than once.*

Nick Arison, CEO
Pat Riley, Pres.
Raquel Libman, General Counsel
Eric Woolworth, Pres., Bus. Oper.
Tim Donovan, VP-Sports Media Rel.
Jeff Morris, VP-Finance
Micky Arison, Managing Gen. Partner
Kim Stone, Exec. VP
Mike Walker, Exec. VP-Heat Group Enterprises
Erik Spoelstra, Head Coach
Micky Arison, Managing Gen. Partner

GROWTH PLANS/SPECIAL FEATURES:

The Miami HEAT is a professional basketball franchise owned by Carnival Chairman Micky Arison. The team entered the NBA in 1988. Although the ball club struggled in its initial seasons, it has missed the playoffs only a few times since 1991 and won its first NBA championship in 2005-06. In total, Miami HEAT has clenched three NBA Championships, the latest in 2013; seven Conference titles, the latest in 2023; and 16 division titles, most recently in 2022 and 2023. The Miami HEAT faced the Denver Nuggets in the 2023 NBA playoffs, but ended up losing 1-4. Notable players that have been on the team include Tim Hardaway, Shaquille O'Neal, Dwayne Wade and Alonzo Mourning. Additionally, LeBron James joined the team from 2010-2014, before returning to the Cleveland Cavaliers. The HEAT's home stadium is the Kaseya Center, with a seating capacity of 19,600 and more than 20,000 for other events. Home game attendance averaged 19,687 per game for the HEAT in its 2022-23 season. The HEAT supports community outreach programs and provides educational services such as HEAT Academy, Miami Heat Learn & Play Center, and the HEAT Youth Basketball League. Forbes estimated the team to be worth $3 billion in October 2022.

FINANCIAL DATA: *Note: Data for latest year may not have been available at press time.*

In U.S. $	2022	2021	2020	2019	2018	2017
Revenue	314,600,000					
R&D Expense						
Operating Income						
Operating Margin %						
SGA Expense						
Net Income						
Operating Cash Flow						
Capital Expenditure						
EBITDA						
Return on Assets %						
Return on Equity %						
Debt to Equity						

CONTACT INFORMATION:

Phone: 786-777-1000   Fax: 786-777-1615
Toll-Free:
Address: 601 Biscayne Blvd., Miami, FL 33132 United States

STOCK TICKER/OTHER:

Stock Ticker: Private   Exchange:
Employees: 550   Fiscal Year Ends: 06/30
Parent Company:

SALARIES/BONUSES:

Top Exec. Salary: $ Bonus: $
Second Exec. Salary: $ Bonus: $

OTHER THOUGHTS:

Estimated Female Officers or Directors: 9
Hot Spot for Advancement for Women/Minorities: Y

Sales, profits and employees may be estimates. Financial information, benefits and other data can change quickly and may vary from those stated here.

Miami Marlins

NAIC Code: 711211A

www.mlb.com/marlins

TYPES OF BUSINESS:

Professional Baseball Team
Team Management and Operations

BRANDS/DIVISIONS/AFFILIATES:

Florida Marlins
Jacksonville Jumbo Shrimp
Pensacola Blue Wahoos
Beloit Sky Carp
Jupiter Hammerheads

CONTACTS: *Note: Officers with more than one job title may be intentionally listed here more than once.*

Kim Ng, Gen. Mngr.
Caroline O'Connor, COO
Derek Jackson, General Counsel
Larry Beinfest, Pres., Baseball Oper.
Brendan Cunningham, Sr. VP-Corp. Partnerships
Alexander Buznego, Mgr.-Digital & Social Media
P. J. Loyello, Sr. VP-Comm. & Broadcasting
Susan Jaison, Sr. VP-Finance
Claude Delorme, Exec. VP-Oper. & Events
Michael Hill, VP
Matt Roebuck, Dir.-Media Rel.
Angela Smith, Dir.-Community Outreach
Bruce Sherman, Chmn.
Albert Gonzalez, Dir.-Int'l Oper.

GROWTH PLANS/SPECIAL FEATURES:

The Miami Marlins, previously the Florida Marlins, joined Major League Baseball (MLB) as an expansion team in 1993. Though winning two World Series championships (in 1997 and 2003), the club has struggled to maintain consistent success as well as attracting a wide fan base. Following both of its World Series victories, the front office drastically reconfigured the team, either trading away its marquee players (known as a fire sale) or allowing them to leave via free agency. These moves have widely served to alienate a fan base already more committed to other sports. The Marlins play in the LoanDepot Park, a retractable roof stadium in Miami with a seating capacity of 37,442 (including standing room). The team averaged 11,203 in home game attendance during the 2022 season. In 2020, the team earned a wild card berth, its third since inception. Minor league affiliations include the Jacksonville Jumbo Shrimp, Pensacola Blue Wahoos, Beloit Sky Carp and Jupiter Hammerheads. In March 2023, Forbes estimated the team to be worth $1 billion, 30th in the league.

FINANCIAL DATA: *Note: Data for latest year may not have been available at press time.*

In U.S. $	2022	2021	2020	2019	2018	2017
Revenue	300,300,000					
R&D Expense						
Operating Income						
Operating Margin %						
SGA Expense						
Net Income						
Operating Cash Flow						
Capital Expenditure						
EBITDA						
Return on Assets %						
Return on Equity %						
Debt to Equity						

CONTACT INFORMATION:

Phone: 305-480-1300   Fax:
Toll-Free:
Address: 501 Marlins Way, Miami, FL 33125 United States

STOCK TICKER/OTHER:

Stock Ticker: Private   Exchange:
Employees: 390   Fiscal Year Ends: 10/31
Parent Company:

SALARIES/BONUSES:

Top Exec. Salary: $ Bonus: $
Second Exec. Salary: $ Bonus: $

OTHER THOUGHTS:

Estimated Female Officers or Directors: 6
Hot Spot for Advancement for Women/Minorities: Y

Middlesbrough Football Club

www.mfc.co.uk

NAIC Code: 711211D

TYPES OF BUSINESS:

Soccer Team
Team Management and Operations

BRANDS/DIVISIONS/AFFILIATES:

Middlesbrough Cricket Club

CONTACTS: *Note: Officers with more than one job title may be intentionally listed here more than once.*

Michael Carrick, Head Coach
Karen Nelson, Head-Admin.
David Allan, Mgr.-Media & Comm.
Ron Bone, Head-Academy Recruitment
David Parnaby, Mgr.-Academy
Wendy Thomas, Head-Academy Oper.
Steve Gibson, Chmn.

GROWTH PLANS/SPECIAL FEATURES:

Middlesbrough Football Club was founded by members of the Middlesbrough Cricket Club in 1876 and is now owned by Steve Gibson and plays in the EFL Championship league, the second tier of English football. Throughout the 1970s and 1980s, the soccer club was promoted and relegated up and down the English Football League System's three divisions. It was an inaugural team in the English Premiership League, the most lucrative and prestigious football league in England. Middlesbrough FC hit bottom in 1986 when it was both relegated to the Third Division and facing bankruptcy. That year, Steve Gibson, founder and chairman of Bulkhaul Limited, purchased the team. Throughout the mid-1990s and into the 2000s, the team's star has been rising. In 1994, under player-manager Bryan Robson, Middlesbrough FC solidified its place in the Premiership League; it also signed star players Nick Barmby and Juninho. The team won the Football League First Division in the 1994-95 season and won the League Cup in the 2003-04 season. In 2005-06, the Middlesbrough FC was a finalist in the UEFA Cup. The club plays at Riverside Stadium in Middlesbrough, which seats approximately 34,000 spectators. Middlesbrough FC's kit manufacturer is Errea, and its shirt sponsor is Unibet. The team's average attendance was 26,234 per home game during the 2022-23 season.

FINANCIAL DATA: *Note: Data for latest year may not have been available at press time.*

In U.S. $	2022	2021	2020	2019	2018	2017
Revenue	30,000,000	20,034,108	23,896,636	81,188,300	156,921,000	156,921,000
R&D Expense						
Operating Income						
Operating Margin %						
SGA Expense						
Net Income		-37,758,186	-37,550,977	2,623,210	14,895,800	14,895,800
Operating Cash Flow						
Capital Expenditure						
EBITDA						
Return on Assets %						
Return on Equity %						
Debt to Equity						

CONTACT INFORMATION:

Phone: 44-1642-757-656   Fax: 44-1642-757-697
Toll-Free:
Address: The Riverside Stadium, Middlesbrough, TS3 6RS United Kingdom

STOCK TICKER/OTHER:

Stock Ticker: Private
Employees: 214
Parent Company:

Exchange:
Fiscal Year Ends: 06/30

SALARIES/BONUSES:

Top Exec. Salary: $ Bonus: $
Second Exec. Salary: $ Bonus: $

OTHER THOUGHTS:

Estimated Female Officers or Directors: 3
Hot Spot for Advancement for Women/Minorities: Y

Milwaukee Brewers

www.mlb.com/brewers

NAIC Code: 711211A

TYPES OF BUSINESS:

Professional Baseball Team
Team Management and Operations

BRANDS/DIVISIONS/AFFILIATES:

CONTACTS: *Note: Officers with more than one job title may be intentionally listed here more than once.*

Rick Schlesinger, Pres.-Bus. Oper.
David Stearns, Pres.-Baseball Oper.
Daniel Fumai, CFO
Sharon McNally, VP-Mktg.
Cas Castro, VP-Human Resources
Karl Mueller, Dir.-Baseball Research & Video Scouting
Derek Hyde, VP-IT
Jill Aronoff, Sr. Dir.-Merch. Branding
Bob Quinn, Exec. VP-Admin.
Marti Wronski, General Counsel
Teddy Werner, Sr. Dir.-Bus. Oper.
Tyler Barnes, VP-Comm.
Bob Quinn, Exec. VP-Finance
Tom Flanagan, Sr. Dir.-Baseball Oper.
Regis Bane, Sr. Dir.-Ticket Oper.
Tom Hecht, VP-Corp. Mktg.
Aleta Mercer, VP-Entertainment & Broadcasting
Mark Attanasio, Chmn.
Eduardo Brizuela, Dir.-Latin American Oper. & Scouting

GROWTH PLANS/SPECIAL FEATURES:

The Milwaukee Brewers is a franchise within Major League Baseball (MLB) that plays in the Central Division of the National League. The third professional baseball team to play in Milwaukee and the second to carry the Brewers name, the current incarnation originated in 1970 when the Seattle Pilots, an expansion franchise started in 1969, moved to Milwaukee. The team's most successful years were 1981 and 1982, with a lineup that featured such notable players as Robin Yount, Rollie Fingers and Paul Molitor, making the playoffs both years only to fall one game short of winning the World Series in 1982. In the years following, the Brewers were mostly a mediocre team, with relatively strong showings in 1987, 1988 and 1992. In 1994, when MLB adopted an expanded playoff system, the team transferred from the American League to the National League. In the NL central division, the Brewers have clenched three division titles, 2011, 2018 and 2021. The Brewers play their home games and the American Family Field, which features a retractable roof and seating for about 42,000 spectators. Average attendance for home games was 30,155 during the 2022 season. In late 2004, the team was sold to Los Angeles investment banker Mark Attanasio, ending over three decades of ownership by current MLB commissioner Bud Selig and his family. Forbes estimated the club's value at $1.605 billion in March 2023.

FINANCIAL DATA: *Note: Data for latest year may not have been available at press time.*

In U.S. $	2022	2021	2020	2019	2018	2017
Revenue	366,600,000					
R&D Expense						
Operating Income						
Operating Margin %						
SGA Expense						
Net Income						
Operating Cash Flow						
Capital Expenditure						
EBITDA						
Return on Assets %						
Return on Equity %						
Debt to Equity						

CONTACT INFORMATION:

Phone: 414-902-4400   Fax: 414-902-4053
Toll-Free:
Address: 1 Brewers Way, Milwaukee, WI 53214 United States

STOCK TICKER/OTHER:

Stock Ticker: Private   Exchange:
Employees: 615   Fiscal Year Ends: 10/31
Parent Company:

SALARIES/BONUSES:

Top Exec. Salary: $ Bonus: $
Second Exec. Salary: $ Bonus: $

OTHER THOUGHTS:

Estimated Female Officers or Directors: 8
Hot Spot for Advancement for Women/Minorities: Y

Milwaukee Bucks

www.nba.com/bucks

NAIC Code: 711211B

TYPES OF BUSINESS:

Professional Basketball Team
Team Management and Operations

BRANDS/DIVISIONS/AFFILIATES:

CONTACTS: *Note: Officers with more than one job title may be intentionally listed here more than once.*

Jon Horst, General Mngr.
Mike McCarthy, COO
Patrick McDonough, CFO
Ron Walter, Exec. VP-Bus. Admin.
John Steinmiller, VP-Bus. Oper.
Michael Grahl, Mgr.-Interactive Mktg.
Dan Smyczek, VP-Public Rel.
Jim Woloszyk, Dir.-Finance
John Hammond, Gen. Mgr.
Theodore Loehrke, Chief Revenue Officer
Larry Drew, Head Coach
Dave Babcock, Dir.-Player Personnel

GROWTH PLANS/SPECIAL FEATURES:

The Milwaukee Bucks is a professional basketball franchise playing in the National Basketball Association (NBA). The team was established in the NBA in 1968 when the franchise was awarded to a group of Milwaukee investors named Milwaukee Professional Sports and Services. By 1971, the team won its first championship under the leadership of the legendary Kareem Abdul-Jabbar (then known as Lew Alcindor). Other notable players in the Bucks include Oscar Robertson in the late 1970s and Sidney Moncrief, who played throughout the 1980s. The Milwaukee Bucks clenched their second NBA championship in 2021, defeating the HEAT in a four-game playoff sweep, then defeating the Nets in seven games in the conference semifinals, and defeating the Phoenix Suns in the finals. In all, the Bucks have three conference titles and 18 division titles (most recently from 2019-2023). Wisconsin senator Herb Kohl, whose family founded Kohl's department stores, sold the Bucks to hedge fund managers Marc Lasry of Avenue Capital and Wes Edens of Fortress Investment Group in May 2014. That October 2014, York Capital Milwaukee founder and investor Jamie Dinan, joined hedge Lasry and Edens as a substantial owner of the team. The Bucks play in the Fiserv Forum, a multi-purpose arena in downtown Milwaukee with a seating capacity of 17,341, with home game attendance averaging 17,531 for the 2022-23 season. The Bucks' main sponsor is Motorola. Forbes estimated the team to be worth $2.3 billion in October 2022.

FINANCIAL DATA: *Note: Data for latest year may not have been available at press time.*

In U.S. $	2022	2021	2020	2019	2018	2017
Revenue	293,150,000					
R&D Expense						
Operating Income						
Operating Margin %						
SGA Expense						
Net Income						
Operating Cash Flow						
Capital Expenditure						
EBITDA						
Return on Assets %						
Return on Equity %						
Debt to Equity						

CONTACT INFORMATION:

Phone: 414-227-0500   Fax: 414-227-0543
Toll-Free:
Address: 1542 N. 2nd St., Fl. 6, Milwaukee, WI 53212 United States

STOCK TICKER/OTHER:

Stock Ticker: Private   Exchange:
Employees: 510   Fiscal Year Ends: 06/30
Parent Company:

SALARIES/BONUSES:

Top Exec. Salary: $ Bonus: $
Second Exec. Salary: $ Bonus: $

OTHER THOUGHTS:

Estimated Female Officers or Directors: 4
Hot Spot for Advancement for Women/Minorities: Y

Minnesota Lynx

www.wnba.com/lynx

NAIC Code: 711211E

TYPES OF BUSINESS:

Women's Basketball Team
Team Management and Operations

BRANDS/DIVISIONS/AFFILIATES:

Minnesota Timberwolves
Pack Gives Back

CONTACTS: *Note: Officers with more than one job title may be intentionally listed here more than once.*

Cheryl Reeve, Pres.-Basketball Oper.
Clare Duwelius, Gen. Mngr.
Carley Knox, Mgr.-Bus. Oper.
Alex King, Coordinator-Public Rel.
Glen Taylor, Owner
Cheryl Reeve, Head Coach
Roger Griffith, Exec. VP
Erin Henning, Sr. Accounts Exec.
Glen Taylor, Owner

GROWTH PLANS/SPECIAL FEATURES:

The Minnesota Lynx is a Women's National Basketball Association (WNBA) team that came into existence in 1999, two years after the WNBA's inception. The team plays in the Western Conference of the WNBA, along with the Dallas Wings, Los Angeles Sparks, Las Vegas Aces, Phoenix Mercury and Seattle Storm. The Lynx are owned by Glen Taylor, a businessman and former state senator who also has a majority ownership in the Minnesota Timberwolves (NBA). The team plays its games at the Target Center in downtown Minneapolis, which has the capacity to seat approximately 18,800 basketball spectators. Home game attendance averaged 7,444 in the 2022 season for the Lynx. The team holds six Western Conference titles in 2011, 2012, 2013, 2015, 2016 and 2017. In 2011, the Minnesota Lynx won its first WNBA Championship by defeating the Atlanta Dream. To date, the team has won a total of four WNBA Championships (2011, 2013, 2015 and 2017). Pack Gives Back is a community platform in which the Minnesota Lynx are involved, supporting communities year-round through NBA, WNBA, NBA2K League and G-League teams.

FINANCIAL DATA: *Note: Data for latest year may not have been available at press time.*

In U.S. $	2022	2021	2020	2019	2018	2017
Revenue						
R&D Expense						
Operating Income						
Operating Margin %						
SGA Expense						
Net Income						
Operating Cash Flow						
Capital Expenditure						
EBITDA						
Return on Assets %						
Return on Equity %						
Debt to Equity						

CONTACT INFORMATION:

Phone: 612-673-8400   Fax:
Toll-Free:
Address: 600 1st Ave. N., Minneapolis, MN 55403 United States

STOCK TICKER/OTHER:

Stock Ticker: Private   Exchange:
Employees: 46   Fiscal Year Ends:
Parent Company:

SALARIES/BONUSES:

Top Exec. Salary: $ Bonus: $
Second Exec. Salary: $ Bonus: $

OTHER THOUGHTS:

Estimated Female Officers or Directors: 8
Hot Spot for Advancement for Women/Minorities: Y

Minnesota Timberwolves

www.nba.com/timberwolves

NAIC Code: 711211B

TYPES OF BUSINESS:

Professional Basketball Team
Team Management and Operations

BRANDS/DIVISIONS/AFFILIATES:

Minnesota Lynx
Iowa Wolves

CONTACTS: *Note: Officers with more than one job title may be intentionally listed here more than once.*

Ethan Casson, CEO
Ryan Tanke, COO
Pete Stene, CFO
Mike Grahl, CMO
Sianneh Mulbah, Chief People Officer
Brett Kahnke, Dir.-Analytics & Research
Ted Johnson, Chief Strategy Officer
Greg Jackson, General Counsel
Rob Babcock, Dir.-Basketball Oper.
Glen A. Taylor, Owner
Rick Adelman, Head Coach
Glen Taylor, Owner

GROWTH PLANS/SPECIAL FEATURES:

The Minnesota Timberwolves, founded in 1988, is a team playing in the National Basketball Association (NBA). The franchise is majority-owned by Glen Taylor, a former Minnesota senator and chairman of the Taylor Corporation. The team plays in the Northwest Division of the NBA's Western Conference, alongside the Denver Nuggets, Portland Trail Blazers, Oklahoma City Thunder and Utah Jazz. Despite some regular season success beginning in the mid-90s, including eight straight playoff appearances from 1997-2004, the franchise has failed to win an NBA championship. Its lineup during these years featured league stars such as Kevin Garnett, Stephon Marbury and Sam Cassell. The team plays home games in the Target Center, a 20,050-seat arena in downtown Minneapolis that also serves the Timberwolves' WNBA sister team the Minnesota Lynx. Home game attendance averaged 16,768 during the 2022-23 season. The club's main sponsor is Aura. Iowa Wolves are affiliates of the Timberwolves, playing in the NBA G League and based in Des Moines. In October 2022, Forbes estimated the Timberwolves to be worth $1.67 billion.

FINANCIAL DATA: *Note: Data for latest year may not have been available at press time.*

In U.S. $	2022	2021	2020	2019	2018	2017
Revenue	268,450,000					
R&D Expense						
Operating Income						
Operating Margin %						
SGA Expense						
Net Income						
Operating Cash Flow						
Capital Expenditure						
EBITDA						
Return on Assets %						
Return on Equity %						
Debt to Equity						

CONTACT INFORMATION:

Phone: 612-673-1600   Fax: 612-673-1699
Toll-Free:
Address: 600 Hennepin Ave., Ste. 300, Minneapolis, MN 55403 United States

STOCK TICKER/OTHER:

Stock Ticker: Private   Exchange:
Employees: 300   Fiscal Year Ends:
Parent Company:

SALARIES/BONUSES:

Top Exec. Salary: $ Bonus: $
Second Exec. Salary: $ Bonus: $

OTHER THOUGHTS:

Estimated Female Officers or Directors:
Hot Spot for Advancement for Women/Minorities: Y

Sales, profits and employees may be estimates. Financial information, benefits and other data can change quickly and may vary from those stated here.

Minnesota Twins

NAIC Code: 711211A

www.mlb.com/twins

TYPES OF BUSINESS:

Professional Baseball Team
Team Management and Operations

BRANDS/DIVISIONS/AFFILIATES:

CONTACTS: *Note: Officers with more than one job title may be intentionally listed here more than once.*

Dave St. Peter, CEO
Matt Hoy, Sr. VP-Oper.
Kip Elliott, CFO
Heather Hinkel, VP-Brand Mktg.
Leticia Silva, Sr. VP-Human Resources
John Avenson, CTO
Kip Elliott, Exec. VP-Bus. Admin.
Matt Hoy, Sr. VP-Oper.
Laura Day, Exec. VP-Bus. Dev.
Kevin Smith, Sr. Dir.-Corp. Comm. & Broadcasting
Andy Weinstein, Sr. Dir.-Finance
Terry Ryan, Exec. VP
Mike Radcliff, VP-Player Personnel
Jeff Jurgella, Sr. Dir.-Corp. Partnerships
Mike Clough, Sr. Dir.-Ticket Sales & Service
Jim Pohlad, Chmn.
Bud Hanley, Sr. Dir.-Procurement

GROWTH PLANS/SPECIAL FEATURES:

The Minnesota Twins are a Major League Baseball (MLB) team based in Minneapolis, playing in the Central Division of the American League (AL). The club was originally established in 1901 as the Washington Senators, but declining fan attendance and poor performance caused the organization to be moved to Minneapolis in 1961. In 1924, 1987 and 1991 the Twins won World Series championships playing in the AL West Division, but went on to eight straight losing seasons from 1993-2000. Since 2002, the team has won the AL Central Division title eight times, including back-to-back wins in 2009 and 2010 as well as in 2019 and 2020. In all, the franchise has won three World Series, six pennants and 12 division titles. In 2002, the team was nearly disbanded, as MLB voted to contract two teams, including the Twins. However, the franchise avoided contraction as they were forced to play out their lease in the Hubert H. Humphrey Metrodome, which they shared with the Minnesota Vikings. In 2005, the Twins won a court decision that allowed them to escape their lease, and a stadium financing deal was approved in May 2006. The club played its first game in the newly constructed Target Field in 2010. The open-air park has a capacity of approximately 38,545, and average attendance for Twins' home games was 22,514 during the 2022 season. Several former Twins players have been inducted into the Baseball Hall of Fame, including Rod Carew, Jim Kaat, Harmon Killebrew, Tony Oliva and Kirby Puckett. In March 2023, Forbes valued the team at $1.39 billion.

FINANCIAL DATA: *Note: Data for latest year may not have been available at press time.*

In U.S. $	2022	2021	2020	2019	2018	2017
Revenue	367,250,000					
R&D Expense						
Operating Income						
Operating Margin %						
SGA Expense						
Net Income						
Operating Cash Flow						
Capital Expenditure						
EBITDA						
Return on Assets %						
Return on Equity %						
Debt to Equity						

CONTACT INFORMATION:

Phone: 612-659-3400   Fax:
Toll-Free:
Address: 1 Twins Way, Minneapolis, MN 55403 United States

STOCK TICKER/OTHER:

Stock Ticker: Private
Employees: 700
Parent Company:

Exchange:
Fiscal Year Ends: 12/31

SALARIES/BONUSES:

Top Exec. Salary: $ Bonus: $
Second Exec. Salary: $ Bonus: $

OTHER THOUGHTS:

Estimated Female Officers or Directors: 5
Hot Spot for Advancement for Women/Minorities: Y

Minnesota United FC

www.mnufc.com

NAIC Code: 711211D

TYPES OF BUSINESS:

Major League Soccer Team
Team Management and Operations

BRANDS/DIVISIONS/AFFILIATES:

Loons (The)
Minnesota United FC 2

CONTACTS: *Note: Officers with more than one job title may be intentionally listed here more than once.*

Shari Ballard, CEO
Maureen Smith, COO
Bryant Pfeiffer, Chief Revenue Officer
John Guagliano, CMO
Chelsea Radfor, Sr. Dir.-People Oper.
Alec Hill, Mngr.-IT
Bill McGuire, Managing Dir.

GROWTH PLANS/SPECIAL FEATURES:

The Minnesota United FC is a Major League Soccer (MLS) club located in the Minneapolis-Saint Paul area of Minnesota. The team is also known as The Loons (a nickname) and is owned by Bill McGuire. Minnesota United was founded in 2015, playing in the Western Conference of the MLS alongside the Austin FC, Colorado Rapids, FC Dallas, Houston Dynamo FC, LA Galaxy, Los Angeles FC, Portland Timbers, Real Salt Lake, San Jose Earthquakes, Seattle Sounders FC, Sporting Kansas City, St. Louis City SC and Vancouver Whitecaps FC. The team is the sixth MLS expansion team to join the league from a lower division, the North American Soccer League (NASL). As a NASL team, the Minnesota United FC played as the Minnesota Stars FC. The current team plays their homes games at the Allianz Field, a soccer-specific stadium in Saint Paul comprising 19,400 seats. Minnesota United averaged 19,555 in attendance per home game during the 2022 season. Minnesota United FC 2 was founded in 2021 as the reserve team of the Minnesota United FC, and also plays its games in the Allianz Field. FC 2 is one of 27 clubs that fields a team in the new MLS Next Pro league (third tier U.S. soccer league system) that began in the 2022 season.

FINANCIAL DATA: *Note: Data for latest year may not have been available at press time.*

In U.S. $	2022	2021	2020	2019	2018	2017
Revenue	7,711,200					
R&D Expense						
Operating Income						
Operating Margin %						
SGA Expense						
Net Income						
Operating Cash Flow						
Capital Expenditure						
EBITDA						
Return on Assets %						
Return on Equity %						
Debt to Equity						

CONTACT INFORMATION:

Phone: 763-476-2237   Fax: 763-331-8788
Toll-Free:
Address: 4150 Olson Memorial Hwy., Ste. 300, Golden Valley, MN 55422
United States

STOCK TICKER/OTHER:

Stock Ticker: Private   Exchange:
Employees: Fiscal Year Ends:
Parent Company:

SALARIES/BONUSES:

Top Exec. Salary: $ Bonus: $
Second Exec. Salary: $ Bonus: $

OTHER THOUGHTS:

Estimated Female Officers or Directors:
Hot Spot for Advancement for Women/Minorities:

Minnesota Vikings

NAIC Code: 711211C

TYPES OF BUSINESS:

Professional Football Team
Team Management and Operations

BRANDS/DIVISIONS/AFFILIATES:

Minnesota Sports Facilities Authority
Vikings Childrens Fund

CONTACTS: *Note: Officers with more than one job title may be intentionally listed here more than once.*

Leonark Wilf, Vice Chmn.
Mark Wilf, Pres.
Kate Shibilski, CFO
Martin Nance, CMO
Lara Juras, Chief People Officer
Andrew Miller, COO
Kevin Warren, Chief Admin. Officer
Kevin Warren, VP-Legal Affairs
Rob Brzezinski, VP-Football Oper.
Dannon Hulskotter, Dir.-Bus. Dev. & Mktg.
Lester Bagley, VP-Public Affairs & Stadium Dev.
Carl Miklas, Controller
Leonard Wilf, Vice Chmn.
Jonathan Wilf, VP-Strategic Planning & Bus. Initiatives
Zygi Wilf, Chmn.

GROWTH PLANS/SPECIAL FEATURES:

The Minnesota Vikings is a professional football team in the National Football League (NFL) based in Minneapolis, Minnesota. The team entered the NFL in 1961 and made it to the Super Bowl on four occasions, all unsuccessful. The Vikings transferred from the National Football Conference (NFC) Central division to the North division in the 2002 season and has remained in NFC North ever since. In all, the Vikings have clenched four conference championships (most recently in 1976) and 21 division championships (most recent in 2022), and have appeared in the playoffs 31 times (most recently in 2022). Well-known team members include Fran Tarkenton, Warren Moon and former head coach Bud Grant. The team is family-owned by businessmen Zygi, Leonard and Mark Wilf. The team plays its home games at the 66,860-football-capacity U.S. Bank Stadium, which features a retractable roof stadium and facilities such as retail shops, restaurants, residential housing and space for small business and corporate offices. U.S. Bank Stadium is owned by the Minnesota Sports Facilities Authority. Average home game attendance for the Vikings was 66,687 for the 2022-23 season. The Vikings hosts several community football programs for youth, high school and college-level participants. The Vikings Children's Fund (VCF) supports pediatric research and child-related wellness programs. Forbes estimated the team to be worth $3.925 billion in 2022.

FINANCIAL DATA: *Note: Data for latest year may not have been available at press time.*

In U.S. $	2022	2021	2020	2019	2018	2017
Revenue	528,450,000					
R&D Expense						
Operating Income						
Operating Margin %						
SGA Expense						
Net Income						
Operating Cash Flow						
Capital Expenditure						
EBITDA						
Return on Assets %						
Return on Equity %						
Debt to Equity						

CONTACT INFORMATION:

Phone: 952-828-6500   Fax: 952-828-6540
Toll-Free:
Address: 2600 Vikings Cir., Eagan, MN 55121 United States

STOCK TICKER/OTHER:

Stock Ticker: Private   Exchange:
Employees: 300   Fiscal Year Ends: 01/31
Parent Company:

SALARIES/BONUSES:

Top Exec. Salary: $ Bonus: $
Second Exec. Salary: $ Bonus: $

OTHER THOUGHTS:

Estimated Female Officers or Directors: 2
Hot Spot for Advancement for Women/Minorities: Y

Minnesota Wild

www.nhl.com/wild

NAIC Code: 711211F

TYPES OF BUSINESS:

Professional Hockey Team (NHL)
Team Management and Operations

BRANDS/DIVISIONS/AFFILIATES:

Minnesota North Stars
Iowa Wild
Iowa Heartlanders

CONTACTS: Note: Officers with more than one job title may be intentionally listed here more than once.

Bill Guerin, Gen. Mgr.
Matt Majka, Pres.
Jeff Pellegrom, CFO
Mitch Helgerson, Sr. VP-Mktg. & Broadcasting
JaAn Scofield-Meche, VP-People Strategy & Experience
Maria Troje, VP-Sales & Service
Craig Leipold, Governor

GROWTH PLANS/SPECIAL FEATURES:

The Minnesota Wild is a National Hockey League (NHL) team that entered the league as an expansion team in 2000 along with the Columbus Blue Jackets. Presently, the team plays in the Central division of the Western Conference along with the Arizona Coyotes, Chicago Blackhawks, Colorado Avalanche, Dallas Stars, Nashville Predators, St. Louis Blues and Winnipeg Jets. Wild is the spiritual successor to the Minnesota North Stars, which moved to Texas in 1993. The creation of the new team set NHL records for ticket sales by an expansion team. Minnesota Wild plays home games at the Xcel Energy Center, a multipurpose sports and entertainment facility owned by the city of Saint Paul. The arena's official hockey capacity is approximately 18,000, with the ability to increase to over 20,000. The team averaged 18,454 in home game attendance during the 2022-23 season. Wild has yet to clench a conference championship, but did win a division title in 2007-08. The team maintains affiliations with the Iowa Wild in the American Hockey League (AHL) and the Iowa Heartlanders in the ECHL. Forbes estimated Minnesota Wild's value at $850 million in December 2022.

FINANCIAL DATA: Note: Data for latest year may not have been available at press time.

In U.S. $	2022	2021	2020	2019	2018	2017
Revenue	124,800,000					
R&D Expense						
Operating Income						
Operating Margin %						
SGA Expense						
Net Income						
Operating Cash Flow						
Capital Expenditure						
EBITDA						
Return on Assets %						
Return on Equity %						
Debt to Equity						

CONTACT INFORMATION:

Phone: 651-602-6000   Fax: 651-222-1055
Toll-Free:
Address: 317 Washington St., St. Paul, MN 55102 United States

STOCK TICKER/OTHER:

Stock Ticker: Private   Exchange:
Employees: 300   Fiscal Year Ends: 06/30
Parent Company:

SALARIES/BONUSES:

Top Exec. Salary: $ Bonus: $
Second Exec. Salary: $ Bonus: $

OTHER THOUGHTS:

Estimated Female Officers or Directors: 2
Hot Spot for Advancement for Women/Minorities: Y

Minor League Baseball
NAIC Code: 711211

www.minorleaguebaseball.com

TYPES OF BUSINESS:
Minor League Baseball Association
Rookie Baseball League

BRANDS/DIVISIONS/AFFILIATES:
Minor League Baseball Umpire Development
MiLB.TV

CONTACTS: *Note: Officers with more than one job title may be intentionally listed here more than once.*
Tim Brunswick, Sr. VP-Bus. Oper.
Scott Poley, Sr. VP-Legal Affairs
Tim Brunswick, VP-Baseball & Bus. Oper.
Tina Gust, VP-Bus. Dev.
Steve Densa, Exec. Dir.-Comm.
Sean Brown, Dir.-Finance
Stan Brand, VP
Sandie Hebert, Dir.-Licensing
Randy Mobley, Pres., Int'l

GROWTH PLANS/SPECIAL FEATURES:
Minor League Baseball (MiLB) is the governing body for 11 leagues with a total of 120 revenue-generating teams in the U.S. and Canada, and operates additional MLB-affiliated rookie league in Arizona, Florida and the Dominican Republic each summer. The minor league system is divided into four classes: Triple-A (AAA), Double-A (AA), High-A (A+) and Single-A (A). MLB franchises may also maintain one or two complex-based rookie teams in the Arizona Complex League or Florida Complex League, and international summer baseball teams in the Dominican Summer League. Minor league seasons consist of 150 games in AAA, 138 games in AA, and 132 games each for A+ and A. Rookies play a shortened season of approximately 60 games starting in mid-June and ending in late-August or early-September. Umpires at the minor league level are overseen by Minor League Baseball Umpire Development, which trains, evaluates and recommends for promotion and retention or release of umpires. Nearly every minor league has its own local radio contract and many have contracts with local television channels. MiLB.TV is the minor leagues' online video streaming service, which offers games for all Triple-A and Double-A teams, and select games from the other classifications.

FINANCIAL DATA: *Note: Data for latest year may not have been available at press time.*

In U.S. $	2022	2021	2020	2019	2018	2017
Revenue						
R&D Expense						
Operating Income						
Operating Margin %						
SGA Expense						
Net Income						
Operating Cash Flow						
Capital Expenditure						
EBITDA						
Return on Assets %						
Return on Equity %						
Debt to Equity						

CONTACT INFORMATION:
Phone: 727-822-6937   Fax: 727-821-5819
Toll-Free: 866-644-2687
Address: 9550 16th St. North, St. Petersburg, FL 33716 United States

STOCK TICKER/OTHER:
Stock Ticker: Private   Exchange:
Employees: Fiscal Year Ends: 12/31
Parent Company:

SALARIES/BONUSES:
Top Exec. Salary: $ Bonus: $
Second Exec. Salary: $ Bonus: $

OTHER THOUGHTS:
Estimated Female Officers or Directors: 15
Hot Spot for Advancement for Women/Minorities: Y

MLS NEXT Pro (Pro Soccer Development LP)

mlsnextpro.com

NAIC Code: 711211D

TYPES OF BUSINESS:

Soccer (Futbol/Football) Teams League
Team Management and Operations

BRANDS/DIVISIONS/AFFILIATES:

Major League Soccer

CONTACTS: *Note: Officers with more than one job title may be intentionally listed here more than once.*

Charles Altchek, Pres.
Ali Curtis, Sr. VP-Oper. & Competition
Jason Tutt, Dir.-Oper.
Sarah Jamieson, Dir.-Communications
Jovina Johnson, VP-Human Resources
Joe Rodriguez, Dir.-Digital Content

GROWTH PLANS/SPECIAL FEATURES:

Pro Soccer Development LP operates MLS NEXT Pro, a professional soccer league inaugurated in 2022 and formed to complete an integrated player pathway from MLS NEXT through to Major League Soccer (MLS) first teams. The new reserve league offers young players and experienced professionals the opportunity to develop and showcase their talents while competing for an MLS NEXT Pro championship. There are 27 clubs in the 2023 season, all affiliated with MLS clubs. MLS NEXT is divided into two conferences: Western Conference includes Colorado Rapids 2, Whitecaps FC 2, Austin FC II, Tacoma Defiance, Houston Dynamo 2, Minnesota United FC 2, North Texas SC, Sporting Kansas City II, St. Louis City SC 2, San Jose Earthquakes II, Real Monarchs, LA Galaxy II, Portland Timbers 2 and Los Angeles FC 2; and Eastern Conference includes Crown Legacy FC, New England Revolution II, Orlando City B, Columbus Crew 2, New York Red Bulls II, New York City FC II, Atlanta United 2, Philadelphia Union II, Inter Miami CF II, FC Cincinnati 2, Chicago Fire FC II, Huntsville City FC and Toronto FC II. The third-tier league will also provide opportunities for coaches, referees and sports business professionals throughout North America. The MLS NEXT league offers 28 matches, with each conference divided into divisions of six or seven teams for scheduling. The top seven teams in each conference will qualify for the playoffs, with the best record in each conference earning a first-round bye. The second and third seeds in each conference choose which of the remaining teams they will play. The top seed in the conference semifinals will also get to choose who they will play. Columbus Crew 2 were the champions in the inaugural 2022 season. Adidas is the kit manufacturer for all MLS NEXT Pro teams.

FINANCIAL DATA: *Note: Data for latest year may not have been available at press time.*

In U.S. $	2022	2021	2020	2019	2018	2017
Revenue						
R&D Expense						
Operating Income						
Operating Margin %						
SGA Expense						
Net Income						
Operating Cash Flow						
Capital Expenditure						
EBITDA						
Return on Assets %						
Return on Equity %						
Debt to Equity						

CONTACT INFORMATION:

Phone: 212 540-1200 Fax:
Toll-Free: 855-657-2245
Address: 420 Fifth Ave., Fl. 7, New York, NY 10018 United States

STOCK TICKER/OTHER:

Stock Ticker: Private Exchange:
Employees: Fiscal Year Ends:
Parent Company:

SALARIES/BONUSES:

Top Exec. Salary: $ Bonus: $
Second Exec. Salary: $ Bonus: $

OTHER THOUGHTS:

Estimated Female Officers or Directors:
Hot Spot for Advancement for Women/Minorities:

Montreal Canadiens

NAIC Code: 711211F

www.nhl.com/canadiens

TYPES OF BUSINESS:

Professional Hockey Team (NHL)
Team Management and Operations

BRANDS/DIVISIONS/AFFILIATES:

Les Canadiens de Montreal
Laval Rocket
Trois-Rivieres Lions

CONTACTS: *Note: Officers with more than one job title may be intentionally listed here more than once.*

Kent Hughes, Gen. Mngr.
Jeff Gorton, Exec. VP-Hockey Oper.

GROWTH PLANS/SPECIAL FEATURES:

The Montreal Canadiens, in French known as Les Canadiens de Montreal, is a professional ice hockey team and Quebec's only National Hockey League (NHL) team. Founded in 1909, the Canadiens are the oldest team in the NHL, and currently play in the Atlantic division of the Eastern conference. The Canadiens have won 24 Stanley Cups, the first of which was in 1916, before the NHL existed, and the most recent of which was in 1993. The team proved to be a dominant force throughout the 1940s, 1950s, 1960s and 1970s. Over 50 former Canadiens players have been inducted into the Hockey Hall of Fame. In 1995, the team began a general decline when it missed the playoffs for the first time in 25 years, and then did so again for three straight seasons between 1999 and 2001. The Canadiens have seen relatively more success in recent years, making the playoffs every year between 2007-2017, and returned in 2019-20 and 2020-21. In fact, Montreal made it to the 2021 Stanley Cup Finals, but lost to Tampa Bay Lightning 1-4. The Molson family formally took ownership of the team in 2009 after purchasing it from George Gillett. The Canadiens play home games at the Bell Centre, one of the largest arenas in the NHL, with an arena capacity of 21,288. The hockey team averaged 21,078 in home game attendance during the 2022-23 season. Minor league affiliations include the Laval Rocket in the American Hockey League (AHL), and the Trois-Rivieres Lions in the ECHL. Forbes estimated the Canadiens' value at $1.85 billion in December 2022.

FINANCIAL DATA: *Note: Data for latest year may not have been available at press time.*

In U.S. $	2022	2021	2020	2019	2018	2017
Revenue	220,000,000	105,000,000	219,000,000	243,000,000	236,000,000	236,000,000
R&D Expense						
Operating Income						
Operating Margin %						
SGA Expense						
Net Income		-18,000,000	87,000,000	106,000,000	92,000,000	92,000,000
Operating Cash Flow						
Capital Expenditure						
EBITDA						
Return on Assets %						
Return on Equity %						
Debt to Equity						

CONTACT INFORMATION:

Phone: 514-932-2582   Fax: 514-932-8736
Toll-Free:
Address: 1260 Ave. des Canadiens-de-Montreal, Montreal, QC H3C 5L2 Canada

STOCK TICKER/OTHER:

Stock Ticker: Private   Exchange:
Employees: Fiscal Year Ends: 08/31
Parent Company:

SALARIES/BONUSES:

Top Exec. Salary: $ Bonus: $
Second Exec. Salary: $ Bonus: $

OTHER THOUGHTS:

Estimated Female Officers or Directors: 1
Hot Spot for Advancement for Women/Minorities:

Motivate LLC

www.motivateco.com

NAIC Code: 532292

TYPES OF BUSINESS:

Bike Sharing Services
Mobile App Booking
Online Management

BRANDS/DIVISIONS/AFFILIATES:

Lyft Inc
Bikeshare Holdings LLC
Capital Bikeshare

CONTACTS: *Note: Officers with more than one job title may be intentionally listed here more than once.*

Matthew Parker, CEO
Grant Barkey, Chief Admin. Officer
Kenneth Ezeadichie, CFO
Troy Poe, Chief People Officer
Matthew Baker, VP-Global Development
Albert Grice, Chief of Staff

GROWTH PLANS/SPECIAL FEATURES:

Motivate, LLC is a global full-service bikeshare operator and technology innovator. The firm offers a full suite of services that help plan, launch, operate and grow bikeshare systems (micromobility). Each Motivate system is run by a local general manager responsible for day-to-day operations; and each general manager is supported by corporate resources such as business intelligence, and a peer-network experienced in bike share. Regional bike share programs serve as a transportation option, and Motivate contracts and operates multi-jurisdiction systems. Many of its systems operate in multiple U.S. cities and some span state lines. Capital Bikeshare is the company's multi-jurisdiction system that operates multiple municipalities. Currently, Motivate operates in the metro areas of Chicago, New York, Washington DC, Boston, San Francisco Bay area, Minneapolis, Columbus and Portland. Motivate takes a data-driven approach to maintenance and repair, keeping bikes and docks in good repair, safe and available for riders. Customer service support teams work 24/7 by phone, email and social media to troubleshoot problems. Motivate's bike valets and corrals help increase capacity at high-demand locations during peak hours by providing staff to receive or supply bikes from strategically-located bike corrals. Motivate operates as a subsidiary of Bikeshare Holdings, LLC, itself a subsidiary of Lyft, Inc.

Motivate offers full-time employees health benefits, 401(k) and paid time off.

FINANCIAL DATA: *Note: Data for latest year may not have been available at press time.*

In U.S. $	2022	2021	2020	2019	2018	2017
Revenue	62,500,000	60,000,000	44,100,000	110,250,000	100,000,000	100,000,000
R&D Expense						
Operating Income						
Operating Margin %						
SGA Expense						
Net Income						
Operating Cash Flow						
Capital Expenditure						
EBITDA						
Return on Assets %						
Return on Equity %						
Debt to Equity						

CONTACT INFORMATION:

Phone: 503-482-7042   Fax:
Toll-Free:
Address: 353 West St., Unit 225, New York, NY 10014 United States

STOCK TICKER/OTHER:

Stock Ticker: Subsidiary   Exchange:
Employees: 800   Fiscal Year Ends:
Parent Company: Lyft Inc

SALARIES/BONUSES:

Top Exec. Salary: $ Bonus: $
Second Exec. Salary: $ Bonus: $

OTHER THOUGHTS:

Estimated Female Officers or Directors:
Hot Spot for Advancement for Women/Minorities:

NASCAR

NAIC Code: 711211

www.nascar.com

TYPES OF BUSINESS:

Professional Stock Car Racing Association
Auto Racing Sanctioning
eRacing

BRANDS/DIVISIONS/AFFILIATES:

Cup Series
Xfinity Series
Craftsman Truck Series
ARCA Menards Series
eNASCAR
NASCAR Digital Media LLC
Automobile Racing Club of America (ARCA)
NASCAR Technical Institute

CONTACTS: *Note: Officers with more than one job title may be intentionally listed here more than once.*

Jim France, CEO
Gary Crotty, General Counsel
Leslie Maxie, Head-Public Rel.

GROWTH PLANS/SPECIAL FEATURES:

National Association for Stock Car Auto Racing, LLC (NASCAR) is an American auto racing sanctioning and operating company. The organization runs more than 1,500 races at 100+ tracks each year throughout the U.S. as well as in Canada, Mexico, Brazil and Europe. Sanctioned series include: National Series, comprised of the Cup Series, Xfinity Series, Craftsman Truck Series and ARCA Menards Series; International Series, comprised of Pinty's Series, Mexico Series, Brasil Sprint Race and Whelen Euro Series; Regional Series, comprised of Weekly Series, Whelen Modified Tour, ARCA Menards Series East and West, and AutoZone Elite and other divisions; and Online Series, comprised of eNASCAR Coca-Cola iRacing Series, eNASCAR College iRacing Series, D-Box NASCAR International iRacing Series and NASCAR Fantasy Live. Subsidiaries and sister organizations include: NASCAR Digital Media LLC, a television production company that produces programs designed to promote professional stock car racing, and manages the NASCAR and related websites; International Speedway Corporation, which constructs and manages tracks at which NASCAR holds competitions; Automobile Racing Club of America (ARCA), an auto racing sanctioning body in the U.S.; Grand American Road Racing Association (Grand-Am), a sanctioning body of sports car racing; International Motor Sports Association (IMSA), a North American sports car racing sanctioning body; and NASCAR Technical Institute, a technical training school based in North Carolina that combines a complete automotive technology program and a NASCAR-specific motor sports program.

FINANCIAL DATA: *Note: Data for latest year may not have been available at press time.*

In U.S. $	2022	2021	2020	2019	2018	2017
Revenue	900,000,000	712,500,000				
R&D Expense						
Operating Income						
Operating Margin %						
SGA Expense						
Net Income						
Operating Cash Flow						
Capital Expenditure						
EBITDA						
Return on Assets %						
Return on Equity %						
Debt to Equity						

CONTACT INFORMATION:

Phone: 386-253-0611   Fax: 386-681-4041
Toll-Free:
Address: 1801 W. International Speedway Blvd., Daytona Beach, FL 32114 United States

STOCK TICKER/OTHER:

Stock Ticker: Private   Exchange:
Employees: 2,000   Fiscal Year Ends: 12/31
Parent Company:

SALARIES/BONUSES:

Top Exec. Salary: $ Bonus: $
Second Exec. Salary: $ Bonus: $

OTHER THOUGHTS:

Estimated Female Officers or Directors: 1
Hot Spot for Advancement for Women/Minorities:

Nashville Predators

www.nhl.com/predators

NAIC Code: 711211F

TYPES OF BUSINESS:

Professional Hockey Team (NHL)
Team Management and Operations

BRANDS/DIVISIONS/AFFILIATES:

Predators Holdings LLC
Preds
Milwaukee Admirals

CONTACTS: Note: Officers with more than one job title may be intentionally listed here more than once.

Sean Henry, CEO
Michelle Kennedy, COO
Keith Hegger, CFO
Bill Wickett, CMO
Courtni Mosley, Sr. VP-Human Resources
Michael Paul, Dir.-IT
Michelle Kennedy, General Counsel
David Poile, Pres., Hockey Oper.
Chris Junghans, Sr. VP-Corp. Dev.
Gerry Helper, Sr. VP-Hockey Comm. & Public Rel.
Beth Snider, Sr. VP-Finance
Barry Trotz, Head Coach
Brian Poile, Dir.-Hockey Oper.
Nat Harden, VP-Ticket Sales
Herbert Fritch, Chmn.

GROWTH PLANS/SPECIAL FEATURES:

The Nashville Predators is a National Hockey League (NHL) team started in 1998 as an expansion team and is popularly known as the Preds. The team plays in the Central division of the Western conference along with the Arizona Coyotes, Chicago Blackhawks, Colorado Avalanche, Dallas Stars, Minnesota Wild, St. Louis Blues and Winnipeg Jets. Although the franchise struggled at first, it won a place in the 2003-04 Conference Quarterfinals, but lost to the Detroit Red Wings. In total, the Predators have won two division titles (2107-18 and 2018-19). The 2017-18 season also saw the team clench its first Presidents' Trophy. Home games are played in Bridgestone Arena, which seats over 20,000 for hockey games and is owned by the Sports Authority of Nashville and Davidson County. The Predators averaged 17,361 in home attendance in the 2022-23 season. The franchise is owned by a consortium of local businessmen operating under the Predators Holdings LLC banner. The group acquired the team and Powers Management from majority owner and former Chairman Craig Leipold for $193 million after Mr. Leipold contemplated moving the team to a different city. The Preds' minor league affiliate is the Milwaukee Admirals in the American Hockey League (AHL). Forbes estimated the Predators to be valued at $810 million in December 2022.

FINANCIAL DATA: Note: Data for latest year may not have been available at press time.

In U.S. $	2022	2021	2020	2019	2018	2017
Revenue	124,150,000					
R&D Expense						
Operating Income						
Operating Margin %						
SGA Expense						
Net Income						
Operating Cash Flow						
Capital Expenditure						
EBITDA						
Return on Assets %						
Return on Equity %						
Debt to Equity						

CONTACT INFORMATION:

Phone: 615-770-2300   Fax: 615-770-2309
Toll-Free:
Address: 501 Broadway, Bridgestone Arena, Nashville, TN 37203 United States

STOCK TICKER/OTHER:

Stock Ticker: Private   Exchange:
Employees: 340   Fiscal Year Ends:
Parent Company:

SALARIES/BONUSES:

Top Exec. Salary: $ Bonus: $
Second Exec. Salary: $ Bonus: $

OTHER THOUGHTS:

Estimated Female Officers or Directors: 3
Hot Spot for Advancement for Women/Minorities: Y

Sales, profits and employees may be estimates. Financial information, benefits and other data can change quickly and may vary from those stated here.

National Basketball Association (NBA)   **www.nba.com**
NAIC Code: 711211

TYPES OF BUSINESS:
Professional Basketball League

BRANDS/DIVISIONS/AFFILIATES:
Basketball Association of America
National Basketball League
WNBA
NBA Cares
NBA G League
NBA TV

CONTACTS: *Note: Officers with more than one job title may be intentionally listed here more than once.*
Adam Silver, Commissioner
Jace Provo, Chief Medical Officer
Chris Brennan, Sr. VP-Retail Dev.
Robert Criqui, Pres., Admin.
Richard Buchanan, General Counsel
Joel M. Litvin, Pres., League Oper.
Rachel Jacobson, Sr. VP-Bus. Dev.
Michael Bass, Exec. VP-Comm.
Michael Whitehead, Sr. VP-Team Finance
Stu Jackson, Exec. VP-Basketball Oper.
Ski Austin, Exec. VP-Events & Attractions
Dan Reed, Pres., NBA Dev. League
Steven M. Angel, Sr. VP-League Oper. & Officiating
Heidi J. Ueberroth, Pres., NBA Int'l

GROWTH PLANS/SPECIAL FEATURES:
The National Basketball Association (NBA) is a world-leading professional basketball league. Formed in 1946 as the Basketball Association of America, the organization adopted its current name in 1949 after merging with rival National Basketball League. David Stern, the league's commissioner from 1984 to 2014, oversaw the creation of the now-independent WNBA; created the NBA Cares social programs; introduced a strict dress code for players; and introduced a new microfiber ball, which he promptly recalled after mounting player concerns. The league is currently composed of 30 teams, 29 in the U.S. and one in Toronto, Canada, as well as 30 in the NBA minor organization NBA G League. The NBA's regular season begins in the last week of October and ends in April. In a regular season, each team plays 82 games, 41 home and 41 away. In the playoffs, eight teams from each conference enter a bracket that consists of four rounds of best-of-seven games. The NBA finals pit the winner of the eastern conference bracket against the winner of the west. The league owns and operates a television network called NBA TV, which is dedicated to showing live and classic basketball games and promoting the sport. The league has additional TV partnerships with ABC/ESPN, TNT and NBA TV in the U.S., as well as international broadcasters. The NBA is an active member of USA Basketball, the national governing body for basketball in the U.S.

FINANCIAL DATA: *Note: Data for latest year may not have been available at press time.*

In U.S. $	2022	2021	2020	2019	2018	2017
Revenue	10,100,000,000	9,600,000,000	8,300,000,000	8,760,000,000	7,400,000,000	7,400,000,000
R&D Expense						
Operating Income						
Operating Margin %						
SGA Expense						
Net Income						
Operating Cash Flow						
Capital Expenditure						
EBITDA						
Return on Assets %						
Return on Equity %						
Debt to Equity						

CONTACT INFORMATION:
Phone: 212-515-6221   Fax: 212-832-3861
Toll-Free:
Address: 645 5th Ave., Olympic Tower, New York, NY 10022 United States

STOCK TICKER/OTHER:
Stock Ticker: Private   Exchange:
Employees: 6,000   Fiscal Year Ends:
Parent Company:

SALARIES/BONUSES:
Top Exec. Salary: $ Bonus: $
Second Exec. Salary: $ Bonus: $

OTHER THOUGHTS:
Estimated Female Officers or Directors: 16
Hot Spot for Advancement for Women/Minorities: Y

National Football League (NFL)

www.nfl.com

NAIC Code: 711211

TYPES OF BUSINESS:

Professional Football League

BRANDS/DIVISIONS/AFFILIATES:

NFL Network
American Football Conference
National Football Conference
Super Bowl

CONTACTS: *Note: Officers with more than one job title may be intentionally listed here more than once.*

Roger Goodell, Commissioner
John Buzzeo, VP-Admin.
Adolpho Birch, VP-Law & Labor Policy
John Buzzeo, VP-Bus. Oper.
Greg Isaacs, VP-Digital Media
Brian Rolapp, COO-NFL Media
Steven M. Bornstein, CEO
Brian McCarthy, VP-Corp. Comm.
Frank Supovitz, Sr. VP-Events

GROWTH PLANS/SPECIAL FEATURES:

The National Football League (NFL), an unincorporated organization controlled by its members, is one of the largest and most popular professional sports leagues in the U.S. Founded in 1920, the modern NFL was born when the league merged with the American Football League (AFL) in 1966. An echo of the two leagues still exists in the NFL's two conferences, the American Football Conference (AFC) and the National Football Conference (NFC). The NFL's 32 franchised teams are equally divided between the two conferences, which are each subdivided into four divisions. NFL matches draw average crowds of approximately 69,400 per game (per the 2022 season). The NFL season begins on the Thursday after Labor Day and runs until late December or early January. About half of the 16 games played by each team in a regular season are against its division rivals, with the remainder consisting of inter-division and inter-conference games. Every year at the end of the season, there are 12 inner-conference playoff games played by the top six teams in each conference, consisting of the four division champions and the top two remaining non-division champion teams with the best record. The resulting AFC champion then plays the NFC champion in the Super Bowl, one of the most-watched television events of the year. The Super Bowl is among the largest sporting events in the world. The league owns the NFL Network, a cable and satellite television network dedicated to the NFL and the sport of football. Although individual league teams act as separate businesses, the NFL maintains a revenue-sharing plan aimed at promoting greater parity between various franchises. In November 2022, Bayern Munich's Allianz Arena was the first venue to host a regular-season NFL game in Germany, with the Tampa Bay Buccaneers playing the Seattle Seahawks before a crowd of 69,811.

FINANCIAL DATA: *Note: Data for latest year may not have been available at press time.*

In U.S. $	2022	2021	2020	2019	2018	2017
Revenue	16,000,000,000	12,200,000,000	14,820,000,000	15,600,000,000	14,500,000,000	14,500,000,000
R&D Expense						
Operating Income						
Operating Margin %						
SGA Expense						
Net Income						
Operating Cash Flow						
Capital Expenditure						
EBITDA						
Return on Assets %						
Return on Equity %						
Debt to Equity						

CONTACT INFORMATION:

Phone: 212-867-2010   Fax:
Toll-Free:
Address: 345 Park Ave., New York, NY 10154 United States

STOCK TICKER/OTHER:

Stock Ticker: Private   Exchange:
Employees: 4,100   Fiscal Year Ends: 03/31
Parent Company:

SALARIES/BONUSES:

Top Exec. Salary: $ Bonus: $
Second Exec. Salary: $ Bonus: $

OTHER THOUGHTS:

Estimated Female Officers or Directors:
Hot Spot for Advancement for Women/Minorities:

National Hockey League (NHL)

www.nhl.com

NAIC Code: 711211

TYPES OF BUSINESS:

Professional Ice Hockey League

BRANDS/DIVISIONS/AFFILIATES:

Stanley Cup
Eastern Conference
Western Conference

CONTACTS: *Note: Officers with more than one job title may be intentionally listed here more than once.*

Gary Bettman, Commissioner
Colin Campbell, Dir.-Hockey Oper.
William L. Daly, Deputy Commissioner
Terry Gregson, Sr. VP
Brendan Shanahan, Sr. VP-Player Safety

GROWTH PLANS/SPECIAL FEATURES:

The National Hockey League (NHL) is the largest professional ice hockey league in North America. It currently includes 32-member teams throughout the U.S. (25) and Canada (7). The firm's teams are divided into two conferences, the Eastern Conference (EC) and the Western Conference (WC), each of which has two divisions that are composed of eight teams. EC's two divisions are Atlantic (Boston Bruins, Buffalo Sabres, Detroit Red Wings, Florida Panthers, Montreal Canadiens, Ottawa Senators, Tampa Bay Lightning and Toronto Maple Leafs) and Metropolitan (Carolina Hurricanes, Columbus Blue Jackets, New Jersey Devils, New York Islanders, New York Rangers, Philadelphia Flyers, Pittsburgh Penguins and Washington Capitals). WC's two divisions are Central (Arizona Coyotes, Chicago Blackhawks, Colorado Avalanche, Dallas Stars, Minnesota Wild, Nashville Predators, St. Louis Blues and Winnipeg Jets) and Pacific (Anaheim Ducks, Calgary Flames, Edmonton Oilers, Los Angeles Kings, San Jose Sharks, Seattle Kraken, Vancouver Canucks and Vegas Golden Knights). Each season, the teams within a division play elimination games against each other to produce a division champion. The division champions in each conference then play each other until one remains. The victors go on to play each other for the Stanley Cup. Every year the NHL awards the Stanley Cup to the champion of its playoff tournament. The company sets the rules, regulates team ownership, governs the game and collects licensing fees for merchandise as well as negotiating fees for national broadcasting rights.

FINANCIAL DATA: *Note: Data for latest year may not have been available at press time.*

In U.S. $	2022	2021	2020	2019	2018	2017
Revenue	5,400,000,000	4,800,000,000	4,000,000,000	4,540,000,000	4,100,000,000	4,100,000,000
R&D Expense						
Operating Income						
Operating Margin %						
SGA Expense						
Net Income						
Operating Cash Flow						
Capital Expenditure						
EBITDA						
Return on Assets %						
Return on Equity %						
Debt to Equity						

CONTACT INFORMATION:

Phone: 212-789-2000   Fax: 212-789-2020
Toll-Free:
Address: 1185 Ave. of the Americas, Fl. 12, New York, NY 10036 United States

STOCK TICKER/OTHER:

Stock Ticker: Private   Exchange:
Employees: 620   Fiscal Year Ends: 06/30
Parent Company:

SALARIES/BONUSES:

Top Exec. Salary: $ Bonus: $
Second Exec. Salary: $ Bonus: $

OTHER THOUGHTS:

Estimated Female Officers or Directors:
Hot Spot for Advancement for Women/Minorities:

Sales, profits and employees may be estimates. Financial information, benefits and other data can change quickly and may vary from those stated here.

National Thoroughbred Racing Association

www.ntra.com

NAIC Code: 711211

TYPES OF BUSINESS:

Thoroughbred Racing Association
Horse Racing Marketing
Branding Campaigns
Media Polling
Sponsorship Programs
Political Action Committee

BRANDS/DIVISIONS/AFFILIATES:

Go Baby Go
NTRA Safety and Integrity Alliance
NTRA.com
NTRA Top Thoroughbred
NTRA Top-3-Year-Old
Eclipse Awards
National Horseplayers Championship
NTRA Advantage

CONTACTS: *Note: Officers with more than one job title may be intentionally listed here more than once.*

Thomas J. Rooney, CEO
Keith Chamblin, COO
Lori Tackett, Accounting
Meghan Rodgers, Sr. VP-Communications
Casey Hamilton, Dir.-Exec. Admin.
Holly Short, Dir.-Mktg. & Events
Stephen Panus, VP-Comm. Affairs
Amber Florence, Dir.-Finance
Bryan Pettigrew, Sr. VP-NTRA Advantage
Mike Ziegler, Exec. VP-Safety & Integrity Alliance
Steve Driskill, Sr. Dir.-Sales

GROWTH PLANS/SPECIAL FEATURES:

The National Thoroughbred Racing Association (NTRA) is a non-profit coalition of more than 100 horse racing interests and thousands of individual stakeholders consisting of horseplayers, racetrack operators, owners, breeders, trainers and affiliated horse racing associations. NTRA focuses on increasing public awareness, creating a centralized national structure, implementing comprehensive marketing strategies and enhancing the industry's economic condition. NTRA markets the sport through various initiatives, including a Go Baby Go branding campaign tied to advertising and merchandising. The NTRA owns and manages the NTRA Safety and Integrity Alliance; NTRA.com; the NTRA Top Thoroughbred and NTRA Top 3-Year-Old weekly media polls; the Eclipse Awards; the National Horseplayers Championship; NTRA Advantage, a corporate partner sales and sponsorship program; and HORSE PAC, a federal political action committee.

FINANCIAL DATA: *Note: Data for latest year may not have been available at press time.*

In U.S. $	2022	2021	2020	2019	2018	2017
Revenue		1,526,366	1,481,909	7,409,546	387,902	387,902
R&D Expense						
Operating Income						
Operating Margin %						
SGA Expense						
Net Income						
Operating Cash Flow						
Capital Expenditure						
EBITDA						
Return on Assets %						
Return on Equity %						
Debt to Equity						

CONTACT INFORMATION:

Phone: 859-245-6872   Fax:
Toll-Free: 800-792-6872
Address: 401 W. Main St., Ste. 222, Lexington, KY 40507 United States

STOCK TICKER/OTHER:

Stock Ticker: Private   Exchange:
Employees: Fiscal Year Ends: 03/31
Parent Company:

SALARIES/BONUSES:

Top Exec. Salary: $ Bonus: $
Second Exec. Salary: $ Bonus: $

OTHER THOUGHTS:

Estimated Female Officers or Directors: 5
Hot Spot for Advancement for Women/Minorities: Y

Sales, profits and employees may be estimates. Financial information, benefits and other data can change quickly and may vary from those stated here.

NBA G League
NAIC Code: 711211

TYPES OF BUSINESS:
Minor League Basketball
Professional Basketball League

BRANDS/DIVISIONS/AFFILIATES:
National Basketball Association (NBA)

CONTACTS: *Note: Officers with more than one job title may be intentionally listed here more than once.*
Shareef Abdur-Rahim, Pres.
Chris Alpert, VP-Basketball Oper.
Jill Olickan, Dir.-Bus. Dev.

GROWTH PLANS/SPECIAL FEATURES:
The NBA G League (G League), a division of the National Basketball Association (NBA), was founded in 2001 by the NBA to act as its in-house minor league. Several current NBA players are former NBA G Leaguers. The league has 30 teams lined up for the 2023-24 season, of which 28 have one-to-one affiliations with NBA franchises. NBA G League Ignite also plays against G League competition. G league is divided into two conferences, East and West. Teams in the Eastern Conference include Long Island Nets, Delaware Blue Coats, Capital City Go-Go, Maine Celtics, Cleveland Charge, Fort Wayne Mad Ants, Windy City Bulls, Lakeland Magic, Motor City Cruise, Raptors 905, College Park Skyhawks, Greensboro Swarm, Wisconsin Herd, Grand Rapids Gold and Westchester Knicks. Teams in the Western Conference include Stockton Kings, Memphis Hustle, South Bay Lakers, Salt Lake City Stars, Sioux Falls Skyforce, Rio Grande Valley Vipers, Santa Cruz Warriors, Mexico City Capitanes, Ontario Clippers, Oklahoma City Blue, G League Ignite, Birmingham Squadron, Iowa Wolves, Austin Spurs and Texas Legends. Players are eligible for the league if they are aged 18 and have passed the tryout as well as those players who were drafted into the NBA. The G League season lasts roughly 20 weeks and teams play a 50-game schedule. The Delaware Blue Coats were the 2022-23 NBA G League champions, and are affiliated with the Philadelphia 76ers.

FINANCIAL DATA: *Note: Data for latest year may not have been available at press time.*

In U.S. $	2022	2021	2020	2019	2018	2017
Revenue						
R&D Expense						
Operating Income						
Operating Margin %						
SGA Expense						
Net Income						
Operating Cash Flow						
Capital Expenditure						
EBITDA						
Return on Assets %						
Return on Equity %						
Debt to Equity						

CONTACT INFORMATION:
Phone: 212-407-8700   Fax: 212-759-1412
Toll-Free:
Address: 477 Madison Ave., Fl. 3, New York, NY 10022 United States

STOCK TICKER/OTHER:
Stock Ticker: Private   Exchange:
Employees: 380   Fiscal Year Ends: 08/31
Parent Company: National Basketball Association (NBA)

SALARIES/BONUSES:
Top Exec. Salary: $ Bonus: $
Second Exec. Salary: $ Bonus: $

OTHER THOUGHTS:
Estimated Female Officers or Directors: 1
Hot Spot for Advancement for Women/Minorities: Y

NBCUniversal Media LLC

www.nbcuniversal.com

NAIC Code: 515120

TYPES OF BUSINESS:

Television Broadcasting
Online News & Information
Resorts
Entertainment Parks
Television Content
Streaming
Television Studios
Media Production and Distribution

BRANDS/DIVISIONS/AFFILIATES:

Comcast Corporation
Universal Pictures Home Entertainment
DreamWorks
NBC News
MSNBC
Universal Studios Hollywood
NBC Sports
peacock

CONTACTS: Note: Officers with more than one job title may be intentionally listed here more than once.

Jeff Shell, CEO
Anand Kini, CFO
Jeff Shell, Chmn.-Universal Filmed Entertainment
Kimberley D. Harris, General Counsel
Maggie McLean Suniewick, Sr. VP-Strategic Integration
Cameron Blanchard, Exec. VP-Comm.
Patricia Fili-Krushel, Chmn.-NBCUniversal News Group
Robert Greenblatt, Chmn., NBC Entertainment
Bonnie Hammer, Chmn., NBCUniversal Cable Entertainment Group
Ted Harbert, Chmn., NBC Broadcasting
Steve Burke, Chmn.
Kevin MacLellan, Chmn., NBCUniversal Int'l
Matt Bond, Exec. VP-Content Dist.

GROWTH PLANS/SPECIAL FEATURES:

NBCUniversal Media, LLC is a world-leading entertainment and media company engaged in related development, production and marketing activities. NBCUniversal is a product of a 2004 merger of Vivendi Universal Entertainment and National Broadcasting Company (NBC). The firm now operates as a wholly-owned subsidiary of Comcast Corporation. NBCUniversal has five divisions: film, news, parks and resorts, tv and streaming, and tv studios. The film division comprises five brands: Universal Pictures Home Entertainment, DreamWorks, Focus Features-A Comcast Company, Universal-A Comcast Company, and Universal Pictures International. The news division comprises NBC News, MSNBC, CNBC and CNBC International. Parks and Resorts consists of five destinations under the Universal Studios brand name, including Hollywood, Orlando Resort, Japan, Singapore and Beijing Resort. TV and streaming brands include NBC, NBC Sports, Telemundo, peacock, NBC, GOLF, Oxygen, NBCUniversal Local, Universal Kids, USA, SyFy, GolfNow, Sports Engine, hayu., bravo, E!, and Fandango. Last, the tv studios division comprises the Universal Television, UCP, Universal Television Alternative and Universal International brands.

NBCUniversal offers its employees health benefits, 401(k) and stock options, and employee assistance programs.

FINANCIAL DATA: Note: Data for latest year may not have been available at press time.

In U.S. $	2022	2021	2020	2019	2018	2017
Revenue	36,000,000,000	34,319,000,000	27,211,000,000	33,958,000,000	32,997,000,000	32,997,000,000
R&D Expense						
Operating Income						
Operating Margin %						
SGA Expense						
Net Income		5,675,000,000	5,355,000,000	8,711,000,000	5,080,000,000	5,080,000,000
Operating Cash Flow						
Capital Expenditure						
EBITDA						
Return on Assets %						
Return on Equity %						
Debt to Equity						

CONTACT INFORMATION:

Phone: 212-664-4444   Fax: 212-664-4085
Toll-Free:
Address: 30 Rockefeller Plz., New York, NY 10112 United States

STOCK TICKER/OTHER:

Stock Ticker: Subsidiary
Employees: 65,700
Parent Company: Comcast Corporation

Exchange:
Fiscal Year Ends: 12/31

SALARIES/BONUSES:

Top Exec. Salary: $ Bonus: $
Second Exec. Salary: $ Bonus: $

OTHER THOUGHTS:

Estimated Female Officers or Directors: 12
Hot Spot for Advancement for Women/Minorities: Y

New Balance Athletic Shoe Inc

www.newbalance.com

NAIC Code: 424340

TYPES OF BUSINESS:

Footwear Distribution
Sports Equipment
Leather Boots
Lacrosse Equipment
Manufacturing
Technology

BRANDS/DIVISIONS/AFFILIATES:

Warrior Sports
Brine

CONTACTS: *Note: Officers with more than one job title may be intentionally listed here more than once.*

Joe Preston, CEO
Peter Zappala, VP-Specialty Sales
Duncan Scott, VP-External Prod.
Edith Harmon, VP-R&D Wellness
John Wilson, Exec. VP-Mfg.
Anne Davis, Exec. VP-Admin.
Christine Madigan, VP-Responsible Leadership
Jim Connors, VP-Global Design & Dev.
Dave Crosier, Exec. VP-Value Chain
Bill Hayden, VP-Finance
James. S. Davis, Chmn.
Alan Hed, Exec. VP-Int'l
Kevin Holian, VP-Global Logistics

GROWTH PLANS/SPECIAL FEATURES:

New Balance Athletic Shoe, Inc. is an athletic footwear and apparel company, which began as an arch-support firm in the early 1900s. New Balance manufactures men's and women's shoes for running, cross training, basketball, tennis, baseball, cheerleading, hiking, golf and more. The company also offers fitness apparel and kids' shoes. In addition, New Balance owns Warrior Sports (which encompasses the Brine brand), a cutting-edge global manufacturer of lacrosse equipment. New Balance makes use of advanced technology in the production of its shoes, using products like Abzorb foam, a complex blend of rubber and proprietary materials which provide extra cushioning, and compression properties. The company is also known for its wide selection of shoe widths. It is the only major maker of athletic shoes that still has plants only in the U.S. New Balance sells its products in over 120 countries, and maintains numerous licensees, joint ventures and distributors worldwide.

New Balance offers its employees medical and dental coverage, a 401(k), flexible spending accounts, tuition reimbursement, a college saving plan and more.

FINANCIAL DATA: *Note: Data for latest year may not have been available at press time.*

In U.S. $	2022	2021	2020	2019	2018	2017
Revenue	5,300,000,000	6,799,650,000	5,230,500,000	4,755,000,000	4,500,000,000	4,500,000,000
R&D Expense						
Operating Income						
Operating Margin %						
SGA Expense						
Net Income						
Operating Cash Flow						
Capital Expenditure						
EBITDA						
Return on Assets %						
Return on Equity %						
Debt to Equity						

CONTACT INFORMATION:

Phone: 617-783-4000   Fax: 617-787-9355
Toll-Free: 800-622-1218
Address: 20 Guest St., Brighton Landing, Boston, MA 02135 United States

STOCK TICKER/OTHER:

Stock Ticker: Private   Exchange:
Employees: 5,500   Fiscal Year Ends: 12/31
Parent Company:

SALARIES/BONUSES:

Top Exec. Salary: $ Bonus: $
Second Exec. Salary: $ Bonus: $

OTHER THOUGHTS:

Estimated Female Officers or Directors: 5
Hot Spot for Advancement for Women/Minorities: Y

New England Patriots

www.patriots.com

NAIC Code: 711211C

TYPES OF BUSINESS:

Professional Football Team
Team Management and Operations

BRANDS/DIVISIONS/AFFILIATES:

Gillette Stadium
Kraft Group (The)
New England Patriots LP

CONTACTS: Note: Officers with more than one job title may be intentionally listed here more than once.

Robert Kraft, CEO
Jonathan A. Kraft, Pres.
Ernie Adams, Dir.-Football Research
Stacey James, VP-Media Rel.
Bill Belichick, Head Coach
Jon Robinson, Dir.-College Scouting
Robert Kraft, Chmn.

GROWTH PLANS/SPECIAL FEATURES:

The New England Patriots is a professional football team playing in the Eastern Division of the American Football Conference (AFC) of the National Football League (NFL). The team formed in 1960 as an original member of the American Football League under the Boston Patriots name. From its inception in 1960 through the early 1990s, the team underwent many changes of ownership, coaching turnovers and poor seasons. In 1994, Robert Kraft obtained full ownership of the administrative New England Patriots LP through his company The Kraft Group, beginning a move toward stability and positive play on the field. In 1996, the team reached Super Bowl XXXI but lost to the Green Bay Packers. Beginning in 2001, the organization completed a turnaround that resulted in five Super Bowl titles in 17 years (2001, 2003, 2004, 2014, 2016 and 2018), a new stadium (Gillette Stadium, privately funded, owned and operated by Robert Kraft) and a revitalized fan base. The Patriots were undefeated through much of the 2007-08 football season, losing in the Super Bowl to the New York Giants; however, in the 2008-09 season, the team failed to make the playoffs despite an 11-5 record, breaking a five-year streak of postseason appearances. In total, the Patriots have 11 conference championships, 22 division championships and have made the playoffs 28 times (most recently in 2021). Notable players have included Tom Brady, Andre Tippett and Mike Haynes. Forbes valued the team at $6.4 billion in 2022. The team averaged 65,878 fans in attendance per home game for the 2022-23 season, selling out each game at Gillette Stadium.

FINANCIAL DATA: Note: Data for latest year may not have been available at press time.

In U.S. $	2022	2021	2020	2019	2018	2017
Revenue	720,200,000					
R&D Expense						
Operating Income						
Operating Margin %						
SGA Expense						
Net Income						
Operating Cash Flow						
Capital Expenditure						
EBITDA						
Return on Assets %						
Return on Equity %						
Debt to Equity						

CONTACT INFORMATION:

Phone: 508-543-8200   Fax: 508-543-0285
Toll-Free: 800-543-1776
Address: 1 Patriot Pl., Foxborough, MA 02035 United States

STOCK TICKER/OTHER:

Stock Ticker: Private   Exchange:
Employees: 550   Fiscal Year Ends: 12/31
Parent Company:

SALARIES/BONUSES:

Top Exec. Salary: $ Bonus: $
Second Exec. Salary: $ Bonus: $

OTHER THOUGHTS:

Estimated Female Officers or Directors:
Hot Spot for Advancement for Women/Minorities:

New England Revolution

NAIC Code: 711211D

TYPES OF BUSINESS:

Major League Soccer Team
Team Management and Operations

BRANDS/DIVISIONS/AFFILIATES:

Revolution Academy

CONTACTS: *Note: Officers with more than one job title may be intentionally listed here more than once.*

Brian Bilello, Pres.
Lizz Summers, Dir.-Comm.
Robert K. Kraft, Operator
Jonathan A. Kraft, Operator
Michael Burns, Gen. Mgr.
Jay Heaps, Head Coach

GROWTH PLANS/SPECIAL FEATURES:

The New England Revolution is a Major League Soccer (MLS) team based in Massachusetts. Revolution was one of the 10 founding teams of the MLS and has fielded star players such as defender Alexi Lalas, midfielder Clint Dempsey, defender Mike Burns and forward Joe-Max Moore. The team plays in the Eastern Conference of the MLS along with the Atlanta United FC, Chicago Fire FC, Columbus Crew, FC Cincinnati, D.C. United, Inter Miami CF, Charlotte FC, CF Montreal, New York City FC, New York Red Bulls, Orlando City SC, Philadelphia Union and Toronto FC. The team has made it to the MLS championship game five times, most recently in 2014, but has thus far failed to win the MLS Cup. However, the team won the US Open Cup in 2007, the SuperLiga Championship in 2008, and the Supporters' Shield in 2021. The New England Revolution is actively devoted to the development of youth soccer, and it runs various training camps and programs tailored to specific age groups and skill sets such as the Revolution Academy. Regular season home game attendance averaged 20,319 in 2022, and the Revolution play in the Kraft-owned Gillette Stadium.

FINANCIAL DATA: *Note: Data for latest year may not have been available at press time.*

In U.S. $	2022	2021	2020	2019	2018	2017
Revenue	9,446,220					
R&D Expense						
Operating Income						
Operating Margin %						
SGA Expense						
Net Income						
Operating Cash Flow						
Capital Expenditure						
EBITDA						
Return on Assets %						
Return on Equity %						
Debt to Equity						

CONTACT INFORMATION:

Phone: 508-543-8200   Fax:
Toll-Free:
Address: 1 Patriot Place, Gillette Stadium, Foxborough, MA 02035 United States

STOCK TICKER/OTHER:

Stock Ticker: Private   Exchange:
Employees: Fiscal Year Ends:
Parent Company:

SALARIES/BONUSES:

Top Exec. Salary: $ Bonus: $
Second Exec. Salary: $ Bonus: $

OTHER THOUGHTS:

Estimated Female Officers or Directors: 5
Hot Spot for Advancement for Women/Minorities: Y

New Jersey Devils

www.nhl.com/devils

NAIC Code: 711211F

TYPES OF BUSINESS:

Professional Hockey Team (NHL)
Team Management and Operations

BRANDS/DIVISIONS/AFFILIATES:

New Jersey Devils LLC
Utica Comets
Adirondack Thunder

CONTACTS: *Note: Officers with more than one job title may be intentionally listed here more than once.*

Tad Brown, CEO
Jake Reynolds, Pres.
David Collins, CFO
Jillian Frechette, Sr. VP-Mktg.
Elizabeth Berman, Chief People Officer
Sasha Puric Mimi Verna, CTO
David Conte, Exec. VP-Hockey Oper.
David Blitzer, Managing Partner

GROWTH PLANS/SPECIAL FEATURES:

The New Jersey Devils franchise, administered through New Jersey Devils, LLC, is a professional ice hockey team playing in the Metropolitan division of the Eastern conference within the National Hockey League (NHL). The team was founded in 1974 in Kansas City, Missouri as the Kansas City Scouts, which it remained until 1976. The franchise then moved to Denver, Colorado and changed its name to the Colorado Rockies. The team became the New Jersey Devils when it moved to East Rutherford, New Jersey in 1982. The Devils had a general losing streak until 1990. Between 1990 and 1993, the team made the playoffs each year, only to lose in the first round. During the 1994-95 season, the franchise won its first Stanley Cup. The Devils went on to make four more consecutive Stanley Cup finals appearances, winning in 1999-00 and in 2002-03 for a total of three Stanley Cups. The Devils maintained a streak of making the playoffs for every year from 1997 to 2011, when the streak was broken. The team's home arena is the Prudential Center, locally known as The Rock. The arena has a seating capacity of 19,500, and the New Jersey Devils averaged 15,207 fans in attendance per home game during the 2022-23 season. The team maintains minor league affiliations with the Utica Comets in the American Hockey League (AHL) and the Adirondack Thunder in the ECHL. Forbes valued the Devils at $960 million in December 2022.

FINANCIAL DATA: *Note: Data for latest year may not have been available at press time.*

In U.S. $	2022	2021	2020	2019	2018	2017
Revenue	149,500,000					
R&D Expense						
Operating Income						
Operating Margin %						
SGA Expense						
Net Income						
Operating Cash Flow						
Capital Expenditure						
EBITDA						
Return on Assets %						
Return on Equity %						
Debt to Equity						

CONTACT INFORMATION:

Phone: 973-757-6100   Fax:
Toll-Free:
Address: Prudential Center, 25 Lafayette St., Newark, NJ 07102 United States

STOCK TICKER/OTHER:

Stock Ticker: Private
Employees: 300
Parent Company:

Exchange:
Fiscal Year Ends: 06/30

SALARIES/BONUSES:

Top Exec. Salary: $ Bonus: $
Second Exec. Salary: $ Bonus: $

OTHER THOUGHTS:

Estimated Female Officers or Directors:
Hot Spot for Advancement for Women/Minorities:

Sales, profits and employees may be estimates. Financial information, benefits and other data can change quickly and may vary from those stated here.

New Orleans Pelicans

NAIC Code: 711211B

www.nba.com/pelicans

TYPES OF BUSINESS:

Professional Basketball Team
Team Management and Operations

BRANDS/DIVISIONS/AFFILIATES:

Birmingham Squadron

CONTACTS: *Note: Officers with more than one job title may be intentionally listed here more than once.*

Dennis Laischa, Pres.
Ben Hales, COO
Ed Lang, CFO
Michael Stanfield, Sr. VP-Sales
Greg Rouchell, Sr. VP-Human Resources
Jody Barbier, Sr. Dir.-IT Oper.
Richard House, General Counsel
Sam Russo, Exec. VP-Oper.
Tom Ward, Sr. VP-Corp. Partnerships
Matt Rose, Dir.-Digital Mktg.
Harold Kaufman, VP-Comm.
Diane North, Controller
Dell Demps, Sr. VP-Basketball Oper.
Monty Williams, Head Coach
Bill Bailey, Sr. VP-Ticket Sales & Service
Shelly Cayette, Dir.-Community Investment
Gayle Benson, Governor

GROWTH PLANS/SPECIAL FEATURES:

The New Orleans Pelicans, formerly the Hornets, began as an NBA expansion team in Charlotte, North Carolina in 1988. Due to poor attendance, the team relocated to New Orleans in 2002. The Pelicans play in the Smoothie King Center (originally New Orleans Arena), with a capacity to seat 16,867 basketball spectators. The team's home attendance average was 16,772 fans per game for the 2022-23 season. The Hornets won their first division title (Southwest Division) in the 2008 playoffs, beating the Dallas Mavericks in the first round, but lost to the defending champion San Antonio Spurs in seven games in the conference semifinals. As the Pelicans, the team qualified for the NBA playoffs during the 2014-15 season as the eighth seed in the Western Conference, but were swept by the Warriors in four games. Noteworthy players of the Pelicans include Larry Johnson, Muggsy Bogues, Alonzo Mourning and Glen Rice. Following the 2005 Hurricane Katrina disaster, the team was temporarily relocated to Oklahoma City for the 2005-06 and 2006-07 seasons. The NBA, which purchased the team in 2010 from George Shinn, sold the organization to Tom Benson two years later for $338 million. Benson changed the team's name from the Hornets to the Pelicans beginning with the 2013-14 season, inspired by Louisiana's state bird, the brown pelican. Birmingham Squadron is the Pelicans' affiliate team, playing in the NBA G League. Forbes Magazine estimated the Pelicans' value at $1.6 billion in October 2022.

FINANCIAL DATA: *Note: Data for latest year may not have been available at press time.*

In U.S. $	2022	2021	2020	2019	2018	2017
Revenue	253,500,000					
R&D Expense						
Operating Income						
Operating Margin %						
SGA Expense						
Net Income						
Operating Cash Flow						
Capital Expenditure						
EBITDA						
Return on Assets %						
Return on Equity %						
Debt to Equity						

CONTACT INFORMATION:

Phone: 504-593-4700   Fax: 504-593-4702
Toll-Free:
Address: 5800 Airline Dr., Metairie, LA 70003 United States

STOCK TICKER/OTHER:

Stock Ticker: Private   Exchange:
Employees: 300   Fiscal Year Ends: 06/30
Parent Company:

SALARIES/BONUSES:

Top Exec. Salary: $ Bonus: $
Second Exec. Salary: $ Bonus: $

OTHER THOUGHTS:

Estimated Female Officers or Directors: 5
Hot Spot for Advancement for Women/Minorities: Y

New Orleans Saints

www.neworleanssaints.com

NAIC Code: 711211C

TYPES OF BUSINESS:

Professional Football Team
Team Management and Operations

BRANDS/DIVISIONS/AFFILIATES:

CONTACTS: *Note: Officers with more than one job title may be intentionally listed here more than once.*

Gayle Benson, CEO
Dennis Lauscha, Pres.
Ed Lang, CFO
Greg Bensel, Sr. VP-Communications
Greg Rouchell, Sr. VP-Human Resources
Jody Barbier, Sr. Dir.-IT Oper.
Vicky Neumeyer, General Counsel
James Nagaoka, Dir.-Football Oper.
Ben Hales, VP-Bus. Dev.
Greg Bensel, VP-Comm.
Charleen Sharpe, Comptroller
Mickey Loomis, Exec. VP
Rita Benson LeBlanc, Vice Chmn.
Sean Payton, Head Coach
Doug Miller, Sr. Dir.-Public Rel.
Ben Hales, COO

GROWTH PLANS/SPECIAL FEATURES:

The New Orleans Saints, owned and operated by New Orleans Saints, L.P., is a professional football team playing in the National Football League (NFL), National Football Conference (NFC) based in New Orleans, Louisiana. The team was founded as an expansion team on All Saints' Day in 1966. Led by coach Jim Haslett, the team won its first playoff game at the end of the 2000 season. In 2006, Sean Payton took over as the Saints head coach, leading the team to its best record, the league's top-ranked offense and an appearance in the NFC Championship game. Following mixed performances in 2007 and 2008, the team achieved their best season ever in 2009, winning 13 out of 16 regular season games, eventually riding the tide all the way to their first Super Bowl victory in a 31-17 game against the Indianapolis Colts. In all, the Saints have clenched one conference championship and nine division championships (2020 most recently), and have made 14 playoff appearances (most recently in 2020). The Saints play their home games in the Caesars Superdome, the largest fixed domed structure in the world. Damaged by Hurricane Katrina in 2005, New Orleans spent $185 million to repair and refurbish the stadium. It seats approximately 76,400 spectators for football games and is owned by the Louisiana Stadium/Expo District. The team averaged 68,987 in home game attendance during the 2022-23 season. The Saints have contributed several former players to the Pro Football Hall of Fame, including Doug Atkins, Earl Campbell, Jim Finks, Jim Taylor, Morten Andersen and Sam Mills, as well as former coach Hank Stram. Forbes valued the team at $3.575 billion in 2022.

FINANCIAL DATA: *Note: Data for latest year may not have been available at press time.*

In U.S. $	2022	2021	2020	2019	2018	2017
Revenue	550,550,000					
R&D Expense						
Operating Income						
Operating Margin %						
SGA Expense						
Net Income						
Operating Cash Flow						
Capital Expenditure						
EBITDA						
Return on Assets %						
Return on Equity %						
Debt to Equity						

CONTACT INFORMATION:

Phone: 504-733-0255   Fax:
Toll-Free:
Address: 5800 Airline Dr., Metairie, LA 70003 United States

STOCK TICKER/OTHER:

Stock Ticker: Private   Exchange:
Employees: 300   Fiscal Year Ends: 03/31
Parent Company:

SALARIES/BONUSES:

Top Exec. Salary: $ Bonus: $
Second Exec. Salary: $ Bonus: $

OTHER THOUGHTS:

Estimated Female Officers or Directors: 2
Hot Spot for Advancement for Women/Minorities: Y

New York City FC

www.nycfc.com

NAIC Code: 711211D

TYPES OF BUSINESS:

Major League Soccer Team
Team Management and Operations

BRANDS/DIVISIONS/AFFILIATES:

City Football Group
Yankee Global Enterprises

CONTACTS: *Note: Officers with more than one job title may be intentionally listed here more than once.*

Brad Sims, CEO
Jennifer O'Sullivan, COO
Andrew Widdowson, CFO
Sam Cooke, VP-Communications
Christina King, VP-Human Resources
Jose Paolini Neto, VP-Technology
Lauren Scrima, VP-Mktg.

GROWTH PLANS/SPECIAL FEATURES:

The New York City FC is a Major League Soccer (MLS) club based in New York, New York. The team has several nicknames, including The Pigeons, The Bronx Blues, The Boys in Blue and Cityzens. It is 80% owned by the City Football Group and 20% owned by Yankee Global Enterprises. New York City FC was founded in 2013 and swiftly made it to the conference semifinals in 2016, but did not win. They were the runners up in the Supporters' Shield in 2017 and 2019, and clenched the MLS Cup in 2021 defeating the Portland Timbers 2-4 in penalty shootouts with a 1-1 score before going into extra time, in which neither team scored. The New York City FC is a member of the Eastern Conference (EC) of the MLS. The EC is also composed of the Atlanta United FC, Charlotte FC, Chicago Fire FC, FC Cincinnati, Columbus Crew, DC United, Inter Miami CF, CF Montreal, Nashville SC, New England Revolution, New York Red Bulls, Orlando City SC, Philadelphia Union and Toronto FC. The team primarily plays its home games in Yankee Stadium, which has a normal soccer capacity of 30,321 but is expandable to 47,422; but has also been playing in the Red Bull Arena since 2020 when scheduling conflicts arise. NYC FC's average home game attendance during the 2022 season was 17,180.

FINANCIAL DATA: *Note: Data for latest year may not have been available at press time.*

In U.S. $	2022	2021	2020	2019	2018	2017
Revenue	33,736,500					
R&D Expense						
Operating Income						
Operating Margin %						
SGA Expense						
Net Income						
Operating Cash Flow						
Capital Expenditure						
EBITDA						
Return on Assets %						
Return on Equity %						
Debt to Equity						

CONTACT INFORMATION:

Phone: 212-738-5900   Fax: 212-738-5901
Toll-Free: 855-776-9232
Address: 600 Third Ave., Fl. 30, New York, NY 10016 United States

STOCK TICKER/OTHER:

Stock Ticker: Private   Exchange:
Employees: Fiscal Year Ends:
Parent Company:

SALARIES/BONUSES:

Top Exec. Salary: $ Bonus: $
Second Exec. Salary: $ Bonus: $

OTHER THOUGHTS:

Estimated Female Officers or Directors:
Hot Spot for Advancement for Women/Minorities:

New York Giants
www.giants.com

NAIC Code: 711211C

TYPES OF BUSINESS:
Professional Football Team
Team Management and Operations

BRANDS/DIVISIONS/AFFILIATES:

CONTACTS: *Note: Officers with more than one job title may be intentionally listed here more than once.*
John K. Mara, CEO
Joe Schoen, Sr. VP
Christine Procops, CFO
Pete Guellt, Chief Business Officer
Celeste Bell, Sr. VP-Human Resources
Justin Warren, VP-IT
Jim Phelan, Dir.-Admin.
William J. Heller, General Counsel
Doug Smoyer, VP-Bus. Dev.
Nilay Shah, Dir.-Digital & Social Media Strategy
Pat Hanlon, Sr. VP-Comm.
Jonathan Tisch, Treas.
Jerry Reese, Sr. VP
Tom Coughlin, Head Coach
Chris Mara, Sr. VP-Player Personnel
John Gorman, Dir.-Ticketing
Steve Tisch, Chmn.

GROWTH PLANS/SPECIAL FEATURES:
The New York Giants is a professional football team in the National Football League (NFL). The franchise plays in the Eastern Division of the National Football Conference (NFC). The team joined the NFL in 1925 along with four other teams, and it is the only remaining team from that year. The Giants won its first title in 1927. Since then, the team has won seven more NFL Championships, four being Super Bowls (1986, 1990, 2007 and 2011). The franchise achieved one of the greatest upsets in NFL Super Bowl history when it beat the previously undefeated New England Patriots in 2007. In total, the Giants have won 11 conference championships and 16 division championships, and have made 33 playoff appearances (most recently in 2022). Notable Giants of the past include Lawrence Taylor, Jim Thorpe, Vince Lombardi, Larry Csonka, Frank Gifford and Tom Landry. In 1991, 50% of the ownership of the team passed from the Mara family, who had owned the team since its 1925 inception, to Preston Robert Tisch, a successful businessman whose operations included the Loews Corporation and Diamond Offshore Drilling. The Tisch and Mara families continue to co-own the New York Giants. Beginning with the 2010 season, the team has played in the MetLife Stadium in East Rutherford, New Jersey, which has a capacity of about 82,500. The team shares the facility with the New York Jets, and averaged 76,474 in home game attendance during the 2022-23 season. Forbes valued the team at $6 billion in 2022.

FINANCIAL DATA: *Note: Data for latest year may not have been available at press time.*

In U.S. $	2022	2021	2020	2019	2018	2017
Revenue	570,000,000					
R&D Expense						
Operating Income						
Operating Margin %						
SGA Expense						
Net Income						
Operating Cash Flow						
Capital Expenditure						
EBITDA						
Return on Assets %						
Return on Equity %						
Debt to Equity						

CONTACT INFORMATION:
Phone: 201-935-8222   Fax: 201-935-8493
Toll-Free:
Address: 1925 Giants Dr., East Rutherford, NJ 07073-2140 United States

STOCK TICKER/OTHER:
Stock Ticker: Private   Exchange:
Employees: 185   Fiscal Year Ends: 02/28
Parent Company:

SALARIES/BONUSES:
Top Exec. Salary: $ Bonus: $
Second Exec. Salary: $ Bonus: $

OTHER THOUGHTS:
Estimated Female Officers or Directors: 7
Hot Spot for Advancement for Women/Minorities: Y

Sales, profits and employees may be estimates. Financial information, benefits and other data can change quickly and may vary from those stated here.

New York Islanders

www.nhl.com/islanders

NAIC Code: 711211F

TYPES OF BUSINESS:

Professional Hockey Team (NHL)
Team Management and Operations

BRANDS/DIVISIONS/AFFILIATES:

New York Islanders Hockey Club LP
UBS Arena
Bridgeport Islanders
Worcester Railers

CONTACTS: *Note: Officers with more than one job title may be intentionally listed here more than once.*

Lou Lamoriello, Gen. Mngr.
Joanne Holewa, Mngr.-Hockey Oper.
Lane Lambert, Head Coach
Joanne Holewa, Mgr.-Hockey Admin.
Tim Beach, VP-Oper.
Kimber Auerbach, Dir.-Comm.
Frank Romano, Controller
Jack Capuano, Head Coach
Garth Snow, Gen. Mgr.
Ken Morrow, Dir.-Pro Scouting
Ralph Sellitti, VP-Ticket Sales
Scott Malkin, Governor
Vellu-Pekka Kautonen, Chief European Scout

GROWTH PLANS/SPECIAL FEATURES:

The New York Islanders franchise is a professional hockey team playing in the Metropolitan division of the Eastern conference within the National Hockey League (NHL). The team was founded in 1972 by William Shea, the originator of the New York Mets major league baseball team. The Islanders started out with one of the worst records in professional hockey history, but by the late 1970s, the team began to improve. The Islanders won four Stanley Cup Championships back-to-back between 1980 and 1983. This period marked the apex of the Islanders' performance, as they won six conference championships in 1977-83 and six division champions in 1977-81, 1983 and 1987. The team has achieved intermittent playoff success in more recent times; it last saw the playoffs in 2006, 2013, 2015 and 2016. The Islanders are owned by the New York Islanders Hockey Club, LP. The Islanders play home games at the UBS Arena, a multi-purpose complex in Elmont that opened in late-2021 and is owned by New York Arena Partners, a joint venture of the New York Islands, Oak View Group, and Sterling Equities. UBS Arena has a 17,255-seat capacity for ice hockey games, and the Islanders averaged 16,912 in home game attendance during the 2022-23 season. The team maintains a minor league affiliation with the Bridgeport Islanders in the American Hockey League (AHL) and the Worcester Railers in the ECHL. Forbes valued the New York Islanders at $1.02 billion in December 2022.

FINANCIAL DATA: *Note: Data for latest year may not have been available at press time.*

In U.S. $	2022	2021	2020	2019	2018	2017
Revenue	107,900,000					
R&D Expense						
Operating Income						
Operating Margin %						
SGA Expense						
Net Income						
Operating Cash Flow						
Capital Expenditure						
EBITDA						
Return on Assets %						
Return on Equity %						
Debt to Equity						

CONTACT INFORMATION:

Phone: 516-501-6700   Fax:
Toll-Free:
Address: 15 Verbena Ave., Floral Park, NY 11001 United States

STOCK TICKER/OTHER:

Stock Ticker: Private   Exchange:
Employees: 240   Fiscal Year Ends: 08/31
Parent Company:

SALARIES/BONUSES:

Top Exec. Salary: $ Bonus: $
Second Exec. Salary: $ Bonus: $

OTHER THOUGHTS:

Estimated Female Officers or Directors: 5
Hot Spot for Advancement for Women/Minorities: Y

New York Jets

www.newyorkjets.com

NAIC Code: 711211C

TYPES OF BUSINESS:

Professional Football Team
Team Management and Operations

BRANDS/DIVISIONS/AFFILIATES:

New York Jets LLC

CONTACTS: Note: Officers with more than one job title may be intentionally listed here more than once.

Joe Douglas, Gen. Mngr.
Hymie Ethai, Pres.
Elaine Chen, VP-Finance
Tim Kemp, VP-Mktg.
Courtney Anderson, VP-Human Resources & Admin.
Brian Friedman, COO
Rex Ryan, Head Coach
John Idzik, Gen. Mgr.
Brendan Phophett, Dir.-Pro Personnel
Jeff Bauer, Dir.-College Scouting
Robert Wood Johnson, Chmn.

GROWTH PLANS/SPECIAL FEATURES:

The New York Jets, owned by Robert (Woody) and Christopher Johnson, and operated by New York Jets LLC, is a professional football team in the National Football League (NFL). The team plays in the Eastern Division of the NFL's American Football Conference (AFC). The Jets originated as the New York Titans, a charter member of the American Football League, in 1960. After a few poor seasons, the team was bought out by a group headed by Sonny Werblin, head of Music Corporation of America (MCA). In 1963, the team's name changed to the Jets due to its new stadium's proximity to LaGuardia Airport. In 1965, the Jets signed Joe Namath, their foremost franchise player and one of the most celebrated quarterbacks of all time. Namath simultaneously propelled the Jets onto the national scene and made them the most beloved football team in New York. He led the Jets to its only Super Bowl win over the then-Baltimore Colts in the 1968-69 season. In 2000, Robert Woody Johnson, IV purchased the team for $635 million. In total, the team has won four division championships and has made 14 playoff appearances. From 1984 to 2009, the Jets played all home games at the Giants Stadium located in East Rutherford, New Jersey. The team shared this venue with the New York Giants. In 2010, the Jets moved to MetLife Stadium, an 82,500-capacity complex that it also shares with the Giants. Average home game attendance was 78,009 during the 2022-23 season. Forbes valued the team at $5.4 billion in 2022.

FINANCIAL DATA: Note: Data for latest year may not have been available at press time.

In U.S. $	2022	2021	2020	2019	2018	2017
Revenue	547,300,000					
R&D Expense						
Operating Income						
Operating Margin %						
SGA Expense						
Net Income						
Operating Cash Flow						
Capital Expenditure						
EBITDA						
Return on Assets %						
Return on Equity %						
Debt to Equity						

CONTACT INFORMATION:

Phone: 973-549-4800   Fax:
Toll-Free: 800-469-5387
Address: One Jets Dr., Florham Park, NJ 07932 United States

STOCK TICKER/OTHER:

Stock Ticker: Private   Exchange:
Employees: 435   Fiscal Year Ends: 02/28
Parent Company:

SALARIES/BONUSES:

Top Exec. Salary: $ Bonus: $
Second Exec. Salary: $ Bonus: $

OTHER THOUGHTS:

Estimated Female Officers or Directors:
Hot Spot for Advancement for Women/Minorities:

New York Knickerbockers

www.nba.com/knicks

NAIC Code: 711211B

TYPES OF BUSINESS:

Professional Basketball Team
Team Management and Operations

BRANDS/DIVISIONS/AFFILIATES:

Madison Square Garden Company (The)
Madison Square Garden
Knicks City Dancers
Knicks City Kids

CONTACTS: *Note: Officers with more than one job title may be intentionally listed here more than once.*

Leon Rose, Pres.
David Hopkinson, COO
Victoria Mink, CFO
Jeremy Watkins, Sr. VP-Communications
Jamaal Lesane, Exec. VP-Gen. Counsel
Daniel Fleeter, Sr. VP-Bus. Oper.
Glen Grunwald, Sr. VP
Marc Schoenfeld, Sr. VP-Legal & Bus. Affairs, Team Oper.
Mark Piazza, Sr. VP-Sports Team Oper.
Jonathan Supranowitz, VP-Public Rel.
John Cudmore, Sr. VP-Finance
John Master, Sr. VP-Legal & Bus. Affairs, Sports Oper.
Mike Woodson, Head Coach
James L. Dolan, Chmn.

GROWTH PLANS/SPECIAL FEATURES:

The New York Knickerbockers (NY Knicks) is a professional basketball team playing in the National Basketball Association (NBA). Uncommonly, the Knicks is a charter member of the NBA still playing in its original city. The franchise was founded in 1946 by The Madison Square Garden Company (MSGI) president Ned Irish. The NBA team has won two championships, four conference titles and eight division titles (most recently in 2013). MSGI also owns the New York Rangers hockey club. The Knicks have played its homes games in the fourth version of Madison Square Garden since 1968. The current arena features a capacity to seat 19,812 spectators per game. Game night entertainment includes the Knicks City Dancers and the Knicks City Kids. The team has risen to NBA prominence in three different decades: the early 50s, when the team played for the NBA title three times; the 70s, when it won two NBA championships with a roster including Willis Reed, Walt Frazier, Dave DeBusschere, Earl Monroe and Bill Bradley; and the 90s, with center Patrick Ewing leading a team that advanced to the NBA finals in 1994 and 1999. Forbes estimated the team to be the most valuable franchise in the NBA, at approximately $5.8 billion, in October 2021. Home attendance average was 18,527 during the 2021-22 season.

FINANCIAL DATA: *Note: Data for latest year may not have been available at press time.*

In U.S. $	2022	2021	2020	2019	2018	2017
Revenue	467,300,000	298,000,000	421,000,000			
R&D Expense						
Operating Income						
Operating Margin %						
SGA Expense						
Net Income						
Operating Cash Flow						
Capital Expenditure						
EBITDA						
Return on Assets %						
Return on Equity %						
Debt to Equity						

CONTACT INFORMATION:

Phone: 212-465-6471   Fax: 212-465-6498
Toll-Free:
Address: 2 Pennsylvania Plz., Madison Square Garden, New York, NY 10121-0091 United States

STOCK TICKER/OTHER:

Stock Ticker: Subsidiary   Exchange:
Employees: Fiscal Year Ends: 12/31
Parent Company: MSG Sports

SALARIES/BONUSES:

Top Exec. Salary: $ Bonus: $
Second Exec. Salary: $ Bonus: $

OTHER THOUGHTS:

Estimated Female Officers or Directors: 15
Hot Spot for Advancement for Women/Minorities: Y

New York Liberty

NAIC Code: 711211E

TYPES OF BUSINESS:

Women's Professional Basketball Team
Team Management and Operations

BRANDS/DIVISIONS/AFFILIATES:

GROWTH PLANS/SPECIAL FEATURES:

The New York Liberty is a Women's National Basketball Association (WNBA) team that was one of the eight original WNBA teams founded in 1997. NY Liberty plays in the Eastern Conference along with Atlanta Dream, Chicago Sky, Connecticut Sun, Indiana Fever and Washington Mystics. The team has appeared in the Finals several times, but has yet to win a championship. However, Liberty holds four conference championship titles: 1997, 1999, 2000 and 2002. NY Liberty plays in the Barclays Center, a 17,732-basketball-seat multi-purpose area in Brooklyn. The team averaged 5,327 fans in attendance per home game during the 2022 season. NY Liberty was acquired by Joseph Tsai, an Asian Canadian businessman who also owns the Brooklyn Nets.

CONTACTS: Note: Officers with more than one job title may be intentionally listed here more than once.

Keia Clarke, CEO
Morgan Taylor, Dir.-Bus. Oper.
John Master, Sr. VP-Legal Affairs
Kevin Christie, Sr. VP-Bus. Dev.
John Cudmore, Sr. VP-Finance
Greg Economou, Exec. VP-Corp. Sales & Solutions
Justin Johnson, Sr. VP-Partnership Strategy
Hank J. Ratner, CEO
Mark Piazza, Sr. VP-Sports Team Oper.
Joe and Clara Wu Tsai, Governors

FINANCIAL DATA: Note: Data for latest year may not have been available at press time.

In U.S. $	2022	2021	2020	2019	2018	2017
Revenue						
R&D Expense						
Operating Income						
Operating Margin %						
SGA Expense						
Net Income						
Operating Cash Flow						
Capital Expenditure						
EBITDA						
Return on Assets %						
Return on Equity %						
Debt to Equity						

CONTACT INFORMATION:

Phone: 212-465-6000   Fax: 212-465-6073
Toll-Free:
Address: 168 39th St., Brooklyn, NY 11232 United States

STOCK TICKER/OTHER:

Stock Ticker: Private   Exchange:
Employees: 40   Fiscal Year Ends: 12/31
Parent Company:

SALARIES/BONUSES:

Top Exec. Salary: $ Bonus: $
Second Exec. Salary: $ Bonus: $

OTHER THOUGHTS:

Estimated Female Officers or Directors: 14
Hot Spot for Advancement for Women/Minorities: Y

Sales, profits and employees may be estimates. Financial information, benefits and other data can change quickly and may vary from those stated here.

New York Mets
NAIC Code: 711211A

TYPES OF BUSINESS:
Professional Baseball Team
Team Management and Operations

BRANDS/DIVISIONS/AFFILIATES:

CONTACTS: *Note: Officers with more than one job title may be intentionally listed here more than once.*
Steven A. Cohen, CEO
Andy Goldberg, CMO
Steve Canna, CFO
Nance Elder, CCO
Ariel Speicher, Dir.-Human Resources
Mark Brubaker, CTO
David Cohen, General Counsel
Dave Howard, Exec. VP-Bus. Oper.
David Newman, Sr. VP-Mktg. & Comm.
Leonard Labita, Controller
Sandy Alderson, Gen. Mgr.
Mike Landeen, Sr. VP-Venue Svcs. & Oper.
Jay Horwitz, VP-Media Rel.
Terry Collins, Mgr.
Steven A. Cohen, Chmn.

GROWTH PLANS/SPECIAL FEATURES:
The New York Mets entered Major League Baseball (MLB) as an expansion team in 1962. Despite 120 losses in their first season, the Mets went on to win their first World Series in 1969, after only seven years as a franchise. The team won its second World Series in 1986 and has made it to the World Series five times, including the all-New York Subway Series in 2000, which the Mets lost to the Yankees. Former Mets stars include Nolan Ryan, Gil Hodges, Tug McGraw, Tom Seaver, Daryl Strawberry, Dwight Gooden, Yogi Berra and Mike Piazza. Following years of mediocre performance, Sterling Doubleday Enterprises sold the team to Fred Wilpon in 2005, who promised to upgrade the team on the field. He made significant changes in the team's management strategy, including the establishment of their own cable network, SportsNet New York, to broadcast the team's games. He then hired Omar Minaya as general manager, the first Hispanic general manager in MLB history. However, due to a string of lackluster seasons, Minaya was replaced by Sandy Alderson at the end of the 2010 season. For the 2014-15 season, the Mets clinched the Eastern division title, as well as the National League pennant, but lost to the Kansas City Royals in the World Series. In 2020, Steve Cohen became the majority owner of the Mets (95%), with the Wilpon family retaining the other 5%. After years of hosting games at Shea Stadium, the team played its first game at the newly built Citi Field in 2009. The open-air stadium, located in the Queens, holds 41,922 spectators. The Mets averaged 33,308 in home game attendance during the 2022-23 season. Forbes estimated the team to be worth $2.9 billion in March 2023.

FINANCIAL DATA: *Note: Data for latest year may not have been available at press time.*

In U.S. $	2022	2021	2020	2019	2018	2017
Revenue	431,600,000					
R&D Expense						
Operating Income						
Operating Margin %						
SGA Expense						
Net Income						
Operating Cash Flow						
Capital Expenditure						
EBITDA						
Return on Assets %						
Return on Equity %						
Debt to Equity						

CONTACT INFORMATION:
Phone: 718-507-6387   Fax: 718-507-6395
Toll-Free:
Address: 120-01 Roosevelt Ave., Flushing, NY 11368 United States

STOCK TICKER/OTHER:
Stock Ticker: Private   Exchange:
Employees: 595   Fiscal Year Ends: 09/30
Parent Company:

SALARIES/BONUSES:
Top Exec. Salary: $ Bonus: $
Second Exec. Salary: $ Bonus: $

OTHER THOUGHTS:
Estimated Female Officers or Directors: 1
Hot Spot for Advancement for Women/Minorities:

New York Rangers

rangers.nhl.com

NAIC Code: 711211F

TYPES OF BUSINESS:

Professional Hockey Team (NHL)
Team Management and Operations

BRANDS/DIVISIONS/AFFILIATES:

Madison Square Garden Inc
Hartford Wolf Pack
Jacksonville Icemen

CONTACTS: *Note: Officers with more than one job title may be intentionally listed here more than once.*

David Hopkinson, Pres.
Victoria Mink, CFO
Jeremy Watkins, Sr. VP-Communications
John Cudmore, Sr. VP-Sports Strategy & Admin.
Daniel Fleeter, Sr. VP-Bus. Oper.
James L. Dolan, Chmn.

GROWTH PLANS/SPECIAL FEATURES:

The New York Rangers is a professional hockey team playing in the National Hockey League (NHL). The team, though originally incorporated as the New York Giants Hockey Club in 1926, soon became known as Tex's Rangers after initial owner Tex Rickard. In the 1927-28 season, its second year, the team won the Stanley Cup. The early Rangers team also won the Stanley Cup in 1933 and 1940, but for the most part, the team played mediocre hockey until the late 1960s. In 1968, the team moved into Madison Square Garden, marking an era of rejuvenation. The Rangers made the playoffs consistently throughout the modern era, but faced post-season setbacks nonetheless, failing to win a Stanley Cup for over 50 years. Finally, in the 1993-94 season, the Rangers put together a team whose roster featured Mark Messier, Adam Graves, Brian Leetch and Sergei Zubov. The team won the President's Trophy, Leetch became the first American to win the Conn Smythe Trophy and the Rangers again won the Stanley Cup. In the 2014-15 season, the Rangers clinched another President's Trophy and the division title. The franchise maintains a minor league affiliation with the Hartford Wolf Pack in the American Hockey League and the Jacksonville Icemen in the ECHL. The Rangers team is owned by Madison Square Garden, Inc (MSG). Forbes estimated the team at $2.2 billion in December 2022, the most valuable team in the NHL. The team averaged approximately 17,859 fans in attendance per home game in its 2022-23 season. The Rangers currently play in the Eastern Conference of the Atlantic Division alongside the Boston Bruins, Buffalo Sabres, Detroit Red Wings, Florida Panthers, Montreal Canadiens, Ottawa Senators, Tampa Bay Lightning and Toronto Maple Leafs.

FINANCIAL DATA: *Note: Data for latest year may not have been available at press time.*

In U.S. $	2022	2021	2020	2019	2018	2017
Revenue	207,350,000	94,000,000	225,000,000		246,000,000	246,000,000
R&D Expense						
Operating Income						
Operating Margin %						
SGA Expense						
Net Income						
Operating Cash Flow						
Capital Expenditure						
EBITDA						
Return on Assets %						
Return on Equity %						
Debt to Equity						

CONTACT INFORMATION:

Phone: 212-465-6000   Fax: 212-465-6494
Toll-Free:
Address: 2 Pennsylvania Plaza, New York, NY 10121 United States

STOCK TICKER/OTHER:

Stock Ticker: Subsidiary   Exchange:
Employees: 250   Fiscal Year Ends: 12/31
Parent Company: MSG Sports

SALARIES/BONUSES:

Top Exec. Salary: $ Bonus: $
Second Exec. Salary: $ Bonus: $

OTHER THOUGHTS:

Estimated Female Officers or Directors: 10
Hot Spot for Advancement for Women/Minorities: Y

New York Red Bulls

NAIC Code: 711211D

TYPES OF BUSINESS:

Major League Soccer Team
Team Management and Operations

BRANDS/DIVISIONS/AFFILIATES:

Red Bull GmbH
Red Bull Arena
MetroStars
Empire Soccer Club

CONTACTS: *Note: Officers with more than one job title may be intentionally listed here more than once.*

Denis Hamlett, Sporting Dir.
Scott Bernstein, Dir.-Team Oper.
J. Carlos Kuri, General Counsel
Shaun Oliver, VP-Oper.
Paul Hawkins, Dir.-Multimedia
Brian Tsao, Sr. Dir.-Comm.
Greg Domico, VP-Finance
Hans Backe, Head Coach
Fabian Lopez, Dir.-Ticket Oper.
Dan Marrett, Dir.-Mktg.
Melissa Brennan, Dir.-Corp. Sponsorships

GROWTH PLANS/SPECIAL FEATURES:

The New York Red Bulls, formerly the MetroStars and the Empire Soccer Club before that, is one of the founding teams of Major League Soccer (MLS). The club competes in the Eastern Conference of the MLS alongside teams such as Atlanta United FC, Charlotte FC, Chicago Fire FC, FC Cincinnati, Columbus Crew, DC United, Inter Miami CF, CF Montreal, Nashville SC, New England Revolution, New York City FC, Orlando City SC, Philadelphia Union and Toronto FC. The Red Bulls became the first U.S.-based MLS club to win a foreign trophy when it defeated Viking FK of Norway to win the La Manga Cup in 2004. The team's performance on the domestic front has been mixed, with only one appearance in the MLS cup final, which it lost to the Columbus Crew in 2008. The Red Bull's won the Supporters' Shield in 2013, 2015 and 2018, and were the runners-up in the U.S. Open Cup in 2003 and 2017. The Red Bulls are owned and operated by Austrian beverage company Red Bull GmbH, which purchased the company in March 2006 from Anschutz Entertainment Group. As part of the agreement, the two companies have partnered in the development of an outdoor stadium complex, Red Bull Arena, located in Harrison, New Jersey. The stadium opened in 2010 and has a capacity of 25,000. The club's training center is in Hanover, New Jersey, covering about 15 acres of the 73-acre property which includes three fields (two grass and one turf) each the size of the one at Red Bull Arena. Average attendance for home games was 17,002 during the 2022 season.

FINANCIAL DATA: *Note: Data for latest year may not have been available at press time.*

In U.S. $	2022	2021	2020	2019	2018	2017
Revenue	18,100,000	17,836,000	17,150,000		25,000,000	25,000,000
R&D Expense						
Operating Income						
Operating Margin %						
SGA Expense						
Net Income						
Operating Cash Flow						
Capital Expenditure						
EBITDA						
Return on Assets %						
Return on Equity %						
Debt to Equity						

CONTACT INFORMATION:

Phone: 201-583-7000   Fax: 201-583-7055
Toll-Free: 877-727-6223
Address: 600 Cape May St., Harrison, NJ 07029 United States

STOCK TICKER/OTHER:

Stock Ticker: Subsidiary   Exchange:
Employees: 420   Fiscal Year Ends:
Parent Company: Red Bull GmbH

SALARIES/BONUSES:

Top Exec. Salary: $ Bonus: $
Second Exec. Salary: $ Bonus: $

OTHER THOUGHTS:

Estimated Female Officers or Directors: 8
Hot Spot for Advancement for Women/Minorities: Y

New York Yankees

NAIC Code: 711211A

www.mlb.com/yankees

TYPES OF BUSINESS:

Professional Baseball Team
Team Management and Operations

BRANDS/DIVISIONS/AFFILIATES:

Yankee Stadium
Yankees Entertainment & Sports Network (YES)
Yankee Global Enterprises

CONTACTS: Note: Officers with more than one job title may be intentionally listed here more than once.

Hal Steinbrenner, Managing General Partner
Randy Levine, Pres.
Scott M. Krug, CFO
Deborah A. Tymon, Sr. VP-Mktg.
Aryn Sobo, VP-Human Resources
Mike Lane, CIO
Alan Chang, Deputy General Counsel
Mark Newman, Sr. VP-Baseball Oper.
Marty Greenspun, Sr. VP-Strategic Ventures
Brian Smith, Sr. VP-Corp. & Comm. Rel.
Derrick Baio, Controller
Henry G. Steinbrenner, Co-Chmn.
Brian Cashman, Sr. VP
Anthony Bruno, Sr. VP
Michael J. Tusiani, Sr. VP-Corp. Sales & Sponsorships
Lonn A. Trost, COO
Felix M. Lopez, Chief Int'l Officer

GROWTH PLANS/SPECIAL FEATURES:

The New York Yankees are a baseball team playing in Major League Baseball's (MLB) Eastern Division of the American League (AL). The team is one of the most successful and recognizable franchises in the history of professional sports. The venerable club has won 27 World Series titles (most recently in 2009), 40 AL pennants and 20 division titles (most recently in 2022). The Yankees has fielded several legendary players, including Babe Ruth, Mickey Mantle, Joe DiMaggio, Lou Gehrig, Reggie Jackson, Whitey Ford, Mariano Rivera, Derek Jeter and Alex Rodriguez. Opening in 1923, the famed Yankee Stadium was the first triple-decked structure built for baseball. Since 2009, the team has played in the new Yankee Stadium, located across the street from the original park. The current stadium holds over 47,500 baseball spectators and features several restaurants and bars. The club averaged 40,207 fans per home game during the 2022-23 season. Since 1973, the Yankees had been owned by George Steinbrenner, who passed away in 2010. His reign was known for an excessive interest in the team, meddling micromanagement, enormous payrolls and great success. Before his death, he ceded much of the control of the team to his sons Hank and Hal Steinbrenner. The team's games are broadcast on The Yankees Entertainment and Sports Network (YES). Forbes valued the franchise at $7.1 billion in March 2023, the highest in baseball.

FINANCIAL DATA: Note: Data for latest year may not have been available at press time.

In U.S. $	2022	2021	2020	2019	2018	2017
Revenue	378,300,000					
R&D Expense						
Operating Income						
Operating Margin %						
SGA Expense						
Net Income						
Operating Cash Flow						
Capital Expenditure						
EBITDA						
Return on Assets %						
Return on Equity %						
Debt to Equity						

CONTACT INFORMATION:

Phone: 718-293-4300   Fax: 718-293-8431
Toll-Free:
Address: One E. 161st St., Yankee Stadium, Bronx, NY 10451 United States

STOCK TICKER/OTHER:

Stock Ticker: Private   Exchange:
Employees: 900   Fiscal Year Ends: 12/31
Parent Company:

SALARIES/BONUSES:

Top Exec. Salary: $ Bonus: $
Second Exec. Salary: $ Bonus: $

OTHER THOUGHTS:

Estimated Female Officers or Directors: 10
Hot Spot for Advancement for Women/Minorities: Y

Newcastle United Football Club

www.nufc.co.uk

NAIC Code: 711211D

TYPES OF BUSINESS:

Soccer Team
Team Management and Operations

BRANDS/DIVISIONS/AFFILIATES:

Public Investment Fund
RB Sports & Media
PCP Capital Partners

CONTACTS: *Note: Officers with more than one job title may be intentionally listed here more than once.*

Darren Eales, CEO
Eddie Howe, Manager
Claire Alexander, Dir.-Finance
Wendy Taylor, Head-Media
Kate Bradley, Mgr.-Charitable Foundation
Yasir Al-Rumayyan, Chmn.

GROWTH PLANS/SPECIAL FEATURES:

Newcastle United Football Club is a professional English football (soccer) team that plays primarily in the English Premier League. Founded in 1892 through the merger of the Newcastle East End and the Newcastle West End, the team did well throughout the pre-Premiership era, winning four First Division championships, six FA Cups, an Inter-Cities Fairs Cup, two Texaco Cups and an Anglo-Italian Cup. However, by 1992 the club was facing relegation into Division Three. By the 1993-94 season, Newcastle was promoted to the FA Premier League, where it remained for the next 16 seasons. The club invested heavily in international talent, and gained intermittent access to the lucrative UEFA Champions' League competition (the former European Cup). Newcastle plays its home games at St. James' Park in Newcastle upon Tyne. The stadium has been the team's home since its founding in 1891 and, following various expansions, boasts one of the highest U.K. football stadium capacities, at 52,305 seats. As a result of the complex promotion and relegation rules governing the U.K. league system, Newcastle spent the 2009-10 season in the second-tier Championship League, but in April 2010 the team earned its way back into the Premier League, where it returned for the 2010-11 season. Newcastle United ranked 4th in the 2022-23 season. The club is majority-owned (80%) by Public Investment Fund of Saudi Arabia, and 10% each by RB Sports & Media and PCP Capital Partners.

FINANCIAL DATA: *Note: Data for latest year may not have been available at press time.*

In U.S. $	2022	2021	2020	2019	2018	2017
Revenue	220,000,000	194,164,382	188,038,298	240,000,000	111,142,000	111,142,000
R&D Expense						
Operating Income						
Operating Margin %						
SGA Expense						
Net Income		-16,895,902	-27,725,175	79,000,000	-53,560,700	-53,560,700
Operating Cash Flow						
Capital Expenditure						
EBITDA						
Return on Assets %						
Return on Equity %						
Debt to Equity						

CONTACT INFORMATION:

Phone: 44-844-372-1892   Fax:
Toll-Free:
Address: St. James' Park, Strawberry Pl., Newcastle, NE1 4ST United Kingdom

STOCK TICKER/OTHER:

Stock Ticker: Private   Exchange:
Employees: 220   Fiscal Year Ends: 06/30
Parent Company: Public Investment Fund

SALARIES/BONUSES:

Top Exec. Salary: $ Bonus: $
Second Exec. Salary: $ Bonus: $

OTHER THOUGHTS:

Estimated Female Officers or Directors: 2
Hot Spot for Advancement for Women/Minorities:

Newport Sports Management Inc

www.thehockeyagency.com

NAIC Code: 711410

TYPES OF BUSINESS:

Athlete Management Agency
Professional Hockey Representation
Athlete & Corporate Marketing Services
Contract Negotiations & Draft Preparation Services
Financial Management Services
Athlete Training & Development Services

BRANDS/DIVISIONS/AFFILIATES:

CONTACTS: Note: Officers with more than one job title may be intentionally listed here more than once.

Donald E. Meehan, Pres.
Chris Feniak, Dir.-Mktg. & Bus. Dev.
Wade E. Arnott, Mgr.-Oper., US
Rand Simon, Mgr.-Finance
Mark Guy, VP-Recruitment, Player Dev. & Contracts, US & OHL
Patrick J. Morris, Mgr.-Recruitment & Contracts, US & OHL
Craig D. Oster, Mgr.-Recruitment & Mgmt., W. Canada & Europe
Aaron Nagy, Mgr.-Recruitment, Player Dev. & Contracts, OHL

GROWTH PLANS/SPECIAL FEATURES:

Newport Sports Management, Inc. (NSM), based in Canada, is an athlete management and representation agency for professional hockey players. It is one of the largest agencies in professional hockey, with more than 125 National Hockey League (NHL) clients. NSM is headquartered in Mississauga, Ontario and has regional Canadian offices in Alberta and Quebec, as well as network offices in the U.S., Russia, Finland and Sweden. The firm is active in three primary service areas: athlete services, marketing services and consulting & property services. Its athlete services division provides contract negotiations, financial management, tax and estate planning, insurance, training and development as well as draft preparation. NSM's athlete marketing division provides clients with additional revenue opportunities such as promotional assignments, endorsements and spokesperson roles. The division specializes in sponsorship sales, corporate sponsorship programs and the evaluation of hockey properties to meet the needs and goals of corporate sponsors. NSM's consulting & property services division provides property representation, corporate consultation, sales promotion, IT and event management services. This division specializes in sponsorship sales, development of corporate sponsorship packages, media exposure, onsite recognition, pre- and post-event publicity, corporate hospitality, logo usage rights, licensing rights, merchandising rights, creating web sites for athletes and cross promotions.

FINANCIAL DATA: Note: Data for latest year may not have been available at press time.

In U.S. $	2022	2021	2020	2019	2018	2017
Revenue						
R&D Expense						
Operating Income						
Operating Margin %						
SGA Expense						
Net Income						
Operating Cash Flow						
Capital Expenditure						
EBITDA						
Return on Assets %						
Return on Equity %						
Debt to Equity						

CONTACT INFORMATION:

Phone: 905-275-2800   Fax: 905-275-4025
Toll-Free:
Address: 201 City Centre Dr., Ste. 400, Mississauga, ON L5B 2T4 Canada

STOCK TICKER/OTHER:

Stock Ticker: Private   Exchange:
Employees: Fiscal Year Ends:
Parent Company:

SALARIES/BONUSES:

Top Exec. Salary: $ Bonus: $
Second Exec. Salary: $ Bonus: $

OTHER THOUGHTS:

Estimated Female Officers or Directors:
Hot Spot for Advancement for Women/Minorities:

Nike Inc

NAIC Code: 424340

www.nike.com

TYPES OF BUSINESS:

Footwear Distribution
Athletic Equipment
Sports Accessories
Retail Stores
Sports Apparel
Plastic Products
Hockey Products
Swimwear

BRANDS/DIVISIONS/AFFILIATES:

Converse Inc
Jordan
NIKE IHM Inc (Air Manufacturing Innovation)
Datalogue
Chuck Taylor
All Star
One Star
Jack Purcell

CONTACTS: Note: Officers with more than one job title may be intentionally listed here more than once.

John Donahoe, CEO
Matthew Friend, CFO
Mark Parker, Chairman of the Board
Chris Abston, Chief Accounting Officer
Hilary Krane, Chief Administrative Officer
Andrew Campion, COO
Monique Matheson, Executive VP, Divisional
Heidi ONeill, President, Divisional

GROWTH PLANS/SPECIAL FEATURES:

Nike is the largest athletic footwear and apparel brand in the world. It designs, develops, and markets athletic apparel, footwear, equipment, and accessories in six major categories: running, basketball, football (soccer), training, sportswear, and Jordan. Footwear generates about two thirds of its sales. Nike's brands include Nike, Jordan, and Converse (casual footwear). Nike sells products worldwide and outsources its production to more than 300 factories in more than 30 countries. Nike was founded in 1964 and is based in Beaverton, Oregon.

FINANCIAL DATA: Note: Data for latest year may not have been available at press time.

In U.S. $	2022	2021	2020	2019	2018	2017
Revenue	46,710,000,000	44,538,000,000	37,403,000,000	39,117,000,000	34,350,000,000	34,350,000,000
R&D Expense						
Operating Income	6,675,000,000	6,937,000,000	3,115,000,000	4,772,000,000	4,749,000,000	4,749,000,000
Operating Margin %	.14%	.16%	.08%	.12%	.14%	.14%
SGA Expense	14,804,000,000	13,025,000,000	13,126,000,000	12,702,000,000	10,563,000,000	10,563,000,000
Net Income	6,046,000,000	5,727,000,000	2,539,000,000	4,029,000,000	4,240,000,000	4,240,000,000
Operating Cash Flow	5,188,000,000	6,657,000,000	2,485,000,000	5,903,000,000	3,846,000,000	3,846,000,000
Capital Expenditure	758,000,000	695,000,000	1,086,000,000	1,119,000,000	1,105,000,000	1,105,000,000
EBITDA	7,515,000,000	7,734,000,000	4,234,000,000	5,492,000,000	5,465,000,000	5,465,000,000
Return on Assets %	.15%	.17%	.09%	.17%	.19%	.19%
Return on Equity %	.43%	.55%	.30%	.43%	.34%	.34%
Debt to Equity	.77%	.97%	1.529	0.383	0.28	0.28

CONTACT INFORMATION:

Phone: 503 671-6453   Fax: 503 671-6300
Toll-Free: 800-344-6453
Address: 1 Bowerman Dr., Beaverton, OR 97005 United States

STOCK TICKER/OTHER:

Stock Ticker: NKE   Exchange: NYS
Employees: 79,100   Fiscal Year Ends: 05/31
Parent Company:

SALARIES/BONUSES:

Top Exec. Salary: $1,221,154   Bonus: $1,200,000
Second Exec. Salary: Bonus: $1,200,000
$1,221,154

OTHER THOUGHTS:

Estimated Female Officers or Directors: 2
Hot Spot for Advancement for Women/Minorities: Y

North Face Inc (The)

www.thenorthface.com

NAIC Code: 424300

TYPES OF BUSINESS:

Outdoor Apparel & Equipment
Footwear
Eyewear
Tents
Sleeping Bags
Backpacks
Outdoor Apparel
Innovative Fabrics and Technology

BRANDS/DIVISIONS/AFFILIATES:

VF Corporation
VECTIV
FUTURELIGHT
ThermoBall Eco
FlashDry
Polartec
TKA
WindWall

CONTACTS: *Note: Officers with more than one job title may be intentionally listed here more than once.*

Nicole Otto, Pres.
Karl Heinz Salzburger, VP-Int'l VF Corp

GROWTH PLANS/SPECIAL FEATURES:

The North Face, Inc., a subsidiary of VF Corporation, is a leading designer, distributor and marketer of technically sophisticated outdoor apparel and equipment. Founded in 1966, the firm has decades of experience as a provider of equipment to many of the world's most challenging high-altitude and polar expeditions. The North Face offers a broad range of outerwear, sportswear, footwear, eyewear, snow sports gear, bicycles, tents, sleeping bags and backpacks. Many of the company's products are designed for extreme activities such as mountaineering, rock and ice climbing, endurance running, backcountry skiing and snowboarding. The North Face puts extensive effort into the research and development of new products. The company employs or sponsors numerous world-class mountaineers and athletes to test its gear in the field, including snowboarders, skiers, rock climbers, mountaineers and endurance runners. The North Face innovative technology brands include: VECTIV, which minimizes the impact of each stride in footwear, reducing tibial stresses; FUTURELIGHT, offering nano structure membrane to allow air to pass through fabrics for better venting and breathability without sacrificing waterproofness and durability; ThermoBall Eco, a sustainable synthetic alternative to down; FlashDry, a fabric technology that repels body moisture to keep the wearer dry; Polartec, offering thermal fabrics designed to enhance performance in a variety of environments; TKA, providing fleece fabrics for insulation and wear-resistant purposes; WindWall, which are fabrics that reduce the effects of wind chill while continuing to be flexible and breathable without over-heating; and DryVent, offering fully waterproof fabrics that are windproof and yet breathable. North Face products are distributed to thousands of wholesale customers worldwide: through retail and outlet locations in the U.S., Canada and the U.K., as well as several others worldwide.

FINANCIAL DATA: *Note: Data for latest year may not have been available at press time.*

In U.S. $	2022	2021	2020	2019	2018	2017
Revenue	2,600,000,000	2,457,400,000	2,920,565,000	2,835,500,000	2,500,000,000	2,500,000,000
R&D Expense						
Operating Income						
Operating Margin %						
SGA Expense						
Net Income						
Operating Cash Flow						
Capital Expenditure						
EBITDA						
Return on Assets %						
Return on Equity %						
Debt to Equity						

CONTACT INFORMATION:

Phone: 510-618-3500   Fax: 510-618-3531
Toll-Free:
Address: 1551 Wewatta St., Denver, CO 80202 United States

STOCK TICKER/OTHER:

Stock Ticker: Subsidiary
Employees: 2,400
Parent Company: VF Corporation

Exchange:
Fiscal Year Ends: 03/31

SALARIES/BONUSES:

Top Exec. Salary: $ Bonus: $
Second Exec. Salary: $ Bonus: $

OTHER THOUGHTS:

Estimated Female Officers or Directors:
Hot Spot for Advancement for Women/Minorities:

Sales, profits and employees may be estimates. Financial information, benefits and other data can change quickly and may vary from those stated here.

Norwich City Football Club

www.canaries.co.uk

NAIC Code: 711211D

TYPES OF BUSINESS:

Soccer Team
Team Management and Operations

BRANDS/DIVISIONS/AFFILIATES:

Canaries (The)
Yellows (The)

CONTACTS: *Note: Officers with more than one job title may be intentionally listed here more than once.*

Stuart Webber, Sporting Dir.
David Wagner, Head Coach
Andrew Blofeld, Sec.
Joe Ferrari, Head-Media
Sam Gordon, Dir.-Finance
Jamie Arnall, Head-Legal
Andy Batley, Mgr.-Safety & Security

GROWTH PLANS/SPECIAL FEATURES:

Norwich City Football Club, known as The Canaries as well as The Yellows, is an English soccer team that competes in the EFL Championship (2022-23 season), the second tier of the English football league system. Established in 1902, Norwich City has played home games at Carrow Road stadium since 1935. Carrow Road has held, at its highest, nearly 44,000 fans, but currently comprises a seating capacity of just over 27,300. Norwich City FC averaged 26,631 in home game attendance during the 2022-23 season. Championships Norwich FC have clenched include five Second Division/Level 2 Championships (2020-21 most recently), two Third Division/League One championships (in 1933-34 and 2009-10), and two Football League Cups (1961-62 and 1984-850. The club is owned by Delia Smith and Michael Wynn-Jones. David Wagner is the head coach.

FINANCIAL DATA: *Note: Data for latest year may not have been available at press time.*

In U.S. $	2022	2021	2020	2019	2018	2017
Revenue		79,187,769				
R&D Expense						
Operating Income						
Operating Margin %						
SGA Expense						
Net Income		21,761,091	2,571,190	-40,164,100	-3,562,500	-3,562,500
Operating Cash Flow						
Capital Expenditure						
EBITDA						
Return on Assets %						
Return on Equity %						
Debt to Equity						

CONTACT INFORMATION:

Phone: 44 1603-76-0760   Fax:
Toll-Free:
Address: Carrow Rd., Norwich, Norfolk NR1 1JE United Kingdom

STOCK TICKER/OTHER:

Stock Ticker: Private
Employees: 265
Parent Company:

Exchange:
Fiscal Year Ends: 06/30

SALARIES/BONUSES:

Top Exec. Salary: $ Bonus: $
Second Exec. Salary: $ Bonus: $

OTHER THOUGHTS:

Estimated Female Officers or Directors:
Hot Spot for Advancement for Women/Minorities:

Oak View Group

www.oakviewgroup.com

NAIC Code: 541611

TYPES OF BUSINESS:

Administrative Management and General Management Consulting
Services
Sport Events
Sports Scheduling
Sport Venues
Hospitality and Food Services
Venue Safety and Security Services
Brand Strategy
Consulting Services

BRANDS/DIVISIONS/AFFILIATES:

OVG Business Development
OVG Global Partnership
OVG Media & Conferences
OVG Arena Alliance
OVG 360
Prevent Advisors
OVG Hospitality
OVG Canada

CONTACTS: Note: Officers with more than one job title may be intentionally listed here more than once.

Tim Leiweke, CEO
Steve Selcer, CFO
Ann Jackson, Chief People Officer

GROWTH PLANS/SPECIAL FEATURES:

Oak View Group is a family of companies engaged in alliance, consulting, sponsorship, partnership and facilities businesses within the sports and live entertainment industry. OVG Business Development offers services and solutions for venue design, venue construction, brand strategy, premium seating strategy/execution, ticketing, team operations, marketing, social media campaign analysis, event bids and media rights. OVG Global Partnership creates and connects people with sports and entertainment brands via storytelling, sponsorship sales and partnership consulting. OVG Media & Conferences communicates relevant industry information and builds innovative experiences in order to move this industry forward. OVG Arena Alliance provides consulting services to each venue member, including business review, negotiations, ticketing strategy, pricing, sales, inventory optimization, evaluation of current processes, operating expenses, database management/utilization, evaluation of event scheduling, venue security, media rights and labor negotiations (unions). This company also offers provision services such as establishing artist residencies at the venue, packaging Alliance members together for entertainment tours, activating reality television and social media brands and providing member access. OVG360 manages, operates and provides hospitality services for over 400 venues worldwide. Prevent Advisors provide safety and security services at sport and entertainment venues. OVG Hospitality offers culinary and food services, serving more than 250,000 events and 40 million guests each year. OVG Canada focuses on Canadian sports and entertainment, offering services in venue development and management, booking and content development, sponsorship consulting and third-party sales. OVG International focuses on growing the firm's core business globally, with an international office in London, U.K. Based in Los Angeles, California, Oak View Group has offices in New York, Philadelphia, Seattle, London and Toronto.

FINANCIAL DATA: Note: Data for latest year may not have been available at press time.

In U.S. $	2022	2021	2020	2019	2018	2017
Revenue						
R&D Expense						
Operating Income						
Operating Margin %						
SGA Expense						
Net Income						
Operating Cash Flow						
Capital Expenditure						
EBITDA						
Return on Assets %						
Return on Equity %						
Debt to Equity						

CONTACT INFORMATION:

Phone: 310-954-4800   Fax:
Toll-Free:
Address: 1100 Glendon Ave., Ste. 2100, Los Angeles, CA 90024 United States

STOCK TICKER/OTHER:

Stock Ticker: Private   Exchange:
Employees: Fiscal Year Ends:
Parent Company:

SALARIES/BONUSES:

Top Exec. Salary: $ Bonus: $
Second Exec. Salary: $ Bonus: $

OTHER THOUGHTS:

Estimated Female Officers or Directors:
Hot Spot for Advancement for Women/Minorities:

Oakland Athletics

www.mlb.com/athletics

NAIC Code: 711211A

TYPES OF BUSINESS:
Professional Baseball Team
Team Management and Operations

BRANDS/DIVISIONS/AFFILIATES:
As

CONTACTS: *Note: Officers with more than one job title may be intentionally listed here more than once.*
John Fisher, Managing Dir.
David Kaval, Pres.
Kasey Jarcik, Sr. Dir.-Finance
Pamela Pitts, Dir.-Baseball Admin.
Neil Kraetsch, General Counsel
Billy Beane, VP-Baseball Oper.
Travis LoDolce, Sr. Mgr.-Digital Mktg.
Ken Pries, VP-Comm. & Broadcasting
Paul Wong, VP-Finance
Bob Melvin, Mgr.
Bob Rose, Dir.-Public Rel.
Keith Lieppman, Dir.-Player Dev.
Farhan Zaidi, Dir.-Baseball Oper.
Lew Wolff, Chmn.

GROWTH PLANS/SPECIAL FEATURES:
The Oakland Athletics (also known as the A's) are a Major League Baseball (MLB) team principally owned by American businessman John J. Fisher. The team was a charter member of the American League (AL) in 1901. For its first fifty years, the club played in Philadelphia under owner and manager Connie Mack. During Mack's tenure, the club won five World Series championships. The A's moved from Philadelphia to Kansas City in 1955 and to Oakland in 1968. The team plays its home games in Oakland's coliseum currently branded as RingCentral, which was built in 1966 and has a baseball seating capacity of 46,847 and expandable to 56,782. The Athletics averaged 9,973 in home game attendance during the 2021-22 season. In the 70s and 80s, The A's won three straight championships in '72, '73 and '74, and again in 1989, for a total of nine World Series titles. A new era for the A's began in 1997 when Billy Beane took over as general manager. Beane brought a level of success to the team through the application of sabermetrics, the analysis of baseball through objective statistical evidence. Sabermetrics allows small market teams such as the A's to compete with large-market teams like the Yankees by identifying undervalued and overvalued commodities in the baseball market. In total, the team has clenched 15 AL pennants and 17 West Division titles (most recently in 2020). Despite this success, the franchise has struggled to attract a large fan base, and it consistently draws low home game attendance figures. Forbes estimated the team worth at $1.18 billion in March 2023.

FINANCIAL DATA: *Note: Data for latest year may not have been available at press time.*

In U.S. $	2022	2021	2020	2019	2018	2017
Revenue	281,450,000					
R&D Expense						
Operating Income						
Operating Margin %						
SGA Expense						
Net Income						
Operating Cash Flow						
Capital Expenditure						
EBITDA						
Return on Assets %						
Return on Equity %						
Debt to Equity						

CONTACT INFORMATION:
Phone: 510-638-4900   Fax: 510-562-1633
Toll-Free:
Address: 7000 Coliseum Way, Oakland, CA 94621 United States

STOCK TICKER/OTHER:
Stock Ticker: Private   Exchange:
Employees: 405   Fiscal Year Ends: 10/31
Parent Company:

SALARIES/BONUSES:
Top Exec. Salary: $ Bonus: $
Second Exec. Salary: $ Bonus: $

OTHER THOUGHTS:
Estimated Female Officers or Directors: 4
Hot Spot for Advancement for Women/Minorities: Y

Octagon Worldwide

www.octagon.com

NAIC Code: 711410

TYPES OF BUSINESS:

Sports Marketing
Athlete Representation
Consulting Services
Event Management
Media Services
Licensing & Merchandising

BRANDS/DIVISIONS/AFFILIATES:

Interpublic Group of Companies Inc

GROWTH PLANS/SPECIAL FEATURES:

Octagon Worldwide, a unit of the Interpublic Group of Companies, Inc., is a global provider of sports and entertainment marketing services. With 32 offices in 18 countries across Asia Pacific, Africa, Europe and the Americas, the firm's services span celebrity strategy, content, creative, digital media, social media, eSports, event management, experiential activation, measurement, analytic insights, media rights, merchandise, mindset/culture, sponsorship consulting and more. Octagon manages/influences billions in worldwide sponsorship rights fees and activation. The company works with hundreds of blue-chip corporate clients, and manage more than 13,000 events each year. Noteworthy clients have included John Elway, Emmitt Smith, Randy Johnson, Chien-Ming Wang, Anna Kournikova, Mia Hamm and Michael Phelps. Current corporate clients include MasterCard, Budweiser, Delta, Siemens, Stella Artois, PlayStation, JBL, Doosan, CISCO and Taco Bell.

CONTACTS:
Note: Officers with more than one job title may be intentionally listed here more than once.

John Shea, CEO
Phil De Picciotto, Pres.
Lisa Murray, CMO
Sarah Knight, Dir.-People & Culture
Simon Wardle, Chief Strategy Officer
Jeff Shifrin, Pres., Octagon Mktg., North America
Phil de Picciotto, Pres., Octagon Worldwide
Joan Cusco, Pres., Octagon Spain
Sean Nicholls, Managing Dir.-Asia, Australia & New Zealand
Franco Barocas, Chmn.
Alexandre Leitao, Pres., Octagon Brazil

FINANCIAL DATA:
Note: Data for latest year may not have been available at press time.

In U.S. $	2022	2021	2020	2019	2018	2017
Revenue						
R&D Expense						
Operating Income						
Operating Margin %						
SGA Expense						
Net Income						
Operating Cash Flow						
Capital Expenditure						
EBITDA						
Return on Assets %						
Return on Equity %						
Debt to Equity						

CONTACT INFORMATION:

Phone: 203-354-7400   Fax: 203-354-7401
Toll-Free:
Address: 290 Harbor Dr., Fl. 2, Stamford, CT 06902 United States

STOCK TICKER/OTHER:

Stock Ticker: Private   Exchange:
Employees: 815   Fiscal Year Ends: 12/31
Parent Company: Interpublic Group of Companies Inc

SALARIES/BONUSES:

Top Exec. Salary: $ Bonus: $
Second Exec. Salary: $ Bonus: $

OTHER THOUGHTS:

Estimated Female Officers or Directors: 1
Hot Spot for Advancement for Women/Minorities: Y

Oklahoma City Thunder

NAIC Code: 711211B

www.nba.com/thunder

TYPES OF BUSINESS:

Professional Basketball Team
Team Management and Operations

BRANDS/DIVISIONS/AFFILIATES:

Professional Basketball Club LLC
Oklahoma City Blue

CONTACTS: *Note: Officers with more than one job title may be intentionally listed here more than once.*

Danny Barth, Chief Admin. Officer
Dan Mahoney, VP-Broadcasting & Corp. Communications
Brian M. Byrnes, Sr. VP-Sales & Mktg.
Tyler Lane, VP-Tech.
Danny Barth, Chief Admin. Officer
Sam Presti, Gen. Mgr.-Basketball Oper.
Jay Ory, Dir-Bus. Dev.
Ron Matthews, Dir.-Digital Media & Publications
Dan Mahoney, VP-Corp. Comm. & Community Rel.
Scott Brooks, Head Coach
Scott Loft, VP-Ticket Sales, Retention & Data Base Oper.
Kelly McKeown, Dir.-Mktg. & Brand Mgmt.
Pete Winemiller, Sr. VP-Guest Rel.
Scott Loft, VP-Ticket Sales & Bus. Intelligence

GROWTH PLANS/SPECIAL FEATURES:

The Oklahoma City Thunder is a National Basketball Association (NBA) team created in 1967 as Seattle's first professional sports team. Formerly as the SuperSonics, the team made several appearances in the NBA finals, but only succeeded in winning one championship in the 1978-79 season. In Seattle, the SuperSonics qualified for the NBA playoffs 22 times and clenched six division titles. After relocating to Oklahoma City in 2008, the Thunder won their first division title in the 2010-11 season and their first Western Conference championship in 2011-12. In total, the club has clenched four conference titles and 11 division titles (2016 most recently). Professional Basketball Club, LLC, a private Oklahoma City-based group led by businessman Clayton Bennett, is the present owner of the organization. The team's current home court is the Paycom Center in Oklahoma City, which seats approximately 18,200 fans for basketball games. Home game attendance averaged 15,534 during the 2022-23 season. The Thunders own NBA G-league team Oklahoma City Blue, which acts as a feeder for Thunder. Forbes estimated the team to be worth $1.875 billion in October 2022.

FINANCIAL DATA: *Note: Data for latest year may not have been available at press time.*

In U.S. $	2022	2021	2020	2019	2018	2017
Revenue	272,350,000					
R&D Expense						
Operating Income						
Operating Margin %						
SGA Expense						
Net Income						
Operating Cash Flow						
Capital Expenditure						
EBITDA						
Return on Assets %						
Return on Equity %						
Debt to Equity						

CONTACT INFORMATION:

Phone: 405-208-4800   Fax:
Toll-Free:
Address: 208 Thunder Dr., Oklahoma City, OK 73102 United States

STOCK TICKER/OTHER:

Stock Ticker: Private   Exchange:
Employees: 450   Fiscal Year Ends: 12/31
Parent Company:

SALARIES/BONUSES:

Top Exec. Salary: $ Bonus: $
Second Exec. Salary: $ Bonus: $

OTHER THOUGHTS:

Estimated Female Officers or Directors: 2
Hot Spot for Advancement for Women/Minorities: Y

Olympiacos Football Club

www.olympiacos.org

NAIC Code: 711211D

TYPES OF BUSINESS:

Soccer Team
Team Management and Operations

BRANDS/DIVISIONS/AFFILIATES:

GROWTH PLANS/SPECIAL FEATURES:

Olympiacos Football Club, also known as Olympiacos Piraeus, is a professional football club in Greece, playing in the Super League Greece, the highest professional association football league in the country. Founded in 1925, Olympiacos plays its home games in the Karaiskakis Stadium, which has a seating capacity of over 32,000. The Olympiacos averaged 19,688 in attendance during the 2022-23 season. Domestically, the club has won 47 Super League Greece titles (winning three in a row in 2019-20, 2020-21 and 2021-22), 28 Greek Cups, four Greek Super Cups and three Greater Greece Cups. Internationally, the team won a Balkans Cup in 1963. Adidas is Olympiacos FC's kit manufacturer and Stoiximan.gr is its shirt sponsor.

CONTACTS: *Note: Officers with more than one job title may be intentionally listed here more than once.*

Jose Anigo, Manager
Evangelos Marinakis, Pres.

FINANCIAL DATA: *Note: Data for latest year may not have been available at press time.*

In U.S. $	2022	2021	2020	2019	2018	2017
Revenue						
R&D Expense						
Operating Income						
Operating Margin %						
SGA Expense						
Net Income						
Operating Cash Flow						
Capital Expenditure						
EBITDA						
Return on Assets %						
Return on Equity %						
Debt to Equity						

CONTACT INFORMATION:

Phone: 30 210-4143000   Fax: 30 210-4143113
Toll-Free:
Address: Alexandra Sq., Piraeus, 185 34 Greece

STOCK TICKER/OTHER:

Stock Ticker: Private   Exchange:
Employees: Fiscal Year Ends:
Parent Company:

SALARIES/BONUSES:

Top Exec. Salary: $ Bonus: $
Second Exec. Salary: $ Bonus: $

OTHER THOUGHTS:

Estimated Female Officers or Directors:
Hot Spot for Advancement for Women/Minorities:

Sales, profits and employees may be estimates. Financial information, benefits and other data can change quickly and may vary from those stated here.

Olympique de Marseille

NAIC Code: 711211D

www.om.fr

TYPES OF BUSINESS:

Professional Soccer Team
Team Management and Operations

BRANDS/DIVISIONS/AFFILIATES:

Marseille
OM

CONTACTS: *Note: Officers with more than one job title may be intentionally listed here more than once.*

Pablo Longoria, Pres.
Elie Baup, Mgr.

GROWTH PLANS/SPECIAL FEATURES:

Olympique de Marseille, usually referred to as either Marseille or OM, is a French professional soccer team that plays in Ligue 1, the top tier of the French soccer league system. The team was founded in 1899 and plays its home games at Stade Velodrome, which is also known as Orange Velodrome. The stadium is owned by the city of Marseille and has a seating capacity of over 67,300. Marseille is the only French team to win the Union of European Football Associations (UEFA) Champions League, having done so in 1992-93. In international play, the club has also clenched the UEFA Intertoto Cup in 2005. In domestic play, Marseille has done considerably well, having won Division 1/Ligue 1 nine times, most recently in 2009-10 and not counting the 1992-1993 title that was stripped for bribery; Ligue 2 once; Coupe de France 10 times; Coupe de la Ligue three times; Trophee des champions three times; and the Coupe Charles Drago in 1957. Marseille placed second in the 2021-22 season of Ligue 1, which has a total of 20 teams. American businessman Frank McCourt is the majority owner (95%) the club, with Margarita Louis-Dreyfus owning the remaining 5%.

FINANCIAL DATA: *Note: Data for latest year may not have been available at press time.*

In U.S. $	2022	2021	2020	2019	2018	2017
Revenue	170,000,000	164,725,698	146,015,628	145,104,740	130,300,815	130,300,815
R&D Expense						
Operating Income						
Operating Margin %						
SGA Expense						
Net Income		-86,506,301	-120,174,686	-102,375,361	-50,825,200	-50,825,200
Operating Cash Flow						
Capital Expenditure						
EBITDA						
Return on Assets %						
Return on Equity %						
Debt to Equity						

CONTACT INFORMATION:

Phone: 33-49-176-5609   Fax: 33-49-176-9129
Toll-Free:
Address: La Commanderie, 33, traverse de La Martine, Marseille, 13012 France

STOCK TICKER/OTHER:

Stock Ticker: Private   Exchange:
Employees: 380   Fiscal Year Ends: 12/31
Parent Company:

SALARIES/BONUSES:

Top Exec. Salary: $ Bonus: $
Second Exec. Salary: $ Bonus: $

OTHER THOUGHTS:

Estimated Female Officers or Directors: 1
Hot Spot for Advancement for Women/Minorities:

Olympique Lyonnais Groupe

www.olweb.fr/en

NAIC Code: 711211D

TYPES OF BUSINESS:

Professional Soccer Team
Team Management and Operations

BRANDS/DIVISIONS/AFFILIATES:

Olympique Lyonnais Groupe
IDG Capital Partners
Lyon
OL

GROWTH PLANS/SPECIAL FEATURES:

Olympique Lyonnais Groupe is a holding company. It is engaged in sporting events, entertainment and media sector in France. This company has a club which owns private and modern stadium connected to it. Olympique earns its revenue through various resources which include ticketing, sponsoring and advertising, media and marketing rights, brand-related revenue and player trading. It sells a various range of products such as watches, goodies, car accessories and others. Nearly large parts of its revenue are generated through the ticketing. Other revenue gets generated through the sale of merchandising products, use of licenses and infrastructure, as well as signing fees.

CONTACTS: Note: Officers with more than one job title may be intentionally listed here more than once.

Jean-Michel Aulas, CEO
Thierry Sauvage, Gen. Mngr.
Jean-Michel Aulas, Pres.
Emmanuelle Sarrabay, CFO
Harry Moyal, Gen. Mngr.-Mktg. & Digital
Vincent Ponsot, Gen. Mngr.-Human Resources
Marino Faccioli, Dir.-Sporting
Mathieu Giraud, VP-Special Oper.
Olivier Blanc, Dir.-Comm.
Remi Garde, Mgr.
Olivier Bernardeau, Dir.-Commercial
Jean-Michel Aulas, Chmn.

FINANCIAL DATA: Note: Data for latest year may not have been available at press time.

In U.S. $	2022	2021	2020	2019	2018	2017
Revenue	171,368,900	126,185,600	192,959,400	235,846,800	211,720,000	211,720,000
R&D Expense						
Operating Income	-100,931,200	-150,599,600	-107,788,100	-58,223,260	-7,917,303	-7,917,303
Operating Margin %	-.59%	-1.19%	-.56%	-.25%	-.04%	-.04%
SGA Expense	42,732,510	34,992,470	39,366,530	37,198,720	31,892,400	31,892,400
Net Income	-57,761,930	-114,231,700	-38,956,460	6,605,940	4,989,161	4,989,161
Operating Cash Flow	-57,619,900	-17,165,190	-46,331,280	2,767,959	-16,903,560	-16,903,560
Capital Expenditure	73,286,850	90,679,500	71,453,290	63,395,020	49,220,980	49,220,980
EBITDA	22,850,610	-19,916,060	56,878,790	78,126,500	63,991,970	63,991,970
Return on Assets %	-.08%	-.15%	-.05%	.01%	.01%	.01%
Return on Equity %	-.56%	-.62%	-.15%	.02%	.02%	.02%
Debt to Equity	4.90%	2.90%	1.188	0.838	0.865	0.865

CONTACT INFORMATION:

Phone: 33-42-629-6700   Fax:
Toll-Free:
Address: 10 avenue Simone Veil, Decines-Charpieu, 29150 France

SALARIES/BONUSES:

Top Exec. Salary: $ Bonus: $
Second Exec. Salary: $ Bonus: $

STOCK TICKER/OTHER:

Stock Ticker: OQLGF
Employees: 293
Parent Company:

Exchange: PINX
Fiscal Year Ends:

OTHER THOUGHTS:

Estimated Female Officers or Directors:
Hot Spot for Advancement for Women/Minorities:

OneTeam Partners LLC

www.joinoneteam.com

NAIC Code: 711400

TYPES OF BUSINESS:

Sports Marketing
Athlete Marketing Services
Athlete Rights Services and Solutions
Investment
Digital Marketing Solutions

BRANDS/DIVISIONS/AFFILIATES:

National Football League Players Association
Major League Baseball Players Association
HPS Investment Partners
Atlantic Park Strategic Capital Fund
Morgan Stanley Tactical Value.

CONTACTS: Note: Officers with more than one job title may be intentionally listed here more than once.

Malaika Underwood, Interim CEO

GROWTH PLANS/SPECIAL FEATURES:

OneTeam Partners, LLC helps athletes maximize the value of their name, image and likeness rights. OneTeam manages the commercial licensing rights of athletes across a diverse cross-section of properties, creates new marketing opportunities through its athlete marketing business and generates unique deal flow and investment opportunities through its venture investment capabilities. The company develops relationships between athletes and brands and delivers integrated solutions across sponsorship, athlete marketing, content and digital marketing. Partners of the firm include MLS Players Association, WNB Players Association, NFL Players Association, MLB Players, USWNT Players and U.S. Rugby Players Association. During 2022, OneTeam Partners announced the sale of RedBird Capital's stake to HPS Investment Partners, Atlantic Park Strategic Capital Fund, and Morgan Stanley Tactical Value. The syndicate replaces RedBird and provides opportunities for OneTeam to diversify its business and expand into new areas.

FINANCIAL DATA: Note: Data for latest year may not have been available at press time.

In U.S. $	2022	2021	2020	2019	2018	2017
Revenue						
R&D Expense						
Operating Income						
Operating Margin %						
SGA Expense						
Net Income						
Operating Cash Flow						
Capital Expenditure						
EBITDA						
Return on Assets %						
Return on Equity %						
Debt to Equity						

CONTACT INFORMATION:

Phone: Fax:
Toll-Free: 844 451-8326
Address: 900 19th St. NW, Washington, DC 20036 United States

SALARIES/BONUSES:

Top Exec. Salary: $ Bonus: $
Second Exec. Salary: $ Bonus: $

STOCK TICKER/OTHER:

Stock Ticker: Private   Exchange:
Employees: Fiscal Year Ends:
Parent Company:

OTHER THOUGHTS:

Estimated Female Officers or Directors:
Hot Spot for Advancement for Women/Minorities:

Orlando City SC

NAIC Code: 711211D

www.orlandocitysc.com

TYPES OF BUSINESS:
Major League Soccer Team
Team Management and Operations

BRANDS/DIVISIONS/AFFILIATES:
Lions (The)

GROWTH PLANS/SPECIAL FEATURES:
The Orlando City SC Is a Major League Soccer (MLS) club based in Orlando, Florida. The team is family-owned by Zygi, Leonard and Mark Wilf, which purchased the team in July 2021 for an estimated $400-450 million. Nicknamed The Lions, Orlando City was founded in 2013 and began play in 2015 as a member of the Eastern Conference (EC) of the MLS. The EC currently comprises the Atlanta United FC, Charlotte FC, Chicago Fire FC, FC Cincinnati, Columbus Crew, DC United, Inter Miami CF, CF Montreal, Nashville SC, New England Revolution, New York City FC, New York Red Bulls, Philadelphia Union and Toronto FC. In the 2022 season, Orlando City won their first Open Cup title, defeating Sacramento Republic FC 3-0 in the final. The team plays its home games in the soccer-specific Exploria Stadium, which has a seating capacity of 25,500. Orlando City SC averaged 17,261 fans in 2022.

CONTACTS:
Note: Officers with more than one job title may be intentionally listed here more than once.

Jarrod Dillon, Pres.-Bus. Oper.
Carlos Osorio, CFO
Pedro Araujo, CMO
Monica Nieves, Dir.-People
Jackie Maynard, Sr. Dir.-Communications & PR
Tony Husenaj, Mngr.-IT Infrastructure

FINANCIAL DATA:
Note: Data for latest year may not have been available at press time.

In U.S. $	2022	2021	2020	2019	2018	2017
Revenue	14,779,800					
R&D Expense						
Operating Income						
Operating Margin %						
SGA Expense						
Net Income						
Operating Cash Flow						
Capital Expenditure						
EBITDA						
Return on Assets %						
Return on Equity %						
Debt to Equity						

CONTACT INFORMATION:
Phone: 407 478-4007   Fax: 407-745-5376
Toll-Free: 855-675-2489
Address: 655 W. Church St., Orlando, FL 32805 United States

STOCK TICKER/OTHER:
Stock Ticker: Private
Employees:
Parent Company:

Exchange:
Fiscal Year Ends:

SALARIES/BONUSES:
Top Exec. Salary: $ Bonus: $
Second Exec. Salary: $ Bonus: $

OTHER THOUGHTS:
Estimated Female Officers or Directors:
Hot Spot for Advancement for Women/Minorities:

Sales, profits and employees may be estimates. Financial information, benefits and other data can change quickly and may vary from those stated here.

Orlando Magic

NAIC Code: 711211B

TYPES OF BUSINESS:

Professional Basketball Team
Team Management and Operations

BRANDS/DIVISIONS/AFFILIATES:

RDV Sports Inc
Orlando Magic Basketball Camp
Orlando Magic Youth Foundation
Lakeland Magic

CONTACTS: *Note: Officers with more than one job title may be intentionally listed here more than once.*

Alex Martins, CEO
Charles Freeman, Pres.-Bus. Oper.
Jim Fritz, CFO
Michael Forde, Chief Sales Officer
Shelly Wilkes, Sr. VP-Mktg.
Joel Glass, CCO
Dan Savage, Mgr.-Web Svcs.
Joel Glass, Sr. VP-Comm.
Charles Freeman, Chief Revenue Officer
Linda Landman Gonzalez, VP-Community Rel.
Jacque Vaughn, Head Coach
Pat Willaims, Sr. VP
Chris D'Orso, VP-Sales & Ticket Oper.
Dan DeVos, Chmn.

GROWTH PLANS/SPECIAL FEATURES:

The Orlando Magic, owned by RDV Sports, Inc., joined the National Basketball Association (NBA) in 1989. Though the first several years of the organization were mainly lackluster, the team saw a rise in its standings when it drafted NBA star Shaquille O'Neal in 1992. O'Neal played in Orlando for four years, leading the team to its first playoff appearances and its first Finals appearance, before leaving for the Los Angeles Lakers in 1996. Other notable players include Anfernee (Penny) Hardaway, Grant Hill, Tracy McGrady, Steve Francis, Rashard Lewis and Dwight Howard. In 2016 and 2017, respectively, Shaquille O'Neal, an Orlando Magic from 1992-1996, and Tracy McGrady (2000-2004) were inducted into the Basketball Hall of Fame. Since its establishment in the NBA, the franchise has won two conference titles (1995 and 2009) and six division titles (1995, 1996, 2008, 2009, 2010 and 2019), but has yet to win an NBA championship. The team's D-League affiliate is the Lakeland Magic. The team plays its home games in the Amway Center in downtown Orlando, Florida, comprising a seating capacity of 20,000, with home attendance averaging 17,765 during the 2022-23 season. Forbes estimated the team to be worth $1.85 billion in October 2022.

FINANCIAL DATA: *Note: Data for latest year may not have been available at press time.*

In U.S. $	2022	2021	2020	2019	2018	2017
Revenue	263,900,000					
R&D Expense						
Operating Income						
Operating Margin %						
SGA Expense						
Net Income						
Operating Cash Flow						
Capital Expenditure						
EBITDA						
Return on Assets %						
Return on Equity %						
Debt to Equity						

CONTACT INFORMATION:

Phone: 407-916-2400   Fax: 407-916-2830
Toll-Free:
Address: 8701 Maitland Summit Blvd., Orlando, FL 32801 United States

STOCK TICKER/OTHER:

Stock Ticker: Private   Exchange:
Employees: 670   Fiscal Year Ends: 06/30
Parent Company:

SALARIES/BONUSES:

Top Exec. Salary: $ Bonus: $
Second Exec. Salary: $ Bonus: $

OTHER THOUGHTS:

Estimated Female Officers or Directors: 1
Hot Spot for Advancement for Women/Minorities: Y

Orvis Company Inc (The)

www.orvis.com

NAIC Code: 451110

TYPES OF BUSINESS:

Outdoor Apparel, Retail
Fly-Fishing & Hunting Equipment
Outdoor Apparel
Sports and Hiking Accessories
Luggage and Travel Goods
Home Goods
Fishing and Shooting Training
Log Home Design & Construction

BRANDS/DIVISIONS/AFFILIATES:

Orvis Travel
Orvis Log Homes
Orvis Shooting Grounds at Pursell Farms

CONTACTS: Note: Officers with more than one job title may be intentionally listed here more than once.

Simon Perkins, Pres.
Robert Bean, CFO
Sheila Shekar Pollak, Chief Brand Experience Officer
Rebecca Jones, Chief People Officer
Reenie Benziger, Chief Product Officer
David Perkins, Vice Chmn.
Marka Hansen, Chmn.

GROWTH PLANS/SPECIAL FEATURES:

The Orvis Company, Inc. was founded in 1856, offering fly-fishing equipment. Today, the firm continues to offer fly fishing equipment, as well as hunting equipment and a wide range of outdoor apparel, packs and bags, dog products, home products and more through retailers, outlets and authorized dealers in the U.S. and the U.K. The company's apparel includes men's and women's clothing, footwear, activity wear, outerwear and accessories such as hats, belts, socks, eye/sunglasses, luggage and wallets. Its fly-fishing products include waders/boots, lines, leaders, rods, reels, vests, packs and fly-fishing apparel. The firm's hunting products include shotguns, shotgun accessories and hunting apparel. In addition, Orvis runs fly-fishing and shooting schools and seminars; guided fishing and hunting trips through its series of lodges; and Orvis Travel helps customers plan international vacations with a focus on outdoor activities. The company's home furnishings include bedding, lighting, dining furniture, kitchen furniture, bedroom furniture, tables, chairs, desks, tableware, outdoor furniture and fireplace accessories. Dog products include beds, collars/leashes, crates, health and grooming supplies, bird dog supplies, toys, treats and more. The firm operates retail stores across the U.S. and U.K., and maintains a network of over 400 independent dealers worldwide, which primarily sell fly-fishing products and apparel. Orvis also markets products through catalogs and an ecommerce website. Other activities include: Orvis Log Homes, a division that offers log home design packages and complete construction options through Rocky Mountain Log Homes Co.; and with partner Pursell Farms LLC, owns Orvis Shooting Grounds at Pursell Farms, comprising 3,200 acres in Alabama with sporting clays, wingshooting and fly-fishing schools.

FINANCIAL DATA: Note: Data for latest year may not have been available at press time.

In U.S. $	2022	2021	2020	2019	2018	2017
Revenue	370,000,000	405,080,000	389,500,000	380,000,000	357,000,000	357,000,000
R&D Expense						
Operating Income						
Operating Margin %						
SGA Expense						
Net Income						
Operating Cash Flow						
Capital Expenditure						
EBITDA						
Return on Assets %						
Return on Equity %						
Debt to Equity						

CONTACT INFORMATION:

Phone: 802-362-1300   Fax: 802-362-0141
Toll-Free: 888-235-9763
Address: 178 Conservation Way, Sunderland, VT 05250 United States

STOCK TICKER/OTHER:

Stock Ticker: Private
Employees: 1,700
Parent Company:

Exchange:
Fiscal Year Ends: 09/30

SALARIES/BONUSES:

Top Exec. Salary: $ Bonus: $
Second Exec. Salary: $ Bonus: $

OTHER THOUGHTS:

Estimated Female Officers or Directors:
Hot Spot for Advancement for Women/Minorities:

Ottawa Senators

NAIC Code: 711211F

senators.nhl.com

TYPES OF BUSINESS:

Professional Hockey Team (NHL)
Team Management and Operations

BRANDS/DIVISIONS/AFFILIATES:

Canadian Tire Centre
Belleville Senators
Allen Americans

CONTACTS: *Note: Officers with more than one job title may be intentionally listed here more than once.*

Pierre Dorion, General Mngr.
Tim Pattyson, Dir.-Hockey Oper.
Cyril M. Leeder, Pres.

GROWTH PLANS/SPECIAL FEATURES:

The Ottawa Senators Hockey Club, based in Ottawa, Ontario, is a professional hockey team playing in the Atlantic division of the Eastern conference within the National Hockey League (NHL). The original Ottawa Senators franchise, first named the Ottawa Silver Seven, was founded in 1883. The team competed in the National Hockey Association and the NHL, winning nine Stanley Cups between 1903 and 1927 before moving to St. Louis, Missouri and changing its name to the St. Louis Eagles in 1934. The team folded a year later in bankruptcy. The modern-day Senators franchise entered the NHL as an expansion team in 1992. The Senators play at Canadian Tire Centre, with a seating capacity of 19,153 and a total capacity, including standing room, of 20,500. The Senators averaged 16,757 fans per home game during the 2022-23 season. The team's current owner is the estate of the late Toronto pharmaceutical billionaire Eugene Melnyk, who purchased the Canadian Tire Centre and the Senators after they declared bankruptcy in 2003. Since then, the Ottawa Senators clenched a Conference Championship in 2006-07, a Presidents' Trophy in 2002-03 and four division championships (2005-06 most recently). Minor league affiliates of the Senators include the Belleville Senators of the American Hockey League (AHL) and the Allen Americans of the ECHL. Forbes estimated the team's value at $800 million in December 2022.

FINANCIAL DATA: *Note: Data for latest year may not have been available at press time.*

In U.S. $	2022	2021	2020	2019	2018	2017
Revenue	130,000,000	67,000,000	115,000,000	127,000,000	135,000,000	135,000,000
R&D Expense						
Operating Income						
Operating Margin %						
SGA Expense						
Net Income		-30,000,000	-2,900,000	3,600,000	10,000,000	10,000,000
Operating Cash Flow						
Capital Expenditure						
EBITDA						
Return on Assets %						
Return on Equity %						
Debt to Equity						

CONTACT INFORMATION:

Phone: 613-599-0250   Fax: 613-599-0358
Toll-Free:
Address: 1000 Palladium Dr., Ottawa, ON K2V 1A5 Canada

STOCK TICKER/OTHER:

Stock Ticker: Private   Exchange:
Employees: 200   Fiscal Year Ends: 06/30
Parent Company:

SALARIES/BONUSES:

Top Exec. Salary: $ Bonus: $
Second Exec. Salary: $ Bonus: $

OTHER THOUGHTS:

Estimated Female Officers or Directors: 3
Hot Spot for Advancement for Women/Minorities: Y

Pacific Cycle Inc

www.pacific-cycle.com

NAIC Code: 336991

TYPES OF BUSINESS:

Bicycles & Scooters
Electric Toys
Juvenile Recreation Equipment
Jogging Strollers
Home Fitness Equipment

BRANDS/DIVISIONS/AFFILIATES:

Dorel Industries Inc
Schwinn
Mongoose
Kid Trax
InSTEP

GROWTH PLANS/SPECIAL FEATURES:

Pacific Cycle, Inc. designs, manufactures, markets and distributes a variety of branded bicycles as well as other recreational products, such as jogging strollers, scooters, backyard toys and bicycle trailers. The company is a leading worldwide bicycle supplier. Its brands include: Schwinn, which encompasses both recreational and off-road mountain bikes; Mongoose, which includes BMX, freestyle, hardtail and full-suspension mountain bikes targeted at male consumers age 7-17; and InSTEP, which consists of jogging strollers and bicycle trailers. Pacific Cycle's products are sold throughout the U.S. through mass-market merchandisers such as Walmart and Target as well as major sporting goods chains, as well as internationally. Headquartered in Madison, Wisconsin, Pacific Cycle has other U.S. offices in California and Illinois, as well as in Canada, the U.K. and China. Pacific Cycle operates as a subsidiary of Dorel Industries, Inc.

CONTACTS: *Note: Officers with more than one job title may be intentionally listed here more than once.*

Martin Schwartz, CEO
Joe Werwie, Global Brand Dir.-Schwinn
Ellen Johnson, VP-Bus. Dev.
Jim Slattery, VP-Sourcing & Purchasing

FINANCIAL DATA: *Note: Data for latest year may not have been available at press time.*

In U.S. $	2022	2021	2020	2019	2018	2017
Revenue						
R&D Expense						
Operating Income						
Operating Margin %						
SGA Expense						
Net Income						
Operating Cash Flow						
Capital Expenditure						
EBITDA						
Return on Assets %						
Return on Equity %						
Debt to Equity						

CONTACT INFORMATION:

Phone: 608-268-2468   Fax: 608-268-2466
Toll-Free: 800-666-8813
Address: 4902 Hamersley Rd., Madison, WI 53711 United States

STOCK TICKER/OTHER:

Stock Ticker: Subsidiary   Exchange:
Employees: 200   Fiscal Year Ends: 12/31
Parent Company: Dorel Industries Inc

SALARIES/BONUSES:

Top Exec. Salary: $ Bonus: $
Second Exec. Salary: $ Bonus: $

OTHER THOUGHTS:

Estimated Female Officers or Directors: 2
Hot Spot for Advancement for Women/Minorities:

Palace Sports & Entertainment Inc

www.313presents.com

NAIC Code: 711310

TYPES OF BUSINESS:

Sports Stadium Operator
Professional Basketball Team Ownership
Music & Events Venues
Venue Management and Operation

BRANDS/DIVISIONS/AFFILIATES:

Detroit Pistons
313 Presents LLC

GROWTH PLANS/SPECIAL FEATURES:

Palace Sports & Entertainment, Inc. (PS&E) is an American sports and entertainment company. The firm's largest subsidiary is the Detroit Pistons, a National Basketball Association (NBA) team. In addition, 313 Presents, LLC is a joint venture between PS&E and Olympia Entertainment, and responsible for the company's entertainment bookings, event production, and promotion of the venues owned or managed by the two companies, including the Little Caesars Arena and Fox Theatre. 313 stands for the area code for Detroit. Other venues between the two firms include Pine Knob Music Theatre, Michigan Lottery Amphitheatre, Meadow Brook Amphitheatre, Comerica Park and Sound Board at Motorcity Casino Hotel.

CONTACTS: Note: Officers with more than one job title may be intentionally listed here more than once.

Howard Handler, Pres.
Keith Dowdican, VP-Finance & Admin.
Kim Klein, VP-Mktg. & Communications
Megan King, Dir.-Human Resources
Michael Donnay, Sr. Dir.-Brand Networks
Sean Hodgson, Dir.-Digital Content
Charles Metzger, Chief Comm. Officer
Dennis Mannion, VP-Ticketing, Consumer Sales & Svcs.

FINANCIAL DATA: Note: Data for latest year may not have been available at press time.

In U.S. $	2022	2021	2020	2019	2018	2017
Revenue						
R&D Expense						
Operating Income						
Operating Margin %						
SGA Expense						
Net Income						
Operating Cash Flow						
Capital Expenditure						
EBITDA						
Return on Assets %						
Return on Equity %						
Debt to Equity						

CONTACT INFORMATION:

Phone: 248-377-0100   Fax: 248-377-3260
Toll-Free:
Address: 6 Championship Dr., Auburn Hills, MI 48326 United States

STOCK TICKER/OTHER:

Stock Ticker: Private   Exchange:
Employees: 550   Fiscal Year Ends:
Parent Company:

SALARIES/BONUSES:

Top Exec. Salary: $ Bonus: $
Second Exec. Salary: $ Bonus: $

OTHER THOUGHTS:

Estimated Female Officers or Directors:
Hot Spot for Advancement for Women/Minorities:

Paramount Global

NAIC Code: 515210

TYPES OF BUSINESS:

Cable TV Networks
Media and Entertainment
Television
Streaming Services
Direct-to-Consumer Services
Studio Production
Live Events
Cable Networks

BRANDS/DIVISIONS/AFFILIATES:

CBS Television Network
Showtime
Nickelodeon
CBS Studios
CBS Stations
Paramount+
BET+
Paramount Pictures

GROWTH PLANS/SPECIAL FEATURES:

Paramount Global is the rebranded recombination of CBS and Viacom that has created a media conglomerate with global scale. CBS contributed Showtime in addition to its television assets--the CBS television network, 28 local TV stations, and 50% of CW, a joint venture between CBS and WarnerMedia. Viacom brought several leading cable network properties, including Nickelodeon, MTV, BET, Comedy Central, VH1, CMT, and Paramount. Paramount Pictures produces original motion pictures and owns a library of 2,500 films, including the Mission: Impossible and Transformers series. Paramount operates a number of streaming services, most notably Paramount+ and Pluto TV.

Paramount Global offers its employees health and wellness programs, retirement plans and other benefits.

CONTACTS: Note: Officers with more than one job title may be intentionally listed here more than once.

Probert M. Bakish, CEO
Naveen Chopra, CFO
Julia Phelps, CCO
Nancy Phillips, Chief People Officer
Doretha Lea, Executive VP, Divisional
Christa D'Alimonte, Executive VP
Julia Phelps, Executive VP
Richard Jones, Executive VP
Nancy Phillips, Executive VP

FINANCIAL DATA: Note: Data for latest year may not have been available at press time.

In U.S. $	2022	2021	2020	2019	2018	2017
Revenue	30,154,000,000	28,586,000,000	25,285,000,000	26,998,000,000	26,535,000,000	26,535,000,000
R&D Expense						
Operating Income	2,806,000,000	4,011,000,000	4,474,000,000	4,267,000,000	5,101,000,000	5,101,000,000
Operating Margin %	.09%	.14%	.18%	.16%	.19%	.19%
SGA Expense	7,098,000,000	6,441,000,000	5,389,000,000	5,580,000,000	5,508,000,000	5,508,000,000
Net Income	1,104,000,000	4,543,000,000	2,422,000,000	3,308,000,000	2,321,000,000	2,321,000,000
Operating Cash Flow	219,000,000	953,000,000	2,294,000,000	1,230,000,000	2,439,000,000	2,439,000,000
Capital Expenditure	358,000,000	354,000,000	324,000,000	345,000,000	356,000,000	356,000,000
EBITDA	2,602,000,000	6,582,000,000	4,608,000,000	4,623,000,000	5,651,000,000	5,651,000,000
Return on Assets %	.02%	.08%	.05%	.07%	.10%	.10%
Return on Equity %	.05%	.24%	.17%	.28%	.82%	.82%
Debt to Equity	.74%	.86%	1.386	1.492	4.785	4.785

CONTACT INFORMATION:

Phone: 212 258-6000   Fax: 212 258-6100
Toll-Free:
Address: 1515 Broadway, New York, NY 10036 United States

STOCK TICKER/OTHER:

Stock Ticker: PARA   Exchange: NAS
Employees: 24,500   Fiscal Year Ends: 09/30
Parent Company:

SALARIES/BONUSES:

Top Exec. Salary: $3,100,000   Bonus: $
Second Exec. Salary: Bonus: $
$1,400,000

OTHER THOUGHTS:

Estimated Female Officers or Directors: 7
Hot Spot for Advancement for Women/Minorities: Y

Paris Saint-Germain Football Club (PSG)   www.psg.fr

NAIC Code: 711211D

TYPES OF BUSINESS:

Soccer Team
Team Management and Operations

BRANDS/DIVISIONS/AFFILIATES:

Qatar Sports Investments
Parc des Princes

GROWTH PLANS/SPECIAL FEATURES:

Paris Saint-Germain Football Club (PSG) is a professional football club in France, playing in the Ligue 1 top-tier division of French football. Founded in 1970, PSG plays its home games in the Parc des Princes stadium, which has a seating capacity of nearly 48,000, of which the team nearly sells out in home game attendance. Domestically, the club has won 11 Ligue 1 titles (most recently in 2021-22 and 2022-23), one Ligue 2 title, 14 Coupe de France titles, nine Coupe de la Ligue titles and 11 Trophee des Champions titles (most recently in 2022). Internationally, PSG has won one UEFA Cup Winners' Cup and one UEFA Intertoto Cup. PSG is owned by Qatar Sports Investments.

CONTACTS: *Note: Officers with more than one job title may be intentionally listed here more than once.*

Nasser Al-Khelaifi, Pres.

FINANCIAL DATA: *Note: Data for latest year may not have been available at press time.*

In U.S. $	2022	2021	2020	2019	2018	2017
Revenue	710,000,000	645,122,618	687,625,251	737,626,025	602,559,516	602,559,516
R&D Expense						
Operating Income						
Operating Margin %						
SGA Expense						
Net Income		-253,981,466	-152,552,321	30,938,372	-22,568,880	-22,568,880
Operating Cash Flow						
Capital Expenditure						
EBITDA						
Return on Assets %						
Return on Equity %						
Debt to Equity						

CONTACT INFORMATION:

Phone: 33 1-41-41-61-00   Fax:
Toll-Free: 800-399-9665
Address: 24, rue du Commandant Guilbaud, Paris, 75016 France

STOCK TICKER/OTHER:

Stock Ticker: Private   Exchange:
Employees: Fiscal Year Ends: 12/31
Parent Company: Qatar Sports Investments

SALARIES/BONUSES:

Top Exec. Salary: $ Bonus: $
Second Exec. Salary: $ Bonus: $

OTHER THOUGHTS:

Estimated Female Officers or Directors:
Hot Spot for Advancement for Women/Minorities:

Sales, profits and employees may be estimates. Financial information, benefits and other data can change quickly and may vary from those stated here.

Patagonia Inc

www.patagonia.com

NAIC Code: 424300

TYPES OF BUSINESS:

Apparel and Clothing Brands, Designers, Importers and Distributors
Outdoor Equipment Sales
Catalog Sales
Surfing Apparel
Surfing Equipment
Retail Stores
Ecommerce
Used Apparel

BRANDS/DIVISIONS/AFFILIATES:

Patagonia Works Inc
Regulator
WornWear.Patagonia.com

CONTACTS: *Note: Officers with more than one job title may be intentionally listed here more than once.*

Ryan Gellert, CEO
Rob BonDurant, VP-Merch.
Dmitri Siegel, VP-Global e-commerce
Jenn Rapp, Dir.-Comm. & Public Rel.
John Collins, VP-Sales, Americas & Asia Pacific

GROWTH PLANS/SPECIAL FEATURES:

Patagonia, Inc. was founded in 1973 in California, USA and markets and sells outdoor clothing and equipment. Patagonia's products are developed and designed for a broad range of extreme sports, such as rock climbing, mountaineering, white-water kayaking, mountain biking, surfing and skiing. The company sells its products through owned retail outlets worldwide as well as through hundreds of other outdoor gear and clothing stores. The firm has pioneered many materials now considered essential for outdoor enthusiasts, such as polypropylene, Capilene and Synchilla, which are designed to retain warmth even when the material becomes moist from precipitation or sweat. Its Regulator system combines soft shells, insulation and moisture transition layers into jackets and pants to create an integrated clothing system designed to keep people warm and dry even in the most adverse weather conditions. Patagonia also introduced t-shirts made from organically grown cotton, and a fleece product line made from recycled plastic soda bottles. The firm is committed to promoting and helping conserve nature and contributes its time, services and at least 1% of its sales to hundreds of global environmental initiatives. Patagonia uses 100% traceable down and not blended with down from unknown sources. Patagonia operates as a subsidiary of venture capital firm Patagonia Works, Inc. Patagonia merchandise can be returned for new merchandise credits; the used merchandise gets cleaned and repaired and sold on the company's Worn Wear website, WornWear.Patagonia.com.

FINANCIAL DATA: *Note: Data for latest year may not have been available at press time.*

In U.S. $	2022	2021	2020	2019	2018	2017
Revenue	1,000,000,000	1,166,300,000	1,090,000,000	1,000,000,000	800,000,000	800,000,000
R&D Expense						
Operating Income						
Operating Margin %						
SGA Expense						
Net Income						
Operating Cash Flow						
Capital Expenditure						
EBITDA						
Return on Assets %						
Return on Equity %						
Debt to Equity						

CONTACT INFORMATION:

Phone: 805-643-8616   Fax: 800-543-5522
Toll-Free: 800-638-6464
Address: 259 W. Santa Clara St., Ventura, CA 93001 United States

STOCK TICKER/OTHER:

Stock Ticker: Subsidiary   Exchange:
Employees: 2,300   Fiscal Year Ends: 04/30
Parent Company: Patagonia Works Inc

SALARIES/BONUSES:

Top Exec. Salary: $ Bonus: $
Second Exec. Salary: $ Bonus: $

OTHER THOUGHTS:

Estimated Female Officers or Directors: 2
Hot Spot for Advancement for Women/Minorities:

Peloton Interactive Inc

NAIC Code: 713940

www.onepeloton.com

TYPES OF BUSINESS:
Interactive Online Cycling Classes
Stationary Bikes
Treadmills
Clothing and Accessories
Retail Stores

GROWTH PLANS/SPECIAL FEATURES:
Peloton Interactive Inc operates an interactive fitness platform. It operates its business in two reportable segments: Connected Fitness Products and Subscription. Connected Fitness Product revenue consists of sales of bike and tread and related accessories, associated fees for delivery and installation, and extended warranty agreements. Subscription revenue consists of revenue generated from monthly Connected Fitness Subscription and Digital Subscription. The company generates the majority of the revenue from the sale of Connected Fitness Products.

BRANDS/DIVISIONS/AFFILIATES:
Peloton Bike

CONTACTS: *Note: Officers with more than one job title may be intentionally listed here more than once.*
John Foley, CEO
Jill Woodworth, CFO
Allen Klingsick, Chief Accounting Officer
Hisao Kushi, Chief Legal Officer
Thomas Cortese, Co-Founder
Mariana Garavaglia, COO
William Lynch, Director
Kevin Cornils, Other Executive Officer

FINANCIAL DATA: *Note: Data for latest year may not have been available at press time.*

In U.S. $	2022	2021	2020	2019	2018	2017
Revenue	3,582,200,000	4,021,800,000	1,825,900,000	915,000,000	218,600,000	218,600,000
R&D Expense	359,500,000	247,600,000	89,100,000	54,800,000	13,000,000	13,000,000
Operating Income	-1,643,400,000	-183,300,000	-79,500,000	-202,200,000	-70,700,000	-70,700,000
Operating Margin %	-.46%	-.05%	-.04%	-.22%		
SGA Expense	1,982,300,000	1,390,100,000	828,100,000	531,000,000	131,600,000	131,600,000
Net Income	-2,827,700,000	-189,000,000	-71,600,000	-195,600,000	-71,100,000	-71,100,000
Operating Cash Flow	-2,020,000,000	-239,700,000	376,400,000	-108,600,000	-18,600,000	-18,600,000
Capital Expenditure	337,300,000	252,300,000	156,500,000	83,600,000	10,200,000	10,200,000
EBITDA	-2,622,300,000	-119,600,000	-26,200,000	-172,200,000	-67,000,000	-67,000,000
Return on Assets %	-.66%	-.05%	-.04%	-.43%		
Return on Equity %	-2.41%	-.11%	-.13%			
Debt to Equity	3.84%	.83%	0.303			

CONTACT INFORMATION:
Phone: 646-277-4497   Fax:
Toll-Free: 866-679-9129
Address: 158 W. 27th St., New York, NY 10001 United States

STOCK TICKER/OTHER:
Stock Ticker: PTON   Exchange: NAS
Employees: 3,723   Fiscal Year Ends: 06/30
Parent Company:

SALARIES/BONUSES:
Top Exec. Salary: $1,000,000   Bonus: $
Second Exec. Salary: Bonus: $
$750,000

OTHER THOUGHTS:
Estimated Female Officers or Directors:
Hot Spot for Advancement for Women/Minorities: Y

Penn National Gaming Inc

www.pngaming.com

NAIC Code: 713210

TYPES OF BUSINESS:

Horse Racetracks
Casinos
Online Wagering
Mobile Gaming

BRANDS/DIVISIONS/AFFILIATES:

Hollywood Casino
Meadows Casino (The)
LAuberge Lake Charles
Boomtown Casino Biloxi
Argosy Casino Riverside
Tropicana Las Vegas
Pennwood Racing Inc
Barstool Sports

CONTACTS: *Note: Officers with more than one job title may be intentionally listed here more than once.*

Jay Snowden, CEO
Felicia Hendrix, CFO
David Handler, Chairman of the Board
Christine LaBombard, Chief Accounting Officer
Harper Ko, Chief Legal Officer
Todd George, Executive VP, Divisional

GROWTH PLANS/SPECIAL FEATURES:

PENN Entertainment Inc provides integrated entertainment, sports content, and casino gaming experiences. It is the operator of gaming and racing properties and video gaming terminal operations in the U.S. It operates retail sports betting across the company's portfolio, as well as online sports betting, online social casino, bingo, and online casinos. The five geographical segments include the Northeast segment, South segment, West segment, Midwest segment and Interactive segment, out of which the majority is from the Northeast segment.

Penn National offers comprehensive medical benefits, 401(k) and a variety of employee assistance programs.

FINANCIAL DATA: *Note: Data for latest year may not have been available at press time.*

In U.S. $	2022	2021	2020	2019	2018	2017
Revenue	6,401,700,000	5,905,000,000	3,578,700,000	5,301,400,000	3,148,000,000	3,148,000,000
R&D Expense						
Operating Income	1,092,200,000	1,059,600,000	213,200,000	745,000,000	463,700,000	463,700,000
Operating Margin %	.17%	.18%	.06%	.14%	.15%	.15%
SGA Expense	1,110,400,000	1,352,900,000	1,130,800,000	1,187,700,000	514,500,000	514,500,000
Net Income	222,100,000	420,800,000	-669,500,000	43,900,000	473,400,000	473,400,000
Operating Cash Flow	878,200,000	896,100,000	338,800,000	703,900,000	477,800,000	477,800,000
Capital Expenditure	272,400,000	268,300,000	141,800,000	202,300,000	100,900,000	100,900,000
EBITDA	1,501,000,000	1,446,400,000	76,600,000	1,035,900,000	708,800,000	708,800,000
Return on Assets %	.01%	.03%	-.05%	.00%	.09%	.09%
Return on Equity %	.06%	.12%	-.30%	.03%		
Debt to Equity	3.52%	2.78%	4.142	5.988		

CONTACT INFORMATION:

Phone: 610 373-2400   Fax: 610 376-4966
Toll-Free:
Address: 825 Berkshire Blvd., Ste. 200, Wyomissing, PA 19610 United States

STOCK TICKER/OTHER:

Stock Ticker: PENN
Employees: 21,875
Parent Company:

Exchange: NAS
Fiscal Year Ends: 12/31

SALARIES/BONUSES:

Top Exec. Salary: $1,786,154   Bonus: $
Second Exec. Salary: $537,500   Bonus: $375,000

OTHER THOUGHTS:

Estimated Female Officers or Directors: 1
Hot Spot for Advancement for Women/Minorities:

PGA European Tour (bda DP World Tour)

www.europeantour.com/dpworld-tour
NAIC Code: 711211

TYPES OF BUSINESS:

Professional Golf Association
Event Sponsorship

BRANDS/DIVISIONS/AFFILIATES:

DP World Tour
European Senior Tour
Challenge Tour
Ryder Cup Europe

GROWTH PLANS/SPECIAL FEATURES:

The PGA European Tour (PGAET), b/d/a DP World Tour, is the leading men's professional golf tour in Europe. The organization also operates the European Senior Tour (for players aged 50 or older) and the developmental Challenge Tour; the second tier of men's professional golf in Europe. The PGAET is the lead partner in Ryder Cup Europe, a joint venture also including the PGA of Great Britain and Ireland and PGA of Europe that operates the Ryder Cup Matches in cooperation with the PGA of America. The organization has a 60% interest in Ryder Cup Europe, with each of its junior partners holding 20%. In June 2023, PGAET announced that it would merge with PGA Tour and LIV Golf to form a single organization. The transaction is still waiting regulatory approval.

CONTACTS: Note: Officers with more than one job title may be intentionally listed here more than once.

Keith W. Pelley, CEO
David Williams, Chmn.

FINANCIAL DATA: Note: Data for latest year may not have been available at press time.

In U.S. $	2022	2021	2020	2019	2018	2017
Revenue						
R&D Expense						
Operating Income						
Operating Margin %						
SGA Expense						
Net Income						
Operating Cash Flow						
Capital Expenditure						
EBITDA						
Return on Assets %						
Return on Equity %						
Debt to Equity						

CONTACT INFORMATION:

Phone: 44-1344-840400   Fax:
Toll-Free:
Address: European Tour Bldg., Wentworth Dr., Virginia Water, Surrey GU25 4LX United Kingdom

STOCK TICKER/OTHER:

Stock Ticker: Private   Exchange:
Employees: Fiscal Year Ends:
Parent Company:

SALARIES/BONUSES:

Top Exec. Salary: $ Bonus: $
Second Exec. Salary: $ Bonus: $

OTHER THOUGHTS:

Estimated Female Officers or Directors:
Hot Spot for Advancement for Women/Minorities:

Philadelphia 76ers

www.nba.com/sixers

NAIC Code: 711211B

TYPES OF BUSINESS:

Professional Basketball Team
Team Management and Operations

BRANDS/DIVISIONS/AFFILIATES:

Syracuse Nationals
Delaware Blue Coats

CONTACTS: *Note: Officers with more than one job title may be intentionally listed here more than once.*

Josh Harris, Managing Dir.
Daryl Morey, Pres.-Basketball Oper.
Elton Brand, Gen. Mngr.
Lara Price, Sr. VP-Bus. Oper.
Nick Gesacion, Dir.-New Media
Michael Preston, Dir.-Public Rel.
Andy Speiser, Sr. VP-Finance
Tom Ward, Sr. VP-Partnerships & Broadcasting
Joe Ondrejko, VP-Ticket Sales & Customer Svcs.
Tina Szwak, Controller
Larry Meli, VP-Fan Experience & Ticket Oper.

GROWTH PLANS/SPECIAL FEATURES:

The Philadelphia 76ers is a professional basketball team playing in the National Basketball Association (NBA) Eastern Atlantic division. The team began as the Syracuse Nationals and relocated to Pennsylvania in 1963. The 76ers have won three championships: one in 1955, one under the lead of the legendary Wilt Chamberlain in 1967 and the third in 1983 with Julius Erving. The team experienced some measure of success throughout the 1980s, gaining several playoff berths throughout the decade, thanks to stars such as Erving, Moses Malone and Charles Barkley. This success was short lived, as the 76ers stumbled throughout the first half of the 1990s. While the franchise has not had championship success in recent years, it has a total of five conference titles and 12 division titles (most recently in 2021). Wells Fargo Center is where the 76ers play their home games, with a 20,478 capacity to seat basketball spectators. The team's home attendance averaged 20,469 in the 2022-23 season. The 76ers maintain an affiliation with the Delaware Blue Coats of the NBA G League. Forbes estimated the 76ers' value at $3.15 billion in October 2022.

FINANCIAL DATA: *Note: Data for latest year may not have been available at press time.*

In U.S. $	2022	2021	2020	2019	2018	2017
Revenue	321,750,000					
R&D Expense						
Operating Income						
Operating Margin %						
SGA Expense						
Net Income						
Operating Cash Flow						
Capital Expenditure						
EBITDA						
Return on Assets %						
Return on Equity %						
Debt to Equity						

CONTACT INFORMATION:

Phone: 215-339-7676   Fax: 215-339-7632
Toll-Free:
Address: 3601 S. Broad St., Philadelphia, PA 19148 United States

STOCK TICKER/OTHER:

Stock Ticker: Private
Employees: 400
Parent Company:

Exchange:
Fiscal Year Ends: 12/31

SALARIES/BONUSES:

Top Exec. Salary: $ Bonus: $
Second Exec. Salary: $ Bonus: $

OTHER THOUGHTS:

Estimated Female Officers or Directors: 5
Hot Spot for Advancement for Women/Minorities: Y

Philadelphia Eagles

NAIC Code: 711211C

www.philadelphiaeagles.com

TYPES OF BUSINESS:

Professional Football Team
Team Management and Operations

BRANDS/DIVISIONS/AFFILIATES:

CONTACTS: *Note: Officers with more than one job title may be intentionally listed here more than once.*

Jeffrey Lurie, CEO
Don Smolenski, Pres.
Greg McDonald, VP-Financial Oper.
Jen Kavanagh, Sr. VP-Mktg. & Media
Kristie Pappal, VP-Human Resources
John Pawling, VP-IT
Brendan McQuillan, Dir.-Merch.
James Harris, Chief of Staff
Aileen Daly, General Counsel
Ari Roitman, Sr. VP-Bus.
Maggie Arganbright, Dir.-Digital & Social Media
Anne Gordan, Sr. VP-Media & Comm.
Greg McDonald, Controller-Oper.
Howie Roseman, Gen. Mgr.
Chip Kelly, Head Coach
Leonard Bonacci, VP-Event Oper. & Event Svcs.
Jason Miller, VP-Facility Oper.
Jeffrey Lurie, Chmn.

GROWTH PLANS/SPECIAL FEATURES:

The Philadelphia Eagles is a professional football team in the Eastern Division of the National Football League's (NFL) National Football Conference (NFC) along with the New York Giants, Dallas Cowboys and Washington Commanders. The franchise has won four NFL titles (three NFL Pre-1970 AFL-NFL merger championships and one Super Bowl championship), five conference championships (most recently in 2022), 16 division championships (most recently in 2022), and 29 playoff appearances (most recently in 2021 and 2022). Struggling at first, the Eagles appeared in three consecutive NFL championship games during the 1940s, winning two of them in 1948 and 1949. The team won its third NFL championship in 1960. However, since then, the Eagles' performance on the field has been plagued by difficulties. Between 1988 and 1996 the team qualified for the playoffs six times. In 1999, the Eagles hired head coach Andy Reid, who drafted quarterback superstar Donovan McNabb. This new era of Eagles football achieved five consecutive trips to the NFC conference championship between 2000 and 2004, but the team only reached the Super Bowl once, losing to the New England Patriots. In 2017 not only did the team make the playoffs, it defeated the New England Patriots to win Super Bowl LII. The Eagles are owned by Jeffrey Lurie, a former Hollywood producer, who bought the team for $195 million in 1994. The Eagles play at Lincoln Financial Field, which holds 69,796 spectators, and usually sells out each home game. The stadium is owned by the City of Philadelphia. Forbes estimated the value of the Eagles at $4.9 billion in 2022.

FINANCIAL DATA: *Note: Data for latest year may not have been available at press time.*

In U.S. $	2022	2021	2020	2019	2018	2017
Revenue	572,000,000					
R&D Expense						
Operating Income						
Operating Margin %						
SGA Expense						
Net Income						
Operating Cash Flow						
Capital Expenditure						
EBITDA						
Return on Assets %						
Return on Equity %						
Debt to Equity						

CONTACT INFORMATION:

Phone: 215-463-2500   Fax: 215-339-5464
Toll-Free:
Address: One NovaCare Way, Philadelphia, PA 19145 United States

STOCK TICKER/OTHER:

Stock Ticker: Private   Exchange:
Employees: 770   Fiscal Year Ends: 12/31
Parent Company:

SALARIES/BONUSES:

Top Exec. Salary: $ Bonus: $
Second Exec. Salary: $ Bonus: $

OTHER THOUGHTS:

Estimated Female Officers or Directors: 8
Hot Spot for Advancement for Women/Minorities: Y

Sales, profits and employees may be estimates. Financial information, benefits and other data can change quickly and may vary from those stated here.

Philadelphia Flyers

flyers.nhl.com

NAIC Code: 711211F

TYPES OF BUSINESS:

Professional Hockey Team (NHL)
Team Management and Operations

BRANDS/DIVISIONS/AFFILIATES:

Compcast Corporation
Comcast Spectacor
Lehigh Valley Phantoms
Reading Royals

CONTACTS: *Note: Officers with more than one job title may be intentionally listed here more than once.*

Dan Hilferty, CEO
Valerie Camillo, Pres.-Bus. Oper.
Blair Listino, CFO
Cynthia Punsalan, Sr. VP-Bus. Admin.
Lauren McNally, VP-Human Resources
Mike Shane, Chief Business Officer
Craig Berube, Head Coach
Bryan Anton, VP-Sales
Dan Hilferty, Chmn.

GROWTH PLANS/SPECIAL FEATURES:

The Philadelphia Flyers is a National Hockey League (NHL) team that plays in the Metropolitan Division of the Eastern Conference. The team is owned by Comcast Spectacor, a subsidiary of Comcast Corporation. The Flyers were founded in 1967 as part of the NHL's expansion. The team was hampered early-on by league restrictions that kept major talent with the original six NHL teams. The Flyers play at the Wells Fargo Center, which it shares with the Philadelphia 76ers, and has a hockey seating capacity of 19,306. The team averaged 17,635 fans in attendance per home game during the 2022 season. The Flyers won Stanley Cups in 1973-74 and 1974-75, and have clenched eight Conference Championships (2009-10 most recently) and 16 Division Championships (2010-11 most recently). In a March 2004 game, the Flyers became the first NHL expansion team to score 10,000 total goals. In that same game, the Flyers and the Ottawa Senators got into several brawls and set an NHL record for the most penalty minutes in a game, 419 minutes. The team's NHL Hall of Famers includes Bobby Clarke, Bernie Parent, Bill Barber, Mark Howe and Paul Coffey. The Flyers maintain a minor league affiliation with the Lehigh Valley Phantoms in the American Hockey League and the Reading Royals in the ECHL. Forbes estimated the Flyers' value at $1.25 billion in December 2022.

FINANCIAL DATA: *Note: Data for latest year may not have been available at press time.*

In U.S. $	2022	2021	2020	2019	2018	2017
Revenue	152,750,000	74,000,000	161,000,000		170,000,000	170,000,000
R&D Expense						
Operating Income						
Operating Margin %						
SGA Expense						
Net Income						
Operating Cash Flow						
Capital Expenditure						
EBITDA						
Return on Assets %						
Return on Equity %						
Debt to Equity						

CONTACT INFORMATION:

Phone: 215-465-4500   Fax: 215-389-9403
Toll-Free:
Address: 3601 S. Broad St., Philadelphia, PA 19148 United States

STOCK TICKER/OTHER:

Stock Ticker: Subsidiary
Employees: 230
Parent Company: Comcast Corporation

Exchange:
Fiscal Year Ends: 06/30

SALARIES/BONUSES:

Top Exec. Salary: $ Bonus: $
Second Exec. Salary: $ Bonus: $

OTHER THOUGHTS:

Estimated Female Officers or Directors: 10
Hot Spot for Advancement for Women/Minorities: Y

Philadelphia Phillies

NAIC Code: 711211A

www.mlb.com/phillies

TYPES OF BUSINESS:

Professional Baseball Team
Team Management and Operations

BRANDS/DIVISIONS/AFFILIATES:

Citizens Bank Park
Lehigh Valley IronPigs
Reading Fightin Phils
Clearwater Threshers

CONTACTS: *Note: Officers with more than one job title may be intentionally listed here more than once.*

John Middleton, CEO
David Dombrowski, Pres.-Baseball Oper.
John Nickolas, CFO
Kurt Funk, VP-Mktg. & Events
Jon Madden, Dir.-Human Resources
Sean Walker, CTO
Scott Brandreth, Dir.-Merch.
Michael Stiles, Sr. VP-Admin.
Rick Strouse, General Counsel
Michael Stiles, Sr. VP-Oper.
Bonnie Clark, VP-Comm.
Mike Carson, Controller
Richard Deats, VP-Phillies Enterprises
Ruben Amaro, Jr., Gen Mgr.
John Weber, VP-Ticket Sales & Oper.
Charlie Manuel, Mgr.
Bill Giles, Chmn. Emeritus

GROWTH PLANS/SPECIAL FEATURES:

The Philadelphia Phillies is a Major League Baseball (MLB) franchise, playing in the East Division of the National League. The team is owned by a limited partnership, with John S. Middleton serving as the managing partner. The organization was founded as the Philadelphia Quakers in 1883 but was soon renamed the Phillies. It is the oldest continuous one-name, one-city franchise in all of American professional sports. The team has won two World Series titles, seven National League Pennants and 11 Division titles (most recently in 2011), but has a reputation for futility and failure, especially in crucial moments. The franchise saw success in the early 2000's, winning five consecutive division titles (2007-2011) and making two successive trips to the World Series in 2008 and 2009 that resulted in its 2008 championship. The club plays home games at the Citizens Bank Park, a baseball-only field with room for approximately 43,651 spectators, built in 2004. Average home attendance for the team was 28,459 during the 2022-23 season. The team has several minor league affiliations, including the Lehigh Valley IronPigs, the Reading Fightin' Phils, the Jersey Shore BlueClaws, and the Clearwater Threshers. Forbes estimated the value of the team at $2.575 billion in March 2023.

FINANCIAL DATA: *Note: Data for latest year may not have been available at press time.*

In U.S. $	2022	2021	2020	2019	2018	2017
Revenue	464,750,000					
R&D Expense						
Operating Income						
Operating Margin %						
SGA Expense						
Net Income						
Operating Cash Flow						
Capital Expenditure						
EBITDA						
Return on Assets %						
Return on Equity %						
Debt to Equity						

CONTACT INFORMATION:

Phone: 215-463-6000   Fax: 215-389-3050
Toll-Free:
Address: One Citizens Bank Way, Philadelphia, PA 19148 United States

STOCK TICKER/OTHER:

Stock Ticker: Private   Exchange:
Employees: 515   Fiscal Year Ends: 10/31
Parent Company:

SALARIES/BONUSES:

Top Exec. Salary: $ Bonus: $
Second Exec. Salary: $ Bonus: $

OTHER THOUGHTS:

Estimated Female Officers or Directors: 5
Hot Spot for Advancement for Women/Minorities: Y

Philadelphia Union

www.philadelphiaunion.com

NAIC Code: 711211D

TYPES OF BUSINESS:

Major League Soccer Team
Team Management and Operations

BRANDS/DIVISIONS/AFFILIATES:

CONTACTS: *Note: Officers with more than one job title may be intentionally listed here more than once.*

Tim McDermott, Pres.
Dave Debusschere, COO
Charlie Slonaker, Chief Revenue Officer
Amanda Young Curtis, VP-Mktg. & Communications
Ashlee Maunz, Sr. Dir.-Human Resources
Tom Via II, Sr. Mngr.-Digital
Rob Parker, Sr. VP-Bus. Dev.
Kerith Gabriel, Mgr.-Digital Media
Cara Joftis, VP-Comm.
Dave Rowan, Chief Revenue Officer
John Hackworth, Team Mgr.
Mike Quarino, VP-Ticket Sales & Fan Svcs.
Dennis Carroll, VP-Finance
Carl Cherkin, VP-Bus. Rel.
Jay Sugarman, Chmn.

GROWTH PLANS/SPECIAL FEATURES:

The Philadelphia Union is a Major League Soccer (MLS) team based in Philadelphia, Pennsylvania. The team plays in the Eastern Conference, along with the Atlanta United FC, Charlotte FC, Chicago Fire FC, FC Cincinnati, Columbus Crew, DC United, Inter Miami CF, CF Montreal, Nashville SC, New England Revolution, New York City FC, New York Red Bulls, Orlando City SC and Toronto FC. The club was founded as an expansion team in 2008 and played its inaugural game against the Seattle Sounders in 2010. At the end of the 2014 MLS season, the team was awarded the MLS Fair Play for being the club with the fewest fouls that season. It finished as runners-up in the 2014, 2015 and 2018 U.S. Open Cup tournaments. The Philadelphia Union won their first trophy, the Supporters' Shield champions in 2020. The team clenched their first Conference title in 2022, and placed second overall in the conference playoffs. Union plays in the Subaru Park, an 18,500-seat soccer specific stadium located in Chester, Pennsylvania. The team's average home game attendance was 18,126 during the 2022 season. The arrival of an MLS in Philadelphia was aided in no small part by the fan group Sons of Ben, who helped lobby local investors and soccer officials to support an expansion. The team's jersey, sleeve and kit are sponsored by Bimbo, Subaru and Adidas, respectively.

FINANCIAL DATA: *Note: Data for latest year may not have been available at press time.*

In U.S. $	2022	2021	2020	2019	2018	2017
Revenue	8,996,400					
R&D Expense						
Operating Income						
Operating Margin %						
SGA Expense						
Net Income						
Operating Cash Flow						
Capital Expenditure						
EBITDA						
Return on Assets %						
Return on Equity %						
Debt to Equity						

CONTACT INFORMATION:

Phone: 610-497-1657   Fax: 610-497-3309
Toll-Free: 877-218-6466
Address: 2501 Seaport Dr., BH Ste. 100, Chester, PA 19013 United States

STOCK TICKER/OTHER:

Stock Ticker: Private   Exchange:
Employees: 170   Fiscal Year Ends:
Parent Company:

SALARIES/BONUSES:

Top Exec. Salary: $ Bonus: $
Second Exec. Salary: $ Bonus: $

OTHER THOUGHTS:

Estimated Female Officers or Directors: 6
Hot Spot for Advancement for Women/Minorities: Y

Philips Sport Vereniging (PSV Eindhoven)

www.psv.nl/psv/home.htm

NAIC Code: 711211D

TYPES OF BUSINESS:

Soccer Team
Team Management and Operations

BRANDS/DIVISIONS/AFFILIATES:

Foundation PSV Football
Philips Stadion

GROWTH PLANS/SPECIAL FEATURES:

Philips Sport Vereniging (PSV Eindhoven) is a professional football club in the Netherlands, playing in the Eredivisie league, the top-tier in Dutch football. Founded in 1913, PSV Eindhoven plays its home games in Philips Stadion, which is owned by PSV Eindhoven and has a seating capacity of approximately 35,000. Nationally, PSV Eindhoven has won 24 Eredivisie titles, 11 KNVB Cups (most recently in 2021-22 and 2022-23) and 13 Johan Cruyff Shield titles (most recently in 2021 and 2022). Internationally, the club has won one European Cup (UEFA Champions League) and one UEFA Cup (UEFA Europa League). Since 2019, PSV Eindhoven's sponsors have been a combined entity known as Metropoolregio Brainport Eindhoven, which is displayed on the team's shirts. The football club is 99%-owned by Foundation PSV Football.

CONTACTS: *Note: Officers with more than one job title may be intentionally listed here more than once.*

Fred Rutten, Head Coach
Robert van der Wallen, Chmn.

FINANCIAL DATA: *Note: Data for latest year may not have been available at press time.*

In U.S. $	2022	2021	2020	2019	2018	2017
Revenue						
R&D Expense						
Operating Income						
Operating Margin %						
SGA Expense						
Net Income						
Operating Cash Flow						
Capital Expenditure						
EBITDA						
Return on Assets %						
Return on Equity %						
Debt to Equity						

CONTACT INFORMATION:

Phone: 3140 2505505   Fax: 3140 2505696
Toll-Free:
Address: Fredriklaan 10a, Eindhoven, 5616 NH Netherlands

STOCK TICKER/OTHER:

Stock Ticker: Subsidiary   Exchange:
Employees: Fiscal Year Ends:
Parent Company: Foundation PSV Football

SALARIES/BONUSES:

Top Exec. Salary: $ Bonus: $
Second Exec. Salary: $ Bonus: $

OTHER THOUGHTS:

Estimated Female Officers or Directors:
Hot Spot for Advancement for Women/Minorities:

Phoenix Mercury

www.wnba.com/mercury

NAIC Code: 711211E

TYPES OF BUSINESS:

Women's Professional Basketball Team
Team Management and Operations

BRANDS/DIVISIONS/AFFILIATES:

Phoenix Suns

CONTACTS: Note: Officers with more than one job title may be intentionally listed here more than once.

Jim Pitman, General Mngr.
Amber Cox, Pres.
Lesley Factor, Dir.-Public & Community Rel.
Corey Gaines, Head Coach
Robert Sarver, Managing Partner

GROWTH PLANS/SPECIAL FEATURES:

The Phoenix Mercury, founded in 1997, is one of the eight original teams to join the Women's National Basketball Association (WNBA). The franchise plays in the Western Conference along with the Dallas Wings, Los Angeles Sparks, Las Vegas Aces, Minnesota Lynx and Seattle Storm. It is the sister team to the Phoenix Suns, a National Basketball Association (NBA) team. Both teams play home games in the Footprint Center, a multi-purpose arena in Phoenix that seats 16,645 spectators. The stadium, which was built through the efforts of former Mercury chairman Jerry Colangelo, is now owned by the City of Phoenix. Average attendance for the Phoenix Mercury was nearly 8,000 during the 2022 season. Although the team made it to the playoffs in 1997, 1998 and 2000, they didn't win their first WNBA Championship until 2007. The Mercury beat the Detroit Shock, the defending champion, in the Shock's home stadium, making the Mercury the first WNBA team to win a championship on the road. The team repeated as WNBA champions with a win over the Indiana Fever in 2009, and again in 2014 with a win over the Chicago Sky. They've clenched five conference titles, with the most recent being in 2021. Mercury Hall-of-Fame members have included player Nancy Lieberman, former coach Cheryl Miller, Linda Sharp and Michele Timms. The franchise has four retired numbers: 7-Michele Timms, 22-Jennifer Gillom, 32-Bridget Pettis and 13-Penny Taylor.

FINANCIAL DATA: Note: Data for latest year may not have been available at press time.

In U.S. $	2022	2021	2020	2019	2018	2017
Revenue						
R&D Expense						
Operating Income						
Operating Margin %						
SGA Expense						
Net Income						
Operating Cash Flow						
Capital Expenditure						
EBITDA						
Return on Assets %						
Return on Equity %						
Debt to Equity						

CONTACT INFORMATION:

Phone: 602-379-7900   Fax: 602-379-7540
Toll-Free:
Address: 201 E. Jefferson St., Phoenix, AZ 85004 United States

STOCK TICKER/OTHER:

Stock Ticker: Private
Employees: 30
Parent Company:

Exchange:
Fiscal Year Ends:

SALARIES/BONUSES:

Top Exec. Salary: $ Bonus: $
Second Exec. Salary: $ Bonus: $

OTHER THOUGHTS:

Estimated Female Officers or Directors: 3
Hot Spot for Advancement for Women/Minorities: Y

Phoenix Suns

NAIC Code: 711211B

TYPES OF BUSINESS:

Professional Basketball Team
Team Management and Operations

BRANDS/DIVISIONS/AFFILIATES:

CONTACTS: *Note: Officers with more than one job title may be intentionally listed here more than once.*

Josh Bartelstein, CEO
Aarom Jerz, Sr. VP-Bus. Oper.
Jim Pitman, CFO
Graham Wincott, Sr. Dir.-Mktg.
Kim Corbitt, Sr. VP-People & Culture
Tramon Thomas, VP-Brand Digital & Social
Jim Pitman, Exec. VP-Admin.
Lon Babby, Pres., Basketball Oper.
Jay Parry, Sr. VP-Bus. & Brand Dev.
Jeramie McPeek, VP-Digital
Tanya Wheeless, Sr. VP-Comm. & Public Affairs
Jim Pitman, Exec. VP-Finance
Robert Sarver, Managing Partner
Lance Blanks, Gen. Mgr.
Ralph Marchetta, Sr. VP-Ticket Oper.
Al McCoy, Sr. VP-Broadcasting
James Jones, Pres.-Basketball Oper.

GROWTH PLANS/SPECIAL FEATURES:

The Phoenix Suns is a professional basketball team in the National Basketball Association (NBA) based in Phoenix, Arizona, playing in the Pacific Division of the Western Conference. The franchise was founded in 1968 by a group of investors in Tucson, Arizona. It played well throughout the 1970s, reaching the NBA Finals in 1976 only to lose to the Boston Celtics. In the mid-1980s, on and off court problems dirtied the reputation of the team, which in 1987 led to the team being sold for $44 million to an investor group led by Jerry Colangelo. Beginning with the 1988 season, the team built a streak of 13 consecutive playoff appearances, which ended in the 2002 season. During that span, the Suns' lineup featured several of the league's star players, including Charles Barkley and Jason Kidd. Despite its performance, the team has failed to collect an NBA Finals championship in its two series appearances. Nonetheless, the Suns have clenched three Conference titles (most recently in 2021) and eight division titles (2021 and 2022 most recently). Former majority owner Jerry Colangelo sold the team to an investment group headed by Robert Sarver, a real estate executive, for $401 million in 2004. The Suns play at the Footprint Center, which has the capacity to seat 16,645 spectators. The team's home attendance average was 17,071 per game during the 2022-23 season. Forbes estimated the value of the Phoenix Suns at $2.7 billion in October 2022.

FINANCIAL DATA: *Note: Data for latest year may not have been available at press time.*

In U.S. $	2022	2021	2020	2019	2018	2017
Revenue	278,200,000					
R&D Expense						
Operating Income						
Operating Margin %						
SGA Expense						
Net Income						
Operating Cash Flow						
Capital Expenditure						
EBITDA						
Return on Assets %						
Return on Equity %						
Debt to Equity						

CONTACT INFORMATION:

Phone: 602-379-2000   Fax: 602-379-7990
Toll-Free:
Address: 201 E. Jefferson St., Phoenix, AZ 85004 United States

STOCK TICKER/OTHER:

Stock Ticker: Private   Exchange:
Employees: 470   Fiscal Year Ends:
Parent Company:

SALARIES/BONUSES:

Top Exec. Salary: $ Bonus: $
Second Exec. Salary: $ Bonus: $

OTHER THOUGHTS:

Estimated Female Officers or Directors: 3
Hot Spot for Advancement for Women/Minorities: Y

Pittsburgh Penguins

penguins.nhl.com

NAIC Code: 711211F

TYPES OF BUSINESS:

Professional Hockey Team (NHL)
Team Management and Operations

BRANDS/DIVISIONS/AFFILIATES:

Fenway Sports Group Holdings LLC
Wilkes-Barre/Scranton Penguins
Wheeling Nailers

CONTACTS: *Note: Officers with more than one job title may be intentionally listed here more than once.*

Kevin Acklin, Pres.-Bus. Oper.
Mike Dillon, CFO
James Santilli, CMO
Tracey McCants Lewis, Chief People Officer
Chris Zaber, Chief Revenue Officer
Jennifer Bullano, Dir.-Comm.
Jason Botterill, Assistant Gen. Mgr.
Ray Shero, Gen. Mgr.
Ron Burkle, Co-Owner
Dan Bylsma, Head Coach
Jennifer Bullano Ridgley, Sr. VP-Communications
Patrik Allvin, Head Scout-Europe

GROWTH PLANS/SPECIAL FEATURES:

The Pittsburgh Penguins franchise is a professional hockey team that has played in the National Hockey League (NHL) since 1967. In its early years, the team met with mixed results on the ice due to a strong offense and weak defense. In 1984, the team drafted Mario Lemieux, who would go on to become one of the greatest players in the NHL and an integral part of the Penguins franchise. Along with Jaromir Jagr, Lemieux led the team to two Stanley Cups in the 1990-91 and 1991-92 seasons. However, with the team facing bankruptcy, and by virtue of his being owed millions of dollars by the Penguins in deferred salary, Lemieux became owner of the hockey club through Lemieux Group LP. Lemieux began playing for the team again in 2000 and led it to the playoffs. The Penguins experienced financial difficulties throughout the early 2000s, forcing it to trade away its talent. The team overcame these troubles by winning consecutive conference championships in 2007-08 and 2008-09, as well as Stanley Cups in the 2008-09, 2015-16 and 2016-17 seasons. In late-2021, Lemieux sold the Penguins to Fenway Sports Group Holdings, LLC. The team plays in the Metropolitan division of the Eastern conference at the PPG Paints Arena. PPG is a multi-purpose arena that seats approximately 19,000 spectators, and the Penguins averaged 17,816 in home game attendance during the 2022-23 season. Minor league affiliations of the Penguins include the Wilkes-Barre/Scranton Penguins in the American Hockey League (AHL), and the Wheeling Nailers in the ECHL. Forbes estimated the Pittsburgh Penguins' value at $990 million in December 2022.

FINANCIAL DATA: *Note: Data for latest year may not have been available at press time.*

In U.S. $	2022	2021	2020	2019	2018	2017
Revenue	152,750,000					
R&D Expense						
Operating Income						
Operating Margin %						
SGA Expense						
Net Income						
Operating Cash Flow						
Capital Expenditure						
EBITDA						
Return on Assets %						
Return on Equity %						
Debt to Equity						

CONTACT INFORMATION:

Phone: 412-642-1300   Fax: 412-255-1980
Toll-Free:
Address: 1001 5th Ave., Pittsburgh, PA 15219 United States

STOCK TICKER/OTHER:

Stock Ticker: Private   Exchange:
Employees: 300   Fiscal Year Ends: 06/30
Parent Company:

SALARIES/BONUSES:

Top Exec. Salary: $ Bonus: $
Second Exec. Salary: $ Bonus: $

OTHER THOUGHTS:

Estimated Female Officers or Directors: 1
Hot Spot for Advancement for Women/Minorities:

Pittsburgh Pirates

www.mlb.com/pirates

NAIC Code: 711211A

TYPES OF BUSINESS:

Professional Baseball Team
Team Management and Operations

BRANDS/DIVISIONS/AFFILIATES:

Indianapolis Indians
Altoona Curve
Greensboro Grasshoppers
Bradenton Marauders

CONTACTS: *Note: Officers with more than one job title may be intentionally listed here more than once.*

Travis Williams, Pres.
Libby Waltman, CFO
Stephen Perkins, Exec. VP-Mktg.
Nayli Russo-Long, VP-People & Strategy
Terry Zeigler, VP-IT
Bryan Stroh, General Counsel
Kevan Graves, Dir.-Baseball Oper.
Travis Apple, Dir.-New Bus. Dev.
Patty Paytas, Sr. VP-Community & Public Affairs
Neal Huntington, Gen. Mgr.
Tyrone Brooks, Dir.-Player Personnel
Bob Nutting, Chmn.
Rene Gayo, Dir.-Latin American Scouting

GROWTH PLANS/SPECIAL FEATURES:

The Pittsburgh Pirates is a Major League Baseball (MLB) team in the Central Division of the National League. Playing its first season with the National League as the Pittsburgh Alleghenies in 1887, the team became the Pirates in 1891. Before that, the Pirates played in the American Association from 1882 through 1886. The team's most famous players include Honus Wagner, Pie Traynor, Roberto Clemente, Willie Stargell and Barry Bonds. In 1970, the Pirates fielded what is believed to be the first all-minority lineup in the modern history of the MLB. The team waxed and waned from the 1940s to the 1980s, briefly reaching prominence in 1960 and throughout the 1970s. In total, the Pirates have won five World Series (most recently in 1979), nine pennants and nine eastern division titles (no central division titles). Its World Series victories in 1971 and 1979 were spurred in part by the strong batting performances of Clemente and Stargell. The Pirates were majority-owned by Kevin McClatchy from 1996 to 2006 when he was replaced by current majority owner Robert Nutting. Home games for the team are played at PNC Park, a 38,747-seat stadium and another in the trend of classic-style ballparks opened in recent decades. Average home game attendance was 15,524 during the 2022 season. The team's minor league affiliations include the Indianapolis Indians, the Altoona Curve, the Greensboro Grasshoppers and the Bradenton Marauders. Forbes estimated the value of the Pirates at $1.32 billion in March 2023.

FINANCIAL DATA: *Note: Data for latest year may not have been available at press time.*

In U.S. $	2022	2021	2020	2019	2018	2017
Revenue	345,150,000					
R&D Expense						
Operating Income						
Operating Margin %						
SGA Expense						
Net Income						
Operating Cash Flow						
Capital Expenditure						
EBITDA						
Return on Assets %						
Return on Equity %						
Debt to Equity						

CONTACT INFORMATION:

Phone: 412-323-5000   Fax: 412-325-4410
Toll-Free:
Address: 115 Federal St., Pittsburgh, PA 15212 United States

STOCK TICKER/OTHER:

Stock Ticker: Private   Exchange:
Employees: 720   Fiscal Year Ends: 10/31
Parent Company:

SALARIES/BONUSES:

Top Exec. Salary: $ Bonus: $
Second Exec. Salary: $ Bonus: $

OTHER THOUGHTS:

Estimated Female Officers or Directors: 5
Hot Spot for Advancement for Women/Minorities: Y

PITTSBURGH STEELERS

www.steelers.com

NAIC Code: 711211C

TYPES OF BUSINESS:

Professional Football Team
Team Management and Operations

BRANDS/DIVISIONS/AFFILIATES:

CONTACTS: *Note: Officers with more than one job title may be intentionally listed here more than once.*

Arthur J. Rooney II, Pres.
Arthur J. Rooney, Jr., VP
Doug Stuver, VP-Finance
Ryan Huzjak, VP-Mktg. & Sales
Jenny Shaeffer, Dir.-Human Resources
Scott Phelps, VP-Technology
Tim Carey, Exec. Officer-Merch.
Omar Khan, Dir.-Admin & Bus.
Kevin Colbert, Gen. Mgr.-Football Oper.
Mark Hart, Dir.-Planning & Dev.
Nathan LoCascio, Mgr.-Public Rel. & Media
Bob Tyler, Dir.-Finance
Rodgers Freyvogel, Mgr.-Equipment
Ben Lentz, Mgr.-Tickets
Mike Tomlin, Head Coach
Kathy Wallace, Mgr.-Corp. Sales & Mktg.
Dan Rooney, Dir.-Bus. Dev. & Strategy

GROWTH PLANS/SPECIAL FEATURES:

The Pittsburgh Steelers is a professional football team in the National Football League (NFL). The team has played in the Northern Division of the NFL's American Football Conference (AFC) since 2002, and in the AFC Central Division from 1970 through 2001. The Steelers franchise was founded in 1933 as the Pittsburgh Pirates; its name changed to its current form in 1941. The team reached the playoffs only once before 1972. The Steelers' fortunes turned in 1969 with the hiring of legendary head coach Chuck Noll. Noll possessed an uncanny ability to select premium players in the NFL draft. Between 1969 and 1974, he drafted eight Hall of Fame superstar players. The Steelers made the playoffs every year between 1972 and 1979, winning the Super Bowl four times in that span. The team most recently won the Super Bowl in 2005-06 and 2008-09, and lost to the Green Bay Packers in the 2010-11 championship game. The franchise currently holds six Super Bowl wins, eight Conference championships and 24 Division championships, as well as 33 playoff appearances (most recently in 2020 and 2021). The team plays at the 68,400-seat capacity Acrisure Stadium, which overlooks the Ohio River in downtown Pittsburgh. Home game attendance averaged 66,280 for the Steelers during the 2022-23 season. Prominent Hall of Famers include Terry Bradshaw, Mean Joe Greene, Jack Lambert and Rod Woodson. Forbes estimated the Steelers to be valued at $3.975 billion in 2022.

FINANCIAL DATA: *Note: Data for latest year may not have been available at press time.*

In U.S. $	2022	2021	2020	2019	2018	2017
Revenue	533,650,000					
R&D Expense						
Operating Income						
Operating Margin %						
SGA Expense						
Net Income						
Operating Cash Flow						
Capital Expenditure						
EBITDA						
Return on Assets %						
Return on Equity %						
Debt to Equity						

CONTACT INFORMATION:

Phone: 412-432-7800   Fax: 412-432-7878
Toll-Free:
Address: 3400 S. Water St., Pittsburgh, PA 15203-2349 United States

STOCK TICKER/OTHER:

Stock Ticker: Private   Exchange:
Employees: 325   Fiscal Year Ends: 03/31
Parent Company:

SALARIES/BONUSES:

Top Exec. Salary: $ Bonus: $
Second Exec. Salary: $ Bonus: $

OTHER THOUGHTS:

Estimated Female Officers or Directors: 7
Hot Spot for Advancement for Women/Minorities: Y

Planet Fitness Inc

www.planetfitness.com

NAIC Code: 713940

TYPES OF BUSINESS:

Fitness Centers

BRANDS/DIVISIONS/AFFILIATES:

PF Black Card
Lunk
Judgement Free Zone

GROWTH PLANS/SPECIAL FEATURES:

Planet Fitness Inc is a franchisor and operator of fitness centers in the United States. The company's reportable segments are Franchise, Corporate-owned stores, and Equipment. Franchise segment includes operations related to its franchising business in the United States, Puerto Rico, Canada, Panama, Mexico and Australia, Corporate-owned stores segment includes operations with respect to all corporate-owned stores throughout the United States and Canada, and The Equipment segment includes the sale of equipment to franchisee-owned stores in the U.S. The firm generates a majority of its revenue from the Corporate-owned stores segment.

CONTACTS: Note: Officers with more than one job title may be intentionally listed here more than once.

Christopher Rondeau, CEO
Thomas Fitzgerald, CFO
Stephen Spinelli, Chairman of the Board
Craig Miller, Chief Information Officer
Jeremy Tucker, Chief Marketing Officer
Dorvin Lively, President

FINANCIAL DATA: Note: Data for latest year may not have been available at press time.

In U.S. $	2022	2021	2020	2019	2018	2017
Revenue	936,772,000	587,023,000	406,618,000	688,803,000	429,942,000	429,942,000
R&D Expense						
Operating Income	230,078,000	143,395,000	59,760,000	233,083,000	147,536,000	147,536,000
Operating Margin %	.25%	.24%	.15%	.34%	.34%	.34%
SGA Expense	114,853,000	94,540,000	68,585,000	78,818,000	60,369,000	60,369,000
Net Income	99,402,000	42,774,000	-14,991,000	117,695,000	33,146,000	33,146,000
Operating Cash Flow	240,207,000	189,289,000	31,138,000	204,311,000	131,021,000	131,021,000
Capital Expenditure	524,997,000	55,962,000	52,560,000	110,803,000	37,722,000	37,722,000
EBITDA	374,088,000	195,971,000	121,432,000	278,612,000	496,613,000	496,613,000
Return on Assets %	.04%	.02%	- .01%	.08%	.03%	.03%
Return on Equity %						
Debt to Equity						

CONTACT INFORMATION:

Phone: 603-750-0001   Fax: 603-750-0004
Toll-Free:
Address: 4 Liberty Ln. W., Hampton, NH 03842 United States

STOCK TICKER/OTHER:

Stock Ticker: PLNT   Exchange: NYS
Employees: 3,137   Fiscal Year Ends: 12/31
Parent Company:

SALARIES/BONUSES:

Top Exec. Salary: $940,385   Bonus: $
Second Exec. Salary: Bonus: $
$549,231

OTHER THOUGHTS:

Estimated Female Officers or Directors:
Hot Spot for Advancement for Women/Minorities:

Portland Timbers

www.timbers.com

NAIC Code: 711211D

TYPES OF BUSINESS:

Major League Soccer Team
Team Management and Operations

GROWTH PLANS/SPECIAL FEATURES:

The Portland Timbers is a Major League Soccer (MLS) club based in Portland, Oregon. The Timbers originally entered the North American Soccer League in 1975, where the team produced three playoff seasons in 1975, 1978 and 1981. The club was also a part of the Western Soccer Alliance League for two seasons, which later turned into the United Soccer Leagues First Division in 1997. In 2009, the Portland Timbers were acquired by Merritt Paulson, owner of Peregrine Sports, LLC, which propelled the team into the MLS Western Conference by 2011. The team plays at Providence Park, a 25,218-seating outdoor arena. Average attendance for the Timbers during 2022 home games was 23,841. The Portland Timbers plays in the MLS Western Conference along with the Austin FC, Colorado Rapids, FC Dallas, Houston Dynamo FC, LA Galaxy, Los Angeles FC, Minnesota United FC, Real Salt Lake, San Jose Earthquakes, Seattle Sounders FC, Sporting Kansas City, St. Louis City SC and Vancouver Whitecaps FC. The team won two Western Conference Regular Season titles, won three Western Conference Championships (2015, 2018 and 2021), and clenched its first and only MLS Cup in 2015. In addition, the Timbers won the one-off MLS is Back Tournament in 2020, defeating Orlando City SC in the final. Notable players have included Clive Charles, Timber Jim, John Bain, Jimmy Conway and Mick Hoban.

BRANDS/DIVISIONS/AFFILIATES:

Peregrine Sports LLC

CONTACTS: Note: Officers with more than one job title may be intentionally listed here more than once.

Heather Davis, CEO
Ashley Highsmith, COO
Sara Keane, CFO
Jen Mylett, Digital Marketing
Finnian McNeff, VP-Human Resources
Jack Dodd, Dir.-Technical
Ken Puckett, Sr. VP-Operations

FINANCIAL DATA: Note: Data for latest year may not have been available at press time.

In U.S. $	2022	2021	2020	2019	2018	2017
Revenue	35,235,900					
R&D Expense						
Operating Income						
Operating Margin %						
SGA Expense						
Net Income						
Operating Cash Flow						
Capital Expenditure						
EBITDA						
Return on Assets %						
Return on Equity %						
Debt to Equity						

CONTACT INFORMATION:

Phone: 503-553-5400 Fax: 503-553-5405
Toll-Free:
Address: 1844 SW Morrison, Portland, OR 97205 United States

STOCK TICKER/OTHER:

Stock Ticker: Private   Exchange:
Employees: Fiscal Year Ends:
Parent Company:

SALARIES/BONUSES:

Top Exec. Salary: $ Bonus: $
Second Exec. Salary: $ Bonus: $

OTHER THOUGHTS:

Estimated Female Officers or Directors:
Hot Spot for Advancement for Women/Minorities:

Portland Trail Blazers

www.nba.com/blazers

NAIC Code: 711211B

TYPES OF BUSINESS:

Professional Basketball Team
Team Management and Operations

BRANDS/DIVISIONS/AFFILIATES:

Paul G Allen Trust
Moda Center

CONTACTS: *Note: Officers with more than one job title may be intentionally listed here more than once.*

Dewayne Hankins, Pres.-Bus. Oper.
Chris McGowan, Pres.
Bill Christensen, CFO
Kevin Kinghorn, CMO
Miriam Maiden, Sr. VP-People & Culture
Christa Stout, Sr. VP-Tech. & Innovation
Mike Janes, Dir.-Eng.
Ben Lauritsen, General Counsel
Nick West, Dir.-Basketball Oper.
Debbie Chitwood, Dir.-Bus. Oper.
Dan Harbison, Dir.-Digital Mktg. & Media
Traci Rose, VP-Community Rel.
Bill Christensen, VP-Finance
Paul G. Allen, Owner
Linda Glasser, Controller
Terry Stotts, Head Coach
Cheri Hanson, VP-Team Rel.
Jody Allen, Chmn.

GROWTH PLANS/SPECIAL FEATURES:

The Portland Trail Blazers is a National Basketball Association (NBA) team playing in the Northwest Division of the Western Conference. The Trail Blazers entered the league in 1970 as an expansion team and won its first and only NBA championship in 1977. The franchise has historically been a strong contender in the league, and appears frequently in the playoffs, with a streak of 21 consecutive postseason appearances between 1983 and 2003. However, the Trail Blazers' best moments have been shared with the surge of some unusually strong teams. Both the Detroit Pistons in the late 1980s and the Chicago Bulls of the early 1990s prevented the Trail Blazers from recapturing a title. In the 2014-15 season, the team made the playoffs, but were defeated in the first round by the Memphis Grizzlies, 1-4. Overall, the Trail Blazers have clenched three Conference titles and six Division titles (most recently in 2018). Among the Trail Blazer's many great players are Hall-of-Fame inductees Clyde Drexler, Bill Walton and Lenny Wilkens, as well as Scottie Pippen and Arvydas Sabonis. Paul G. Allen, a co-founder of Microsoft, purchased the team from Larry Weinberg in 1988 for $70 million. The team is currently owned and operated by Paul G. Allen Trust. Allen was instrumental in developing and funding the Trail Blazers' home court, Moda Center, which seats 19,393 for basketball games. The team's home attendance average was 18,716 spectators during the 2022-23 season. Forbes estimated the Trail Blazers to be worth $2.1 billion in October 2022.

FINANCIAL DATA: *Note: Data for latest year may not have been available at press time.*

In U.S. $	2022	2021	2020	2019	2018	2017
Revenue	286,650,000					
R&D Expense						
Operating Income						
Operating Margin %						
SGA Expense						
Net Income						
Operating Cash Flow						
Capital Expenditure						
EBITDA						
Return on Assets %						
Return on Equity %						
Debt to Equity						

CONTACT INFORMATION:

Phone: 503-234-9291   Fax: 503-736-2187
Toll-Free:
Address: One Centre Ct., Ste. 200, Portland, OR 97227 United States

STOCK TICKER/OTHER:

Stock Ticker: Private   Exchange:
Employees: 410   Fiscal Year Ends: 06/30
Parent Company:

SALARIES/BONUSES:

Top Exec. Salary: $ Bonus: $
Second Exec. Salary: $ Bonus: $

OTHER THOUGHTS:

Estimated Female Officers or Directors: 45
Hot Spot for Advancement for Women/Minorities: Y

Sales, profits and employees may be estimates. Financial information, benefits and other data can change quickly and may vary from those stated here.

Prince Global Sports LLC

www.princetennis.com

NAIC Code: 339920

TYPES OF BUSINESS:

Manufacturing-Tennis Equipment
Sport Racquets
Sport Footwear
Sport Bags and Accessories
Tennis Racquet Strings
Stringing & Ball Machines

BRANDS/DIVISIONS/AFFILIATES:

Authentic Brands Group LLC

GROWTH PLANS/SPECIAL FEATURES:

Prince Global Sports, LLC is a court sports equipment manufacturer that produces racquets, footwear, tennis balls, sport bags and tennis court machines. The firm sells racquets in several categories, including feel, spin, adaptability, heritage, control, power, comfort, play, stability, maneuverability, all-around and fun. Prince Global's footwear products include men's, women's and junior footwear; and its accessories include strings, stringing tools, replacement grips and sport bags. Tennis machines by the company include electronic stringing machines and tennis ball machines. In addition, the company sponsors several professional tennis players on the ATP and WTA tours. Prince Global and the Prince brand are wholly-owned by Authentic Brands Group, LLC.

CONTACTS: Note: Officers with more than one job title may be intentionally listed here more than once.

Jamie Salter, Chmn.-Authentic Brands

FINANCIAL DATA: Note: Data for latest year may not have been available at press time.

In U.S. $	2022	2021	2020	2019	2018	2017
Revenue						
R&D Expense						
Operating Income						
Operating Margin %						
SGA Expense						
Net Income						
Operating Cash Flow						
Capital Expenditure						
EBITDA						
Return on Assets %						
Return on Equity %						
Debt to Equity						

CONTACT INFORMATION:

Phone: 609-291-5800   Fax: 609-291-5900
Toll-Free:
Address: 3280 Peachtree Road, Ste 2000, Atlanta, GA 30305 United States

STOCK TICKER/OTHER:

Stock Ticker: Subsidiary   Exchange:
Employees: 68   Fiscal Year Ends: 09/30
Parent Company: Authentic Brands Group LLC

SALARIES/BONUSES:

Top Exec. Salary: $ Bonus: $
Second Exec. Salary: $ Bonus: $

OTHER THOUGHTS:

Estimated Female Officers or Directors: 1
Hot Spot for Advancement for Women/Minorities:

Professional Bowlers Association LLC   www.pba.com

NAIC Code: 711211

TYPES OF BUSINESS:

Bowling Association
Professional Bowling Sanctioning
Professional Bowling Tournaments

GROWTH PLANS/SPECIAL FEATURES:

The Professional Bowlers Association, LLC (PBA) is the worldwide governing body for the sport of major league professional bowling. Founded in 1958 with 33 charter members, the PBA currently has about 3,000 members representing more than 30 countries. The organization sanctions for the sport of professional 10-pen bowling in the U.S., overseeing competition between professional bowlers through tours including: PBA Tour, an annual calendar of games running from January to December; PBA Regional Tour, enabling PBA members and qualifying amateurs to compete in weekend events; PBA50/60 Tours, for PBA members aged 50 and older, as well as a tour for members 60 years and older to compete in their own events; and PBA Jr., a club for youth bowlers aged 17 and under, enabling them to compete in regional events with the goal of qualifying for scholarship earnings at the PBA Jr. National Championship. The PBA is currently owned by Bowlero Corporation.

BRANDS/DIVISIONS/AFFILIATES:

Bowlero Corporation
PBA Tour
PBA Regional Tour
PBA50/60 Tours
PBA Jr

CONTACTS: Note: Officers with more than one job title may be intentionally listed here more than once.

Thomas F. Shannon, Chmn.-Bowlero

FINANCIAL DATA: Note: Data for latest year may not have been available at press time.

In U.S. $	2022	2021	2020	2019	2018	2017
Revenue						
R&D Expense						
Operating Income						
Operating Margin %						
SGA Expense						
Net Income						
Operating Cash Flow						
Capital Expenditure						
EBITDA						
Return on Assets %						
Return on Equity %						
Debt to Equity						

CONTACT INFORMATION:

Phone: 804-730-4000   Fax:
Toll-Free:
Address: 7313 Bell Creek, Mechanicsville, VA 23111 United States

STOCK TICKER/OTHER:

Stock Ticker: Subsidiary   Exchange:
Employees: 69   Fiscal Year Ends:
Parent Company: Bowlero Corporation

SALARIES/BONUSES:

Top Exec. Salary: $ Bonus: $
Second Exec. Salary: $ Bonus: $

OTHER THOUGHTS:

Estimated Female Officers or Directors:
Hot Spot for Advancement for Women/Minorities:

Professional Bull Riders Inc

www.pbr.com

NAIC Code: 711211

TYPES OF BUSINESS:

Professional Bull Riding Association
Bull Riding Competition Management
Bull Riding Qualifier Competitions

BRANDS/DIVISIONS/AFFILIATES:

Endeavor Group Holdings Inc
Unleash the Beast
Velocity Tour
Touring Pro Division
PBR World Finals
PBR Team Series
PBR Challenger Series

CONTACTS: *Note: Officers with more than one job title may be intentionally listed here more than once.*

Sean Gleason, CEO
Matthew A. Rivela, General Counsel
Jay Daugherty, Sr. VP-Competition
David Cordovano, Chief Global Events Officer
Terry Bassett, Exec. VP-Sales & Partnerships

GROWTH PLANS/SPECIAL FEATURES:

Professional Bull Riders, Inc. (PBR) was founded in 1992 by 20 celebrated bull riders. The organization now has more than 500 bull-riding members who compete in over 200 PBR competitions throughout the U.S., Australia, Brazil, Canada and Mexico. The company organizes and manages three primary touring competitions: the Unleash the Beast (UTB) series, the Velocity Tour and the Touring Pro Division. UTB is also known as the Premier Series, with competition beginning in January and culminating in the PBR World Finals at the end of the year. The Velocity Tour features young and up-coming talent competing against the established talent of the sport. The Velocity Tour offers the chance to earn points to attempt to qualify for the UTB series and the PBR World Finals. The Touring Pro Division is a minor tour that offers up-and-coming bull riders and others not in UTB events the ability to compete in PBR events so they can attempt to earn money to qualify for elite series and PBR World Finals. In addition, the PBR Team Series debuted in 2022 and features eight teams of bull riders competing against each other; and the Challenger Series also debuted in 2022 and is a way for riders to compete at PBR events in the U.S. as individuals (not as a team) during the Team Series season, and is a way for Team Series managements to scout for riders to add as alternates to their teams. PBR operates as a wholly-owned subsidiary of Endeavor Group Holdings, Inc., an American holding company for talent and media agencies.

FINANCIAL DATA: *Note: Data for latest year may not have been available at press time.*

In U.S. $	2022	2021	2020	2019	2018	2017
Revenue	14,720,000	14,300,000	13,000,000			
R&D Expense						
Operating Income						
Operating Margin %						
SGA Expense						
Net Income						
Operating Cash Flow						
Capital Expenditure						
EBITDA						
Return on Assets %						
Return on Equity %						
Debt to Equity						

CONTACT INFORMATION:

Phone: 719-242-2800   Fax: 719-242-2855
Toll-Free:
Address: 101 W. Riverwalk, Pueblo, CO 81003 United States

STOCK TICKER/OTHER:

Stock Ticker: Subsidiary   Exchange:
Employees: 160   Fiscal Year Ends:
Parent Company: Endeavor Group Holdings Inc

SALARIES/BONUSES:

Top Exec. Salary: $ Bonus: $
Second Exec. Salary: $ Bonus: $

OTHER THOUGHTS:

Estimated Female Officers or Directors:
Hot Spot for Advancement for Women/Minorities:

Professional Golfers Association of America (PGA) www.pga.com

NAIC Code: 711211

TYPES OF BUSINESS:

Professional Golf Association
Event Sponsorship
Junior Tournaments
Golf Instruction
Golf Courses
Hotel Resort

BRANDS/DIVISIONS/AFFILIATES:

PGA Golf Management
PGA Championship
Womens PGA Championship
Senior PGA Championship
PGA Professional Championship
Ryder Cup
PGA Cup
PGA Tour

CONTACTS: Note: Officers with more than one job title may be intentionally listed here more than once.

Seth Waugh, CEO
John Lindert, Pres.
Paul Levy, Sec.
Derek Sprague, VP
Dawes Marlatt, Sr. Dir.-Education & Employment

GROWTH PLANS/SPECIAL FEATURES:

The Professional Golfers Association of America (PGA) is an organization founded in 1916, and comprised of nearly 29,000 men and women golf professional members. Elected members of the PGA must go through three levels of education courses, written exams, simulation testing, seminars and pass the PGA Playing Ability Test. These men and women have the option to pursue the PGA education through self-study, by use of the accredited PGA Golf Management Universities (currently 18 U.S. universities offer a PGA Golf Management program) or through an accelerated PGA Golf Management program. The PGA's function is to conduct major events, including the PGA Tour's PGA Championship, the Women's PGA Championship and the Senior PGA Championship. The organization conducts more than 30 tournaments, including the PGA Professional Championship, and also co-organizes the biennial Ryder Cup, PGA Cup and the Women's PGA Cup. The PGA is organized into 14 districts that encompass 41 geographical sections throughout the U.S. PGA Reach is the charitable foundation of the PGA of America, with a mission to positively impact the lives of youth, military and diverse populations by enabling access to PGA professionals, PGA Sections and the game of golf. From the association's website, golfers can access information concerning golf equipment, tour news, golf travel, rulebooks and golf etiquette. The PGA Shop is available on the association's website, featuring apparel, caps, club head covers, golf bags and other items with logos from the PGA and its major tournaments. During 2022, the PGA moved its headquarters from Florida to Frisco, Texas, along with two championship golf courses (Welling's West and Hanse's East). The Omni PGA Frisco Resort opened in early-2023. In mid-2023, the PGA agreed to merge its PGA Tour operations with LIV, a major golf tour operator. The deal is subject to approval by regulatory authorities.

FINANCIAL DATA: Note: Data for latest year may not have been available at press time.

In U.S. $	2022	2021	2020	2019	2018	2017
Revenue		103,806,699	94,369,726	128,103,651	128,621,234	128,621,234
R&D Expense						
Operating Income						
Operating Margin %						
SGA Expense						
Net Income						
Operating Cash Flow						
Capital Expenditure						
EBITDA						
Return on Assets %						
Return on Equity %						
Debt to Equity						

CONTACT INFORMATION:

Phone: 561-624-8400   Fax:
Toll-Free:
Address: 1916 PGA Pkwy., Frisco, TX 75033 United States

STOCK TICKER/OTHER:

Stock Ticker: Private   Exchange:
Employees: 800   Fiscal Year Ends: 03/31
Parent Company:

SALARIES/BONUSES:

Top Exec. Salary: $ Bonus: $
Second Exec. Salary: $ Bonus: $

OTHER THOUGHTS:

Estimated Female Officers or Directors:
Hot Spot for Advancement for Women/Minorities:

PUMA SE

www.puma.com

NAIC Code: 424340

TYPES OF BUSINESS:

Footwear Distribution
Athletic Apparel
Sports Equipment
Retail Stores
Smart Technology

BRANDS/DIVISIONS/AFFILIATES:

Kering SA
PUMA
stichd
Cobra Puma Golf

GROWTH PLANS/SPECIAL FEATURES:

Puma SE is engaged in footwear, apparel, and accessories business under the Puma and Cobra Golf brand names. Footwear is the company's leading category. Puma also licenses its brand name for fragrances, eyewear, and watches. Nearly a quarter of the company's sales are direct to consumers through Puma's retail stores, factory outlets, and online channels. The remaining sales are wholesale to Puma's retail partners. Most of the company's revenue is generated in the Americas; and Europe, Middle East, and Africa geographic segments.

CONTACTS: Note: Officers with more than one job title may be intentionally listed here more than once.

Bjorn Gulden, CEO
Michael Lammermann, CFO
Michael Lammermann, General Manager-Legal
Michael Lammermann, General Manager-Finance

FINANCIAL DATA: Note: Data for latest year may not have been available at press time.

In U.S. $	2022	2021	2020	2019	2018	2017
Revenue	9,039,757,000	7,267,388,000	5,589,740,000	5,875,720,000	4,416,668,000	4,416,668,000
R&D Expense	87,780,190	65,888,540	60,442,320	65,888,540	57,025,090	57,025,090
Operating Income	683,980,700	595,025,800	222,974,500	465,704,900	261,098,000	261,098,000
Operating Margin %	.08%	.08%	.04%	.08%	.06%	.06%
SGA Expense	3,432,077,000	2,846,342,000	2,358,639,000	2,364,085,000	1,786,039,000	1,786,039,000
Net Income	377,497,500	330,617,300	84,256,170	280,213,200	145,018,800	145,018,800
Operating Cash Flow	446,696,500	491,334,100	450,113,800	586,055,600	255,011,100	255,011,100
Capital Expenditure	281,494,600	216,140,000	161,250,700	233,226,200	131,243,100	131,243,100
EBITDA	1,104,300,000	913,576,100	570,250,900	760,120,900	337,345,000	337,345,000
Return on Assets %	.06%	.06%	.02%	.07%	.05%	.05%
Return on Equity %	.15%	.16%	.04%	.15%	.08%	.08%
Debt to Equity	.42%	.38%	0.45	0.321		

CONTACT INFORMATION:

Phone: 49 09132810   Fax: 49 09132812246
Toll-Free:
Address: Puma Way 1, Herzogenaurach, BY 91074 Germany

STOCK TICKER/OTHER:

Stock Ticker: PMMAF   Exchange: PINX
Employees: 16,669   Fiscal Year Ends: 12/31
Parent Company:

SALARIES/BONUSES:

Top Exec. Salary: $ Bonus: $
Second Exec. Salary: $ Bonus: $

OTHER THOUGHTS:

Estimated Female Officers or Directors:
Hot Spot for Advancement for Women/Minorities:

Rawlings Sporting Goods Company Inc

www.rawlings.com

NAIC Code: 339920

TYPES OF BUSINESS:

Sporting Goods & Equipment
Baseballs, Softballs & Helmets
Football Apparel
Ball Equipment
Protective Gear
Product Manufacturing
Ecommerce

BRANDS/DIVISIONS/AFFILIATES:

Seidler Equity Partners
MLB Properties LLC
Rawlings
Easton
Miken
Worth

CONTACTS: Note: Officers with more than one job title may be intentionally listed here more than once.

Michael F. Zlaket, CEO
Robert M. Parish, Pres.
Kurt Hunzeker, Sr. Dir.-Brand Mktg.

GROWTH PLANS/SPECIAL FEATURES:

Rawlings Sporting Goods Company, Inc. is a leading manufacturer, marketer and distributor of equipment and protective gear for baseball and softball throughout the U.S. Product categories by Rawlings include gloves, bats, balls, helmets, catcher's gear, bags, apparel and accessories. The company also offers customized gloves and helmets, as well as personalized gloves and engraved gloves and helmets. Apparel categories span sport (baseball, softball and football), outerwear, pants, jerseys, shirts, shorts, hats, footwear, masks/gaiters, belts and socks. Apparel is offered for men, women, youth and children. Accessories include, but are not limited to, wallets, backpacks, tote and duffle bags, batting gloves, training equipment and supplies, and tailgating supplies. Products can be ordered online, and the Rawlings site offers sizing charts, a rewards program, order status, affiliate programs, warranty information and instructions for product returns and exchanges. Brands of the firm include Rawlings, Easton, Miken and Worth. Rawlings Sporting Goods operates as a subsidiary of Seidler Equity Partners and MLB Properties LLC.

FINANCIAL DATA: Note: Data for latest year may not have been available at press time.

In U.S. $	2022	2021	2020	2019	2018	2017
Revenue		394,680,000	379,500,000	345,000,000	330,000,000	330,000,000
R&D Expense						
Operating Income						
Operating Margin %						
SGA Expense						
Net Income						
Operating Cash Flow						
Capital Expenditure						
EBITDA						
Return on Assets %						
Return on Equity %						
Debt to Equity						

CONTACT INFORMATION:

Phone: 314-819-2800   Fax: 314-819-2988
Toll-Free: 800-729-5464
Address: 510 Maryville University Dr., Ste. 110, St. Louis, MO 63141
United States

STOCK TICKER/OTHER:

Stock Ticker: Joint Venture   Exchange:
Employees: 1,200   Fiscal Year Ends: 12/31
Parent Company: Seidler Equity Partners

SALARIES/BONUSES:

Top Exec. Salary: $ Bonus: $
Second Exec. Salary: $ Bonus: $

OTHER THOUGHTS:

Estimated Female Officers or Directors: 2
Hot Spot for Advancement for Women/Minorities:

Real Madrid Club de Futbol

www.realmadrid.com

NAIC Code: 711211D

TYPES OF BUSINESS:

Professional Soccer Team
Team Management and Operations

BRANDS/DIVISIONS/AFFILIATES:

Real Madrid
Estadio Santiago Bernabeu
Realmadrid Foundation

CONTACTS: *Note: Officers with more than one job title may be intentionally listed here more than once.*

Florentino Perez Rodriguez, Pres.
Carlo Ancelotti, Head Coach
Enrique Sanchez Gonzalez, Sec.
Carlo Ancelotti, Mgr.
Fernando Fernandez Tapias, 1st VP
Eduardo Fernandez de Blas, 2nd VP
Pedro Lopez Jimenez, 3rd VP

GROWTH PLANS/SPECIAL FEATURES:

Real Madrid Club de Futbol, commonly known as Real Madrid, is a Spanish professional soccer team based in Madrid and playing in La Liga, the top tier of the Spanish soccer league system. Real Madrid was founded in 1902 and is owned and operated by the club's members. The club plays in the wholly-owned Estadio Santiago Bernabeu in Madrid, with a seating capacity of over 81,000. Real Madrid is one of three clubs that have never been relegated out of the top tier of play, sharing this honor with its long-time rival Barcelona. The club has found great success both domestically and abroad. Domestically, Real Madrid has won La Liga 35 times, most recently in 2021-22; the Copa del Rey 20 times (most recently in 2022-23); the Supercopa de Espana 12 times, most recently in 2021-22; and both the Copa Eva Duarte and Copa de la Liga once. In international play, the club has won 14 European Cup/Union of European Football Associations (UEFA) Champions League titles (2021-22 most recent); five FIFA Club World Cups (2022); five European Super Cups (2022); three Intercontinental Cups; and two UEFA Cups. Real Madrid is currently sponsored by Adidas (kit manufacturer), a German sports paraphernalia manufacturer; and by Emirates (shirt), an airline based out of Dubai. The club's charitable foundation is the Realmadrid Foundation, which promotes the values inherent in sports and uses sports as an educational tool. Forbes ranked Real Madrid at $6.07 billion in May 2023.

FINANCIAL DATA: *Note: Data for latest year may not have been available at press time.*

In U.S. $	2022	2021	2020	2019	2018	2017
Revenue		771,814,759	778,922,000	848,071,000	808,558,000	808,558,000
R&D Expense						
Operating Income						
Operating Margin %						
SGA Expense						
Net Income		1,040,427	352,038	43,002,700	25,155,100	25,155,100
Operating Cash Flow						
Capital Expenditure						
EBITDA						
Return on Assets %						
Return on Equity %						
Debt to Equity						

CONTACT INFORMATION:

Phone: 34-91-398-4300   Fax: 34-91-398-4382
Toll-Free:
Address: Santiago Bernabeu Stadium, Avenida Concha Espina, N.-Degree 1, #44, Madrid, 28036 Spain

STOCK TICKER/OTHER:

Stock Ticker: Cooperative
Employees: 819
Parent Company:

Exchange:
Fiscal Year Ends: 06/30

SALARIES/BONUSES:

Top Exec. Salary: $ Bonus: $
Second Exec. Salary: $ Bonus: $

OTHER THOUGHTS:

Estimated Female Officers or Directors:
Hot Spot for Advancement for Women/Minorities:

Real Salt Lake

NAIC Code: 711211D

TYPES OF BUSINESS:

Major League Soccer Team
Team Management and Operations

BRANDS/DIVISIONS/AFFILIATES:

Utah Royals FC

GROWTH PLANS/SPECIAL FEATURES:

Real Salt Lake (RSL) is a Major League Soccer's (MLS) team playing in the Western Conference. The team was formed in 2004 and commenced playing in April 2005. RSL has fielded former greats including midfielder/forward Clint Mathis and forward Jason Kreis. The team won the MLS Cup Championship in 2009, and were runners-up in the 2011 CONCACAF Champions League, the 2013 MLS Cup, the 2010 Supporters' Shield and the 2013 Lamar Hunt U.S. Open Cup. RSL plays its home games at the America First Field, located in Sandy, with a capacity of roughly 20,213. The team averaged 20,470 spectators per home game during the 2022 season. The team also runs Utah Royals FC, a women's soccer team that plays in the National Women's Soccer League (NWSL). Real Salt Lake is owned by David S. Blitzer and Ryan Smith's Smith Entertainment Group.

CONTACTS: *Note: Officers with more than one job title may be intentionally listed here more than once.*

John Kimball, Pres.
Tara Cupello, CFO
Tyler Gibbons, VP-Mktg.
Lita Quero, Dir.-Human Resources
John Genna, VP-Communications
Elliot Fall, Team Admin.
Garth Lagerwey, Gen. Mgr.
Trey Fitz-Gerald, VP-Comm. & Broadcasting
Tara Silcox, VP-Finance
John Kimball, Sr. VP-RSL Media & ESPN 700 GM
Jason Kreis, Head Coach
Justin Weidauer, Mgr.-Gen. Sales
Blake Beyer, Controller
Justin Nelson, Gen. Mngr.

FINANCIAL DATA: *Note: Data for latest year may not have been available at press time.*

In U.S. $	2022	2021	2020	2019	2018	2017
Revenue	7,426,125					
R&D Expense						
Operating Income						
Operating Margin %						
SGA Expense						
Net Income						
Operating Cash Flow						
Capital Expenditure						
EBITDA						
Return on Assets %						
Return on Equity %						
Debt to Equity						

CONTACT INFORMATION:

Phone: 801-727-2700   Fax: 801-727-1469
Toll-Free:
Address: 9256 S. State St., Sandy, UT 84070 United States

STOCK TICKER/OTHER:

Stock Ticker: Private   Exchange:
Employees: 138   Fiscal Year Ends:
Parent Company:

SALARIES/BONUSES:

Top Exec. Salary: $ Bonus: $
Second Exec. Salary: $ Bonus: $

OTHER THOUGHTS:

Estimated Female Officers or Directors: 5
Hot Spot for Advancement for Women/Minorities: Y

Reebok International Limited

www.reebok.com

NAIC Code: 424340

TYPES OF BUSINESS:

Footwear Distribution
Apparel
Sports Footwear
Athletic Equipment
Ecommerce
Retail Stores
Product Manufacturing
Product Design

BRANDS/DIVISIONS/AFFILIATES:

Authentic Brands Group LLC

GROWTH PLANS/SPECIAL FEATURES:

Reebok International Limited designs, manufactures, distributes and sells fitness apparel for men, women and children marketed under the Reebok brand name, as well as the CrossFit brand name through a partnership agreement. The company's apparel offerings include tops, shirts, hoodies, sweats, jackets, shorts, pants, joggers, sports bras, capris, leggings, footwear, bags, socks and hats. Reebok's products serve the training, running, walking, CrossFit, basketball, combat and dance sports markets. Reebok also offers an apparel, footwear and accessories collection by Victoria Beckham, featuring a high performance meets minimalism design. Other artists that have signed endorsement agreements with Reebok over the years include Ariana Grande, Gal Gadot, Cardi B, Victoria Beckham and Camille Kostek, among others. Reebok is a subsidiary of Authentic Brands Group, LLC.

CONTACTS: Note: Officers with more than one job title may be intentionally listed here more than once.

Todd Krinsky, CEO
David Mischler, Head-Brand Oper.
David Baxter, Pres., Sports Licensed Div.
John Warren, Gen. Mgr.-Sports Licensed Div.
Chris Froio, Head-Fitness & Training
Charlie Maurath, Head-Latin America

FINANCIAL DATA: Note: Data for latest year may not have been available at press time.

In U.S. $	2022	2021	2020	2019	2018	2017
Revenue	2,510,000,000	2,422,840,000	1,730,600,000	1,955,280,000	2,194,490,000	2,194,490,000
R&D Expense						
Operating Income						
Operating Margin %						
SGA Expense						
Net Income						
Operating Cash Flow						
Capital Expenditure						
EBITDA						
Return on Assets %						
Return on Equity %						
Debt to Equity						

CONTACT INFORMATION:

Phone: 781-401-5000   Fax: 781-401-7402
Toll-Free:
Address: 1895 J. W. Foster Blvd., Canton, MA 02021 United States

STOCK TICKER/OTHER:

Stock Ticker: Subsidiary   Exchange:
Employees: 9,000   Fiscal Year Ends: 12/31
Parent Company: Authentic Brands Group LLC

SALARIES/BONUSES:

Top Exec. Salary: $ Bonus: $
Second Exec. Salary: $ Bonus: $

OTHER THOUGHTS:

Estimated Female Officers or Directors:
Hot Spot for Advancement for Women/Minorities:

REI (Recreational Equipment Inc)

www.rei.com

NAIC Code: 451110

TYPES OF BUSINESS:

Outdoor Gear & Clothing, Retail
Sporting Equipment Retail & Rental
Adventure Travel Services
Catalog Sales
Ecommerce

BRANDS/DIVISIONS/AFFILIATES:

REI
REI Adventures
REI Gear and Apparel
www.rei.com
www.rei.com/rei-garage

CONTACTS: Note: Officers with more than one job title may be intentionally listed here more than once.

Eric Artz, CEO
Chris Speyer, Chief Merchandising Officer
Kelley Hall, CFO
Vivienne Long, CMO
Apple Musni, Chief People Officer
Dan Shull, CTO
Susan Viscon, VP-Merch.
Catherine Walker, General Counsel
Brad Brown, Sr. VP-e-Commerce & Direct Sales
Michael Collins, VP-Public Affairs
Sue Sallee, VP-Finance & Acct.
Tim Spangler, Sr. VP-Retail
Kathleen Peterson, VP-REI Private Brands
Beth Newlands Campbell, Chmn.
Rick Bingle, VP-Supply Chain

GROWTH PLANS/SPECIAL FEATURES:

Recreational Equipment, Inc. (REI) is one of the largest consumer cooperatives in the U.S. The firm offers quality outdoor gear, clothing and footwear selected for performance and durability in outdoor recreation, including hiking, climbing, camping, bicycling, paddling and winter sports. Today, REI has approximately 23 million lifetime members served by over 180 retail stores across the U.S. states and Washington DC, as well as ecommerce sites www.rei.com and www.rei.com/rei-garage (outlet). Stores include a variety of facilities for testing equipment, including bike test trails, climbing pinnacles and camp stove demonstration tables. While anyone may shop at the stores, customers who pay a small fee to become members receive special discounts and a share in the company's profits through an annual patronage refund based on their purchases. REI's ecommerce sites offer a comprehensive library of product information, expert gear advice and outdoor recreation information. In addition to nationally-recognized brands, the company sells private label apparel and accessories under the REI Gear and Apparel brand. It also offers mountain, road, specialty, hybrid, electric and kid's bikes under various brand names. Through REI Adventures, the company has been operating small group tours throughout the world for decades, avoiding standard tourist routes and emphasizing outdoor activities. Each year, REI Adventures plans domestic and international bicycling, trekking, kayaking, hiking, camping and mountaineering adventures. The firm invests millions of dollars on an annual basis to build trails, clean up the environment and teach children outdoor ethics.

REI offers its employees comprehensive health benefits, retirement and profit-sharing plans, tuition reimbursement and a variety of assistance plans and programs.

FINANCIAL DATA: Note: Data for latest year may not have been available at press time.

In U.S. $	2022	2021	2020	2019	2018	2017
Revenue	3,850,174,000	3,739,259,000	2,754,714,000	3,122,994,000	2,622,776,000	2,622,776,000
R&D Expense						
Operating Income						
Operating Margin %						
SGA Expense						
Net Income	-164,712,000	97,660,000	-33,543,000	22,137,000	30,525,000	30,525,000
Operating Cash Flow						
Capital Expenditure						
EBITDA						
Return on Assets %						
Return on Equity %						
Debt to Equity						

CONTACT INFORMATION:

Phone: 253-891-2500   Fax: 253-891-2523
Toll-Free: 800-426-4840
Address: 6750 S. 228th St., Kent, WA 98032 United States

STOCK TICKER/OTHER:

Stock Ticker: Private   Exchange:
Employees: 15,000   Fiscal Year Ends: 01/02
Parent Company:

SALARIES/BONUSES:

Top Exec. Salary: $ Bonus: $
Second Exec. Salary: $ Bonus: $

OTHER THOUGHTS:

Estimated Female Officers or Directors: 7
Hot Spot for Advancement for Women/Minorities: Y

Rogers Communications Inc

www.rogers.com

NAIC Code: 517110

TYPES OF BUSINESS:

Cable TV Service
Internet Services
Wireless Phone Service
5G Technology
Wireless Services
Connected Home
Internet of Things
Media Services

BRANDS/DIVISIONS/AFFILIATES:

Rogers
Fido
chatr

GROWTH PLANS/SPECIAL FEATURES:

Rogers is the largest wireless service provider in Canada, with its more than 10 million subscribers equating to one third of the total Canadian market. Rogers' wireless business accounted for 60% of the company's total sales in 2021 and has increasingly provided a bigger portion of total company sales over the last several years. Rogers' cable segment, which provides about one fourth of total sales, offers home internet, television, and landline phone service to consumers and businesses. Remaining sales come from Rogers' media unit, which owns and operates various television and radio stations and the Toronto Blue Jays. Rogers' significant exposure to sports also includes ownership stakes in the Toronto Maple Leafs, Raptors, FC, and Argonauts.

CONTACTS: Note: Officers with more than one job title may be intentionally listed here more than once.

Alan Horn, CEO, Subsidiary
Jordan Banks, Pres., Divisional
Joseph Natale, CEO
Anthony Staffieri, CFO
Edward Rogers, Chairman of the Board
Jorge Fernandes, Chief Information Officer
Graeme McPhail, Chief Legal Officer
Melinda Rogers-Hixon, Deputy Chairman
Philip Lind, Director
Lisa Durocher, Executive VP, Divisional
James Reid, Other Executive Officer
Eric Agius, Other Executive Officer
Sevaun Palvetzian, Other Executive Officer
Dean Prevost, President, Divisional
Brent Johnston, President, Divisional

FINANCIAL DATA: Note: Data for latest year may not have been available at press time.

In U.S. $	2022	2021	2020	2019	2018	2017
Revenue	11,229,920,000	10,689,430,000	10,150,400,000	10,994,330,000	10,480,820,000	10,480,820,000
R&D Expense						
Operating Income	2,784,140,000	2,408,496,000	2,362,544,000	2,716,305,000	2,450,802,000	2,450,802,000
Operating Margin %	.25%	.23%	.23%	.25%	.23%	.23%
SGA Expense						
Net Income	1,225,401,000	1,136,413,000	1,161,213,000	1,490,175,000	1,345,753,000	1,345,753,000
Operating Cash Flow	3,277,218,000	3,035,055,000	3,151,760,000	3,301,288,000	2,872,398,000	2,872,398,000
Capital Expenditure	2,277,203,000	2,072,970,000	1,727,961,000	2,091,205,000	1,819,866,000	1,819,866,000
EBITDA	4,446,454,000	4,081,752,000	4,165,633,000	4,463,230,000	3,989,847,000	3,989,847,000
Return on Assets %	.03%	.04%	.04%	.06%	.06%	.06%
Return on Equity %	.16%	.15%	.17%	.23%	.27%	.27%
Debt to Equity	3.13%	1.78%	1.912	1.855	1.693	1.693

CONTACT INFORMATION:

Phone: 416 935-2303   Fax: 416 935-3548
Toll-Free:
Address: 333 Bloor St. E., Fl. 10, Toronto, ON M4W 1G9 Canada

STOCK TICKER/OTHER:

Stock Ticker: RCI
Employees: 25,300
Parent Company:

Exchange: NYS
Fiscal Year Ends: 12/31

SALARIES/BONUSES:

Top Exec. Salary: $1,293,048   Bonus: $
Second Exec. Salary: $756,731   Bonus: $

OTHER THOUGHTS:

Estimated Female Officers or Directors: 6
Hot Spot for Advancement for Women/Minorities: Y

Roush Fenway Keselowski Racing (RFK Racing)

www.rfkracing.com

NAIC Code: 711219

TYPES OF BUSINESS:

NASCAR Racing Teams

BRANDS/DIVISIONS/AFFILIATES:

RFK Racing

CONTACTS: Note: Officers with more than one job title may be intentionally listed here more than once.

Jack Roush, Co-Owner
John W. Henry, Co-Owner
Steve Newmark, Pres.
Brad Keselowski, Co-Owner
Sam Belnavis, Chief Diversity Officer

GROWTH PLANS/SPECIAL FEATURES:

Roush Fenway Keselowski Racing does business as RFK Racing is an American professional stock car organization that competes in the NASCAR Cup Series. The company was established in 1988 as Roush Racing and was renamed Roush Fenway Racing in 2007 when John W. Henry and the Fenway Sports Group became co-owners. Then in 2022, professional stock car racing driver Brad Keselowski became a co-owner of the firm, which was subsequently renamed Roush Fenway Keselowski Racing (RFK Racing). Current race drivers (2023) include Brad Keselowski, Chris Buescher, Matt McCall and Scott Graves, each driving Ford race cars. As for the current RFK Racing organization, it has competed in 2,315 total races, including the Cup Series, the Xfinity Series, the Camping World Truck Series and the ARCA Re/Max Series. The group has clenched eight driver's championships, 329 race victories and 235 pole positions (as of June 1, 2023). Partners of RFK Racing include Fastenal, Castrol, Fifth Third Bank, King's Hawaiian, Solomon Plumbing, Esperion, Violet Defense, Wyndham Rewards, Socios.com, Makers Wanted, Pala Casino, Titan Fitness, and many others.

FINANCIAL DATA: Note: Data for latest year may not have been available at press time.

In U.S. $	2022	2021	2020	2019	2018	2017
Revenue		11,096,800	11,440,000	52,000,000	62,000,000	62,000,000
R&D Expense						
Operating Income						
Operating Margin %						
SGA Expense						
Net Income				3,000,000		
Operating Cash Flow						
Capital Expenditure						
EBITDA						
Return on Assets %						
Return on Equity %						
Debt to Equity						

CONTACT INFORMATION:

Phone: 704-720-4600   Fax: 704-720-4605
Toll-Free:
Address: 4600 Roush Pl. NW, Concord, NC 28027 United States

STOCK TICKER/OTHER:

Stock Ticker: Joint Venture   Exchange:
Employees: 160   Fiscal Year Ends: 12/31
Parent Company:

SALARIES/BONUSES:

Top Exec. Salary: $ Bonus: $
Second Exec. Salary: $ Bonus: $

OTHER THOUGHTS:

Estimated Female Officers or Directors:
Hot Spot for Advancement for Women/Minorities:

Russell Brands LLC

www.russellathletic.com

NAIC Code: 339920

TYPES OF BUSINESS:

Athletic Apparel & Equipment
Active Apparel
Apparel Manufacturing
Bags and Backpacks
Footwear

BRANDS/DIVISIONS/AFFILIATES:

Berkshire Hathaway Inc
Fruit of the Loom Inc
Russell Athletic

GROWTH PLANS/SPECIAL FEATURES:

Russell Brands, LLC, a subsidiary of Fruit of the Loom, Inc., itself a subsidiary of Berkshire Hathaway, Inc., is a leading manufacturer of activewear and related accessories. The company's primary brand is Russell Athletic, with product offered for men, women and youth, including t-shirts, hoodies and sweatshirts, performance shirts, sleeveless and tank tops, polos, pullovers, jackets, fleece tops, pants, sweatpants, fleece bottoms and shorts. Accessories include bags and backpacks, hats, beanies and slide sandals. The Athletic Club is the company's membership program that offers exclusive Russell Athletic perks, such as discounts, free ground shipping on orders over $50, first access to new Russell Athletic products, access to limited edition releases and more. Russellathletic.com and mobile app provide size charts, shipping and delivery information, order status and info regarding merchandise returns.

CONTACTS: Note: Officers with more than one job title may be intentionally listed here more than once.

Victoria W. Beck, Principal Acct. Officer
Warren Buffett, Chmn.-Berkshire Hathaway

FINANCIAL DATA: Note: Data for latest year may not have been available at press time.

In U.S. $	2022	2021	2020	2019	2018	2017
Revenue	2,900,000,000	2,835,308,000	2,025,220,000	1,858,000,000	1,750,000,000	1,750,000,000
R&D Expense						
Operating Income						
Operating Margin %						
SGA Expense						
Net Income						
Operating Cash Flow						
Capital Expenditure						
EBITDA						
Return on Assets %						
Return on Equity %						
Debt to Equity						

CONTACT INFORMATION:

Phone: 270-781-6400   Fax: 270-781-6588
Toll-Free: 877-879-8410
Address: 1 Fruit of the Loom Dr., Bowling Green, KY 42103 United States

STOCK TICKER/OTHER:

Stock Ticker: Subsidiary   Exchange:
Employees: 1,000   Fiscal Year Ends: 12/31
Parent Company: Berkshire Hathaway Inc

SALARIES/BONUSES:

Top Exec. Salary: $ Bonus: $
Second Exec. Salary: $ Bonus: $

OTHER THOUGHTS:

Estimated Female Officers or Directors: 1
Hot Spot for Advancement for Women/Minorities:

Sacramento Kings

www.nba.com/kings

NAIC Code: 711211B

TYPES OF BUSINESS:

Professional Basketball Team
Team Management and Operations

BRANDS/DIVISIONS/AFFILIATES:

CONTACTS: *Note: Officers with more than one job title may be intentionally listed here more than once.*

John Rinehart, Pres., Bus. Oper.
Martina Kolokotronis, COO
Mike Whitehead, Sr. VP-Finance
Ryan Spillers, Sr. Dir.-Mktg.
Stacy Wegzyn, Sr. VP-Human Resources
Eric King, VP-Technology
John Rinehart, Exec. VP-Bus. Oper.
Andrew Nicholson, Dir.-New Media
Chris Clark, Dir.-Public Rel.
Gerri Guzman, Dir.-Finance
Matina Kolokotronis, Pres., Bus. Oper.
Craig Amazeen, Sr. VP-Broadcasting & Brand Dev.
Wayne Cooper, VP
Phil Horn, VP-Ticket Sales & Service
Vivek Ranadive, Chmn.
Andrea Gracis, Int'l Scout

GROWTH PLANS/SPECIAL FEATURES:

The Sacramento Kings franchise is a professional basketball team playing in the National Basketball Association (NBA) and based in Sacramento, California. After its founding as the Rochester Seagrams in 1923 in New York as a member of the National Basketball League, the club moved to Cincinnati, where it remained from 1957-72. From 1972-85, the club was based in Kansas City, and since 1985, it has been in Sacramento. The Kings did very poorly in the NBA until the 1998-99 season, when it acquired Jason Williams, Vlade Divac, Chris Webber and Peja Stojakovic. This improvement of performance coincided with the team's acquisition by the Maloof family. The Kings play in the Pacific Division of the Western Conference along with the Golden State Warriors, Los Angeles Clippers, Los Angeles Lakers and Phoenix Suns. The team plays in the Golden 1 Center, which has a basketball seating capacity of 17,608. Average home game attendance for the Kings was 17,451 during the 2022-23 season. The organization has won two league championships (1945-46 and 1950-51) and has clenched six division titles (2023 most recently). The Maloof family sold the Kings (in 2013) to an ownership group lead by entrepreneur Vivek Ranadive. The team's main sponsor is Dialpad. Forbes estimated the Sacramento Kings to be worth $2.03 billion in October 2022.

FINANCIAL DATA: *Note: Data for latest year may not have been available at press time.*

In U.S. $	2022	2021	2020	2019	2018	2017
Revenue	284,050,000					
R&D Expense						
Operating Income						
Operating Margin %						
SGA Expense						
Net Income						
Operating Cash Flow						
Capital Expenditure						
EBITDA						
Return on Assets %						
Return on Equity %						
Debt to Equity						

CONTACT INFORMATION:

Phone: 916-701-5400   Fax:
Toll-Free:
Address: 500 David J. Stern Walk, Golden 1 Center, Sacramento, CA 95814 United States

STOCK TICKER/OTHER:

Stock Ticker: Private
Employees: 315
Parent Company:

Exchange:
Fiscal Year Ends: 06/30

SALARIES/BONUSES:

Top Exec. Salary: $ Bonus: $
Second Exec. Salary: $ Bonus: $

OTHER THOUGHTS:

Estimated Female Officers or Directors: 8
Hot Spot for Advancement for Women/Minorities: Y

San Antonio Spurs

www.nba.com/spurs

NAIC Code: 711211B

TYPES OF BUSINESS:

Professional Basketball Team
Team Management and Operations

BRANDS/DIVISIONS/AFFILIATES:

CONTACTS: *Note: Officers with more than one job title may be intentionally listed here more than once.*

Julianna Hawn Holt, CEO
Brian Wright, Gen. Mngr.
Lori Warren, Exec. VP-Finance & Admin.
Jeanne Garza, VP-Mktg.
Jaimi Martinez, Dir.-Human Resources
Nguyen, Dir.-IT
Lori Warren, Sr. VP-Corp. Admin.
Rick Pych, Pres., Bus. Oper.
Lori Warren, Sr. VP-Finance
R. C. Buford, Gen. Mgr.
Gregg Popovich, Head Coach
Tom Paquette, VP
Lawrence Payne, Exec. VP-Corp. Partnerships & Broadcasting
Peter J. Holt, Managing Partner

GROWTH PLANS/SPECIAL FEATURES:

The San Antonio Spurs have historically been one of the top teams in the National Basketball Association's (NBA) Western Conference. Founded in 1967 as the Dallas Chaparrals in the American Basketball Association (ABA), the club moved to San Antonio in 1973 and was renamed the Spurs. The team has won five championships since 1999, with victories in 1999, 2003, 2005, 2007 and 2014. The Spurs have also clenched six conference titles and 22 division titles (most recently in 2017). Legendary duo David Robinson and Tim Duncan led the Spurs to two of its championships. Prior to the arrivals of Robinson and Duncan, San Antonio's most famed player was George Gervin, or Iceman, who led the Spurs to five division titles in the 1970s and 80s. The club plays its home games at the 18,581-seat capacity AT&T Center. Home attendance for the Spurs averaged 16,937 in the 2022-23 season. Spurs Sports & Entertainment LLC owns the team. Forbes estimated the Spurs to be worth $2 billion in October 2022.

FINANCIAL DATA: *Note: Data for latest year may not have been available at press time.*

In U.S. $	2022	2021	2020	2019	2018	2017
Revenue	299,000,000					
R&D Expense						
Operating Income						
Operating Margin %						
SGA Expense						
Net Income						
Operating Cash Flow						
Capital Expenditure						
EBITDA						
Return on Assets %						
Return on Equity %						
Debt to Equity						

CONTACT INFORMATION:

Phone: 210-444-5000   Fax: 210-444-5100
Toll-Free:
Address: 1 AT&T Center Pkwy., San Antonio, TX 78219-3604 United States

STOCK TICKER/OTHER:

Stock Ticker: Private   Exchange:
Employees: 490   Fiscal Year Ends: 06/30
Parent Company:

SALARIES/BONUSES:

Top Exec. Salary: $ Bonus: $
Second Exec. Salary: $ Bonus: $

OTHER THOUGHTS:

Estimated Female Officers or Directors: 2
Hot Spot for Advancement for Women/Minorities: Y

San Diego Padres

NAIC Code: 711211A

www.mlb.com/padres

TYPES OF BUSINESS:

Professional Baseball Team
Team Management and Operations

BRANDS/DIVISIONS/AFFILIATES:

El Paso Chihuahuas
San Antonio Missions
Fort Wayne TinCaps
Lake Elsinore Storm

CONTACTS: *Note: Officers with more than one job title may be intentionally listed here more than once.*

Erik Greupner, CEO
A.J. Preller, Pres.-Baseball Oper. & Gen. Mngr.
Tom Garfinkle, Pres.
Caroline Perry, COO
Chris Connolly, CMO
Sara Greenspan, Sr. VP-People & Culture
Ray Chan, VP-IT
Erik Greupner, Sr. VP-Bus. Admin.
Erik Greupner, General Counsel
Omar Minaya, Sr. VP-Baseball Oper.
Tyler Epp, Sr. VP-Bus. Dev.
Sarah Farnsworth, Sr. VP-Public Affairs
Todd Bollman, Dir.-Acct.
Josh Byrnes, Gen. Mgr.
Jarrod Dillon, VP-Corp. Partnerships
Sue Botos, VP-Community Rel.
Mark Guglielmo, VP-Ballpark Oper.
Peter Seidler, Chmn.

GROWTH PLANS/SPECIAL FEATURES:

The San Diego Padres are a Major League Baseball (MLB) team playing in the Western Division of the National League. Founded in 1969, the Padres struggled as a young team, beginning with nine straight losing seasons. In 1984, the Padres appeared in the first of its two World Series, losing to the Tigers. The Padres made it to the postseason three more times, losing another World Series in 1998. The Padres' most famous players include Tony Gwynn, who won eight batting titles with the team and was inducted to the Hall of Fame in 2007; and Dave Winfield, who is now an executive and a special advisor in the team's front office. In 2004, the Padres changed playing facilities from Qualcomm Stadium, which they shared with the San Diego Chargers, to their own $450-million stadium, PETCO Park, which seats 41,164. With this change of address and the team's first winning season since 1998, came the franchise's highest attendance numbers, topping 3 million tickets sold. Average home game attendance for the Padres was 36,931 during the 2022 season. The team maintains several minor league affiliations, including the El Paso Chihuahuas, San Antonio Missions, Fort Wayne TinCaps and Lake Elsinore Storm. The club has a 20-year, $1.4 billion broadcasting contract with Fox, creating a San Diego County regional sports network (RSN) in which the team owns a 20% equity interest. The Padres are owned by a group of investors, including Ron Fowler, as well as relatives of former Los Angeles Dodgers owner Peter O'Malley. Forbes estimated the franchise to be worth $1.75 billion in March 2023.

FINANCIAL DATA: *Note: Data for latest year may not have been available at press time.*

In U.S. $	2022	2021	2020	2019	2018	2017
Revenue	377,650,000					
R&D Expense						
Operating Income						
Operating Margin %						
SGA Expense						
Net Income						
Operating Cash Flow						
Capital Expenditure						
EBITDA						
Return on Assets %						
Return on Equity %						
Debt to Equity						

CONTACT INFORMATION:

Phone: 619-795-5000   Fax:
Toll-Free:
Address: 100 Park Blvd., San Diego, CA 92101 United States

STOCK TICKER/OTHER:

Stock Ticker: Private   Exchange:
Employees: 625   Fiscal Year Ends: 10/31
Parent Company:

SALARIES/BONUSES:

Top Exec. Salary: $ Bonus: $
Second Exec. Salary: $ Bonus: $

OTHER THOUGHTS:

Estimated Female Officers or Directors: 5
Hot Spot for Advancement for Women/Minorities: Y

San Francisco 49ers

www.49ers.com

NAIC Code: 711211C

TYPES OF BUSINESS:

Professional Football Team
Team Management and Operations

BRANDS/DIVISIONS/AFFILIATES:

49ers Enterprises

CONTACTS: Note: Officers with more than one job title may be intentionally listed here more than once.

Jed York, CEO
Al Guido, Pres.
Peter Wilhelm, CFO
Alex Chang, CMO
Hapreet Basran, Chief People Officer
John York, Co-Chmn.
Kunal Malik, CTO
Hannah Gordon, Dir.-Legal Affairs
Jim Mercurio, VP-Stadium Oper. & Security
Larry MacNeil, Exec. VP-Dev.
Scott Sabatino, Dir.-Finance
Keena Turner, VP-Football Affairs
Ethan Casson, VP-Corp. Sales
Jim Harbaugh, Head Coach
John York, Co-Chmn.
Denise DeBartolo York, Co-Chmn.
Steve Risser, Mgr.-Team Logistics

GROWTH PLANS/SPECIAL FEATURES:

The San Francisco 49ers is a National Football League (NFL) team in the National Football Conference (NFC). The team was the first major league professional sports franchise on the West Coast. Brothers Anthony and Victor Morabito founded the franchise in 1946 as part of the All American Football Conference (AAFC). The team joined the NFL in 1950 when the AAFC collapsed. In 1977, the brothers sold the franchise to Edward DeBartolo. The 49ers have won 21 division titles (2022 most recently) and seven conference championships, and it was the first franchise in NFL history to win five Super Bowl titles, which occurred in 1994. The 49ers dominated the 1980s when they won four of their five Super Bowl Championships (1981, 1984, 1988 and 1989). San Francisco was able to produce 10 or more wins for 16 consecutive seasons, from 1983 to 1998. After Edward DeBartolo's death in 1994, his children contended for control of DeBartolo Corporation. They finally split the company's assets in 1999, when daughter Denise DeBartolo York gained full control of the 49ers. The team is now owned by the York family's 49ers Enterprises company. Nearly 30 former 49ers are in the Pro Football Hall of Fame, including head coach Bill Walsh, who led the 49ers to three Super Bowl titles; quarterback Joe Montana, who retired with the highest quarterback rating in NFL history; Jerry Rice, who holds a number of wide receiver records; and Steve Young, who won six NFL passing titles. The 49ers currently play in the Levi's Stadium in Santa Clara, which seats 68,500 spectators, with the team averaging 71,629 per home game attendance in the 2022-23 season. Forbes estimated the team to be valued at $5.2 billion in 2022.

FINANCIAL DATA: Note: Data for latest year may not have been available at press time.

In U.S. $	2022	2021	2020	2019	2018	2017
Revenue	587,600,000					
R&D Expense						
Operating Income						
Operating Margin %						
SGA Expense						
Net Income						
Operating Cash Flow						
Capital Expenditure						
EBITDA						
Return on Assets %						
Return on Equity %						
Debt to Equity						

CONTACT INFORMATION:

Phone: 408-562-4949   Fax: 408-727-4937
Toll-Free:
Address: 4949 Centennial Blvd., Santa Clara, CA 95054 United States

SALARIES/BONUSES:

Top Exec. Salary: $ Bonus: $
Second Exec. Salary: $ Bonus: $

STOCK TICKER/OTHER:

Stock Ticker: Private   Exchange:
Employees: 550   Fiscal Year Ends: 12/31
Parent Company:

OTHER THOUGHTS:

Estimated Female Officers or Directors: 7
Hot Spot for Advancement for Women/Minorities: Y

San Francisco Giants

www.mlb.com/giants

NAIC Code: 711211A

TYPES OF BUSINESS:

Professional Baseball Team
Team Management and Operations

BRANDS/DIVISIONS/AFFILIATES:

Sacramento River Cats
Richmond Flying Squirrels
Eugene Emeralds
San Jose Giants
San Francisco Baseball Associates LLC

CONTACTS: *Note: Officers with more than one job title may be intentionally listed here more than once.*

Larry Baer, CEO
Farhan Zaidi, Pres.-Baseball Oper.
Lisa Pantages, CFO
Rachel Heit, CMO
Jose Martin, Chief People Officer
Bill Schlough, CIO
Alfonso G. Felder, Sr. VP-Admin.
Jack F. Bair, General Counsel
Mario Alioto, Sr. VP-Bus. Oper.
Bryan Srabian, Dir.-Social Media
Staci Slaughter, Sr. VP-Comm.
Lisa Pantages, VP-Finance
Brian R. Sabean, Gen. Mgr.
Jorge Costa, Sr. VP-Ballpark Oper.
Shana Daum, VP-Public Affairs & Community Rel.
Jeff Tucker, VP-Ticket Sales
Greg Johnson, Chmn.
Pablo Peguero, Dir.-Dominican Oper.

GROWTH PLANS/SPECIAL FEATURES:

The San Francisco Giants are a professional baseball team playing in the National League West Division within Major League Baseball (MLB). The club began in New York as the Gothams in 1883 and became the New York Giants in 1885 before moving west in 1958. During its New York years, the team played at the famed Polo Grounds, which witnessed the Shot Heard Round the World homerun by Bobby Thomson on October 3, 1951 that won the pennant against the Brooklyn Dodgers. The Giants now play their home games at Oracle Park, situated on the San Francisco Bay and seats nearly 42,000 fans. The team averaged 30,650 in attendance per home game in the 2022 season. Oracle Park was privately financed by Giants owner Peter McGowan, replacing the much-maligned Candlestick Park. Famous Giants players have included Willie Mays, Willie McCovey, Juan Marichal, Will Clark and Barry Bonds, who broke the single-season home run record in 2001 and the all-time home run record in 2007. In all, the franchise has won eight World Series titles, including the 2014 series against the Kansas City Royals (4-3), as well as 23 pennants and nine division titles. The Giants are owned by San Francisco Baseball Associates, LLC. The team maintains minor league affiliations Sacramento River Cats, Richmond Flying Squirrels, Eugene Emeralds, and San Jose Giants. In March 2023, Forbes valued the Giants to be worth $3.7 billion.

FINANCIAL DATA: *Note: Data for latest year may not have been available at press time.*

In U.S. $	2022	2021	2020	2019	2018	2017
Revenue	543,400,000					
R&D Expense						
Operating Income						
Operating Margin %						
SGA Expense						
Net Income						
Operating Cash Flow						
Capital Expenditure						
EBITDA						
Return on Assets %						
Return on Equity %						
Debt to Equity						

CONTACT INFORMATION:

Phone: 415-972-2000   Fax: 415-947-2800
Toll-Free:
Address: 24 Willie Mays Plz., AT&T Park, San Francisco, CA 94107
United States

STOCK TICKER/OTHER:

Stock Ticker: Private   Exchange:
Employees: 850   Fiscal Year Ends: 12/31
Parent Company:

SALARIES/BONUSES:

Top Exec. Salary: $ Bonus: $
Second Exec. Salary: $ Bonus: $

OTHER THOUGHTS:

Estimated Female Officers or Directors: 14
Hot Spot for Advancement for Women/Minorities: Y

San Jose Earthquakes

www.sjearthquakes.com

NAIC Code: 711211D

TYPES OF BUSINESS:

Major League Soccer Team
Team Management and Operations

BRANDS/DIVISIONS/AFFILIATES:

Earthquakes Soccer LLC

CONTACTS: *Note: Officers with more than one job title may be intentionally listed here more than once.*

John Fisher, Managing Partner
Jared Shawlee, Pres.
Kashmira Bhathena, VP-Finance
Peggy O'Halloran, VP-Human Resources
John Doyle, Gen. Mgr.-Soccer Oper.
Jed Mettee, VP-Corp. Comm.
Anthony Perry, Sr. Exec.-Acct.
Jose Vega, Mgr.-Equipment
Frank Yallop, Head Coach
Lew Wolff, Owner
Richard Fedesco, Sr. Dir.-Ticket Oper.
Chris Leitch, Gen. Mngr.

GROWTH PLANS/SPECIAL FEATURES:

The San Jose Earthquakes is a Major League Soccer (MLS) team playing in the Western Conference alongside the Austin FC, Colorado Rapids, FC Dallas, Houston Dynamo FC, LA Galaxy, Los Angeles FC, Minnesota United FC, Portland Timbers, Real Salt Lake, Seattle Sounders FC, Sporting Kansas City, St. Louis City SC and Vancouver Whitecaps FC. The organization, which was an inaugural MLS club, returned in 2008 from a two-year hiatus that saw the team's entire operations moved to Houston, Texas to form the Houston Dynamo. The team resumed play as an expansion team owned by Lewis Wolff through Earthquakes Soccer, LLC. Because the Earthquakes have retained the former team's records, colors and logos, the team bears the odd distinction of being both an MLS founding member and one of the league's most recent expansion teams. The first iteration of the team, as the Houston Dynamo, won the MLS Cup in 2001 and 2003. The Earthquakes have also won the Supporters' Shield in 2005 and 2012. The club plays its home games at PayPal Park in Santa Clara, California, which has a seating capacity of 18,000. During the 2022 season, the Earthquakes averaged 15,260 per home game attendance.

FINANCIAL DATA: *Note: Data for latest year may not have been available at press time.*

In U.S. $	2022	2021	2020	2019	2018	2017
Revenue	11,245,500					
R&D Expense						
Operating Income						
Operating Margin %						
SGA Expense						
Net Income						
Operating Cash Flow						
Capital Expenditure						
EBITDA						
Return on Assets %						
Return on Equity %						
Debt to Equity						

CONTACT INFORMATION:

Phone: 408-556-7700   Fax: 408-796-5242
Toll-Free:
Address: 1123 Coleman Ave, San Jose, CA 95110 United States

SALARIES/BONUSES:

Top Exec. Salary: $ Bonus: $
Second Exec. Salary: $ Bonus: $

STOCK TICKER/OTHER:

Stock Ticker: Private
Employees: 180
Parent Company:

Exchange:
Fiscal Year Ends:

OTHER THOUGHTS:

Estimated Female Officers or Directors: 3
Hot Spot for Advancement for Women/Minorities: Y

San Jose Sharks

NAIC Code: 711211F

TYPES OF BUSINESS:

Professional Hockey Team (NHL)
Team Management and Operations

BRANDS/DIVISIONS/AFFILIATES:

San Jose Sports & Entertainment Enterprises
San Jose Barracuda

CONTACTS: *Note: Officers with more than one job title may be intentionally listed here more than once.*

Mike Grier, Gen. Mngr.
Jonathan Becher, Pres.
Greg Matthews, CFO
Doug Bentz, CMO
Cassie McBride, Sr. VP-Gen. Counsel
Scott Emmert, VP-Communications
John Tortora, General Counsel
Malcolm Bordelon, Exec. VP-Bus. Oper.
Michael T. Lehr, Exec. VP-Bus. Dev.
Doug Bentz, Dir.-Digital Media
Ken Caveney, VP-Finance
Jim Goddard, Exec. VP
Doug Wilson, Exec. VP
Rich Sotelo, VP-Building Oper.
Todd McLellan, Head Coach
Neda Tabatabaie, Sr. VP-Business Analytics & Technology

GROWTH PLANS/SPECIAL FEATURES:

The San Jose Sharks is a professional ice hockey team playing in the Pacific division of the Western conference of the National Hockey League (NHL). The team was founded in 1991 by Cleveland businessmen George and Gordon Gund. In its early years, the franchise was a relatively poor team on the ice. At the beginning of its third season, the Sharks moved to their current home, the SAP Center (also known as the San Jose Arena and The Shark Tank). This move marked a turnaround in the team's performance, with the Sharks not only making the playoffs, but also upsetting the heavily favored Detroit Red Wings in the first round. Average home game attendance was 13,912 during the 2022-23 season. After years of mixed results, a local group of investors headed by team president Greg Jamison bought out the team in 2002. San Jose Sports & Entertainment Enterprises currently owns and manages the Sharks. The Sharks won their first conference championship in 2015-16, but lost in the finals for the Stanley Cup to the Pittsburgh Penguins, 1-3. In total, the team has clenched six division championships, a president's trophy and the conference championship. Minor league affiliates of the San Jose Sharks include the San Jose Barracuda in the American Hockey League (AHL), and the Wichita Thunder in the East Coast Hockey League (ECHL). In December 2022, Forbes valued the team at $740 million.

FINANCIAL DATA: *Note: Data for latest year may not have been available at press time.*

In U.S. $	2022	2021	2020	2019	2018	2017
Revenue	118,950,000					
R&D Expense						
Operating Income						
Operating Margin %						
SGA Expense						
Net Income						
Operating Cash Flow						
Capital Expenditure						
EBITDA						
Return on Assets %						
Return on Equity %						
Debt to Equity						

CONTACT INFORMATION:

Phone: 408-287-7070   Fax: 408-999-5797
Toll-Free: 800-366-4423
Address: 525 W. Santa Clara St., San Jose, CA 95113 United States

STOCK TICKER/OTHER:

Stock Ticker: Private   Exchange:
Employees: 275   Fiscal Year Ends: 07/31
Parent Company:

SALARIES/BONUSES:

Top Exec. Salary: $ Bonus: $
Second Exec. Salary: $ Bonus: $

OTHER THOUGHTS:

Estimated Female Officers or Directors: 7
Hot Spot for Advancement for Women/Minorities: Y

Santos Futebol Clube

www.santosfc.com.br

NAIC Code: 711211D

TYPES OF BUSINESS:

Soccer Team
Team Management and Operations

BRANDS/DIVISIONS/AFFILIATES:

Estadio Urbano Caldeira

GROWTH PLANS/SPECIAL FEATURES:

Santos Futebol Clube is a professional football club in Brazil, playing in the Paulisao premier state league as well as the Serie A top-tier Brazilian football league system. Founded in 1912, Santos FC plays its home games in the Estadio Urbano Caldeira stadium (also known as Vila Belmiro), which has a seating capacity of over 16,000. The stadium is also owned by Santos FC. Average attendance for the Serie A league in 2022 was 11,844. Regionally, the club has won 22 Campeonato Paulista titles, five Torneio Rio-Sao Paulo titles and one Copa Paulista de Futebol title. Nationally, Santos FC has clenched eight Campeonato Brasileiro Serie A titles. Internationally, the team has won two Intercontinental Cups, one Intercontinental Supercup, three Copa Libertadores, one Copa CONMEBOL title and one Recopa Sudamerica title. Santos FC is currently sponsored by kit manufacturer Umbro, as well as financial sponsors.

CONTACTS: Note: Officers with more than one job title may be intentionally listed here more than once.

Andres Rueda, Pres.

FINANCIAL DATA: Note: Data for latest year may not have been available at press time.

In U.S. $	2022	2021	2020	2019	2018	2017
Revenue	80,000,000	50,713,183	46,102,894	98,988,864	86,600,844	86,600,844
R&D Expense						
Operating Income						
Operating Margin %						
SGA Expense						
Net Income			-23,038,950	5,818,331	-4,276,302	-4,276,302
Operating Cash Flow						
Capital Expenditure						
EBITDA						
Return on Assets %						
Return on Equity %						
Debt to Equity						

CONTACT INFORMATION:

Phone: 55 13 3257-4000   Fax:
Toll-Free:
Address: Rua Princesa Isabel, s / n, Vila Belmiro, Santos, SP 11075-500 Brazil

STOCK TICKER/OTHER:

Stock Ticker: Private
Employees:
Parent Company:

Exchange:
Fiscal Year Ends: 12/31

SALARIES/BONUSES:

Top Exec. Salary: $ Bonus: $
Second Exec. Salary: $ Bonus: $

OTHER THOUGHTS:

Estimated Female Officers or Directors:
Hot Spot for Advancement for Women/Minorities:

Sales, profits and employees may be estimates. Financial information, benefits and other data can change quickly and may vary from those stated here.

Sao Paulo Futebol Clube

www.saopaulofc.net/spfc

NAIC Code: 711211D

TYPES OF BUSINESS:

Soccer Team
Team Management and Operations

BRANDS/DIVISIONS/AFFILIATES:

Estadio do Morumbi
Tricolor Paulista

GROWTH PLANS/SPECIAL FEATURES:

Sao Paulo Futebol Clube is a professional football club in the Morumbi district of Sao Paulo, Brazil. Founded in 1930, the team plays in the Campeonato Paulista premier Brazilian state league and the Campeonato Brasileiro Serie A (the top-tier of the football league system in Brazil). Home games occur in the Estadio do Morumbi which seats 72,039, among the largest private stadiums in Brazil and owned by Sao Paulo FC. Sao Paulo FC averaged 30,132 in Serie A attendance for the 2022 season. Nicknamed Tricolor Paulista, the club has won 12 international titles, including two Intercontinental Cups and a FIFA Club World Cup, as well as six Campeonato Brasileiro titles, 22 Campeonato Paulista titles, and a Supercampeonato Paulista and Torneio Rio-Sao Paulo title.

CONTACTS: *Note: Officers with more than one job title may be intentionally listed here more than once.*

Dorival Junior, Head Coach
Julio Casares, Pres.

FINANCIAL DATA: *Note: Data for latest year may not have been available at press time.*

In U.S. $	2022	2021	2020	2019	2018	2017
Revenue						
R&D Expense						
Operating Income						
Operating Margin %						
SGA Expense						
Net Income						
Operating Cash Flow						
Capital Expenditure						
EBITDA						
Return on Assets %						
Return on Equity %						
Debt to Equity						

CONTACT INFORMATION:

Phone: 55 11 37498000   Fax:
Toll-Free:
Address: Praca Roberto Gomez Pedrosa 1, Morumbi, Sao Paulo, SP 05653 Brazil

STOCK TICKER/OTHER:

Stock Ticker: Private   Exchange:
Employees: Fiscal Year Ends:
Parent Company:

SALARIES/BONUSES:

Top Exec. Salary: $ Bonus: $
Second Exec. Salary: $ Bonus: $

OTHER THOUGHTS:

Estimated Female Officers or Directors:
Hot Spot for Advancement for Women/Minorities:

Score Media Ventures Inc

www.scoremediaandgaming.com

NAIC Code: 519130

TYPES OF BUSINESS:

Mobile Sports News
Digital Sports Media
Sports Betting App
Innovative Technology
Online Sports Betting
Sportsbook

BRANDS/DIVISIONS/AFFILIATES:

PENN National Gaming Inc
theScore
theScore Bet
theScore Bet Sportsbook and Casino

CONTACTS: Note: Officers with more than one job title may be intentionally listed here more than once.

John Levy, CEO
Benjie Levy, Pres.
Tom Hearne, CFO

GROWTH PLANS/SPECIAL FEATURES:

Score Media Ventures, Inc. is a technology company that has developed theScore, which offers digital media and sports betting products via online and mobile applications. theScore delivers highly personalized live scores, news, stats and betting information to fans, who can choose their favorite teams, leagues and players to follow. The application's sports betting app, theScore Bet, delivers an immersive and holistic mobile sports betting experience across categories including NBA, NHL, MLB, NFL, MLS, beach volleyball, boxing, cricket, cycling, golf, MMA, motorsports, table tennis and more. theScore also creates and distributes innovative digital content through its web, social and eSports platforms. Score Media Ventures operates as a wholly-owned subsidiary of PENN Entertainment, Inc., a public entity that provides omnichannel retail and online gaming, live racing and sports betting entertainment. Score Media has offices in Toronto, Ontario, Canada and in Hoboken, New Jersey, USA. During 2022, Score Media launched theScore Bet Sportsbook and Casino in Ontario, and then expanded it with the launch of a web version in March 2023.

FINANCIAL DATA: Note: Data for latest year may not have been available at press time.

In U.S. $	2022	2021	2020	2019	2018	2017
Revenue	16,900,000	16,449,388	15,816,719	23,208,866	18,795,834	18,795,834
R&D Expense						
Operating Income						
Operating Margin %						
SGA Expense						
Net Income			-28,955,459	-7,019,860	-6,588,672	-6,588,672
Operating Cash Flow						
Capital Expenditure						
EBITDA						
Return on Assets %						
Return on Equity %						
Debt to Equity						

CONTACT INFORMATION:

Phone: 416-479-8812   Fax: 416-361-2045
Toll-Free:
Address: 500 King St. West, Fl. 4, Toronto, ON M5V 1L9 Canada

STOCK TICKER/OTHER:

Stock Ticker: Subsidiary   Exchange:
Employees: 216   Fiscal Year Ends: 12/31
Parent Company: PENN National Gaming Inc

SALARIES/BONUSES:

Top Exec. Salary: $ Bonus: $
Second Exec. Salary: $ Bonus: $

OTHER THOUGHTS:

Estimated Female Officers or Directors: 1
Hot Spot for Advancement for Women/Minorities:

Sales, profits and employees may be estimates. Financial information, benefits and other data can change quickly and may vary from those stated here.

Seattle Mariners

www.mlb.com/mariners

NAIC Code: 711211A

TYPES OF BUSINESS:

Professional Baseball Team
Team Management and Operations

BRANDS/DIVISIONS/AFFILIATES:

First Avenu Entertaintment LP
Nintendo of America
Baseball Club of Seattle LP (The)
Tacoma Rainiers
Arkansas Travelers
Everett AquaSox
Modesto Nuts

CONTACTS: *Note: Officers with more than one job title may be intentionally listed here more than once.*

Jerry Dipoto, Pres.-Baseball Oper.
Catie Griggs, Pres.-Bus. Oper.
Tim Kornegay, CFO
Kevin Martinez, Sr. VP-Mktg. & Communications
Lisa Winsby, Sr. VP-People & Culture
Kari Escobedo, Sr. VP-IT
Julie McGillivray, Dir.-Retail Merch.
Bart Waldman, General Counsel
Bob Aylward, Exec. VP-Bus. Oper.
Randy Adamack, Sr. VP-Comm.
Kevin Mather, Exec. VP-Finance & Ballpark Oper.
Jack Zduriencik, Exec. VP-Baseball Oper.
Eric Wedge, Mgr.
Tim Kornegay, VP-Finance
Kevin Martinez, VP-Mktg.
John Stanton, Chmn.
Tim Kissner, Dir.-Int'l Oper.
Sandy Fielder, Sr. Dir.-Procurement

GROWTH PLANS/SPECIAL FEATURES:

The Seattle Mariners, operated by The Baseball Club of Seattle, LP, is an organization founded in 1977 within Major League Baseball (MLB), playing in the West Division. The team struggled in its early years, with a string of 14 losing seasons from 1977 to 1990. The Mariners have clenched division titles three times, but have been unable to advance to the World Series despite a successful 2001 season in which the team won an impressive 116 games. The Mariners has featured superstars such as Randy Johnson, Ken Griffey, Jr. and Alex Rodriguez, as well as Japanese import Ichiro Suzuki. First Avenue Entertainment LP is the majority-owner of the Mariners, with Nintendo of America holding a 10% share. The team maintains a number of minor league affiliations, including the Tacoma Rainiers, the Arkansas Travelers, the Everett AquaSox, and the Modesto Nuts. The Mariners and DIRECTV Sports Networks established a regional sports network (RSN) to broadcast the team's games through 2030 for roughly $2 billion over the life of its contract. The club has played its home games at the 47,574-seat capacity T-Mobile Park since 1999, with attendance averaging 28,590 per home game in the 2022 season. In March 2023, Forbes valued the team at $2.2 billion.

FINANCIAL DATA: *Note: Data for latest year may not have been available at press time.*

In U.S. $	2022	2021	2020	2019	2018	2017
Revenue	408,200,000					
R&D Expense						
Operating Income						
Operating Margin %						
SGA Expense						
Net Income						
Operating Cash Flow						
Capital Expenditure						
EBITDA						
Return on Assets %						
Return on Equity %						
Debt to Equity						

CONTACT INFORMATION:

Phone: 206-346-4001   Fax: 206-346-4100
Toll-Free:
Address: 1250 First Ave. S., Seattle, WA 98134 United States

STOCK TICKER/OTHER:

Stock Ticker: Private   Exchange:
Employees: 620   Fiscal Year Ends: 10/31
Parent Company:

SALARIES/BONUSES:

Top Exec. Salary: $ Bonus: $
Second Exec. Salary: $ Bonus: $

OTHER THOUGHTS:

Estimated Female Officers or Directors: 13
Hot Spot for Advancement for Women/Minorities: Y

Seattle Seahawks

www.seahawks.com

NAIC Code: 711211C

TYPES OF BUSINESS:

Professional Football Team
Team Management and Operations

BRANDS/DIVISIONS/AFFILIATES:

Paul G Allen Trust

CONTACTS: Note: Officers with more than one job title may be intentionally listed here more than once.

John Schneider, Gen. Mngr.
Chuck Arnold, Pres.
Karen Spencer, CFO
Dave Pearson, CCO
Cindy Kelley, Chief Human Resources Officer
David Young, COO
Matt Thomas, VP-Football Admin.
Lance Lopes, General Counsel
Pete Carroll, Exec. VP-Football Oper.
Kenton Olson, Dir.-Digital & Emerging Media
Dave Pearson, VP-Comm., Broadcasting & Website Content
Karen Beckman, VP-Finance
John Schneider, Gen. Mgr.
Eric Mastalir, Chief Commercial Officer
Tag Ribary, Dir.-Pro Personnel
Mike Flood, VP-Community Rel. & Special Projects
Jody Allen, Chmn.

GROWTH PLANS/SPECIAL FEATURES:

The Seattle Seahawks is a National Football League (NFL) team playing in the Western Division of the National Football Conference. The team was established in 1974 and entered the league in 1976 as an NFL expansion along with the Tampa Bay Buccaneers. During its early years, the Seahawks played mediocre football with highlights provided by Hall of Fame receiver Steve Largent. The team made its first playoff appearance in 1983 when they reached the conference championship game. In total, the Seahawks have made the playoffs 20 times (2022 most recently), and has also clenched 11 division championships (two AFC West and nine NFC West). The team reached the Super Bowl in the 2005, 2013 and 2014 seasons, but won its first and only Super Bowl championship (XLVIII) in 2013 against the Denver Broncos, 43-8. The Seahawks is owned by Paul G. Allen Trust. The team plays in Lumen Field, owned by the City of Seattle through the Washington State Public Stadium Authority. The stadium seats approximately 67,000 spectators (72,000 for special events), with the Seahawks averaging 68,832 fans in home game attendance during the 2022-23 season. Forbes estimated the value of the team at $4.5 billion in 2022.

FINANCIAL DATA: Note: Data for latest year may not have been available at press time.

In U.S. $	2022	2021	2020	2019	2018	2017
Revenue	542,100,000					
R&D Expense						
Operating Income						
Operating Margin %						
SGA Expense						
Net Income						
Operating Cash Flow						
Capital Expenditure						
EBITDA						
Return on Assets %						
Return on Equity %						
Debt to Equity						

CONTACT INFORMATION:

Phone: 425-203-8000 Fax:
Toll-Free: 888-635-4295
Address: 12 Seahawks Way, Renton, WA 98056 United States

SALARIES/BONUSES:

Top Exec. Salary: $ Bonus: $
Second Exec. Salary: $ Bonus: $

STOCK TICKER/OTHER:

Stock Ticker: Private Exchange:
Employees: 380 Fiscal Year Ends: 01/31
Parent Company:

OTHER THOUGHTS:

Estimated Female Officers or Directors: 16
Hot Spot for Advancement for Women/Minorities: Y

Sales, profits and employees may be estimates. Financial information, benefits and other data can change quickly and may vary from those stated here.

Seattle Sounders FC

www.soundersfc.com

NAIC Code: 711211D

TYPES OF BUSINESS:

Major League Soccer Team
Team Management and Operations

BRANDS/DIVISIONS/AFFILIATES:

CONTACTS: *Note: Officers with more than one job title may be intentionally listed here more than once.*

Hugh Weber, Pres.-Bus. Oper.
Maya Mendoza-Exstrom, COO
Peter McLoughlin, Pres.
Tom Riley, CFO
Taylor Graham, CMO
Erin Vagley, Sr. VP-People & Culture
Joe Welsh, Dir.-IT
Cindy Kelley, VP-Admin.
Lance Lopes, General Counsel
Gary Wright, Sr. VP-Bus. Oper.
Dave Pearson, VP-Broadcasting & Website Content
Dave Pearson, VP-Comm.
Karen Beckman, VP-Finance
Joe Roth, Majority Owner
Bart Wiley, VP-Bus. Oper.
Mike Flood, VP-Community Rel.
Eric Mastalir, Chief Commercial Officer
Mikaela Purvis, VP-Bus. Oper.

GROWTH PLANS/SPECIAL FEATURES:

Seattle Sounders FC is a Major League Soccer (MLS) soccer franchise based out of Washington state. The team celebrated its inaugural season in 2009, and is the third to bear the Sounders name. The original Sounders played from 1974-83 in the North American Soccer League (NASL), and the second played from 1994-2008 in the United Soccer Leagues First Division. The franchise plays in the Western Conference alongside Austin FC, Colorado Rapids, FC Dallas, Houston Dynamo FC, LA Galaxy, Los Angeles FC, Minnesota United FC, Portland Timbers, Real Salt Lake, San Jose Earthquakes, Sporting Kansas City, St. Louis City SC and Vancouver Whitecaps FC. Its official home is Lumen Field, featuring an MLS seating capacity of 37,722, with the Sounders averaging 33,607 in home game attendance during the 2022 season. The team is owned by a consortium of businessmen and entertainers, with Adrian Hanauer holding the majority stake, and minority owners including the Paul Allen estate, Drew Carey and 14 families from the Seattle area. The Sounders have proven to be highly successful for a young team, winning the U.S. Open Cup and making a playoff appearance in its first season. In 2011, the team won its third consecutive US Open Cup and its fourth in 2014. The Sounders placed 4th in the Western Conference in 2016, qualifying for the MLS Cup Playoffs and defeated Toronto 5-4 in a penalty shootout and clenched their first MLS championship in franchise history. In 2019, the Sounders defeated the Los Angeles FC in the conference finals, leading them to face Toronto FC in the MLS Cup final for the third time in four years. The Sounders won the game 3-1, obtaining their second MLS Cup title. The Seattle Sounders clenched their first CONCACAF Champions League title in 2022, defeating UNAM in the final.

FINANCIAL DATA: *Note: Data for latest year may not have been available at press time.*

In U.S. $	2022	2021	2020	2019	2018	2017
Revenue	15,101,100					
R&D Expense						
Operating Income						
Operating Margin %						
SGA Expense						
Net Income						
Operating Cash Flow						
Capital Expenditure						
EBITDA						
Return on Assets %						
Return on Equity %						
Debt to Equity						

CONTACT INFORMATION:

Phone: 206-512-1200   Fax:
Toll-Free: 877-657-4625
Address: 159 S. Jackson St. #200, Seattle, WA 98104 United States

STOCK TICKER/OTHER:

Stock Ticker: Private   Exchange:
Employees: 290   Fiscal Year Ends:
Parent Company:

SALARIES/BONUSES:

Top Exec. Salary: $ Bonus: $
Second Exec. Salary: $ Bonus: $

OTHER THOUGHTS:

Estimated Female Officers or Directors: 8
Hot Spot for Advancement for Women/Minorities: Y

Seattle Storm

www.wnba.com/storm

NAIC Code: 711211E

TYPES OF BUSINESS:

Women's Basketball Team
Team Management and Operations

BRANDS/DIVISIONS/AFFILIATES:

Force 10 Hoops LLC

CONTACTS: *Note: Officers with more than one job title may be intentionally listed here more than once.*

Alisha Valavanis, CEO
Tricia McLean, CFO
Kenny Dow, Sr. VP-Mktg. & Communications
Kyle Waters, Chief Sales Officer
Kris Kolehmain, Sr. Mgr.-Research & Analytics
Nate Silverman, Chief Commercial Officer
Heather Saldivar, Mgr.-Merch. Oper.
Navreet Gill, Mgr.-Bus. Oper.
Sarah Scott, Mgr.-Acct. & Human Resources
Brian Agler, Head Coach
Jenny Boucek, Assistant Coach
Nancy Darsch, Assistant Coach
Tom Spencer, Head-Athletic Trainer

GROWTH PLANS/SPECIAL FEATURES:

The Seattle Storm, owned by Force 10 Hoops, LLC, is a Women's National Basketball Association (WNBA) team based in Seattle, Washington. The team plays in the Western Conference of the WNBA along with the Dallas Wings, Los Angeles Sparks, Las Vegas Aces, Minnesota Lynx and Phoenix Mercury. Home games take place at the Climate Pledge Arena, a multipurpose arena in Seattle that seats 18,100 basketball fans, with the Storm averaging 10,631 for the 2022 season. Founded in 2000, the Storm quickly reached prominence with a 2004 WNBA championship. Though the franchise had been a regular contender in the WNBA playoffs, reaching the semifinals every year since 2004, it did not claim another championship until the 2010 season. The team's 2010 championship year set the record for most home wins in a WNBA season, with a perfect 17-0 record. In the 2016 and 2017 seasons, Seattle made the playoffs but lost to Atlanta and Phoenix, respectively. In 2018, the Seattle Storm clenched the Conference Finals against Phoenix as well as the WNBA Finals, beating the Washington Mystics 3-0. Again in 2020, The Seattle Storm did not lose a single game and defeated the Las Vegas Aces in three games, clenching their fourth WNBA championship. The team has featured notable players such as the two-time WNBA MVP Lauren Jackson, the three-time WNBA All-Star Swim Cash and the two-time Olympic Gold Medalist Sue Bird.

FINANCIAL DATA: *Note: Data for latest year may not have been available at press time.*

In U.S. $	2022	2021	2020	2019	2018	2017
Revenue						
R&D Expense						
Operating Income						
Operating Margin %						
SGA Expense						
Net Income						
Operating Cash Flow						
Capital Expenditure						
EBITDA						
Return on Assets %						
Return on Equity %						
Debt to Equity						

CONTACT INFORMATION:

Phone: 206-217-9622   Fax:
Toll-Free:
Address: 3411 Thorndyke Ave. W., Seattle, WA 98119 United States

STOCK TICKER/OTHER:

Stock Ticker: Private   Exchange:
Employees: 73   Fiscal Year Ends:
Parent Company: Force 10 Hoops LLC

SALARIES/BONUSES:

Top Exec. Salary: $ Bonus: $
Second Exec. Salary: $ Bonus: $

OTHER THOUGHTS:

Estimated Female Officers or Directors: 18
Hot Spot for Advancement for Women/Minorities: Y

Sirius XM Holdings Inc

www.siriusxm.com

NAIC Code: 515111

TYPES OF BUSINESS:

Satellite and Online Radio
Mobile Television Content

BRANDS/DIVISIONS/AFFILIATES:

SiriusXM
Pandora Media LLC

GROWTH PLANS/SPECIAL FEATURES:

Sirius XM Holdings is composed of two businesses: SiriusXM and Pandora. SiriusXM transmits music, talk shows, sports, and news via its two satellite radio networks, primarily to consumers in vehicles who pay a subscription fee. The firm's radios come preinstalled on a wide range of light vehicles in the U.S. and Canada. The firm acquired Pandora Media in February 2019 via an all-stock transaction. Pandora is a streaming music platform that offers an ad-supported radio option and a paid on-demand service as well as a robust and growing podcast library. Liberty Media owns 81% of SiriusXM, traded through its Liberty SiriusXM Group tracking stock.

Sirius XM offers comprehensive benefits, retirement and savings options and employee assistance programs.

CONTACTS: *Note: Officers with more than one job title may be intentionally listed here more than once.*

Jennifer Witz, CEO
Sean Sullivan, CFO
Gregory Maffei, Chairman of the Board
Thomas Barry, Chief Accounting Officer
Dara Altman, Chief Administrative Officer
James Meyer, Director
Patrick Donnelly, Executive VP
Scott Greenstein, Other Executive Officer

FINANCIAL DATA: *Note: Data for latest year may not have been available at press time.*

In U.S. $	2022	2021	2020	2019	2018	2017
Revenue	9,003,000,000	8,696,001,000		7,794,000,000	5,425,000,000	5,425,000,000
R&D Expense	285,000,000	265,000,000		280,000,000	112,000,000	112,000,000
Operating Income	2,100,000,000	2,035,000,000		1,731,000,000	1,641,000,000	1,641,000,000
Operating Margin %	.23%	.23%		.22%	.30%	.30%
SGA Expense	1,600,000,000	1,570,000,000		1,461,000,000	773,000,000	773,000,000
Net Income	1,213,000,000	1,314,000,000		914,000,000	648,000,000	648,000,000
Operating Cash Flow	1,976,000,000	1,998,000,000	2,018,000,000	2,017,000,000	1,856,000,000	1,856,000,000
Capital Expenditure	426,000,000	388,000,000	350,000,000	363,000,000	288,000,000	288,000,000
EBITDA	2,612,000,000	2,524,000,000		2,111,000,000	1,909,000,000	1,909,000,000
Return on Assets %	.12%	.13%		.09%	.08%	.08%
Return on Equity %						
Debt to Equity						

CONTACT INFORMATION:

Phone: 212 584-5100   Fax:
Toll-Free:
Address: 1221 Ave. of the Americas, Fl. 36, New York, NY 10020 United States

STOCK TICKER/OTHER:

Stock Ticker: SIRI   Exchange: NAS
Employees: 5,869   Fiscal Year Ends: 12/31
Parent Company:

SALARIES/BONUSES:

Top Exec. Salary: $1,741,539   Bonus: $6,100,000
Second Exec. Salary: $1,628,616   Bonus: $3,050,000

OTHER THOUGHTS:

Estimated Female Officers or Directors: 3
Hot Spot for Advancement for Women/Minorities: Y

Skis Rossignol SA

www.rossignol.com

NAIC Code: 339920

TYPES OF BUSINESS:

Ski Equipment
Winter Sports Accessories
Outerwear & Apparel
Product Manufacturing
Bikes
Sport Racing

BRANDS/DIVISIONS/AFFILIATES:

Altor Equity Partners
Rossignol
Dynastar
Lange
Look
Kerma
Risport
Heretic

CONTACTS: Note: Officers with more than one job title may be intentionally listed here more than once.

Vincent Wauters, CEO

GROWTH PLANS/SPECIAL FEATURES:

Skis Rossignol SA, majority-owned by Swedish private equity group Altor Equity Partners, is a leading manufacturer of winter sports goods as well as products designed for year-round mountain sports and the lifestyle associated with such sports. The company owns several brands. The Rossignol brand is a winter sports brand, offering an array of products for both amateurs and experts in alpine skiing, Nordic skiing and snowboarding. Rossignol's apparel includes high-end sportswear, active and contemporary fashion, all of which display the company's three-color rooster logo, an emblem they've had for more than 100 years. Dynastar is a specialist ski brand that provides high-tech products for demanding ski experiences. Lange produces high-end winter sports boots, primarily for snow skiing. Look is a bindings manufacturer. Kerma specializes in alpine ski poles. Risport manufactures ice skates. In addition, the Rossignol Factory Team is a bike racing team that participates in the Enduro World Series, and race on the Rossignol Heretic brand of bikes.

FINANCIAL DATA: Note: Data for latest year may not have been available at press time.

In U.S. $	2022	2021	2020	2019	2018	2017
Revenue	320,000,000	309,875,280	409,109,000	280,000,000	275,000,000	275,000,000
R&D Expense						
Operating Income						
Operating Margin %						
SGA Expense						
Net Income						
Operating Cash Flow						
Capital Expenditure						
EBITDA						
Return on Assets %						
Return on Equity %						
Debt to Equity						

CONTACT INFORMATION:

Phone: 33-4-38-03-80-38   Fax: 33-4-38-03-80-00
Toll-Free:
Address: 98 rue Louis Barran, Saint-Jean de Moirans, 38430 France

STOCK TICKER/OTHER:

Stock Ticker: Private
Employees: 1,310
Parent Company: Altor Equity Partners

Exchange:
Fiscal Year Ends: 03/31

SALARIES/BONUSES:

Top Exec. Salary: $ Bonus: $
Second Exec. Salary: $ Bonus: $

OTHER THOUGHTS:

Estimated Female Officers or Directors:
Hot Spot for Advancement for Women/Minorities:

Snap Fitness Inc

www.snapfitness.com

NAIC Code: 713940

TYPES OF BUSINESS:

Fitness Clubs

BRANDS/DIVISIONS/AFFILIATES:

Lift Brands Inc
easyFIT

CONTACTS: *Note: Officers with more than one job title may be intentionally listed here more than once.*

Ty Menzies, CEO
Peter Taunton, Pres.
Bill Rodriguez, Sr. VP-Bus. Dev.
Brant Schmitz, Mgr.-Online Mktg.
Ryan Kalinowski, Dir.-Franchise Support
Chad Vinson Ruf, Dir.-Personal Training

GROWTH PLANS/SPECIAL FEATURES:

Snap Fitness, Inc., a subsidiary of Lift Brands, Inc., is a franchisor of 24/7 fitness centers in more than 20 countries. Clubs are relatively small and feature cardio and strength training equipment as well as value-added fitness services such as personal training and tanning. The firm has more than 1,000 clubs and more than 1 million members worldwide. Snap members pay on a month-to-month basis and have access to all clubs in North America. Customers are able to freeze their accounts for up to three months annually. Additionally, gym memberships allow clients access to numerous discounts on services and apparel from companies such as Costco and T-Mobile. Snap, in collaboration with Rolling Strong, also launched workout centers at nationwide Pilot Flying J Travel Centers. The company's Corporate Wellness program enables employers to add discounted membership rates to their corporate benefits packages. Its proprietary easyFIT program features a wearable body motion monitor that converts the user's daily activity and calorie burn into a point score, allowing the user to track their fitness levels. Franchisees receive support throughout the process, including planning and securing finance, sourcing property, recruiting and training, pre-sales and launch, ongoing growth and personal contact. Snap Fitness offers a free app for members, enabling them to customize goals, track fitness activities in and out of the gym, and access on-demand workouts, nutritional guidance, mindfulness programming and tips for healthy living and more.

FINANCIAL DATA: *Note: Data for latest year may not have been available at press time.*

In U.S. $	2022	2021	2020	2019	2018	2017
Revenue	50,000,000	46,307,999	44,102,856	74,750,603	67,801,000	67,801,000
R&D Expense						
Operating Income						
Operating Margin %						
SGA Expense						
Net Income						
Operating Cash Flow						
Capital Expenditure						
EBITDA						
Return on Assets %						
Return on Equity %						
Debt to Equity						

CONTACT INFORMATION:

Phone: 952-474-5422   Fax: 952-474-5416
Toll-Free: 877-474-5422
Address: 2411 Galpin Ct., Ste. 110, Chanhassen, MN 55317 United States

STOCK TICKER/OTHER:

Stock Ticker: Subsidiary   Exchange:
Employees: 500   Fiscal Year Ends:
Parent Company: Lift Brands Inc

SALARIES/BONUSES:

Top Exec. Salary: $ Bonus: $
Second Exec. Salary: $ Bonus: $

OTHER THOUGHTS:

Estimated Female Officers or Directors:
Hot Spot for Advancement for Women/Minorities:

Sociedade Esportiva Palmeiras

www.palmeiras.com.br

NAIC Code: 711211D

TYPES OF BUSINESS:

Soccer Team
Team Management and Operations

BRANDS/DIVISIONS/AFFILIATES:

Allianz Parque

CONTACTS: *Note: Officers with more than one job title may be intentionally listed here more than once.*

Abel Ferreira, Head Coach
Leila Pereira, Pres.

GROWTH PLANS/SPECIAL FEATURES:

Sociedade Esportiva Palmeiras is a professional football club in Brazil, playing in the Campeonato Brasileiro Serie A and Campeonato Paulista leagues. Founded in 1914, Palmeiras plays its home games in Allianz Parque, a multi-purpose stadium in Sao Paulo with a seating capacity of nearly 44,000, and the team averaging 35,943 in attendance during the 2022 Serie A season. The stadium is owned by Palmeiras. Nationally, Palmeiras has won 11 Campeonato Brasileiro Seire A titles (most recently in 2022), four Copa do Brasil titles, one Copa dos Campeoes title, two Campeonato Brasileiro Seire B titles, its first Supercopa do Brasil in 2023. Interstate titles by Palmeiras include five Torneio Rio-Sao Paulo titles and four Taca dos Campeoes Estaduais Rio-Sao Paulo titles. Statesde, the Palmerias have clenched 25 Campeonato Paulista titles (most recently in 2022 and 2023). Internationally, the club won the Copa Rio Championship in 1951, has won three Copa Libertadores titles (most recently in 2021), its first Recopa Sudamericana in 2022, and one Copa Mercosul title. Puma is the team's kit manufacturer, and Crefisa is its shirt sponsor.

FINANCIAL DATA: *Note: Data for latest year may not have been available at press time.*

In U.S. $	2022	2021	2020	2019	2018	2017
Revenue						
R&D Expense						
Operating Income						
Operating Margin %						
SGA Expense						
Net Income						
Operating Cash Flow						
Capital Expenditure						
EBITDA						
Return on Assets %						
Return on Equity %						
Debt to Equity						

CONTACT INFORMATION:

Phone: 55 11 3874 6500   Fax:
Toll-Free:
Address: Rua Palestra Italia, #214 - Perdizes, Sao Paulo, SP 05005-030 Brazil

STOCK TICKER/OTHER:

Stock Ticker: Private
Employees:
Parent Company:

Exchange:
Fiscal Year Ends:

SALARIES/BONUSES:

Top Exec. Salary: $ Bonus: $
Second Exec. Salary: $ Bonus: $

OTHER THOUGHTS:

Estimated Female Officers or Directors:
Hot Spot for Advancement for Women/Minorities:

Sales, profits and employees may be estimates. Financial Pinformation, benefits and other data can change quickly and may vary from those stated here.

Societa Sportiva Calcio Napoli (SSC Napoli)   www.sscnapoli.it

NAIC Code: 711211D

TYPES OF BUSINESS:

Soccer Team
Team Management and Operations

BRANDS/DIVISIONS/AFFILIATES:

Stadio Diego Armando Maradona

GROWTH PLANS/SPECIAL FEATURES:

Societa Sportiva Calcio Napoli (SSC Napoli) is a professional
football club playing in the Serie A league, an Italian premier
football league system. Founded in 1926, SSC Napoli is owned
by Filmauro S.r.l. and plays its home games at Stadio Diego
Armando Maradona (also referred to as Stadio San Paolo),
which has a seating capacity of over 54,500. The stadium is
owned by the community of Napoli. SCC has won the Serie A
national title three times (2022-23 most recently), with other
national titles including the Coppa Italia (6 titles) and the
Supercoppa Italian (2 titles). SSC Napoli also won the
European UEFA Cup in 1988-89. Emporio Armani is SSC
Napoli's kit manufacturer, with Lete/MSC Cruises, Floki Inu and
Amazon also sponsoring the team.

CONTACTS: Note: Officers with more than one job title may be intentionally listed here more than once.

Aurelio De Laurentis, Pres.

FINANCIAL DATA: Note: Data for latest year may not have been available at press time.

In U.S. $	2022	2021	2020	2019	2018	2017
Revenue	230,000,000	207,728,290	308,960,584	221,500,000		
R&D Expense						
Operating Income						
Operating Margin %						
SGA Expense						
Net Income			-21,335,938	32,500,000		
Operating Cash Flow						
Capital Expenditure						
EBITDA						
Return on Assets %						
Return on Equity %						
Debt to Equity						

CONTACT INFORMATION:

Phone: 39 081 5095344   Fax: 39 081 5093917
Toll-Free:
Address: Via del Maio di Porto, 9, Campania, 80133 Italy

STOCK TICKER/OTHER:

Stock Ticker: Private   Exchange:
Employees: Fiscal Year Ends: 06/30
Parent Company: Filmauro Srl

SALARIES/BONUSES:

Top Exec. Salary: $ Bonus: $
Second Exec. Salary: $ Bonus: $

OTHER THOUGHTS:

Estimated Female Officers or Directors:
Hot Spot for Advancement for Women/Minorities:

Sodexo Live!

NAIC Code: 722310

us.sodexo.com/industry/sodexo-live.html

TYPES OF BUSINESS:

Food & Beverage Concessions
Conference and Venue Management
Catering Services
Sales Services
Event Management
Food and Beverage Services
Construction and Technical Venue Services

BRANDS/DIVISIONS/AFFILIATES:

Sodexo SA

GROWTH PLANS/SPECIAL FEATURES:

Sodexo Live! Is owned by Sodexo SA, and is a leading manager of conference, cultural and sporting venues and major events throughout the world. With 500 sites, Sodexo Live! offers clients a range of bespoke catering, sales and event management services. Events managed by the firm have included the Royal Ascot, Tour de France, and Rugby World Cup, and will manage the Paris 2024 Games. Sodexo Live! range of services include food services, convenience food and beverage services, office coffee and micro-market services, concierge services, construction and technical services, employee benefits and rewards services, facilities management services, procurement services and customized/bespoke services. Industries served by Sodexo Live! span airport lounges, conference centers, cultural destinations, convention centers, global events, stadiums and arenas.

CONTACTS: *Note: Officers with more than one job title may be intentionally listed here more than once.*

Belinda Oakley, CEO
Desmond Hague, Pres.
Hadi Monavar, CFO
Ashley Brown, VP-Retail Merch.
Keith B.W. King, General Counsel
Michael Kaufman, Pres., Centerplate Restaurant Group
Adam Elliot, Pres., The Lindley Group
Paul Daly, Sr. VP-Procurement

FINANCIAL DATA: *Note: Data for latest year may not have been available at press time.*

In U.S. $	2022	2021	2020	2019	2018	2017
Revenue	221,867,100	184,889,250	142,222,500	948,150,000	860,000,000	860,000,000
R&D Expense						
Operating Income						
Operating Margin %						
SGA Expense						
Net Income						
Operating Cash Flow						
Capital Expenditure						
EBITDA						
Return on Assets %						
Return on Equity %						
Debt to Equity						

CONTACT INFORMATION:

Phone: 301-987-4000   Fax:
Toll-Free:
Address: 9801 Washingtonian Blvd., Gaithersburg, MD 20878 United States

STOCK TICKER/OTHER:

Stock Ticker: Private
Employees: 1,550
Parent Company: Sodexo SA

Exchange:
Fiscal Year Ends: 12/31

SALARIES/BONUSES:

Top Exec. Salary: $ Bonus: $
Second Exec. Salary: $ Bonus: $

OTHER THOUGHTS:

Estimated Female Officers or Directors: 1
Hot Spot for Advancement for Women/Minorities:

SoulCycle Inc

NAIC Code: 713940

www.soul-cycle.com

TYPES OF BUSINESS:

Physical Fitness Centers
Fitness Biking Studios
At-Home Fitness Bikes
Fitness Apparel
Fitness Accessories
Franchising

BRANDS/DIVISIONS/AFFILIATES:

GROWTH PLANS/SPECIAL FEATURES:

SoulCycle, Inc. is a chain of fitness centers that offer indoor cycling classes. Each 45-minute class features high-intensity cardio, muscle-sculpting strength training and rhythm-based choreography to benefit the body and the mind. The bikes are custom designed to fit every person's body. Having opened its first studio on the Upper West Side of New York, the firm has more than 80 studios across the U.S., Canada and the U.K. Corporate partnerships are offered to companies. Advanced group booking and private ride booking (one-on-one within the studio) are also available. SoulCycle also offers at-home biking workout, including immersive on-demand and live classes through stationary fitness bikes. Finance and upgrade options are available for the company's stationary bikes. SoulCycle also offers fitness apparel and accessories for men and women, and can be purchased online.

CONTACTS: *Note: Officers with more than one job title may be intentionally listed here more than once.*

Evelyn Webster, CEO

FINANCIAL DATA: *Note: Data for latest year may not have been available at press time.*

In U.S. $	2022	2021	2020	2019	2018	2017
Revenue	1,250,000,000	82,069,000	76,700,000	130,000,000	130,000,000	130,000,000
R&D Expense						
Operating Income						
Operating Margin %						
SGA Expense						
Net Income						
Operating Cash Flow						
Capital Expenditure						
EBITDA						
Return on Assets %						
Return on Equity %						
Debt to Equity						

CONTACT INFORMATION:

Phone: 212-787-7685   Fax:
Toll-Free:
Address: 609 Greenwich St., New York, NY 10014 United States

STOCK TICKER/OTHER:

Stock Ticker: Private   Exchange:
Employees: 1,600   Fiscal Year Ends:
Parent Company:

SALARIES/BONUSES:

Top Exec. Salary: $ Bonus: $
Second Exec. Salary: $ Bonus: $

OTHER THOUGHTS:

Estimated Female Officers or Directors:
Hot Spot for Advancement for Women/Minorities:

Southampton Football Club

www.saintsfc.co.uk

NAIC Code: 711211D

TYPES OF BUSINESS:
Professional Soccer Team
Team Management and Operations

BRANDS/DIVISIONS/AFFILIATES:
Sport Repbublic
Saints
Saints Foundation

CONTACTS:
Note: Officers with more than one job title may be intentionally listed here more than once.
Ruben Selles, Managing Dir.
Mauricio Pochettino, First Team Mgr.
Miguel D'Agostino, First Team Coach

GROWTH PLANS/SPECIAL FEATURES:
The Southampton Football Club, also called the Saints, is an English professional football team. The club lost its place in the English Premier League in 2005 and played in the English Championship League from 2005 to 2012. A win over Coventry City in April 2012 led to the team's return to the Premier League, the top in the English football system. Southampton finished seventh, their highest ever Premier League rank, with 60 points (2015); qualified for the 2015-16 UEFA Europa League in the 2015 FA Cup Final, but failed to make it past the playoff stage. In the 2022-23 season, the Saints came in last place in the Premier League, and were therefore relegated to the EFL Championship League. The team plays at the St. Mary's Stadium, with a seating capacity of 32,505. Southampton averaged approximately 30,388 fans in attendance per home game in the 2022-23 season. Fans may purchase paving stones or bricks with personalized engraved messages, which then become part of the stadium. Notable former Saints players include fullback Micky Adams, fullback Reuben Agboola, Derek Allan and Paul Allen. To support its community, the club provides coaching sessions for its disability football program and operates the Saints Foundation, which supports disadvantaged youth and adults. Southampton FC is 80%-owned by Sport Republic, with Katharina Liebherr owning the remaining 20%.

FINANCIAL DATA:
Note: Data for latest year may not have been available at press time.

In U.S. $	2022	2021	2020	2019	2018	2017
Revenue	220,000,000	217,628,912	155,855,000	188,424,000	231,276,000	231,276,000
R&D Expense						
Operating Income						
Operating Margin %						
SGA Expense						
Net Income		-15,152,300	-76,447,800	-42,709,400	4,378,200	4,378,200
Operating Cash Flow						
Capital Expenditure						
EBITDA						
Return on Assets %						
Return on Equity %						
Debt to Equity						

CONTACT INFORMATION:
Phone: 08-45-688-9448   Fax: 08-45-688-9445
Toll-Free:
Address: Britannia Rd., St. Mary's Stadium, Southampton, SO14 5FP United Kingdom

STOCK TICKER/OTHER:
Stock Ticker: Private
Employees: 340
Parent Company: Sport Repbublic

Exchange:
Fiscal Year Ends: 06/30

SALARIES/BONUSES:
Top Exec. Salary: $ Bonus: $
Second Exec. Salary: $ Bonus: $

OTHER THOUGHTS:
Estimated Female Officers or Directors:
Hot Spot for Advancement for Women/Minorities:

Specialized Bicycle Components Inc

www.specialized.com

NAIC Code: 336991

TYPES OF BUSINESS:

Bicycles
Biking Accessories
Biking Apparel
Bicycle Manufacture
Road and Mountain Bikes
Active Bikes
Electric Bikes
Kids Bikes

BRANDS/DIVISIONS/AFFILIATES:

Stumpjumper
Globe
Specialized Ride App

CONTACTS: *Note: Officers with more than one job title may be intentionally listed here more than once.*

Mike Sinyard, Pres.
Eric Edgecumbe, Chief Prod. Officer
Mike Sinyard, Chmn.

GROWTH PLANS/SPECIAL FEATURES:

Specialized Bicycle Components, Inc., based in California, is a manufacturer of bicycles, bike parts, accessories and related apparel. The firm's original Stumpjumper, introduced in 1981, was displayed in the Smithsonian Museum and became one of the first mass-produced mountain bikes, establishing the company as a top-seller. Today, Specialized groups its bikes into five categories: mountain, road, active, electric and kids. Mountain bikes span cross country, trail, downhill, BMX and dirt jump, along with a series of frame options. Road bikes span performance, gravel, cyclocross and triathlon, along with frame options. Active bikes are categorized into fitness, transport and comfort. Electric bikes include eBikes for the road, mountain, active cycling and the Globe active/road bike for hauling things and for recreational purposes. Kids bikes are designed for toddlers, little kids aged four through seven, and bigger kids aged seven through 10+. Innovative bike features and technology utilized by Specialized include aerodynamics, turbo-technology, FACT carbon fiber, a Specialized Ride app and more. In addition to bikes, Specialized provides related apparel, footwear, gear and components. Apparel includes jerseys, bibs, shorts, jackets, vests, base layers, warmers, tights, gloves, shirts, hats, socks and hoodies. Gear includes shoes, helmets, lights, pumps, tools, grips, tape, storage, bags, bottle cages, water bottles, commute gear and turbo extras. Components consist of tires, tubes, wheels, saddles, power meters, drivetrain, handlebars, pedals, seat posts, stems and suspension. Innovation utilized with these products encompass ANGi helmet technology, body geometry, S-Works cycling shoes and more. Specialized has worldwide retail and facility locations, including the Americas, Africa, Middle East, Europe, Asia and Asia Pacific.

Specialized Bicycle offers its employees medical, dental and vision benefits; 401(k) options; profit sharing and 529 college savings plan; and a variety of employee programs and perks.

FINANCIAL DATA: *Note: Data for latest year may not have been available at press time.*

In U.S. $	2022	2021	2020	2019	2018	2017
Revenue	660,000,000	652,365,000	621,300,000	570,000,000	560,000,000	560,000,000
R&D Expense						
Operating Income						
Operating Margin %						
SGA Expense						
Net Income						
Operating Cash Flow						
Capital Expenditure						
EBITDA						
Return on Assets %						
Return on Equity %						
Debt to Equity						

CONTACT INFORMATION:

Phone: 408-779-6229   Fax: 408-779-1631
Toll-Free: 877-808-8154
Address: 15130 Concord Cir., Morgan Hill, CA 95037 United States

STOCK TICKER/OTHER:

Stock Ticker: Private   Exchange:
Employees: 1,000   Fiscal Year Ends: 12/31
Parent Company:

SALARIES/BONUSES:

Top Exec. Salary: $ Bonus: $
Second Exec. Salary: $ Bonus: $

OTHER THOUGHTS:

Estimated Female Officers or Directors:
Hot Spot for Advancement for Women/Minorities:

Speedway Motorsports LLC

www.speedwaymotorsports.com

NAIC Code: 711212

TYPES OF BUSINESS:

Automobile Race Tracks
Motorsports Entertainment
Motorsports Sponsoring
Motorsports Marketing
Speedway Operations
Merchandising
Modified Race Car Manufacture

BRANDS/DIVISIONS/AFFILIATES:

Atlanta Motor Speedway
Bristol Motor Speedway
Charlotte Motor Speedway
Dover Motor Speedway
Kentucky Speedway
North Wilkesboro Speedway
Sonoma Raceway
Texas Motor Speedway

GROWTH PLANS/SPECIAL FEATURES:

Speedway Motorsports, LLC markets, promotes and sponsors motorsports entertainment in the U.S. Wholly-owned by Sonic Financial Corporation, the company, through its own subsidiaries, owns and operates the following facilities: Atlanta Motor Speedway, Bristol Motor Speedway, Charlotte Motor Speedway, Dover Motor Speedway, Kentucky Speedway, Las Vegas Motor Speedway, Nashville Superspeedway, New Hampshire Motor Speedway, North Wilkesboro Speedway, Sonoma Raceway, and Texas Motor Speedway. The firm provides souvenir merchandising services through SMI Properties; manufactures and distributes smaller-scale, modified racing cars and parts through U.S. Legend Cars International; and produces and broadcasts syndicated motorsports programming to radio stations through Performance Racing Network.

CONTACTS: Note: Officers with more than one job title may be intentionally listed here more than once.

Marcus G. Smith, CEO
William Brooks, CFO
Gregory Walter, Executive VP, Subsidiary
D. Hutchison, Executive VP, Subsidiary
Jerry Caldwell, Executive VP, Subsidiary
Mark Simendinger, Executive VP, Subsidiary
David McGrath, Executive VP, Subsidiary
Steve Page, General Manager, Subsidiary
William Gossage, General Manager, Subsidiary
R. Powell, President, Subsidiary

FINANCIAL DATA: Note: Data for latest year may not have been available at press time.

In U.S. $	2022	2021	2020	2019	2018	2017
Revenue	300,000,000	117,372,343	106,702,130	485,009,683	453,588,992	453,588,992
R&D Expense						
Operating Income						
Operating Margin %						
SGA Expense						
Net Income						
Operating Cash Flow						
Capital Expenditure						
EBITDA						
Return on Assets %						
Return on Equity %						
Debt to Equity						

CONTACT INFORMATION:

Phone: 704 455-3239   Fax: 704 455-2547
Toll-Free:
Address: 5555 Concord Pkwy. S., Concord, NC 28027 United States

STOCK TICKER/OTHER:

Stock Ticker: Private   Exchange:
Employees: 1,070   Fiscal Year Ends: 12/31
Parent Company: Sonic Financial Corporation

SALARIES/BONUSES:

Top Exec. Salary: $ Bonus: $
Second Exec. Salary: $ Bonus: $

OTHER THOUGHTS:

Estimated Female Officers or Directors: 1
Hot Spot for Advancement for Women/Minorities:

Sport Maska Inc (CCM Hockey)

us.ccmhockey.com

NAIC Code: 339920

TYPES OF BUSINESS:

Hockey Equipment & Apparel
Hockey Skates and Equipment
Product Manufacture
Innovation
Skate Design and Production
Skate Blade Manufacture
Metals and Finishes
Inline Skates

BRANDS/DIVISIONS/AFFILIATES:

Birch Hill Equity Partners Management Inc
CCM Hockey
STEP Skate Blades Inc
Tournament Sports Marketing Inc
Jackson
Atom

CONTACTS: *Note: Officers with more than one job title may be intentionally listed here more than once.*

Marrouane Nabih, CEO
Igor Landau, Chmn.-Adidas AG
Herbert Hainer, CEO-Adidas AG
Uli Becker, Pres., Reebok

GROWTH PLANS/SPECIAL FEATURES:

Sport Maska, Inc. operates as CCM Hockey and is a designer, manufacturer and marketer of hockey equipment and related apparel. For hockey players, the firm offers ice skates, sticks, helmets, gloves, protective gear, pucks and referee gear. For goalies, it offers skates, sticks, masks, cages and protective gear. CCM's apparel offerings include shirts, pants, tracksuits, training wear and hats, as well as team apparel. In addition, CCM designs, manufactures and sells in-line roller skates, as well as wheels and related accessories and in-line pants and padded shirts. CCM subsidiary STEP Skate Blades, Inc. specializes in the design and manufacture of blades for skates, as well as in skate blade metals and finishes; and subsidiary Tournament Sports Marketing, Inc. manufactures figure skating boots, blades and skates through its Jackson brand, and makes roller and in-line skates through its Atom brand. CCM is based in Canada and has operations in the U.S., Sweden, Finland and Taiwan. Sport Maska is privately-owned by Birch Hill Equity Partners Management, Inc., which is based in Toronto, Ontario, Canada.

CCM offers its employees benefits including health coverage, disability and life insurance and an employee pension plan, which may vary per location.

FINANCIAL DATA: *Note: Data for latest year may not have been available at press time.*

In U.S. $	2022	2021	2020	2019	2018	2017
Revenue	466,000,000	457,600,000	440,000,000	400,000,000	380,000,000	380,000,000
R&D Expense						
Operating Income						
Operating Margin %						
SGA Expense						
Net Income						
Operating Cash Flow						
Capital Expenditure						
EBITDA						
Return on Assets %						
Return on Equity %						
Debt to Equity						

CONTACT INFORMATION:

Phone: 514-461-8000   Fax:
Toll-Free:
Address: 3400 Rue Raymond Lasnier, Montreal, QC H4R 3L3 Canada

STOCK TICKER/OTHER:

Stock Ticker: Private   Exchange:
Employees: 1,303   Fiscal Year Ends: 12/31
Parent Company: Birch Hill Equity Partners Management Inc

SALARIES/BONUSES:

Top Exec. Salary: $ Bonus: $
Second Exec. Salary: $ Bonus: $

OTHER THOUGHTS:

Estimated Female Officers or Directors:
Hot Spot for Advancement for Women/Minorities:

Sporting Kansas City

www.sportingkc.com

NAIC Code: 711211D

TYPES OF BUSINESS:

Major League Soccer Team
Team Management and Operations

BRANDS/DIVISIONS/AFFILIATES:

Sporting Club
MLS Next Pro
Sporting Kansas City II

CONTACTS: *Note: Officers with more than one job title may be intentionally listed here more than once.*

Peter Vermes, Managing Dir.
Brian Bliss, Technical Dir.
Benny Feilhaber, Head Coach
Greg Cotton, General Counsel
Chris Wyche, Exec. VP-Stadium Oper.
David Ficklin, VP-Dev.
Rob Thomson, Exec. VP-Comm.
Shawn Quesnell C, Controller
Peter Vermes, Head Coach
Jamie Guin, VP-Corp. Partnerships
Jake Reid, Chief Revenue Officer
Kristin Bock, Mgr.-Sporting Club Network

GROWTH PLANS/SPECIAL FEATURES:

Sporting Kansas City is a Major League Soccer (MLS) club owned and operated by the Sporting Club group of investors. The team plays in the Western Conference of the MLS. Established in 1995 as the Kansas City Wiz, the franchise is one of the league's 10 charter members. After the 1996 season, the team officially extended its name to the Kansas City Wizards. In 2010, to coincide with the franchise's relocation to then soccer-specific Sporting Park in Kansas City, Kansas, the team took the European style moniker Sporting Kansas City. Sporting Park is now known as Children's Mercy Park, and comprises an 18,467-soccer-game seating capacity, with the team averaging 18,365 in home game attendance during the 2022 season. Over the course of the club's history, its lineup has featured star players such as Preki, Diego Guitierrez, Josh Wolff and Diego Walsh. Sporting KC won the MLS Cup in 2000 and 2013, the MLS Supporters' Shield in 2000 and the U.S. Open Cup in 2004, 2012, 2015 and 2017. In KC's 2017-18 season, they placed first in the Western Division, but lost 2-3 to the Portland Timbers in the Conference final. In 2015, the league moved the team from the Eastern Conference to the Western Conference, along with the Houston Dynamo. In addition, Sporting KC has a reserve team, Sporting Kansas City II, that began play in the second-tier USL Championship and switched to MLS Next Pro in 2022. MLS Next Pro is classified as part of the third tier of the U.S. soccer league system.

FINANCIAL DATA: *Note: Data for latest year may not have been available at press time.*

In U.S. $	2022	2021	2020	2019	2018	2017
Revenue	13,883,625					
R&D Expense						
Operating Income						
Operating Margin %						
SGA Expense						
Net Income						
Operating Cash Flow						
Capital Expenditure						
EBITDA						
Return on Assets %						
Return on Equity %						
Debt to Equity						

CONTACT INFORMATION:

Phone: 913-387-3400   Fax: 913-387-3401
Toll-Free: 888-452-4625
Address: 2020 Baltimore Ave., Kansas City, MO 64108 United States

STOCK TICKER/OTHER:

Stock Ticker: Private   Exchange:
Employees: 260   Fiscal Year Ends:
Parent Company:

SALARIES/BONUSES:

Top Exec. Salary: $ Bonus: $
Second Exec. Salary: $ Bonus: $

OTHER THOUGHTS:

Estimated Female Officers or Directors: 4
Hot Spot for Advancement for Women/Minorities: Y

Sports Illustrated

NAIC Code: 511120

TYPES OF BUSINESS:

Sports Magazine
Ecommerce Merchandising
Online Journalism
Sports Magazine
Sports Content
Sports Ticketing

BRANDS/DIVISIONS/AFFILIATES:

Authentic Brands Group LLC
Arena Group Holdings Inc (The)
SI
Fannation
SI Swimsuit
Spun (The)
SI Sportsbook
SI Tickets

CONTACTS: *Note: Officers with more than one job title may be intentionally listed here more than once.*

Ryan Hunt, Co-Editor in Chief
Stephen Cannella, Co-Editor in Chief
Mark Ford, Pres.
Scott Smith, Sr. Dir.-Tech. Solutions
Craig Coffey, Dir.-Magazine & Digital Eng.
Joan Rosinsky, Dir.-Admin.
Judith R. Margolin, Dir.-Legal
Luisa Durante, Dir.-Oper
Julie Souza, VP-Bus. Dev.
Vivek Shah, Pres., SI Digital
Emily Christopher, Associate Dir.-Communications
Elissa Fishman, Sr. VP-Finance
Martha Nelson, Editor-in-Chief
Paul Fichtenbaum, Managing Editor-SI.com
David Clarke, Managing Editor-SI Golf Group
Brad Smith, Dir.-Photography

GROWTH PLANS/SPECIAL FEATURES:

Sports Illustrated (SI) is an American sports magazine owned by Authentic Brands Group, LLC and published by The Arena Group Holdings, Inc. Originally published in 1954, SI has evolved from being a weekly print-only magazine into an ecosystem of print and digital sports-related content, media, live events and sports betting, as well as interests in other industries including hospitality, tourism and fashion/apparel. As for sports, SI covers the NFL, NBA, MLB, NCAAF, Soccer, Golf, NHL, NCAAB, WNBA and MMA, as well as fantasy sports. The company's si.com website also offers links for fans (Fannation), the popular SI Swimsuit issue, The Spun sport stories and interviews, the SI Sportsbook, the SI Tickets link for purchasing tickets to games, and the SI Shop which offers SI apparel, accessories and other merchandise.

FINANCIAL DATA: *Note: Data for latest year may not have been available at press time.*

In U.S. $	2022	2021	2020	2019	2018	2017
Revenue	625,000,000	610,500,000	555,000,000	600,000,000	575,000,000	575,000,000
R&D Expense						
Operating Income						
Operating Margin %						
SGA Expense						
Net Income						
Operating Cash Flow						
Capital Expenditure						
EBITDA						
Return on Assets %						
Return on Equity %						
Debt to Equity						

CONTACT INFORMATION:

Phone: 212-522-1212   Fax: 212-522-0475
Toll-Free: 800-528-5000
Address: 1271 Avenue of the Americas, Fl. 32, New York, NY 10020
United States

STOCK TICKER/OTHER:

Stock Ticker: Subsidiary   Exchange:
Employees: 625   Fiscal Year Ends: 12/31
Parent Company: Authentic Brands Group LLC

SALARIES/BONUSES:

Top Exec. Salary: $ Bonus: $
Second Exec. Salary: $ Bonus: $

OTHER THOUGHTS:

Estimated Female Officers or Directors: 8
Hot Spot for Advancement for Women/Minorities: Y

Sportsmans Guide Inc (The)

www.sportsmansguide.com

NAIC Code: 451110

TYPES OF BUSINESS:

Outdoor & Hunting Products
Online & Catalog Sales
Outdoor Apparel & Footwear
Boating Supplies
Military Surplus Gear

BRANDS/DIVISIONS/AFFILIATES:

Northern Tool & Equipment Company Inc
SportsmansGuide.com
Buyers Club (The)
Buyers Advantage Catalog
Guide Gear
Bolderton
HQ Issue
Castle Creek

CONTACTS: *Note: Officers with more than one job title may be intentionally listed here more than once.*

Franz Weiglein, CEO
Tim Arland, Sr. VP-e-commerce

GROWTH PLANS/SPECIAL FEATURES:

The Sportsman's Guide, Inc. is a multi-channel direct marketer of value-priced outdoor gear and clothing, golf equipment and general merchandise. The company sells its products through main and specialty catalogs and ecommerce site, SportsmansGuide.com. The firm's main catalog is mailed monthly and offers merchandise across a broad range of categories. Additional specialized catalogs are also offered during the course of each year and focus on individual categories such as camping, government surplus, ammunition and shooting supplies, gifts and hunting. The Buyers' Club, which customers can join for an annual fee, offers discounts on most merchandise; a monthly Buyer's Advantage Catalog; and exclusive special offers, discounts and coupons. The Sportsman's Guide e-commerce site offers a selection similar to its print catalog in addition to certain specialty categories available exclusively online. An online resource center features a variety of articles, advice columns and information about outdoor lifestyles and pursuits, including a section specifically aimed at female outdoor enthusiasts. In addition, customers can find maps, fish and game forecasts, local guide and outfitter listings, ballistics charts, useful links and other information on the website. Merchandise orders can be placed 24-hours-a-day by phone or online, and the company ships all orders directly from its 591,000-square-foot warehouse. The Sportsman's Guide operates as a subsidiary of Northern Tool & Equipment Company, Inc.

FINANCIAL DATA: *Note: Data for latest year may not have been available at press time.*

In U.S. $	2022	2021	2020	2019	2018	2017
Revenue						
R&D Expense						
Operating Income						
Operating Margin %						
SGA Expense						
Net Income						
Operating Cash Flow						
Capital Expenditure						
EBITDA						
Return on Assets %						
Return on Equity %						
Debt to Equity						

CONTACT INFORMATION:

Phone: 651-451-3030   Fax: 651-450-6130
Toll-Free: 800-888-3006
Address: 411 Farwell Ave. S., St. Paul, MN 55075-0239 United States

STOCK TICKER/OTHER:

Stock Ticker: Subsidiary   Exchange:
Employees: 755   Fiscal Year Ends: 12/31
Parent Company: Northern Tool & Equipment Company Inc

SALARIES/BONUSES:

Top Exec. Salary: $ Bonus: $
Second Exec. Salary: $ Bonus: $

OTHER THOUGHTS:

Estimated Female Officers or Directors:
Hot Spot for Advancement for Women/Minorities:

Sportverein Werder Bremen von 1899 eV
NAIC Code: 711211D

www.werder.de/en

TYPES OF BUSINESS:
Soccer Team
Team Management and Operations

BRANDS/DIVISIONS/AFFILIATES:

GROWTH PLANS/SPECIAL FEATURES:
Sportverein Werder Bremen von 1899 eV (Werder Bremen) is a professional sports club in Germany. Werder Bremen is primarily known for their team that plays in the Bundesliga league, the second division of professional football in Germany. The football club plays its home games at Weserstadion, a multi-purpose stadium in Bremen, Germany, with a seating capacity of over 42,000. Werder Bremen averaged 41,526 in attendance during the 2022-23 season. Weserstadion is owned and operated by Bremer Weser-Stadion GmbH. Domestically, Werder Bremen has won 4 Bundesliga titles, one 2. Bundesliga Nord title, six DFB-Pokal titles, one DFL-Ligapokal title, three DFL-Supercups, and one DFB-Hallenpokal title. Internationally, the club won the European Cup Winners' Cup in 1991-92, and won the UEFA Intertoto Cup in 1998. Other sports via Werder Bremen include baseball, chess, cricket, tennis and various types of athletics.

CONTACTS: *Note: Officers with more than one job title may be intentionally listed here more than once.*
Ole Werner, Head Coach
Hubertus hess-Grunewald, Pres.

FINANCIAL DATA: *Note: Data for latest year may not have been available at press time.*

In U.S. $	2022	2021	2020	2019	2018	2017
Revenue						
R&D Expense						
Operating Income						
Operating Margin %						
SGA Expense						
Net Income						
Operating Cash Flow						
Capital Expenditure						
EBITDA						
Return on Assets %						
Return on Equity %						
Debt to Equity						

CONTACT INFORMATION:
Phone: 49 0180 5937337   Fax:
Toll-Free:
Address: Franz-Bohmert-StraÃŸe 1c, Bremen, 28205 Germany

STOCK TICKER/OTHER:
Stock Ticker: Private   Exchange:
Employees: Fiscal Year Ends:
Parent Company:

SALARIES/BONUSES:
Top Exec. Salary: $ Bonus: $
Second Exec. Salary: $ Bonus: $

OTHER THOUGHTS:
Estimated Female Officers or Directors:
Hot Spot for Advancement for Women/Minorities:

St Louis Blues

blues.nhl.com

NAIC Code: 711211F

TYPES OF BUSINESS:

Professional Hockey Team (NHL)
Team Management and Operations

BRANDS/DIVISIONS/AFFILIATES:

SLB Acquisition Holdings LLC
Springfield Thunderbirds

GROWTH PLANS/SPECIAL FEATURES:

The St. Louis Blues franchise is a Missouri-based professional ice hockey team owned by SLB Acquisition Holdings, LLC. Founded in 1967, the team was one of the six expansion teams during the year, and was named after W. C. Handy's Saint Louis Blues song. The hockey club plays in the Central division of the Western conference within the National Hockey League (NHL). The Blues' home arena is Enterprise Center, an 18,096-seat arena in downtown St. Louis, with the team averaging 18,075 fans in attendance during the 2022-23 season. The hockey team clenched its first and only Stanley Cup and conference championship in 2018-19 after defeating Eastern conference champion Boston Bruins in four out of seven games. The St. Louis Blues have a total of 10 division titles. The team is affiliated with the Springfield Thunderbirds of the American Hockey League (AHL). In December 2022, Forbes estimated the Blues' value to be $880 million.

CONTACTS: Note: Officers with more than one job title may be intentionally listed here more than once.

Chris Zimmerman, Pres.
Doug Armstrong, Pres.-Hockey Oper.
Phil Siddle, CFO
Steve Chapman, CMO
Jamie Sackman, Chief People Officer
Matt Gardner, VP-Innovation & Digital Strategy
Dave Taylor, Pres., Hockey Oper.
Michael Caruso, VP-Public Rel.
Keith Hegger, Controller
Todd Lambert, Sr. VP-Sales
John Urban, Sr. VP-Events and Booking
Ken Hitchcock, Head Coach
Eric Stisser, Sr. VP-Corporate Sponsorship
Tom Stillman, Chmn.

FINANCIAL DATA: Note: Data for latest year may not have been available at press time.

In U.S. $	2022	2021	2020	2019	2018	2017
Revenue	129,350,000					
R&D Expense						
Operating Income						
Operating Margin %						
SGA Expense						
Net Income						
Operating Cash Flow						
Capital Expenditure						
EBITDA						
Return on Assets %						
Return on Equity %						
Debt to Equity						

CONTACT INFORMATION:

Phone: 314-622-2500   Fax: 314-622-2582
Toll-Free:
Address: 1401 Clark Ave., St. Louis, MO 63103-2709 United States

STOCK TICKER/OTHER:

Stock Ticker: Private   Exchange:
Employees: 190   Fiscal Year Ends: 06/30
Parent Company:

SALARIES/BONUSES:

Top Exec. Salary: $ Bonus: $
Second Exec. Salary: $ Bonus: $

OTHER THOUGHTS:

Estimated Female Officers or Directors: 34
Hot Spot for Advancement for Women/Minorities: Y

Sales, profits and employees may be estimates. Financial information, benefits and other data can change quickly and may vary from those stated here.

St Louis Cardinals

www.mlb.com/cardinals

NAIC Code: 711211A

TYPES OF BUSINESS:

Professional Baseball Team
Team Management and Operations

BRANDS/DIVISIONS/AFFILIATES:

St Louis Brown Stockings

CONTACTS: *Note: Officers with more than one job title may be intentionally listed here more than once.*

William O. DeWitt, Jr., CEO
Dan Good, VP-Bus. Dev.
Brad Wood, CFO
Dan Farrell, Sr. VP-Mktg. & Sales
Felicia Lamar, Mngr.-Human Resources
Perry Yee, Dir.-IT
Vicki Bryant, VP-Merch. & Event Svcs.
Mike Whittle, General Counsel
Joe Abernathy, VP-Stadium Oper.
Ron Watermon, Dir.-Public Rel. & Civic Affairs
John Lowry, Dir.-Acct.
John Mozeliak, Sr. VP
Frederick O. Hanser, Vice Chmn.
Joe Strohm, VP-Ticket Sales
Mike Matheny, Mgr.
William O. DeWitt, Jr., Chmn.
Moises Rodriguez, Dir.-Int'l Oper.
Mark Murray, Dir.-Purchasing & Cost Analysis

GROWTH PLANS/SPECIAL FEATURES:

The St. Louis Cardinals are one of the oldest teams in Major League Baseball (MLB), playing in the Central Division of the National League. The franchise began as the St. Louis Brown Stockings of the American Association in 1882 and has played under its current name since 1900. A long-time rival of the Chicago Cubs, the Cardinals have been far more successful, with a total of 11 World Series victories, 19 NL pennants, four AA pennants, and 15 division titles (East-1960-1993 and Central-1994 to present). Led by player/manager Rogers Hornsby, the team shocked the world in 1926 by beating the New York Yankees in the World Series. The team was a contender for many years to come, and in the 1930s had a group of players known as the Gashouse Gang, which featured such legends as Dizzy Dean, Joe Medwick, Pepper Martin and Leo Durocher. The 1940s were its best decade by far, as the team won three World Series and featured star player Stan Musial. The team won three more pennants in the 1960s and three in the 1980s. In the latter decade, the Cardinals were noted for speedy runners and a sparkling defense, with a roster featuring Vince Coleman, Ozzie Smith, Willie McGee, Jack Clark, Bruce Sutter and others. In 2006, the Cardinals began playing in a new $365 million facility, the third to be named Busch Stadium III. Home game attendance averaged 40,994 in the 2022 season. Current owner, William DeWitt, Jr., purchased the ballclub in 1996 for $150 million. Forbes estimated the team's worth at $2.55 billion in March 2023. The organization's Ballpark Village is a commercial use development located next to the stadium, featuring retail shops, restaurants and sports viewing experiences.

FINANCIAL DATA: *Note: Data for latest year may not have been available at press time.*

In U.S. $	2022	2021	2020	2019	2018	2017
Revenue	502,500,000					
R&D Expense						
Operating Income						
Operating Margin %						
SGA Expense						
Net Income						
Operating Cash Flow						
Capital Expenditure						
EBITDA						
Return on Assets %						
Return on Equity %						
Debt to Equity						

CONTACT INFORMATION:

Phone: 314-345-9600   Fax: 314-345-9523
Toll-Free:
Address: 700 Clark St., St. Louis, MO 63102 United States

STOCK TICKER/OTHER:

Stock Ticker: Private   Exchange:
Employees: 500   Fiscal Year Ends: 10/31
Parent Company:

SALARIES/BONUSES:

Top Exec. Salary: $ Bonus: $
Second Exec. Salary: $ Bonus: $

OTHER THOUGHTS:

Estimated Female Officers or Directors: 6
Hot Spot for Advancement for Women/Minorities: Y

St Louis City SC

NAIC Code: 711211D

www.stlcitysc.com

TYPES OF BUSINESS:

Soccer (Futbol/Football) Teams
Team Management and Operations

BRANDS/DIVISIONS/AFFILIATES:

GROWTH PLANS/SPECIAL FEATURES:

St. Louis City SC is an American professional men's soccer club based in Missouri, playing in the Western Conference of Major League Soccer (MLS). Founded in 2019, St. Louis City joined the MLS in 2023 as an expansion team. The club plays its home games at CityPark, a soccer-specific stadium nearby Union Station in downtown St. Louis, with a capacity to seat 22,500 fans. As of June 2023, St. Louis City was averaging 22,423 in home game attendance for the 2023 season. The team played its first MLS match against Austin FC, winning 3-2; and played its first home game against Charlotte FC before a sold-out crowd, winning 3-1. Adidas is St. Louis City's kit manufacturer, and Purina and BJC HealthCare are the shirt and sleeve sponsors, respectively. St. Louis City is privately-owned by Carolyn Kindle, Jo Ann Taylor Kindle and Jim Kavanaugh.

CONTACTS: *Note: Officers with more than one job title may be intentionally listed here more than once.*

Bradley Carnell, Head Coach
Carolyn Kindle, Chmn.

FINANCIAL DATA: *Note: Data for latest year may not have been available at press time.*

In U.S. $	2022	2021	2020	2019	2018	2017
Revenue						
R&D Expense						
Operating Income						
Operating Margin %						
SGA Expense						
Net Income						
Operating Cash Flow						
Capital Expenditure						
EBITDA						
Return on Assets %						
Return on Equity %						
Debt to Equity						

CONTACT INFORMATION:

Phone: 314-339-7128   Fax:
Toll-Free:
Address: 326 S. 21st St., St. Louis, MO 63103 United States

STOCK TICKER/OTHER:

Stock Ticker: Private   Exchange:
Employees: Fiscal Year Ends:
Parent Company:

SALARIES/BONUSES:

Top Exec. Salary: $ Bonus: $
Second Exec. Salary: $ Bonus: $

OTHER THOUGHTS:

Estimated Female Officers or Directors:
Hot Spot for Advancement for Women/Minorities:

Sales, profits and employees may be estimates. Financial information, benefits and other data can change quickly and may vary from those stated here.

Tampa Bay Buccaneers
www.buccaneers.com

NAIC Code: 711211C

TYPES OF BUSINESS:

Professional Football Team
Team Management and Operations

BRANDS/DIVISIONS/AFFILIATES:

CONTACTS: *Note: Officers with more than one job title may be intentionally listed here more than once.*

Jason Licht, General Mngr.
Edward Glazer, Co-Chmn.
Joe Fada, CFO
James Ruth, CMO
Kristin Hamwey, VP-Human Resources
Todd Toriscelli, Dir.-Sports Medicine & Performance
Joel Glazer, Co-Chmn.
Spencer Dille, Dir.-Football Tech.
Jim Pyne, Chief Partnership Officer
Andres Trescastro, Dir.-Corp. Security & Facilities
Connie Mojallal, Dir.-Special Events & Game Oper.
Matt Kaiser, Dir.-New Bus. Dev.
Clark Moss, Dir.-Creative Svcs.
Jeff Ryan, Dir.-Broadcast Oper.
Greg Schiano, Head Coach
Edward Glazer, Co-Chmn.
Joel Glazer, Co-Chmn.
Mark Dominik, Gen. Mgr.
Bryan Glazer, Co-Chmn.

GROWTH PLANS/SPECIAL FEATURES:

The Tampa Bay Buccaneers franchise is a professional football team playing in the National Football League (NFL) as part of the Southern Division of the National Football Conference (NFC). Professional football came to Tampa as part of the 1976 NFL expansion. Nicknamed the Bucs by fans, the team had a bumpy start, losing every game its first season and all but two the next. The team was able to turn these poor records around quickly, earning a spot in the playoffs for the first time in its fourth season. The Buccaneers' success was short-lived, as the team only managed two winning seasons between 1980 and 1996. The team's rosters have included many football greats, such as Vinny Testaverde, Warrick Dunn, Steve Young, Keyshawn Johnson, Warren Sapp, Tom Brady and Rob Gronkowski. In 1996, Malcolm Glazer, owner of Manchester United (a top club in England's FA Premier League) bought the team for $192 million, the highest sum paid for a professional sports franchise at that time. The introduction of new head coach Tony Dungy brought the team back to respectability, achieving a division title in 1999. Under the ownership of the Glazer family, the Buccaneers has reached the playoffs several times (2020, 2021 and 2022 most recently) and won the Super Bowl in seasons 2001-02 and 2020-21. The Buccaneers have eight division championships, three in NFC Central and five in NFC South (2021 and 2022 most recently). The team plays in the 65,618-seat Raymond James Stadium, which opened in 1998, and share the stadium with the University of South Florida football team. The Buccaneers averaged 68,988 in home game attendance during the 2022-23 season. Forbes estimated the Tampa Bay Buccaneers' value to be $3.675 billion in 2022.

FINANCIAL DATA: *Note: Data for latest year may not have been available at press time.*

In U.S. $	2022	2021	2020	2019	2018	2017
Revenue	508,950,000					
R&D Expense						
Operating Income						
Operating Margin %						
SGA Expense						
Net Income						
Operating Cash Flow						
Capital Expenditure						
EBITDA						
Return on Assets %						
Return on Equity %						
Debt to Equity						

CONTACT INFORMATION:

Phone: 813-870-2700   Fax: 813-878-0813
Toll-Free:
Address: 1 Buccaneer Pl., Tampa, FL 33607 United States

STOCK TICKER/OTHER:

Stock Ticker: Private   Exchange:
Employees: 450   Fiscal Year Ends: 12/31
Parent Company:

SALARIES/BONUSES:

Top Exec. Salary: $ Bonus: $
Second Exec. Salary: $ Bonus: $

OTHER THOUGHTS:

Estimated Female Officers or Directors: 5
Hot Spot for Advancement for Women/Minorities: Y

Tampa Bay Lightning
NAIC Code: 711211F

lightning.nhl.com

TYPES OF BUSINESS:
Professional Hockey Team (NHL)
Team Management and Operations

BRANDS/DIVISIONS/AFFILIATES:
VSG Enterprises LLC
Syracuse Crunch
Orlando Solar Bears

CONTACTS: *Note: Officers with more than one job title may be intentionally listed here more than once.*
Steve Griggs, CEO
Mark Pitts, COO
Casey Rodgers, CFO
Matt Corey, CMO
Nicole Parente, VP-People Operations
Andrew McIntyre, Sr. VP-Technology & Innovation
Jim Shimberg, General Counsel
Bill Wickett, Exec. VP-Mktg. & Comm.
Doug Riefler, VP-Finance
Lynn Wittenburg, Sr. VP-Mktg.
Phil Esposito, VP-Corp. Relations
Dave Andreychuk, VP-Corp & Community Affairs
Jeff Vinik, Chmn.

GROWTH PLANS/SPECIAL FEATURES:
The Tampa Bay Lightning hockey club is a National Hockey League (NHL) team that plays in the Atlantic division of the Eastern conference. The team was founded in 1992 by former NHL player Phil Esposito as an expansion franchise. Although the Lightning met with success in its early years, it floundered in the following years due to mismanagement and financial troubles from its backing by a consortium of Japanese businesses headed by Kokusai Green, a Japanese golf course and resort operator. When Kokusai Green decided to sell the Lightning in 1997, the team had debt equaling 236% of its value. The team's ownership has changed hands several times since. Currently, the team is owned by investment banker Jeff Vinik through his company, VSG Enterprises LLC. In 2003-04, Tampa Bay Lightning clenched its first Stanley Cup after beating the Calgary Flames in seven games. The Lightning club won two more Stanley Cups in 2019-20 and 2020-21, and has also earned four Conference championships (most recently in 2021-22), and a President's Trophy (2018-19). Lightning home games are usually sold out at the Amalie Arena, which has a hockey seating capacity of about 19,092. Minor league affiliates include the Syracuse Crunch of the American Hockey League (AHL), and the Orlando Solar Bears of the ECHL. In December 2022, Forbes estimated Tampa Bay Lightning's value to be $1 billion.

FINANCIAL DATA: *Note: Data for latest year may not have been available at press time.*

In U.S. $	2022	2021	2020	2019	2018	2017
Revenue	133,250,000					
R&D Expense						
Operating Income						
Operating Margin %						
SGA Expense						
Net Income						
Operating Cash Flow						
Capital Expenditure						
EBITDA						
Return on Assets %						
Return on Equity %						
Debt to Equity						

CONTACT INFORMATION:
Phone: 813-301-6500   Fax: 813-301-1487
Toll-Free:
Address: 401 Channelside Dr., Tampa, FL 33602 United States

STOCK TICKER/OTHER:
Stock Ticker: Private
Employees: 390
Parent Company:

Exchange:
Fiscal Year Ends: 06/30

SALARIES/BONUSES:
Top Exec. Salary: $ Bonus: $
Second Exec. Salary: $ Bonus: $

OTHER THOUGHTS:
Estimated Female Officers or Directors: 9
Hot Spot for Advancement for Women/Minorities: Y

Tampa Bay Rays

NAIC Code: 711211A

www.mlb.com/rays

TYPES OF BUSINESS:

Professional Baseball Team
Team Management and Operations

BRANDS/DIVISIONS/AFFILIATES:

Durham Bulls
Montgomery Biscuits
Bowling Green Hot Rods
Charleston RiverDogs

CONTACTS: *Note: Officers with more than one job title may be intentionally listed here more than once.*

Brian Auld, Co-Pres.
Matthew Silverman, Co-Pres.
Rob Gagliardi, CFO
Patrick Abts, VP-Mktg.
Jennifer Lyn Tran, Chief People & Culture Officer
Juan Ramirez, CTO
Darcy Raymond, VP-Branding & Fan Experience
John Higgins, Sr. VP-Admin.
John Higgins, General Counsel
Brian Auld, Sr. VP-Bus. Oper.
Michael Kalt, Sr. VP-Dev. & Bus. Affairs
Rick Vaughn, VP-Comm.
Rob Gagliardi, VP-Finance
Andrew Friedman, Exec. VP-Baseball Oper.
Rick Nafe, VP-Oper. & Facilities
Brian Richeson, VP-Sales & Svcs.
Joe Maddon, Mgr.
Stuart Sternberg, Principal
Carlos Alfonso, Dir.-Latin American Scouting
Bill Wiener, Jr., Sr. Dir.-Procurement & Bus. Svcs.

GROWTH PLANS/SPECIAL FEATURES:

The Tampa Bay Rays is a team within Major League Baseball (MLB) that was formed as part of the 1998 league expansion. The genesis of the Rays was difficult, with many bids to place a team in St. Petersburg, Florida (the team's home) but none panning out until a group led by Vince Naimoli gained approval in the 1998 expansion. Once the team was off the ground, it finished in last place in its division every season from 1998 to 2003. The Rays signed legendary manager Lou Piniella during the 2003 off-season, and in 2004, finished with a 70-91 record. In 2005, Stuart Sternberg led a group that purchased a controlling interest of the team from Naimoli. In 2008, the club won the American League Pennant for the first time in club history and advanced to the World Series, where it was defeated by the Philadelphia Phillies. The Rays clenched another AL Pennant in 2020, but lost to the Los Angeles Dodgers in the World Series. The club has four AL East Division titles, most recently in seasons 2020 and 2021. The Rays is affiliated with several minor league teams, including the Durham Bulls, the Montgomery Biscuits, the Bowling Green Hot Rods and the Charleston RiverDogs. The team plays at Tropicana Field, an artificial turf stadium with a 42,735-spectator capacity. Average home attendance for the Rays was 13,927 during the 2022 season. Forbes estimated the team to be worth $1.25 billion in March 2023.

FINANCIAL DATA: *Note: Data for latest year may not have been available at press time.*

In U.S. $	2022	2021	2020	2019	2018	2017
Revenue	250,000,000					
R&D Expense						
Operating Income						
Operating Margin %						
SGA Expense						
Net Income						
Operating Cash Flow						
Capital Expenditure						
EBITDA						
Return on Assets %						
Return on Equity %						
Debt to Equity						

CONTACT INFORMATION:

Phone: 727-825-3137   Fax: 727-825-3111
Toll-Free: 888-326-7297
Address: 1 Tropicana Dr., St. Petersburg, FL 33705 United States

STOCK TICKER/OTHER:

Stock Ticker: Private   Exchange:
Employees: 550   Fiscal Year Ends: 10/31
Parent Company:

SALARIES/BONUSES:

Top Exec. Salary: $ Bonus: $
Second Exec. Salary: $ Bonus: $

OTHER THOUGHTS:

Estimated Female Officers or Directors: 8
Hot Spot for Advancement for Women/Minorities: Y

Team Penske

NAIC Code: 711219

TYPES OF BUSINESS:

Racing Teams
Race Cars

BRANDS/DIVISIONS/AFFILIATES:

Penske Corporation
Porsche Penske Motorsport

CONTACTS: *Note: Officers with more than one job title may be intentionally listed here more than once.*

Tim Cindric, Pres.
Ron Ruzewski, Race Eng.
Roger S. Penske, Chmn.

GROWTH PLANS/SPECIAL FEATURES:

Team Penske was founded in 1966 and is an American professional auto racing organization owned by Penske Corporation. Team Penske competes in the IndyCar Series, NASCAR Cup Series, IMSA SportsCar Championship and FIA World Endurance Championship. The organization has also competed in various types of professional racing such as Formula One, Can-Am, Trans-Am and Australian Supercars. Cars owned and prepared by Team Penske have produced more than 610 major race wins, over 670 pole positions and 43 championships across open-wheel, stock car and sports car racing competition. The team has also earned 19 Indianapolis 500 victories, three Daytona 500 Championships, a Formula 1 win, victories in the 24 Hours of Daytona and the 12 Hours of Sebring, along with a win in Australia's Bathurst 1000 race. For the 2023 season, Team Penske competes in the NTT IndyCar Series and the NASCAR Cup Series. In addition, the organization has a new global partnership with Porsche, enabling Porsche Penske Motorsport to compete in the IMSA WeatherTech SportsCar Championship and the World Endurance Championship for the 2023 season.

FINANCIAL DATA: *Note: Data for latest year may not have been available at press time.*

In U.S. $	2022	2021	2020	2019	2018	2017
Revenue	15,100,000	14,729,000	14,300,000	65,000,000	63,000,000	63,000,000
R&D Expense						
Operating Income						
Operating Margin %						
SGA Expense						
Net Income						
Operating Cash Flow						
Capital Expenditure						
EBITDA						
Return on Assets %						
Return on Equity %						
Debt to Equity						

CONTACT INFORMATION:

Phone: 704-664-2300   Fax:
Toll-Free:
Address: 200 Penske Way, Mooresville, NC 28115 United States

STOCK TICKER/OTHER:

Stock Ticker: Subsidiary   Exchange:
Employees: 170   Fiscal Year Ends:
Parent Company: Penske Corporation

SALARIES/BONUSES:

Top Exec. Salary: $ Bonus: $
Second Exec. Salary: $ Bonus: $

OTHER THOUGHTS:

Estimated Female Officers or Directors:
Hot Spot for Advancement for Women/Minorities:

Tecnica Group SpA

www.tecnicagroup.com

NAIC Code: 339920

TYPES OF BUSINESS:

Sports Equipment
Ski & Snowboard Equipment
Technical Clothing
In-Line Skates
Outdoor Footwear
Ski Boots
Ski Manufacture
Research and Development

BRANDS/DIVISIONS/AFFILIATES:

Blizzard
Nordica
Lowa
Moon Boot
Rollerblade
Tecnica

CONTACTS: *Note: Officers with more than one job title may be intentionally listed here more than once.*

Giovanni Zoppas, CEO
Giancarlo Zanatta, Pres.
Maurizio Di Trani, Dir.-Comm.
Alberto Zanatta, Chmn.

GROWTH PLANS/SPECIAL FEATURES:

Tecnica Group SpA is an Italian manufacturer and marketer of active sports products, primarily footwear. Tecnica utilizes innovation and technology to develop and manufacture its footwear products, which span trekking, hiking and ski boots, as well as outdoor shoes and inline skates. The company's trekking and hiking footwear solutions include customized shapes for each foot. The measurements take about 20-minutes' time, from which the company uses to tailor-make the shoes. The shoes offer a high level of foothold, support and comfort. Ski boots are designed for racing, all-mountain performance, sport performance, mountain freeriding, touring and more. Boots are made for men, women and kids. Inline skates can include innovations and features such as brake systems, toolless adjustable kids skates, and closure systems. Skates are made for every type of skater and every type of skate discipline. Tecnica also offers an array of related accessories, including socks, face guards, apparel, hats, backpacks, sole kits, fit kits, ski boot liners, ski boot buckles and other components. Blizzard and Nordica are subsidiaries of Tecnica Group that specialize in the manufacture of skis, including alpine skis. Other brands of Tecnica include Lowa, Moon Boot, Rollerblade and Tecnica. Tecnica Group is headquartered in Italy, and has an international office in Germany, as well as research and development, modeling and prototype, and logistics and warehousing locations throughout the world.

FINANCIAL DATA: *Note: Data for latest year may not have been available at press time.*

In U.S. $	2022	2021	2020	2019	2018	2017
Revenue	475,000,000	468,000,000	450,000,000	474,800,000		
R&D Expense						
Operating Income						
Operating Margin %						
SGA Expense						
Net Income						
Operating Cash Flow						
Capital Expenditure						
EBITDA						
Return on Assets %						
Return on Equity %						
Debt to Equity						

CONTACT INFORMATION:

Phone: 39-0422-8841   Fax: 39-0422-775-178
Toll-Free:
Address: Via Fante D'Italia 56, Giavera del Montello, 31040 Italy

STOCK TICKER/OTHER:

Stock Ticker: Private   Exchange:
Employees: 3,150   Fiscal Year Ends: 12/31
Parent Company:

SALARIES/BONUSES:

Top Exec. Salary: $ Bonus: $
Second Exec. Salary: $ Bonus: $

OTHER THOUGHTS:

Estimated Female Officers or Directors:
Hot Spot for Advancement for Women/Minorities:

Tennessee Titans

www.titansonline.com

NAIC Code: 711211C

TYPES OF BUSINESS:

Professional Football Team
Team Management and Operations

BRANDS/DIVISIONS/AFFILIATES:

Houston Oilers

CONTACTS: *Note: Officers with more than one job title may be intentionally listed here more than once.*

Burke Nihill, CEO
Daniel Werly, COO
Shannon Myers, CFO
Gil Beverly, CMO
Allie Lessmiller, VP-People & Culture
Kenneth S. Adams, IV, Co-Chmn.
Don MacLachlan, Exec. VP-Admin. & Facilities
Elza Bullock, General Counsel
Stuart Spears, VP-Bus. Oper. & Sales
Gary Glenn, Dir.-Internet Oper. & Publications
Robbie Bohren, Dir.-Media Rel.
Ruston Webster, Exec. VP
Mike Munchak, Head Coach
Vincent Marino, VP-Football Admin.
Tina Tuggle, Dir.-Player Dev.
Amy Adams Strunk, Co-Chmn.

GROWTH PLANS/SPECIAL FEATURES:

The Tennessee Titans is a National Football League (NFL) team owned by the family of the late K.S. (Bud) Adams. Established in 1959, the Titans were originally known as the Houston Oilers and played in the American Football League, but moved to Nashville in 1996 after local voters approved the use of public funding to construct a new stadium downtown. The team began to play at the stadium in 1999, which was called the Adelphia Coliseum until 2002 and became the Nissan Stadium in 2016. It is a multi-purpose stadium is owned by the Metropolitan Government of Nashville and Davidson County, with a seating capacity of 69,143. The Titans averaged 68,616 fans in attendance per home game during the 2022-23 season. The football team won two AFL championships (1960 and 1961), but has yet to win an NFL Superbowl title. In total, the Titans have clenched one AFC Conference championship, 11 AFL and AFC Division championships (most recently in 2020 and 2021 AFC), and have made the playoffs 25 times (AFL and NFL), most recently in 2019, 2020 and 2021 NFL. The team currently plays in the AFC South conference, alongside the Jacksonville Jaguars, Indianapolis Colts and Houston Texans. Notable players have included Steve McNair, Eddie George, Frank Wycheck, Drew Bennett and Samari Rolle. Forbes estimated the Titans at $3.5 billion in 2022.

FINANCIAL DATA: *Note: Data for latest year may not have been available at press time.*

In U.S. $	2022	2021	2020	2019	2018	2017
Revenue	504,400,000					
R&D Expense						
Operating Income						
Operating Margin %						
SGA Expense						
Net Income						
Operating Cash Flow						
Capital Expenditure						
EBITDA						
Return on Assets %						
Return on Equity %						
Debt to Equity						

CONTACT INFORMATION:

Phone: 615-565-4000   Fax:
Toll-Free:
Address: 460 Great Circle Rd., Nashville, TN 37228 United States

STOCK TICKER/OTHER:

Stock Ticker: Private   Exchange:
Employees: 220   Fiscal Year Ends: 03/31
Parent Company:

SALARIES/BONUSES:

Top Exec. Salary: $ Bonus: $
Second Exec. Salary: $ Bonus: $

OTHER THOUGHTS:

Estimated Female Officers or Directors: 4
Hot Spot for Advancement for Women/Minorities: Y

Sales, profits and employees may be estimates. Financial information, benefits and other data can change quickly and may vary from those stated here.

Texas Rangers

NAIC Code: 711211A

www.mlb.com/rangers

TYPES OF BUSINESS:

Professional Baseball Team
Team Management and Operations

BRANDS/DIVISIONS/AFFILIATES:

Rangers Baseball Express LLC
Round Rock Express
Frisco RoughRidgers
Hickory Crawdads
Down East Wood Ducks

CONTACTS: *Note: Officers with more than one job title may be intentionally listed here more than once.*

Chris Young, General Manager
Neil Leibman, Pres.
Kellie Fischer, CFO
Travis Dillon, Sr. VP-Mktg.
Jeff Miller, VP-Human Resources
Mike Bullock, Sr. VP-IT
Kate Cassidy, Associate Counsel
Rick George, Pres., Bus. Oper.
Joe Januszewski, Exec. VP-Bus. Partnerships & Dev.
Kaylan Eastepp, Dir.-Interactive & Social Media Mktg.
John Blake, Exec. VP-Comm.
Starr Gulledge, Controller
Bob Simpson, Co-Chmn.
Jim Sundberg, Sr. Exec. VP
Rob Matwick, Exec. VP-Ballpark & Event Oper.
Ron Washington, Mgr.
Ray C. Davis, Managing Partner
Mike Daly, Dir.-Int'l Oper.

GROWTH PLANS/SPECIAL FEATURES:

The Texas Rangers are a Major League Baseball (MLB) team based in Arlington, Texas, playing in the East Division of the American League (AL). The team began as the third incarnation of the Washington Senators in 1961, but moved to Texas and became the Rangers in 1972. Despite three previous postseason appearances, in 1996, 1998 and 1999, the club finally made it to the World Series in 2010, but lost to the San Francisco Giants in five games. The team repeated its success in 2011, winning the AL West crown and advancing to the World Series, only to fall short of the championship for a second straight year. In total, the club has clenched seven Western Division titles (2016 most recently) as well as the two American League Pennants. Popular ex-players include shortstop Alex Rodriguez, Sammy Sosa and Hall-of-Fame pitcher Nolan Ryan (former Rangers CEO). The team plays at the Globe Life Park in Arlington, a 48,114-seat open-air ballpark. The Rangers averaged 24,831 in home game attendance during the 2022 season. Minor league affiliates include the Round Rock Express, Frisco RoughRiders, Hickory Crawdads, and Down East Wood Ducks. After former team owner Hicks Sports Group Holdings LLC (an entity controlled by Thomas O. Hicks) filed for bankruptcy in 2010, the club was sold to Rangers Baseball Express, LLC, an investor group that includes Ray Davis and Bob Simpson. Forbes valued the team at $2.225 billion in March 2023.

FINANCIAL DATA: *Note: Data for latest year may not have been available at press time.*

In U.S. $	2022	2021	2020	2019	2018	2017
Revenue	541,500,000					
R&D Expense						
Operating Income						
Operating Margin %						
SGA Expense						
Net Income						
Operating Cash Flow						
Capital Expenditure						
EBITDA						
Return on Assets %						
Return on Equity %						
Debt to Equity						

CONTACT INFORMATION:

Phone: 817-273-5222   Fax: 817-273-5174
Toll-Free:
Address: 1000 Ballpark Way, Ste. 400, Arlington, TX 76011 United States

STOCK TICKER/OTHER:

Stock Ticker: Private   Exchange:
Employees: 625   Fiscal Year Ends: 12/31
Parent Company:

SALARIES/BONUSES:

Top Exec. Salary: $ Bonus: $
Second Exec. Salary: $ Bonus: $

OTHER THOUGHTS:

Estimated Female Officers or Directors: 10
Hot Spot for Advancement for Women/Minorities: Y

Topgolf Callaway Brands Corp

www.callawaygolf.com

NAIC Code: 339920

TYPES OF BUSINESS:

Golf Equipment
Custom Club Fitting
Golf Apparel
Golf Entertainment

BRANDS/DIVISIONS/AFFILIATES:

Callaway Golf
Odyssey
CallawayGolfPreOwned.com
Topgolf International Inc

GROWTH PLANS/SPECIAL FEATURES:

Topgolf Callaway Brands Corp is a modern golf and active lifestyle company that provides world-class golf entertainment experiences, designs and manufactures premium golf equipment, and sells golf and active lifestyle apparel and other accessories. It operates in the below segments: Topgolf; Golf Equipment and Active Lifestyle. Some of its brands are Odyssey, OGIO, TravisMathew, and Jack Wolfskin. Its geographical segments are the United States, Europe, Japan, and the Rest of the World. Majority of the revenue is earned from United States.

Callaway offers medical, dental, vision, prescription and life insurance; and employee assistance plans.

CONTACTS: Note: Officers with more than one job title may be intentionally listed here more than once.

Oliver Brewer, CEO
Brian Lynch, CFO
John Lundgren, Chairman of the Board
Jennifer Thomas, Chief Accounting Officer
Erik Anderson, Director
Mark Leposky, Executive VP, Divisional
Glenn Hickey, Executive VP, Divisional
Joseph Flannery, Executive VP, Divisional

FINANCIAL DATA: Note: Data for latest year may not have been available at press time.

In U.S. $	2022	2021	2020	2019	2018	2017
Revenue	3,995,700,000	3,133,400,000	1,589,500,000	1,701,063,000	1,048,736,000	1,048,736,000
R&D Expense	76,400,000	68,000,000	46,300,000	50,579,000	36,568,000	36,568,000
Operating Income	256,800,000	204,700,000	68,800,000	132,668,000	78,837,000	78,837,000
Operating Margin %	.06%	.07%	.04%	.08%	.08%	.08%
SGA Expense	2,047,500,000	1,581,200,000	542,500,000	583,540,000	365,043,000	365,043,000
Net Income	157,900,000	322,000,000	-126,900,000	79,408,000	40,806,000	40,806,000
Operating Cash Flow	-35,100,000	278,300,000	228,200,000	86,550,000	117,699,000	117,699,000
Capital Expenditure	535,500,000	322,300,000	39,200,000	54,702,000	26,203,000	26,203,000
EBITDA	477,500,000	622,000,000	-41,100,000	169,213,000	90,025,000	90,025,000
Return on Assets %	.02%	.07%	-.06%	.05%	.05%	.05%
Return on Equity %	.04%	.15%	-.18%	.11%	.07%	.07%
Debt to Equity	.87%	.78%	1.226	0.757	0.015	0.015

CONTACT INFORMATION:

Phone: 760 931-1771   Fax: 760 931-8013
Toll-Free:
Address: 2180 Rutherford Rd., Carlsbad, CA 92008 United States

STOCK TICKER/OTHER:

Stock Ticker: MODG   Exchange: NYS
Employees: 32,000   Fiscal Year Ends: 12/31
Parent Company:

SALARIES/BONUSES:

Top Exec. Salary: $1,000,000   Bonus: $
Second Exec. Salary: Bonus: $
$547,883

OTHER THOUGHTS:

Estimated Female Officers or Directors:
Hot Spot for Advancement for Women/Minorities:

Topps Company Inc (The)

www.topps.com

NAIC Code: 311351

TYPES OF BUSINESS:

Candy & Gum Manufacturing
Collectibles
Trading Cards
Promotional Products
Marketing Products
Rewards Program
Digital Trading

BRANDS/DIVISIONS/AFFILIATES:

Fanatics Inc

CONTACTS: *Note: Officers with more than one job title may be intentionally listed here more than once.*

Michael Brandstaedter, CEO
Michael Bramlage, VP-Digital

GROWTH PLANS/SPECIAL FEATURES:

The Topps Company, Inc. is a producer and marketer of sport and entertainment products, as well as chewing gum. Product categories include trading cards, collectibles, memorabilia and cards that can be customized. Topps' website also provides a range of digital apps, NTF digital collectibles, and offers promotional events spanning areas such as major league baseball, international card trading, social media contests and marketing opportunities for consumers. Topps partners include iPlayers, Major League Baseball, Disney, Star Wars, Marvel, National Hockey League, NHL Players' Association, UEFA Champions League, Bundesliga, Major League Soccer and UEFA Europa League. Topps also offers collectibles and products that are not related to sports, including Elvis Presley and Garbage Pail Kids. Topps offers a rewards program in which consumers earn points that can be redeemed for Topps merchandise. Fanatics, Inc. owns The Topps Company, Inc. In early-2023, Topps released art work from original race posters from 1923 to the present for their partner's 24 Hours of Le Mans Motorsport event (24H of Le Mans), and are currently obtainable through Topps' U.K. platform.

FINANCIAL DATA: *Note: Data for latest year may not have been available at press time.*

In U.S. $	2022	2021	2020	2019	2018	2017
Revenue						
R&D Expense						
Operating Income						
Operating Margin %						
SGA Expense						
Net Income						
Operating Cash Flow						
Capital Expenditure						
EBITDA						
Return on Assets %						
Return on Equity %						
Debt to Equity						

CONTACT INFORMATION:

Phone: 212-376-0300   Fax: 212-376-0573
Toll-Free:
Address: One Whitehall St., New York, NY 10004 United States

STOCK TICKER/OTHER:

Stock Ticker: Joint Venture   Exchange:
Employees: 422   Fiscal Year Ends: 02/28
Parent Company: Fanatics Inc

SALARIES/BONUSES:

Top Exec. Salary: $ Bonus: $
Second Exec. Salary: $ Bonus: $

OTHER THOUGHTS:

Estimated Female Officers or Directors:
Hot Spot for Advancement for Women/Minorities:

Sales, profits and employees may be estimates. Financial information, benefits and other data can change quickly and may vary from those stated here.

Toronto Blue Jays

www.mlb.com/bluejays

NAIC Code: 711211A

TYPES OF BUSINESS:

Professional Baseball Team
Team Management and Operations

BRANDS/DIVISIONS/AFFILIATES:

Rogers Communications Inc
Buffalo Bisons
New Hampshire Fisher Cats
Vancouver Canadians
Dunedin Blue Jays

CONTACTS: *Note: Officers with more than one job title may be intentionally listed here more than once.*

Mark A. Shapiro, CEO
Paul Beeston, Pres.
Ben Colabrese, Exec. VP.-Finance
Ben Sibley, Dir.-Mktg., Communications & Lotteries
Matt Phinney, VP-People Operations
Anthony Miranda, VP-Technology
Anthony Partipilo, VP-Merch.
Matthew Shuber, Legal Counsel
Stephen R. Brooks, Sr. VP-Bus. Oper.
John Griffin, Dir.-Bus. Dev. & Corp. Partnerships
Jay Stenhouse, VP-Comm.
Lynda Kolody, Controller
Alex Anthopoulos, Gen. Mgr.
Howard Starkman, VP-Special Projects
Mark Ditmars, VP-Corp. Partnerships
Mario Coutinho, VP-Stadium Oper. & Security
Edward Rogers, Chmn.
Helen Maunder, Dir.-Purchasing

GROWTH PLANS/SPECIAL FEATURES:

The Toronto Blue Jays are a Major League Baseball (MLB) team playing in the Eastern Division of the American League (AL). The club was founded in 1976 as the second MLB expansion team in Canada (the now defunct Montreal Expos were the first). The original owners of the franchise consisted of Imperial Trust Ltd., Labatt's Breweries and the Canadian Imperial Bank of Commerce. Today, the team is owned by Rogers Communications Inc., a leading cable television and wireless phone service provider in Canada. The Blue Jays had a strong run of postseason play in the late '80s and early '90s, including consecutive World Series victories in 1992 and 1993. Beyond its World Series and AL Pennants, the Blue Jays have six AL East Division titles, most recently in 2015. The club's home stadium is the Rogers Centre, which is situated next to the CN Tower in downtown Toronto and features a 348-room hotel in center field; a capacity to seat 49,282 spectators; one of the largest Jumbotron scoreboards in the world; and a VIP seating section with amenities including a gourmet restaurant, in-seat food service, a wine lounge and a high-end bar. The team averaged 32,763 fans in attendance per home game during the 2022 season. Minor League affiliations include the Buffalo Bisons, New Hampshire Fisher Cats, Vancouver Canadians, and Dunedin Blue Jays. Forbes estimated the value of the Blue Jays at $2.1 billion in March 2023.

FINANCIAL DATA: *Note: Data for latest year may not have been available at press time.*

In U.S. $	2022	2021	2020	2019	2018	2017
Revenue	255,000,000	238,000,000	265,000,000	265,000,000	278,000,000	278,000,000
R&D Expense						
Operating Income						
Operating Margin %						
SGA Expense						
Net Income		-52,000,000	16,000,000	-16,000,000	22,900,000	22,900,000
Operating Cash Flow						
Capital Expenditure						
EBITDA						
Return on Assets %						
Return on Equity %						
Debt to Equity						

CONTACT INFORMATION:

Phone: 416-341-1000   Fax:
Toll-Free:
Address: 1 Blue Jays Way, Ste. 3200, Toronto, ON M5V 1J1 Canada

STOCK TICKER/OTHER:

Stock Ticker: Subsidiary   Exchange:
Employees: 585   Fiscal Year Ends: 12/31
Parent Company: Rogers Communications Inc

SALARIES/BONUSES:

Top Exec. Salary: $ Bonus: $
Second Exec. Salary: $ Bonus: $

OTHER THOUGHTS:

Estimated Female Officers or Directors: 14
Hot Spot for Advancement for Women/Minorities: Y

Sales, profits and employees may be estimates. Financial information, benefits and other data can change quickly and may vary from those stated here.

Toronto FC

NAIC Code: 711211D

TYPES OF BUSINESS:

Major League Soccer Team
Team Management and Operations

BRANDS/DIVISIONS/AFFILIATES:

Maple Leaf Sports & Entertainment Ltd

CONTACTS: *Note: Officers with more than one job title may be intentionally listed here more than once.*

Bill Manning, Pres.
Chris Shewfelt, VP-Bus. Oper.
Damien Hall, Sr. Dir.-Finance
Corey Wray, Mgr.-Team Oper.
Earl Cochrane, Dir.-Team & Player Oper.
Paul Beirne, VP-Bus. Oper.
Cesar Velasco, Sr. Dir.-Comm.
Ryan Nelsen, Head Coach
Pat Onstead, Chief Scout
Breagha Carr-Harris, Mgr.-Community Sports Partnerships

GROWTH PLANS/SPECIAL FEATURES:

Toronto FC, established in 2005, is a Canadian soccer franchise that plays in the Major League Soccer (MLS) organization. The club was the first Canadian team to enter MLS, extending the league's reach outside of the U.S. The team is owned and operated by Maple Leaf Sports & Entertainment Ltd. The Toronto FC moniker is a throwback to the European tradition of calling city football clubs by the initials FC. Home games are played at the soccer-specific BMO Field (short for Bank of Montreal), with a seating capacity of 30,991. Toronto FC averaged 25,427 in home game attendance during the 2022 season. The MLS club plays in the Eastern Conference along with Atlanta United FC, Charlotte FC, Chicago Fire FC, FC Cincinnati, Columbus Crew, DC United, Inter Miami CF, CF Montreal, Nashville SC, New England Revolution, New York City FC, New York Red Bulls, Orlando City SC and Philadelphia Union. The team won the Canadian Championship four consecutive years (2009-2012) and three consecutive years (2016-2018). In the 2016 season, Toronto FC were the Cup Playoffs Eastern Conference champions, obtaining its first MLS cup appearance, but lost in the final game at home to the Seattle Sounders, 4-5. During the 2017 season, the team returned to the MLS Cup finals and clenched the win after defeating the Sounders 2-0. That same season (2017), Toronto FC won the Supporters' Shield and the Canadian Championship. In fact, Toronto FC has eight Canadian Championship titles (2020 most recently).

FINANCIAL DATA: *Note: Data for latest year may not have been available at press time.*

In U.S. $	2022	2021	2020	2019	2018	2017
Revenue	41,000,000	24,230,500	21,070,000	43,000,000	48,000,000	48,000,000
R&D Expense						
Operating Income						
Operating Margin %						
SGA Expense						
Net Income				-19,000,000		
Operating Cash Flow						
Capital Expenditure						
EBITDA						
Return on Assets %						
Return on Equity %						
Debt to Equity						

CONTACT INFORMATION:

Phone: 416-360-4625　　　Fax: 416-815-6050
Toll-Free:
Address: 170 Princes' Blvd., Toronto, ON M6K 3C3 Canada

STOCK TICKER/OTHER:

Stock Ticker: Private　　　　　Exchange:
Employees: 100　　　　　　　Fiscal Year Ends: 06/30
Parent Company: Maple Leaf Sports & Entertainment Ltd

SALARIES/BONUSES:

Top Exec. Salary: $　　　Bonus: $
Second Exec. Salary: $　　Bonus: $

OTHER THOUGHTS:

Estimated Female Officers or Directors: 2
Hot Spot for Advancement for Women/Minorities:

Toronto Maple Leafs

www.nhl.com/mapleleafs

NAIC Code: 711211F

TYPES OF BUSINESS:

Professional Hockey Team (NHL)
Team Management and Operations

BRANDS/DIVISIONS/AFFILIATES:

Maple Leaf Sports & Entertainment Ltd
Toronto Marlies
Newfoundland Growlers

CONTACTS: *Note: Officers with more than one job title may be intentionally listed here more than once.*

Brendan Shanahan, Pres.
Brad Treliving, General Mngr.

GROWTH PLANS/SPECIAL FEATURES:

The Toronto Maple Leafs hockey club is an ice hockey team playing in the Atlantic division of the Eastern conference within the National Hockey League (NHL). The team was founded in 1917 as one of the original six NHL clubs. The Maple Leafs started out as the Toronto Arenas, but due to financial difficulties, the Arenas withdrew from the NHL shortly after their first season. The team reemerged in the 1919-20 season, this time as the Toronto St. Patricks. In 1927, Conn Smythe purchased the team and re-christened them the Maple Leafs, and in 1931, he gave the team a new stadium, Maple Leaf Gardens. The franchise (while still the Arenas) won the Stanley Cup in its first season (1917), and would do so 12 more times (most recently in 1966-67). During the 1970s and 80s, the Maple Leafs wallowed in relative obscurity and failure, but in the 90s, the club looked primed to bounce back into contention, clenching the division title in 2020-21, but lost to the Montreal Canadiens in the first round of the playoffs. The Leafs play their home games in the Scotiabank Arena, which seats 18,800 hockey spectators and 20,270 with standing room. The franchise averaged 18,753 in home game attendance during the 2022-23 season. Maple Leaf Sports & Entertainment Ltd. owns the franchise as well as the NBA's Toronto Raptors. The team's minor league affiliations are the Toronto Marlies in the American Hockey League (AHL), and the Newfoundland Growlers in the ECHL. In December 2022, Forbes estimated the Leafs' value at $2 billion.

FINANCIAL DATA: *Note: Data for latest year may not have been available at press time.*

In U.S. $	2022	2021	2020	2019	2018	2017
Revenue	210,000,000	101,000,000	223,000,000	243,000,000	211,000,000	211,000,000
R&D Expense						
Operating Income						
Operating Margin %						
SGA Expense						
Net Income		-32,000,000	56,000,000	101,000,000	76,000,000	76,000,000
Operating Cash Flow						
Capital Expenditure						
EBITDA						
Return on Assets %						
Return on Equity %						
Debt to Equity						

CONTACT INFORMATION:

Phone: 416-703-5323   Fax: 416-359-9205
Toll-Free:
Address: 50 Bay St., Ste. 500, Toronto, ON M5J 2L2 Canada

STOCK TICKER/OTHER:

Stock Ticker: Private   Exchange:
Employees: 90   Fiscal Year Ends: 06/30
Parent Company: Maple Leaf Sports & Entertainment Ltd

SALARIES/BONUSES:

Top Exec. Salary: $ Bonus: $
Second Exec. Salary: $ Bonus: $

OTHER THOUGHTS:

Estimated Female Officers or Directors: 1
Hot Spot for Advancement for Women/Minorities:

Toronto Raptors

www.nba.com/raptors

NAIC Code: 711211B

TYPES OF BUSINESS:

Professional Basketball Team
Team Management and Operations

BRANDS/DIVISIONS/AFFILIATES:

Maple Leaf Sports & Entertainment Ltd
Welcome Toronto

CONTACTS: *Note: Officers with more than one job title may be intentionally listed here more than once.*

Masai Ujiri, Pres.
Bobby Webster, Gen. Mngr.
Peter Miller, General Counsel
Ed Stefanski, Exec. VP-Basketball Oper.
Ian Clarke, Exec. VP-Bus. Dev.
Jim LaBumbard, Dir.-Media Rel.
Kevin Nonomura, Sr. VP-Finance
Dwayne Casey, Head Coach
Beth Robertson, Sr. VP-Ticket Sales & Service
Chris Hebb, Sr. VP-Content & Comm.
Maurizio Gherardini, VP-Intl. Scouting

GROWTH PLANS/SPECIAL FEATURES:

The Toronto Raptors, established as an expansion franchise in 1995, is a professional basketball team playing in the National Basketball Association (NBA) and based in Toronto, Ontario. The Raptors have won the Atlantic Division seven times in 2007, 2014, 2015, 2016, 2018, 2019 and 2020. The team clenched its first and only Conference title (Eastern) and NBA Championship in 2019. The club's standout players have included Damon Stoudamire, Chris Bosh, DeMar DeRozan, Kyle Lowry and Hakeem Olajuwon; and Vince Carter, who led the team from his 1998-99 rookie season until being traded in 2004. Maple Leaf Sports & Entertainment Ltd. owns the Raptors. The franchise plays its home games at the Scotiabank Arena, which is also owned by Maple Leaf and holds more than 19,800 basketball fans. The Raptors averaged 19,786 in home game attendance during the 2022-23 season. Raptors 905 is an affiliate of the Toronto Raptors, playing in the NBA G League based in Ontario. In October 2022, Forbes estimated the Toronto Raptors to be worth $3.1 billion.

FINANCIAL DATA: *Note: Data for latest year may not have been available at press time.*

In U.S. $	2022	2021	2020	2019	2018	2017
Revenue	300,000,000	194,000,000	264,000,000	334,000,000	250,000,000	250,000,000
R&D Expense						
Operating Income						
Operating Margin %						
SGA Expense						
Net Income		2,100,000	79,000,000	79,000,000	51,000,000	51,000,000
Operating Cash Flow						
Capital Expenditure						
EBITDA						
Return on Assets %						
Return on Equity %						
Debt to Equity						

CONTACT INFORMATION:

Phone: 416-815-5600   Fax: 416-359-9213
Toll-Free:
Address: 40 Bay St., Air Canada Centre, Ste. 500, Toronto, ON M5J 2L2 Canada

STOCK TICKER/OTHER:

Stock Ticker: Private   Exchange:
Employees: 150   Fiscal Year Ends: 06/30
Parent Company: Maple Leaf Sports & Entertainment Ltd

SALARIES/BONUSES:

Top Exec. Salary: $ Bonus: $
Second Exec. Salary: $ Bonus: $

OTHER THOUGHTS:

Estimated Female Officers or Directors: 3
Hot Spot for Advancement for Women/Minorities: Y

Tottenham Hotspur Football Club

www.tottenhamhotspur.com

NAIC Code: 711211D

TYPES OF BUSINESS:

Soccer Team
Team Management and Operations

BRANDS/DIVISIONS/AFFILIATES:

ENIC Group
ENIC International Limited
Spurs

CONTACTS: *Note: Officers with more than one job title may be intentionally listed here more than once.*

Matthew J. Collecott, Dir.-Finance
Andre Villas-Boas, Mgr.
Daniel P. Levy, Chmn.

GROWTH PLANS/SPECIAL FEATURES:

Tottenham Hotspur Football Club, founded in 1882, is an English Premier League soccer team. ENIC International Limited, a subsidiary of ENIC Group, is the majority-owner (approximately 85%) of the team. The name Hotspur is thought to come from Sir Henry Percy, immortalized as Harry Hotspur in Shakespeare's King Henry IV, Part I. The team, also known as the Spurs, plays their home games at the Tottenham Hotspur Stadium, a multi-purpose stadium that seats more than 62,000 spectators, one of the largest in the Premier League. The club averaged 60,094 spectators at home games during the 2022-23 season. In 1960-61, the Spurs became the first team in the 20th century to win the both the Football League Cup and Football Association (FA) Cup, sometimes called a Double. The franchise has consistently been one of London's top soccer teams and has enjoyed a long-standing rivalry with nearby competitors Arsenal. Domestically, the Spurs have won two First Division Premier League and two Second Division Championship titles, eight FA Cups, four League Cups and seven FA Charity Shields/Community Shields. Internationally, they've won the UEFA Cup Winners' Cup once and the UEFA Cup twice. Beyond the men's professional soccer team, the franchise sponsors youth feeder teams, a semi-professional women's team, and development courses for improving soccer techniques and abilities for local youth. Forbes valued Hotspur FC at $2.803 billion in May 2023.

FINANCIAL DATA: *Note: Data for latest year may not have been available at press time.*

In U.S. $	2022	2021	2020	2019	2018	2017
Revenue	485,000,000	461,060,082	359,680,544	604,256,000	397,259,000	397,259,000
R&D Expense						
Operating Income						
Operating Margin %						
SGA Expense						
Net Income		-140,461,727	-117,208,485	89,976,100	53,440,100	53,440,100
Operating Cash Flow						
Capital Expenditure						
EBITDA						
Return on Assets %						
Return on Equity %						
Debt to Equity						

CONTACT INFORMATION:

Phone: 44 844499500   Fax: 1992761608
Toll-Free:
Address: 782 High Rd., Tottenham, N17 OBX United Kingdom

STOCK TICKER/OTHER:

Stock Ticker: Private   Exchange:
Employees: 541   Fiscal Year Ends: 06/30
Parent Company: ENIC Group

SALARIES/BONUSES:

Top Exec. Salary: $ Bonus: $
Second Exec. Salary: $ Bonus: $

OTHER THOUGHTS:

Estimated Female Officers or Directors:
Hot Spot for Advancement for Women/Minorities:

Trek Bicycle Corporation

NAIC Code: 336991

www.trekbikes.com

TYPES OF BUSINESS:

Bicycles
Cycling Accessories and Apparel
Bicycle Manufacturing
Bicycle Design and Development

BRANDS/DIVISIONS/AFFILIATES:

Roth Distributing Co Inc
IsoSpeed
Madone
Super
Bontrager
Electra
Trek Factory Racing
Fuel EX

CONTACTS: *Note: Officers with more than one job title may be intentionally listed here more than once.*

John Burke, Pres.
Denise DeMarb, Dir.-Finance
Maureen Muldoon, Dir.-Int'l Sales

GROWTH PLANS/SPECIAL FEATURES:

Trek Bicycle Corporation is a designer and manufacturer of high-performance bicycles and cycling products for men, women and children. The company manufactures a variety of bicycles such as electric, electric mountain, mountain, cross country, trail, downhill, fat bikes, road, cyclocross, gravel, hybrid, urban/commuter, fitness, triathlon, adventure, touring, and customized. The firm has consistently been engaged in innovation and technology, introducing OCLV carbon bikes in 1992, Alpha Aluminum bikes, Active Braking Pivot rear suspension, RE:aktiv rear suspension, full floater shocks, IsoSpeed decoupler, Fuel Exe pin ring motor, and more. Some of Trek's best-known bike models are the Madone, Super Commuter+, Domane, Top Fuel, 1120, Marlin, CrossRip+, Roscoe, FX 3 Disc, Remedy, Session, Emonda ALR, Fuel EX/EXe, among others. Equipment offered by Trek include tires, wheels, helmets, lights, saddles, related computers/global positioning systems (GPS), handlebars, grips, brakes, levers, cables, stems & seat posts, water bottles & cages, pedals, tubes, tubeless accessories, pumps, bags, baskets, racks, fenders, locks, mirrors, bells, horns, cycling glasses, trailers, car racks, bike storage, kickstands, protective gear, nutrition, skin care products and more. Apparel includes arm/leg warmers, base layers, booties and toe covers, casual wear, cycling caps, headwear, gloves, jackets, jerseys, shoes, shorts, bibs, socks, tights/pants, t-shirts and team wear. Trek retailers are located worldwide, including North America, South America, the U.K., Europe and Asia. Primary brands of the company include Trek, Bontrager, Electra and Trek Travel. The firm is privately owned by Roth Distributing Co., Inc.

FINANCIAL DATA: *Note: Data for latest year may not have been available at press time.*

In U.S. $	2022	2021	2020	2019	2018	2017
Revenue	1,290,000,000	1,280,000,000	1,362,500,000	1,250,000,000	1,100,000,000	1,100,000,000
R&D Expense						
Operating Income						
Operating Margin %						
SGA Expense						
Net Income						
Operating Cash Flow						
Capital Expenditure						
EBITDA						
Return on Assets %						
Return on Equity %						
Debt to Equity						

CONTACT INFORMATION:

Phone: 920-478-2191   Fax: 920-478-2774
Toll-Free:
Address: 801 W. Madison St., Waterloo, WI 53594 United States

STOCK TICKER/OTHER:

Stock Ticker: Private   Exchange:
Employees: 2,000   Fiscal Year Ends: 09/30
Parent Company: Roth Distributing Co Inc

SALARIES/BONUSES:

Top Exec. Salary: $ Bonus: $
Second Exec. Salary: $ Bonus: $

OTHER THOUGHTS:

Estimated Female Officers or Directors: 3
Hot Spot for Advancement for Women/Minorities: Y

Under Armour Inc

www.underarmour.com

NAIC Code: 424300

TYPES OF BUSINESS:

Apparel and Clothing Brands, Designers, Importers and Distributors
Outdoor and Sports Apparel
Shirts
Footwear
Gloves

BRANDS/DIVISIONS/AFFILIATES:

HEATGEAR
COLDGEAR
UA HOVR
UA Micro G
UA Flow
Charged Cushioning

GROWTH PLANS/SPECIAL FEATURES:

Under Armour develops, markets, and distributes athletic apparel, footwear, and accessories in North America, Asia-Pacific, Europe, and other regions. Consumers of its apparel include professional and amateur athletes, sponsored college and professional teams, and people with active lifestyles. The company sells merchandise through direct-to-consumer, including e-commerce and more than 400 combined factory house and brand house stores, and wholesale channels. Under Armour also operates a digital fitness app called MapMyFitness. The Baltimore-based company was founded in 1996.

CONTACTS: Note: Officers with more than one job title may be intentionally listed here more than once.

Patrik Frisk, CEO
David Bergman, CFO
Kevin Plank, Chairman of the Board
Aditya Maheshwari, Chief Accounting Officer
Tchernavia Rocker, Chief Administrative Officer
Alessandro de Pestel, Chief Marketing Officer
Colin Browne, COO
John Stanton, Executive VP
Lisa Collier, Other Executive Officer
Stephanie Pugliese, President, Geographical

FINANCIAL DATA: Note: Data for latest year may not have been available at press time.

In U.S. $	2022	2021	2020	2019	2018	2017
Revenue		5,683,466,000	4,474,667,000	5,267,132,000	4,989,244,000	4,989,244,000
R&D Expense						
Operating Income		526,808,000	-11,839,000	236,770,000	151,892,000	151,892,000
Operating Margin %		.09%	.00%	.04%	.03%	.03%
SGA Expense		2,334,691,000	2,171,934,000	2,233,763,000	2,099,522,000	2,099,522,000
Net Income		360,060,000	-549,177,000	92,139,000	-48,260,000	-48,260,000
Operating Cash Flow		664,829,000	212,864,000	509,031,000	237,460,000	237,460,000
Capital Expenditure		69,759,000	92,291,000	145,802,000	281,339,000	281,339,000
EBITDA		667,952,000	153,145,000	423,195,000	197,976,000	197,976,000
Return on Assets %		.07%	-.11%	.02%	-.01%	-.01%
Return on Equity %		.19%	-.29%	.04%	-.02%	-.02%
Debt to Equity		.65%	1.10	0.546	0.379	0.379

CONTACT INFORMATION:

Phone: 410 454-6428   Fax: 410 367-2400
Toll-Free: 888-727-6687
Address: 1020 Hull St., Baltimore, MD 21230 United States

STOCK TICKER/OTHER:

Stock Ticker: UA
Employees: 16,400
Parent Company:

Exchange: NYS
Fiscal Year Ends: 12/31

SALARIES/BONUSES:

Top Exec. Salary: $1,286,539   Bonus: $
Second Exec. Salary: $754,808   Bonus: $

OTHER THOUGHTS:

Estimated Female Officers or Directors:
Hot Spot for Advancement for Women/Minorities:

Underdog Sports Inc

NAIC Code: 519130

underdogfantasy.com

TYPES OF BUSINESS:

Fantasy Sports Leagues
Online Sports Betting
Fantasy Sports Platform Development
Fantasy Sports Platform Management

BRANDS/DIVISIONS/AFFILIATES:

Underdog Fantasy

GROWTH PLANS/SPECIAL FEATURES:

Underdog Sports, Inc. has developed and operates the Underdog Fantasy online and mobile fantasy sports platform. Daily, weekly, seasonal and pick'em fantasy sport options are available, with prize pools into the million-dollar category. Types of sports offered include NFL, NBA, NHL, MLB, PGA and others. Information regarding lobby badges, experience, ties, multiple entries, scoring, lineup restrictions, ineligible states, non-guaranteed contests, multiple accounts and contests, suspended accounts, cancelling entries, traded/injured players, swapping and contest integrity are provided on the Underdog Fantasy platform. Rules are also provided, such as best ball, Battle Royale, pick'em, promotions, withdrawals, privacy policy and terms. Underdog offers 24/7 support and secure payment services.

CONTACTS: *Note: Officers with more than one job title may be intentionally listed here more than once.*

Brandon Stakenborg, CEO

FINANCIAL DATA: *Note: Data for latest year may not have been available at press time.*

In U.S. $	2022	2021	2020	2019	2018	2017
Revenue						
R&D Expense						
Operating Income						
Operating Margin %						
SGA Expense						
Net Income						
Operating Cash Flow						
Capital Expenditure						
EBITDA						
Return on Assets %						
Return on Equity %						
Debt to Equity						

CONTACT INFORMATION:

Phone: 443-917-0080   Fax:
Toll-Free: 800-426-2537
Address: 150 Waterbury St., Brooklyn, NY 11206 United States

STOCK TICKER/OTHER:

Stock Ticker: Private   Exchange:
Employees: Fiscal Year Ends:
Parent Company:

SALARIES/BONUSES:

Top Exec. Salary: $ Bonus: $
Second Exec. Salary: $ Bonus: $

OTHER THOUGHTS:

Estimated Female Officers or Directors:
Hot Spot for Advancement for Women/Minorities:

Union of European Football Associations (UEFA) www.uefa.com

NAIC Code: 711211

TYPES OF BUSINESS:

Professional Soccer Association
Professional European Football Administration
European Football Governing Organization
Men's and Women's Professional European Football
Youth Football Championships
Amateur Football Championship

BRANDS/DIVISIONS/AFFILIATES:

Federation Internationale de Football Association
UEFA Champions League
UEFA Europa League
UEFA Super Cup
UEFA Youth League
UEFA Womens Champions League
UEFA Futsal Champions League
UEFA Under-19 Futsal Championship

CONTACTS: *Note: Officers with more than one job title may be intentionally listed here more than once.*

Aleksander Ceferin, Pres.
Gianni Infantino, Sec.
Senes Erzik, VP-UEFA Exec. Committee
Geoffrey Thompson, VP-UEFA Exec. Committee
Marios N. Lefkaritis, VP-UEFA Exec. Committee
Giancarlo Abete, VP-UEFA Exec. Committee

GROWTH PLANS/SPECIAL FEATURES:

The Union of European Football Associations (UEFA) is the administrative body for association football, futsal and beach soccer in Europe. It is one of six continental confederations of world football's governing body Federation Internationale de Football Association (FIFA). UEFA represents more than 50 national football association members in Europe, running national, youth/amateur, women's, club and Futsal competitions. Futsal is a type of indoor five-a-side (named because each team fields five players instead of the normal 11) soccer officially sanctioned by FIFA. The organization's main competitions include the UEFA Champions League, for national league champions, one of the most prestigious club trophies; the UEFA Europa League, a second-tier invitational for top positioned national teams in most leagues and in select leagues up to the fifth place in the standings; the UEFA Europa Conference League, an annual football club competition for eligible European football clubs; the UEFA Super Cup, a game between the winners of the Championships League and the UEFA Europa League; the UEFA Youth League, an annual competition for youth teams (under 19 years of age) of the clubs competing in the UEFA Champions League; the UEFA Women's Champions League; and the UEFA Futsal Champions League. National competitions consist of European qualifiers, UEFA Euro, UEFA Nations League, UEFA Women's Championship, championships for players under 21 years of age (male and female), UEFA Futsal Championship, UEFA Women's Futsal Championship, and UEFA Under-19 Futsal Championship. In addition, the UEFA Region's Cup is for amateur players.

FINANCIAL DATA: *Note: Data for latest year may not have been available at press time.*

In U.S. $	2022	2021	2020	2019	2018	2017
Revenue	7,100,000,000	6,814,559,290	3,417,124,304	4,384,360,000	3,395,710,000	3,395,710,000
R&D Expense						
Operating Income						
Operating Margin %						
SGA Expense						
Net Income		26,308,282	83,116,808	-52,741,500	-8,020,890	-8,020,890
Operating Cash Flow						
Capital Expenditure						
EBITDA						
Return on Assets %						
Return on Equity %						
Debt to Equity						

CONTACT INFORMATION:

Phone: 41-848-00-2727   Fax: 41-848-01-2727
Toll-Free:
Address: Route de Geneve 46, Case Postale, Nyon 2, CH-1260 Switzerland

STOCK TICKER/OTHER:

Stock Ticker: Private
Employees: 549
Parent Company:

Exchange:
Fiscal Year Ends: 06/30

SALARIES/BONUSES:

Top Exec. Salary: $ Bonus: $
Second Exec. Salary: $ Bonus: $

OTHER THOUGHTS:

Estimated Female Officers or Directors:
Hot Spot for Advancement for Women/Minorities:

United Soccer League

NAIC Code: 711211

www.uslsoccer.com

TYPES OF BUSINESS:

Soccer League
Amateur Soccer Leagues
Youth Soccer Leagues
Men's and Women's Soccer Leagues

BRANDS/DIVISIONS/AFFILIATES:

USL Championship
USL Super League
USL League One
USL League Two
USL W League
USL Super Y League
USL Academy

CONTACTS: *Note: Officers with more than one job title may be intentionally listed here more than once.*

Alec Papadakis, CEO
Justin Papadakis, COO
Karen Gittens, CFO
Greg Lalas, CMO
Rachel Bukszar, Sr. VP-People
Julie Fogarty, Dir.-Technology & Data Strategy
Peter Mellor, Dir.-National Tech.
David Wagner, Dir.-Legal Counsel
David Wagner, Dir.-Pro League Oper.
Seth Witkowicz, Dir.-New Media
Jay Preble, Dir.-Comm.
Brad Freeman, Controller
Ryan Brooks, Sr. Dir.-Premier Dev. League
Amanda Duffy, Sr. Dir.-W-League
Natalie Akula, Dir.-Youth League Oper.
Robert Hoskins, Chmn.

GROWTH PLANS/SPECIAL FEATURES:

United Soccer League (USL) is the organizer of several soccer leagues with teams in the U.S. and Canada. USL includes men's and women's leagues, both professional and amateur. The organization oversees the USL Championship (USSF Division II), USL Super League (USSF Division II women's league expected to begin play in 2024), USL League One (USSF Division III), and USL League Two (pre-professional. Women's pre-professional soccer league, USL W League, began its first season in 2022, with approximately 30 teams. USL W League is directly affiliated with the United States Soccer Federation and the United States Adult Soccer Association. USL Super Y League is a youth soccer league with teams in the U.S. and Canada, and is dedicated to the progression of future professional players. In addition, USL announced the launch of USL Academy, an elite youth platform to offer clubs in the Championship, League One and League Two, enabling the development of a soccer path for top youth prospects to reach the professional level and to sign directly with their senior team. The USL Academy is composed of four key components: Standards, USL Academy Contracts, USL Academy Cup and USL Academy League. USL is sanctioned by the U.S. Soccer Federation and Canadian Soccer Association.

FINANCIAL DATA: *Note: Data for latest year may not have been available at press time.*

In U.S. $	2022	2021	2020	2019	2018	2017
Revenue						
R&D Expense						
Operating Income						
Operating Margin %						
SGA Expense						
Net Income						
Operating Cash Flow						
Capital Expenditure						
EBITDA						
Return on Assets %						
Return on Equity %						
Debt to Equity						

CONTACT INFORMATION:

Phone: 813-963-3909   Fax: 813-963-3807
Toll-Free:
Address: 1715 N. Westshore Blvd., Ste. 825, Tampa, FL 33607 United States

STOCK TICKER/OTHER:

Stock Ticker: Private   Exchange:
Employees: Fiscal Year Ends:
Parent Company:

SALARIES/BONUSES:

Top Exec. Salary: $ Bonus: $
Second Exec. Salary: $ Bonus: $

OTHER THOUGHTS:

Estimated Female Officers or Directors: 4
Hot Spot for Advancement for Women/Minorities: Y

United States Golf Association (USGA)   www.usga.org

NAIC Code: 711211

TYPES OF BUSINESS:

Golf Association
Golf Tournaments
Youth Programs
Turf Grass Research
Golf Museum
Men's and Women's Golf
Senior Golf

BRANDS/DIVISIONS/AFFILIATES:

US Womens Open
US Open
US Senior Open
US Senior Womens Open
US Womens Amateur Four-Ball
US Amateur Four-Ball
Curtis Cup
US Junior Amateur

CONTACTS: Note: Officers with more than one job title may be intentionally listed here more than once.

Mike Whan, CEO
Susan Pikitch, CFO
Jon Podany, CCO
Chris Fraser, Chief Legal and Human Resources Officer
Ernest J. Getto, General Counsel
Jessica Carroll, Managing Dir.-Digital Media
Joe Goode, Managing Dir.-Comm.
Diana M. Murphy, Treas.
Thomas J. O'Toole, Jr., VP
Daniel R. Burton, VP
William L. Katz, Sec.
John M. Bodenhamer, Sr. Managing Dir.-Rules, Competition & Equipment

GROWTH PLANS/SPECIAL FEATURES:

The United States Golf Association (USGA) is a nonprofit national governing body for the game of golf in the U.S. and Mexico. The association was founded in 1894 to write formal rules, conduct national championships and establish a national system of handicapping; it continues to perform these duties and also supports course maintenance practices, funds grassroots programs and preserves the history of the sport in its Museum and Archives in Far Hills, New Jersey. The USGA is supported significantly by its members. The nonprofit is perhaps best known for the professional and amateur tournaments it conducts in the U.S. and internationally. USGA conducts annual national championships in addition to international and team competitions. These championships and competitions include the U.S. Women's Open, U.S. Open, U.S. Senior Open, U.S. Senior Women's Open, U.S. Adaptive Open, U.S. Women's Amateur Four-Ball, U.S. Amateur Four-Ball, Curtis Cup, U.S. Girls' Junior, U.S. Junior Amateur, U.S. Women's Amateur, U.S. Amateur, U.S. Senior Amateur, U.S. Mid-Amateur, U.S. Senior Women's Amateur, U.S. Women's Mid-Amateur and Walker Cup. Partners of the USGA include American Express, Cisco, Deloitte, Lexus, Sentry and Rolex.

FINANCIAL DATA: Note: Data for latest year may not have been available at press time.

In U.S. $	2022	2021	2020	2019	2018	2017
Revenue		566,751,050	492,827,000	210,911,000	214,999,503	214,999,503
R&D Expense						
Operating Income						
Operating Margin %						
SGA Expense						
Net Income						
Operating Cash Flow						
Capital Expenditure						
EBITDA						
Return on Assets %						
Return on Equity %						
Debt to Equity						

CONTACT INFORMATION:

Phone: 908-234-2300   Fax: 908-234-9687
Toll-Free:
Address: P.O. Box 708, Far Hills, NJ 07931 United States

STOCK TICKER/OTHER:

Stock Ticker: Private   Exchange:
Employees: 370   Fiscal Year Ends: 11/30
Parent Company:

SALARIES/BONUSES:

Top Exec. Salary: $ Bonus: $
Second Exec. Salary: $ Bonus: $

OTHER THOUGHTS:

Estimated Female Officers or Directors: 6
Hot Spot for Advancement for Women/Minorities: Y

United States Olympic & Paralympic Committee (USOPC)

www.teamusa.org
NAIC Code: 711211

TYPES OF BUSINESS:
Olympic Association
Athletic Training
Olympic Committee
Training Facilities

BRANDS/DIVISIONS/AFFILIATES:

CONTACTS: *Note: Officers with more than one job title may be intentionally listed here more than once.*
Kirsten Volpi, Chief Admin. Officer
Rana Dershowitz, General Counsel
Mike English, Chief-Sport Oper.
Patrick Sandusky, Chief Comm. Officer
Christopher G. Sullivan, Chief Bid & Protocol Officer
Charlie Huebner, Chief-U.S. Paralympics
Alan Ashley, Chief-Sport Performance
John Ruger, Athlete Ombudsman
Gene Sykes, Chmn.

GROWTH PLANS/SPECIAL FEATURES:
United States Olympic & Paralympic Committee (USOPC) was founded in 1894 and operates as a nonprofit group that serves the National Olympic Committee and the National Paralympic Committee for the U.S. The USOPC is responsible for the training, entering and funding of U.S. teams for the Olympic, Paralympic, Youth Olympic, Pan American and Parapan American Games. The committee also aids the nation's Olympic and Paralympic athletes via national governing bodies, financial support and jointly working to develop customized athlete support and coaching education programs. The USOPC supports U.S. Olympic and Paralympic on and off the playing field through programming such as direct athlete funding, health insurance, tuition grants, media/marketing opportunities, career services and performance-based monetary rewards. Olympic Training Center facilities provide athletes with performance services, including sports medicine, strength/conditioning, psychology assistance, physiology assistance, nutrition assistance and performance technology. The USOPC also oversees the process by which U.S. cities bid to host the Olympic/Paralympic Games, the Youth Olympic Games or the Pan/Parapan American Games, as well as bidding/hosting other international competitions. Therefore, the USOPC approves the U.S. trials sites and procedures for the games' team selections.

FINANCIAL DATA: *Note: Data for latest year may not have been available at press time.*

In U.S. $	2022	2021	2020	2019	2018	2017
Revenue	297,000,000	228,995,800	208,178,000	332,431,050	183,732,740	183,732,740
R&D Expense						
Operating Income						
Operating Margin %						
SGA Expense						
Net Income	-30,000,000				-30,838,170	-30,838,170
Operating Cash Flow						
Capital Expenditure						
EBITDA						
Return on Assets %						
Return on Equity %						
Debt to Equity						

CONTACT INFORMATION:
Phone: 719-866-4444   Fax:
Toll-Free: 888-222-2313
Address: One Olympic Plaza, Colorado Springs, CO 80909 United States

STOCK TICKER/OTHER:
Stock Ticker: Private   Exchange:
Employees: 675   Fiscal Year Ends: 12/31
Parent Company:

SALARIES/BONUSES:
Top Exec. Salary: $ Bonus: $
Second Exec. Salary: $ Bonus: $

OTHER THOUGHTS:
Estimated Female Officers or Directors: 12
Hot Spot for Advancement for Women/Minorities: Y

United States Tennis Association (USTA)

www.usta.com

NAIC Code: 711211

TYPES OF BUSINESS:

Tennis Association
Tennis Facilities
Sports Marketing
Amateur Tennis Organization
Professional Tennis Organization

BRANDS/DIVISIONS/AFFILIATES:

USTA Billie Jean King National Tennis Center

CONTACTS: Note: Officers with more than one job title may be intentionally listed here more than once.

Lew Sherr, CEO
Dave Haggerty, Pres.
Andrea Hirsch, Chief Admin. Officer
Andrea Hirsch, General Counsel
Carlos Lakomy, Dir.-Oper. & Tech.
Chris Widmaier, Managing Dir.-Corp. Comm.
Joseph Healy, Controller
D.A. Abrams, Chief Diversity & Inclusion Officer
Kurt Kamperman, CEO-Community Tennis Dev.
Patrick McEnroe, Gen. Mgr.-Player Dev.
Rich Coiro, Sr. Dir.-Finance
Ed Brandt, Dir.-Purchasing

GROWTH PLANS/SPECIAL FEATURES:

The United States Tennis Association (USTA), a nonprofit organization, is the U.S. governing body for the sport of tennis and one of the largest tennis organizations in the world. USTA comprises individual members of all age and skill levels, as well as organizational members. The organization sets the rules of tennis and develops and promotes the sport at the local and professional level. At the local level, USTA supports a wide range of programs designed to help people learn and play tennis, including a flex league, where players play matches in their spare time. At the professional level, the organization operates as a sports marketing, entertainment and media group that generates revenue through television, sponsorship, ticket sales, merchandising, membership and advanced media. Generated revenue supports related community initiatives and promotes the sport of tennis. USTA runs the USTA Billie Jean King National Tennis Center, which hosts the U.S. Open each year. The organization also hosts tournaments across the country throughout the year for club players and professionals. USTA is made up of 17 individual sections, each representing distinct geographic locations, and include Caribbean, Eastern, Florida, Hawaii Pacific, InterMountain, MidAtlantic, Middle States, MidWest, Missouri Valley, New England, Northern, Northern California, Pacific Northwest, Southern, Southern California, Southwest and Texas.

FINANCIAL DATA: Note: Data for latest year may not have been available at press time.

In U.S. $	2022	2021	2020	2019	2018	2017
Revenue		111,542,410	96,993,400	332,162,497	291,915,411	291,915,411
R&D Expense						
Operating Income						
Operating Margin %						
SGA Expense						
Net Income						
Operating Cash Flow						
Capital Expenditure						
EBITDA						
Return on Assets %						
Return on Equity %						
Debt to Equity						

CONTACT INFORMATION:

Phone: 914-696-7000 Fax:
Toll-Free:
Address: 70 W. Red Oak Ln., White Plains, NY 10604 United States

STOCK TICKER/OTHER:

Stock Ticker: Private Exchange:
Employees: 400 Fiscal Year Ends: 12/31
Parent Company:

SALARIES/BONUSES:

Top Exec. Salary: $ Bonus: $
Second Exec. Salary: $ Bonus: $

OTHER THOUGHTS:

Estimated Female Officers or Directors: 9
Hot Spot for Advancement for Women/Minorities: Y

Sales, profits and employees may be estimates. Financial information, benefits and other data can change quickly and may vary from those stated here.

US Figure Skating

www.usfsa.org

NAIC Code: 711211

TYPES OF BUSINESS:

Figure Skating Association
Figure Skating Government
Olympic Committee Member
Skating Union Member
Governing Figure Skating Committees
Skating Program Development

BRANDS/DIVISIONS/AFFILIATES:

United States Olympic & Paralympic Committee
International Skating Union

CONTACTS: *Note: Officers with more than one job title may be intentionally listed here more than once.*

Samuel Auxier, Pres.
Samuel Auxier, Sec.
Warren Napthal, Treasurer

GROWTH PLANS/SPECIAL FEATURES:

U.S. Figure Skating is the official national governing body for figure skating in the U.S., and is a member of the United States Olympic & Paralympic Committee (USOPC) and International Skating Union (ISU). Established in 1921, the nonprofit's mission is to create and cultivate opportunities for participation and achievement in figure skating. With more than 750 members, school-affiliated and collegiate clubs, U.S. Figure Skating is comprised of 26 committees organized into five groups. Each committee has a specific role to play in supporting the organization as it carries out its mission. Responsibilities of each committee group is detailed in the U.S. Figure Skating Committee Handbook. The committee oversees, interprets and adjust rules under their jurisdiction to ensure their part of the sport is relevant, current and in support of the national governing body. Committees evaluate, develop and implement programs to support members in their respective areas; and each committee is represented by a group coordinator on the Board of Directors. More than 500 volunteers filling various positions serve on U.S. Figure Skating's Board of Directors and numerous committees. Thousands of volunteers dedicate their time to club activities, judging, officiating and competition management. In May 2023, U.S. Figure Skating announced the addition of a coaching membership category to launch July 1, 2023. The category would include establishing coaches for council for governance and building a headquarters team to lead in the area of coaching education, certification and development.

FINANCIAL DATA: *Note: Data for latest year may not have been available at press time.*

In U.S. $	2022	2021	2020	2019	2018	2017
Revenue		38,108,439	27,353,224	24,126,447	20,481,288	20,481,288
R&D Expense						
Operating Income						
Operating Margin %						
SGA Expense						
Net Income		18,893,332	6,656,872	2,036,226	4,088,470	4,088,470
Operating Cash Flow						
Capital Expenditure						
EBITDA						
Return on Assets %						
Return on Equity %						
Debt to Equity						

CONTACT INFORMATION:

Phone: 719-635-5200   Fax: 719-635-9548
Toll-Free:
Address: 20 First St., Colorado Springs, CO 80906 United States

STOCK TICKER/OTHER:

Stock Ticker: Private   Exchange:
Employees: 475   Fiscal Year Ends: 06/30
Parent Company:

SALARIES/BONUSES:

Top Exec. Salary: $ Bonus: $
Second Exec. Salary: $ Bonus: $

OTHER THOUGHTS:

Estimated Female Officers or Directors: 8
Hot Spot for Advancement for Women/Minorities: Y

US Soccer Federation

www.ussoccer.com

NAIC Code: 711211

TYPES OF BUSINESS:

Soccer League Organization
Youth Soccer Programs
Men's & Women's US National Soccer Teams
International Soccer Tournaments
Soccer Governing Body

BRANDS/DIVISIONS/AFFILIATES:

CONTACTS: *Note: Officers with more than one job title may be intentionally listed here more than once.*

Cindy Parlow Cone, Pres.
Dan Flynn, Sec. Gen.
Mike Edwards, Exec. VP

GROWTH PLANS/SPECIAL FEATURES:

The U.S. Soccer Federation (USCF) is a nonprofit organization and the governing body of soccer in the U.S., designed to promote soccer on competitive as well as recreational levels. The federation has overseen the operation of several international tournaments, including the Lamar Hunt U.S. Open Cup, which was first held in 1914. USCF is primarily a volunteer organization administered through a national council of elected officials. This council represents the organization's four administrative branches: youth players, adult players, the professional division and athletes. The U.S men's national team was advanced through the coaching of Bora Milutinovic in the early 1990s, Steve Sampson in the mid-1990s and Bruce Arena in the late 1990s and early 2000s. The men's soccer team is currently coached by Gregg Berhalter. Priorities of the organization also include promoting youth soccer organizations, funding facilities and camps; initiating Major League Soccer (MLS) in the U.S. as a training ground for the country's best players; and promoting the U.S. Women's National Team. Teams affiliated with the USCF include U.S. men's national soccer team, U.S. women's national soccer team, Under-23 men's/women's national soccer team, Under-20 men's/women's national soccer teams, Under-19 men's/women's national soccer teams, Under-18 men's/women's national soccer teams, Under-17 men's/women's national soccer teams, Under-16 boys'/girls' soccer teams, Under-15 boys'/girls' soccer teams and Under-14 NDP (National Development Program) for boys and girls. Affiliated leagues under the professional council include MLS National Women's Soccer League (NWSL), MLS and United Soccer League (USL). Additional affiliates include those within the Youth Council, the Adult Council and others.

FINANCIAL DATA: *Note: Data for latest year may not have been available at press time.*

In U.S. $	2022	2021	2020	2019	2018	2017
Revenue		61,223,417	135,444,082	108,660,552	152,393,266	152,393,266
R&D Expense						
Operating Income						
Operating Margin %						
SGA Expense						
Net Income		-1,708,000	-28,169,946	-17,108,899	46,308,114	46,308,114
Operating Cash Flow						
Capital Expenditure						
EBITDA						
Return on Assets %						
Return on Equity %						
Debt to Equity						

CONTACT INFORMATION:

Phone: 312-808-1300   Fax: 312-808-1301
Toll-Free:
Address: 1801 S. Prairie Ave., Chicago, IL 60616 United States

STOCK TICKER/OTHER:

Stock Ticker: Private   Exchange:
Employees: 1,500   Fiscal Year Ends: 03/31
Parent Company:

SALARIES/BONUSES:

Top Exec. Salary: $ Bonus: $
Second Exec. Salary: $ Bonus: $

OTHER THOUGHTS:

Estimated Female Officers or Directors: 2
Hot Spot for Advancement for Women/Minorities:

USA Basketball

NAIC Code: 711211

TYPES OF BUSINESS:

Basketball Association
Basketball Governing Organization
Basketball Training
Basketball Team Fielding

BRANDS/DIVISIONS/AFFILIATES:

CONTACTS: *Note: Officers with more than one job title may be intentionally listed here more than once.*

Jim Tooley, CEO
Heather Mosher Awtrey, Assistant Dir.-Admin.
Craig Miller, Chief Comm. & Media Officer
Heather Mosher Awtrey, Assistant Dir.-Finance
Carol Callan, Dir.-Women's National Team
Sean Ford, Dir.-Men's National Team
Caroline Williams, Dir.-Comm.
Ellis Dawson, Mgr.-Competitive Programs
Martin E. Dempsey, Chmn.

GROWTH PLANS/SPECIAL FEATURES:

USA Basketball, based in Colorado Springs, Colorado, is a nonprofit organization and the national governing body for men's and women's basketball in the U.S. The organization is the recognized as such by the International Basketball Federation (FIBA) and the United States Olympic & Paralympic Committee (USOPC), and is responsible for the selection, training and fielding of U.S. teams that compete in FIBA-sponsored international basketball competitions, as well as some national competitions. USA Basketball ranks Number One in all five of FIBA's world-ranking categories: combined, men's, women's, boys and girls. Competitions in which USA teams compete regularly include the Olympics, FIBA Basketball World Cups, FIBA AmeriCups, Pan American Games, FIBA U19 and U17 World Cups, FIBA Americas U18 and U16 Championships, Nike Hoop Summit, Youth Olympic Games, FIBA 3x3 World cups, FIBA 3x3 U23 World Cups and FIBA 3x3 U18 World Cups. USA Basketball is made up of organizations grouped into five categories: Professional, including National Basketball Association, National Basketball Association G League and Women's National Basketball Association; Collegiate, including National Association of Intercollegiate Athletics, National Collegiate Athletic Association and National Junior College Athletic Association; Scholastic, including National Federation of State High School Association; Youth, including Amateur Athletic Union; and Associate, including but not limited to, Athletes in Action, Harlem Globetrotters, Latin-American Basketball League of Los Angeles CA Inc., National Basketball Players Association, National Wheelchair Basketball Association, USA Deaf Basketball, and Women's Basketball Coaches Association.

FINANCIAL DATA: *Note: Data for latest year may not have been available at press time.*

In U.S. $	2022	2021	2020	2019	2018	2017
Revenue		14,313,296	12,446,344	15,359,351	10,923,502	10,923,502
R&D Expense						
Operating Income						
Operating Margin %						
SGA Expense						
Net Income			3,254,316	-567,227	2,690,424	2,690,424
Operating Cash Flow						
Capital Expenditure						
EBITDA						
Return on Assets %						
Return on Equity %						
Debt to Equity						

CONTACT INFORMATION:

Phone: 719-590-4800   Fax: 719-590-4811
Toll-Free:
Address: 27 S. Tejont St., Ste. 100, Colorado Springs, CO 80903 United States

STOCK TICKER/OTHER:

Stock Ticker: Private   Exchange:
Employees: 90   Fiscal Year Ends: 09/30
Parent Company:

SALARIES/BONUSES:

Top Exec. Salary: $ Bonus: $
Second Exec. Salary: $ Bonus: $

OTHER THOUGHTS:

Estimated Female Officers or Directors: 8
Hot Spot for Advancement for Women/Minorities: Y

USA Cycling

NAIC Code: 711211

www.usacycling.org

TYPES OF BUSINESS:

Cycling Organization
Cycling Governing Body
Cycling Sport Development
Cycling Sport Racing

BRANDS/DIVISIONS/AFFILIATES:

GROWTH PLANS/SPECIAL FEATURES:

USA Cycling (USAC) is a national non-profit governing body for the sport of cycling in the U.S. USAC oversees the disciplines of road, track, mountain bike, cyclocross and BMX. The organization's mission is to develop the sport of cycling at all levels and to achieve sustained international racing success by supporting cyclists ranging from beginner enthusiasts to seasoned professionals. USAC identifies, develops and selects cyclists to represent the U.S. in international competition. It also supports amateur bike racing via grassroots development programs and the provision of infrastructure to run organized racing, as well as fun rides. USAC began in 1920 and is currently comprised of about 60,000 member racers, cyclists, coaches, officials, mechanics and race directors. USAC funds its operations via member-generated revenue, sponsorships, U.S. Olympic Committee funding and donations from the USA Cycling Foundation.

CONTACTS: *Note: Officers with more than one job title may be intentionally listed here more than once.*

Brendan Quirk, CEO
Shawn Farrell, Dir.-Tech.
Katey Price, Staff Attorney
Steve McCauley, Dir.-Dev.
Jesse Hammond, Mgr.-New Media
Bill Kellick, Dir.-Comm.
Bob Plutt, Mgr.-Acct.
Nancy Cowan, Mgr.-Member Benefits Provider
Jim Miller, VP-Athletics
Micah Rice, Managing Dir.-National Events
Jeffrey Hansen, Mgr.-Collegiate & High School Cycling
Cari Higgins, Chmn.
Sean Perry, Chief-Domestic & Int'l Affairs

FINANCIAL DATA: *Note: Data for latest year may not have been available at press time.*

In U.S. $	2022	2021	2020	2019	2018	2017
Revenue		13,092,650	11,384,913	16,744,891	14,562,584	14,562,584
R&D Expense						
Operating Income						
Operating Margin %						
SGA Expense						
Net Income			113,353	-323,577	-597,524	-597,524
Operating Cash Flow						
Capital Expenditure						
EBITDA						
Return on Assets %						
Return on Equity %						
Debt to Equity						

CONTACT INFORMATION:

Phone: 719-434-4200   Fax: 719-434-4300
Toll-Free:
Address: 210 USA Cycling Point, Ste. 100, Colorado Springs, CO 80919
United States

STOCK TICKER/OTHER:

Stock Ticker: Private
Employees:
Parent Company:

Exchange:
Fiscal Year Ends: 12/31

SALARIES/BONUSES:

Top Exec. Salary: $ Bonus: $
Second Exec. Salary: $ Bonus: $

OTHER THOUGHTS:

Estimated Female Officers or Directors: 10
Hot Spot for Advancement for Women/Minorities: Y

Sales, profits and employees may be estimates. Financial information, benefits and other data can change quickly and may vary from those stated here.

USA Gymnastics

NAIC Code: 711211

TYPES OF BUSINESS:

Gymnastics Association
Gymnastic Sports
Gymnastic Governing Body

BRANDS/DIVISIONS/AFFILIATES:

USA Gymnastics University

CONTACTS: *Note: Officers with more than one job title may be intentionally listed here more than once.*

Li Li Leung, CEO
Lauryn Turner, COO
Jill Geer, CMO
Matt Steinke, Mgr.-Web Content
Leslie King, VP-Comm.
Cheryl Jarrett, VP-Member Svcs.
Renee Posan, Dir.-Business Affairs & Olympic Relations

GROWTH PLANS/SPECIAL FEATURES:

USA Gymnastics is a nonprofit organization that serves as the national governing body for gymnastics within the U.S. The U.S. Olympic Committee and the International Gymnastics Federation (IGF) designate the organization. Early U.S. gymnastics pioneers, such as Frank Bare, Arthur Gander, Gene Wettstone, George Gulack, and Dean McCoy, helped gain membership into the IGF in the 1970s. The organization sets the rules and policies that govern gymnastics. USA Gymnastics encompasses six disciplines: women's gymnastics, men's gymnastics, trampoline and tumbling, rhythmic gymnastics, acrobatic gymnastics and gymnastics for all (group gymnastics). It also trains and selects the U.S. gymnastics teams for the Olympics and World Championships. Currently, USA Gymnastics has over 200,000 members. The organization annually sanctions approximately 4,000 competitions and events throughout the U.S. USA Gymnastics itself conducts and produces five to six nationally televised annual events for national championships and international invitational competitions, including U.S. Olympic Team Trials. Some of the programs that the firm supports include TOPs (Talent Opportunity Program), an educational and talent search program for female gymnasts ages 7-11 and their coaches; USA Gymnastics University, which provides gymnastics education for instructors, coaches, teachers and judges; Future Stars, a men's program designed to identify talented athletes and to get them started on the right developmental path; and the JumpStart program, which helps talented athletes between the ages 7 and 12 years old. In addition, the firm organizes fundraiser events, membership clubs, training and scholarships to further promote the sport of gymnastics.

FINANCIAL DATA: *Note: Data for latest year may not have been available at press time.*

In U.S. $	2022	2021	2020	2019	2018	2017
Revenue		24,751,048	23,572,427	26,492,612	25,057,726	25,057,726
R&D Expense						
Operating Income						
Operating Margin %						
SGA Expense						
Net Income			2,502,068	-4,887,770	-1,493,546	-1,493,546
Operating Cash Flow						
Capital Expenditure						
EBITDA						
Return on Assets %						
Return on Equity %						
Debt to Equity						

CONTACT INFORMATION:

Phone: 317-237-5050   Fax: 317-237-5069
Toll-Free: 800-345-4719
Address: 1099 N. Meridian St., Ste. 800, Indianapolis, IN 46204 United States

STOCK TICKER/OTHER:

Stock Ticker: Private   Exchange:
Employees: 240   Fiscal Year Ends: 12/31
Parent Company:

SALARIES/BONUSES:

Top Exec. Salary: $ Bonus: $
Second Exec. Salary: $ Bonus: $

OTHER THOUGHTS:

Estimated Female Officers or Directors: 17
Hot Spot for Advancement for Women/Minorities: Y

USA Hockey Inc

www.usahockey.com

NAIC Code: 711211

TYPES OF BUSINESS:

Amateur Hockey Association
Ice Hockey Governing Body
Ice Hockey Organization
Ice Hockey Training and Development

BRANDS/DIVISIONS/AFFILIATES:

USA Hockey Foundation
National Team Development Program

CONTACTS: *Note: Officers with more than one job title may be intentionally listed here more than once.*

Mike Trimboli, Pres.
Pat Kelleher, Exec. Dir.
Kelly Mahncke, Dir.-Finance
Tony Driscoll, Dir.-Mktg. & Communications
Amber Rayfield, Dir.-Human Resources
Mark Hilberg, Sr. Dir.-IT
Bob Weldon, Assistant Exec. Dir.-Admin.
Jim Johannson, Assistant Exec. Dir.-Hockey Oper.
Pat Kelleher, Assistant Exec. Dir.-Dev.
Eddie Olson, Dir.-Internet Dev.
Dave Fischer, Sr. Dir.-Comm.
Bob Weldon, Assistant Exec. Dir.-Finance
Lou Vairo, Dir.-Special Projects
Rae Briggle, Assistant Exec. Dir.-Member Svcs.
Kevin McLaughlin, Sr. Dir.-Hockey Dev.
John Vanbiesbrouck, Exec. Dir.-Hockey Oper.

GROWTH PLANS/SPECIAL FEATURES:

USA Hockey, Inc. (USAH) is the national governing body for ice hockey in the U.S., as well as an official representative to the United States Olympic & Paralympic Committee (USOPC) and the International Ice Hockey Federation. USAH is responsible for organizing and training men's and women's teams for international tournaments, including the IIHF World Championships and the Olympic and Paralympic Winter Games. It is a membership service organization with more than 1 million members, including ice and inline hockey players, coaches, officials and volunteers. The organization is divided into 12 geographical districts throughout the U.S., each comprising a registrar to register teams, a referee-in-chief, a coach-in-chief, a risk manager and a skill development program administrator. Within USA Hockey's 12 districts, a total of 34 affiliates provide the formal governance for the sport. USAH's member services include standardizing playing rules, streamlining league and tournament sanctioning procedures, providing comprehensive insurance coverage benefits, providing training clinics for coaching and officiating, offering resource materials for all participants and organizing special events and tournaments. The USA Hockey Foundation is a nonprofit organization dedicated to promoting the sport, as well as providing financial support for USAH. The organization's National Team Development Program, based in Michigan, is operated by USAH and prepares student-athletes under the age of 18 for participation on U.S. national teams and continued success throughout their hockey careers. The organization also promotes the sport of ice hockey and its development through its affiliation with over 30 amateur leagues throughout the U.S. USAH holds several adult tournaments every year, including recreational, non-checking tournaments which are open to registered teams in 30+ and 40+ age brackets and novice, intermediate, advanced and women's divisions, and supports a disabled hockey program. It also holds youth ice hockey national championships for boys' and girls' hockey.

FINANCIAL DATA: *Note: Data for latest year may not have been available at press time.*

In U.S. $	2022	2021	2020	2019	2018	2017
Revenue		43,371,923	46,204,122	43,625,921	44,446,718	44,446,718
R&D Expense						
Operating Income						
Operating Margin %						
SGA Expense						
Net Income		2,358,855	7,617,227	-3,296,252	309,460	309,460
Operating Cash Flow						
Capital Expenditure						
EBITDA						
Return on Assets %						
Return on Equity %						
Debt to Equity						

CONTACT INFORMATION:

Phone: 719-576-8724   Fax: 719-538-1160
Toll-Free:
Address: 1775 Bob Johnson Dr., Colorado Springs, CO 80906-4090 United States

STOCK TICKER/OTHER:

Stock Ticker: Private   Exchange:
Employees: Fiscal Year Ends: 08/31
Parent Company:

SALARIES/BONUSES:

Top Exec. Salary: $ Bonus: $
Second Exec. Salary: $ Bonus: $

OTHER THOUGHTS:

Estimated Female Officers or Directors: 7
Hot Spot for Advancement for Women/Minorities: Y

Sales, profits and employees may be estimates. Financial information, benefits and other data can change quickly and may vary from those stated here.

USA Swimming

NAIC Code: 711211

TYPES OF BUSINESS:
Swimming Association
Swimming Sport Governing Body
Swimming Competition Opportunities
Swimming Training
Swimming Education
Swimming Events

BRANDS/DIVISIONS/AFFILIATES:

CONTACTS: *Note: Officers with more than one job title may be intentionally listed here more than once.*
Tim Hinchey, CEO
Eric Skufca, CFO
Guillermo Rojas, Dir.-Mktg. & Bus.
Josh Fowler, Mgr.-Special Projects
Lindsay Mintenko, Managing Dir.-National Team
Pat Hogan, Managing Dir.-Club Dev.
Tom Avischious, Dir.-Field Svcs.

GROWTH PLANS/SPECIAL FEATURES:
USA Swimming is the national governing body for the sport of swimming. Founded in 1981, USA Swimming creates opportunities for athletes and coaches of all backgrounds to participate and advanced the sport via clubs, events and education. Today, the organization has more than 3,100 clubs/teams that provide service to 400,000+ members. Membership is comprised of swimmers of all ages and abilities, coaches, officials and volunteers. USA Swimming is responsible for selecting and training teams for international competition, including the Olympic Games, and administer competitive swimming in accordance with the Ted Stevens Olympic & Amateur Sports Act. Local Swim Communities (LSCs) are groups that act as representatives for specific swimming committees throughout the country. There are approximately 60 LSCs with defined boundaries unique to an area of the country, and are tasked with registering members, scheduling competitions and leading clubs on behalf of USA Swimming. The nation is divided into western, central, eastern and southern zones, each responsible for representing the LSCs in their regional area and for conducting zone-level championship meets.

FINANCIAL DATA: *Note: Data for latest year may not have been available at press time.*

In U.S. $	2022	2021	2020	2019	2018	2017
Revenue		41,848,707	36,390,180	46,484,011	36,171,850	36,171,850
R&D Expense						
Operating Income						
Operating Margin %						
SGA Expense						
Net Income			3,605,354	3,300,085	-1,279,913	-1,279,913
Operating Cash Flow						
Capital Expenditure						
EBITDA						
Return on Assets %						
Return on Equity %						
Debt to Equity						

CONTACT INFORMATION:
Phone: 719-866-4578   Fax: 719-866-4669
Toll-Free:
Address: 1 Olympic Plaza, Colorado Springs, CO 80909 United States

STOCK TICKER/OTHER:
Stock Ticker: Private   Exchange:
Employees: 80   Fiscal Year Ends: 12/31
Parent Company:

SALARIES/BONUSES:
Top Exec. Salary: $ Bonus: $
Second Exec. Salary: $ Bonus: $

OTHER THOUGHTS:
Estimated Female Officers or Directors: 3
Hot Spot for Advancement for Women/Minorities: Y

USA Track & Field Inc

www.usatf.org

NAIC Code: 711211

TYPES OF BUSINESS:

Track & Field Organization
Track and Field Sports Governing Body
Track and Field Sport Rules and Regulations
Track and Field Sport Training
Sporting Events

BRANDS/DIVISIONS/AFFILIATES:

CONTACTS: Note: Officers with more than one job title may be intentionally listed here more than once.

Max Siegel, CEO
Vin Lananna, Pres.
Neale Johantgen, Tech. Coordinator
Blake Roebuck, Dir.-Merch.
Norman Wain, General Counsel
Blake Roebuck, Dir.-Oper.
Blake Facey, Webmaster
Jill Geer, Chief Public Affairs Officer
Melissa Bowlby, Mgr.-Acct.
Patty Hogan, Exec. Mgr.-Office
Sarah Austin, Mgr.-Legal Affairs
Benita Fitzgerald Mosley, Chief-Sport Performance
Susan Hazzard, Dir.-Public Rel.
Michael Conley, Chmn.
Sandy Snow, Dir.-Int'l & Championship Teams
Dorothy Hawkins, Travel Svcs.

GROWTH PLANS/SPECIAL FEATURES:

USA Track & Field, Inc. (USATF), a nonprofit organization, is the U.S. national governing body for the sports of track and field, race walking and long-distance running. It sets and enforces rules and regulations; selects the U.S. track and field teams for the Olympics, world championships and other international events each year; and promotes the sport through programs of training and competition for people of all ages. Thousands of coaches have been educated through USATF instructional programs, which are designed to elevate and standardize the level of coaching throughout the country. Athlete clinics are held nationwide, covering a wide range of disciplines, from race walking to pole vault. USATF sanctions more than 8,000 events annually throughout the U.S., certifies race courses for accuracy, validates records and provides insurance to sanctioned events, member clubs and member-athletes. The organization provides administration and financial sponsorship support in connection with certain USATF national championship events. More than 130,000 Americans are members of USATF, which includes organizations such as the NCAA, NAIA, Road Runners Club of America, Running USA and the National Federation of State High School Associations.

FINANCIAL DATA: Note: Data for latest year may not have been available at press time.

In U.S. $	2022	2021	2020	2019	2018	2017
Revenue		35,341,321	32,128,474	35,809,490	32,417,015	32,417,015
R&D Expense						
Operating Income						
Operating Margin %						
SGA Expense						
Net Income			8,853,997	-1,424,800	1,417,892	1,417,892
Operating Cash Flow						
Capital Expenditure						
EBITDA						
Return on Assets %						
Return on Equity %						
Debt to Equity						

CONTACT INFORMATION:

Phone: 317-261-0500   Fax: 317-261-0481
Toll-Free:
Address: 130 E. Washington St., Ste. 800, Indianapolis, IN 46204 United States

STOCK TICKER/OTHER:

Stock Ticker: Private
Employees: 330
Parent Company:

Exchange:
Fiscal Year Ends: 12/31

SALARIES/BONUSES:

Top Exec. Salary: $ Bonus: $
Second Exec. Salary: $ Bonus: $

OTHER THOUGHTS:

Estimated Female Officers or Directors: 13
Hot Spot for Advancement for Women/Minorities: Y

USL Championship League (USL Pro LLC)www.uslchampionship.com

NAIC Code: 711211D

TYPES OF BUSINESS:
Soccer (Futbol/Football) Teams League
Team Management and Operations

BRANDS/DIVISIONS/AFFILIATES:
United Soccer League

CONTACTS: *Note: Officers with more than one job title may be intentionally listed here more than once.*
Alec Papadakis, CEO
Jake Edwards, Pres.
Justin Papadakis, COO
Robert Hoskins, Chmn.

GROWTH PLANS/SPECIAL FEATURES:
USL Pro, LLC operates the USL Championship League, a second-tier North American professional soccer league founded in 2010. Sanctioned by the United Soccer League as a Division II professional league, the USL Championship comprised 24 clubs throughout the U.S. and in Canada during the 2023 season. Member clubs are provided with support via professionals across department categories, ranging from operations to marketing, communications and sponsorship. USL Pro has a media partnership with ESPN, which broadcasts all league matches through its various channels. The pinnacle of the USL Championship's season consists of the 24 teams (as of the 2023 season) playing their conference opponents twice, and one game each with the teams in the opposite conference. The top eight from the Eastern Conference and the top eight from the Western Conference compete in the USL Cup Playoffs, a four-week period of post-season play that determines the champion team of the league. The San Antonio FC were the champions for the 2022 season, which was the 12th season of the USL Championship and the sixth season under Division II sanctioning. 27 teams participated in the two conferences of the 2022 regular season.

FINANCIAL DATA: *Note: Data for latest year may not have been available at press time.*

In U.S. $	2022	2021	2020	2019	2018	2017
Revenue						
R&D Expense						
Operating Income						
Operating Margin %						
SGA Expense						
Net Income						
Operating Cash Flow						
Capital Expenditure						
EBITDA						
Return on Assets %						
Return on Equity %						
Debt to Equity						

CONTACT INFORMATION:
Phone: 813 963-3909   Fax:
Toll-Free:
Address: 1715 N Westshore Blvd., Ste. 825, Tampa, FL 33607 United States

STOCK TICKER/OTHER:
Stock Ticker: Private   Exchange:
Employees: Fiscal Year Ends:
Parent Company:

SALARIES/BONUSES:
Top Exec. Salary: $ Bonus: $
Second Exec. Salary: $ Bonus: $

OTHER THOUGHTS:
Estimated Female Officers or Directors:
Hot Spot for Advancement for Women/Minorities:

Utah Jazz

NAIC Code: 711211B

www.nba.com/jazz

TYPES OF BUSINESS:

Professional Basketball Team
Team Management and Operations

BRANDS/DIVISIONS/AFFILIATES:

CONTACTS: *Note: Officers with more than one job title may be intentionally listed here more than once.*

Danny Ainge, CEO-Basketball Oper.
Jim Olson, Pres.
John Larson, CFO
Elaina Pappas, Sr. VP-Mktg.
Alejandra Montoya, Dir.-People & Culture
Josh Ziska, Sr. VP-Technology
Robert Tingey, General Counsel
Dan Knight, Dir.-Oper.
Brendan Burke, Dir.-Mktg. & New Media
Linda Luchetti, VP-Comm.
Randy Wright, VP-Finance
Dennis Linsey, Gen. Mgr.
Tyrone Corbin, Head Coach
Walt Perrin, VP-Player Personnel
Doug Jardine, Controller
Ryan Smith, Chmn.
Rich Sheubrooks, Exec. Dir.-Global & Pro Scouting

GROWTH PLANS/SPECIAL FEATURES:

The Utah Jazz is a professional basketball team in the National Basketball Association (NBA) based in Salt Lake City, Utah. The franchise originated in the NBA as the New Orleans Jazz in 1974, and relocated to Salt Lake City in 1979. While the team has never won a championship, it has had made numerous playoff appearances, including back-to-back NBA Finals appearances in 1997 and 1998. The team's success throughout the 90s was due in large part to the Hall of Fame duo of point guard Jon Stockton and power forward Karl Malone as well as former head coach Jerry Sloan. During the 2000's, the Utah Jazz captured division titles in 2000, 2007, 2008, 2017, 2021 and 2022. The team plays in the Western Conference, Northwest Division. In 2020, billionaire businessman and Utah native Ryan Smith purchased the Utah Jazz from the Miller family; and in 2021, former professional player Dwyane Wade purchased a minority share in the team. The team averaged 18,206 in home game attendance during the 2022-23 season, playing at the Vivint Arena with a basketball seating capacity of 18,306. The Salt Lake City Stars are affiliated with the Utah Jazz, playing in the NBA G League. Forbes estimated Utah Jazz to be worth $2.025 billion in October 2022.

FINANCIAL DATA: *Note: Data for latest year may not have been available at press time.*

In U.S. $	2022	2021	2020	2019	2018	2017
Revenue	317,200,000					
R&D Expense						
Operating Income						
Operating Margin %						
SGA Expense						
Net Income						
Operating Cash Flow						
Capital Expenditure						
EBITDA						
Return on Assets %						
Return on Equity %						
Debt to Equity						

CONTACT INFORMATION:

Phone: 801-325-2500   Fax: 801-325-2578
Toll-Free:
Address: 301 W. S. Temple, Salt Lake City, UT 84101 United States

STOCK TICKER/OTHER:

Stock Ticker: Private   Exchange:
Employees: 250   Fiscal Year Ends: 06/30
Parent Company:

SALARIES/BONUSES:

Top Exec. Salary: $ Bonus: $
Second Exec. Salary: $ Bonus: $

OTHER THOUGHTS:

Estimated Female Officers or Directors: 5
Hot Spot for Advancement for Women/Minorities: Y

Vail Resorts Inc

NAIC Code: 713920

www.vailresorts.com

TYPES OF BUSINESS:

Ski Resorts
Luxury Hotels & Lodging
Real Estate Development
Golf Courses

BRANDS/DIVISIONS/AFFILIATES:

Vail Resorts Development Company
Whistler Blackcomb
Heavenly
Park City
Stowe
Liberty Mountain
RockResorts
Grand Teton Lodge Company

GROWTH PLANS/SPECIAL FEATURES:

Vail Resorts Inc is a resorts and casinos company that operates mountain resorts and ski areas. The company has three business segments that include Mountain, Lodging, and Real Estate. The Mountain segment operates numerous ski resort properties that offer a variety of winter and summer activities, such as skiing, snowboarding, snowshoeing, hiking, and mountain biking. The Lodging segment owns and operates hotels and condominiums. The Real Estate segment owns, develops, and leases real estate, typically near its other properties. The company generates the vast majority of its revenue within the United States.

CONTACTS: *Note: Officers with more than one job title may be intentionally listed here more than once.*

Robert Katz, CEO
Michael Barkin, CFO
Nathan Gronberg, Chief Accounting Officer
Kirsten Lynch, Chief Marketing Officer
David Shapiro, Executive VP
James O'Donnell, President, Divisional
Gregory Sullivan, Senior VP, Divisional
Ryan Bennett, Vice President, Divisional

FINANCIAL DATA: *Note: Data for latest year may not have been available at press time.*

In U.S. $	2022	2021	2020	2019	2018	2017
Revenue	2,525,912,000	1,909,710,000	1,963,704,000	2,271,575,000	1,907,218,000	1,907,218,000
R&D Expense						
Operating Income	576,740,000	280,467,000	247,752,000	481,720,000	395,220,000	395,220,000
Operating Margin %	.23%	.15%	.13%	.21%	.21%	.21%
SGA Expense	347,493,000	296,993,000	278,695,000	274,415,000	236,799,000	236,799,000
Net Income	347,923,000	127,850,000	98,833,000	301,163,000	210,553,000	210,553,000
Operating Cash Flow	710,499,000	525,250,000	394,950,000	634,231,000	470,983,000	470,983,000
Capital Expenditure	192,817,000	115,097,000	172,334,000	192,035,000	144,432,000	144,432,000
EBITDA	857,735,000	529,167,000	472,726,000	696,578,000	591,695,000	591,695,000
Return on Assets %	.06%	.02%	.02%	.07%	.06%	.06%
Return on Equity %	.22%	.09%	.07%	.19%	.17%	.17%
Debt to Equity	1.76%	1.84%	1.978	1.031	0.801	0.801

CONTACT INFORMATION:

Phone: 303 404-1800   Fax: 303 404-6415
Toll-Free:
Address: 390 Interlocken Crescent, Broomfield, CO 80021 United States

STOCK TICKER/OTHER:

Stock Ticker: MTN   Exchange: NYS
Employees: 6,900   Fiscal Year Ends: 07/31
Parent Company:

SALARIES/BONUSES:

Top Exec. Salary: $1,000,320   Bonus: $
Second Exec. Salary: Bonus: $
$885,999

OTHER THOUGHTS:

Estimated Female Officers or Directors: 3
Hot Spot for Advancement for Women/Minorities: Y

Valencia Club de Futbol (Valencia CF/Valencia)

www.valenciacf.com/en
NAIC Code: 711211D

TYPES OF BUSINESS:

Soccer Team
Team Management and Operations

BRANDS/DIVISIONS/AFFILIATES:

Mestalla

GROWTH PLANS/SPECIAL FEATURES:

Valencia Club de Futbol (also referred to as Valencia CF and Valencia) is a professional football club in Spain, playing in La Liga, the top professional division of the Spanish football league system. Founded in 1919, Valencia CF plays its home games at Mestalla stadium in Valencia, Spain, which has a seating capacity of 49,430. Average home game attendance was 40,602 for Valencia CF's 2022-23 season. Domestically, the football club has won six La Liga titles, two Segunda Division titles, eight Copa del Rey titles, one Supercopa de Espana titles and one Copa Eva Duarte title. Internationally, Valencia CF won the European Cup Winners' Cup in the 1979-80 season, has one UEFA Cup, two Inter-Cities Fairs Cups, two European Super Cups (UEFA Super Cup) and one UEFA Intertoto Cup. Puma is Valencia CF's kit manufacturer and Cazoo is its shirt sponsor.

CONTACTS: Note: Officers with more than one job title may be intentionally listed here more than once.

Layhoon Chan, Pres.

FINANCIAL DATA: Note: Data for latest year may not have been available at press time.

In U.S. $	2022	2021	2020	2019	2018	2017
Revenue						
R&D Expense						
Operating Income						
Operating Margin %						
SGA Expense						
Net Income						
Operating Cash Flow						
Capital Expenditure						
EBITDA						
Return on Assets %						
Return on Equity %						
Debt to Equity						

CONTACT INFORMATION:

Phone: 34 96 337 2626   Fax: 34 96 337 2335
Toll-Free:
Address: Plaza del Valencia CF, 2, Valencia, 46010 Spain

STOCK TICKER/OTHER:

Stock Ticker: Private   Exchange:
Employees: Fiscal Year Ends:
Parent Company:

SALARIES/BONUSES:

Top Exec. Salary: $ Bonus: $
Second Exec. Salary: $ Bonus: $

OTHER THOUGHTS:

Estimated Female Officers or Directors:
Hot Spot for Advancement for Women/Minorities:

Vancouver Canucks

canucks.nhl.com

NAIC Code: 711211F

TYPES OF BUSINESS:

Professional Hockey Team (NHL)
Team Management and Operations

BRANDS/DIVISIONS/AFFILIATES:

Canucks Sports and Entertainment
Aquilini Investment Group
Abbotsford Canucks

CONTACTS: *Note: Officers with more than one job title may be intentionally listed here more than once.*

Michael Doyle, Pres.
Todd Kobus, CFO
Kelsey Philpott, Sr. VP-Mktg.
Dana Clark, VP-People
Derek Boyd, Dir.-Tech.
Janeil Mackay, Dir.-Consumer Prod. Mktg. & Retail
Al Hutchings, Dir.-Eng.
Jonathan Wall, Dir.-Hockey Admin.
Chris Gear, General Counsel
Laurence Gilman, VP-Hockey Oper.
David Comuzzi, Sr. Dir.-Bus. Dev.
Kevin Kinghorn, Dir.-Website & New Media
T.C. Carling, VP-Comm. & Community Partnerships
Todd Kobus, VP-Finance
Michael Doyle, Gen. Mgr.-Arena
Michael Cassidy, Gen. Mgr.-Aramark Food Svcs.
Lorne Henning, VP-Player Personnel
Harvey Jones, VP-Construction
Francesco Aquilini, Chmn.

GROWTH PLANS/SPECIAL FEATURES:

The Vancouver Canucks have been a National Hockey League (NHL) team since 1970. The Canucks play in the Pacific division of the NHL's Western Conference, along with the Anaheim Ducks, Calgary Flames, Edmonton Oilers, Los Angeles Kings, San Jose Sharks, Seattle Kraken and Vegas Golden Knights. Although named the Canucks, the team's logo and mascot is an orca whale, with Johnny Canuck, a Canadian lumberjack cartoon superhero, being adopted as the unofficial second team mascot. Its home stadium is the Rogers Arena in Vancouver, British Columbia, which features an 18,910-seating capacity for hockey games and plays hosts to a myriad of events such as concerts, basketball games and entertainment shows. Average home game attendance for the Canucks was 18,702 during the 2022-23 season. Both the Canucks and Rogers Arena are owned and operated by Canucks Sports and Entertainment, which is run by Aquilini Investment Group, a Vancouver-based company led by Francesco Aquilini. The team made it to the Stanley Cup Finals three times in 1982, 1994 and 2011, and earned the Presidents' Trophy for both the 2010-11 and 2011-12 seasons. Additionally, the Canucks have won three conference and ten division championships. One of the Canucks' most memorable players was Stan Smyl, nicknamed the Steamer, who joined the team in 1978 and played for it throughout his entire 13 season professional career until he retired in 1991. The Canucks maintain a minor league affiliation with the Abbotsford Canucks of the American Hockey League (AHL). In December 2022, Forbes estimated the Canucks' value to be $1.01 billion.

FINANCIAL DATA: *Note: Data for latest year may not have been available at press time.*

In U.S. $	2022	2021	2020	2019	2018	2017
Revenue	130,000,000	68,000,000	146,000,000	167,000,000	156,000,000	156,000,000
R&D Expense						
Operating Income						
Operating Margin %						
SGA Expense						
Net Income		-35,000,000	2,900,000	31,000,000	22,000,000	22,000,000
Operating Cash Flow						
Capital Expenditure						
EBITDA						
Return on Assets %						
Return on Equity %						
Debt to Equity						

CONTACT INFORMATION:

Phone: 604-899-7400   Fax: 604-899-7401
Toll-Free: 855-462-8257
Address: 800 Griffiths Way, Vancouver, BC V6B 6G1 Canada

STOCK TICKER/OTHER:

Stock Ticker: Private   Exchange:
Employees: 480   Fiscal Year Ends: 06/30
Parent Company: Canucks Sports & Entertainment

SALARIES/BONUSES:

Top Exec. Salary: $ Bonus: $
Second Exec. Salary: $ Bonus: $

OTHER THOUGHTS:

Estimated Female Officers or Directors: 9
Hot Spot for Advancement for Women/Minorities: Y

Vancouver Whitecaps FC

www.whitecapsfc.com

NAIC Code: 711211D

TYPES OF BUSINESS:

Professional Soccer Team
Team Management and Operations

BRANDS/DIVISIONS/AFFILIATES:

Vancouver 86ers
Southsiders

CONTACTS: *Note: Officers with more than one job title may be intentionally listed here more than once.*

Axel Schuster, CEO
Vanni Sartini, Head Coach
Lisa Abbate, Dir.-Finance
Erin Mathany, Sr. VP-Mktg.
Jennifer Fong, Dir.-People & Culture
Aditi Bhatt, CCO
Danielle Gorgerat, Mgr.-Ticket Oper.
Dan Lendarduzzi, Dir.-Soccer Dev.
Carly Thorson Jokic, Dir.-Comm. & Broadcast
Don Ford, Dir.-Finance
Kim Jackman, Dir.-Mktg.
Hillary Campbell, Dir.-Event Oper.
Tom Soehn, Head Coach-Men
Greg Anderson, Dir.-Professional Teams
Jeff Mallett, Chmn.

GROWTH PLANS/SPECIAL FEATURES:

Vancouver Whitecaps FC is a Major League Soccer (MLS) team based in Vancouver, Canada, playing in the Western Conference. The club is the spiritual successor to a team which held the same name in the North American Soccer League until 1984. The team was reborn as the Vancouver 86ers and played in various leagues over the next two and a half decades until it was renewed as an MLS expansion team in 2009 (and later began playing in the 2011 season). Despite the changes, the club has maintained some traditions, including the Southsiders fan group. The team's name alludes to the mountains around Vancouver and the waves in the Pacific Ocean. Domestically, the Whitecaps won their first Canadian Championship in 2015, and were runners-up in 2011, 2012, 2013, 2016 and 2018. The team clenched its second Canadian Championship in 2022, defeating the Valour FC 2-0. Home games are played at BC Place in Vancouver, with a 22,120-seat MLS capacity. Average home game attendance for the Whitecaps was 16,399 during the 2022 season. Adidas is the Whitecap's kit manufacturer and Telus is its shirt sponsor. The Vancouver Whitecaps have also won three Cascadia Cups, in 2013, 2014 and 2016, respectively.

FINANCIAL DATA: *Note: Data for latest year may not have been available at press time.*

In U.S. $	2022	2021	2020	2019	2018	2017
Revenue	50,000,000	4,830,000	4,200,000	20,000,000	22,000,000	22,000,000
R&D Expense						
Operating Income						
Operating Margin %						
SGA Expense						
Net Income				-5,000,000		
Operating Cash Flow						
Capital Expenditure						
EBITDA						
Return on Assets %						
Return on Equity %						
Debt to Equity						

CONTACT INFORMATION:

Phone: 604-669-9283   Fax: 604-684-5173
Toll-Free:
Address: 201 - 788 Beatty St., Vancouver, BC V6B 2M1 Canada

STOCK TICKER/OTHER:

Stock Ticker: Private   Exchange:
Employees: Fiscal Year Ends:
Parent Company:

SALARIES/BONUSES:

Top Exec. Salary: $ Bonus: $
Second Exec. Salary: $ Bonus: $

OTHER THOUGHTS:

Estimated Female Officers or Directors: 8
Hot Spot for Advancement for Women/Minorities: Y

Sales, profits and employees may be estimates. Financial information, benefits and other data can change quickly and may vary from those stated here.

Varsity Brands Holding Co Inc

www.varsitybrands.com

NAIC Code: 424300

TYPES OF BUSINESS:

Apparel and Clothing Brands, Designers, Importers and Distributors
Training Camps
Cheerleading Uniforms
Dance Team Uniforms
Team Events & Competitions
Athletic Gear
Graduation Products
Product Design

BRANDS/DIVISIONS/AFFILIATES:

Bain Capital LP
Varsity.com
Varsity TV
Universal Dance Association
Varsity Spirit
BSN Sports
Herff Jones

CONTACTS: *Note: Officers with more than one job title may be intentionally listed here more than once.*

Adam Blumenfeld, CEO
Jeffrey G. Webb, Pres.
Marlene Cota, VP-Bus. Dev. & Corp. Alliances
Jackie Martin, Mgr.-Content, Varsity.com
Nicole Lauchaire, VP-Comm.
Gregory C. Webb, Sr. VP-Camps & Events
Kimberly Williams, VP-Design
J. Kristyn Shepherd, Sr. VP-Special Events
Sheila Noone, VP-Public Rel.

GROWTH PLANS/SPECIAL FEATURES:

Varsity Brands, Inc. is a top designer, marketer and supplier of cheerleader and dance team uniforms and accessories. Thousands of catalogs featuring the firm's uniforms and accessories are mailed annually to schools, school spirit advisors and coaches. Company website, Varsity.com, enables customers to design uniforms via numerous colors and styles. The site also features Varsity TV, a library for online videos from competitions and events. Varsity promotes its products through active association with championships and specials, including Varsity All Star, National Cheerleaders Association, Universal Cheerleaders Association, The American Championships, All Star Challenge, Spirit Cheer and CHEERSPORT. Varsity is also a leading operator of cheerleading and dance team training camps, competitions and clinics. Most of its dance team camps and competitions are operated through division Universal Dance Association. Besides training camps, the firm also offers various educational materials through its website, such as online articles featuring information on topics including becoming a cheerleader, being a male cheerleader, the history of cheerleading, being the parent of a cheerleader, coaching cheerleaders, transitioning from high school to college cheerleading squads, being on a dance team, practical tips on developing cheerleading skills, cheerleading safety and other issues. Varsity's primary brands include: Varsity Spirit, engaged in cheerleading and dance; BSN Sports, offering athletic gear; and Herff Jones, a provider of graduation and recognition products and services designed to inspire student achievement. Varsity Brands is privately-owned by Bain Capital LP.

FINANCIAL DATA: *Note: Data for latest year may not have been available at press time.*

In U.S. $	2022	2021	2020	2019	2018	2017
Revenue	801,000,000	795,558,400	764,960,000	1,366,000,000	1,352,000,000	1,352,000,000
R&D Expense						
Operating Income						
Operating Margin %						
SGA Expense						
Net Income				2,100,000,000	1,700,000,000	1,700,000,000
Operating Cash Flow						
Capital Expenditure						
EBITDA						
Return on Assets %						
Return on Equity %						
Debt to Equity						

CONTACT INFORMATION:

Phone: 972-496-3477   Fax: 972-247-0650
Toll-Free:
Address: 14460 Varsity Brands Way, Farmers Branch, TX 75244 United States

STOCK TICKER/OTHER:

Stock Ticker: Subsidiary   Exchange:
Employees: 4,000   Fiscal Year Ends: 12/31
Parent Company: Bain Capital LP

SALARIES/BONUSES:

Top Exec. Salary: $ Bonus: $
Second Exec. Salary: $ Bonus: $

OTHER THOUGHTS:

Estimated Female Officers or Directors: 6
Hot Spot for Advancement for Women/Minorities: Y

Vegas Golden Knights

www.nhl.com/goldenknights

NAIC Code: 711211F

TYPES OF BUSINESS:

Professional Hockey Team (NHL)
Team Management and Operations

BRANDS/DIVISIONS/AFFILIATES:

Henderson Silver Knights
Savannah Ghost Pirates

CONTACTS: *Note: Officers with more than one job title may be intentionally listed here more than once.*

Bill Foley, CEO
Kerry Bubolz, Pres.
Heather Clayton, CFO
Eric Tosi, CMO
Robert Foley, Chief Business Officer
George McPhee, Pres.-Hockey Oper.

GROWTH PLANS/SPECIAL FEATURES:

Vegas Golden Knights are an ice hockey team based in the Las Vegas metropolitan area that began playing in the 2017-18 National Hockey League (NHL) season and won its division (Pacific) and conference (Western) championships that same season. The Golden Knights became the third NHL team to advance to the Stanley Cup Finals in its inaugural season. The team snatched additional division titles in 2019-20 and 2022-23, and won its second Conference Championship in 2022-23, sending them to the Stanley Cup playoffs against the Florida Panthers. The Golden Knights defeated the Panthers in five games and won the 2023 Stanley Cup. The Golden Knights play at the T-Mobile Arena in Paradise, Nevada, which seats 17,500 for hockey games, and up to 20,000 for other events. Average attendance for the team's home games during the 2022-23 season was 18,024. Minor league affiliates include the Henderson Silver Knights of the American Hockey League (AHL) and the Savannah Ghost Pirates of the ECHL. In December 2022, Forbes valued the Knights at $965 million.

FINANCIAL DATA: *Note: Data for latest year may not have been available at press time.*

In U.S. $	2022	2021	2020	2019	2018	2017
Revenue	150,800,000					
R&D Expense						
Operating Income						
Operating Margin %						
SGA Expense						
Net Income						
Operating Cash Flow						
Capital Expenditure						
EBITDA						
Return on Assets %						
Return on Equity %						
Debt to Equity						

CONTACT INFORMATION:

Phone: 702-790-2663   Fax:
Toll-Free:
Address: 1550 S. Pavillion Center Dr., Las Vegas, NV 89135 United States

STOCK TICKER/OTHER:

Stock Ticker: Private   Exchange:
Employees: Fiscal Year Ends:
Parent Company:

SALARIES/BONUSES:

Top Exec. Salary: $ Bonus: $
Second Exec. Salary: $ Bonus: $

OTHER THOUGHTS:

Estimated Female Officers or Directors:
Hot Spot for Advancement for Women/Minorities:

Verein fur Bewegungsspiele Stuttgart 1893 eV (VfB Stuttgart)

NAIC Code: 711211D

www.vfb.de

TYPES OF BUSINESS:

Soccer Team
Team Management and Operations
Professional Hockey Team
Tennis
Athletics

BRANDS/DIVISIONS/AFFILIATES:

Mercedes-Benz Arena

GROWTH PLANS/SPECIAL FEATURES:

Verein fur Bewegungsspiele Stuttgart 1893 ev (VfB Stuttgart) is a sports club in Germany, primarily known for its football team that plays in Germany's premier division, the Bundesliga. Founded in 1893, VfB Stuttgart plays its home games at the Mercedes-Benz Arena, which has a seating capacity of over 60,000. During the 2022-23 season, VfB Stuttgart averaged 46,430 in home game attendance. Nationally, VfB Stuttgart has won the Bundesliga championship five times, the 2 Bundesliga twice, the DFB-Pokal three times and the German Super Cup once. Internationally, the club has won the UEFA Intertoto Cup two times. Jako is the team's kit manufacturer. Other sports through VfB Stuttgart include hockey, tennis and general athletics.

CONTACTS:
Note: Officers with more than one job title may be intentionally listed here more than once.

Claus Vogt, Pres.
Tobias Keller, Dir.-Finance
Alexander Wehrle, Chmn.

FINANCIAL DATA:
Note: Data for latest year may not have been available at press time.

In U.S. $	2022	2021	2020	2019	2018	2017
Revenue						
R&D Expense						
Operating Income						
Operating Margin %						
SGA Expense						
Net Income						
Operating Cash Flow						
Capital Expenditure						
EBITDA						
Return on Assets %						
Return on Equity %						
Debt to Equity						

CONTACT INFORMATION:

Phone: 49 1806 991893   Fax:
Toll-Free:
Address: MercedesstraÃŸe 109, Stuttgart, 70372 Germany

STOCK TICKER/OTHER:

Stock Ticker: Private   Exchange:
Employees: Fiscal Year Ends:
Parent Company:

SALARIES/BONUSES:

Top Exec. Salary: $ Bonus: $
Second Exec. Salary: $ Bonus: $

OTHER THOUGHTS:

Estimated Female Officers or Directors:
Hot Spot for Advancement for Women/Minorities:

VF Corporation
www.vfc.com
NAIC Code: 424300

TYPES OF BUSINESS:
Apparel and Clothing Brands, Designers, Importers and Distributors
Swimsuits
Outdoor Gear & Apparel
Image Wear
Outlet Stores
Footwear

BRANDS/DIVISIONS/AFFILIATES:
North Face (The)
Timberland
SmartWool
Vans
Eastpak
JanSport
Dickies
Timberland PRO

CONTACTS: Note: Officers with more than one job title may be intentionally listed here more than once.
Steven Rendle, CEO
Matthew Puckett, CFO
Bryan McNeill, Chief Accounting Officer
Laura Meagher, Executive VP
Curtis Holtz, Executive VP
Stephen Murray, Executive VP
Martino Guerrini, Executive VP
Kevin Bailey, Executive VP

GROWTH PLANS/SPECIAL FEATURES:
VF designs, produces, and distributes branded apparel and accessories. Its largest apparel categories include action sports, outdoor, and workwear. Its portfolio of about a dozen brands includes Vans, The North Face, Timberland, Supreme, and Dickies. VF markets its products in the Americas, Europe, and Asia-Pacific through wholesale sales to retailers, e-commerce, and branded stores owned by the company and partners. The company has grown through multiple acquisitions and traces its roots to 1899.

FINANCIAL DATA: Note: Data for latest year may not have been available at press time.

In U.S. $	2022	2021	2020	2019	2018	2017
Revenue	11,841,840,000	9,238,830,000	10,488,560,000	10,266,890,000	8,394,684,000	8,394,684,000
R&D Expense						
Operating Income	1,632,204,000	627,992,000	1,251,028,000	1,190,182,000	883,374,000	883,374,000
Operating Margin %	.14%	.07%	.12%	.12%	.11%	.11%
SGA Expense	4,823,243,000	4,240,058,000	4,547,008,000	4,420,379,000	3,662,062,000	3,662,062,000
Net Income	1,386,941,000	407,869,000	679,449,000	1,259,792,000	614,923,000	614,923,000
Operating Cash Flow	864,288,000	1,313,225,000	874,527,000	1,664,223,000	1,474,660,000	1,474,660,000
Capital Expenditure	328,320,000	274,200,000	333,836,000	269,002,000	203,818,000	203,818,000
EBITDA	1,926,654,000	861,208,000	1,086,869,000	1,401,780,000	1,128,173,000	1,128,173,000
Return on Assets %	.10%	.03%	.06%	.12%	.06%	.06%
Return on Equity %	.42%	.13%	.18%	.32%	.14%	.14%
Debt to Equity	1.59%	2.27%	1.081	0.492	0.588	0.588

CONTACT INFORMATION:
Phone: 720-778-4000   Fax:
Toll-Free:
Address: 1551 Wewatta St., Denver, CO 80202 United States

STOCK TICKER/OTHER:
Stock Ticker: VFC   Exchange: NYS
Employees: 35,000   Fiscal Year Ends: 12/31
Parent Company:

SALARIES/BONUSES:
Top Exec. Salary: $1,400,000   Bonus: $
Second Exec. Salary: Bonus: $
$739,789

OTHER THOUGHTS:
Estimated Female Officers or Directors: 5
Hot Spot for Advancement for Women/Minorities: Y

Sales, profits and employees may be estimates. Financial information, benefits and other data can change quickly and may vary from those stated here.

Vista Outdoor Inc

NAIC Code: 332992

TYPES OF BUSINESS:

Small Arms Ammunition Manufacturing
Shotguns and Rifles Manufacturing
Archery Equipment Manufacturing
Golf Rangefinder Manufacturing
Rifle and Spotting Scope Manufacturing

BRANDS/DIVISIONS/AFFILIATES:

Alliant Powder
Bee Stinger
Bell
CamelBak
American Eagle
Blazer
CCI
Estate Cartridge

CONTACTS: Note: Officers with more than one job title may be intentionally listed here more than once.

Christopher Metz, CEO
Sudhanshu Priyadarshi, CFO
Michael Callahan, Chairman of the Board
Mark Kowalski, Chief Accounting Officer
Tig Krekel, Director
Dylan Ramsey, General Counsel
Kelly Reisdorf, Other Executive Officer
Brad Crandell, Other Executive Officer
Jason Vanderbrink, President, Divisional

GROWTH PLANS/SPECIAL FEATURES:

Vista Outdoor Inc designs, develops, and manufactures outdoor sports and recreation products, and is domiciled in the United States. The company organizes itself into two segments: Shooting sports and Outdoor products. Shooting sports, which contributes the largest proportion of company revenue, includes ammunition, long guns, and related equipment under brands such as Federal Premium, Blackhawk, and Hoppe's. Outdoor products include archery and hunting accessories, eyewear, golf products, hydration products, and stand-up paddle boards under brands including CamelBak and Bushnell. The company derives the vast majority of revenue domestically.

FINANCIAL DATA: Note: Data for latest year may not have been available at press time.

In U.S. $	2022	2021	2020	2019	2018	2017
Revenue	3,044,621,000	2,225,522,000	1,755,871,000	2,058,528,000	2,546,892,000	2,546,892,000
R&D Expense	28,737,000	22,538,000	22,998,000	27,742,000	32,769,000	32,769,000
Operating Income	646,222,000	272,962,000	33,214,000	10,897,000	212,148,000	212,148,000
Operating Margin %	.21%	.12%	.02%	.01%	.08%	.08%
SGA Expense	434,273,000	337,460,000	302,554,000	377,049,000	424,269,000	424,269,000
Net Income	473,226,000	266,012,000	-155,079,000	-648,443,000	-274,454,000	-274,454,000
Operating Cash Flow	318,311,000	345,374,000	76,745,000	97,475,000	158,401,000	158,401,000
Capital Expenditure	42,782,000	30,166,000	23,768,000	42,242,000	90,665,000	90,665,000
EBITDA	718,562,000	350,068,000	-64,378,000	-539,578,000	-113,245,000	-113,245,000
Return on Assets %	.23%	.17%	-.10%	-.30%	-.09%	-.09%
Return on Equity %	.51%	.45%	-.29%	-.71%	-.19%	-.19%
Debt to Equity	.66%	.78%	1.331	1.124	0.875	0.875

CONTACT INFORMATION:

Phone: 763-433-1000   Fax:
Toll-Free:
Address: 1 Vista Way, Anoka, MN 55303 United States

STOCK TICKER/OTHER:

Stock Ticker: VSTO   Exchange: NYS
Employees: 6,900   Fiscal Year Ends: 12/31
Parent Company:

SALARIES/BONUSES:

Top Exec. Salary: $1,096,154   Bonus: $
Second Exec. Salary: Bonus: $
$539,399

OTHER THOUGHTS:

Estimated Female Officers or Directors:
Hot Spot for Advancement for Women/Minorities:

Walt Disney Company (The)

NAIC Code: 515210

corporate.disney.go.com

TYPES OF BUSINESS:

Cable TV Networks, Broadcasting & Entertainment
Film Media
Television Media
Content Production and Distribution
Content Sales and Licensing
Theme Parks, Resorts & Cruise Lines
Book and Comic Book Publishing
Branded Merchandise

BRANDS/DIVISIONS/AFFILIATES:

Disney
ESPN
Freeform
National Geographic
A+E Television Networks
Disney+
Star+
Disney Cruise Line

CONTACTS: Note: Officers with more than one job title may be intentionally listed here more than once.

Robert Chapek, CEO
Christine Mccarthy, CFO
Robert Iger, Chairman of the Board
Brent Woodford, Executive VP, Divisional
Alan Braverman, General Counsel
Paul Richardson, Other Executive Officer
Zenia Mucha, Senior Executive VP, Divisional

GROWTH PLANS/SPECIAL FEATURES:

Walt Disney owns the rights to some of the most globally recognized characters, from Mickey Mouse to Luke Skywalker. These characters and others are featured in several Disney theme parks around the world. Disney makes live-action and animated films under studios such as Pixar, Marvel, and Lucasfilm and also operates media networks including ESPN and several TV production studios. Disney shifted into a more streaming-focused firm by acquiring the remainder of Hulu and launching Disney+ and ESPN+. Across its streaming platforms, Disney had over 235 million subscribers as of September 2022, up sharply from under 64 million in December 2019.

FINANCIAL DATA: Note: Data for latest year may not have been available at press time.

In U.S. $	2022	2021	2020	2019	2018	2017
Revenue	82,722,000,000	67,418,000,000	65,388,000,000	69,607,000,000	55,137,000,000	55,137,000,000
R&D Expense						
Operating Income	6,770,000,000	3,659,000,000	3,794,000,000	11,830,000,000	13,873,000,000	13,873,000,000
Operating Margin %	.08%	.05%	.06%	.17%	.25%	.25%
SGA Expense	16,388,000,000	13,517,000,000	12,369,000,000	11,549,000,000	8,176,000,000	8,176,000,000
Net Income	3,145,000,000	1,995,000,000	-2,864,000,000	11,054,000,000	8,980,000,000	8,980,000,000
Operating Cash Flow	6,010,000,000	5,567,000,000	7,618,000,000	6,606,000,000	12,343,000,000	12,343,000,000
Capital Expenditure	4,943,000,000	3,578,000,000	4,022,000,000	4,876,000,000	3,623,000,000	3,623,000,000
EBITDA	11,997,000,000	9,218,000,000	5,093,000,000	19,068,000,000	17,077,000,000	17,077,000,000
Return on Assets %	.02%	.01%	-.01%	.08%	.10%	.10%
Return on Equity %	.03%	.02%	-.03%	.16%	.21%	.21%
Debt to Equity	.51%	.58%	0.668	0.429	0.463	0.463

CONTACT INFORMATION:

Phone: 818 5601000 Fax:
Toll-Free:
Address: 500 S. Buena Vista St., Burbank, CA 91521 United States

STOCK TICKER/OTHER:

Stock Ticker: DIS Exchange: NYS
Employees: 220,000 Fiscal Year Ends: 09/30
Parent Company:

SALARIES/BONUSES:

Top Exec. Salary: $3,000,000 Bonus: $
Second Exec. Salary: Bonus: $
$2,500,000

OTHER THOUGHTS:

Estimated Female Officers or Directors: 7
Hot Spot for Advancement for Women/Minorities: Y

Sales, profits and employees may be estimates. Financial information, benefits and other data can change quickly and may vary from those stated here.

Washington Capitals
NAIC Code: 711211F

TYPES OF BUSINESS:
Professional Hockey Team (NHL)
Team Management and Operations

BRANDS/DIVISIONS/AFFILIATES:
Monumental Sports & Entertainment
Hershey Bears
South Carolina Stingrays

CONTACTS: Note: Officers with more than one job title may be intentionally listed here more than once.
Ted Leonsis, CEO
Dick Patrick, Pres.
Barry Trotz, Head Coach
Brian ManLellan, Sr. VP-Hockey Oper.

GROWTH PLANS/SPECIAL FEATURES:
The Washington Capitals is a Washington DC-based National Hockey League (NHL) team that plays in the Metropolitan division of the Eastern conference. The Capitals played its first season in 1974 and is owned and operated by Monumental Sports & Entertainment. Home games take place in the Capital One Arena, which seats 18,506 patrons for hockey events and are usually sold out. The NHL franchise has won two conference championship (1997-98, 2017-18), three Presidents' Trophy (2009-10, 2015-16, 2016-17) and 13 division championships (most recently in 2019-20). The team has historically seen a good deal of success, completing 14 consecutive playoff appearances from 1982-1996. The Capitals clenched their first and only Stanley Cup in 2017-18, beating the Vegas Golden Knights in five games. Notable Washington Capital players of the past include Denis Dupere, Bengt Gustafsson, Mike Gartner, Dennis Maruk and Calle Johansson. The team is affiliated with the Hershey Bears of the American Hockey League (AHL) and the South Carolina Stingrays of the ECHL. In December 2022, Forbes valued the Capitals at $1.2 billion.

FINANCIAL DATA: Note: Data for latest year may not have been available at press time.

In U.S. $	2022	2021	2020	2019	2018	2017
Revenue	142,350,000					
R&D Expense						
Operating Income						
Operating Margin %						
SGA Expense						
Net Income						
Operating Cash Flow						
Capital Expenditure						
EBITDA						
Return on Assets %						
Return on Equity %						
Debt to Equity						

CONTACT INFORMATION:
Phone: 202-266-2200   Fax: 202-266-2360
Toll-Free:
Address: 627 N. Glebe Rd., Ste. 850, Arlington, VA 22203 United States

STOCK TICKER/OTHER:
Stock Ticker: Private   Exchange:
Employees: 148   Fiscal Year Ends: 07/31
Parent Company: Monumental Sports & Entertainment

SALARIES/BONUSES:
Top Exec. Salary: $ Bonus: $
Second Exec. Salary: $ Bonus: $

OTHER THOUGHTS:
Estimated Female Officers or Directors: 3
Hot Spot for Advancement for Women/Minorities: Y

Washington Commanders

www.commanders.com

NAIC Code: 711211C

TYPES OF BUSINESS:

Professional Football Team
Team Management and Operations

BRANDS/DIVISIONS/AFFILIATES:

Washington Redskins
Washington Football Team

CONTACTS: *Note: Officers with more than one job title may be intentionally listed here more than once.*

Daniel M. Snyder, Co-CEO
Tanya Snyder, Co-CEO
Jason Wright, Pres.
John Winborn, VP-IT
Andre Chambers, Chief People Officer
Lauren John, VP-Finance
Eric Shaffer, VP-Football Admin.
Lon Rosenberg, Sr. VP-Oper.
Mike Shanahan, Head Coach
Bruce Allen, Gen. Mgr.
Tony Wyllie, Sr. VP
Paul Kelly, Dir.-Football Oper.
Martin Mayhew, Gen. Mngr.

GROWTH PLANS/SPECIAL FEATURES:

The Washington Commanders is a professional football team based in Washington DC, playing in the Eastern conference of the National Football League (NFL). The team has been in the NFL since 1932, tracing its origins to Boston, Massachusetts, where it played in Fenway Park (home of the Boston Red Sox). Due to poor attendance in the Boston area, the team was moved in 1937 to Washington DC. Over the course of the team's history, the Commanders have won five NFL Championships, including three of the five Super Bowls in which they have played. In 1999, as the club was sold to Daniel Snyder, chairman of Six Flags, Inc. and founder of Snyder Communications, Inc. Under terms of the deal, Snyder purchased the team and their then two-year-old stadium, FedEx Field, for $800 million following the death of previous owner Jack Kent Cooke. Under Snyder's ownership, team revenues have increased significantly, and Forbes valued the team at $5.6 billion in 2022, sixth within the NFL. Despite the team's lucrative financial run under Snyder, its on-field performance has been mediocre, with recent division championships occurring in 2012, 2015 and 2020. The Commanders have contributed more than 30 former players and coaching staff to the Pro Football Hall of Fame, including George Allen, Cliff Battles, Sammy Baugh, Turk Edwards, Darrell Green, Sonny Jurgensen and Art Monk. In 2020, the Washington Redskins changed its name to Washington Football Team, which played under the moniker for two seasons until it rebranded again in 2022 as the Washington Commanders.

FINANCIAL DATA: *Note: Data for latest year may not have been available at press time.*

In U.S. $	2022	2021	2020	2019	2018	2017
Revenue	579,800,000					
R&D Expense						
Operating Income						
Operating Margin %						
SGA Expense						
Net Income						
Operating Cash Flow						
Capital Expenditure						
EBITDA						
Return on Assets %						
Return on Equity %						
Debt to Equity						

CONTACT INFORMATION:

Phone: 703-726-7000   Fax: 703-726-7086
Toll-Free:
Address: 21300 Redskins Park Dr., Ashburn, VA 20147 United States

STOCK TICKER/OTHER:

Stock Ticker: Private   Exchange:
Employees: 490   Fiscal Year Ends: 01/31
Parent Company:

SALARIES/BONUSES:

Top Exec. Salary: $ Bonus: $
Second Exec. Salary: $ Bonus: $

OTHER THOUGHTS:

Estimated Female Officers or Directors: 1
Hot Spot for Advancement for Women/Minorities:

Washington Mystics
NAIC Code: 711211E

www.wnba.com/mystics

TYPES OF BUSINESS:
Women's Basketball Team
Team Management and Operations

BRANDS/DIVISIONS/AFFILIATES:
Monumental Sports & Entertainment

GROWTH PLANS/SPECIAL FEATURES:
The Washington Mystics is a Women's National Basketball Association (WNBA) team based in Washington DC. The Mystics, sister team to National Basketball Association's (NBA) Washington Wizards, play in the Eastern Conference along with the Atlanta Dream, Chicago Sky, Connecticut Sun, Indiana Fever and New York Liberty. Monumental Sports & Entertainment owns the Mystics. Home games are played at the Entertainment and Sports Arena, an 118,000-square-foot multi-purpose facility that seats 4,200. The Mystics' home game attendance average was 3,983 during the 2022 season. The Mystics qualified for the WNBA Playoffs in 2018 after clenching a Conference title, reaching the WNBA finals for the first time in franchise history. They played against the Seattle Storm, but were swept 0-3. Then in 2019, the Mystics returned to the WNBA finals and earned their first-ever championship with an 89-78 victory against Connecticut Sun.

CONTACTS:
Note: Officers with more than one job title may be intentionally listed here more than once.

Jim Van Stone, Pres.-Bus. Oper.
Hunter Lochmann, CMO
Thomas Glasgow, Sr. Dir.-Digital Mktg.
Kate Layman, Dir.-Game Oper.
Scott Hall, Sr. Dir.-Comm.
Mike Thibault, Gen. Mgr.
Maria Giovannetti, Dir.-Basketball Oper.
Jim Van Stone, Sr. VP-Ticket Sales & Svcs.
Tom Hunt, Sr. VP-Corp. Partnerships

FINANCIAL DATA:
Note: Data for latest year may not have been available at press time.

In U.S. $	2022	2021	2020	2019	2018	2017
Revenue						
R&D Expense						
Operating Income						
Operating Margin %						
SGA Expense						
Net Income						
Operating Cash Flow						
Capital Expenditure						
EBITDA						
Return on Assets %						
Return on Equity %						
Debt to Equity						

CONTACT INFORMATION:
Phone: 202-527-7540   Fax: 202-527-7539
Toll-Free:
Address: 601 F St. NW, Fl. 3, Washington, DC 20004 United States

STOCK TICKER/OTHER:
Stock Ticker: Private   Exchange:
Employees: 107   Fiscal Year Ends: 01/31
Parent Company: Monumental Sports & Entertainment

SALARIES/BONUSES:
Top Exec. Salary: $ Bonus: $
Second Exec. Salary: $ Bonus: $

OTHER THOUGHTS:
Estimated Female Officers or Directors: 15
Hot Spot for Advancement for Women/Minorities: Y

Washington Nationals

www.mlb.com/nationals

NAIC Code: 711211A

TYPES OF BUSINESS:

Professional Baseball Team
Team Management and Operations

BRANDS/DIVISIONS/AFFILIATES:

Montreal Expos

CONTACTS: *Note: Officers with more than one job title may be intentionally listed here more than once.*

Mark D. Lerner, Managing Principal
Mike Rizzo, Pres.-Baseball Oper.
Ted Towne, VP-Finance
Elise Holman, Sr. VP-Admin.
Damon T. Jones, General Counsel
Mike Rizzo, Exec. VP-Baseball Oper.
John Knebel, Managing Dir.-Bus. Dev. & Corp. Partnerships
Chad Kurz, Dir.-New Media & Creative Svcs.
Lara Potter, Managing Dir.-Comm. & Brand Dev.
Ted Towne, VP-Finance
Bob Boone, Assistant Gen. Mgr.
Roy Clark, Assistant Gen. Mgr.
Chris Gargani, VP
Gregory McCarthy, VP-Gov't & Municipal Affairs
Johnny DiPuglia, Dir.-Int'l Scouting

GROWTH PLANS/SPECIAL FEATURES:

The Washington Nationals is a professional baseball team based in Washington DC. The franchise was founded in 1969 as the Montreal Expos as part of a four-team expansion, and were later purchased by Major League Baseball (MLB) which relocated the team to Washington DC. As the Montreal Expos, the team obtained a division title in 1981, but struggled throughout its formative years. Eventually, the Washington Nationals was established in 2005, and continues to compete in the Eastern Division of the National League and has since clenched another four division titles (most recently in 2016 and 2017), as well as a World Series title in 2019. The Nationals began the 2019 season with a 19-31 record, but turned things around with a 74-38 win/loss record across the remaining 112 games, earning a wild card game. The Nationals won the wild card game against the Brewers, then defeated the Dodgers in five games, propelling them beyond the divisional round for the first time ever. The Nationals defeated the Houston Astros in game seven, clenching the 2019 World Series. Former players and managers inducted into the Baseball Hall of Fame include Tony Perez, Gary Carter, Randy Johnson, Pedro Martinez, Frank Robinson and Ivan Rodriguez. The Washington Nationals plays in the 41,339-seat National Park, and averaged 25,017 fans per home game during the 2022-23 season. Forbes valued the Nationals at $2.5 billion in March 2023.

FINANCIAL DATA: *Note: Data for latest year may not have been available at press time.*

In U.S. $	2022	2021	2020	2019	2018	2017
Revenue	519,000,000					
R&D Expense						
Operating Income						
Operating Margin %						
SGA Expense						
Net Income						
Operating Cash Flow						
Capital Expenditure						
EBITDA						
Return on Assets %						
Return on Equity %						
Debt to Equity						

CONTACT INFORMATION:

Phone: 202-675-6287   Fax: 202-640-7999
Toll-Free:
Address: 1500 S. Capitol St. SE, Washington, DC 20003 United States

STOCK TICKER/OTHER:

Stock Ticker: Private   Exchange:
Employees: 1,130   Fiscal Year Ends: 10/31
Parent Company:

SALARIES/BONUSES:

Top Exec. Salary: $ Bonus: $
Second Exec. Salary: $ Bonus: $

OTHER THOUGHTS:

Estimated Female Officers or Directors: 12
Hot Spot for Advancement for Women/Minorities: Y

Washington Wizards

www.nba.com/wizards

NAIC Code: 711211B

TYPES OF BUSINESS:

Professional Basketball Team
Team Management and Operations

BRANDS/DIVISIONS/AFFILIATES:

Monumental Sports & Entertainment
Capital One Arena
Capital City Go-Go

CONTACTS: *Note: Officers with more than one job title may be intentionally listed here more than once.*

Ted Leonsis, CEO
Tommy Sheppard, VP-Basketball Admin.
Greg Bibb, Exec. VP-Bus. Oper.
Sashia Jones, Sr. Dir.-Community Rel.
Keith Burrows, VP-Finance
Milt Newton, VP-Player Personnel
Derric Whitfield, Dir.-Dance Team
Tom Hunt, Sr. VP-Corp. Partnerships & Monumental Sports
Randy Wittman, Head Coach

GROWTH PLANS/SPECIAL FEATURES:

The Washington Wizards is a Washington DC-based National Basketball Association (NBA) team owned by Monumental Sports & Entertainment. Since its 1961 creation, the team has undergone numerous name changes, including Chicago Packers, Chicago Zephyrs, Baltimore Bullets, Capital Bullets, Washington Bullets and then the Washington Wizards from 1997 onward. Throughout its franchise history, the team has won one championship in 1978, under the leadership of Wes Unseld and Phil Chenier. The rest of the team's achievements, including four conference titles and eight division titles, primarily occurred in the 1970s, except for its most recent division title in 2017. The Wizards received major publicity coverage when former Chicago Bulls star Michael Jordan returned from retirement and played on the team during the 2001-02 and 2002-03 seasons. In 2014-15, the Wizards made it to the semifinals in the Playoffs, but were defeated by the Atlanta Hawks, 2-4. In 2017, the team won the division title (southeast, within the Eastern conference) for the first time since 1979. Jordan briefly managed the team, but failed to have a significant immediate impact. All home games are played at the Capital One Arena, which is also owned by Monumental Sports & Entertainment, and has seating capacity for 20,356 basketball fans. Wizard home game attendance averaged 17,328 during the 2022-23 season. Capital City Go-Go is an affiliate team of the Wizards, playing in the NBA G League. Forbes estimated the Washington Wizards worth $2.5 billion in October 2022.

FINANCIAL DATA: *Note: Data for latest year may not have been available at press time.*

In U.S. $	2022	2021	2020	2019	2018	2017
Revenue	288,600,000					
R&D Expense						
Operating Income						
Operating Margin %						
SGA Expense						
Net Income						
Operating Cash Flow						
Capital Expenditure						
EBITDA						
Return on Assets %						
Return on Equity %						
Debt to Equity						

CONTACT INFORMATION:

Phone: 202-628-3200   Fax: 202-661-5101
Toll-Free:
Address: 601 F St. NW, Washington, DC 20004 United States

STOCK TICKER/OTHER:

Stock Ticker: Private   Exchange:
Employees: 470   Fiscal Year Ends: 06/30
Parent Company: Monumental Sports & Entertainment

SALARIES/BONUSES:

Top Exec. Salary: $ Bonus: $
Second Exec. Salary: $ Bonus: $

OTHER THOUGHTS:

Estimated Female Officers or Directors: 12
Hot Spot for Advancement for Women/Minorities: Y

Sales, profits and employees may be estimates. Financial information, benefits and other data can change quickly and may vary from those stated here.

Wasserman Media Group LLC

www.teamwass.com

NAIC Code: 711410

TYPES OF BUSINESS:

Sports Management Agency
Marketing and Branding Services
Talent Agency
Consultancy
Media Network
Sports and Entertainment Agency

BRANDS/DIVISIONS/AFFILIATES:

Laundry Service
Cycle
Riddle & Bloom
Collective (The)
Athlete Exchange
Jet Sports Management

CONTACTS: *Note: Officers with more than one job title may be intentionally listed here more than once.*

Casey Wasserman, CEO
Trista Schroeder, General Counsel
Stephanie Rudnick, VP-Corp. Comm.
Arn Tellem, Head-Team Sports Div.
Sara Munds, Co-Pres., Global Media Div.-London
Malcolm Turner, Pres., Golf Div.
Fahri Ecvet, COO-Global Football
David Kogan, Co-Pres., Global Media Div.-London

GROWTH PLANS/SPECIAL FEATURES:

Wasserman Media Group, LLC is a full-service agency that serves talent and brands worldwide. The company's agency expertise spans sports, entertainment, music, social, media, consultancy, culture and more. Wasserman represents thousands of athletes, broadcasters, coaches and social media influencers, supporting their careers, business and brand opportunities. Its brands division offers consultancy services and solutions, and its properties division provides ways to capitalize the commercial landscape for marketing purposes. Wasserman's family of brands include: Laundry Service, a full-service agency offering creative, production and media buying; Cycle, an influencer and branded content company designed to give brands premium content, cultural relevance and to reach audiences; Riddle & Bloom, an ideas and access agency that connects brands to the next generation of consumers through cultural experiences; The Collective, which empowers women to elevate brands, businesses and careers; and Athlete Exchange, a media network that combines talent endorsement, branded content creation and targeted distribution. Wasserman is based in the U.S. and has office locations throughout the world. During 2022, Wasserman acquired Jet Sports Management, a sports talent agency with a focus on Major League Baseball.

FINANCIAL DATA: *Note: Data for latest year may not have been available at press time.*

In U.S. $	2022	2021	2020	2019	2018	2017
Revenue	130,000,000	127,968,750	121,875,000	125,000,000	114,000,000	114,000,000
R&D Expense						
Operating Income						
Operating Margin %						
SGA Expense						
Net Income						
Operating Cash Flow						
Capital Expenditure						
EBITDA						
Return on Assets %						
Return on Equity %						
Debt to Equity						

CONTACT INFORMATION:

Phone: 310-407-0200   Fax:
Toll-Free:
Address: 10900 Wilshire Blvd., Ste. 1200, Los Angeles, CA 90024
United States

STOCK TICKER/OTHER:

Stock Ticker: Private   Exchange:
Employees: 500   Fiscal Year Ends:
Parent Company:

SALARIES/BONUSES:

Top Exec. Salary: $ Bonus: $
Second Exec. Salary: $ Bonus: $

OTHER THOUGHTS:

Estimated Female Officers or Directors: 5
Hot Spot for Advancement for Women/Minorities: Y

West Bromwich Albion Football Club   www.wba.co.uk

NAIC Code: 711211D

TYPES OF BUSINESS:

Soccer Team
Team Management and Operations

BRANDS/DIVISIONS/AFFILIATES:

Baggies
Albion Foundation

CONTACTS: *Note: Officers with more than one job title may be intentionally listed here more than once.*

Ron Gourlay, CEO
Mark Miles, Dir.-Operations
John G. Silk, Pres.
Xiao Pu, Dir.-Finance
Ian Skidmore, Dir.-Communications
Mark Miles, Head-Facility Oper. & Dev.
John Simpson, Press Officer
Guochuan Lai, Chmn.

GROWTH PLANS/SPECIAL FEATURES:

West Bromwich Albion Football Club (Albion) is a professional English football team based in the U.K. Formed in 1878, Albion has played at its current home stadium, The Hawthorns, since the stadium's completion in 1900. It seats roughly 26,850 and was one of the first to feature big screens in widescreen format, which were added at the beginning of the 2002-03 season. Average home attendance for the Ablions was 22,844 during the 2022-23 season. Albion was the first U.K. professional team to win in Soviet Russia, in 1957, as well as the first British team to play in China, in 1978. The team was originally nicknamed the Throstles after the thrush on their jerseys, but in 1905 earned the nickname the Baggies, the origin of which is uncertain. Albion has earned a number of honors over the course of the club's history, including one Football League First Division/Premier League championship, three Football League Second Division/EFL Championships, five FA Cups, one Football League Cup, two FA Charity Shields and one FA Youth Cup. The team has been in and out of the Premier League several times since the 2002-03 season. The 2017-2018 season saw Albion finish last in the Premier League and was regulated to the Championship League. The team also runs the Albion Foundation, a registered charity that sponsors various after-school clubs for children and offers a range of sports and education programs.

FINANCIAL DATA: *Note: Data for latest year may not have been available at press time.*

In U.S. $	2022	2021	2020	2019	2018	2017
Revenue	85,000,000	76,940,447	69,945,861	92,861,600	178,838,000	178,838,000
R&D Expense						
Operating Income						
Operating Margin %						
SGA Expense						
Net Income			-26,959,766	-9,181,230	41,874,600	41,874,600
Operating Cash Flow						
Capital Expenditure						
EBITDA						
Return on Assets %						
Return on Equity %						
Debt to Equity						

CONTACT INFORMATION:

Phone: 44-121-524-3470   Fax:
Toll-Free:
Address: 9 Birmingham Rd, West Bromwich, B71 4LF United Kingdom

STOCK TICKER/OTHER:

Stock Ticker: Private   Exchange:
Employees: 200   Fiscal Year Ends: 06/30
Parent Company:

SALARIES/BONUSES:

Top Exec. Salary: $ Bonus: $
Second Exec. Salary: $ Bonus: $

OTHER THOUGHTS:

Estimated Female Officers or Directors: 1
Hot Spot for Advancement for Women/Minorities:

West Ham United Football Club
www.whufc.com

NAIC Code: 711211D

TYPES OF BUSINESS:
English Premiere Soccer Team
Team Management and Operations

BRANDS/DIVISIONS/AFFILIATES:
Thames Ironworks
Hammers
Members Club

CONTACTS: Note: Officers with more than one job title may be intentionally listed here more than once.
David Sullivan, Co-Chmn.
David Gold, Co-Chmn.
David Moyes, Mngr.

GROWTH PLANS/SPECIAL FEATURES:
West Ham United Football Club is a professional English football club based in London, England, playing in the top-tier Premier League. Founded in 1895 as the Thames Ironworks, the club was given its current West Ham United name in 1900 and is often called the Hammers. West Ham has won many honors throughout its history. Domestically, these include two second-tier Football League titles, a Western Football League championship, three FA Cups (most recent in 1979-80), an FA Charity Shield, a Football League War Cup, a Southern Floodlit Cup, nine London Challenge Cups, and others. West Ham clenched a European Cup, a UEFA Intertoto Cup, and an International Soccer League title. The team plays at the 62,500-capacity London Stadium, which was built for the 2012 London Olympics, and averaged 58,990 per home game attendance during the 2022-23 season. West Ham offers seasonal memberships, giving members access to the Members' Club, a ticket to the game as well as lounge access, complimentary drinks, legend appearances, priority tickets for away games and more. West Ham United runs the West Ham United Foundation, a social and community outreach organization that provides opportunities for the residents of Eats London and Essex.

FINANCIAL DATA: Note: Data for latest year may not have been available at press time.

In U.S. $	2022	2021	2020	2019	2018	2017
Revenue	285,000,000	272,451,678	171,108,066	250,123,000	235,396,000	235,396,000
R&D Expense						
Operating Income						
Operating Margin %						
SGA Expense						
Net Income		-31,371,599	-79,916,756	36,987,200	25,732,500	25,732,500
Operating Cash Flow						
Capital Expenditure						
EBITDA						
Return on Assets %						
Return on Equity %						
Debt to Equity						

CONTACT INFORMATION:
Phone: 44 20 8548 2748   Fax: 020 8548 2758
Toll-Free:
Address: London Stadium, Queen Elizabeth Olympic Park, London, E20 2ST United Kingdom

STOCK TICKER/OTHER:
Stock Ticker: Private
Employees: 652
Parent Company:

Exchange:
Fiscal Year Ends: 05/31

SALARIES/BONUSES:
Top Exec. Salary: $ Bonus: $
Second Exec. Salary: $ Bonus: $

OTHER THOUGHTS:
Estimated Female Officers or Directors:
Hot Spot for Advancement for Women/Minorities:

Sales, profits and employees may be estimates. Financial information, benefits and other data can change quickly and may vary from those stated here.

West Marine Inc

NAIC Code: 441222

TYPES OF BUSINESS:

Boating Supplies, Retail
Catalog & Online Sales
Marine Products
Anchor and Docking Products
Boats and Motor Parts
Marine Electronics
Marine Apparel
Ecommerce

BRANDS/DIVISIONS/AFFILIATES:

L Catterton

GROWTH PLANS/SPECIAL FEATURES:

West Marine, Inc. is a specialty retailer of recreational and commercial boating supplies in North America. The company operates approximately 235 stores in 38 U.S. states and Puerto Rico under the brand name West Marine, as well as ecommerce websites, reaching domestic, international and professional customers. The firm offers a selection of marine products, with categories including anchor and docking, boats/motors/parts, electrical, electronics and navigation, fishing, galley and outdoor, maintenance and hardware, men's, women's paddling, plumbing and ventilation, safety, sailing, shoes and water sports. West Marine sells directly through its catalogs and website as well as through its virtual call center, allowing customers access to technical product advice through trained sales representatives. West Marine is privately-owned by L Catterton.

CONTACTS: Note: Officers with more than one job title may be intentionally listed here more than once.

Chuck Rubin, CEO
Calvin Hollinger, COO
Jim Grady, CFO
Paulee Day, Chief Human Resources Officer
Barbara Rambo, Director
Randolph Repass, Director
Barry Kelley, Executive VP, Divisional
Paul Rutenis, Executive VP, Divisional

FINANCIAL DATA: Note: Data for latest year may not have been available at press time.

In U.S. $	2022	2021	2020	2019	2018	2017
Revenue	765,000,000	757,506,750	721,435,000	715,000,000	705,000,000	705,000,000
R&D Expense						
Operating Income						
Operating Margin %						
SGA Expense						
Net Income						
Operating Cash Flow						
Capital Expenditure						
EBITDA						
Return on Assets %						
Return on Equity %						
Debt to Equity						

CONTACT INFORMATION:

Phone: 831-728-2700   Fax:
Toll-Free:
Address: 500 Westridge Dr., Watsonville, CA 95076 United States

STOCK TICKER/OTHER:

Stock Ticker: Private   Exchange:
Employees: 5,000   Fiscal Year Ends: 12/31
Parent Company: L Catterton

SALARIES/BONUSES:

Top Exec. Salary: $ Bonus: $
Second Exec. Salary: $ Bonus: $

OTHER THOUGHTS:

Estimated Female Officers or Directors: 6
Hot Spot for Advancement for Women/Minorities: Y

WHOOP Inc

www.whoop.com

NAIC Code: 334118

TYPES OF BUSINESS:

Health Tracking & Monitoring Devices
Fitness Technology
Data Analytics
Human Performance Optimization
Wearable Fitness Tracker

BRANDS/DIVISIONS/AFFILIATES:

WHOOP

CONTACTS: *Note: Officers with more than one job title may be intentionally listed here more than once.*

Will Ahmed, CEO

GROWTH PLANS/SPECIAL FEATURES:

WHOOP, Inc. is a technology and data analytics company with a focus on human performance optimization. The firm has developed a system that offers an approach to understanding the body in order to prevent over-training, under-training, injury and/or fatigue. WHOOP as a company is made up of athletes, mechanical engineers, designers and data scientists that have collaborated, tested and developed a wearable fitness tracker for transforming behavior and fitness, and for injury reduction. The WHOOP platform also offers athletes tangible performance data such as wins/losses, batting average, time trials and more, across sport types. How it works: members receive WHOOP hardware for every generation released, which can be worn non-stop due (on wrist or off via body apparel), contains five LEDs and four photodiodes for capturing data, and can be charged wirelessly with a waterproof battery pack. All information is displayed through the WHOOP app. The strap's core analytics monitors trends for evaluation and insight purposes. The WHOOP app community (available for iOS, Android and desktop) enables users to create or join like-minded teams, based on features such as activities, interests, training groups and more. Significant improvements include reduced resting heart rate, increased heart rate variability, better sleep, fewer injuries, less consumed alcohol before bed and minimized symptoms of exhaustion due to traveling. Daily behaviors can be tracked through the app, such as type of diet, stress levels and caffeine intake for navigating which behaviors affect sleep, recovery and more. WHOOP also serves organizations with its performance products, including athletic, business and government/defense entities.

WHOOP offers its employees health benefits, life and disability insurance, a 401(k) and company perks.

FINANCIAL DATA: *Note: Data for latest year may not have been available at press time.*

In U.S. $	2022	2021	2020	2019	2018	2017
Revenue						
R&D Expense						
Operating Income						
Operating Margin %						
SGA Expense						
Net Income						
Operating Cash Flow						
Capital Expenditure						
EBITDA						
Return on Assets %						
Return on Equity %						
Debt to Equity						

CONTACT INFORMATION:

Phone: 844 490-1593   Fax:
Toll-Free:
Address: 1325 Boylston St., Ste. 401, Boston, MA 02215 United States

STOCK TICKER/OTHER:

Stock Ticker: Private   Exchange:
Employees: 500   Fiscal Year Ends:
Parent Company:

SALARIES/BONUSES:

Top Exec. Salary: $ Bonus: $
Second Exec. Salary: $ Bonus: $

OTHER THOUGHTS:

Estimated Female Officers or Directors:
Hot Spot for Advancement for Women/Minorities:

Wilson Sporting Goods Co

www.wilson.com

NAIC Code: 339920

TYPES OF BUSINESS:

Sporting Goods
Sports Apparel
Sports Accessories
Pitching Machines
Golf Equipment
Balls
Product Manufacturing
Retail Stores and Ecommerce

BRANDS/DIVISIONS/AFFILIATES:

Amer Sports Corporation
Wilson Staff
Ultra
ProStaff
Wilson.com
Louisville
DeMarini
ATEC

CONTACTS: Note: Officers with more than one job title may be intentionally listed here more than once.

Joe Dudy, Pres.
Susie White, Dir.-Oper.
Molly Wallace, Dir.-Comm.
Mike Kuehne, Gen. Mgr.-Inflates Mktg.
Chris Rusin, Mgr.-Golf National Sales

GROWTH PLANS/SPECIAL FEATURES:

Wilson Sporting Goods Co., a subsidiary of Finland-based Amer Sports Corporation, is one of the world's leading manufacturers and marketers of ball sports equipment. The company serves customers in over 100 countries and its products are used by the National Football League (NFL), National Collegiate Athletic Association (NCAA), Championship Volleyball, Inc. and numerous collegiate and professional tennis and soccer teams. Wilson's products include sports-related equipment and apparel for team sports, such as baseball, fast pitch/slow pitch softball, basketball, volleyball, football and soccer; racquet sports, such as tennis, racquetball, badminton and squash; and golf. The firm's golf division, Wilson Staff, designs and manufactures golf equipment such as drivers, irons, putters, balls and bags under the Wilson Staff, Ultra and ProStaff brand names. Products are sold globally through an extensive sales network with specialty stores and chain sporting goods stores, as well as a few Wilson branded retail stores located in the U.S. Wilson's website features a section that helps customers choose the right gear by age, position and type of play. Additionally, Wilson.com offers a Players & Coaches section, allowing readers to locate statistics on numerous players and coaches in different sports and to view the products that they use. Wilson's family of brands encompass Louisville, DeMarini, ATEC, EvoShield and Luxilon.

Wilson Sporting Goods offers its employees medical and dental insurance, and a 401(k).

FINANCIAL DATA: Note: Data for latest year may not have been available at press time.

In U.S. $	2022	2021	2020	2019	2018	2017
Revenue						
R&D Expense						
Operating Income						
Operating Margin %						
SGA Expense						
Net Income						
Operating Cash Flow						
Capital Expenditure						
EBITDA						
Return on Assets %						
Return on Equity %						
Debt to Equity						

CONTACT INFORMATION:

Phone: 773 714-6400   Fax:
Toll-Free: 800-401-7967
Address: 1 Prudential Plaza, 130 E. Randolph St., Ste. 600, Chicago, IL 60601 United States

STOCK TICKER/OTHER:

Stock Ticker: Subsidiary   Exchange:
Employees: 1,500   Fiscal Year Ends: 12/31
Parent Company: Amer Sports Corporation

SALARIES/BONUSES:

Top Exec. Salary: $ Bonus: $
Second Exec. Salary: $ Bonus: $

OTHER THOUGHTS:

Estimated Female Officers or Directors: 2
Hot Spot for Advancement for Women/Minorities: Y

Winnipeg Jets

NAIC Code: 711211F

TYPES OF BUSINESS:
Professional Hockey Team (NHL)
Team Management and Operations

BRANDS/DIVISIONS/AFFILIATES:
True North Sports & Entertainment
Manitoba Moose

CONTACTS: Note: Officers with more than one job title may be intentionally listed here more than once.
Kevin Cheveldayoff, General Mngr.
John Olfert, Pres.
Lorna Daniels, CFO
Dorian Morphy, VP-Mktg.
Dawn Haus, VP-People & Culture
Christina Litz, CCO
Craig Heisinger, Sr. VP-Hockey Oper.
Scott Brown, Sr. Dir.-Corp. Comm.
Mark Chipman, Chmn.

GROWTH PLANS/SPECIAL FEATURES:
The Winnipeg Jets is a National Hockey League (NHL) professional hockey team based in Manitoba, playing in the Central division of the Western conference. Beginning as an expansion franchise based in Atlanta, Georgia in June 1997, the team is one of the newest in the NHL. Atlanta Spirit purchased the franchise from Time Warner in 2004; then True North Sports & Entertainment purchased the franchise from Atlanta Spirit in 2011 and later moved the team to Winnipeg, hence the Winnipeg Jets. The franchise has found little success since its inception. The team's home venue is the Canada Life Centre, which comprises approximately 15,320 seats for ice hockey games. The Jets averaged 14,045 in home game attendance during the 2022-23 season. The Manitoba Moose are a minor league affiliate of the Winnipeg Jets, and play in the American Hockey League (AHL). In December 2022, Forbes estimated the team's value to be $650 million.

FINANCIAL DATA: Note: Data for latest year may not have been available at press time.

In U.S. $	2022	2021	2020	2019	2018	2017
Revenue	130,000,000	68,000,000	117,000,000	127,000,000	119,000,000	119,000,000
R&D Expense						
Operating Income						
Operating Margin %						
SGA Expense						
Net Income		-46,000,000	-7,600,000	-7,700,000	10,000,000	10,000,000
Operating Cash Flow						
Capital Expenditure						
EBITDA						
Return on Assets %						
Return on Equity %						
Debt to Equity						

CONTACT INFORMATION:
Phone: 204-987-7825　　　Fax:
Toll-Free:
Address: 600-223 Carlton St., Winnipeg, MB R3C 0V4 Canada

STOCK TICKER/OTHER:
Stock Ticker: Private　　　Exchange:
Employees: 150　　　Fiscal Year Ends: 12/31
Parent Company: True North Sports & Entertainment Limited

SALARIES/BONUSES:
Top Exec. Salary: $　　　Bonus: $
Second Exec. Salary: $　　　Bonus: $

OTHER THOUGHTS:
Estimated Female Officers or Directors: 6
Hot Spot for Advancement for Women/Minorities: Y

Sales, profits and employees may be estimates. Financial information, benefits and other data can change quickly and may vary from those stated here.

Winter Sports Inc
www.skiwhitefish.com
NAIC Code: 713920

TYPES OF BUSINESS:
Ski Resorts
Property Management
Hotel and Lodging
Restaurant and Dining
Retail Shops
Repair Shops

BRANDS/DIVISIONS/AFFILIATES:
Whitefish Mountain Resort

CONTACTS: *Note: Officers with more than one job title may be intentionally listed here more than once.*
Nick Polumbus, CEO
Daniel Graves, Pres.
Riley Polumbus, Mgr.-Public Rel.
Bill Cubbage, Dir.-Snow Sports
Bill Foley, Chmn.

GROWTH PLANS/SPECIAL FEATURES:
Winter Sports, Inc. owns and operates the Whitefish Mountain Resort, a ski resort located on 3,000 acres around Big Mountain in the Rocky Mountains of Montana. The company's ski facilities include: high-speed quads, fixed-grips, triples, T-bars and a carpet conveyor. The ski terrain's difficulty is around 15% beginner, 35% intermediate, 40% advanced and 10% expert. It has more than 100 marked trails, with Hellfire being the longest at 3.3 miles. Winter Sports also operates: a lodging and hotel facility; restaurant/dining options; a ski rental, retail and repair shop; a ski school; a retail store at the mountain's peak; a day spa; and a ski shop and services operation. Associated recreational opportunities include snowshoeing, Nordic skiing, tubing, snowmobiling, dog sledding, ice-skating and winter tours of nearby Glacier National Park. In addition, Winter Sports operates a property management business, as well as a real estate brokerage business that leases and sells condos, townhomes and single-family homes within the mountain village area. Nearly half of company revenues come from lease arrangements via other companies who use this land. The firm also operates on a limited basis between June and October, offering chairlift and gondola rides to the summit for sightseeing, hiking, mountain biking, zip lining and other recreational activities.

FINANCIAL DATA: *Note: Data for latest year may not have been available at press time.*

In U.S. $	2022	2021	2020	2019	2018	2017
Revenue						
R&D Expense						
Operating Income						
Operating Margin %						
SGA Expense						
Net Income						
Operating Cash Flow						
Capital Expenditure						
EBITDA						
Return on Assets %						
Return on Equity %						
Debt to Equity						

CONTACT INFORMATION:
Phone: 406 862-1900   Fax: 406 862-2955
Toll-Free:
Address: 3889 Big Mountain Rd., Whitefish, MT 59937 United States

STOCK TICKER/OTHER:
Stock Ticker: Private   Exchange:
Employees: 80   Fiscal Year Ends: 05/31
Parent Company:

SALARIES/BONUSES:
Top Exec. Salary: $ Bonus: $
Second Exec. Salary: $ Bonus: $

OTHER THOUGHTS:
Estimated Female Officers or Directors: 1
Hot Spot for Advancement for Women/Minorities:

Wolverhampton Wanderers Football Club

www.wolves.co.uk

NAIC Code: 711211D

TYPES OF BUSINESS:

English Premiere Soccer Team
Team Management and Operations

BRANDS/DIVISIONS/AFFILIATES:

Fosun International Limited
Wolverhampton Wanderers
Wolves
Under-23
Wolverhampton Wanderers Womens FC

CONTACTS: *Note: Officers with more than one job title may be intentionally listed here more than once.*

Jenny Wilkes, Chmn.

GROWTH PLANS/SPECIAL FEATURES:

Wolverhampton Wanderers Football Club, owned by Fosun International Limited, is a professional English football club based in England. Located in Wolverhampton, West Midlands, the Wanderers play in the top-tier Premier League. Also nicknamed as the Wolves, the club also has a second-tier Under-23 team and a professional women's team, known as Wolves Women. Founded in 1877, the club has a successful domestic history, with three Football League First Division championships, four EFL Championship/Football League Second Division championships, four FA Cups, two Football League Cups, four FA Charity Shields, a Football League Trophy, a Football League War Cup and a Texaco Cup. The Wanderers have played at Molineux Stadium since 1889, and had an average of 31,477 fans in home game attendance during the 2022-23 season. The club finished 7th in the 2018-2019 Premier League season, allowing the club to play in the 2019-2020 UEFA Europa League for the first time. The Under-23 team and youth academy give young players a chance to hone their skills in hopes of making the first team. Wolverhampton Wanderers Women's Football Club (also known as Wolves Women) currently play in the third level of English women's football in the FA Women's National League North, with home games at the New Bucks Head stadium in Shropshire, England.

FINANCIAL DATA: *Note: Data for latest year may not have been available at press time.*

In U.S. $	2022	2021	2020	2019	2018	2017
Revenue	300,000,000	275,288,298	163,685,919	226,199,000	30,480,500	30,480,500
R&D Expense						
Operating Income						
Operating Margin %						
SGA Expense						
Net Income		29,940,524	-45,264,849	-79,858,635	-26,744,300	-26,744,300
Operating Cash Flow						
Capital Expenditure						
EBITDA						
Return on Assets %						
Return on Equity %						
Debt to Equity						

CONTACT INFORMATION:

Phone: 0371 222 2220   Fax: 0371 222 1877
Toll-Free:
Address: Molineux Stadium, Waterloo Rd., Wolverhampton, WV1 4QR United Kingdom

STOCK TICKER/OTHER:

Stock Ticker: Subsidiary   Exchange:
Employees: 379   Fiscal Year Ends: 05/31
Parent Company: Fosun International Limited

SALARIES/BONUSES:

Top Exec. Salary: $ Bonus: $
Second Exec. Salary: $ Bonus: $

OTHER THOUGHTS:

Estimated Female Officers or Directors:
Hot Spot for Advancement for Women/Minorities:

Womens National Basketball Association (WNBA)

www.wnba.com
NAIC Code: 711211

TYPES OF BUSINESS:

Professional Women's Basketball League

BRANDS/DIVISIONS/AFFILIATES:

National Basketball Association

CONTACTS: *Note: Officers with more than one job title may be intentionally listed here more than once.*

Jamin S. Dershowitz, General Counsel
Renee Brown, Chief-Basketball Oper. & Player Rel.
Rachel Jacobson, Sr. VP-Bus. Dev.
Dina Skokos, Dir.-WNBA Comm.
Michael Whitehead, Sr. VP-Finance
Todd Harris, VP-Broadcasting
Melissa Brenner, VP-Mktg.
Donna Daniels, VP-Team Mktg. & Bus. Dev.
Cathy Engelbert, Commissioner

GROWTH PLANS/SPECIAL FEATURES:

The Women's National Basketball Association (WNBA) operates the first women's professional basketball league fully supported by the National Basketball Association (NBA), which owned the WNBA until 2002. The WNBA is currently a privately-owned entity. The league plays from May to September, after the NBA regular season, allowing many WNBA players to use the off-season to play for teams overseas. League games are broadcast via partnerships, including ABC, ESPN, CBS, NBA TV in the U.S. and several international partners. The WNBA began with just eight teams in 1997, and through a series of expansions, contractions and relocations, the league currently consists of 12 teams; but there has been a total of 18 franchises in WNBA history. Current teams play within two conferences: Eastern, which includes the Atlanta Dream, Chicago Sky, Connecticut Sun, Indiana Fever, New York Liberty and Washington Mystics; and Western, including the Dallas Wings, Las Vegas Aces, Los Angeles Sparks, Minnesota Lynx, Phoenix Mercury and Seattle Storm. Since 2022, the playoffs have been held in a standard knockout format, with the first round consisting of a best-of-three series, and the semi-finals and finals being a best-of-five. The Las Vegas Aces were the champions in 2022, beating the Connecticut Sun 3-1.

FINANCIAL DATA: *Note: Data for latest year may not have been available at press time.*

In U.S. $	2022	2021	2020	2019	2018	2017
Revenue						
R&D Expense						
Operating Income						
Operating Margin %						
SGA Expense						
Net Income						
Operating Cash Flow						
Capital Expenditure						
EBITDA						
Return on Assets %						
Return on Equity %						
Debt to Equity						

CONTACT INFORMATION:

Phone: 212-688-9622   Fax: 212-750-9622
Toll-Free:
Address: 645 5th Ave., Olympic Tower, New York, NY 10022 United States

STOCK TICKER/OTHER:

Stock Ticker: Private   Exchange:
Employees: Fiscal Year Ends: 06/30
Parent Company:

SALARIES/BONUSES:

Top Exec. Salary: $ Bonus: $
Second Exec. Salary: $ Bonus: $

OTHER THOUGHTS:

Estimated Female Officers or Directors: 25
Hot Spot for Advancement for Women/Minorities: Y

Womens Tennis Association (WTA)

www.wtatennis.com

NAIC Code: 711211

TYPES OF BUSINESS:

Tennis Association
Women's Professional Tennis Organization
Tennis Tournaments
Tennis Professional Ranking System
Professional Sport Awards

BRANDS/DIVISIONS/AFFILIATES:

WTA Tour
Grand Slam
WTA 1000
WTA 500
WTA 250
Billie Jean King Cup
WTA Finals
WTA Elite Trophy

CONTACTS: *Note: Officers with more than one job title may be intentionally listed here more than once.*

Steve Simon, CEO
Micky Lawler, Pres.
Matthew Cenedella, COO
Diana Myers, General Counsel
Joan Pennello, Sr. VP-Oper.
Chris Wallace, Sr. VP-Comm.
John Learing, VP-Broadcast
Ashley Keber, Sr. Dir.-Player Rel. & Player Dev.
Kirsten Fisher, VP-Sales & Sponsorship Mktg.
Jean Nachand, VP-Competition & On-site Oper.
Steve Simon, Chmn.
Peter Johnston, Managing Dir.-Asia Pacific

GROWTH PLANS/SPECIAL FEATURES:

The Women's Tennis Association (WTA) manages the WTA Tour, an international professional tennis organization with more than 1,650 female athletes representing approximately 85 countries. The association was founded in 1970, with only nine players inspired to build a future for women's tennis. The WTA Tour comprises over 50 events and four Grand Slam tournaments (supervised by the International Tennis Federation, ITF), spanning six continents and nearly 30 countries and regions. The WTA Tour culminates with the WTA Finals, comprised of the season's top singles and doubles players based on the final standings of the Race to WTA Finals leaderboard. WTA awards points to players, including singles and doubles as well as qualification players and doubles teams. The rankings are based on a rolling 52-week, cumulative system, and ranks determine how far a player will advance in a tournament. As of May 29, 2023, Iga Swiatek of Poland was the highest ranking singles player in the WTA, and Katerina Siniakova was the highest ranking individual doubles player in the WTA.

FINANCIAL DATA: *Note: Data for latest year may not have been available at press time.*

In U.S. $	2022	2021	2020	2019	2018	2017
Revenue		87,800,000	30,000,000	109,700,000	78,000,000	78,000,000
R&D Expense						
Operating Income						
Operating Margin %						
SGA Expense						
Net Income						
Operating Cash Flow						
Capital Expenditure						
EBITDA						
Return on Assets %						
Return on Equity %						
Debt to Equity						

CONTACT INFORMATION:

Phone: 727-895-5000
Fax: 727-894-1982
Toll-Free:
Address: 100 Second Ave. S., Ste 1100-S, St. Petersburg, FL 33701 United States

STOCK TICKER/OTHER:

Stock Ticker: Private
Employees: 88
Parent Company:

Exchange:
Fiscal Year Ends: 08/31

SALARIES/BONUSES:

Top Exec. Salary: $
Second Exec. Salary: $

Bonus: $
Bonus: $

OTHER THOUGHTS:

Estimated Female Officers or Directors: 8
Hot Spot for Advancement for Women/Minorities: Y

Sales, profits and employees may be estimates. Financial information, benefits and other data can change quickly and may vary from those stated here.

World Boxing Association (The)

NAIC Code: 711211

www.wbaboxing.com

TYPES OF BUSINESS:

Boxing Association
Professional Boxing Sanctioning Organization
Boxing Tournaments
Boxing Ranking System
Professional Weight Classification

BRANDS/DIVISIONS/AFFILIATES:

World Champions
Continental Champions
Intercontinental Champions
International Champions
National Boxing Association (NBA)

CONTACTS: *Note: Officers with more than one job title may be intentionally listed here more than once.*

Gilberto Jesus Mendoza, Pres.
Alberto Sarmiento, Dir.-Treasury
Gilberto Jesus Mendoza, Jr., Exec. VP
George Martinez, Vice Chmn.

GROWTH PLANS/SPECIAL FEATURES:

The World Boxing Association (WBA) sanctions professional boxing matches alongside the World Boxing Council (WBC), International Boxing Federation (IBF) and World Boxing Organization (WBO). Founded in 1921 by 13 U.S. state representatives as the National Boxing Association (NBA), in 1962 the organization changed its name to World Boxing Association due to becoming popular throughout the world. Members from other nations began to join the organization. As a result, the WBA began awarding its world championship title at the professional level. Weight classes including minimumweight, light flyweight, flyweight, super flyweight, bantamweight, featherweight, super featherweight, lightweight, super lightweight, welterweight, super welterweight, middleweight, super middleweight, light heavyweight, cruiserweight and heavyweight. These class weight range from 105 to more than 200 pounds for male boxers and from 102 to more than 168 pounds for female boxers. Championship boxing matches include the World Champions, Continental Champions, Intercontinental Champions and International Champions. Tournaments and boxers are ranked by the WBA per weight class.

FINANCIAL DATA: *Note: Data for latest year may not have been available at press time.*

In U.S. $	2022	2021	2020	2019	2018	2017
Revenue						
R&D Expense						
Operating Income						
Operating Margin %						
SGA Expense						
Net Income						
Operating Cash Flow						
Capital Expenditure						
EBITDA						
Return on Assets %						
Return on Equity %						
Debt to Equity						

CONTACT INFORMATION:

Phone: 507-203-7680   Fax:
Toll-Free:
Address: Av. Aquilino de la Guardia & Calle 47, Fl. 14, Office 14-05, Marbella, Panama, 0819-01091 Panama

STOCK TICKER/OTHER:

Stock Ticker: Private
Employees:
Parent Company:

Exchange:
Fiscal Year Ends:

SALARIES/BONUSES:

Top Exec. Salary: $ Bonus: $
Second Exec. Salary: $ Bonus: $

OTHER THOUGHTS:

Estimated Female Officers or Directors:
Hot Spot for Advancement for Women/Minorities:

World Boxing Council

www.wbcboxing.com

NAIC Code: 711211

TYPES OF BUSINESS:
Boxing Association
Boxing Tournaments
Weight Class Ranking

BRANDS/DIVISIONS/AFFILIATES:
North American Boxing Federation
Oriental and Pacific Boxing Federation
European Boxing Union
African Boxing Council

CONTACTS: *Note: Officers with more than one job title may be intentionally listed here more than once.*
Mauricio Sulaiman, Pres.
Avel Gonzalez, General Counsel
Kovid Bhakdibhumi, VP-Thailand
Houcine Houichi, VP-Tunisia
Rex Walker, VP-USA
Soohwan Hong, VP-Korea
Charles Giles, VP-Great Britain

GROWTH PLANS/SPECIAL FEATURES:
The World Boxing Council (WBC) is an international professional boxing organization that hosts and officiates boxing matches throughout the world. Founders from eleven countries (the U.S., Argentina, the U.K., France, Mexico, the Philippines, Panama, Chile, Peru, Venezuela and Brazil) created the council in 1963. The group's mission was to create an international boxing organization and control the expansion of the sport. WBC's green championship belt portrays the flags of all the member countries of the organization. All WBC world-title belts look identical, regardless of weight class. The WBC has nine regional governing body affiliates, such as the North American Boxing Federation, the Oriental and Pacific Boxing Federation, the European Boxing Union and the African Boxing Council. There are seven primary rules for the boxers during a match: retreat to your corner of the ring before a fallen opponent; a half-minute count after a fall and the ability to get back to the center of the ring and restart the fight or be considered a man out of action; only the boxers and their seconds can climb into the ring; private arrangements between boxers in terms of money is prohibited; referees settle disputes between boxers; hitting an opponent when down is prohibited; and locks can only be used above the waistline. Matches are provided for men and women, and classes include atomweight, strawweight, light flyweight, flyweight, super flyweight, bantamweight, super bantamweight, featherweight, super featherweight, lightweight, super lightweight, welterweight, super welterweight, middleweight, super middleweight, light heavyweight, cruiserweight, bridgerweight and heavyweight. These weights range from 105 to over 200 pounds for males, and from 102 to over 168 pounds for females.

FINANCIAL DATA: *Note: Data for latest year may not have been available at press time.*

In U.S. $	2022	2021	2020	2019	2018	2017
Revenue						
R&D Expense						
Operating Income						
Operating Margin %						
SGA Expense						
Net Income						
Operating Cash Flow						
Capital Expenditure						
EBITDA						
Return on Assets %						
Return on Equity %						
Debt to Equity						

CONTACT INFORMATION:
Phone: 52-555-119-5274   Fax: 525-5119-5293
Toll-Free:
Address: Riobamba 835, Col. Lindavista, 07300 Mexico

STOCK TICKER/OTHER:
Stock Ticker: Private   Exchange:
Employees: 120   Fiscal Year Ends:
Parent Company:

SALARIES/BONUSES:
Top Exec. Salary: $ Bonus: $
Second Exec. Salary: $ Bonus: $

OTHER THOUGHTS:
Estimated Female Officers or Directors:
Hot Spot for Advancement for Women/Minorities:

World Triathlon Corporation (Ironman, WTC) www.ironman.com

NAIC Code: 711300

TYPES OF BUSINESS:

Triathlon Events
Professional Running Events
Professional Triathlons
Running Events
Triathlon Events
Sport Equipment
Cycling Events
Cycling App

BRANDS/DIVISIONS/AFFILIATES:

Advance Publications Inc
Ironman
Ironman 70.2
Ironman World Championship
5150 Triathlon
UTMB World Series
Epic Series
FulGaz

CONTACTS: *Note: Officers with more than one job title may be intentionally listed here more than once.*

Andrew Messick, CEO
Shane Facteau, Pres.
Bill Potts, VP-Global Licensing & Partner Services

GROWTH PLANS/SPECIAL FEATURES:

World Triathlon Corporation (Ironman, WTC) owns and organizes Ironman-branded racing events, including the Ironman and the Ironman 70.3 triathlon series. Ironman sports span more than 250 events throughout the world. Some races qualify competitors for the Ironman World Championship held annually in Kona, Hawaii every October. Ironman-branded events, including the Ironman World Championship, consist of a 2.4-mile ocean swim, 112-mile bike race and 26.2-mile run, with an allowed race time of 17 hours. The Ironman World Championship generally hosts approximately 2,000 competitors. Ironman 70.3 races comprise a 1.2-mile swim, a 56-mile bike race and a 13.1-mile run, which is half of an Ironman World Champion race. The 5150 Triathlon Series consists of an approximate 1-mile swim, 25-mile bike and 6-mile run. The UTMB World Series offers 36 international trail running events across 22 countries in Asia, Oceania, Europe and the Americas (for the 2023 series), and consists of three levels including the UTMB World Series Events, the UTMB World Series Majors and the UTMB World Series Finals. Epic Series offers mountain bike stage races in which teams of two riders take on the trails; Haute Route offers mountain and road cycling events. FulGaz is an app that brings realistic riding experiences to cyclists, featuring a library of 1,500+ routes from over 40 countries, including 100 official Ironman bike courses. IronKids offers more than 80 triathlon events worldwide, ranging from fun runs to competitions.

FINANCIAL DATA: *Note: Data for latest year may not have been available at press time.*

In U.S. $	2022	2021	2020	2019	2018	2017
Revenue						
R&D Expense						
Operating Income						
Operating Margin %						
SGA Expense						
Net Income						
Operating Cash Flow						
Capital Expenditure						
EBITDA						
Return on Assets %						
Return on Equity %						
Debt to Equity						

CONTACT INFORMATION:

Phone: 813-868-5940   Fax:
Toll-Free:
Address: 3407 W. Dr. Martin Luther King Jr Blvd., Tampa, FL 33607 United States

STOCK TICKER/OTHER:

Stock Ticker: Subsidiary   Exchange:
Employees: 525   Fiscal Year Ends:
Parent Company: Advance Publications Inc

SALARIES/BONUSES:

Top Exec. Salary: $ Bonus: $
Second Exec. Salary: $ Bonus: $

OTHER THOUGHTS:

Estimated Female Officers or Directors: 1
Hot Spot for Advancement for Women/Minorities:

Xtep International Holdings Limited

www.xtep.com.hk

NAIC Code: 423910

TYPES OF BUSINESS:

Sporting and Recreational Goods and Supplies Merchant Wholesalers
Apparel
Sportswear
Footwear
Manufacturing
Distribution
Retail
Ecommerce

BRANDS/DIVISIONS/AFFILIATES:

Xtep
K-Swiss
Palladium
Saucony
Merrell
Xtep Dry
Xtep Cool
Xtep Shield

GROWTH PLANS/SPECIAL FEATURES:

Xtep International Holdings Ltd owns the Chinese sportswear brand XTEP. The company markets its brand as a stylish professional sports brand with a focus on running gear. Footwear accounts for more than half of the company's revenue. The most remaining revenue comes from apparel sales. The company has thousands of XTEP retail stores in China that are primarily operated by the company's distributors or authorized retailers. It also sells online through its own website and third-party e-commerce platforms. In addition to China, Xtep has distributors in the Middle East, Europe, and Southeast Asia.

CONTACTS: Note: Officers with more than one job title may be intentionally listed here more than once.

Ding Shui Po, CEO
Ding Shui Po, Chmn.

FINANCIAL DATA: Note: Data for latest year may not have been available at press time.

In U.S. $	2022	2021	2020	2019	2018	2017
Revenue	1,877,752,000	1,454,124,000	1,186,727,000	1,188,295,000	742,573,300	742,573,300
R&D Expense						
Operating Income	192,540,200	184,141,800	113,469,000	152,775,300	94,704,700	94,704,700
Operating Margin %		.13%	.10%	.13%	.13%	.13%
SGA Expense	601,805,500	447,362,100	375,769,300	381,160,200	243,721,600	243,721,600
Net Income	133,848,500	131,909,100	74,502,260	105,669,700	59,269,980	59,269,980
Operating Cash Flow	83,041,500	101,849,700	46,485,970	112,992,300	81,050,230	81,050,230
Capital Expenditure	55,010,390	96,917,710	30,647,390	14,495,140	27,333,620	27,333,620
EBITDA	250,472,400	224,487,300	151,588,600	202,420,100	122,355,200	122,355,200
Return on Assets %		.07%	.04%	.07%	.05%	.05%
Return on Equity %		.12%	.07%	.12%	.08%	.08%
Debt to Equity		.28%	0.228	0.20	0.195	0.195

CONTACT INFORMATION:

Phone: 852-2152-0333   Fax:
Toll-Free:
Address: Unit A, 27/Fl, Tower A, 1 Wang Kwong Rd., Kowloon Bay, Kowloon, 999077 Hong Kong

STOCK TICKER/OTHER:

Stock Ticker: XTEPY   Exchange: PINX
Employees: 8,000   Fiscal Year Ends: 12/31
Parent Company:

SALARIES/BONUSES:

Top Exec. Salary: $ Bonus: $
Second Exec. Salary: $ Bonus: $

OTHER THOUGHTS:

Estimated Female Officers or Directors:
Hot Spot for Advancement for Women/Minorities:

Zumba Fitness LLC   **www.zumba.com**

NAIC Code: 713940

TYPES OF BUSINESS:

Dance Fitness Classes
Fitness Programs
Fitness Training
Fitness Apparel and Accessories

BRANDS/DIVISIONS/AFFILIATES:

Zumba Academy

CONTACTS: *Note: Officers with more than one job title may be intentionally listed here more than once.*

Alberto Perlman, CEO

GROWTH PLANS/SPECIAL FEATURES:

Zumba Fitness, LLC produces the dance fitness program called Zumba, which combines dance and aerobics to create a full-body fitness routine. Zumba incorporates moves from a variety of dances, including hip-hop, samba, salsa, mambo and belly dancing in addition to martial arts moves. The fitness routines are led by instructors to the backdrop of globally-influenced music. Zumba classes, taught by licensed instructors trained at the Zumba Academy, are available in more than 180 countries and 200,000 locations across the world. An estimated 15 million people engage in Zumba classes worldwide. Zumba Academy offers a variety of training options, with training sessions lasting one to two days for a one-year instructor license. Once licensed, instructors can teach Zumba at any venue. Zumba instructors can also join the paid membership Zumba Instructor Network (ZIN), which allows special access to training classes and other benefits. In addition to its basic fitness classes, the firm offers a variety of specialty courses including body toning, water aerobics, classes for toddlers/kids/seniors, fitness routines that utilize the stability of a chair, step aerobics, circuit aerobics and more. Zumba Fitness also offers a variety of merchandise, including its own clothing line, DVDs, exercise equipment such as toning sticks, music, video games and fitness magazine.

Zumba employees receive benefits including healthcare, 401(k), free instructor trainings and other company incentives and perks.

FINANCIAL DATA: *Note: Data for latest year may not have been available at press time.*

In U.S. $	2022	2021	2020	2019	2018	2017
Revenue	80,000,000	75,264,000	71,680,000	128,000,000	120,000,000	120,000,000
R&D Expense						
Operating Income						
Operating Margin %						
SGA Expense						
Net Income						
Operating Cash Flow						
Capital Expenditure						
EBITDA						
Return on Assets %						
Return on Equity %						
Debt to Equity						

CONTACT INFORMATION:

Phone: 954-925-3755   Fax:
Toll-Free:
Address: 800 Silks Run, Ste. 2310, Hallandale, FL 33009 United States

STOCK TICKER/OTHER:

Stock Ticker: Private   Exchange:
Employees: 225   Fiscal Year Ends:
Parent Company:

SALARIES/BONUSES:

Top Exec. Salary: $ Bonus: $
Second Exec. Salary: $ Bonus: $

OTHER THOUGHTS:

Estimated Female Officers or Directors:
Hot Spot for Advancement for Women/Minorities:

ADDITIONAL INDEXES

Contents:

Index of Firms Noted as "Hot Spots for Advancement" for Women/Minorities   **506**

Index by Subsidiaries, Brand Names and Selected Affiliations   **508**

INDEX OF FIRMS NOTED AS HOT SPOTS FOR ADVANCEMENT FOR WOMEN & MINORITIES

Altice USA Inc
American Golf Corporation
American Hockey League Inc
Anaheim Ducks
Arizona Cardinals
Arizona Coyotes
Arizona Diamondbacks
Associazione Calcio Milan spa
Aston Villa Football Club
Atlanta Braves
Atlanta Dream
Atlanta Falcons
Atlanta Hawks
Baltimore Orioles
Baltimore Ravens
BDA Sports Management
Boston Celtics
Boston Red Sox
BRG Sports Inc
Brooklyn Nets
Brunswick Corporation
Buffalo Bills
Buffalo Sabres
Calgary Flames
Canadian Football League
Carolina Hurricanes
Carolina Panthers
Charlotte Hornets
Chicago Bears
Chicago Blackhawks
Chicago Bulls
Chicago Cubs
Chicago Fire Soccer Club
Chicago White Sox
Cincinnati Bengals
Cincinnati Reds
Cleveland Browns
Cleveland Cavaliers
Cleveland Guardians
Colorado Rapids
Colorado Rockies
Columbia Sportswear Company
Columbus Blue Jackets
Columbus Crew
Comcast Corporation
Connecticut Sun
Cox Communications Inc
Dallas Mavericks
Dallas Stars
Dallas Wings
DC United
Delaware North Companies Inc
Delta Apparel Inc

Denver Broncos
Detroit Lions
Detroit Pistons
Detroit Red Wings
Detroit Tigers
Dicks Sporting Goods Inc
Disney Media & Entertainment Distribution
ECHL
ESPN Inc
FC Dallas
Fila USA Inc
Florida Panthers
Fox Broadcasting Company
Golden State Warriors
Green Bay Packers
HealthFitness Corporation
Hibbett Sports Inc
Houston Astros
Houston Dynamo FC
Houston Rockets
Houston Texans
Ilitch Holdings Inc
Indiana Fever
Indiana Pacers
Indianapolis Colts
Jacksonville Jaguars
Johnson Outdoors Inc
Kansas City Chiefs
Kansas City Royals
Kellwood Company LLC
Ladies Professional Golf Association (LPGA)
Las Vegas Aces
Las Vegas Raiders
Levy Restaurants
Li Ning Company Limited
Life Time Inc
Los Angeles Angels
Los Angeles Chargers
Los Angeles Clippers
Los Angeles Dodgers
Los Angeles Galaxy
Los Angeles Kings
Los Angeles Lakers
Los Angeles Rams
Los Angeles Sparks
lululemon athletica inc
Major League Soccer (MLS)
Maple Leaf Sports & Entertainment Ltd
Memphis Grizzlies
Miami Dolphins
Miami HEAT
Miami Marlins
Middlesbrough Football Club
Milwaukee Brewers
Milwaukee Bucks
Minnesota Lynx
Minnesota Timberwolves
Minnesota Twins

Minnesota Vikings
Minnesota Wild
Minor League Baseball
Nashville Predators
National Basketball Association (NBA)
National Thoroughbred Racing Association
NBA G League
NBCUniversal Media LLC
New Balance Athletic Shoe Inc
New England Revolution
New Orleans Pelicans
New Orleans Saints
New York Giants
New York Islanders
New York Knickerbockers
New York Liberty
New York Rangers
New York Red Bulls
New York Yankees
Nike Inc
Oakland Athletics
Octagon Worldwide
Oklahoma City Thunder
Orlando Magic
Ottawa Senators
Paramount Global
Peloton Interactive Inc
Philadelphia 76ers
Philadelphia Eagles
Philadelphia Flyers
Philadelphia Phillies
Philadelphia Union
Phoenix Mercury
Phoenix Suns
Pittsburgh Pirates
Pittsburgh Steelers
Portland Trail Blazers
Real Salt Lake
REI (Recreational Equipment Inc)
Rogers Communications Inc
Sacramento Kings
San Antonio Spurs
San Diego Padres
San Francisco 49ers
San Francisco Giants
San Jose Earthquakes
San Jose Sharks
Seattle Mariners
Seattle Seahawks
Seattle Sounders FC
Seattle Storm
Sirius XM Holdings Inc
Sporting Kansas City
Sports Illustrated
St Louis Blues
St Louis Cardinals
Tampa Bay Buccaneers
Tampa Bay Lightning

Tampa Bay Rays
Tennessee Titans
Texas Rangers
Toronto Blue Jays
Toronto Raptors
Trek Bicycle Corporation
United Soccer League
United States Golf Association (USGA)
United States Olympic & Paralympic Committee
(USOPC)
United States Tennis Association (USTA)
US Figure Skating
USA Basketball
USA Cycling
USA Gymnastics
USA Hockey Inc
USA Swimming
USA Track & Field Inc
Utah Jazz
Vail Resorts Inc
Vancouver Canucks
Vancouver Whitecaps FC
Varsity Brands Holding Co Inc
VF Corporation
Walt Disney Company (The)
Washington Capitals
Washington Mystics
Washington Nationals
Washington Wizards
Wasserman Media Group LLC
West Marine Inc
Wilson Sporting Goods Co
Winnipeg Jets
Womens National Basketball Association (WNBA)
Womens Tennis Association (WTA)

INDEX OF SUBSIDIARIES, BRAND NAMES AND AFFILIATIONS

Brand or subsidiary, followed by the name of the related corporation

24GO; **24 Hour Fitness**
24GO Plus; **24 Hour Fitness**
24GO TV; **24 Hour Fitness**
313 Presents; **Ilitch Holdings Inc**
313 Presents LLC; **Palace Sports & Entertainment Inc**
49ers Enterprises; **San Francisco 49ers**
5150 Triathlon; **World Triathlon Corporation (Ironman, WTC)**
A+E Television Networks; **Walt Disney Company (The)**
a4; **Altice USA Inc**
Abbotsford Canucks; **Vancouver Canucks**
ABC Inc; **ESPN Inc**
Aberdeen IronBirds; **Baltimore Orioles**
Abernethys; **Levy Restaurants**
Abu Dhabi United Group; **Manchester City Football Club**
Access Industries Inc; **DAZN Group Limited**
adidas; **adidas AG**
adidas Body; **adidas AG**
Adirondack Thunder; **New Jersey Devils**
Adult Safe Hockey League; **Canlan Ice Sports Corp**
Advance Publications Inc; **World Triathlon Corporation (Ironman, WTC)**
Advantage Club; **Golf Galaxy Inc**
AEG; **Anschutz Entertainment Group Inc**
AEG 1Earth; **Anschutz Entertainment Group Inc**
AEG 1Source; **Anschutz Entertainment Group Inc**
AEG Community Foundation; **Anschutz Entertainment Group Inc**
AEG Global Partners; **Anschutz Entertainment Group Inc**
AEG Real Estate; **Anschutz Entertainment Group Inc**
AEG Worldwide; **Anschutz Entertainment Group Inc**
AFC Ajax Vrouwen; **AFC Ajax NV**
African Boxing Council; **World Boxing Council**
AIGLE; **Li Ning Company Limited**
Akron RubberDucks; **Cleveland Guardians**
Albion Foundation; **West Bromwich Albion Football Club**
Albuquerque Isotopes; **Colorado Rockies**
All Star; **Nike Inc**
Allen Americans; **Ottawa Senators**
Alliant Powder; **Vista Outdoor Inc**
Allianz Parque; **Sociedade Esportiva Palmeiras**
All-Star Game; **Major League Baseball (MLB)**
Alpine Design; **Dicks Sporting Goods Inc**
Altice Mobile; **Altice USA Inc**
Altoona Curve; **Pittsburgh Pirates**
Altor Equity Partners; **Skis Rossignol SA**
Amer Sports Corporation; **Wilson Sporting Goods Co**
American Eagle; **Vista Outdoor Inc**

American Football Conference; **National Football League (NFL)**
American League; **Major League Baseball (MLB)**
American Rod & Gun; **BPS Direct LLC (Bass Pro Shops)**
AMF; **Bowlero Corp**
Anaheim Arena Management LLC; **Anaheim Ducks**
AND 1 Mix Tape Tour; **AND 1**
AND 1 Streetball; **AND 1**
Anfield; **Liverpool Football Club**
Anfield; **Fenway Sports Group LLC**
Anschutz Corporation (The); **Anschutz Entertainment Group Inc**
Anschutz Entertainment Group; **Los Angeles Galaxy**
Anschutz Entertainment Group Inc; **ASM Global**
Anshutz Entertainment Group; **Los Angeles Kings**
ANTA; **ANTA Sports Products Limited**
ANTA Kids; **ANTA Sports Products Limited**
Anta Sports Products Limited; **Amer Sports Corporation**
Apex Legends; **Electronic Arts Inc (EA)**
Aquilini Investment Group; **Vancouver Canucks**
ARCA Menards Series; **NASCAR**
Arena Group Holdings Inc (The); **Sports Illustrated**
Argosy Casino Riverside; **Penn National Gaming Inc**
Arkansas Travelers; **Seattle Mariners**
Arrowhead Stadium; **Kansas City Chiefs**
Arsenal Academy; **Arsenal Football Club Plc**
Arsenal Holdings Limited; **Arsenal Football Club Plc**
Arsenal Women; **Arsenal Football Club Plc**
art+commerce; **Endeavor Group Holdings Inc**
As; **Oakland Athletics**
AS Roma Femminile; **AS Roma (Associazione Sportiva Roma)**
ASICS America Corp; **ASICS Corp**
ASICS Europe BV; **ASICS Corp**
Aspen Highlands; **Aspen Skiing Company**
Aspen Mountain; **Aspen Skiing Company**
At Bat; **Major League Baseball Advanced Media LP (MLBAM)**
ATEC; **Wilson Sporting Goods Co**
Athlete Exchange; **Wasserman Media Group LLC**
Athletic Club Femenino; **Athletic Club (Athletic Bilbao)**
Atlanta Falcons Youth Foundation; **Atlanta Falcons**
Atlanta Gladiators; **Arizona Coyotes**
Atlanta Motor Speedway; **Speedway Motorsports LLC**
Atlantic Park Strategic Capital Fund; **OneTeam Partners LLC**
Atom; **Sport Maska Inc (CCM Hockey)**
ATP Challenger Tour; **Association of Tennis Professionals (ATP Tour Inc)**
ATP Tour; **Association of Tennis Professionals (ATP Tour Inc)**
ATP Tour 250; **Association of Tennis Professionals (ATP Tour Inc)**
ATP Tour 500; **Association of Tennis Professionals (ATP Tour Inc)**
ATP Tour Masters 1000; **Association of Tennis Professionals (ATP Tour Inc)**

INDEX OF SUBSIDIARIES, BRAND NAMES AND AFFILIATIONS, CONT.

Augusta GreenJackets; **Atlanta Braves**
Authentic Brands Group LLC; **Prince Global Sports LLC**
Authentic Brands Group LLC; **Reebok International Limited**
Authentic Brands Group LLC; **Sports Illustrated**
Automobile Racing Club of America (ARCA); **NASCAR**
Avalanche Bay Indoor Waterpark; **Boyne Resorts**
B/R Gaming; **Bleacher Report Inc (B/R)**
B/R Gridiron; **Bleacher Report Inc (B/R)**
B/R Kicks; **Bleacher Report Inc (B/R)**
Baggies; **West Bromwich Albion Football Club**
Baillabong; **Boardriders Inc**
Bain Capital LP; **Varsity Brands Holding Co Inc**
Bakersfield Condors; **Edmonton Oilers**
Ball Arena; **Denver Nuggets**
Ball Arena; **Kroenke Sports & Entertainment LLC**
Barca; **Futbol Club Barcelona**
Barstool Sports; **Penn National Gaming Inc**
Baseball Club of Seattle LP (The); **Seattle Mariners**
Basketball Association of America; **National Basketball Association (NBA)**
Bass Pro Shops; **BPS Direct LLC (Bass Pro Shops)**
Battlefield; **Electronic Arts Inc (EA)**
Bayern Munich; **Football-Club Bayern Munchen eV**
Bayliner; **Brunswick Corporation**
Bear Creek Country Club; **American Golf Corporation**
Bee Stinger; **Vista Outdoor Inc**
Bell; **Vista Outdoor Inc**
Belleville Senators; **Ottawa Senators**
Beloit Sky Carp; **Miami Marlins**
Berkshire Hathaway Inc; **Russell Brands LLC**
BET+; **Paramount Global**
Big 5 Services Corporation; **Big 5 Sporting Goods Corporation**
Big Bear Mountain Resort; **Alterra Mountain Company**
Big Cedar Lodge; **BPS Direct LLC (Bass Pro Shops)**
Big Sky Resort; **Boyne Resorts**
Big Ten Network; **Fox Sports (Fox Sports Media Group)**
BigShots; **ClubCorp Holdings Inc (Invited)**
Bikeshare Holdings LLC; **Motivate LLC**
Billie Jean King Cup; **Womens Tennis Association (WTA)**
Birch Hill Equity Partners Management Inc; **Sport Maska Inc (CCM Hockey)**
Birmingham Barons; **Chicago White Sox**
Birmingham Squadron; **New Orleans Pelicans**
Black-and-Red; **DC United**
Blazer; **Vista Outdoor Inc**
Blizzard; **Tecnica Group SpA**
Bluebirds; **Cleveland Guardians**
Blues Partners Limited; **Chelsea Football Club**
Bolderton; **Sportsmans Guide Inc (The)**
Bontrager; **Trek Bicycle Corporation**
Boomtown Casino Biloxi; **Penn National Gaming Inc**
BOOTCAMP; **Golds Gym International Inc**

Booth Creek Ski Group Inc; **Booth Creek Ski Holdings Inc**
Boston Basketball Partners LLC; **Boston Celtics**
Boston Bruins Foundation; **Boston Bruins**
Boston Holdings; **Delaware North Companies Inc**
Boston Red Sox; **Fenway Sports Group LLC**
Boston Whaler; **Brunswick Corporation**
Bowie Baysox; **Baltimore Orioles**
Bowlero; **Bowlero Corp**
Bowlero Corporation; **Professional Bowlers Association LLC**
Bowling Green Hot Rods; **Tampa Bay Rays**
Bowlmor Lanes; **Bowlero Corp**
Boyne Country Sports; **Boyne Resorts**
BPS Direct LLC (Bass Pro Shops); **Cabelas Inc**
Bradenton Marauders; **Pittsburgh Pirates**
Bridgeport Islanders; **New York Islanders**
Briggs New York; **Kellwood Company LLC**
Brine; **New Balance Athletic Shoe Inc**
Bristol Motor Speedway; **Speedway Motorsports LLC**
BSN Sports; **BSN Sports Inc**
BSN Sports; **Varsity Brands Holding Co Inc**
BSN Sports Direct; **BSN Sports Inc**
BSNSPORTS Equipment; **BSN Sports Inc**
Buffalo Bisons; **Toronto Blue Jays**
Build & Play; **Little Gym International Inc (The)**
Buttermilk Mountain; **Aspen Skiing Company**
Buyers Advantage Catalog; **Sportsmans Guide Inc (The)**
Buyers Club (The); **Sportsmans Guide Inc (The)**
Buzztime Bar; **eGames.com Holdings LLC (Buzztime)**
BVB; **Borussia Dortmund GmbH & Co KGaA**
Cabelas; **BPS Direct LLC (Bass Pro Shops)**
Cabelas.ca; **Cabelas Inc**
Cabelas.com; **Cabelas Inc**
Calder Casino and Racing; **Churchill Downs Incorporated**
Calgary Sports and Entertainment Corporation; **Calgary Flames**
Calgary Wranglers; **Calgary Flames**
CALIA; **Dicks Sporting Goods Inc**
Callaway Golf; **Topgolf Callaway Brands Corp**
CallawayGolfPreOwned.com; **Topgolf Callaway Brands Corp**
CamelBak; **Vista Outdoor Inc**
Camp Nou; **Futbol Club Barcelona**
Canadian Tire Centre; **Ottawa Senators**
Canaries (The); **Norwich City Football Club**
Canes (The); **Carolina Hurricanes**
Canlan Classic Tournaments; **Canlan Ice Sports Corp**
Canlan Youth Hockey League; **Canlan Ice Sports Corp**
Canucks Sports and Entertainment; **Vancouver Canucks**
Capital Bikeshare; **Motivate LLC**
Capital City Go-Go; **Washington Wizards**
Capital One Arena; **Washington Wizards**
Castle Creek; **Sportsmans Guide Inc (The)**
CBS Stations; **Paramount Global**

INDEX OF SUBSIDIARIES, BRAND NAMES AND AFFILIATIONS, CONT.

CBS Studios; **Paramount Global**
CBS Television Network; **Paramount Global**
CCI; **Vista Outdoor Inc**
CCM Hockey; **Sport Maska Inc (CCM Hockey)**
Challenge Tour; **PGA European Tour (bda DP World Tour)**
Championnat National; **Ligue de Football Professionnel**
Chaparral; **Marine Products Corporation**
Chaparral Boats Inc; **Marine Products Corporation**
Charged Cushioning; **Under Armour Inc**
Charleston RiverDogs; **Tampa Bay Rays**
Charlotte Bobcats; **Charlotte Hornets**
Charlotte Checkers; **Florida Panthers**
Charlotte Honey Bees; **Charlotte Hornets**
Charlotte Knights; **Chicago White Sox**
Charlotte Motor Speedway; **Speedway Motorsports LLC**
chatr; **Rogers Communications Inc**
Chattanooga Lookouts; **Cincinnati Reds**
Cheddar; **Altice USA Inc**
Chicago White Stockings; **Chicago Cubs**
Chicago Wolves; **Carolina Hurricanes**
Chip Ganassi Racing; **Chip Ganassi Racing With Felix Sabates Inc**
Chivas; **Club Deportivo Guadalajara SA de CV (Chivas)**
Chuck Taylor; **Nike Inc**
Chuck Taylor All Star Classic; **Converse Inc**
Churchill Downs Racetrack; **Churchill Downs Incorporated**
Cincinnati Cyclones; **Buffalo Sabres**
CITIC Group Corporation Ltd; **Manchester City Football Club**
Citizens Bank Park; **Philadelphia Phillies**
City Football Group; **New York City FC**
City Football Group Limited; **Manchester City Football Club**
City Gear; **Hibbett Sports Inc**
City Sports Club; **LA Fitness (LA Fitness International LLC)**
Classics Country Club (The); **American Golf Corporation**
Clearwater Threshers; **Philadelphia Phillies**
Cleveland Forest Citys; **Cleveland Guardians**
Cleveland Indians; **Cleveland Guardians**
Cleveland Monsters; **Columbus Blue Jackets**
Cleveland Rams; **Los Angeles Rams**
CMH Heli Skiing & Summer Adventures; **Alterra Mountain Company**
Coast; **Delta Apparel Inc**
Cobra Puma Golf; **PUMA SE**
COLDGEAR; **Under Armour Inc**
Coleman; **Coleman Company Inc (The)**
Collective (The); **Wasserman Media Group LLC**
Colorado Avalanche; **Kroenke Sports & Entertainment LLC**

Colorado Avalanche LLC; **Colorado Avalanche**
Colorado Eagles; **Colorado Avalanche**
Colorado Mammoth; **Kroenke Sports & Entertainment LLC**
Colorado Rapids; **Kroenke Sports & Entertainment LLC**
Columbia; **Columbia Sportswear Company**
Columbia Fireflies; **Kansas City Royals**
Columbus Clippers; **Cleveland Guardians**
Comcast Corporation; **NBCUniversal Media LLC**
Comcast Spectacor; **Philadelphia Flyers**
Compass Group plc; **Levy Restaurants**
Compcast Corporation; **Philadelphia Flyers**
Continental Champions; **World Boxing Association (The)**
Converse Inc; **Nike Inc**
Copa del Rey; **Campeonato Nacional de Liga Primera Division (La Liga)**
Cox Enterprises Inc; **Cox Communications Inc**
Cozmo; **Los Angeles Galaxy**
Craftsman Truck Series; **NASCAR**
Crestliner; **Brunswick Corporation**
Cruisers Yachts; **MarineMax Inc**
Crystal Mountain; **Alterra Mountain Company**
Cup Series; **NASCAR**
Curiouser Products Inc; **lululemon athletica inc**
Curtis Cup; **United States Golf Association (USGA)**
Cuves On the Go; **Curves NA**
Cycle; **Wasserman Media Group LLC**
Cypress Cay; **Brunswick Corporation**
Cypress Mountain; **Boyne Resorts**
Cyrus Capital Partners LP; **24 Hour Fitness**
D&E Retail; **Aspen Skiing Company**
Daily Fantasy Sports; **DraftKings Inc**
DAK Capital; **Katz Group Of Companies (The)**
Dallas Burn; **FC Dallas**
Dark Castle Entertainment; **Katz Group Of Companies (The)**
Datalogue; **Nike Inc**
Dayton Tortugas; **Cincinnati Reds**
Daytona Dragons; **Cincinnati Reds**
DAZN; **DAZN Group Limited**
DAZN Bet; **DAZN Group Limited**
DAZN Boxing.io; **DAZN Group Limited**
DAZN Moments; **DAZN Group Limited**
DAZN Pay-Per-View; **DAZN Group Limited**
DAZN Store; **DAZN Group Limited**
DBA Studio; **Levy Restaurants**
DC; **Boardriders Inc**
DC United Holdings; **DC United**
Deer Valley Resort; **Alterra Mountain Company**
Delaware Blue Coats; **Philadelphia 76ers**
Delaware North Companies; **Boston Bruins**
Delmarva Shorebirds; **Baltimore Orioles**
Delta; **Delta Apparel Inc**
DeMarini; **Wilson Sporting Goods Co**

INDEX OF SUBSIDIARIES, BRAND NAMES AND AFFILIATIONS, CONT.

Democracy; **Kellwood Company LLC**
Denver Nuggets; **Kroenke Sports & Entertainment LLC**
Derby City Gaming; **Churchill Downs Incorporated**
DESCENTE; **ANTA Sports Products Limited**
Detroit Pistons; **Palace Sports & Entertainment Inc**
Detroit Red Wings; **Ilitch Holdings Inc**
Detroit Tigers; **Ilitch Holdings Inc**
Dickies; **VF Corporation**
Dicks Sporting Goods; **Dicks Sporting Goods Inc**
Dicks Sporting Goods Inc; **Field & Stream**
Dicks Sporting Goods Inc; **Golf Galaxy Inc**
Dicks Sporting Goods Park; **Kroenke Sports & Entertainment LLC**
Disney; **Walt Disney Company (The)**
Disney Cruise Line; **Walt Disney Company (The)**
Disney+; **Walt Disney Company (The)**
dixon talent inc; **Endeavor Group Holdings Inc**
Dodgers Stadium; **Los Angeles Dodgers**
Donnelley Sports; **BSN Sports Inc**
Dorel Industries Inc; **Cannondale Bicycle Corporation**
Dorel Industries Inc; **Pacific Cycle Inc**
Dover Motor Speedway; **Speedway Motorsports LLC**
Down East Wood Ducks; **Texas Rangers**
DP World Tour; **PGA European Tour (bda DP World Tour)**
dreamstock inc; **ASICS Corp**
DreamWorks; **NBCUniversal Media LLC**
Drive Shack Inc; **American Golf Corporation**
DSG; **Dicks Sporting Goods Inc**
DSL Braves; **Atlanta Braves**
DTG2Go LLC; **Delta Apparel Inc**
Dunedin Blue Jays; **Toronto Blue Jays**
Durham Bulls; **Tampa Bay Rays**
Dynastar; **Skis Rossignol SA**
E15; **Levy Restaurants**
Earthquakes Soccer LLC; **San Jose Earthquakes**
Eastern Conference; **Major League Soccer (MLS)**
Eastern Conference; **National Hockey League (NHL)**
Eastern Mountain Sports Schools; **Eastern Mountain Sports Inc**
Easton; **Rawlings Sporting Goods Company Inc**
Eastpak; **VF Corporation**
easyFIT; **Snap Fitness Inc**
Eclipse Awards; **National Thoroughbred Racing Association**
Edmonton Oilers; **Katz Group Of Companies (The)**
El Paso Chihuahuas; **San Diego Padres**
Electra; **Trek Bicycle Corporation**
element; **Boardriders Inc**
Eleven Group; **DAZN Group Limited**
Elliott Management Corporation; **Associazione Calcio Milan spa**
Emirates ATP Rankings; **Association of Tennis Professionals (ATP Tour Inc)**

Emirates ATP Rankings Race to London; **Association of Tennis Professionals (ATP Tour Inc)**
Empire Soccer Club; **New York Red Bulls**
EMS; **Eastern Mountain Sports Inc**
EMS Rewards; **Eastern Mountain Sports Inc**
eNASCAR; **NASCAR**
Endeavor; **Endeavor Group Holdings Inc**
Endeavor Group Holdings Inc; **BDA Sports Management**
Endeavor Group Holdings Inc; **Professional Bull Riders Inc**
Endeavor Streaming; **Endeavor Group Holdings Inc**
ENIC Group; **Tottenham Hotspur Football Club**
ENIC International Limited; **Tottenham Hotspur Football Club**
Epic Series; **World Triathlon Corporation (Ironman, WTC)**
Epson Tour; **Ladies Professional Golf Association (LPGA)**
Equinox Hotel; **Equinox Fitness**
Eqx; **Equinox Fitness**
Erie SeaWolves; **Detroit Tigers**
ESPN; **Walt Disney Company (The)**
ESPN; **ESPN Inc**
ESPN Radio; **ESPN Inc**
ESPN.com; **ESPN Inc**
ESPN+; **ESPN Inc**
Esporta Fitness; **LA Fitness (LA Fitness International LLC)**
Estadio Azteca; **Club de Futbol America SA de CV (America)**
Estadio do Morumbi; **Sao Paulo Futebol Clube**
Estadio Governador Magalhaes Pinto; **Cruzeiro Esporte Clube**
Estadio Nemesio Diez; **Deportivo Toluca Futbol Club SA de CV**
Estadio Olimpico Universitario; **Club Universidad Nacional-Asociacion Civil (UNAM/Pumas)**
Estadio Santiago Bernabeu; **Real Madrid Club de Futbol**
Estadio Urbano Caldeira; **Santos Futebol Clube**
Estate Cartridge; **Vista Outdoor Inc**
Eugene Emeralds; **San Francisco Giants**
Eureka!; **Johnson Outdoors Inc**
European Boxing Union; **World Boxing Council**
European Senior Tour; **PGA European Tour (bda DP World Tour)**
Everett AquaSox; **Seattle Mariners**
Everlast; **Everlast Worldwide Inc**
Evolution Bike Park; **Crested Butte Mountain Resort Inc**
Exor SpA; **Juventus Football Club SpA**
Fanatics Betting & Gaming; **Fanatics Inc**
Fanatics Collectibles; **Fanatics Inc**
Fanatics Commerce; **Fanatics Inc**
Fanatics Inc; **Majestic Athletic**
Fanatics Inc; **Topps Company Inc (The)**

INDEX OF SUBSIDIARIES, BRAND NAMES AND AFFILIATIONS, CONT.

Fanautic Club; **Brunswick Corporation**
FanDuel; **FanDuel Group**
Fannation; **Sports Illustrated**
FanZones; **Majestic Athletic**
FC Bayern; **Football-Club Bayern Munchen eV**
FCL Braves; **Atlanta Braves**
Federation Internationale de Football Association; **Union of European Football Associations (UEFA)**
FedExForum; **Memphis Grizzlies**
Fenerbahce Futbol AS; **Fenerbahce Spor Kulubu**
Fenerbahce SA; **Fenerbahce Spor Kulubu**
Fenerbahce Sukru Saracoolu Stadium; **Fenerbahce Spor Kulubu**
Fenway Park; **Fenway Sports Group LLC**
Fenway Partners LLC; **BRG Sports Inc**
Fenway Sports Group Holdings LLC; **Liverpool Football Club**
Fenway Sports Group Holdings LLC; **Pittsburgh Penguins**
Fenway Sports Group LLC; **Boston Red Sox**
Fenway Sports Group Real Estate; **Fenway Sports Group LLC**
Fenway Sports Management; **Fenway Sports Group LLC**
Fido; **Rogers Communications Inc**
Field & Stream; **Field & Stream**
Field & Stream; **Dicks Sporting Goods Inc**
FIFA Council; **FIFA (Federation Internationale de Football Association)**
FIFA Museum; **FIFA (Federation Internationale de Football Association)**
FIFA Statutes; **FIFA (Federation Internationale de Football Association)**
FIFA World Cup; **FIFA (Federation Internationale de Football Association)**
FILA; **ANTA Sports Products Limited**
Fila Holdings Corp; **Fila USA Inc**
FILA Kids; **ANTA Sports Products Limited**
First Avenu Entertaintment LP; **Seattle Mariners**
Fitkidz; **Grupo Sports World SAB de CV**
FitReserve; **HealthFitness Corporation**
FlashDry; **North Face Inc (The)**
Florida Marlins; **Miami Marlins**
Flutter Entertainment plc; **FanDuel Group**
Fomento Economico Mexicano SAB de CV; **Club de Futbol Monterrey**
Force 10 Hoops LLC; **Seattle Storm**
Ford Field; **Detroit Lions**
Formula One Licensing BV; **Formula One Group (F1)**
Formula One Management; **Formula One Group (F1)**
Formula One Paddock Club; **Formula One Group (F1)**
Formula One Promotions and Administration; **Formula One Group (F1)**
Fort Wayne Komets; **Edmonton Oilers**
Fort Wayne TinCaps; **San Diego Padres**

Fosun International Limited; **Wolverhampton Wanderers Football Club**
Foundation PSV Football; **Philips Sport Vereniging (PSV Eindhoven)**
Four Mountain Sports; **Aspen Skiing Company**
FOX Business; **Fox Broadcasting Company**
Fox Corporation; **Fox Broadcasting Company**
Fox Corporation; **Fox Sports (Fox Sports Media Group)**
Fox Deportes; **Fox Sports (Fox Sports Media Group)**
FOX News; **Fox Broadcasting Company**
FOX NOW; **Fox Broadcasting Company**
Fox Soccer Plus; **Fox Sports (Fox Sports Media Group)**
FOX Sports; **Fox Broadcasting Company**
Fox Sports 1 (FS1); **Fox Sports (Fox Sports Media Group)**
Fox Sports 2 (FS2); **Fox Sports (Fox Sports Media Group)**
Fox Sports Racing; **Fox Sports (Fox Sports Media Group)**
Fox Television Stations Inc; **Fox Broadcasting Company**
Foxes (The); **Leicester City Football Club**
FoxSports.com; **Fox Sports (Fox Sports Media Group)**
Fraser Yachts Group; **MarineMax Inc**
Frasers Group plcs; **Everlast Worldwide Inc**
Freddy Fever; **Indiana Fever**
Freeform; **Walt Disney Company (The)**
French Connection; **Buffalo Sabres**
Fresno Grizzlies; **Colorado Rockies**
Friedkin Group (The); **AS Roma (Associazione Sportiva Roma)**
Frisco RoughRidgers; **Texas Rangers**
Fruit of the Loom Inc; **Russell Brands LLC**
Fuel EX; **Trek Bicycle Corporation**
FulGaz; **World Triathlon Corporation (Ironman, WTC)**
Furthermore From Equinox; **Equinox Fitness**
FUTURELIGHT; **North Face Inc (The)**
Gainbridge Fieldhouse; **Indiana Pacers**
Gainline Capital Partners LP; **AND 1**
Galaxy Universal LLC; **AND 1**
GameChanger; **Dicks Sporting Goods Inc**
Gatlinburg SkyLift Park; **Boyne Resorts**
Get Pacers Fit; **Indiana Pacers**
Gillette Stadium; **New England Patriots**
Globe; **Specialized Bicycle Components Inc**
GMS Racing; **Legacy Motor Club**
Go Baby Go; **National Thoroughbred Racing Association**
GoDigital Media Group; **Eastern Mountain Sports Inc**
Golden Bear; **Big 5 Sporting Goods Corporation**
GOLDS AMP; **Golds Gym International Inc**
GOLDS BURN; **Golds Gym International Inc**
GOLDS CYCLE; **Golds Gym International Inc**
GOLDS FIT; **Golds Gym International Inc**
Golds Gym; **Golds Gym International Inc**
Golf Alliance Co Ltd; **Accordia Golf Co Ltd**

INDEX OF SUBSIDIARIES, BRAND NAMES AND AFFILIATIONS, CONT.

Golf Galaxy; **Dicks Sporting Goods Inc**
GolfGalaxy.com; **Golf Galaxy Inc**
Grand Lodge Crested Butte Hotel & Suites (The); **Crested Butte Mountain Resort Inc**
Grand Rapids Griffins; **Detroit Red Wings**
Grand Slam; **Womens Tennis Association (WTA)**
Grand Teton Lodge Company; **Vail Resorts Inc**
Green Bay Packers Inc; **Green Bay Packers**
Greensboro Grasshoppers; **Pittsburgh Pirates**
Greensboro Swarm; **Charlotte Hornets**
Greenville Swamp Rabbits; **Florida Panthers**
Grizzlies Hoops Camp Series; **Memphis Grizzlies**
Grizzlies Read to Achieve Program; **Memphis Grizzlies**
Grupo Omnilife; **Club Deportivo Guadalajara SA de CV (Chivas)**
Grupo Televisa SAB; **Club de Futbol America SA de CV (America)**
Guggenheim Baseball; **Los Angeles Dodgers**
Guide Gear; **Sportsmans Guide Inc (The)**
Gwinnett Stripers; **Atlanta Braves**
GX24; **24 Hour Fitness**
Hammers; **West Ham United Football Club**
Harsh; **Big 5 Sporting Goods Corporation**
Hartford Wolf Pack; **New York Rangers**
Hartford Wolf Pack; **Madison Square Garden Sports Corp**
Hartford Yard Goats; **Colorado Rockies**
Hearst Corporation; **ESPN Inc**
Heartwell Golf Course; **American Golf Corporation**
HEAT Academy; **Miami HEAT**
HEAT Youth Basketball League; **Miami HEAT**
HEATGEAR; **Under Armour Inc**
Heavenly; **Vail Resorts Inc**
Helmet Technology Center; **BRG Sports Inc**
Henderson Silver Knights; **Vegas Golden Knights**
Hendrick Automotive Group; **Hendrick Motorsports**
Heretic; **Skis Rossignol SA**
Herff Jones; **Varsity Brands Holding Co Inc**
Herff Jones Inc; **BSN Sports Inc**
Hershey Bears; **Washington Capitals**
Heyday; **Brunswick Corporation**
Hibbett Sports; **Hibbett Sports Inc**
Hickory Crawdads; **Texas Rangers**
Hollywood Casino; **Penn National Gaming Inc**
Honda Center; **Anaheim Ducks**
Houston Oilers; **Tennessee Titans**
HPS Investment Partners; **OneTeam Partners LLC**
HQ Issue; **Sportsmans Guide Inc (The)**
Huffy Corporation; **Huffy Bicycle Co**
Hugo the Hornet; **Charlotte Hornets**
Hulu Theater at Madison Square Garden; **Madison Square Garden Sports Corp**
Hummingbird; **Johnson Outdoors Inc**
Hunt Sports Group; **FC Dallas**
Hyperflame; **Coleman Company Inc (The)**

i24NEWS; **Altice USA Inc**
Idaho Steelheads; **Dallas Stars**
IDG Capital Partners; **Olympique Lyonnais Groupe**
Ilitch Holdings Inc; **Detroit Tigers**
Ilitch Sports + Entertainment; **Ilitch Holdings Inc**
IMG; **Endeavor Group Holdings Inc**
Impact Guide System; **ASICS Corp**
In Shape; **Grupo Sports World SAB de CV**
Indiana Fever; **Indiana Pacers**
Indianapolis Indians; **Pittsburgh Pirates**
Indianapolis Motor Speedway; **IndyCar LLC**
Individual Champion; **LIV Golf Inc**
Indy Fuel; **Chicago Blackhawks**
Indy NXT; **IndyCar LLC**
Indy Pro 2000 Championship; **IndyCar LLC**
IndyCar Radio; **IndyCar LLC**
Inferno Dance Team; **Indiana Fever**
InSTEP; **Pacific Cycle Inc**
Inter Milan; **Football Club Internazionale Milano SpA**
Intercontinental Champions; **World Boxing Association (The)**
International Champions; **World Boxing Association (The)**
International Paralympic Committee; **International Olympic Committee (IOC)**
International Skating Union; **US Figure Skating**
Interpublic Group of Companies Inc; **Octagon Worldwide**
Intrepid; **MarineMax Inc**
Invited; **ClubCorp Holdings Inc (Invited)**
Iowa Cubs; **Chicago Cubs**
Iowa Heartlanders; **Minnesota Wild**
Iowa Wild; **Minnesota Wild**
Iowa Wolves; **Minnesota Timberwolves**
Ironman; **World Triathlon Corporation (Ironman, WTC)**
Ironman 70.2; **World Triathlon Corporation (Ironman, WTC)**
Ironman World Championship; **World Triathlon Corporation (Ironman, WTC)**
IsoSpeed; **Trek Bicycle Corporation**
ITF Mens Circuit; **Association of Tennis Professionals (ATP Tour Inc)**
J Medical; **Juventus Football Club SpA**
Jack Purcell; **Nike Inc**
Jackson; **Sport Maska Inc (CCM Hockey)**
Jacksonville Icemen; **New York Rangers**
Jacksonville Jumbo Shrimp; **Miami Marlins**
Jake Melnicks Corner Tap; **Levy Restaurants**
JanSport; **VF Corporation**
Jet Sports Management; **Wasserman Media Group LLC**
Jetboil; **Johnson Outdoors Inc**
Jolt; **Kellwood Company LLC**
Jong Ajax; **AFC Ajax NV**
Jordan; **Nike Inc**
Judgement Free Zone; **Planet Fitness Inc**

INDEX OF SUBSIDIARIES, BRAND NAMES AND AFFILIATIONS, CONT.

Jupiter Hammerheads; **Miami Marlins**
Juventus; **Juventus Football Club SpA**
Juventus Stadium; **Juventus Football Club SpA**
Kalamazoo Wings; **Columbus Blue Jackets**
Kannapolis Cannon Ballers; **Chicago White Sox**
Kason; **Li Ning Company Limited**
Katz Group Real Estate; **Katz Group Of Companies (The)**
Kauffman Stadium; **Kansas City Royals**
Kentucky Speedway; **Speedway Motorsports LLC**
Kering SA; **PUMA SE**
Kerma; **Skis Rossignol SA**
Kid Trax; **Pacific Cycle Inc**
Kids Klub; **LA Fitness (LA Fitness International LLC)**
King Power International Group; **Leicester City Football Club**
King Power Stadium; **Leicester City Football Club**
Knicks City Dancers; **New York Knickerbockers**
Knicks City Kids; **New York Knickerbockers**
Kolon Sport; **ANTA Sports Products Limited**
Kraft Group (The); **New England Patriots**
Kroenke Sports & Entertainment; **Arsenal Football Club Plc**
Kroenke Sports & Entertainment; **Colorado Avalanche**
Kroenke Sports & Entertainment; **Colorado Rapids**
K-Swiss; **K-Swiss Inc**
K-Swiss; **Xtep International Holdings Limited**
L Catterton; **West Marine Inc**
LA Fitness; **LA Fitness (LA Fitness International LLC)**
Lady Luck Casino Nemacolin; **Churchill Downs Incorporated**
LAFC; **Los Angeles Football Club**
LAFC Academy; **Los Angeles Football Club**
Lake County Captains; **Cleveland Guardians**
Lake Elsinore Storm; **San Diego Padres**
Lakeland Flying Tigers; **Detroit Tigers**
Lakeland Magic; **Orlando Magic**
Lakers Read to Achieve; **Los Angeles Lakers**
Lakewood Country Club; **American Golf Corporation**
Lange; **Skis Rossignol SA**
LAuberge Lake Charles; **Penn National Gaming Inc**
Laundry Service; **Wasserman Media Group LLC**
Laval Rocket; **Montreal Canadiens**
LCFC Women; **Leicester City Football Club**
Lehigh Valley IronPigs; **Philadelphia Phillies**
Lehigh Valley Phantoms; **Philadelphia Flyers**
Leicester City FC Academy; **Leicester City Football Club**
Les Canadiens de Montreal; **Montreal Canadiens**
Liberty Media Corporation; **Atlanta Braves**
Liberty Media Corporation; **Formula One Group (F1)**
Liberty Mountain; **Vail Resorts Inc**
Life Time Group Holdings Inc; **Life Time Inc**
Lift Brands Inc; **Snap Fitness Inc**
Ligue 1; **Ligue de Football Professionnel**

Ligue 2; **Ligue de Football Professionnel**
Limelight Hotel Aspen; **Aspen Skiing Company**
Line & Lure Seafood Kitchen and Tap; **Levy Restaurants**
LI-NING; **Li Ning Company Limited**
LionRock Capital; **Football Club Internazionale Milano SpA**
Lions (The); **Orlando City SC**
Little Caesars Arena; **Detroit Red Wings**
Little Caesars Pizza; **Ilitch Holdings Inc**
Little Gym Camps; **Little Gym International Inc (The)**
Little Nell (The); **Aspen Skiing Company**
LIV Golf League; **LIV Golf Inc**
Liverpool FC; **Fenway Sports Group LLC**
Loarre Investments Sarl; **Campeonato Nacional de Liga Primera Division (La Liga)**
Lodge at Mountaineer Square (The); **Crested Butte Mountain Resort Inc**
Long Island Nets; **Brooklyn Nets**
Look; **Skis Rossignol SA**
Loon Mountain Resort; **Boyne Resorts**
Loons (The); **Minnesota United FC**
Los Angeles Lakers Inc; **Los Angeles Lakers**
Los Angeles Lakers Youth Foundation; **Los Angeles Lakers**
Los Angeles Rams; **Kroenke Sports & Entertainment LLC**
Louisville; **Wilson Sporting Goods Co**
Louisville Bats; **Cincinnati Reds**
Lowa; **Tecnica Group SpA**
LPGA Foundation; **Ladies Professional Golf Association (LPGA)**
LPGA Professionals; **Ladies Professional Golf Association (LPGA)**
LPGA Tour; **Ladies Professional Golf Association (LPGA)**
lululemon; **lululemon athletica inc**
Lund; **Brunswick Corporation**
Lunk; **Planet Fitness Inc**
Lyft Inc; **Motivate LLC**
Lynchburg Hillcats; **Cleveland Guardians**
Lyon; **Olympique Lyonnais Groupe**
Madison Square Garden; **Madison Square Garden Sports Corp**
Madison Square Garden; **New York Knickerbockers**
Madison Square Garden Company (The); **New York Knickerbockers**
Madison Square Garden Inc; **New York Rangers**
Madone; **Trek Bicycle Corporation**
Maine Mariners; **Boston Bruins**
MajesticAthletic.com; **Majestic Athletic**
Major League Baseball Players Association; **OneTeam Partners LLC**
Major League Baseball Players Association; **Major League Baseball (MLB)**

INDEX OF SUBSIDIARIES, BRAND NAMES AND AFFILIATIONS, CONT.

Major League Soccer; **MLS NEXT Pro (Pro Soccer Development LP)**
Mammoth Mountain; **Alterra Mountain Company**
Manchester City Womens Football Club; **Manchester City Football Club**
Manchester United Football Club; **Manchester United plc**
Manitoba Moose; **Winnipeg Jets**
Maple Leaf Sports & Entertainment Ltd; **Toronto FC**
Maple Leaf Sports & Entertainment Ltd; **Toronto Maple Leafs**
Maple Leaf Sports & Entertainment Ltd; **Toronto Raptors**
Mares; **Head Sport GmbH**
MarineMax Vacations; **MarineMax Inc**
Marseille; **Olympique de Marseille**
Matmut Atlantique; **Football Club des Girondins de Bordeaux (Bordeaux)**
Meadows Casino (The); **Penn National Gaming Inc**
Members Club; **West Ham United Football Club**
Memphis Basketball LLC; **Memphis Grizzlies**
Mercedes-Benz Arena; **Verein fur Bewegungsspiele Stuttgart 1893 eV (VfB Stuttgart)**
Merrell; **Xtep International Holdings Limited**
Mestalla; **Valencia Club de Futbol (Valencia CF/Valencia)**
MetroStars; **New York Red Bulls**
Miami Heat Learn & Play Center; **Miami HEAT**
Michael Jordan; **Charlotte Hornets**
Michael Jordans Steak House; **Levy Restaurants**
Middlesbrough Cricket Club; **Middlesbrough Football Club**
Mighty Ducks; **Anaheim Ducks**
Miken; **Rawlings Sporting Goods Company Inc**
MiLB.TV; **Minor League Baseball**
Milwaukee Admirals; **Nashville Predators**
Minn Kota; **Johnson Outdoors Inc**
Minnesota Lynx; **Minnesota Timberwolves**
Minnesota North Stars; **Minnesota Wild**
Minnesota Sports Facilities Authority; **Minnesota Vikings**
Minnesota Timberwolves; **Minnesota Lynx**
Minnesota United FC 2; **Minnesota United FC**
Minor League Baseball Umpire Development; **Minor League Baseball**
MIPS; **BRG Sports Inc**
MIRROR; **lululemon athletica inc**
Mississippi Braves; **Atlanta Braves**
Missy; **Kellwood Company LLC**
MJ Soffe LLC; **Delta Apparel Inc**
MLB Advanced Media LP; **Major League Baseball (MLB)**
MLB Network; **Major League Baseball Advanced Media LP (MLBAM)**
MLB Productions; **Major League Baseball Advanced Media LP (MLBAM)**
MLB Productions; **Major League Baseball (MLB)**

MLB Properties LLC; **Rawlings Sporting Goods Company Inc**
MLB.com; **Major League Baseball Advanced Media LP (MLBAM)**
MLB.com; **Major League Baseball (MLB)**
MLS Cup; **Major League Soccer (MLS)**
MLS Next Pro; **Sporting Kansas City**
Moda Center; **Portland Trail Blazers**
Modesto Nuts; **Seattle Mariners**
Mohegan Sun Arena; **Connecticut Sun**
Mohegan Sun Casino; **Connecticut Sun**
Mohegan Tribal Gaming Authority; **Connecticut Sun**
Monarch Alternative Capital LP; **24 Hour Fitness**
Mongoose; **Pacific Cycle Inc**
Montgomery Biscuits; **Tampa Bay Rays**
Montreal Expos; **Washington Nationals**
Monumental Sports & Entertainment; **Washington Capitals**
Monumental Sports & Entertainment; **Washington Mystics**
Monumental Sports & Entertainment; **Washington Wizards**
Moon Boot; **Tecnica Group SpA**
Morgan Stanley Tactical Value.; **OneTeam Partners LLC**
Motor City Casino and Hotel; **Ilitch Holdings Inc**
Motor City Cruise; **Detroit Pistons**
Mountain Hardwear; **Columbia Sportswear Company**
MSG Sports & Entertainment LLC; **Madison Square Garden Sports Corp**
MSNBC; **NBCUniversal Media LLC**
Mullett Arena; **Arizona Coyotes**
MUTV; **Manchester United plc**
My LAFitness; **LA Fitness (LA Fitness International LLC)**
MyCurves On Demand; **Curves NA**
MyNetworkTV; **Fox Broadcasting Company**
Myrtle Beach Pelicans; **Chicago Cubs**
MYZone; **LA Fitness (LA Fitness International LLC)**
NASCAR Digital Media LLC; **NASCAR**
NASCAR Technical Institute; **NASCAR**
National Basketball Association; **Womens National Basketball Association (WNBA)**
National Basketball Association (NBA); **NBA G League**
National Basketball League; **National Basketball Association (NBA)**
National Boxing Association (NBA); **World Boxing Association (The)**
National Football Conference; **National Football League (NFL)**
National Football League Players Association; **OneTeam Partners LLC**
National Geographic; **Walt Disney Company (The)**
National Golf Club (The); **American Golf Corporation**
National Horseplayers Championship; **National Thoroughbred Racing Association**

INDEX OF SUBSIDIARIES, BRAND NAMES AND AFFILIATIONS, CONT.

National League; **Major League Baseball (MLB)**
National Team Development Program; **USA Hockey Inc**
NBA Cares; **National Basketball Association (NBA)**
NBA G League; **National Basketball Association (NBA)**
NBA TV; **National Basketball Association (NBA)**
NBC News; **NBCUniversal Media LLC**
NBC Sports; **NBCUniversal Media LLC**
Need for Speed; **Electronic Arts Inc (EA)**
New England Patriots LP; **New England Patriots**
New England Sports Network; **Boston Red Sox**
New England Sports Network; **Fenway Sports Group LLC**
New Hampshire Fisher Cats; **Toronto Blue Jays**
New Jersey Devils LLC; **New Jersey Devils**
New York Interconnect; **Altice USA Inc**
New York Islanders Hockey Club LP; **New York Islanders**
New York Jets LLC; **New York Jets**
New York KNicks; **Madison Square Garden Sports Corp**
New York LIberty; **Madison Square Garden Sports Corp**
New York Rangers; **Madison Square Garden Sports Corp**
Newell Brands Inc; **Coleman Company Inc (The)**
Newfoundland Growlers; **Toronto Maple Leafs**
Newport; **Churchill Downs Incorporated**
News 12 Networks; **Altice USA Inc**
NFL Network; **National Football League (NFL)**
Nickelodeon; **Paramount Global**
NIKE IHM Inc (Air Manufacturing Innovation); **Nike Inc**
Nike Inc; **Converse Inc**
Nintendo of America; **Seattle Mariners**
Nordica; **Tecnica Group SpA**
Norfolk Admirals; **Carolina Hurricanes**
Norfolk Tides; **Baltimore Orioles**
North American Boxing Federation; **World Boxing Council**
North Face (The); **VF Corporation**
North Wilkesboro Speedway; **Speedway Motorsports LLC**
Northern Tool & Equipment Company Inc; **Sportsmans Guide Inc (The)**
Northwest Arkansas Naturals; **Kansas City Royals**
NRG Stadium; **Houston Texans**
NSWE; **Aston Villa Football Club**
NTRA Advantage; **National Thoroughbred Racing Association**
NTRA Safety and Integrity Alliance; **National Thoroughbred Racing Association**
NTRA Top Thoroughbred; **National Thoroughbred Racing Association**
NTRA Top-3-Year-Old; **National Thoroughbred Racing Association**
NTRA.com; **National Thoroughbred Racing Association**

NTT IndyCar Series; **IndyCar LLC**
Oak Grove; **Churchill Downs Incorporated**
Ocean Kayak; **Johnson Outdoors Inc**
Odyssey; **Topgolf Callaway Brands Corp**
OEG Inc; **Katz Group Of Companies (The)**
Offshore Angler; **BPS Direct LLC (Bass Pro Shops)**
Oklahoma City Blue; **Oklahoma City Thunder**
OL; **Olympique Lyonnais Groupe**
Old Town; **Johnson Outdoors Inc**
Olimpiyskiy National Sports Complex; **Football Club Dynamo Kyiv**
Oliver and Bonacini and Concorde Group; **Katz Group Of Companies (The)**
Olympia Development of Michigan; **Ilitch Holdings Inc**
Olympic Games; **International Olympic Committee (IOC)**
Olympique Lyonnais Groupe; **Olympique Lyonnais Groupe**
OM; **Olympique de Marseille**
Omaha Storm Chasers; **Kansas City Royals**
One Star; **Nike Inc**
Onex Corporation; **ASM Global**
Onitsuka Tiger; **ASICS Corp**
Ontario Clippers; **Los Angeles Clippers**
Ontario Reign; **Los Angeles Kings**
Optimum; **Altice USA Inc**
Oriental and Pacific Boxing Federation; **World Boxing Council**
Oriole Park at Camden Yards; **Baltimore Orioles**
Orlando Magic Basketball Camp; **Orlando Magic**
Orlando Magic Youth Foundation; **Orlando Magic**
Orlando Solar Bears; **Tampa Bay Lightning**
Orvis Log Homes; **Orvis Company Inc (The)**
Orvis Shooting Grounds at Pursell Farms; **Orvis Company Inc (The)**
Orvis Travel; **Orvis Company Inc (The)**
OutDry; **Columbia Sportswear Company**
OVG 360; **Oak View Group**
OVG Arena Alliance; **Oak View Group**
OVG Business Development; **Oak View Group**
OVG Canada; **Oak View Group**
OVG Global Partnership; **Oak View Group**
OVG Hospitality; **Oak View Group**
OVG Media & Conferences; **Oak View Group**
Pacers Learning Center; **Indiana Pacers**
Pacers Sports & Entertainment; **Indiana Pacers**
Pacifica; **Big 5 Sporting Goods Corporation**
Pack Gives Back; **Minnesota Lynx**
Palladium; **Xtep International Holdings Limited**
Pandora Media LLC; **Sirius XM Holdings Inc**
Paralympic Games; **International Olympic Committee (IOC)**
Paramount Pictures; **Paramount Global**
Paramount+; **Paramount Global**

INDEX OF SUBSIDIARIES, BRAND NAMES AND AFFILIATIONS, CONT.

Parc des Princes; **Paris Saint-Germain Football Club (PSG)**
Park City; **Vail Resorts Inc**
Patagonia Works Inc; **Patagonia Inc**
Patina Restaurant Group; **Delaware North Companies Inc**
Paul G Allen Trust; **Portland Trail Blazers**
Paul G Allen Trust; **Seattle Seahawks**
PBA Jr; **Professional Bowlers Association LLC**
PBA Regional Tour; **Professional Bowlers Association LLC**
PBA Tour; **Professional Bowlers Association LLC**
PBA50/60 Tours; **Professional Bowlers Association LLC**
PBR; **Endeavor Group Holdings Inc**
PBR Challenger Series; **Professional Bull Riders Inc**
PBR Team Series; **Professional Bull Riders Inc**
PBR World Finals; **Professional Bull Riders Inc**
PCP Capital Partners; **Newcastle United Football Club**
Peacock; **Comcast Corporation**
peacock; **NBCUniversal Media LLC**
Peloton Bike; **Peloton Interactive Inc**
Penn; **Head Sport GmbH**
PENN National Gaming Inc; **Score Media Ventures Inc**
Pennwood Racing Inc; **Penn National Gaming Inc**
Pensacola Blue Wahoos; **Miami Marlins**
Penske Corporation; **IndyCar LLC**
Penske Corporation; **Team Penske**
Penske Entertainment Corp; **IndyCar LLC**
Peregrine Sports LLC; **Portland Timbers**
Perfect Fit Frame; **Huffy Bicycle Co**
Petty GMS Motorsports; **Legacy Motor Club**
PF Black Card; **Planet Fitness Inc**
PGA Championship; **Professional Golfers Association of America (PGA)**
PGA Cup; **Professional Golfers Association of America (PGA)**
PGA Golf Management; **Professional Golfers Association of America (PGA)**
PGA Professional Championship; **Professional Golfers Association of America (PGA)**
PGA Tour; **Professional Golfers Association of America (PGA)**
Philadelphia Flyers; **Comcast Corporation**
Philips Stadion; **Philips Sport Vereniging (PSV Eindhoven)**
Phoenix Suns; **Phoenix Mercury**
Pirelli & C SpA; **Football Club Internazionale Milano SpA**
Pittsburgh Penguins; **Fenway Sports Group LLC**
Plants vs Zombies; **Electronic Arts Inc (EA)**
Play Forward Pathway; **Canlan Ice Sports Corp**
Plaza (The); **Crested Butte Mountain Resort Inc**
Polartec; **North Face Inc (The)**
Porsche Penske Motorsport; **Team Penske**
prAna; **Columbia Sportswear Company**

Predators Holdings LLC; **Nashville Predators**
Preds; **Nashville Predators**
Prevent Advisors; **Oak View Group**
Professional Basketball Club LLC; **Oklahoma City Thunder**
Professional Bowlers Association (PBA); **Bowlero Corp**
ProStaff; **Wilson Sporting Goods Co**
Providence Bruins; **Boston Bruins**
Public Investment Fund; **LIV Golf Inc**
Public Investment Fund; **Newcastle United Football Club**
Public Lands; **Dicks Sporting Goods Inc**
PUMA; **PUMA SE**
Qatar Sports Investments; **Paris Saint-Germain Football Club (PSG)**
Quad cities River Bandits; **Kansas City Royals**
Quebec Nordiques; **Colorado Avalanche**
Quicksilver; **Boardriders Inc**
Radio City Music Hall; **Madison Square Garden Sports Corp**
Rangers Baseball Express LLC; **Texas Rangers**
Rank + Rally; **Levy Restaurants**
Rapit City Rush; **Calgary Flames**
Raptors 905; **Maple Leaf Sports & Entertainment Ltd**
Rawlings; **Rawlings Sporting Goods Company Inc**
Rayados; **Club de Futbol Monterrey**
RB Sports & Media; **Newcastle United Football Club**
RCVA; **Boardriders Inc**
RDV Sports Inc; **Orlando Magic**
Read to Achieve; **Indiana Pacers**
Reading Fightin Phils; **Philadelphia Phillies**
Reading Royals; **Philadelphia Flyers**
Reading Time-Outs; **Indiana Pacers**
Real Madrid; **Real Madrid Club de Futbol**
Realmadrid Foundation; **Real Madrid Club de Futbol**
reCreation; **Kellwood Company LLC**
Red Bull Arena; **New York Red Bulls**
Red Bull GmbH; **New York Red Bulls**
RedBird Capital Partners; **Associazione Calcio Milan spa**
RedHead; **BPS Direct LLC (Bass Pro Shops)**
Reebok; **adidas AG**
Regulator; **Patagonia Inc**
REI; **REI (Recreational Equipment Inc)**
REI Adventures; **REI (Recreational Equipment Inc)**
REI Gear and Apparel; **REI (Recreational Equipment Inc)**
Related Companies LP (The); **Equinox Fitness**
rEvo; **Head Sport GmbH**
Revolution Academy; **New England Revolution**
Rewind; **Kellwood Company LLC**
RFK Racing; **Roush Fenway Keselowski Racing (RFK Racing)**
Richmond Flying Squirrels; **San Francisco Giants**
Riddell; **BRG Sports Inc**
Riddle & Bloom; **Wasserman Media Group LLC**
Risport; **Skis Rossignol SA**

INDEX OF SUBSIDIARIES, BRAND NAMES AND AFFILIATIONS, CONT.

Riversiders; **Blackburn Rovers Football Club**
Robalo; **Marine Products Corporation**
Robalo Acquisition Company LLC; **Marine Products Corporation**
Rochester Americans; **Buffalo Sabres**
Rockford IceHogs; **Chicago Blackhawks**
RockResorts; **Vail Resorts Inc**
Rogers; **Rogers Communications Inc**
Rogers Communications Inc; **Toronto Blue Jays**
Rollerblade; **Tecnica Group SpA**
Rome Braves; **Atlanta Braves**
Rossignol; **Skis Rossignol SA**
Roth Distributing Co Inc; **Trek Bicycle Corporation**
Round Rock Express; **Texas Rangers**
Roxy; **Boardriders Inc**
Roxy Girl; **Boardriders Inc**
Royal Charities; **Kansas City Royals**
RSG Group GmbH; **Golds Gym International Inc**
Rugged Exposure; **Big 5 Sporting Goods Corporation**
Russell Athletic; **Russell Brands LLC**
Ryder Cup; **Professional Golfers Association of America (PGA)**
Ryder Cup Europe; **PGA European Tour (bda DP World Tour)**
Sacramento River Cats; **San Francisco Giants**
Saints; **Southampton Football Club**
Saints Foundation; **Southampton Football Club**
Salt Life LLC; **Delta Apparel Inc**
San Antonio Missions; **San Diego Padres**
San Antonio Silver Stars; **Las Vegas Aces**
San Antonio Stars; **Las Vegas Aces**
San Diego Chargers; **Los Angeles Chargers**
San Francisco Baseball Associates LLC; **San Francisco Giants**
San Jose Barracuda; **San Jose Sharks**
San Jose Giants; **San Francisco Giants**
San Jose Sports & Entertainment Enterprises; **San Jose Sharks**
San Mames; **Athletic Club (Athletic Bilbao)**
Saucony; **Xtep International Holdings Limited**
Savannah Ghost Pirates; **Vegas Golden Knights**
SBTech Malta Limited; **DraftKings Inc**
Schalke 04; **Football-Club Gelsenkirchen-Schalke 04 eV**
Schwinn; **Pacific Cycle Inc**
Scotiabank Arena; **Maple Leaf Sports & Entertainment Ltd**
SCUBAPRO; **Johnson Outdoors Inc**
Sculptor Capital Investments LLC; **24 Hour Fitness**
Sea Ray; **Brunswick Corporation**
Seidler Equity Partners; **Rawlings Sporting Goods Company Inc**
Self Esteem Brands; **Anytime Fitness LLC**
Senior PGA Championship; **Professional Golfers Association of America (PGA)**
Shows; **Bleacher Report Inc (B/R)**

Showtime; **Paramount Global**
SI; **Sports Illustrated**
SI Sportsbook; **Sports Illustrated**
SI Swimsuit; **Sports Illustrated**
SI Tickets; **Sports Illustrated**
Sierra-at-Tahoe Resort; **Booth Creek Ski Holdings Inc**
Signal Iduna Park (Westfalenstadion); **Borussia Dortmund GmbH & Co KGaA**
Signature; **Marine Products Corporation**
Silver Lake; **Manchester City Football Club**
Sims (The); **Electronic Arts Inc (EA)**
SiriusXM; **Sirius XM Holdings Inc**
Sky Limited; **Comcast Corporation**
Sky News; **Comcast Corporation**
Sky Sports; **Comcast Corporation**
SLB Acquisition Holdings LLC; **St Louis Blues**
SmartWool; **VF Corporation**
Snow Valley; **Alterra Mountain Company**
Snowmass Mountain; **Aspen Skiing Company**
sntv; **Endeavor Group Holdings Inc**
Sodexo SA; **Sodexo Live!**
SoFi Stadium; **Kroenke Sports & Entertainment LLC**
Sonoma Raceway; **Speedway Motorsports LLC**
Sorel; **Columbia Sportswear Company**
South Bend Cubs; **Chicago Cubs**
South Carolina Stingrays; **Washington Capitals**
South Shore Golf Course; **American Golf Corporation**
Southsiders; **Vancouver Whitecaps FC**
Sparks LA Sports LLC; **Los Angeles Sparks**
Specialized Ride App; **Specialized Bicycle Components Inc**
Spokane Indians; **Colorado Rockies**
Sport Repbublic; **Southampton Football Club**
Sporting Club; **Sporting Kansas City**
Sporting Kansas City II; **Sporting Kansas City**
Sporting Life Group Limited; **Golf Town Limited**
Sports Additions; **Hibbett Sports Inc**
Sports World Club; **Grupo Sports World SAB de CV**
Sports World Fit; **Grupo Sports World SAB de CV**
Sportsbook; **DraftKings Inc**
SportsCenter; **ESPN Inc**
SportsmansGuide.com; **Sportsmans Guide Inc (The)**
Springfield Thunderbirds; **St Louis Blues**
Spun (The); **Sports Illustrated**
Spurs; **Tottenham Hotspur Football Club**
SSI; **Head Sport GmbH**
SSi; **Marine Products Corporation**
SSX; **Marine Products Corporation**
St Louis Brown Stockings; **St Louis Cardinals**
St Lous Rams; **Los Angeles Rams**
Stade Geoffroy-Guichard; **Association Sportive de Saint-Etienne Loire (AS Saint-Etienne)**
Stadio Diego Armando Maradona; **Societa Sportiva Calcio Napoli (SSC Napoli)**
Stanley Cup; **National Hockey League (NHL)**

INDEX OF SUBSIDIARIES, BRAND NAMES AND AFFILIATIONS, CONT.

Star+; **Walt Disney Company (The)**
State Farm Stadium; **Arizona Cardinals**
Stay in School Challenge; **Memphis Grizzlies**
Steamboat; **Alterra Mountain Company**
STEP Skate Blades Inc; **Sport Maska Inc (CCM Hockey)**
stichd; **PUMA SE**
Stowe; **Vail Resorts Inc**
Stumpjumper; **Specialized Bicycle Components Inc**
Suddenlink; **Altice USA Inc**
Sugarbush Resort; **Alterra Mountain Company**
Sugarloaf; **Boyne Resorts**
Sunday River Resort; **Boyne Resorts**
Sunesta; **Marine Products Corporation**
Suning Holdings GroupCo Ltd; **Football Club
Internazionale Milano SpA**
Sunrise Sports & Entertainment; **Florida Panthers**
Super; **Trek Bicycle Corporation**
Super Bowl; **National Football League (NFL)**
Supercopa de Espana; **Campeonato Nacional de Liga
Primera Division (La Liga)**
SW Gym; **Grupo Sports World SAB de CV**
SW Gym Plus; **Grupo Sports World SAB de CV**
Syracuse Crunch; **Tampa Bay Lightning**
Syracuse Nationals; **Philadelphia 76ers**
Tacoma Rainiers; **Seattle Mariners**
Tai Chi; **AND 1**
TD Garden; **Delaware North Companies Inc**
Team Champion; **LIV Golf Inc**
Tecnica; **Tecnica Group SpA**
Tennessee Smokies; **Chicago Cubs**
Texas Motor Speedway; **Speedway Motorsports LLC**
Texas Stars; **Dallas Stars**
Thames Ironworks; **West Ham United Football Club**
ThermoBall Eco; **North Face Inc (The)**
theScore; **Score Media Ventures Inc**
theScore Bet; **Score Media Ventures Inc**
theScore Bet Sportsbook and Casino; **Score Media
Ventures Inc**
TIAA Bank Field; **Jacksonville Jaguars**
Timberland; **VF Corporation**
Timberland PRO; **VF Corporation**
TKA; **North Face Inc (The)**
Tokyo Smoke; **Katz Group Of Companies (The)**
Toledo Mud Hens; **Detroit Tigers**
Toledo Walleye; **Detroit Red Wings**
Topgolf International Inc; **Topgolf Callaway Brands
Corp**
Toronto Argonauts; **Maple Leaf Sports & Entertainment
Ltd**
Toronto FC II; **Maple Leaf Sports & Entertainment Ltd**
Toronto Football Club; **Maple Leaf Sports &
Entertainment Ltd**
Toronto Maple Leafs; **Maple Leaf Sports &
Entertainment Ltd**
Toronto Marlies; **Toronto Maple Leafs**

Toronto Marlies; **Maple Leaf Sports & Entertainment
Ltd**
Toronto Raptors; **Maple Leaf Sports & Entertainment
Ltd**
Touring Pro Division; **Professional Bull Riders Inc**
Tournament Sports Marketing Inc; **Sport Maska Inc
(CCM Hockey)**
Trek Factory Racing; **Trek Bicycle Corporation**
Tricolor Paulista; **Sao Paulo Futebol Clube**
Trois-Rivieres Lions; **Montreal Canadiens**
Tropicana Las Vegas; **Penn National Gaming Inc**
True North Sports & Entertainment; **Winnipeg Jets**
Trustmark; **HealthFitness Corporation**
Tucson Roadrunners; **Arizona Coyotes**
Turfway Park; **Churchill Downs Incorporated**
Turkish Airlines EuroLeague; **Endeavor Group Holdings
Inc**
TwinSpires; **Churchill Downs Incorporated**
Tyrolia; **Head Sport GmbH**
UA Flow; **Under Armour Inc**
UA HOVR; **Under Armour Inc**
UA Micro G; **Under Armour Inc**
UBS Arena; **New York Islanders**
UEFA Champions League; **Union of European Football
Associations (UEFA)**
UEFA Champions League; **Campeonato Nacional de
Liga Primera Division (La Liga)**
UEFA Europa Conference League; **Campeonato Nacional
de Liga Primera Division (La Liga)**
UEFA Europa League; **Union of European Football
Associations (UEFA)**
UEFA Europa League; **Campeonato Nacional de Liga
Primera Division (La Liga)**
UEFA Futsal Champions League; **Union of European
Football Associations (UEFA)**
UEFA Super Cup; **Union of European Football
Associations (UEFA)**
UEFA Under-19 Futsal Championship; **Union of
European Football Associations (UEFA)**
UEFA Womens Champions League; **Union of European
Football Associations (UEFA)**
UEFA Youth League; **Union of European Football
Associations (UEFA)**
Ultra; **Wilson Sporting Goods Co**
Under-23; **Wolverhampton Wanderers Football Club**
Underdog Fantasy; **Underdog Sports Inc**
Union of European Football Association; **Campeonato
Nacional de Liga Primera Division (La Liga)**
Unique Image LLC; **BSN Sports Inc**
United Center; **Chicago Bulls**
United Center; **Chicago Blackhawks**
United Center JV; **Chicago Bulls**
United Center JV; **Chicago Blackhawks**
United Soccer League; **USL Championship League (USL
Pro LLC)**

INDEX OF SUBSIDIARIES, BRAND NAMES AND AFFILIATIONS, CONT.

United States Boxing Association (USBA); **International Boxing Federation**
United States Olympic & Paralympic Committee; **US Figure Skating**
Universal Dance Association; **Varsity Brands Holding Co Inc**
Universal Pictures; **Comcast Corporation**
Universal Pictures Home Entertainment; **NBCUniversal Media LLC**
Universal Studios; **Comcast Corporation**
Universal Studios Hollywood; **NBCUniversal Media LLC**
Universidad Nacional Autonoma de Mexico; **Club Universidad Nacional-Asociacion Civil (UNAM/Pumas)**
Unleash the Beast; **Professional Bull Riders Inc**
Unleashed Brands Group; **Little Gym International Inc (The)**
US Amateur Four-Ball; **United States Golf Association (USGA)**
US F2000 National Championship; **IndyCar LLC**
US Junior Amateur; **United States Golf Association (USGA)**
US Open; **United States Golf Association (USGA)**
US Senior Open; **United States Golf Association (USGA)**
US Senior Womens Open; **United States Golf Association (USGA)**
US Womens Amateur Four-Ball; **United States Golf Association (USGA)**
US Womens Open; **United States Golf Association (USGA)**
USA Gymnastics University; **USA Gymnastics**
USA Hockey Foundation; **USA Hockey Inc**
USL Academy; **United Soccer League**
USL Championship; **United Soccer League**
USL League One; **United Soccer League**
USL League Two; **United Soccer League**
USL Super League; **United Soccer League**
USL Super Y League; **United Soccer League**
USL W League; **United Soccer League**
USTA Billie Jean King National Tennis Center; **United States Tennis Association (USTA)**
Utah Grizzlies; **Colorado Avalanche**
Utah Royals FC; **Real Salt Lake**
Utah Starzz; **Las Vegas Aces**
Utica Comets; **New Jersey Devils**
UTMB World Series; **World Triathlon Corporation (Ironman, WTC)**
Vail Resorts Development Company; **Vail Resorts Inc**
Vail Resorts Inc; **Crested Butte Mountain Resort Inc**
Vancouver 86ers; **Vancouver Whitecaps FC**
Vancouver Canadians; **Toronto Blue Jays**
Vans; **VF Corporation**
Varsity Brands Inc; **BSN Sports Inc**
Varsity Spirit; **Varsity Brands Holding Co Inc**
Varsity TV; **Varsity Brands Holding Co Inc**

Varsity.com; **Varsity Brands Holding Co Inc**
VECTIV; **North Face Inc (The)**
Velocity Tour; **Professional Bull Riders Inc**
Venkateshwara Hatcheries Pvt Ltd; **Blackburn Rovers Football Club**
Venkys London Limited; **Blackburn Rovers Football Club**
VF Corporation; **North Face Inc (The)**
Vikings Childrens Fund; **Minnesota Vikings**
Villa Park; **Aston Villa Football Club**
Villains; **Aston Villa Football Club**
Vista Outdoor Inc; **CamelBak Products LLC**
VonZipper; **Boardriders Inc**
VSG Enterprises LLC; **Tampa Bay Lightning**
Walt Disney Company (The); **Disney Media & Entertainment Distribution**
Walt Disney Company (The); **ESPN Inc**
Walton-Penner Family Ownership Group; **Denver Broncos**
Warner Bros Discovery Inc; **Bleacher Report Inc (B/R)**
Warrior Sports; **New Balance Athletic Shoe Inc**
Washington Football Team; **Washington Commanders**
Washington Redskins; **Washington Commanders**
Waterview Golf Club; **American Golf Corporation**
Welcome Toronto; **Toronto Raptors**
West Michigan Whitecaps; **Detroit Tigers**
Western Conference; **Major League Soccer (MLS)**
Western Conference; **National Hockey League (NHL)**
Wheeling Nailers; **Pittsburgh Penguins**
Whistler Blackcomb; **Vail Resorts Inc**
White River Fly Shops; **BPS Direct LLC (Bass Pro Shops)**
Whitefish Mountain Resort; **Winter Sports Inc**
WHOOP; **WHOOP Inc**
Wilkes-Barre/Scranton Penguins; **Pittsburgh Penguins**
Wilson Staff; **Wilson Sporting Goods Co**
Wilson.com; **Wilson Sporting Goods Co**
WindWall; **North Face Inc (The)**
Windy City Bulls; **Chicago Bulls**
Winston-Salem Dash; **Chicago White Sox**
Wirtz Corporation; **Chicago Blackhawks**
Wit & Wisdom; **Kellwood Company LLC**
WME; **BDA Sports Management**
WNBA; **National Basketball Association (NBA)**
Wolverhampton Wanderers; **Wolverhampton Wanderers Football Club**
Wolverhampton Wanderers Womens FC; **Wolverhampton Wanderers Football Club**
Wolves; **Wolverhampton Wanderers Football Club**
Womens PGA Championship; **Professional Golfers Association of America (PGA)**
Wonders of Wildlife; **BPS Direct LLC (Bass Pro Shops)**
Worcester Railers; **New York Islanders**
World Champions; **World Boxing Association (The)**
World Series; **Major League Baseball (MLB)**

INDEX OF SUBSIDIARIES, BRAND NAMES AND AFFILIATIONS, CONT.

WornWear.Patagonia.com; **Patagonia Inc**
Worth; **Rawlings Sporting Goods Company Inc**
WTA 1000; **Womens Tennis Association (WTA)**
WTA 250; **Womens Tennis Association (WTA)**
WTA 500; **Womens Tennis Association (WTA)**
WTA Elite Trophy; **Womens Tennis Association (WTA)**
WTA Finals; **Womens Tennis Association (WTA)**
WTA Tour; **Womens Tennis Association (WTA)**
www.ibf.usba-boxing.com; **International Boxing Federation**
www.rei.com; **REI (Recreational Equipment Inc)**
www.rei.com/rei-garage; **REI (Recreational Equipment Inc)**
XFINITY; **Comcast Corporation**
Xfinity Series; **NASCAR**
Xtep; **Xtep International Holdings Limited**
Xtep Cool; **Xtep International Holdings Limited**
Xtep Dry; **Xtep International Holdings Limited**
Xtep International Holdings Limited; **K-Swiss Inc**
Xtep Shield; **Xtep International Holdings Limited**
Yankee Global Enterprises; **New York City FC**
Yankee Global Enterprises; **New York Yankees**
Yankee Stadium; **New York Yankees**
Yankees Entertainment & Sports Network (YES); **New York Yankees**
Yellows (The); **Norwich City Football Club**
Zumba Academy; **Zumba Fitness LLC**

INDEX OF SUBSIDIARIES, BRAND NAMES AND AFFILIATIONS, CONT.

A Short Sports & Recreation Industry Glossary

Above the Line (ATL) Marketing: Traditional advertising through large media outlets, such as newspapers, radio and television. See "Below the Line (BTL) Marketing."

Above the Line (ATL) Marketing: Traditional advertising through large (mass) media outlets, such as newspapers, radio and television. Also, see "Below the Line (BTL) Marketing."

Activewear: A category of apparel that includes clothing for sports activities, workout and other types of exercises.

Adams Division: Part of the Wales Conference in the National Hockey League prior to the 1994 reorganization. Now called the Northeastern Division of the Eastern Conference.

Affiliate: A broadcast radio or television station that is an "affiliate" of a national network, such as NBC or CBS, contracts with the national network, which provides programming to the affiliate for all or part of each day. In return, the affiliate provides the network with an agreed-upon number of minutes of advertising time, which the network then resells to advertisers.

AFL: Arena Football League. See www.arenafootball.com.

AHL: American Hockey League. See www.theahl.com.

All-Star Game: An exhibition game featuring a sport's star players, usually elected by the fans.

AM: See "Amplitude Modulation (AM)."

American Football Conference (AFC): One of two football conferences in the National Football League. The AFC is divided into four divisions: AFC East, AFC West, AFC North and AFC South. The winner of the AFC playoff plays against the winner of the NFC playoff in the Super Bowl.

American Football Conference (South): One of four divisions that make up the American Football Conference. The division includes the Indianapolis

Colts, Jacksonville Jaguars, Houston Texans and Tennessee Titans.

American Football Conference East (AFC East): One of four divisions that make up the American Football Conference. The division includes the New England Patriots, New York Jets, Buffalo Bills and Miami Dolphins.

American Football Conference North (AFC North): One of four divisions that make up the American Football Conference. The division includes the Pittsburgh Steelers, Baltimore Ravens, Cincinnati Bengals and Cleveland Browns.

American Football League West: One of four divisions that make up the American Football Conference. The division includes the San Diego Chargers, Denver Broncos, Kansas City Chiefs and Oakland Raiders.

American League: One of two leagues in Major League Baseball. The American League is divided into three divisions: East, West and Central. The winner of the National League playoff plays the winner of the American League playoff in the World Series. See www.mlb.com.

American League Central: One of the three divisions of the American League. The division includes the Chicago White Sox, Minnesota Twins, Detroit Tigers, Cleveland Indians and Kansas City Royals.

American League East: One of the three divisions of the American League. The division includes the Baltimore Orioles, Boston Red Sox, Toronto Blue Jays, New York Yankees and Tampa Bay Devil Rays.

American League West: One of the three divisions of the American League. The division includes the Los Angeles Angels, Texas Rangers, Oakland Athletics and Seattle Mariners.

American Research Bureau (ARB): One of several national firms that conduct audience research. ARB is the founder of Arbitron ratings.

America's Cup: A major international yacht race.

Amplitude Modulation (AM): Radio broadcasts in the range of 535 kHz to 1705 kHz.

Area of Dominant Influence (ADI): A market area established by Arbitron that places cities and/or parts of counties into groupings that are reached by the same local radio or television stations. It is similar to Nielsen's "Designated Market Area." For example, advertising on radio stations in Boston will reach listeners far outside of Boston within the surrounding ADI.

Astroturf: An artificial grass used on many professional sports fields.

Atlantic Coast Conference (ACC): An NCAA (National College Athletic Association) Division I-A sports conference including Virginia Tech, Florida State, Miami, Virginia, North Carolina, Clemson, Georgia Tech, Maryland, North Carolina State, Wake Forest, Boston College and Duke.

Audience: Total number of households or individuals that can be reached by a an advertising or media vehicle. See "Vehicle."

Below the Line (BTL) Marketing: Nonstandard (and generally less expensive) advertising and marketing efforts, such as direct mail, sales promotions and public relations activities.

Big 10 Conference: An NCAA (National College Athletic Association) Division I-A sports conference that includes Iowa, Michigan, Wisconsin, Northwestern, Ohio State, Purdue, Michigan State, Minnesota, Penn State, Illinois, Indiana and Nebraska.

Big 12 Conference: An NCAA (National College Athletic Association) Division I-A sports conference including Baylor, Iowa State, Kansas, Kansas State, Missouri, Oklahoma, Oklahoma State, Texas, Texas Tech and Texas Christian University.

Big East Conference: An NCAA (National College Athletic Association) Division I-A sports conference including Cincinnati, Connecticut, Louisville, Pittsburgh, Rutgers, South Florida, West Virginia and Syracuse.

Bowl Game (College Football): An exhibition game played in college football after the end of the regular season. Examples include the Rose Bowl and the Orange Bowl. The BCS (Bowl Championship Series) bowl is played by the two top ranked teams to determine the national championship.

Brand Marketing: A marketing strategy that places a focus on the brand name of a product, service or firm in order to eventually enhance the brand's market share, increase sales, establish credibility, improve satisfaction, raise the profile of the firm and increase profits. Public relations and special events are common methods of brand marketing. In contrast, performance marketing is focused on getting the consumer of a message to take a specific action, such as a click on a link.

Branding: A marketing strategy that places a focus on the brand name of a product, service or firm in order to increase the brand's market share, increase sales, establish credibility, improve satisfaction, raise the profile of the firm and increase profits. Also, see "Brand."

Broadcast: Electronic transmission of media by radio or television: generally refers to wireless methods.

Cable TV: A television system consisting of a local television station that is equipped with an antenna or satellite dish. The antenna or dish receives signals from distant, central network stations and retransmits those signals via TV cable to the local subscriber.

CAFTA-DR: See "Central American-Dominican Republic Free Trade Agreement (CAFTA-DR)."

Call Letters: Letters that identify a station, e.g., KTRU. Call letters are established by the Federal Communications Commission. Each broadcast station has unique letters. The letters may denote whether the station is in the eastern or western U.S.

Central American-Dominican Republic Free Trade Agreement (CAFTA-DR): A trade agreement signed into law in 2005 that aimed to open up the Central American and Dominican Republic markets to American goods. Member nations include Guatemala, Nicaragua, Costa Rica, El Salvador, Honduras and the Dominican Republic. Before the law was signed, products from those countries could enter the U.S. almost tariff-free, while American goods heading into those countries faced stiff tariffs. The goal of this agreement was to create U.S. jobs while at the same time offering the non-U.S. member citizens a chance for a better quality of life through access to U.S.-made goods.

CFL: Canadian Football League. See www.cfl.ca.

Chain Break: A pause in program broadcasting used to identify the television or radio station, and to air additional advertisements.

Champions League: In UEFA European football (soccer), the Champions League consists of 32 teams that have won qualifying rounds.

Commissioner (Sports): The chief executive of a sports league.

CONCACAF: The Confederation Norte-Centroamericana y Del Caribe de Football. CONCACAF is the regional organization of North American and Central American soccer under which World Cup qualifying matches are played.

Conference USA (C-USA): An NCAA (National College Athletic Association) Division I-A sports conference that includes East Carolina, Central Florida, Memphis, Alabama Birmingham, Tulane, Rice, Southern Methodist, Marshall, Texas-El Paso, Southern Mississippi, Tulsa and Houston.

Conferences: Groups of teams in professional or college football, typically based on geographical regions.

CRM: See "Customer Relationship Management (CRM)."

Customer Relationship Management (CRM): Refers to the automation, via sophisticated software, of business processes involving existing and prospective customers. CRM may cover aspects such as sales (contact management and contact history), marketing (campaign management and telemarketing) and customer service (call center history and field service history). Well known providers of CRM software include Salesforce, which delivers via a Software as a Service model (see "Software as a Service (Saas)"), Microsoft and Oracle.

Demographic Segmentation: Dividing a given population into ethnic and cultural groups in order to target different groups with tailored advertisements.

Demographics: The breakdown of the population into statistical categories such as age, income, education and sex.

Draft (NFL Draft): The annual, league-wide system by which teams in the National Football League (NFL) select players who are ready to leave college teams and enter the realm of professional football. The system is designed so that the teams with the worst records in the previous year have preference in making selections.

Echo Boomers: See "Generation Y."

Eco Index: An environmental assessment tool designed to advance sustainability practices. It provides companies throughout the supply chain a way to benchmark and measure their environmental footprint, allowing them to identify areas for improvement and make informed sourcing and product life cycle decisions. Although rooted in the outdoor industry, the project's output and tools have a wide range of applicability to other industries and sectors. The Eco Index initiative is led by Outdoor Industry Association and the European Outdoor Group and has been facilitated by Zero Waste Alliance, a 501(c)(3) non-profit focused on developing standards, tools and practices that lead to a more sustainable future. See www.ecoindexbeta.org.

Enterprise Resource Planning (ERP): An integrated information system that helps manage all aspects of a business, including accounting, ordering and human resources, typically across all locations of a major corporation or organization. ERP is considered to be a critical tool for management of large organizations. Suppliers of ERP tools include SAP and Oracle.

ERP: See "Enterprise Resource Planning (ERP)."

EU: See "European Union (EU)."

EU Competence: The jurisdiction in which the European Union (EU) can take legal action.

European Community (EC): See "European Union (EU)."

European Cup: The championship series for European football (soccer). See "Union of European Football Associations (UEFA)."

European Union (EU): A consolidation of European countries (member states) functioning as one body to facilitate trade. Previously known as the European

Community (EC). The EU has a unified currency, the Euro. See europa.eu.int.

Expansion Team: A new team added to a sports league.

Facilities Management: The management of a company's physical buildings and/or information systems on an outsourced basis.

Fantasy Team: A standardized, Internet-based system that allows individuals who have subscribed to a fantasy league through one of several providers to draft a team of players. An individual's team competes against those of friends or strangers in customizable leagues. Each team accumulates statistics during the season that are reflected in overall standings, eventually leading to a league champion.

Farm Team: In baseball, a minor league team that is owned by a major league team. The farm team is used to develop new talent.

FASB: See "Financial Accounting Standards Board (FASB)."

FC: Football Club.

Federal Communications Commission (FCC): The U.S. Government agency that regulates broadcast television and radio, as well as satellite transmission, telephony and all uses of radio spectrum.

FIFA: Federation International de Football Association. FIFA is the worldwide governing body of soccer and sponsors the World Cup tournament every four years. See www.fifa.com. Note, in Europe and elsewhere, soccer is referred to as "football."

Final Four: The last four teams in the NCAA (National College Athletic Association) championship basketball tournament.

Financial Accounting Standards Board (FASB): An independent organization that establishes the Generally Accepted Accounting Principles (GAAP).

FM: See "Frequency Modulation (FM)."

Franchise: 1) A contractual agreement between a franchisor (for example, a company or organization owning all rights to a brand, type of business, retail operation, restaurant concept or sports league) and a franchisee (person or organization desiring to license the use of those rights for a specific purpose within a specific region) that allows the franchisee to operate a retail outlet or other type of business using a brand, trade secrets, formulas and format developed and supported by the franchisor. Typically, a franchisee pays an upfront fee and then continuing fees to the franchisor. 2) A generic term used to describe a very well established business or brand.

Franchise (in Sports): A team: the legal arrangement that establishes ownership of an individual team within a league. (Also, see "Franchise.")

Franchise Player (in Sports): A star player around which a franchise is built: the most valuable player on a sports team.

Franchisee: See "Franchise."

Franchisor: See "Franchise."

Free Agent: A player whose contract with his most recent team has expired, allowing him to sign a new contract with any team that makes him an offer.

Frequency Modulation (FM): Radio broadcasts in the range of 88 MHz to 108 MHz.

GAAP: See "Generally Accepted Accounting Principles (GAAP)."

GDP: See "Gross Domestic Product (GDP)."

Generally Accepted Accounting Principles (GAAP): A set of accounting standards administered by the Financial Accounting Standards Board (FASB) and enforced by the U.S. Security and Exchange Commission (SEC). GAAP is primarily used in the U.S.

Generation M: A very loosely defined term that is sometimes used to refer to young people who have grown up in the digital age. "M" may refer to any or all of media-saturated, mobile or multi-tasking. The term was most notably used in a Kaiser Family Foundation report published in 2005, "Generation M: Media in the Lives of 8-18 year olds." Also, see "Generation Y" and "Generation Z."

Generation X: A loosely-defined and variously-used term that describes people born between approximately 1965 and 1980, but other time frames are recited. Generation X is often referred to as a group influential in defining tastes in consumer goods, entertainment and/or political and social matters.

Generation Y: Refers to people born between approximately 1982 and 2002. In the U.S., they number more than 90 million, making them the largest generation segment in the nation's history. They are also known as Echo Boomers, Millennials or the Millennial Generation. These are children of the Baby Boom generation who will be filling the work force as Baby Boomers retire.

Generation Z: Some people refer to Generation Z as people born after 1991. Others use the beginning date of 2001, or refer to the era of 1994 to 2004. Members of Generation Z are considered to be natural and rapid adopters of the latest technologies.

Gross Domestic Product (GDP): The total value of a nation's output, income and expenditures produced with a nation's physical borders.

Gross National Product (GNP): A country's total output of goods and services from all forms of economic activity measured at market prices for one calendar year. It differs from Gross Domestic Product (GDP) in that GNP includes income from investments made in foreign nations.

Gross Rating Points (GRPs): Measures the audience share of a television program's audience delivery. GRPs are the sum of individual ratings for all programs in a particular time slot. See "Ratings/Ratings Points/Ratings Share."

Heisman Trophy: An award presented annually by the Downtown Athletic Club of New York to the best college football player in the United States.

IFRS: See "International Financials Reporting Standards (IFRS)."

Image Advertising: Advocating a product based on its affiliation with a particular type of person or activity rather than the properties of the product itself, such as promoting a soda by claiming that basketball players drink it.

Indianapolis 500 (Indy 500): A popular 500-mile car race, first held in 1911, held annually at the Indianapolis Motor Speedway in Speedway, Indiana.

Industry Code: A descriptive code assigned to any company in order to group it with firms that operate in similar businesses. Common industry codes include the NAICS (North American Industrial Classification System) and the SIC (Standard Industrial Classification), both of which are standards widely used in America, as well as the International Standard Industrial Classification of all Economic Activities (ISIC), the Standard International Trade Classification established by the United Nations (SITC) and the General Industrial Classification of Economic Activities within the European Communities (NACE).

Initial Public Offering (IPO): A company's first effort to sell its stock to investors (the public). Investors in an up-trending market eagerly seek stocks offered in many IPOs because the stocks of newly public companies that seem to have great promise may appreciate very rapidly in price, reaping great profits for those who were able to get the stock at the first offering. In the United States, IPOs are regulated by the SEC (U.S. Securities Exchange Commission) and by the state-level regulatory agencies of the states in which the IPO shares are offered.

Intellectual Property (IP): The exclusive ownership of original concepts, ideas, designs, engineering plans or other assets that are protected by law. Examples include items covered by trademarks, copyrights and patents. Items such as software, engineering plans, fashion designs and architectural designs, as well as games, books, songs and other entertainment items are among the many things that may be considered to be intellectual property. (Also, see "Patent.")

International Financials Reporting Standards (IFRS): A set of accounting standards established by the International Accounting Standards Board (IASB) for the preparation of public financial statements. IFRS has been adopted by much of the world, including the European Union, Russia and Singapore.

IOC: International Olympic Committee. See www.olympic.org.

IP: See "Intellectual Property (IP)."

Kentucky Derby (Horse Racing): A 1.25 mile horse race held at the Churchill Downs racetrack in Louisville, Kentucky. Winning the Kentucky Derby is the first step in attaining the Triple Crown.

LAC: An acronym for Latin America and the Caribbean.

LDCs: See "Least Developed Countries (LDCs)."

Least Developed Countries (LDCs): Nations determined by the U.N. Economic and Social Council to be the poorest and weakest members of the international community. There are currently 50 LDCs, of which 34 are in Africa, 15 are in Asia Pacific and the remaining one (Haiti) is in Latin America. The top 10 on the LDC list, in descending order from top to 10th, are Afghanistan, Angola, Bangladesh, Benin, Bhutan, Burkina Faso, Burundi, Cambodia, Cape Verde and the Central African Republic. Sixteen of the LDCs are also Landlocked Least Developed Countries (LLDCs) which present them with additional difficulties often due to the high cost of transporting trade goods. Eleven of the LDCs are Small Island Developing States (SIDS), which are often at risk of extreme weather phenomenon (hurricanes, typhoons, Tsunami): have fragile ecosystems: are often dependent on foreign energy sources: can have high disease rates for HIV/AIDS and malaria: and can have poor market access and trade terms.

Licensed Brands: Brands for which the licensor (the owner of a well-known name) enters a contractual arrangement with a licensee (a retailer or a third party manufacturer or distributor). The licensee either manufactures or contracts with a manufacturer to produce the licensed product and pays a royalty to the licensor. For example, popular movies, such as Star Wars, often license their brand to makers of toys or gifts.

Lifestyle Merchandising: Development of merchandise lines based on consumer living patterns.

Location-Based Entertainment: The use of entertainment themes and attractions to draw consumers to specific locations, such as shopping malls, casinos and restaurants.

Logo/Logotype: The simple mark or picture most often used to indicate a brand (e.g., the stylized GE

that represents General Electric or the multicolored flag that represents Microsoft Windows).

LPGA: Ladies Professional Golf Association. See www.lpga.com.

Market Segmentation: The division of a consumer market into specific groups of buyers based on demographic factors.

Mass Media: Refers to all media that disseminate information throughout the world, including television, radio, film, print, photography and electronic media.

Media: Used loosely to refer to the entire communications system of reporters, editors, producers, print publications, broadcast programs, magazines and online publications.

Media Outlet: A broadcast or publication that brings news and features to the public through a distribution channel.

Medium: Any form of communication on a large scale, seen as a possible avenue for advertising. Different media types include television, radio, the Internet, newspapers and magazines.

Merchandising: Any marketing method utilized to foster sales growth.

Mid-American Conference (MAC): An NCAA (National College Athletic Association) Division I-A sports conference that is divided into two divisions, East and West. The Eastern Division includes Miami (Ohio), Akron, Ohio, Kent State, Bowling Green and Buffalo. The Western Division includes Toledo, Northern Illinois, Eastern Michigan, Central Michigan, Ball State, Temple and Western Michigan.

Millenials: See "Generation Y."

MLB: Major League Baseball. See www.mlb.com.

MLS: Major League Soccer. See www.mlsnet.com.

Mountain West Conference (MWC): An NCAA (National College Athletic Association) Division I-A sports conference that includes New Mexico, Texas Christian, Wyoming, Air Force, Colorado State, San Diego State, Boise State and Nevada-Las Vegas.

MVP: Most Valuable Player.

NAICS: North American Industrial Classification System. See "Industry Code."

National Basketball Association Eastern Conference: One of two conferences in the National Basketball Association. The winner of the Eastern Conference playoff plays the winner of the Western Conference playoff in the NBA Championship. The Eastern Conference is divided into three divisions: Atlantic, Central and Southeast.

National Basketball Association Western Conference: One of two conferences in the National Basketball Association. The winner of the Eastern Conference playoff plays the winner of the Western Conference playoff in the NBA Championship. The Western Conference has three divisions Northwest, Pacific and Southwest.

National Collegiate Athletic Association (NCAA): A voluntary association of over 1,200 colleges and universities in the U.S. whose role is to establish standards and protect the integrity of amateurism for student-athletes. See www2.ncaa.org.

National Football Conference (NFC): One of two football conferences in the National Football League. The NFC is divided into four divisions: NFC East, NFC West, NFC North and NFC South. The winner of the American Football Conference playoff plays the winner of the National Football Conference playoff in the Super Bowl.

National Football Conference East (NFC East): One of four divisions that make up the National Football Conference. The division consists of the Philadelphia Eagles, New York Giants, Dallas Cowboys and Washington Redskins.

National Football Conference North: One of four divisions that make up the National Football Conference. The division includes the Chicago Bears, Detroit Lions, Green Bay Packers and Minnesota Vikings.

National Football Conference South (NFC South): One of four divisions that make up the National Football Conference. The division includes the Atlanta Falcons, Carolina Panthers, New Orleans Saints and Tampa Bay Buccaneers.

National Football Conference West (NFC West): One of four divisions that make up the National Football Conference. The division consists of the Seattle Seahawks, St. Louis Rams, Arizona Cardinals and San Francisco 49ers.

National Invitational Tournament (NIT): A college basketball tournament in which teams that are not selected for the NCAA (National Collegiate Athletic Association) tournament may be invited to play.

National League: One of two leagues in Major League Baseball. The National League is divided into three divisions: East, West and Central. The winner of the National League playoff plays the winner of the American League playoff in the World Series. See www.mlb.com.

National League Central: One of the three divisions of the National League. The division includes the St. Louis Cardinals, Milwaukee Brewers, Chicago Cubs, Houston Astros, Pittsburgh Pirates and Cincinnati Reds.

National League East: One of the three divisions of the National League. The division includes the Florida Marlins, Atlanta Braves, Washington Nationals, New York Mets and Philadelphia Phillies.

National League West: One of the three divisions of the National League. The division includes the Los Angeles Dodgers, Arizona Diamondbacks, San Francisco Giants, San Diego Padres and Colorado Rockies.

NBA: National Basketball Association. See www.nba.com.

NBA Finals: The post-season playoffs in the National Basketball Association.

NCAA: See "National Collegiate Athletic Association (NCAA)."

Newspaper Syndicate: A firm selling features, photos, columns, comic strips or other special material for publication in a large number of newspapers. For example, a typical fee charged by a syndicate to a daily newspaper for a popular comic strip is $10 per day. Generally, the syndicate splits the fee with the author.

NFL: National Football League. See www.nfl.com.

NHL: National Hockey League. See www.nhl.com.

Nielsen Ratings: Ratings created by The Nielsen Corporation, a company engaged in television audience ratings and other market research.

Nielsen Station Index (NSI): An index that rates individual television stations.

Nielsen Television Index (NTI): An index that rates national television network programming.

OECD: See "Organisation for Economic Co-operation and Development (OECD)."

Onshoring: The opposite of "offshoring." Providing or maintaining manufacturing or services within or nearby a company's domestic location. Sometimes referred to as reshoring.

Organisation for Economic Co-operation and Development (OECD): A group of more than 30 nations that are strongly committed to the market economy and democracy. Some of the OECD members include Japan, the U.S., Spain, Germany, Australia, Korea, the U.K., Canada and Mexico. Although not members, Estonia, Israel and Russia are invited to member talks: and Brazil, China, India, Indonesia and South Africa have enhanced engagement policies with the OECD. The Organisation provides statistics, as well as social and economic data: and researches social changes, including patterns in evolving fiscal policy, agriculture, technology, trade, the environment and other areas. It publishes over 250 titles annually, including a corporate magazine, the OECD Observer. It also has radio and TV studios, and has centers in Tokyo, Washington, D.C., Berlin and Mexico City that distribute the Organisation's work and organizes events.

Pacific 10 Conference: An NCAA (National Collegiate Athletic Association) Division I-A sports conference that includes Southern California, California, Arizona State, Oregon State, UCLA, Oregon, Washington State, Stanford, Arizona, Washington, Utah and Colorado.

Patent: An intellectual property right granted by a national government to an inventor to exclude others from making, using, offering for sale, or selling the invention throughout that nation or importing the invention into the nation for a limited time in exchange for public disclosure of the invention when the patent is granted. In addition to national patenting agencies, such as the United States Patent and Trademark Office, and regional organizations such as the European Patent Office, there is a cooperative international patent organization, the World Intellectual Property Organization, or WIPO, established by the United Nations.

Pay-Per-View (PPV): A service that enables television subscribers, including cable and satellite viewers, to order and view events or movies on an individual basis. PPV programming may include sporting events.

PGA: Professional Golfers Association. See www.pga.com. Also see "LPGA."

Ratings/Rating Points/Ratings Share: The rating of a medium is its audience size expressed as a percentage of the measured market, where one rating point is equivalent to 1% of the base. Ratings are often referred to as "percent coverage." A television show with a 22% share has 22 points, or 22% of the total TV audience within its market.

Red Shirt: A designation given to a college athlete who did not play in any games during a particular year due to injury or coach's choice: such a player is permitted to practice with the team during that season and is granted an additional year of eligibility.

Rookie: An athlete in his or her first year of a sport.

SaaS: See "Software as a Service (SaaS)."

Satellite Broadcasting: The use of Earth-orbiting satellites to transmit, over a wide area, TV, radio, telephony, video and other data in digitized format.

Share: In broadcasting, the percentage of television households tuned into a particular program or category of programming. The higher the share, the larger the amount that can be charged for advertising on the program. Also, with regard to the Internet, a web site feature that allows users to share content with others through e-mail or social networks. Content can include video, images, article links or other similar media.

SIC: Standard Industrial Classification. See "Industry Code."

Software as a Service (SaaS): Refers to the practice of providing users with software applications that are hosted on remote servers and accessed via the Internet. Excellent examples include the CRM (Customer Relationship Management) software provided in SaaS format by Salesforce. An earlier technology that operated in a similar, but less sophisticated, manner was called ASP or Application Service Provider.

Southeastern Conference (SEC): An NCAA (National Collegiate Athletic Association) Division I-A sports conference that is divided into two divisions, East and West. The Eastern Conference includes Tennessee, Georgia, Florida, South Carolina, Kentucky and Vanderbilt. The Western Conference includes Auburn, Louisiana State, Alabama, Arkansas, Mississippi, Mississippi State and Texas A&M.

Special Olympics: An international organization dedicated to empowering individuals with intellectual disabilities to become physically fit, productive and respected members of society through sports training and competition. Special Olympics offers children and adults with intellectual disabilities year-round training and competition in 26 Olympic-type summer and winter sports. There is no charge to participate in Special Olympics. See www.specialolympics.org.

Specialty Publication: A trade or professional magazine that is industry- or audience-specific (e.g., Shopping Center World magazine).

Subsidiary, Wholly-Owned: A company that is wholly controlled by another company through stock ownership.

Sun Belt Conference: An NCAA (National Collegiate Athletic Association) Division I-A sports conference that includes North Texas, Troy, Louisiana-Monroe, Middle Tennessee State, Arkansas State, Louisiana-Lafayette, Florida Atlantic, Florida International and Western Kentucky.

Super Bowl: The U.S. national championship game of the National Football League (NFL).

Superstation: A local television station with a signal that is retransmitted via satellite to distant cable systems that cannot be reached by over-the-air signals.

Supply Chain: The complete set of suppliers of goods and services required for a company to operate its business. For example, a manufacturer's supply chain may include providers of raw materials, components, custom-made parts and packaging materials.

Syndicated: A report, story, television program, radio program or graphic that is sold to multiple media outlets simultaneously. For example, popular newspaper columns are commonly syndicated to various newspapers throughout the United States, but only one newspaper per market is allowed to participate.

System (Cable): A facility that provides cable television service in a given geographic area, consisting of one or more headends.

Teqball: A football (soccer)-based sport played on a specially curved table (the Teq Table) that is basically a combination of soccer, pingpong and tennis.

Time Shifting: Services that allow viewers to digitally record television programs for playback at a later, more convenient time. Such services include video-on-demand (VOD) and personal TV services. Time shifting will eventually make up a significant portion of all television viewing.

Triple Crown: Horse racing's greatest prize. To win the Triple Crown, the horse must first win the Kentucky Derby, then the Preakness Stakes and, finally, the Belmont Stakes.

U.S. Open (Golf): First played in 1895 and is considered to be the premier golf tournament in the U.S.

UEFA: See "Union of European Football Associations (UEFA)."

UEFA Cup: In European football (soccer), a competition for the runners up and the cup winners from each nation, along with other selected teams.

UHF: See "Ultra High Frequency (UHF)."

Ultra High Frequency (UHF): The frequency band ranging from 300 MHz to 3,000 MHz, which includes TV channels 14 through 83.

Union of European Football Associations (UEFA): The governing body of European football (soccer). See www.uefa.com.

USCF: United States Cycling Federation. See www.usacycling.org.

USGA: United States Golf Association. See www.usga.org.

USL: United Soccer Leagues. See www.uslsoccer.com.

USOC: United States Olympic Committee. See www.usoc.org.

USTA: United States Tennis Association. See www.usta.com.

Value Added Tax (VAT): A tax that imposes a levy on businesses at every stage of manufacturing based on the value it adds to a product. Each business in the supply chain pays its own VAT and is subsequently repaid by the next link down the chain: hence, a VAT is ultimately paid by the consumer, being the last link in the supply chain, making it comparable to a sales tax. Generally, VAT only applies to goods bought for consumption within a given country: export goods are exempt from VAT, and purchasers from other countries taking goods back home may apply for a VAT refund.

Vehicle: Any particular publication or broadcasting channel that carries advertisements.

Very High Frequency (VHF): The frequency band ranging from 30 MHz to 300 MHz, which includes TV channels 2 through 13 and FM radio.

VHF: See "Very High Frequency (VHF)."

Western Athletic Conference (WAC): An NCAA (National Collegiate Athletic Association) Division I-A sports conference that includes California State-Fresno, Hawaii, Idaho, Louisiana Tech, Nevada-Reno, New Mexico State, San Jose State and Utah State.

Wild Card: A U.S. football team that makes the NFL (National Football League) playoffs by having one of the two best records among non-division winners in its conference.

WNBA: Women's National Basketball Association. See www.wnba.com.

World Cup: The worldwide soccer championship tournament sponsored by FIFA (the Federation International de Football Association).

World Series: The championship series for Major League Baseball (MLB).

World Trade Organization (WTO): One of the only globally active international organizations dealing with the trade rules between nations. Its goal is to assist the free flow of trade goods, ensuring a smooth, predictable supply of goods to help raise the quality of life of member citizens. Members form consensus decisions that are then ratified by their respective parliaments. The WTO's conflict resolution process generally emphasizes interpreting existing commitments and agreements, and discovers how to ensure trade policies to conform to those agreements, with the ultimate aim of avoiding military or political conflict.

WTO: See "World Trade Organization (WTO)."

Milton Keynes UK
Ingram Content Group UK Ltd.
UKHW050638140923
428670UK00012B/473